Weapons of Mass Destruction and Terrorism

Weapons of Mass Destruction and Terrorism

Edited by

Alan O'Day

Greyfriars, University of Oxford, UK

ASHGATE

Published by
Ashgate Publishing Limited
Gower House
Croft Road
Aldershot
Hants GU11 3HR
England

Ashgate Publishing Company
Suite 420
101 Cherry Street
Burlington, VT 05401-4405
USA

Ashgate website: http://www.ashgate.com

British Library Cataloguing in Publication Data
Weapons of mass destruction and terrorism. – (The
 international library of essays in terrorism)
 1. Terrorism – History 2. Weapons of mass destruction
 3. Terrorism – Prevention 4. World politics – 1995–2005
 I. O'Day, Alan
 327.1'745

Library of Congress Control Number: 2004112017

ISBN 0 7546 2425 0

Printed in Great Britain by The Cromwell Press, Trowbridge, Wiltshire

Contents

Acknowledgements

The editor and publishers wish to thank the following for permission to use copyright material.

Blackwell Publishing for the essays: R. Havlak, S.E. Gorman and S.A. Adams (2002), 'Challenges Associated with Creating a Pharmaceutical Stockpile to Respond to a Terrorist Event', *Clinical Microbiology and Infection*, **8**, pp. 529–33. Copyright © 2002 European Society of Clinical Microbiology and Infectious Diseases; R. Roffey, K. Lantorp, A. Tegnell and F. Elgh (2002), 'Biological Weapons and Bioterrorism Preparedness: Importance of Public-Health Awareness and International Cooperation', *Clinical Microbiology and Infection*, **8**, pp. 522–8. Copyright © 2002 European Society of Clinical Microbiology and Infectious Diseases; Joseph W. Foxell, jr (1997), 'The Prospect of Nuclear and Biological Terrorism', *Journal of Contingencies and Crisis Management*, **5**, pp. 98–108; Joseph W. Foxell, jr (1999), 'Trends in Bio-Terrorism: Two Generations of Potential Weapons', *Journal of Contingencies and Crisis Management*, **7**, pp. 102–18.

Bulletin of the Atomic Scientists for the essays: Jeffrey Richelson (2002), 'Defusing Nuclear Terror', *Bulletin of the Atomic Scientists*, **58**, pp. 39–43. Copyright © 2002 Bulletin of Atomic Scientists; Michael Barletta, Amy Sands and Jonathan B. Tucker (2002), 'Keeping Track of Anthrax: The Case of a Biosecurity Convention', *Bulletin of the Atomic Scientists*, **58**, pp. 57–62. Copyright © 2002 Bulletin of Atomic Scientists.

Duke University Press for the essay: Kenneth C. Hyams, Frances M. Murphy and Simon Wessely (2002), 'Responding to Chemical, Biological, or Nuclear Terrorism: The Indirect and Long-Term Health Effects May Present the Greatest Challenge', *Journal of Health Politics, Policy and Law*, **27**, pp. 273–91. Copyright © 2002 Duke University Press.

Elsevier for the essay: Richard J. Whitley (2003), 'Smallpox: A Potential Agent of Bioterrorism', *Antiviral Research*, **57**, pp. 7–12. Copyright © 2003 Elsevier Science, BV.

Frank Cass Publishers for the essay: Daniel S. Gressang IV (2001), 'Audience and Message: Assessing Terrorist WMD Potential', *Terrorism and Political Violence*, **13**, pp. 83–106.

Lawrence Erlbaum Associates for the essay: James A. Romano, jr and James M. King (2002), 'Chemical Warfare and Chemical Terrorism: Psychological and Performance Outcomes', *Military Psychology*, **14**, pp. 85–92.

Maney Publishing for the essay: Jack Harris (1999), 'The Threat of Nuclear Terrorism', *Interdisciplinary Science Reviews*, **24**, pp. 81–84. Copyright © 1999 Iom Communications Ltd.

The volume is made possible through the assistance of staff at the Harmsworth Library, University of Oxford and the aid of Miles L. Bradbury and Col. Helen E. O'Day.

Series Preface

Acts of Terrorism have existed for centuries but since the late 1960s they have become more numerous and wide-ranging, giving terrorism fresh importance in the domestic affairs of countries afflicted and to the international community. Terrorism, or international terrorism, is not a constant but rather an evolving construct, manifesting itself in differing ways over time and in specific geographical contexts. Following the Cold War, terrorism has reared its head in places and in ways that were less common earlier. Presidents Reagan and Clinton in the 1980s and 90s stressed the importance of combating terrorism; President George W. Bush, too, recognised the threat. However, the attacks on the World Trade Center and the Pentagon on 11 September 2001, followed by incidents elsewhere, notably in Madrid on 11 March 2004, have given impetus to the study of terrorism in academic circles, among journalists and a heightened awareness by the general public.

A major problem for rigorous analysis of terrorism has been an absence of readily available, widely disseminated research and serious academic discussion. Many valuable articles have appeared in a range of academic and professional periodicals. Often these journals have limited circulations and even the great academic libraries of the western world, do not posses a full complement of articles. Thus the study of terrorism and the ability to offer university options in the field are frequently hampered by the absence of literature. This problem is vastly greater in the many small educational institutions. Even in libraries that do have a large number of the periodicals, the problem of searching out germane articles is demanding and time-consuming.

The series is directed, towards providing a partial remedy to this problem. It seeks to provide in a number of volumes, pertinent material for the study and understanding of terrorism, making these available to a wider audience. An important feature of the volumes is that the articles selected are intended to reflect various opinions and to afford a glimpse into the controversies about such matters as the very definition of terrorism, its various dimensions and future prospects.

ALAN O'DAY
Series Editor
Greyfriars,
University of Oxford

Introduction

We must realize, however, that the next attacks are likely to be different from those on September 11. Most threatening is the nexus between terrorists and WMD . . . As horrible as September 11 was, the death, destruction, and disruption to U.S. society was minimal compared to what a weapon of mass destruction could have inflicted. (Senator Richard G. Lugar, this volume, p. 225)

Acts of terrorism range from threats of terrorism, assassinations, kidnappings, hijackings, bomb scares and bombings, cyber attacks (computer-based), to the use of chemical, biological and nuclear weapons . . . They are capable of spreading fear by sending explosives or chemical and biological agents through the mail . . . The danger of a massive strategic nuclear attack on the United States involving many weapons receded with the end of the Cold War. However, some terrorists have been supported by nations that have nuclear weapons programs. (White House Press Release, 7 February 2003)

The question of terrorist deployment of weapons of mass destruction (WMD) is causing extensive discussion or at least raising the temperature of the debate, as well as adding to public fears about safety. In Chapter 9 of this volume Richard A. Falkenrath poses one basic question: how serious is the threat of WMD terrorism to the national security of modern liberal democracies? Although the probability of WMD terrorism is low, it is a high-consequence threat because the harm caused by even one successful act would be profound – and not only in terms of lives lost. The conventional, low-technology terrorism of the past has exercised a social and political impact far out of proportion with the casualties it has caused. The massive, indiscriminate destruction caused by an act of WMD terrorism would have similarly disproportionate social, political, economic and strategic effects. James A. Romano, jr and James M. King (Chapter 17) concur, noting that there can be little dispute about the importance of the topic of WMDs even if the likelihood of their use is less than for other modes of terrorist attack. The issue of WMDs subsumes many of the key questions about terrorism – definition, objects, motivation, whether there is a different species of it emerging in the aftermath of the close of the Cold War, preparedness and the means of prevention. WMDs received attention before 9/11. Concerted interest dates back to the attack in March 1995 by Aum Shinrikyo, a Japanese religious cult, on the Tokyo subway, which killed 12 people and injured 5000. But for an element of technical incapacity, the casualty figures would have been very much greater.

The potential for deploying WMDs in crowded urban environments is widely recognized. There is an extensive popular literature using, as its plot, the potential threat of WMDs either by nations or terrorists. In Chapter 7 Jeffrey Richelson notes that the James Bond thriller, *Thunderball*, along with Larry Collins's *The Fifth Horseman*, Tom Clancy's novel, *The Sum of All Fears* and the 1997 film, *The Peacemaker*, represent a handful among the many films and novels that have taken the threatened use of WMDs as a motif. In the present-day world, the belief that WMDs will be used and inflict heavy casualties is prevalent. Jeffrey Boutwell, Francesco Calogero and Jack Harris observe that:

There are many ways that terrorists can wreak death and destruction, including through the use of chemical and biological/bacteriological agents, radiological materials, and the hijacking of airliners and using them as missiles to destroy skyscrapers, or perhaps civilian nuclear power plants. The question of which option may be 'easier' than another is immaterial, as the answer will largely depend on the specific competencies and capabilities (including access to key materials) available to the terrorists, as well as their personal histories and contacts.

What does seem beyond doubt is that acquiring the capability to explode a nuclear device – the 'absolute weapon' – must certainly be very appealing to any terrorist group seeking to cause major damage to society and the governmental and social institutions they opposed. Such a capability is likely to confer on its possessors a great feeling of power, not to mention its value as an effective instrument for blackmail or retaliation.

To the extent that terrorism is a means of levelling the playing field and constitutes a message network, WMDs must be the ultimate equalizer, the supreme conduit for conveying a signal about what the perpetrators want and the methods they are prepared to employ to facilitate their ends. Governments have been actively promoting awareness of the dangers and preparing their respective publics for the prospect of attacks by terrorists employing WMDs. The American administration issued detailed instructions in 2003 about the possibility of an attack and measures to be followed in its eventuality; in July 2004 the UK government followed suit, delivering a pamphlet on emergency procedures to every household. It is reminiscent of the early days of the Cold War when, in Northern America, volunteers passed their evenings surveying the Canadian skies for a sneak attack from the Soviet Union.

Discussion of WMDs largely focuses on the direct consequences for humans. However, Elizabeth L. Chalecki (Chapter 27) usefully identifies another, and possibly more devastating, target – the environment. Environmental terrorism, she notes, is an old type of conflict with a new face. Most recent discussions of terrorism focus on the identity of terrorists, their motivations and the increasingly destructive potential of the weapons at their disposal. However, to date, there is less discussion about their choice of targets. Environmental terrorism, Chalecki points out, is distinct from both eco-terrorism and environmental warfare. Eco-terrorism is the violent destruction of property perpetrated by the radical fringes of environmental groups in the name of saving the environment from further human encroachment and destruction. Based in deep ecology theory, the professed aim of eco-terrorists is to slow or halt exploitation of natural resources and to bring public attention to environmental issues such as unsustainable logging or wildlife habitat loss through development. In contrast, environmental terrorism involves targeting natural resources. It can be more efficacious than either a standard conventional weapon or WMD attack on civil targets, although terrorists might very well make use of the latter as a deliberate choice. The choice of environmental resources as targets or tools of terrorism is consistent with both the increasing lethality of terrorism and growing environmental awareness on the part of the public. At the same time, it presents fewer risks to perpetrators. Chalecki's essay widens the scope of WMD potential in the hands of terrorists. It makes clear that the number of targets is virtually limitless and that the destruction of millions of acres of forest or farmland could have a symbolic or economic impact as large as an attack upon a civilian population.

Brief History

The use of biological and chemical agents in warfare has a lengthy lineage going back over many centuries. In Chapter 19 Steven Kuhr and Jerome M. Hauer report that, during the

First World War, experimentation took place with this form of weaponry, particularly the use of gas. In 1925 the Geneva Protocol prohibited the use of chemical and bacterial agents in war. The convention had little effect, however: governments continued to develop, and sometimes test, such potential weapons. Japan used biological weapons against the Chinese and Americans during the Second World War. Great Britain, and the United States also developed biological and chemical capacity. At Camp Detrick in Maryland deadly viruses were developed and tests were conducted on a cohort of American citizens. Paul F. Deisler, jr (Chapter 25) notes that from 1951 and into the 1960s several American cities were subjected to clandestine releases of Serratia marcenscens by personnel at military facilities in order to assess the dispersal of biological agents under realistic conditions. At least one death and several illness resulted. In 1972 more than 100 nations ratified the Convention on the Prohibition of Development, Production and Stockpiling of Bacteriological and Toxin Weapons and Their Destruction, although it did little to contain work in the area. Actual use of these weapons, however, has been the exception rther than the rule. Falkenrath's list of terrorist incidents taking place between 1925 and 1995 and incurring over 100 casualties per incident reveals only three where such agents were used (see p. 100).

The Likelihood of Terrorists Using WMDs

Speculation on terrorists' deployment of WMDs has the teleology of late-night undergraduate discussions about the existence of God and whether there is a heaven and hell. One can never know for sure until it is too late; belief carries no risk, and absence of faith can consign one for eternity to the everlasting bonfire. This is a powerful tool in the arsenal of religious bodies, and it is an equally compelling idea in the public, and indeed in governmental, consciousness about the outcome of an attack by WMDs. People want certainty, or at least the illusion of it. In the case of a terrorist attack, overcaution and false alarms cause minor inconvenience whereas an error in detection has devastating consequences. If the USA has at times seemed overzealous about terror threats since 9/11, this has had much to do with 'once bitten, twice shy'. The more measured approach taken in the UK reflects, in part, a longer and more intimate exposure to the threat of terrorism. Nevertheless, the number of terror alerts in the Western world is on the increase.

Andrew O'Neil (Chapter 1) observes that there is a tendency among observers to converge on analogous assessments of the threat at the higher end of the threat spectrum. The ease with which such attacks can be carried out has been exaggerated; acquiring WMD capabilities for delivery against targets is much more problematic for terrorists than is generally acknowledged in the literature. However, this is not to say, he pleads, that the possibility of such attacks can or should be ruled out. O'Neil subscribes to the idea that the rise of a 'new' brand of terrorism that operates across transnational networks and whose operations aim to inflict mass casualties, coupled with the destructive threshold crossed on 9/11, mean that terrorist attacks using WMD will continue to be a realistic prospect in the future. Amy Sands (2002) points out that much of the literature is marred by a tendency to 'comfortably reiterate the same threat mantra without examining more closely certain underlying assumptions'. A particularly salient feature has been an assumption that, if terrorist groups are able to get their hands on WMD *materials*, they will, as a matter of course, be capable of fabricating a viable *weapon* to use against a target.

This outlook is fuelled by a prevailing view among policy elites and much of the academic community that large-scale terrorist acts using WMDs are only 'a matter of time'. O'Neill assesses three interrelated propositions:

1   Can terrorists acquire WMDs?
2   What is the likelihood that terrorists will actually use WMDs?
3   Has the threat increased since 9/11?

First, as O'Neil comments, while terrorist attacks involving WMDs remain a real prospect, the ease with which such attacks can be executed has been exaggerated. In particular, the inherent difficulties of actually constructing a WMD, as distinct from merely having access to the materials for one, have often been underestimated. His observation receives endorsement from Aaron Weiss in Chapter 28, who maintains that one main reason why there have been so few examples of successful chemical–biological terrorism is because of its technical complexity. These propositions lie at the heart of the 29 essays in this volume on WMDs and their effects.

To achieve a realistic understanding of the scope of the threat, it is necessary to draw a clear distinction between biological, chemical and nuclear weapons. Furthermore, although it is vital to temper assumptions about the 'inevitability' of WMD terrorism, it is equally important that the pendulum must not swing too far in the other direction. There is abundant evidence that a wide range of terrorist outfits have actively sought WMD materials, and it is very likely that some have obtained them. Documents discovered in Afghanistan link al-Qaeda with the possible acquisition of WMDs. Although, as mentioned earlier, the challenges of constructing WMDs remain formidable, groups that invest enormous amounts of time, energy, and resources in endeavouring to acquire these capabilities have a very strong incentive to succeed. O'Neil believes that, on balance, there can be little doubt that once terrorist groups who are intent on acquiring a WMD do gain that capability, they will seek to use it.

The fact remains, however, that, apart from the use of automatic weapons, the explosive is the commonest form of conventional terrorist weapon, being utilized in over 70 per cent of actions. Weiss draws attention to an investigation by the Center for Nonproliferation Studies in Monterey, California that attempted to bridge the gap between anecdotal and empirical knowledge. The centre compiled a database of 520 global chemical and biological incidents that occurred in the twentieth century, analysing 263 cases that were terrorist, rather than criminal, cases. Contrary to conventional wisdom about the catastrophic nature of biological and chemical terrorism, actual attacks were few in number, small in scale, and generally produced far lower casualties than conventional bombs. Terrorists are likely to continue to use the most available resources, which are conventional weapons and the person prepared to die for the cause.

But when are terrorists likely to use WMDs? The single most important variable that makes terrorist use of WMDs increasingly credible, according to O'Neill, is the changing nature of the underlying philosophy of terrorist groups themselves. Long gone are the days when terrorism was exemplified by the gun-toting anarchist seeking to overturn a corrupt political order within the strict confines of state borders. The terrorists of the twenty-first century are exemplified by operatives who are part of a loose, yet sophisticated, transnational network with the goal to overturn *global* trends that are deemed to be in profound conflict with their core religious or political beliefs. Throughout the final decade of the twentieth century, the capacity of terrorist groups to organize themselves into transnational networks for the purpose of coordinating operations across different continents was significantly enhanced by the rapid globalization of information technologies. However, there is some debate about whether a 'new terrorism' does exist, and this is treated at more length in the companion volume *Dimensions of Terrorism* (O'Day, 2004).

Charles L. Mercier, jr (Chapter 6) concurs with O'Neil that religiously motivated groups are more likely to use chemical or biological weapons than are politically motivated groups. Yet, apart from the attack in Tokyo, there is an absence of direct evidence to support this apparent truism. Daniel S. Gressang IV (Chapter 15) notes that there are two schools of thought: first, that the use of WMDs is inevitable; second, that Aum Shinrikyo was an aberration. He points out that terrorists are rational actors who have specified and identifiable sets of preferences that are driven by cost–benefit calculations. It is his fundamental tenet that all terrorists are alike in at least one important way: they seek to acquire and maintain some degree of influence over an identifiable audience. Combining audience, message and social relationships offers an opportunity to distinguish between terrorist groups most likely to consider the large-scale use of mass-casualty weapons and those that are not. Many terrorists groups use the language of religion, he cautions, but are, despite outward appearances, addressing human audiences more than an ethereal one. This worldly posture places constraints on the choice of weapons. It is noteworthy that al-Qaeda's attacks on 9/11 made imaginative use of makeshift weapons and aircraft, not WMDs.

Biological and Bacterial Weapons

Biological agents are organisms or toxins that can kill or incapacitate people, livestock and crops. Biological weapons are powered by organic agents. Biological terrorists thus have a wealth of source materials to choose from in constructing their weapons. In many types of biological attack people will not know that they have been exposed to an agent. *Bacillus anthracis*, in particular, is the ideal biological warfare agent. It is found worldwide, and vast numbers of spores can be isolated using simple fermentation technology. In 1979 an accidental release of anthrax from a military facility outside Sverdlovsk in Russia resulted in the death of at least 66 individuals. A review of the incident estimated that less than one gram of spores was released. In Chapter 14 Joseph W. Foxell, jr considers the character of more than three dozen potential biological terror agents. To date, there has been very little bio-terrorism – due mainly to the long-standing taboo on the use of such infective substances even in wartime, as well as the inherent difficulties and dangers in handling and deploying such materials. Yet, as Foxell shows, biological devices in the hands of terrorists may very well be the quintessential terror weapons, as they are quite suited to silent attack on extended civilian populations, many of whom could become fatally infected long before the onset of symptoms would reveal the nature of the onslaught against them. Such an event would have a potent psychological impact on the nation attacked, and it would doubtless shatter its citizens' perceptions of their personal, as well as collective, security. Moreover, shortly after such an attack, the victimized locality's ability to provide emergency medical services could become severely eroded due to the sheer numbers of casualties that the incident would generate. The most immediate danger stems from the simplicity of the tasks required for manufacturing a biological terror mass casualty weapon based on either *Bacillus anthracis* or *Clostridium botulinum*, since preparing such devices calls for exponentially lower levels of skills, resources and expertise in comparison to those needed for making chemical or nuclear devices, and the materials are much more readily available.

The first evidence of an attack may be when symptoms of the disease caused by exposure to an agent are noticed. Christopher F. Chyba (Chapter 10) cautions that, too often, thinking about biological terrorism has mimicked that about chemical terrorism, as though the two involved different versions of the same weapon. It is generally accepted that biological agents pose few technical challenges of development and deployment to terrorist groups. Nevertheless, most biological agents are difficult to grow and maintain. Many break down quickly when exposed to sunlight and other environmental factors, whilst others, such as anthrax spores, are very long-lived. They can be dispersed by spraying them into the atmosphere or by infecting animals which then carry the disease to humans through food and water contamination. As the White House circular of 2003 notes, anthrax spores formulated as a white powder were mailed to individuals in the government and media in the autumn of 2001. The action of postal sorting machines and the opening of letters acted as an aerosol and dispersed the spores, resulting in several deaths. The effect was to disrupt mail service and to cause a widespread fear of handling delivered mail among the public. The person-to-person spread of a few infectious agents is also possible. Humans have been the source of infection for smallpox, the plague and the Lassa viruses.

The three basic groups of biological agents which would most likely be used as weapons are bacteria, viruses and toxins. *Bacteria* are small free-living organisms that reproduce by simple division and are easy to grow. The diseases they produce often respond to treatment with antibiotics. *Viruses* are organisms that require living cells in which to reproduce and are intimately dependent on the body they infect. Viruses produce diseases which generally do not respond to antibiotics, although anti-viral drugs are sometimes effective. *Toxins* are poisonous substances found in, and extracted from, living plants, animals or micro-organisms, and some of them can be produced or altered by chemical means. Some toxins can be treated with specific anti-toxins and selected drugs.

Among those agents identified by the Center for Disease Control and Prevention as 'class A bioterrorist threats', smallpox is among the most dangerous reports Richard J. Whitley in Chapter 11. The ease with which this agent is transmitted, the lack of immunity in the population at large to this agent, and the rapidity of its spread if released all generate significant concern about its possible deployment. The problem is particularly acute in the West because natural immunity to smallpox has diminished. Consequently, Whitley urges the development of a vaccine without major side effects.

Biological terrorism challenges three requirements for successful deterrence. First, it may prove difficult to identify the perpetrators of certain biological attacks, especially since some diseases incubate for as long as a week before symptoms become manifest. Second, a terrorist group might hope that its attack would remain completely unrecognized by government officials. History suggests that the origin of some disease outbreaks may remain ambiguous, or only be clarified as natural or intentional after some time. Finally, as with any form of terrorism, some apocalyptic or other non-state groups may not be concerned about punishment. All this means that an appropriate defence has to be based on improved public health surveillance and response. Preparing for biological terrorism has more in common with confronting the threat of emerging infectious diseases than with preparing for chemical or nuclear attacks, a position that is highlighted by R. Roffey, K. Lantorp, A. Tegnell and F. Elgh in Chapter 5.

Chemical Weapons

Second in order of likelihood, if not in potential destructive capacity, are chemical agents in the form of poisonous vapours, aerosols, liquids or solids that have toxic effects on people, animals or plants. These can be released by bombs, sprayed from aircraft, boats or vehicles, or used as a liquid to create a hazard to people and the environment. Some chemical agents may be odourless and tasteless. They can have either an immediate effect (a few seconds to a few minutes) or a delayed effect (several hours to several days). However, chemical agents are difficult to deliver in lethal concentrations as they often dissipate rapidly outdoors. They are also difficult to produce. Nevertheless, technical competence is widespread and, in due course, many of the difficulties of deployment may well be resolved.

Nuclear Weapons

The use of nuclear devices by terrorists has a lower probability than the use of biological and chemical weapons but it provokes an even higher degree of fear. They are the ultimate nightmare scenario although, as Jack Harris proclaims in an editorial (see Chapter 24), there remains a failure to take the threat seriously. The nuclear potential is often viewed as too improbable – something perhaps left to the authors of thrillers. An exchange in *Survival* between Karl-Heinz Kamp, Joseph F. Pilat, Jessica Stern and Richard A. Falkenrath (Chapter 23) brings the question into stark relief. According to the White House press release cited at the beginning of the introduction, nuclear explosions can cause deadly effects – blinding light, intense heat (thermal radiation), initial nuclear radiation, blast, fires started by the heat pulse and secondary fires caused by the destruction. They also produce radioactive particles called fall-out that can be carried by wind for hundreds of miles. Use by terrorists of a radiological dispersion device (RDD) – often called 'dirty nuke' or 'dirty bomb' – is considered far more likely than employment of a nuclear device. These radiological weapons are a combination of conventional explosives and radioactive material designed to scatter dangerous and sub-lethal amounts of radioactive material over a general area. Such radiological weapons appeal to terrorists because they require less technical knowledge to construct and deploy compared to that required for a nuclear device. Also, these radioactive materials, used widely in medicine, agriculture, industry and research, are much more readily available and easy to obtain in comparison with weapons-grade uranium or plutonium. Terrorist use of a nuclear device would probably be limited to a single smaller 'suitcase' weapon. Nonetheless, the strength of such a weapon would be in the range of the bombs used during the Second World War and its effects would be similar in nature to those of a weapon delivered by an intercontinental missile, although the area and severity of the effects would be significantly more limited. There is no way of knowing how much warning would be given before a terrorist nuclear or radiological weapon attack. A surprise attack remains a possibility.

A main concern has been availability of essential materials for a nuclear device. Observers, including Jon B. Wolfsthal and Tom Z. Collina (Chapter 26) point to the relatively low quality of storage in Russia – a reminder that the problem of WMDs is not circumscribed by national borders. In addition, Achilles Skordas (Chapter 29) expresses concern that the international legal system, notably the International Court of Justice, has fudged, rather than addressed, the issue of states' rights to hold and deploy nuclear weapons. As he points out, the nuclear age is still far from being over: for better or for worse, for more peace and stability or for more chaos and destruction – that is the question.

Preparation and Impacts

In Chapter 16, Kenneth C. Hyams, Frances M. Murphy and Simon Wessely point out that even small-scale WMD incidents – like the recent spread of anthrax spores through the mail – can cause widespread confusion, fear and psychological stress that have lasting effects on the health of affected communities and on a nation's sense of well-being. More emphasis therefore needs to be placed on indirect effects and on the medical, social, economic and legal consequences that follow for months or years afterwards. At the same time, they argue, future chemical, biological or nuclear terrorism should be anticipated. In preparing for these attacks, we have to walk a fine line between lack of preparedness and creating undue fear in daily lives. Terrorism is not simply about killing people; it is also about destroying a sense of individual well-being and public trust in government.

   R. Havlak, S.E. Gorman and S.A. Adams (Chapter 4) observe that there are many challenges associated with the creation and use of a pharmaceutical stockpile. They point to the need to prepare for the unexpected. Steven Kuhr and Jerome M. Hauer (Chapter 19) urge that, with forethought and planning, local government agencies can develop programmes that can detect an outbreak early in its progress and implement a response that will reduce morbidity and mortality. However, a less optimistic picture is painted by Charles L. Mercier, jr (Chapter 6) who maintains that, although the US army is now trained to deal with potential WMD emergencies, its reserves are not. In the current state of post-Cold War military organization, more reliance has been placed on these less trained reservists. Moreover, Henry W. Fischer III (Chapter 22) observes that, with reference to Presidential Directive 39 which initiates US plans to enhance mitigation and response activity, anecdotal information suggests that many of the likely behavioural and organizational response challenges are not being addressed. And, in a telling empirical analysis, the study of emergency departments in the greater Philadelphia area by Michael I. Greenberg and Robert G. Hendrickson (Chapter 13) reveals an overall lack of preparedness for a major terrorist incident involving WMDs. It is highly unlikely that this situation differs significantly elsewhere in the USA and abroad. A training exercise in Great Britain in mid-2004 revealed significant deficiencies in emergency procedures and the capacity to cope with a major incident.

   Two other essays consider what can be done at the wider policy level to prepare for, and mitigate, the impact of WMD terrorism. Jeffry L. Anderson, Eric Gordon, Stephen A. Levine, Roger Morrison and Michael E. Rosenbaum (Chapter 2) consider proposed hypothetical protocols addressing both the prevention and treatment of acute anthrax and smallpox. They discuss the potential benefit of additional or 'integrative' modalities with conventional allopathic approaches, with specific emphasis on applied medical nutrition and homeopathy. In Chapter 8 Michael Barletta, Amy Sands and Jonathan B. Tucker discuss the Biological and Toxin Weapons Convention (BWC) that bans development, production, stockpiling and transfer of microbial disease agents and natural poisons (toxins) as weapons, but note that it lacks any formal measures to ensure treaty compliance. The issue is complicated by several factors, including American political and economic concerns. They point out that, in July 2001, the Bush administration rejected the draft protocol to the bio-weapons treaty and withdrew from negotiations, claiming that it allowed determined proliferators to conceal offensive bio-warfare weapons programmes with little risk of detection and pointing out also that on-site inspections would jeopardize the trade secrets of American pharmaceutical and biotech companies. Thus, as usual, numerous complications exist at virtually every level of detection, compliance, preparedness and international cooperation. What seems certain is that the advanced public health programmes of Western nations probably decrease their relative vulnerability compared with, say, the Third World. In most epidemics the affluent West has suffered proportionately less than the poorer regions of the world.

Conclusions

Senator Lugar's words bear emphasis: 'In a world in which terrorist attacks on our country can be planned in Germany, financed in Asia, and carried out in the United States, old distinctions between "in" and "out of area" have become irrelevant' (p. 227). However, recent events have demonstrated the success of terrorism in disrupting society with relatively little investment in raw material. As Jonathan D. Moreno (Chapter 20) observes from the standpoint of bioethics, the emphasis on autonomy and individual rights may come to be tempered by greater concern about the collective good. Increased emphasis on solidarity over autonomy could greatly alter public response to research abuses aimed at defence, ranging from bioterrorism, to privacy of genetic information and to control of private medical resources to protect the public health.

In an intriguing evaluation, Gabrielle Hecht (Chapter 3) seeks deeper reasons for terrorists' resort to WMDs, suggesting that the current shape of global technopolitics has deep roots in the dialectics between nuclear and post-colonial rupture-talk, between nuclear and post-colonial technopolitics. These dialectics have defined the parameters for global power relations and have shaped geopolitical subjectivities in multiple registers and in ways whose significance we have barely begun to grasp. If we are indeed in a 'post' or a 'post-post-'Cold War world, then it's the same kind of 'post-ness' that we find in the 'post-colonial'. The infrastructures and discourses of Cold War technopolitics continue to shape the parameters of global and local action, just as the infrastructures and discourses of colonialism do. Hecht warns that we ignore those roots – and the contradictions they produce – at our peril. The issue of WMDs is not going to disappear; indeed, it seems likely to take on an enhanced importance in the coming years. As commentators warn, there is no simple answer to whether or not a terrorist WMD attack will take place.

[1]

Terrorist use of weapons of mass destruction: how serious is the threat?

ANDREW O'NEIL

This article examines the extent to which terrorist use of nuclear, chemical, and biological weapons poses a tangible threat to international security. In the literature on terrorism and weapons of mass destruction (WMD) some analysts have tended to exaggerate the scope of the threat and assumed that large-scale terrorist acts involving WMD are only 'a matter of time'. In short, there is a tendency among observers to converge on analogous assessments at the higher end of the threat spectrum. In this article I argue that although WMD terrorism remains a real prospect, the ease with which such attacks can be carried out has been exaggerated; acquiring WMD capabilities for delivery against targets is a lot more problematic for terrorists than is generally acknowledged in the literature. However, this is not to say that the possibility of such attacks can (or should) be ruled out. The rise of a 'new' brand of terrorism that operates across transnational networks and whose operations aim to inflict mass casualties, coupled with the destructive threshold crossed on 11 September 2001, mean that terrorist attacks using WMD will continue to be a realistic prospect in the future.

Introduction

Accurately assessing threats is a notoriously problematic undertaking for states. The challenge of itemising and attaching specific priority to tangible and potential threats to national security in a way that is readily accessible for policy makers remains especially difficult. Even generously funded and highly capable intelligence agencies struggle to formulate coherent and timely threat assessments across the security spectrum. Terrorism is a particularly difficult threat to assess. Usually comprised of amorphous associations of highly mobile individuals whose intentions are virtually impossible to gauge without access to reliable (and timely) human intelligence, terrorist groups remain elusive (Hoffman 1996). Nevertheless, in recent years assessing terrorist threats has become the single most salient preoccupation for Western national security agencies. Faced with the most destructive phase of international terrorism in the modern era, critically evaluating the nature and scope of the threat in order to select the most appropriate countermeasures to safeguard the state and its interests has become a fixation for most Western political leaders.

100   *A. O'Neil*

Of the manifold threats posed by terrorist organisations, attacks using nuclear, chemical, or biological weapons against state assets loom especially large. The fear that terrorists will resort to using Weapons of Mass Destruction (WMD) is nothing new. The spectre of terrorist attacks involving WMD has preoccupied security analysts both within and outside official government circles since at least the early 1970s.[1] However, the perceived threat of WMD use by terrorist groups has been magnified dramatically since the end of the Cold War. This can be attributed to three main factors.

The first is the collapse of the USSR in 1991 and attendant concerns about the physical security of WMD assets in the territories of the former Soviet Union (FSU). The primary concern has been that lax security practices in the FSU have made it easier for terrorist organisations to access WMD technologies, either via covert purchasing arrangements or theft. The phenomenon of 'loose nukes' in the FSU has received wide publicity, but less acknowledged are the enormous stocks of unsecured biological and chemical weapons stemming from the massive Soviet Cold War inventory. One authoritative source has identified several dozen repositories in Russia housing BW stocks from the former Soviet program that lack adequate security and tracking arrangements (Cirincione, Wolfsthal, and Rajkumar 2002: 125). The second factor has been the rise of what is generally regarded as a new breed of terrorism worldwide. Prone to using far more lethal and indiscriminate forms of violence than older, more established, terrorist groups, the new terrorist groups are said to covet those weapons that can do the maximum damage to their target set: WMD. The third factor contributing to increased anxiety over the threat of WMD terrorism has been a gradual realisation that, in contrast to the Cold War period when worldwide terrorist attacks were concentrated largely in Europe and the Middle East, terrorism now poses a distinctive security threat to the United States mainland as well as other parts of the globe traditionally regarded as relatively safe. The 1993 attacks on the World Trade Centre, the 1995 Oklahoma City bombing, and the 11 September 2001 attacks each had the effect of dramatically illustrating America's vulnerability to terrorism. While none of these attacks involved the use of WMD, they nevertheless raised fears about the possibility of such an attack on American territory. As a general rule, when the world's sole remaining superpower becomes the target of a specific security danger, this invariably raises the profile of such threats internationally—and so it has been with WMD terrorism.

Over the past decade there has been a surge in the academic literature on the subject of WMD terrorism. Yet, as Amy Sands (2002) has noted, in dealing with this issue much of the literature has been marred by a tendency to 'comfortably reiterate the same threat mantra without examining more closely certain underlying assumptions'. A particularly salient feature has been an assumption that if terrorist groups are able to get their hands on WMD *materials*, they will, as a matter of course, be capable of fabricating a viable *weapon* to use against a target set (for instance, see Laqueur 1996; Falkenrath 1998; and Hoffman 1998: 196–97). One of the unfortunate by-products of this analytical trend among security specialists has been that 'a great deal of reporting on the subject has been careless and exaggerated, creating a mood of political paranoia' (Stern 1998–99: 176). This has been further fuelled by a prevailing view among policy elites and much of the academic community that large-scale terrorist acts using WMD are only 'a matter of time'.

Part of the problem is that insufficient attention has been devoted to assessing dispassionately whether hypothetical scenarios are likely to be transformed into reality. This article is concerned with addressing this issue, along with the broader question of whether the WMD threat has been exaggerated. I address three inter-related propositions that I maintain are central to understanding the degree to which WMD terrorism should be categorised as a security threat: can terrorists acquire WMD; what is the likelihood that terrorists will actually use WMD; has the threat increased since 11 September 2001?

My argument is essentially twofold. First, while terrorist attacks involving WMD remain a real prospect, the ease with which such attacks can be executed has been exaggerated. In particular, the inherent difficulties of weaponising a WMD capability (as distinct from merely having access to WMD materials) has often been underestimated. To achieve a realistic understanding of the scope of the threat it is necessary to draw a clear distinction between nuclear, biological, and chemical weapons. Second, although it is important to temper assumptions about the 'inevitability' of WMD terrorism, it is equally important not to let the pendulum swing too far in the other direction.[2] There is abundant evidence that a wide range of terrorist outfits have actively sought WMD materials, and it is very likely that some have obtained them. While the challenges of weaponising WMD capabilities remain formidable, groups which invest enormous amounts of time, energy, and resources in endeavouring to acquire these capabilities have a very strong incentive to succeed, which itself should not be underestimated as a factor. On balance, there can be little doubt that once terrorist groups who are intent on acquiring a WMD capability gain that capability, they will seek to use it.

Can terrorists acquire WMD?

Starting from scratch

Accounts vary over the ease with which terrorist groups could acquire nuclear, chemical, and biological weapons. Nuclear weapons clearly remain the most powerful of the WMD triad in terms of the sheer destruction they can wreak. The demonstrated blast, heat and longer-term radiation effects of fission and fusion weapons mark them out as unrivalled in the history of warfare. Because of this, they are no doubt attractive from a terrorist standpoint: but how easy are they to acquire?

Those who maintain that nuclear weapons are accessible for terrorist groups point out that knowledge on 'how to build a bomb' is now freely available to anyone who has Internet access. They also point to documented lapses in Russia's nuclear system during the 1990s that indicated a leakage of weapons-grade fissile material on to the black market and a striking level of vulnerability in Russia to theft of tactical nuclear warheads and smaller atomic demolition munitions (Collina and Wolfsthal 2002). However, there is general consensus that nuclear weapons are more difficult to obtain than their chemical and biological counterparts. Despite some claims to the contrary, the core ingredients of weapons grade fissile material—highly enriched uranium and plutonium—are scarce internationally and very expensive to produce in sufficient quantities to manufacture even the crudest of nuclear devices. Moreover, since the mid-1980s, tight export controls have been observed by the small group of countries able to supply nuclear materials and equipment worldwide (Milhollin 2002). Even assuming that a terrorist organisation was able to amass enough fissile material to fabricate a nuclear device, the challenges of secure storage prior to use, the risks of being discovered transporting the device to the target area, and effective delivery would be prohibitive for all but the most sophisticated terrorist group.

A more readily attainable option would be acquiring the requisite materials to fabricate a radiological weapon, or 'dirty bomb' (i.e. conventional explosives laced with radioactive material aimed at propelling the latter across a wide area). There is some indication that elements of theAl Qaeda network have exhibited an interest in obtaining radioactive materials on the Russian black market for possible use in a 'dirty bomb', although it remains unclear whether their quest has been successful (see Warrick 2002; and Stout 2002). While yielding nowhere near the destructive effects of nuclear weapons, terrorist use of a radiological weapon could induce considerable panic among a target population by exploiting fears of radioactive poisoning. And unlike nuclear weapons, the materials required for a radiological weapon are widely used in 'unsecured' civilian applications such as medical imaging equipment. Although not usually included in the WMD threat template, radiological weapons could impose significant financial costs on the target state and would be an ideal terrorist weapon in severely disrupting public health and safety among a target population (Levi and Kelly 2002). As in the case of a complete nuclear warhead, however, terrorist groups would still confront significant challenges in transporting a radiological device over land, sea, or air and delivering that device against an assigned target.

The requisite technologies for manufacturing viable biological warfare (BW) agents and chemical warfare (CW) agents are widely available.[3] The inherent dual-use nature of these technologies means that many of the key ingredients comprising chemical and biological weapons can also be found in perfectly legitimate biotechnology and chemical industry sectors in any number of states around the world.[4] Indeed, it is generally agreed that if a country possesses a functioning civilian chemical or biotechnology industry then it is in a position to acquire the necessary materials to manufacture CW and BW agents. Certainly when compared with the difficulty of obtaining fissile material for manufacturing nuclear weapons, acquiring the requisite materials for constructing chemical and biological weapons is much less challenging for states and non-state entities alike. In many respects, a greater challenge for a terrorist organisation would be choosing the most appropriate CW or BW agent to weaponise for use against their designated target. As one authoritative US report has concluded, 'the ease or difficulty with which terrorists could cause mass casualties with an improvised chemical or biological weapon or device depends on the chemical or biological agent selected' (US General Accounting Office 1999: 10).

The use of CW agents by terrorist groups has provoked serious concern among observers, particularly since the 1995 sarin gas attack by the Aum Shinrikyo sect on the Tokyo subway which killed twelve and injured in excess of five thousand people. If the operation had not been botched, it is estimated that the attack could have killed thousands given the acutely lethal nature of the nerve agent used (Stern 1999: 64). Yet while a terrorist attack using chemical weapons cannot be ruled out, the prospect of terrorists employing biological weapons against population centres is now regarded as the most likely scenario across the entire WMD threat spectrum. Biological weapons are judged to be the ideal terrorist WMD instrument for three key reasons.

First, BW agents are far easier to acquire than nuclear weapons and it takes considerably less BW agent to produce the same killing impact as chemical weapons. Quantum leaps in biotechnology applications may mean revolutionary advances in drug discovery for treatment, but the very same quantum leaps can be used to broaden horizons for acquiring new, and refining existing, BW agents (Wheelis 2002). Moreover, on a pound for pound basis, BW agents are far more potent than any of the most deadly CW agents which must be 'delivered in massive quantities to inflict lethal concentrations over large areas' (Tucker 2000: 5). As Tucker (2000: 5) observes:

> [A] chemical attack that caused 50 per cent casualties over a square kilometre would require about a metric ton of sarin. In contrast, microorganisms infect people in minute doses and then multiply within the host to cause disease. For example, a mere 8,000 anthrax bacteria—an amount smaller than a speck of dust—are sufficient to infect a human being. As a result, a biological attack with a few kilograms of anthrax could inflict the same level of casualties over a square kilometer as a metric ton of sarin—provided that the anthrax was effectively disseminated.

Second, the effects of biological weapons on a target population would be extremely hard to counter. Administering vaccines and rendering more general medical assistance to a widely affected population would place unprecedented strains on emergency authorities (Katz 2002). This is assuming that an attack using BW agents could be detected in a timely fashion. Indeed, one of the major obstacles for state authorities would be detecting that a covert attack using BW agents had actually taken place. For instance, vaccination against the most contagious BW agent, smallpox, is only effective if administered within seven days of exposure to the virus. Yet during the early stages of contracting the virus, individuals merely exhibit flu-like symptoms making prompt diagnosis problematic. Left undetected for even a few days, smallpox has the potential to spread rapidly among the target population, creating an epidemic that could be impossible to contain (Chyba 2002: 134).

Third, the insidious nature of BW agents—composed as they are of living micro-organisms with the capacity to reproduce and mutate—has the potential to

104   *A. O'Neil*

psychologically 'unhinge' target populations. As one analyst has put it, 'because they are silent, stealthy, invisible, and slow acting, germs are capable of inducing levels of anxiety approaching hysteria (Regis 2001: 12). One only has to look at the American public's angst-ridden reaction to the tightly targeted anthrax attacks in October 2001 to appreciate the potential panic induced by a widespread terrorist attack involving BW agents. The fact that these attacks used small, though highly lethal, quantities of anthrax and were carried out by using a highly novel dissemination route (the postal service) merely served to accentuate the sense of vulnerability among the US public.

Although the necessary materials for manufacturing BW agents are relatively easy to acquire, it would be a mistake to assume that these materials can be easily weaponised for use against a target population. In order to ensure effective delivery to inflict mass casualties, a terrorist group would need to develop a powder or aerosol that could be disseminated over a wide geographical radius.[5] This requires considerable scientific skill and expertise that, most analysts agree, is still beyond the reach of most terrorist organisations (see Falkenrath 1998: 47; Chyba 2002: 127; and Parachini 2001: 4). One of the main reasons why the Aum Shinrikyo sect used the CW agent sarin in its 1995 Tokyo subway attack was that it had previously failed to develop sufficiently virulent BW strains of anthrax and botulinum toxin. This was despite the group being generously financed and its employment of some two dozen professionally trained microbiologists working in well-equipped scientific laboratories (Mangold and Goldberg 1999: 335–51).

Alternative avenues?

Given the intrinsic difficulties associated with manufacturing a viable WMD device from scratch, would terrorist groups have alternative avenues for acquiring such a capability? One possible scenario would be the theft of complete or partially complete devices from established state inventories. As noted earlier, the security and tracking systems for all categories of WMD remains woefully underdeveloped in the FSU, especially Russia. But this is not to say that the latter would be the only target for terrorist groups intent on pilfering a WMD device. The 2001 anthrax attacks in the US were carried out with material that appears to have come from the US defence establishment, an establishment that has maintained some of the tightest security and tracking systems in the world (Cirincione, Wolfsthal, and Rajkumar 2002: 181–84).

Another scenario is that a nuclear, biological or chemical weapon could be provided to a terrorist organisation by a state that remains sympathetic to the terrorists' motives and aims. This threat has gained increased currency in US policy-making circles, with the Bush administration linking international terrorist networks with individual states it alleges are actively seeking WMD capabilities— Iran, Iraq, and North Korea (*The Economist* 2002). Yet despite these states having demonstrated a willingness to sponsor terrorist activities in the past, it is doubtful whether any state would transfer WMD to a non-state entity, assuming they were in a position to do so. It is difficult to imagine any state that would be willing to risk being discovered as having links with a terrorist group that had attacked US targets (for instance) with WMD, let alone one that would be willing to furnish such a group with a WMD capability. For as long as regime preservation remains the paramount credo in Iran, Iraq, and North Korea, it is highly improbable that ruling elites would risk certain US retaliation (probably with nuclear weapons) in the wake of a WMD attack on American territory.

However, this cautious approach could be revised if a leadership elite found itself in mortal peril. While regime preservation may be the overriding priority in Baghdad, if the regime judged that its demise was imminent in the latter stages of a war with the United States, then it is entirely plausible that it would attempt to use all the WMD assets at its disposal. This could well include nuclear, biological, or chemical weapons supplied to terrorist groups for use against targets on the American mainland or targets in Israel. With the regime's demise imminent, there would be little, if any, incentive to exercise restraint and no fear of retaliation from the United States and its allies (O'Neil 2002: 14–15). Other countries for whom 'contracting out' WMD terrorism may be an option are US adversaries (possibly including China) who fear the longer term strategic implications of National Missile Defence (NMD). If Washington successfully deploys NMD, these states may be more inclined to consider using terrorists as 'delivery systems' if the option of delivering their WMD payloads against US targets with long range missiles has been effectively nullified (Glaser and Fetter 2001: 54–57). In such a scenario these states may well calculate that they would not be identified as the source of an attack.

What is the likelihood of terrorists using WMD?

Norms and strategic value

Just as the issue of WMD accessibility for terrorist groups is contested, so too is the question of whether such groups would actually use WMD in certain circumstances. Scepticism towards the notion that terrorists will seek to use WMD is largely predicated on accepting the much-quoted observation of US terrorist expert Brian Jenkins that 'terrorists want a lot of people watching and a lot of people listening, not a lot of people dead' (quoted in Hoffman 1998: 198). Traditionalists like Jenkins, who maintain that the WMD threat is exaggerated, point to the fact that historically few terrorist groups have shown an active interest in acquiring a capability to inflict mass casualties in the thousands or tens of thousands. According to this line of thinking, the best assurance we have that a mass casualty terrorist attack involving WMD will not happen is that it hasn't happened yet. While terrorist groups by their very nature aim to effect radical political and social change, an attack on this scale could not be vindicated by any conceivable ideology (see Kamp 1998–99: 170). No terrorist group, so the argument goes, would risk attracting the international opprobrium such a mass casualty attack would provoke. From this perspective, although terrorists may be violent, they are also rational and

106   A. O'Neil

calculating; they understand that a mass casualty attack using WMD would serve no instrumental purpose in propagating their ideology and objectives.

However, this traditionalist argument overlooks several important variables which suggest that, far from being remote, the likelihood of terrorist groups that have acquired nuclear, chemical, or biological weapons using these weapons is increasingly plausible. The most conspicuous of these variables is that non-state actors in international relations do not, as a general rule, operate according to the same normative constraints as sovereign states (Starr 1995: 306). While there is strong circumstantial evidence to support the claim that a norm of WMD non-use has evolved over time among states, there are few grounds for assuming that terrorist organisations will necessarily adhere to this norm. Indeed, the inherent shock value of terrorism is essentially based on the willingness of terrorist groups to flout generally accepted international norms of behaviour. Moreover, the perceived strategic merits of WMD are likely to outweigh any normative considerations for most terrorists. Due to the unprecedented mass casualties that they can cause, nuclear, biological, and chemical weapons are optimal instruments for achieving the asymmetric warfare strategy that lies at the heart of terrorist operations (Lesser 1999: 94–96; for broader discussion of asymmetric warfare strategies, see Arreguin-Toft 2001). Avoiding confrontation with a target state where it is strongest (in conventional military terms), the modus operandi of terrorist groups has been to strike states where they are most vulnerable to attack (in densely populated cities). From a terrorist perspective, using WMD would graphically illustrate a capacity to inflict maximum damage against a stronger power at a time and place of the terrorist group's own choosing.

The rise of 'new' terrorism

But the single most important variable that makes terrorist use of WMD increasingly credible is the changing nature of the underlying philosophy of terrorist groups themselves. International terrorism has, over time, become a more complex phenomenon. Long gone are the days when terrorism was exemplified by the gun-toting anarchist seeking to overturn a corrupt political order within the strict confines of state borders. The terrorist of the twenty-first century is exemplified by the operative who is part of a loose, yet sophisticated, transnational network whose goal is to overturn *global* trends that are deemed to be in profound conflict with their core religious or political beliefs (see Chalk 1999). Throughout the last decade of the twentieth century, the capacity of terrorist groups to organise themselves into transnational networks for the purpose of coordinating operations across different continents was significantly enhanced by the rapid globalisation of information technologies. The most well-known of these groups, Al Qaeda, used coded e-mail communications and posted encrypted messages on various Internet web sites to coordinate several high profile attacks during the 1990s as well as the 11 September attacks on the American mainland (Brownfeld 2001; and Risen and Engelberg 2001).

In the mid to late 1990s, official and non-official analysts began distinguishing between the ideology of 'old' terrorism and 'new' terrorism. Encompassing groups such as ETA, the IRA, and the various 'Red' terrorist cells operating in Western Europe during the Cold War, the 'old' paradigm of terrorism was characterised by a calculation that indiscriminate or excessive violence would have the effect of undermining claims of legitimacy among domestic constituencies and international public opinion more generally. In eschewing mass casualty attacks of the type carried out by Aum Shinrikyo and Al Qaeda, old-style terrorist groups sought to preserve their eligibility for a seat at the post-conflict negotiating table. In short, these groups regarded themselves as fundamentally part of the political process, not separate from it (Stevenson 2001: 153–54).

Examples of the new terrorism include extremist fundamentalist organisations, millenarian and apocalyptic-inspired sects, and radical anti-government 'hate' groups. In marked contrast to the old terrorist groups, who invariably rationalised violence as an instrument for achieving a clear-cut political strategy, the violence employed by new terrorist groups is far less discriminating and far more lethal as a consequence. As evidenced over the last decade, the terrorist operations performed by these groups have frequently (and deliberately) failed to distinguish between 'legitimate' targets symbolising 'corrupt' state authority (such as military installations and police barracks) and civilian sectors of the population. The single most influential element uniting new terrorist groups has been hard-core religious dogma. Groups such as Al Qaeda, Aum Shinrikyo, and the various Christian Identity organisations active in the West are each inspired by the doctrine of 'cosmic war', in which violence is seen as the only means to achieve 'moral restoration' (Juergensmeyer 2001: 145–63). According to this mindset, violent acts 'are 'sanitised' because they are symbolic, enacted on a cosmic stage' (Simon and Benjamin 2000: 66). Engaged in a cosmic struggle where 'a satanic enemy cannot be transformed, only destroyed', the intensity of the violence used in specific terrorist acts is unconstrained by 'worldly' ethical considerations (Juergensmeyer 2001: 217). As Peter Chalk has observed:

> The prevalence of radical religious imperatives [...] has significant implications for the lethality of terrorism. For the religious zealot, there is essentially no reason to show restraint in the perpetration of violence. The main objective is to inflict as much pain and suffering as possible, with the enemy typically denigrated as fundamentally evil and beyond all redemption.

In sum, terrorist groups subscribing to this form of ideology are much more likely to be attracted to the mass destructive properties of WMD than terrorist organisations have been in the past.

Has the WMD terrorist threat increased since 11 September 2001?

Would a terrorist group actively attempt to acquire and use WMD when the events of 11 September 2001 showed that spectacular attacks can be staged using fully fuel-laden hijacked civilian airliners? The short answer is that a successful large-scale use of nuclear, chemical, or biological weapons would make the events of 11 September pale in comparison. The mass casualties resulting from a large-scale WMD attack against US urban centres has been the most important issue exercising the collective minds of American national security agencies post-11 September. A leaked US intelligence report in March 2002 estimated that a ten kiloton nuclear device (of similar yield to the Hiroshima bomb) detonated in lower Manhattan would kill over one hundred thousand people instantly, poison several hundred thousand people with radiation sickness, and level all infrastructure standing within one kilometre of the blast's epicentre (Gellman 2002). An extensive attack against an urban centre with an acutely lethal chemical weapon such as the nerve agent sarin could potentially kill thousands and render the surrounding area a heavily contaminated zone for an extended period of time. While slower in its impact, a successful large-scale attempt to target densely populated centres with a highly contagious BW agent such as smallpox would trigger an epidemic of unparalleled scope in the modern era.

On balance, the likelihood of a terrorist organisation using WMD has increased in the wake of the 11 September attacks for two reasons. First, the events of 11 September exposed—much more dramatically than did the 1993 World Trade Centre attack and the 1995 Oklahoma City bombing—the vulnerability of open societies like the United States to large-scale terrorist strikes. The Al Qaeda operatives who carried out the 11 September attacks were inserted into the US, received flight school training in the US, coordinated their pre-attack planning in the US, hijacked the airliners from US airports, and successfully struck high value targets on American soil without warning. To be sure, any terrorist group with a serious grudge against the United States and its democratic allies will take heart from the events of 11 September. While the United States and allies including Australia have taken some significant steps to bolster early warning and crisis response capabilities (see, for example, Gellman 2002; Connolly 2002; and Hill 2002), their cities will continue to remain extremely vulnerable to terrorist attacks involving WMD.[6]

Second, the events of 11 September set an entirely new benchmark, or threshold, for future terrorist attacks. There can be little doubt that the motivation to 'surpass 11 September' will be a strong incentive for future terrorist groups contemplating the use of WMD. Never before had thousands been killed in a single terrorist attack. That the most powerful country in the international system was the target merely added potency to its psychological impact. As Jenkins (2001: 4) has argued, the events of 11 September created 'a new level of destruction toward which other terrorists will strive'. Rather than being cowed by the 2001 attacks, the Bush administration responded forcefully by declaring a 'War on Terrorism' and expelling Al Qaeda from its home base in Afghanistan. Yet, it is far less certain whether the United States would be able to cope with a massive WMD strike against a key urban centre such as Los Angeles, with fatalities ranging in the tens of thousands. Would the US public be willing to maintain its support for America's global strategic commitments following such an attack? The US public may well conclude that the benefits flowing from American global hegemony are far outweighed by the costs of being a terrorist target. In this scenario, it is certainly conceivable that public pressure for the United States to return to its pre-1941 isolationalist policy would be too intense for any administration to resist. The subsequent unravelling of America's strategic alliances in the Asia-Pacific, Europe, and the Middle East would inject a degree of instability into international relations not witnessed since the end of the Cold War. Some terrorist groups could well judge that this possibility more than justifies any endeavour to launch a large-scale WMD assault along the lines sketched above.

Conclusion

Given the high stakes involved, it is all too easy to exaggerate possible scenarios involving terrorists using WMD. Yet it is equally easy to dismiss possible threat scenarios as being unduly alarmist. As the head of the United Nation's Terrorism Prevention Branch has remarked, the greatest challenge in evaluating the WMD terrorist threat is 'walking the fine line between fear and paranoia on the one hand, and prudence and disbelief on the other' (Schmid 2000: 108).

One of the most prevalent features in mainstream discussions of WMD terrorism has been the conflation of motive and capability. All too often observers assume that simply because terrorist groups are motivated to acquire WMD they will be successful in doing so. A related assumption is that once terrorists gain access to WMD materials they will, ipso facto, be able to build a weapon and deliver it against assigned targets. The prevalence of this approach has meant that insufficient attention has been paid to addressing the key issue of accessibility to nuclear, chemical, and biological weapons on the part of terrorist groups and the likelihood of such groups actually using WMD. Consequently, the challenging nature of assessing the threat of WMD terrorism has frequently been overlooked in much of the academic literature. Simply accepting at face value the hypothesis that WMD terrorism is only 'a matter of time' is no substitute for detailed and measured threat assessment. As I have argued, the issue is complex and not one that lends itself to hard and fast conclusions.

On the one hand, I demonstrated that it remains very difficult for all but the most technologically advanced terrorist organisations to successfully weaponise nuclear material and CW and BW agents for delivery against targets. This is particularly the case with respect to nuclear weapons, but also holds true for chemical and biological weapons. In the case of biological weapons—which have become the most feared category of WMD in terms of likely terrorist use—although the requisite material for devising BW agents is widely available, the skill and expertise for effectively weaponising a BW agent is still seemingly beyond terrorist groups. Overall, acquiring WMD capabilities for delivery against targets is a lot harder for terrorists than is generally acknowledged in the literature.

On the other hand, however, it is clear that contemporary terrorists have fewer moral scruples about initiating mass casualty attacks targeting civilian populations than the terrorists of yesteryear. Since the end of the Cold War, terrorism has become far more lethal in its scope due to the increasingly indiscriminate violence sanctioned by new terrorist groups such as Al Qaeda. In short, contrary to the view

110 *A. O'Neil*

held in some quarters, terrorists of today are far more likely to use WMD (assuming they can weaponise capabilities) than those in the past. As I have argued, this trend will only be strengthened in the wake of the 11 September 2001 attacks which graphically underscored the vulnerability of open societies like the United States to mass casualty attacks, while setting a new threshold for future terrorist attacks worldwide.

Notes

1. Nuclear terrorism was the primary concern during the Cold War period. The United States devoted considerable resources to putting in place contingency plans specifically designed to counter this threat. Between 1975 and 1981 alone it is estimated that the US Nuclear Emergency Search Team (a specialist unit attached to the Department of Energy) was tasked with investigating *plausible* threats involving nuclear devices in no less than eight separate major urban centres. See Richelson (2002).
2. Existing examples of exaggerated scepticism about the WMD terrorist threat range from dismissing the threat as 'somewhat fanciful' (Spear 1997: 114–15) to overlooking it through omission (see, for instance, Butfoy 2001; and Martin 2002).
3. CW agents rely on the toxic properties of chemical substances, rather than explosive properties, to inflict physical and physiological effects on an enemy. Similarly, BW agents rely on their innate properties rather than any explosive power to cause casualties. But unlike CW agents, BW agents exploit naturally occurring and genetically modified infectious diseases by spreading them among the target population.
4. For instance, one of the most basic CW choking agents, phosgene, is widely used in the international chemical industry as a chlorinating substance.
5. This is not to say that much cruder systems of delivery could not be effective in causing significant casualties among a target population. One possible 'delivery system' that has been canvassed in sections of the literature is the 'suicide sneezer' who is deliberately infected with a lethal and highly contagious BW agent and charged with the mission of circulating among the target population. See Zilinskas (2001: 441).
6. A recent study commissioned by the Council on Foreign Relations and chaired by former US Senators Gary Hart and Warren Rudman concluded that 'A year after [11 September], America remains dangerously unprepared to prevent and respond to a catastrophic terrorist attack on US soil'. See Mintz (2002).

References

Arreguin-Toft, A., 2001. 'How the Weak Win Wars: A Theory of Asymmetric Conflict', *International Security*, 26, 1: 93–128.

Brownfeld, A, 2001. 'Bin Ladin's Activities Exposed in New York Trial', *Jane's Terrorism & Security Monitor*, 14 March, http://janes.com/security/international_security/news/jtsm/jtsm010314_1_n.shtml

Butfoy, A., 2001. 'Controlling the Spread of Weapons of Mass Destruction', in M. Hanson and W. Tow (eds), *International Relations in the New Century: An Australian Perspective* (South Melbourne: Oxford University Press): 38–54.

Chalk, P., 1999. 'The Evolving Dynamic of Terrorism in the 1990s', *Australian Journal of International Affairs*, 53, 2: 151–67.

Chyba, C., 2002. 'Toward Biological Security', *Foreign Affairs*, 81, 3: 122–36.

Cirincione, J., J. Wolfsthal, and M. Rajkumar, 2002. *Deadly Arsenals: Tracking Weapons of Mass Destruction* (Washington DC: Carnegie Endowment for International Peace).

Collina, T. and J. Wolfsthal, 2002. 'Nuclear Terrorism and Warhead Control in

Terrorist use of weapons of mass destruction   111

Russia', *Arms Control Today*, April,
http://www.armscontrol.org/act/2002_04/colwolfapril02.asp

Connolly, C., 2002. 'Smallpox Vaccine Program Readied', *Washington Post*, 8 July.

Falkenrath, R., 1998. 'Confronting Nuclear, Biological and Chemical Terrorism', *Survival*, 40, 3: 43–65.

Gellman, B., 2002. 'Fears Prompt US to Beef Up Nuclear Terror Detection', *Washington Post*, 3 March.

Glaser, C. and S. Fetter, 2001. 'National Missile Defence and the Future of US Nuclear Weapons Policy', *International Security*, 26, 1: 40–92.

Hill, R., 2002. 'Defence Recruiting New Scientists to Combat Terrorism', *Media Release, Senator the Hon. Robert Hill, Minister for Defence*, MIN 431/02, 28 August.

Hoffman, B., 1996. 'Intelligence and Terrorism: Emerging Threats and New Security Challenges in the Post-Cold War Era', *Intelligence and National Security*, 11, 2: 207–223.

——1998. *Inside Terrorism* (New York: Columbia University Press).

Jenkins, B., 2001. *Statement of Brian Michael Jenkins, Senior Adviser to the President of the RAND Corporation Before the Senate Armed Services Subcommittee on Emerging Threats, 15 November 2001.*

Juergensmeyer, M., 2001. *Terror in the Mind of God: The Global Rise of Religious Violence* (Berkeley and Los Angeles: University of California Press).

Kamp, K., 1998–99. 'Nuclear Terrorism is Not the Core Problem', *Survival*, 40, 4: 168–71.

Katz, R., 2002. 'Public Health Preparedness: The Best Defence Against Biological Weapons', *The Washington Quarterly*, 25, 3: 69–82.

Laqueur, W., 1996. 'Postmodern Terrorism', *Foreign Affairs*, 75, 5: 24–37.

Lesser, I., 1999. 'Countering the New Terrorism: Implications for Strategy', in I. Lesser *et al.* (eds), *Countering the New Terrorism* (Santa Monica: Rand Corporation): 85–144.

Levi, M. and H. Kelly, 2002. 'Weapons of Mass Disruption', *Scientific American*, November: 77–81.

Mangold, T. and J. Goldberg, 1999. *Plague Wars: A True Story of Biological Warfare* (London: Macmillan).

Martin, S., 2002. 'The Role of Biological Weapons in International Politics: The Real Military Revolution', *The Journal of Strategic Studies*, 25, 1: 63–98.

Milhollin, G., 2002. 'Can Terrorists Get the Bomb?', *Commentary*, 113, 2: 45–49.

Mintz, J., 2002. 'Report: US Still Vulnerable', *Washington Post*, 25 October.

O'Neil, A., 2002. 'Waging War Against Iraq: Rationale, Possibilities, and Risks', *AQ: Journal of Contemporary Analysis*, 74, 4: 12–15.

Parachini, J., 2001. *Combating Terrorism: Assessing the Threat of Biological Terrorism—Testimony Before the Subcommittee on National Security, Veteran's Affairs, and International Relations, Committee on Government Reform, US House of Representatives, 12 October 2001.*

Regis, E. 2001. 'Does Mass Biopanic Portend Mass Destruction?', *Scientific American*, December: 11–13.

Richelson, J., 2002. 'Defusing Nuclear Terror', *Bulletin of the Atomic Scientists*, March-April, http://www.thebulletin.org/issues/2002/ma02/ma02richelson.html

Risen, J. and S. Engelberg, 2001. 'Failure to Heed Signs of Change in Terror Goals', *New York Times*, 14 October.

Sands, A., 2002. 'Deconstructing the Chem-Bio Threat: Testimony for the United States Senate Foreign Relations Committee, 19 March 2002', *CNS Report*, Monterey Institute of International Studies, http://www.cns.miis.edu/pubs/reports/asands.htm

Schmid, A., 2000. 'Terrorism and the Use of Weapons of Mass Destruction: From Where the Risk?', in M. Taylor and J. Horgan (eds), *The Future of Terrorism* (London: Frank Cass): 106–32.

Simon, S. and D. Benjamin, 2000. 'America and the New Terrorism', *Survival*, 42, 1: 59–75.

Spear, J., 1997. 'Arms and Arms Control', in B. White, R. Little and M. Smith (eds), *Issues in World Politics* (London: Macmillan Press): 111–133.

Starr, H., 1995. 'International Law and International Order', in C. Kegley (ed.), *Controversies in*

112   *A. O'Neil*

    International Relations Theory: Realism and the Neoliberal Challenge (St Martin's Press: New York): 299–315.
Stern, J., 1998–99. 'Apocalypse Never, But the Threat is Real', *Survival*, 40, 4: 176–79.
——1999. *The Ultimate Terrorists* (Cambridge: Harvard University Press).
Stevenson, J., 2001. 'Terrorism: New Meets Old', *Survival*, 43, 2: 153–57.
Stout, D., 2002. 'US Arrests American Accused of Planning "Dirty Bomb" Attack', *New York Times*, 10 June.
The Economist, 2002. 'George Bush and the Axis of Evil', 2 February: 13–14.
Tucker, J., 2000. 'Introduction', in J. Tucker (ed.), *Toxic Terror: Assessing Terrorist Use of Chemical and Biological Weapons* (Boston: MIT Press): 1–14.
US General Accounting Office, 1999. *Combating Terrorism: Need for Comprehensive Threat and Risk Assessments of Chemical and Biological Attacks* (Washington DC: US General Accounting Office).
Warrick, J., 2002. 'Hunting a Deadly Soviet Legacy', *Washington Post*, 11 November.
Wheelis, M., 2002. 'Biotechnology and Biochemical Weapons', *The Nonproliferation Review*, 9, 1: 48–53.
Zilinskas, R., 2001. 'Rethinking Bioterrorism', *Current History*, 100, 650: 438–42.

[2]

Hypothetical Integrative Medical Strategies for the Prevention and Treatment of Bio-terrorism Incidents

JEFFRY L. ANDERSON MD,[1] ERIC GORDON MD,[2]
STEPHEN A. LEVINE PhD,[3] ROGER MORRISON MD[4] AND
MICHAEL E. ROSENBAUM MD[1]

[1]*Corte Madera, CA,* [2]*Santa Rosa, CA,* [3]*Kentfield, CA,* [4]*Hahnemann Clinic,
Pt. Richmond, CA, USA*

Abstract
*The authors present proposed hypothetical protocols addressing both the prevention and
treatment of acute anthrax and smallpox, as may occur in relation to bio-terrorism events
or incidents. The potential benefit of additional or 'integrative' modalities with conventional
allopathic approaches is discussed, with specific emphasis on applied medical nutrition and
homeopathy. An in-depth discussion of the pathophysiology of inhalation anthrax and a
unique approach to intervention based on seminal research by Hanna et al. is presented;
the treatment protocol includes aggressive parenteral administration of N-acetyl cysteine
and other nutriceutical antioxidants, as well as inhalation therapy with L-glutathione.*

Keywords: bio-terrorism, anthrax, smallpox, homeopathy, N-acetyl cysteine, L-glutathione, intravenous
therapies.

INTRODUCTION AND SITUATION ANALYSIS

Conventional medical protocols for inhalation anthrax cited by professional publications and
by the news media recommend a course of treatment utilizing aggressive pharmaceutical
intervention with intravenous antibiotic administration of doxycycline, penicillin or
ciprofloxacin, depending on specific strain sensitivities, plus electrolyte and fluid replacement, glucocorticoids and respiratory/life support [1–4]. Because the reported mortality rate
range (depending on the source) is 30–80% in presenting symptomatic patients, regardless
of the time of initiation or the aggressiveness of this approach, this protocol may be 'correct',
but inadequate. In most cases, the pathogenic cascade of events may be irreversible by the
time of symptom onset.

Epidemic smallpox is a more difficult problem to address with respect to both prevention
and treatment. The causative agent, a virus in the orthopoxvirus family, could be disseminated widely through micro-aerosol technology, similar to anthrax; however, unlike anthrax,
it is highly communicable through intrapersonal contact and it poses difficult epidemiological
challenges, e.g. isolation and quarantine procedures. Complicating matters further is the
unfortunate fact that the vast majority of our population is either unvaccinated or experiences
minimal residual immunity from distant vaccination. Finally, the fundamental nature of viral
infections and the lack of any specific antiviral drugs against the smallpox virus markedly
limit treatment options within the conventional medical paradigm [5].

It is imperative to explore the potential efficacy of integrative medical modalities that
combine conventional or traditional medical protocols to improve results and potentially

302   J. L. ANDERSON *ET AL.*

save thousands of lives. The probability of major benefits with low to minimum adverse side-effects is significant. Through the development of integrative medical strategies that address prevention as well as treatment, the intention of this paper is to aid and empower our physicians, healthcare workers, government agencies and postal service in protecting our citizens, our families and our lives.

MEETING THE CHALLENGE

Due to the increasing threat of bio-terrorism and chemo-terrorism, the development of a plan that outlines prospective procedures for medical intervention and interdiction pertaining to potential terrorist events seems prudent. The strategies addressed in this paper support conventional medical modalities and are based on concepts associated with the integrative, complementary and holistic healthcare paradigm. The plan contains both prevention and treatment protocols and specifically addresses the problems of anthrax and smallpox.

The rationale and necessity for these protocols are based on: (1) the possibility of inadequate preparedness of local, state and federal government public health agencies; (2) the possible limited availability of supplies of crucial antibiotics, vaccines, antidotes and other medical materials; (3) the potential that the response capabilities of local and regional medical care facilities may be overwhelmed due to excessive demand; (4) the potential for a significantly high morbidity and failure rate associated with (a) a probable high incidence of adverse effects of vaccines, antiviral and antibiotic pharmaceuticals and (b) the possible emergence of antibiotic resistance.

These problems can be addressed by the judicious use of a multi-disciplined, integrated medical approach that addresses the prevention and treatment of these potentially devastating bio-terrorism incidents.

The issue of chemo-terrorism will not be addressed in this paper. The potential for chemical warfare and terrorism is currently poorly defined, and the list of possible chemical toxic agents that could be utilized is extensive, including pesticides of at least two major categories, nerve gases, heavy metal compounds, common rodenticides and other agents. In addition, the possible routes of introduction and dissemination of chemical weapons are myriad and both the preventative and treatment options (e.g. antidotes) are, at the same time, more limited and more complex.

Sources of research materials for this outline include current and historical peer-reviewed scientific literature and texts, expert opinion and publications generated by specific professional individuals, information from governmental agencies (Centers for Disease Control, National Institutes of Health) and professional medical organizations (American Academy of Environmental Medicine, American Medical Association), as well as personal experience and knowledge. The authors must stress that some of the treatment strategies presented here are in the realm of predictive hypothesis, based on *in vitro* and *in vivo* animal model studies, in particular, a seminal study published by Hanna *et al.* in 1994 [6]. In that and subsequent studies, discussed in more detail later, the similarity of interactive pathophysiological mechanisms between anthrax toxin(s) and both mouse and human macrophages and other immune defense parameters was described, and hypothetical strategies for therapeutic intervention offered [6, 7]. Because there have been no major occurrences of smallpox or human anthrax for many decades, there has been no opportunity for human application of these protocols. Nonetheless, the potential benefit of these protocols and their minimal adverse effects is significant.

PREVENTION: GENERAL MEASURES

Defense against Contamination

Good personal hygiene practices are important. However, with respect to anthrax and smallpox, some significant factors exist. Anthrax is not communicable and it cannot be passed on from one infected person to another; infection only occurs through direct contact with anthrax (*Bacillus anthracis*) spores via (1) inhalation, producing the respiratory and most serious form, (2) ingestion, producing the less serious gastrointestinal form, (3) skin contact, producing the least serious cutaneous form. Therefore, it is paramount to follow published guidelines established by governmental agencies including the Centers for Disease Control, the Surgeon General, and the National Institutes of Health, regarding the handling of mail or other sources of airborne dissemination [1, 3]. Anthrax spores are very hardy and survive extreme conditions of heat, cold, and humidity. Although typical bacteriostatic/bacteriocidal soaps have little effect in killing anthrax spores, it is important to thoroughly irrigate and flush all suspected contact body surfaces at least with water, including the mouth and nose, to minimize the concentration of spores.

In contrast, smallpox is unusually communicable, especially via respiratory droplet broadcast through sneezing, coughing, inhalation or ingestion. The smallpox virus, unlike anthrax spores, is very susceptible to inactivation by air contact, heat, and low humidity. Quarantine and isolation procedures are therefore warranted [5]. The main focus on prevention involves strategies to generally enhance the individual's innate immune system defense mechanisms, which are applicable in both prevention and treatment regardless of the nature of the infecting organism. Some strategies are specifically unique to anthrax and smallpox.

Prevention through Enhancement of the Immune System

Environmental factors. Absorption and accumulation of environmental pollutants and toxins can interfere with the normal function of the immune system and the body's built-in detoxification and cell repair mechanisms [8–10]. Toxins come in many forms and from many sources. They are impossible to avoid entirely as they contaminate our food, water and air supply. In the event of a bio-terrorism incident, measures should be taken to avoid excessive and/or prolonged exposures that can create cellular damage. Important pollutants/ poisons to avoid include (a) pesticides, herbicides, and fungicides that are neurotoxic, (b) oil-based and marine paints containing petrochemicals, (c) chemical solvents and sealers, (d) petroleum distillate and combustion products, (e) heavy metals including mercury, lead and cadmium, and (f) soft synthetic rubber and plastics [8]. Some of this can be accomplished by using less toxic alternative building and decorative materials, non-toxic bio-integral pest/weed management in the home and garden and less toxic materials in hobbies and crafts.

Enhancing the body's ability to mobilize and excrete toxins is extremely beneficial. The most effective methods include: depuration through regular aerobic exercise, saunas or sweat lodges; skin brushing with a lufa or body brush; drinking plenty of pure water (eight or more glasses per day of purified or bottled water), and optimizing bowel elimination. Adhering to a balanced healthy diet and using supportive nutritional supplementation is essential to health enhancement in the event of a bio-terrorism incident [8].

Endogenous toxins generated through metabolic processes and digestive putrefaction can also be very damaging if they accumulate due to inadequate elimination and detoxification and will enhance the effects of a bio-terrorism incident. Poor intestinal health contributes significantly to this problem and is often related to deficient beneficial (bacteria) or excessive pathological (bacteria, yeast/fungi, parasite) intestinal flora. This condition is often caused by or aggravated by factors such as overzealous use of antibiotics, allied constipation, contaminated or poorly cooked/prepared food, excessive dietary sugar and insufficient fiber intake [11–15]. Treatment by healthcare professionals is sometimes necessary in persistent or chronic situations. However, simply cleaning up the diet, avoiding pollutants and additives in food, correcting sluggish elimination/constipation and using probiotics (beneficial flora, e.g. *Lactobacillus acidophilus* and other species) and fiber supplements is often very beneficial. The inclusion of one to two servings of vegetables and fruits per day from each major color group (red, yellow-orange, green, blue-purple) provides a wide variety of important antioxidants and plant sterols/sterolins, which, acting synergistically, enhance immune defense [16–18].

Diet/nutrition. The prevention and treatment of bio-terrorist viral and bacterial infections requires an immune response that is on 'red alert'. Each compartment of the immune system must be able to be readily activated to attain peak performance.

There are two fundamental components of the immune activity: the innate response and the acquired response. Innate immunity represents phylogenetically the oldest immune response and consists of non-specific reactions by macrophages and natural killer cells. The acquired response is mediated by T and B cells and confers specific immunity. The innate response is immediate and non-specific; the acquired response may require several weeks after exposure to a pathogen to evolve and is specific [19]. Diet and specific nutrients play an active role in modulating the immune response [16–18].

General, broad-based supplementation with various nutrient formulas and herbs can support immune system function and metabolic detoxification mechanisms [8–10, 16–18, 20]. The most appropriate approach is to use low doses of multiple factors in combination, to provide the best additive and synergistic beneficial effects with the least chance of side-effects or 'overload' [17, 18]. There are many excellent formulas marketed by numerous manufacturers. The general supplement recommendations of the authors include: B complex vitamins; vitamins A, C, D, E, K; mixed carotenoids; mixed flavones/flavinoids; a balanced array of trace minerals including zinc and selenium; amino acids; essential fatty acids; enzymes and co-enzymes; and herbs or their extracts such as milk thistle weed seed, green tea, astragalus and echinachea (the latter should be used intermittently, no more than 1 week per month separate or mixed with other appropriate herbs). The adjunctive use of digestive enzymes (plant or animal based) can optimize the efficient absorption and assimilation of nutrients.

Individualized supplement programs can be designed to meet unique or specific needs. For instance, for individuals with an impaired immune response due to age, disease states or malnutrition, more aggressive protocols using higher doses of the above listed factors as well as more complex immune potentiating factors can be utilized. Current, state-of-the-art laboratory diagnostic technology can be utilized to measure both cellular and humoral immune response parameters, as well as specific nutritional deficiencies.

There is a variety of specific nutritional factors known to enhance the immune response. The innate immune response is generally activated by antioxidants and by beta-glucans extracted from the cell walls of bakers' yeast, therapeutic mushrooms and micro-algae species such as chlorella and spirulina [21–25]. Plant sterols and sterolins are also very beneficial [26–28].

The T lymphocyte response is directly augmented by zinc—a trace mineral that tends to be deficient in children, pregnant women and in the elderly [29–32]. A zinc deficiency may be readily determined by a red blood cell zinc assay. Other nutritional T cell stimulants include colostrum, typically of bovine origin (goat rarely), which contains a panoply of immune factors including secretory antibodies that confer passive immunity, transfer factors, immune cytokines and lactoferrin. These three components may be fractionated from colostrum and administered individually in much higher doses than that present in the colostrum itself. The donor animals also may be 'hyperimmunized' against a particular pathogen to enrich the content of that particular transfer factor (antigen specific of 'educated' transfer factor). For example, it may be possible to inoculate cows with an attenuated form of anthrax or smallpox to produce specific immune peptides in their colostrum that can transfer that specific immunity to the people who ingest it.

Lactoferrin is an iron-binding protein present in most mammalian exocrine gland secretions. It is present in particularly high concentrations in colostrum where it serves as a potent antibiotic and immune stimulant [33–42]. Lactoferrin:

- acts as a potent antioxidant by sequestering iron which, in its free state, can instigate the production of dangerous hydroxyl free radicals;
- inactivates a wide variety of viruses and bacteria;
- attracts neutrophils to zones of inflammation;
- enhances T cell growth and development;
- inactivates tumor necrosis factor-alpha, a key pro-inflammatory cytokine that may be responsible for much of the symptom complex in anthrax (see below).

Oriental herbs can also be very effective in enhancing immune defenses. Astragalus is one of the best studied herbs known to enhance specific immune response. It stimulates T cells, especially Th1 subsets. A member of the licorice family, astragalus can also markedly enhance cytotoxic and natural killer cell activity [43–49]. Echinachea particularly enhances the innate immune response through stimulation of macrophages and also probably natural killer cells [50–52].

More complex individualized herbal formulas can be prescribed by appropriate practitioners, which may contain more esoteric herbs utilized for different effects, including the synergistic enhancement or modulation of the principal herb(s), detoxifying, cooling, heating, etc. A word of caution: oriental herbs can be very potent, especially when used in complex formulations, and can be potentially toxic, often due to contamination with heavy metals, drug additives and chemicals associated with poor regulation and quality control. Thus, scrupulous investigation regarding the purity and source integrity (growers, packagers, shipping methods, etc.) of herbal medicinals is paramount. Advanced practitioners of oriental medicine are the most appropriate source of pure herbal materials and individualized prescribing.

Lifestyle/the mind–body–spirit connection. Mainstream scientific research has increasingly demonstrated the profound influence of psychological, emotional and spiritual states on the integrity of the body's immune response. Experiences of anger, hate, resentment, fear, despair can measurably impair the body defenses, whereas love, compassion, faith, hope and serenity can enhance the same defenses. Prayer and meditation have been shown to be powerful stimulants to healing and immune system function in several seminal studies [53–59].

In this context, there are many valuable and available approaches to enhance the body's defense/immune system processes. They include various somatic, movement, 'energy', and meditative oriented modalities including advanced osteopathy, structural body work, massage, versions of Qi Gung, Tai Chi and Yoga, transcendental and other meditation practices, etc. The application of one or several of these approaches combined with a daily spiritual practice, as well as involvement in nurturing relationships and community, and the pursuit of one's unique creative expression and regular interaction with nature will serve well in supporting the body's defenses and healing potential.

SPECIFIC TREATMENT PROTOCOLS

Anthrax

Background scientific rationale. Anthrax is caused by the Gram-positive, spore-forming rod, *Bacillus anthracis*. The virulence of this organism is dependent on the presence of a poly-D-glutamic acid capsule and the production of proteinaceous toxins. Production of the toxins and capsule is due to the presence of two genetic plasmids. The capsule is thought to contribute to the virulence by preventing lysis of the organism by cationic host proteins. Major symptoms and death from systemic, usually inhalation/respiratory, anthrax infections are mediated by the action of the pathogen's exo-toxins (discussed below) on the host's neutrophils and macrophages. Neutrophils are disarmed by inhibition of the oxidative burst pathway due to interference of signal transduction by the action of the anthrax toxins. The clinical and symptomatic manifestations of anthrax infection, on the other hand, are mediated by the effects of the toxins on the host macrophages [6, 7].

Bacillus anthracis produces three distinct toxic proteins; the one predominantly responsible for morbidity and mortality in the inhalation (respiratory) form is called the lethal toxin. This toxin is composed of one protein called the lethal factor, bound to the second protein, a 'carrier' protein called the protective antigen. The lethal toxin gains entry into the macrophage when the protective antigen component binds to cell membrane surface receptors and essentially 'tricks' the cell membrane into transporting the lethal factor–protective antigen complex into the cell interior. There, the lethal factor is cleaved from the protective antigen by a protease and begins to exert its pathogenic effects (the *Bacillus anthracis* version of the Trojan Horse story). The third toxic protein of significance, the edema factor, produces swelling and inflammation and contributes to the pulmonary pathology of inhalation anthrax (pneumonitis) [6, 7, 60, 61].

The predominant mechanism utilized by the macrophage in immune surveillance against invading pathogenic organisms following recognition/activation is via phagocytosis succeeded by incapacitation/destruction by bombardment with large amounts of generated reactive oxygen and nitrogen intermediates, commonly referred to as 'free radicals'. The most important of these is the family of reactive oxygen species which includes the superoxide ion (O_2^-), its reduction product's singlet oxygen ($O_2\downarrow$), hydrogen peroxide (H_2O_2), hydroxyl radical ($\cdot OH$), and the halogenated byproduct of peroxide, hypochlorite radical (^-OCl). Macrophages, as well as other types of white blood cell, are also stimulated by invading pathogens to synthesize and secrete an array of immune bio-regulatory molecules, the cytokines, which signal the mobilization of additional immune defense parameters. These include interleukins and interferons. The main cytokines involved in this discussion are interleukin-1-beta and tumor necrosis factor-alpha [6, 7].

This sophisticated defense system, however, teeters on a precarious balance because the same molecules (reactive oxygen and nitrogen intermediates and cytokines) produced by the macrophages in defense against invading organisms also have the potential to cause serious damage and destruction of the macrophages themselves. Furthermore, if excessive amounts of these molecules escape into the extracellular space and general circulation, they can also cause severe damage and inflammation in distant tissues and ultimately cause systemic shock and death [6, 7].

Normally, this potential for self-injury/destruction is well compensated for by an elegant built-in self-protection system, whereby the macrophage (a) simultaneously produces its own free radical scavenger/antioxidant molecules and associated enzyme catalysts, such as glutathione, glutathione peroxidase, and superoxide dismutase; (b) tightly regulates the synthesis/inhibition signaling governing the production and release of these 'double-edged sword' molecules; (c) restricts them to subcellular locales where their effects can be tolerated [6, 7].

The anthrax bacillus, however, has developed through evolutionary stealth, the unique capacity to divert the killing mechanisms towards the macrophages themselves. In the early stages of inhalation anthrax, low levels of the lethal toxin stimulate macrophages to generate large amounts of the cytokines interleukin-1-beta and tumor necrosis factor-alpha. These cytokines contribute to many of the influenza-like symptoms such as fever, myalgia and malaise. In the later stages, as the anthrax bacillus proliferates, large amounts of the lethal toxin are released, which results in extensive macrophage cytolysis. This occurs when high concentrations of the toxin induce the generation of massive levels of reactive oxygen intermediates via activation of the NADPH oxidase complex. The macrophage's auto-protective antioxidant mechanisms are thus overwhelmed and apoptosis/cytolysis results. (This is yet another example of anthrax as an 'evil trickster'. Macrophages undergoing this assault are also incapable of ingesting and destroying the invading bacteria; thus the bacterium has evolved a clever strategy to incapacitate the major obstacle to its proliferation) [6, 7].

As the ultimate catastrophic result of the extensive macrophage cytolysis, massive levels of stored interleukin-1-beta and tumor necrosis factor-alpha are released *en masse*, enter the general circulation and rapidly induce shock and eventually death. Thus, the lethal toxin exerts dual, dose-related effects on macrophages: early stimulation of the production and release of cytokines, and eventual cell death/cytolysis; both effects are mediated through unregulated generation of reactive oxygen intermediates induced by the lethal toxin [6, 7].

As mentioned above, the conventional or standard medical protocol for the treatment of inhalation anthrax is: intravenous administration of appropriate antibiotics depending on specific strain sensitivities, plus electrolyte and fluid replacement, glucocorticoids and respiratory/life support. With this treatment regimen there is a 50–80% mortality rate; therefore, the efficacy remains less than desirable.

Other innovative intervention strategies are currently being researched, including inhibition of anthrax toxin–cell receptor binding by synthetic polyvalent polypeptide moieties; however, clinical application of this and similar technologies is not likely in the near future [62].

The protocols described herein provide sophisticated approaches for intervention by addressing the key pathogenic mechanism of anthrax, the action of the lethal toxin, and predictably should improve overall mortality and morbidity. However, antibiotic administration remains an essential component of the treatment regimen because production of the lethal toxin by the anthrax bacilli will continue as long as they are present in sufficient numbers and/or proliferating; also, theoretically, the effects of this protocol may impair/ delay the phagocytic clearance of the bacilli by macrophages and other white blood cells. The intravenous protocol is based on research described herein and is additionally cited in the bibliography.

Research. After delineating the mechanisms described above, Hanna *et al.* hypothesized that specific antioxidant compounds might significantly attenuate the cascade of events associated with the pathogenesis of the anthrax bacillus [6, 7].

They tested their hypothesis in two ways: (a) *in vitro* studies using harvested mouse and human macrophages treated with a variety of antioxidants then challenged with variable levels of the lethal toxin and (b) *in vivo* studies using groups of live mice treated with the antioxidants preceding challenge with the lethal toxin.

The results confirmed their prediction: specific antioxidant compounds markedly diminished the macrophage response to the lethal toxin with respect to all three parameters, cytokine synthesis, reactive oxygen intermediate production and cytolysis; in the *in vivo* studies, both the mortality rate (time span = 14 days) and the duration of the illness were significantly reduced.

The most effective and applicable antioxidants tested were the sulfhydryl amino acids N-acetyl-L-cysteine and methionine. Vitamins C and E were less effective. N-acetyl-L-cysteine and methionine both function as precursors (building blocks) to the biosynthesis of the key intracellular antioxidant, glutathione in the macrophages; however, N-acetyl-L-cysteine is a much more efficiently utilized substrate in intracellular glutathione biosynthesis. Vitamins C and E function as major nutrient antioxidants [6, 7].

Melatonin and dehydroepiandrosterone (DHEA) have been demonstrated, in many studies, to play a role in immunomodulation and as antioxidants in both animals and humans. An additional clinical study conducted by Shin *et al.* [63] revealed that low doses of DHEA and melatonin produced significant inhibition of the lethal toxin-induced production and release of the cytokine tumor necrosis factor-alpha from mouse macrophages.

In Shin *et al.*'s study, physiological concentrations of DHEA (10^{-8} M) and concentrations 10 times higher protected macrophages by 35%. Previous studies suggested that melatonin at 10^{-7} M could inhibit tumor necrosis factor-alpha in monocytes. In Shin *et al.*'s study, concentrations ranging from 10^{-8} to 10^{-9} mol 1^{-1} reduced tumor necrosis factor-alpha by about 50% [63].

These observations demonstrate that DHEA plays a role as a regulator of the production of various cytokines in macrophages, including anthrax lethal toxin-induced cytokines; it also appears to act as a cytokine buffer to insure homeostasis of the cell during alteration of cytokine production. Melatonin may inhibit tumor necrosis factor-alpha via its antioxidant and/or immunostimulatory activity.

Extrapolating from these data and taking into account the extensive loss due to absorption, hepatic inactivation and distribution factors, the calculated dose range for DHEA would be 1 to 10 mg *per os* and for melatonin a very broad range of 100 μg to 10 mg. Further research evaluating oral dosing in relationship to blood and tissue levels would be required to determine more precisely the dose ranges required to maintain optimal therapeutic tissue concentrations.

Specific prevention and treatment protocols

Prevention protocol (for those with significant potential exposure risk)

(1) N-acetyl-L-cysteine 250–500 mg × 3 per day
(2) Grape seed/bilberry extract 50 mg × 3 per day
(3) Vitamin C 500–1000 mg × 3 per day
(4) Vitamin E 400 u (mixed tocopherols with at least 150 u gamma-tocopherol) 1–2, × 2 per day
(5) Alpha lipoic acid 100 mg × 2 per day
(6) DHEA 5 mg × 2 per day
(7) Melatonin 1–3 mg (sustained release form) at bedtime
(8) Lactoferrin 300–500 mg once per day.

(1) and (2) support the production of intracellular glutathione; vitamin C serves to help regenerate 'spent' or depleted reduced glutathione (see discussion below); lipoic acid and vitamin E enhance general antioxidant function and work synergistically. This protocol will serve to keep the white blood cells, especially the macrophages, 'primed' for reactive oxygen intermediate auto-defense. See text above concerning the effects of lactoferrin.

Persons with a high exposure risk potential, such as postal workers, healthcare and hospital personnel, etc., should use the entire protocol. The known or highly suspect exposure profile should include oral antibiotic prophylaxis with ciprofloxacin, doxycycline or penicillin. Doses have been calculated for an average adult; doses for children would be adjusted according to weight; (6) and (7) should not be given to persons under 16 years of age without medical supervision.

The nutrient supplements listed are all readily available through pharmacies, health food stores and via catalog/websites.

Treatment of active inhalation anthrax. Presenting as fever, chills, sweats, fatigue malaise, nausea/vomiting, minimal or non-productive cough, respiratory distress; diagnosis confirmed by appropriate laboratory and radiographic evaluation.

Intravenous administration

(a) N-acetyl-L-cysteine 200 mg ml^{-1} (20% sol.); 30 mg kg^{-1}, every 8 hours (× 3 per 24 hours); dilute in 250 ml of 5% dextrose; infuse over 1 hour.
(b) L-glutathione 500 mg ml^{-1}; 30 mg kg^{-1}. Sodium ascorbate (vitamin C) 500 mg ml^{-1}; 375 mg kg^{-1}. Magnesium chloride 100 mg ml^{-1}; 3 ml. Selenium (selenous acid)

40 μg ml^{-1}; 10 ml. Vitamin A, emulsified 50,000 u ml^{-1}; 1.0 ml. Administer every 8 hours ($\times 3$ per 24 hours); dilute in 250 ml of sterile water; infuse over 1 hour.

(c) Ciprofloxacin 400 mg every 8 hours, infuse over 60 min (or equivalent protocols for doxycycline and penicillin; see package inserts for preparation and administration information).

Infusions should be given via a pic-line or central venous catheter and kept open with normal saline. Allow a 60–120 min interval between sequential infusions of (a), (b), (c). Preparations should be kept within the desired osmolarity range of 0.280–0.310 mOsm ml^{-1}. Additions and adjustments must be made to address individual electrolyte and fluid volume replacement requirements.

Oral administration (if patient conscious and capable)

(a) Pure silver colloid solution 300 ppm, 1 tsp $\times 3$ per day
(b) Vitamin E, 400 u (as in prevention protocol) every 8 hours.
(c) DHEA 5 mg 8 a.m., 12 p.m., 4 p.m.
(d) Melatonin 1.2–3 mg, sustained release; once between 9 and 11 p.m.
(e) Alpha lipoic acid 200 mg; $\times 3$ per day.
(f) Grape seed/bilberry extract (proanthocyanidins/anthocyanosides)100 mg, $\times 3$ per day.
(g) Homeopathic intervention (see below).
(h) Lactoferrin 500 mg three times per day.

Inhalation therapy

Inhaled glutathione is a powerful antioxidant that should be considered in the treatment of anthrax. Glutathione is found in the epithelial lining of the lower airways [64]. Decreased levels of glutathione have been noted in patients with cystic fibrosis, Chronic Obstructive Pulmonary Disease (COPD), idiopathic pulmonary fibrosis, asymptomatic HIV-positive patients, and patients with asthma [65]. There have been several small studies and multiple case reports of nebulized glutathione being helpful in the treatment of idiopathic pulmonary fibrosis, HIV-positive patients, and patients with COPD [66–68]. Nebulized glutathione has been shown to increase glutathione levels in the epithelial lining fluid of the lower airways and cause a decrease in spontaneous superoxide anion release by alveolar macrophages [69]. The predicted benefit of nebulized glutathione in acute respiratory anthrax is therefore based on several probable mechanisms including: replenishment of glutathione in the epithelial milieu, the stabilization of alveolar macrophages, and antioxidant-mediated attenuation of at least some of the toxic/pro-inflammatory effects of the lethal toxin and edema factor.

There is a study showing exacerbation of symptoms in patients with mild asthma who have been treated with nebulized glutathione [70]. This exacerbation was prevented by pre-treatment with salbutamol. In one author's clinic (Gordon), many patients with post-viral cough, COPD, post-chemical exposure cough, and one patient with long-standing bronchiectasis have been successfully treated with inhaled nebulized glutathione. Much smaller doses than were used in the study that provoked exacerbations of asthmatics were used in these patients. Mild exacerbations have rarely been seen in patients utilizing the lower dose protocol, and have consisted of mostly a slight increase in the cough. The exacerbation reported in asthmatics was somewhat surprising, as they too have been demonstrated to have low glutathione levels. One possibility is that this phenomenon is perhaps due to a problem with sulfite detoxification, as there are multiple sulfite intermediaries produced with glutathione metabolism in the lung [71]. It may also be due to an effect on leukotriene biosynthesis by glutathione [72]. Glutathione is involved in the metabolism of leukotriene A4 which results in the formation of leukotriene C4, and this in turn can be converted to leukotriene D4. Both leukotriene C4 and D4 are well-known potent bronchoconstrictors and increase vascular permeability and have been implicated in the pathogenesis of bronchial asthma. The increase in glutathione concentrations in asthmatics may cause an imbalance in the metabolism of the leukotrienes and therefore trigger an increased inflammatory reaction.

Recommended for anthrax is 600 mg of glutathione powder dissolved in 4 ml of normal saline and then delivered by nebulizer over approximately 25 min. This can be given every 12 hours. If the glutathione concentrate is not available, we would suggest using 3 ml of 100 mg ml^{-1} glutathione given over 10–15 min via a nebulizer every 6 hours. If there is a good clinical response, we would not hesitate to use the higher dose glutathione on an every 4 to 6 hour basis. Studies show that glutathione levels can decrease to pre-treatment levels within 3 hours after treatment.

For patients with a history of asthma, we recommend pre-treatment with 2.5 mg albuterol (salbutamol) via a nebulizer prior to the administration of glutathione.

Discussion. The intravenous protocol is based on research described above and cited in the references. The use of both N-acetyl-L-cysteine and glutathione/ascorbate alternately is because the action of N-acetyl-L-cysteine is predominantly via stimulation of endogenous intracellular glutathione biosynthesis (enhanced by oral grape seed- and bilberry-derived anthocyanosides), and while exogenous glutathione may not contribute to intracellular biosynthesis, it is a very potent extracellular antioxidant and cofactor for glutathione peroxidase and phase II detoxification function [73–77]. Vitamin C (ascorbate) has been shown to exhibit potent *in vivo* antitoxin activity against various protein bio-toxins (such as various snake venoms) and has a key role in the regeneration/recycling of intracellular oxidized (expended) glutathione [82–90].

In addition, the potent antioxidant effects of this regimen would predictably diminish the edema factor-mediated tissue inflammation and edema in pulmonary anthrax. Alpha lipoic acid both enhances the effect of vitamin C and provides additional antioxidant support, as does vitamin E (especially re: lipid peroxidation) [91, 92]. Silver ions, particularly in colloid solution form, have shown ubiquitous antimicrobial effects in a wide variety of prokaryotic organisms (bacteria, fungi) and should provide additional 'insurance' against antibiotic resistance or failure [93–101].

The determination of the dose ranges for intravenous N-acetyl-L-cysteine was difficult. In their seminal paper, Hanna *et al.* failed to discuss the rationale for the dose of N-acetyl-L-cysteine chosen to treat the mice in the *in vivo* studies. They administered one 800 mg dose intravenously to each ~ 20 g mouse. This is equivalent to 40,000 mg kg^{-1}, which would be a massive dose in human terms. They were clear in reporting no apparent toxic effects on the mice from this dose. N-acetyl-L-cysteine has been shown to be generally well tolerated by patients in doses of 10 + g p.o. (140 mg kg^{-1}) and 10.5 + g intravenously (150 mg kg^{-1} infused over 15 min) in the treatment protocols for paracetamol overdosage. Adverse effects are reported in a small but significant percentage of patients treated at these doses, however. These range from erythematous and urticarial rashes, nausea, vomiting, diarrhea and headache to anaphylactoid reactions, the latter especially associated with a higher than recommended intravenous infusion rate [73, 81]. A dose of 40,000 mg kg^{-1} is orders of magnitude higher than that typically administered to human subjects, and furthermore, no human subject to our knowledge has ever received an intravenous dose approaching this level. Also, because the primary mechanism of N-acetyl-L-cysteine interdiction in acute anthrax is partially different than that related to massive paracetamol hepatotoxicity (the latter predictably requiring substantially higher doses), and because the dose levels used to treat paracetamol poisoning are associated with significant adverse effects, we chose a more conservative dose schedule. We believe 30 mg kg^{-1} will, in all probability, be sufficient in producing the desired therapeutic benefit with a very low incidence of appreciable adverse effects. Two other aspects of this protocol which justify a lower dose level are the relatively slow infusion rate, and the interval administration schedule (every 8 hours or three doses per 24 hours), which should produce more sustained cellular and extracellular concentrations than the one large single dose given in the Hanna *et al.* study.

These materials (excluding the antibiotics) are fundamentally non-toxic, used as recommended, and have an extremely low incidence of side-effects or demonstrated hypersensitivity reactions. In addition, N-acetyl-L-cysteine and alpha-lipoic acid have both been demonstrated to prevent or markedly diminish the hepatotoxic and neurotoxic effects of many drugs and chemical agents. Ciprofloxacin (Cipro) is one antibiotic which has a significant incidence of liver damage associated with its use in higher dose ranges.

N-acetyl-L-cysteine for infusion is available through conventional pharmaceutical distributors; L-glutathione and vitamin A micro-emulsion for intravenous administration can be obtained through commercial compounding pharmacies. All other materials listed for the intravenous protocols are available through pharmaceutical suppliers. The oral supplements listed are available through the resources cited previously.

Smallpox

Epidemic smallpox is a more difficult problem to address, both with respect to prevention and treatment. The causative agent, a virus in the orthopoxvirus family, may be disseminated widely through micro-aerosol technology, similar to anthrax; however, unlike anthrax, it is highly communicable through intrapersonal contact and poses difficult epidemiological challenges, e.g. isolation and quarantine procedures. Complicating matters further is the unfortunate fact that the vast majority of our population is either unvaccinated or experiences minimal residual immunity from distant vaccination.

Currently, adequate stores of aged smallpox vaccine allegedly remain in storage, sufficient to vaccinate the entire US population and updated vaccine may become available within the next few years. However, smallpox vaccine administration is more complex than with most other vaccines, and carries a significant risk of serious reactions, often requiring therapeutic intervention with neutralizing antibodies present in vaccinia immune globulin. This is in very short supply and only available through the Centers for Disease Control. Although it appears that vaccination within 4 days of initial exposure may ameliorate the severity of the ensuing disease, it would provide no benefit and is contraindicated beyond that point. Finally, the fundamental nature of viral infections, and the lack of any specific antiviral drugs against the smallpox virus, markedly limit treatment options within the conventional medical paradigm. One antiviral drug, cidofovir, in experimental studies, has shown promise in treating early smallpox infections; however, it must be given intravenously within the first 3–4 days of infection and has a high incidence of kidney damage [5, 102–104].

As stated earlier, smallpox is quite communicable, but fortunately the speed of transmission through the population is slower than for some other epidemic viral diseases such as chickenpox or measles. This is primarily due to the fact that a person with smallpox cannot transmit the virus to another individual until the onset of the rash (skin and mouth/throat lesions); this usually occurs several days after the onset of severe fatigue, malaise, high fever and back/headache, at which point most individuals are bedridden and therefore secondary exposure is usually limited to household members and/or healthcare personnel [5, 102–104].

The virus is shed into saliva (from mucous membrane lesions) and into skin lesion exudate. The rate of transmission of the virus through these sources is very high with close contact via aerosol droplet through sneezing, coughing; clothing and bedding. The incubation period (time between exposure and the onset of symptoms) averages 12–14 days with a 7–17 day range. Infectivity/communicability drops to near zero by the time all skin lesions have scabbed over. Death usually occurs (~30% mortality) in the second week, from toxemia associated with massive viral antigen/immune complex load, complicating encephalitis or hemorrhaging [5, 102–104].

312   J. L. ANDERSON *ET AL.*

Prevention

Higher exposure risk—additional oral supplements

(1) N-acetyl-L-cysteine 250 mg, × 3 per day
(2) Vitamin C 500–1000 mg, × 3 per day
(3) Vitamin E 400 u (see anthrax prevention protocol above)
(4) Alpha lipoic acid 100 mg, × 2 per day
(5) Olive leaf standardized extract 500 mg, × 3 per day
(6) Monolaurin (lauricidic acid) 300 mg, × 2–3 per day
(7) Zinc citrate 50 mg, × 3 per day
(8) Lactoferrin 300–500 mg once per day.

Treatment

Early stage disease (prodromal, mild symptoms)/oral administration

(1) N-acetyl-L-cysteine 500 mg, × 3 per day
(2) Vitamin C 1000 mg every 1–2 hours (10–12 g minimum total)
(3) Olive leaf standardized extract 1000 mg every 4 hours
(4) Monolaurin 300 mg every 4 hours
(5) Zinc citrate 100 mg, × 3 per day
(6) Vitamin E 400 u 1–2, 2 × per day
(7) Alpha lipoic acid 100 mg, × 2 per day
(8) Vitamin A mycelized liquid 100,000 u per day
(9) *Glycyrrhizinate(monoammonium) 75 mg/glycyrrhetinic acid 98% 75 mg; one capsule three times per day
(10) Lactoferrin 500 mg three times per day.

*Contraindicated in patients with hypertension and hypertensive cardiovascular disease.

Later stage disease/severe symptoms

(1) Intravenous infusion

    (a) N-acetyl-L-cysteine 200 mg ml^{-1} (20% sol.); 30 mg kg^{-1}
    (b) Sodium ascorbate 500 mg ml^{-1}; 375 mg kg^{-1}
    (c) Magnesium chloride 100 mg ml^{-1}; 3 ml
    (d) Vitamin A, emulsified 50,000 u ml^{-1}; 0.5 ml
    (e) Zinc sulfate 5 mg
    (f) Selenium (selenous acid) 40 μg ml^{-1}; 20 ml

Dilute contents in 500 ml of sterile water; infuse over 2 hours; administer every 12 hours; treat for 3–5 days as indicated by response. Infusions should be given via upper extremity pic-line or central venous catheter. Keep open with normal saline. Allow a 60–120 min interval between sequential infusions of (a), (b), (c). Preparations should be kept within the desired osmolarity range of 0.280–0.310 mOsm ml^{-1}. Additions and adjustments must be made to address individual electrolyte and fluid volume replacement requirements.

(2) Oral administration

    (a) Olive leaf standardized extract 1000 mg every 4 hours
    (b) Monolaurin 600 mg every 4 hours
    (c) Vitamin E 400 u 1–2, 2 x per day
    (d) Alpha lipoic acid 100 mg every 6 hours
    (e) *Glycyrrhizinate(monoammonium) 75 mg/glycyrrhetinic acid 98% 75 mg; two capsules three times per day.

*Contraindicated in patients with hypertension and hypertensive cardiovascular disease.

Discussion. With the exception of immune compromised individuals and the very aged, the survival rate and severity of illness in individuals treated with the integrative protocols should be substantially improved. In addition to effects mentioned earlier, N-acetyl-L-cysteine also possesses potent antiviral properties [78–80].

High doses of vitamin C, vitamin A and zinc in combination also exhibit significant antiviral effects, at least partially through the enhancement of immune surveillance mechanisms and antioxidant effects [29–32, 84, 88, 89]. Selenium salts have been demonstrated to exert marked antiviral effects against a number of pathogens, including specific retroviruses, hemorrhagic fever (Ebola/Marburg) viruses, coxsackie B strains, and the poxvirus molluscum contagiosum [105–115]. Extracts from olive leaf (oleuropein) [116–123] and specific fractions of coconut oil (the monoglygerol ester of lauric acid, monolaurin) [124–138] have shown marked viral suppression activity. Glycyrrhizin and derivatives have been demonstrated to possess significant antiviral activity, especially against hepatitis-associated viruses (hepatitis B and C) and herpes viruses [139, 140]. The antioxidants are important in modulating the toxemia associated with the disease.

All materials listed above are available through the resources cited in the previous section.

ADDITIONAL MODALITIES

Homeopathic Intervention: Anthrax and Smallpox Nosodes

Currently there are no safe, effective vaccines for anthrax or smallpox currently available to the general healthcare community or general public. Homeopathy can offer protection based on a different principle. Homeopathic nosodes are very diluted extracts from a specific agent or substance (diluted to the point that only the 'subtle energy' or 'resonance' remains) which are given to 'boost' the body's defenses against that agent; in essence, a homeopathic 'vaccination'. Unlike allopathic vaccines produced from killed or live-attenuated bacteria or viruses, homeopathic nosodes have no biological activity in the classic sense, and produce no serious or lasting side-effects. Occasionally, mild and transient constitutional symptoms can be induced, such as fatigue, malaise, or aches. However, it is strongly advised to use these protocols only under the guidance of an experienced practitioner of homeopathic medicine, as modifications may be necessary based on individual needs.

Anthracinum is derived from the sterilized extract of killed anthrax bacilli, variolinum is derived from the sterilized exudate of a variola (smallpox) lesion [141–144].

Remote threat (no known cases in region; as a prophylactic measure)

Anthrax

(1) Anthracinum 30 C once a week × 3 weeks; then interval × 1 week.
(2) Anthracinum 200 C once a week × 3 weeks; then interval × 1 week.
(3) Anthracinum 1 M once a week × 3 weeks. Dose = two to three pellets sublingual.

Smallpox

As long as there are no cases reported in your area, we do not recommend treating.

Potential threat (documented regional cases; exposure to anthrax/smallpox possible)

For both anthracinum and variolinum

(a) 30 C once a day × 5 days; then interval × 1 month.
(b) 200 C × 1 dose; then interval × 1 month.
(c) M × 1 dose. Dose = two to three pellets sublingual.

314   J. L. ANDERSON *ET AL.*

Severe threat [known exposure; cohorts with disease; antibiotics not available (anthrax) or active disease]

For both anthracinum and variolinum

(a) 30 C three times a day, first day.
(b) 200 C three times a day, second day.
(c) M three times a day, third day. Dose = two to three pellets.

Individuals who are under homeopathic treatment with a constitutional remedy should consult with their homeopathic practitioner before instituting this protocol, as the effect of the constitutional remedy may be antidoted. General principals of classic homeopathy should be followed, especially with respect to avoidance of antidoting and interfering substances, e.g. coffee or camphor. Doses should be administered at least 30 min before and/or after eating or drinking [141].

CONCLUSION

As noted in the opening section, the proposed protocols described for the treatment and prevention or attenuation of acute respiratory anthrax and smallpox are based on an integration of published research regarding the pathogenic mechanisms associated with the respective causative agents, the established pathophysiological processes and clinical manifestations characteristic of each disease, the known mechanisms of action of specific protocol components, as well as the combined clinical experience of the authors and their peers. Because, to our knowledge, no human victims of anthrax or smallpox have been treated with these protocols, nor, for obvious reasons, no research on human subjects has been undertaken utilizing these protocols, they remain in the realm of hypotheses. At least with respect to anthrax, however, as Hanna *et al.* and other researchers have pointed out, murine macrophages behave physiologically very similarly, if not identically, to those of human origin; it would be reasonable to assume, therefore, that the pathophysiological effects of the lethal toxin would be equally predictable. Controlled studies of the efficacy of these protocols on animal (preferably primate) subjects would, of course, be most desirable. Nonetheless, we believe that the predicted safety and low probability of adverse effects combined with the high, potentially life-saving benefits of these protocols, may warrant their application in selected clinical settings.

ACKNOWLEDGMENTS

The authors would like to thank Ms Joan Webb for her invaluable contribution in formatting and editing this paper.

REFERENCES

[1] Centers for Disease Control Update. Investigation of anthrax associated with intentional exposure and interim public health guidelines. Centers for Disease Control and Prevention MMWR October 2001; 50: 889–97.
[2] Jernigan JA, Stephens DS, Ashford DA, *et al.* Bioterrorism-related inhalation anthrax: the first 10 cases reported in the United States. Emerg Infect Dis 2001; 7(5): 1–26.
[3] Inglesby TV *et al.* Anthrax as a biological weapon: medical and public health management (Consensus Statement). J Am Med Assoc 1999; 281: 1735–45.
[4] Swartz MN. Recognition and management of anthrax—an update. N Engl J Med 2001; 345(22): 1621–6.
[5] Henderson DA, Inglesby TV, Bartlett JG, *et al.* Smallpox as a biological weapon. Medical and public health management. J Am Med Assoc 1999; 281: 2127–37.
[6] Hanna PC, Kruskal BA, Ezkowitz RA, *et al.* Role of macrophage oxidative burst in the action of anthrax lethal toxin. Mol Med 1994; 1(1): 7–18.
[7] Hanna PC. Understanding *Bacillus anthracis* pathogenicity. Trends Microbiol 1999; 7(5): 180–2.

[8] Rea WJ. Chemical Sensitivity. Lewis Publishers: Boca Raton, 1992–1997.
[9] Jacoby WB (ed.) Enzymatic Basis of Detoxication. Academic Press: New York, 1980.
[10] Scriver CR *et al.* (eds) The Metabolic and Molecular Basis of Inherited Disease, 8th edn. McGraw-Hill: New York, 2000.
[11] Latella G, Caprilli R. Metabolism of large bowel mucosa in health and disease. Int J Colorect Dis 1991; 6: 127–32.
[12] Galland L, Barrie S. Intestinal dysbiosis and the causes of disease. J Adv Med 1993; 6: 67–82.
[13] Lichtman SN, Keku J, Schwab JH, Sartor RB. Hepatic injury associated with small bowel bacterial overgrowth in rats is prevented by metronidazole and tetracycline. Gastroenterology 1991; 100(2): 513–9.
[14] Kirsch M. Bacterial overgrowth. Am J Gastroent 1990; 85: 31–7.
[15] Bjarnason I *et al.* Intestinal permeability: an overview. Gastroenterology 1995; 108: 1566–81.
[16] Shils ME *et al.* Modern Nutrition in Health and Disease, 9th edn. Lippincott, Williams & Wilkins: Philadelphia, 1999.
[17] Werbach MR, Moss J. Textbook of Nutritional Medicine. Third Line Press: Tarzana, CA, 1999.
[18] Werbach MR. Foundations of Nutritional Medicine: a Sourcebook of Clinical Research. Third Line Press: Tarzana, CA, 1997.
[19] Roitt IM, Brostoff J (eds). Immunology, 6th edn. C.V. Mosby: St. Louis, MO, 2001.
[20] Murray RK *et al.* Harper's Biochemistry, 25th edn. McGraw-Hill: New York, 1999.
[21] Suzuki T, Ohno N, Chiba N, Miura NN, Adachi Y, Yadomae T. Immunopharmacological activity of the purified insoluble glucan, zymocel, in mice. J Pharm Pharmacol 1996; 48(12): 1243–8.
[22] Ooi VE, Liu F. Immunomodulation and anti-cancer activity of polysaccharide–protein complexes. Curr Med Chem 2000; 7(7): 715–29.
[23] Bogwald J, Johnson E, Seljelid R. The cytotoxic effect of mouse macrophages stimulated in vitro by a beta-1,3-D glucan from yeast cell walls. Scand J Immunol 1982; 14: 297–304.
[24] Sandula J, Machova E, Hribalova V. Mitogenic activity of particulate yeast beta-1,3-D glucan and its water soluble derivatives. Int J Biol Macromol 1995; 17: 323–6.
[25] Fullerton SA, Samadi AA, Tortorelis DG *et al.* Induction of apoptosis in human prostatic cancer cells with beta-glucan (Maitake mushroom polysaccharide). Mol Urol 2000; 4(1): 7–13.
[26] Pegel KH. The importance of sitosterol and sitosterolin in human and animal nutrition. S Afr J Sci 1997; 93: 263–8.
[27] Bouic PJD, Etsebeth S, Liebenberg RW *et al.* Beta-sitosterol and beta-sitosterol glycoside stimulate human peripheral blood lymphocyte proliferation: implications for their use as an immunomodulatory vitamin combination. Int J Immunopharmacol 1996; 18: 693–700.
[28] Bouic PJD. Plant sterols and sterolins: a review of their immune-modulating properties. Altern Med Rev 1999; 4: 170–7.
[29] Bogden JD *et al.* Effects of one year of supplementation with zinc and other micronutrients on cellular immunity in the elderly. J Am Coll Nutr 1990; 9(3): 214–25.
[30] Wagner PA *et al.* Zinc nutriture and cell-mediated immunity in the aged. Int J Vitam Nutr Res 1983; 53(1): 94–101.
[31] Duchateau J *et al.* Influence of oral zinc supplementation on the lymphocyte response to mitogens of normal subjects. Am J Clin Nutr 1981; 34: 88–93.
[32] Chandra RJ. Nutrition and immunity in serious illness. Proc Nutr Soc 1993; 52: 77–84.
[33] In Vivo Activities of Lactoferrin. NIH Guide, 1994; 23(14).
[34] Zimecki M, Wlasczyk A. LF and its effects on the immune response. Arch Immunol Ther Exp (warsz) 1998; 46(4): 231–40.
[35] Swart PJ, Kuipers EM. (LF and) Anti-viral activity against HIV and CMV in cell culture (fibroblasts). Adv Exp Med Biol 1998; 443: 205–13.
[36] Ikeda M, Sugiyama K. (LF and) Prevention of Hep C in human liver cells in vitro. Biochem Biophys Res Commun 1998; 245(2): 549–53.
[37] Zhang GH, Mann DM, Tsai CM. Neutralization of endotoxin in vitro and in vivo by a human lactoferrin-derived peptide. Infect Immun 1999; 67(3): 1353–8.
[38] Lee WJ, Farmer JL, Hilty M, Kim YB. The protective effects of lactoferrin feeding against endotoxin lethal shock in germfree piglets. Infect Immun 1999; 66(4): 1421–6.
[39] Yamauchi K, Wakabayashi H, Hashimoto S, Teraguchi S, Hayasawa H, Tomita M. Effects of orally administered bovine lactoferrin on the immune system of healthy volunteers. Adv Exp Med Biol 1998; 443: 261–5.
[40] Dial EJ, Hall LR, Serna H, Romero JJ, Fox JG, Lichtenberger LM. Antibiotic properties of bovine lactoferrin on *Helicobacter pylori*. Dig Dis Sci 1998; 43(12): 2750–6.
[41] Bhimani RS, Vendrov Y, Furmanski P. Influence of lactoferrin feeding and injection against systemic staphylococcal infections in mice. J Appl Microbiol 1999; 86(1): 135–44.
[42] Vorland LH, Ulvatne H, Andersen J *et al.* Lactoferricin of bovine origin is more active than lactoferricins of human, murine and caprine origin. Scand J Infect Dis 1998; 30(5): 513–7.
[43] Liang H *et al.* The effect of astragalus polysaccharides on cell mediated immunity (CMI) in burned mice. Chin J Plast Surg Burns 1994; 10(2): 138.

[44] Rittenhouse JR *et al.* Chinese medicinal herbs reverse macrophage suppression induced by urological tumors. J Urol 1991; 146(2): 486.

[45] Sun Y *et al.* Immune restoration and/or augmentation of local graft-versus-host reaction by traditional Chinese medicinal herbs. Cancer 1983; 52(1): 70–3.

[46] Sun Y *et al.* Preliminary observations on the effects of the Chinese medicinal herbs *Astragalus membranaceus* and *Ligustrum lucidum* on lymphocyte blastogenic response. J Biol Respon Modif 1983; 2(3): 227–37.

[47] Hou Y *et al.* Interferon induction and lymphocyte transformation stimulated by *Astragalus membranaceus* in mouse spleen cell cultures. Zhonghua Weisheng Wuxue Hemian Yixue Zazhi 1981; 1(2): 137–9.

[48] Chen LJ, Shen ML, Wang MY, Zhai SK, Liu MZ. Effect of Astragalus polysaccharides on phagocytic function in mice. Chung Kuo I Hsueh Ko Hsueh Yuan Hsueh Pao 1983; 5(4): 231–4 [in Chinese].

[49] Chu DT, Lepe-Zuniga J, Wong WL, LaPushin R, Mavligit GM. Fractionated extract of *Astragalus membranaceus*, a Chinese medicinal herb, potentiates LAK cell cytotoxicity generated by a low dose of recombinant interleukin-2. Chung Kuo Yao Li Hsueh Pao 1981; 2(3): 200–4 [in Chinese].

[50] Steinmuller C, Roesler J *et al.* Application of purified polysaccharides from cell cultures of the plant *Echinacea purpurea* to mice mediates protection against systemic infection with *Listeria monocyogenes* and *Candida albicans*. Int J Immunopharmac 1991; 13: 27–37.

[51] See DM, Broumand N, Sahl L, Tilles JG. In vitro effects of echinacea and ginseng on natural killer and antibody-dependent cell cytotoxicity in healthy subjects and chronic fatigue syndrome or acquired immunodeficiency syndrome patients. Immunopharmacology 1997; 35(3): 229–35.

[52] Luettig B, Steinmüller C, Gifford GE, Wagner H, Lohmann-Matthes ML. Macrophage activation by the polysaccharide arabinogalactan isolated from plant cell cultures of *Echinacea purpurea*. J Natl Cancer Inst 1989; 81(9): 669–75.

[53] Spiegel D *et al.* Mind matters. Coping and cancer progression. J Psychosom Res 2001; 50(5): 287–90.

[54] Schulman R. The Psychology of Chronic Illness. Basic Books/Harper Collins: New York, 1996.

[55] Koenig HG *et al.* Handbook of Religion and Health: a Century of Research Reviewed. Oxford University Press: New York, 2000.

[56] Dossey L. Healing Words: the Power of Prayer and the Practice of Medicine. Harper Collins: San Francisco, 1993.

[57] Dossey L. Recovering the Soul: a Scientific and Spiritual Search. Bantam Books: New York, 1989.

[58] Ornish D. Love and Survival: the Scientific Basis for the Healing Power of Intimacy. Harper Collins: New York, 1998.

[59] Larson DB. The Faith Factor, Vol. 2: An Annotated Bibliography of Systematic Reviews and Clinical Research on Spiritual Subjects. National Institute for Healthcare Research: Bethesda, MD, 1993.

[60] Pannifer AD *et al.* Crystal structure of the anthrax lethal factor. Nature 2001; October.

[61] Bradley KA *et al.* Identification of the cellular receptor for anthrax toxin. Nature 2001; October.

[62] Mourez M *et al.* Designing a polyvalent inhibitor of anthrax toxin. Nature Biotechnology 2001; 19: 958–61.

[63] Shin S *et al.* Dehydroepiandrosterone and melatonin prevent *Bacillus anthracis* lethal toxin-induced TNF production in macrophages. Cell Biol Toxicol 2000; 16: 165–74.

[64] Rahman I. Inflammation and the regulation of glutathione level in lung epithelial cells. Antioid Redox Signal 1999; 1(4): 425–47.

[65] Rahman Q. Glutathione redox system in oxidative lung injury. Crit Rev Toxicol 1999; 29(6): 543–68.

[66] Borok Z. Effect of glutathione aerosol on oxidant–antioxidant imbalance in idiopathic pulmonary fibrosis. Lancet 1991; 338: 215–6.

[67] Holroyd K *et al.* Correction of glutathione deficiency in the lower respiratory tract of HIV seropositive individuals by glutathione aerosol treatment. Thorax 1993; 48: 985–9.

[68] Lamson DW, Brignall MS. The use of nebulized glutathione in the treatment of emphysema: a case report. Altern Med Rev 2000; 5(5): 429–31.

[69] MacNee W. Oxidants and antioxidants as therapeutic targets in COPD. Am J Respir Crit Care Med 1999; 160: 558–65.

[70] Marrades RM *et al.* Nebulized glutathione induces bronchcoconstriction in patients with mild asthma. Am J Respir Crit Care Med 1997; 156(2): 425–30.

[71] Snashall PD, Baldwin C. Mechanisms of sulfur dioxide induced bronchoconstriction in normal and asthmatic men. Thorax 1982; 37: 118–23.

[72] Lewis RR *et al.* Leukotrienes and other products of the 5-lipoxygenase pathway. N Engl J Med 1990; 323: 645–55.

[73] Jones AL. Mechanism of action and value of N-acetylcysteine in the treatment of early and late acetaminophen poisoning: a critical review. J Toxicol Clin Toxicol 1998; 36(4): 277–85.

[74] DeMattia G, Bravi MC, Laurenti O, *et al.* Reduction of oxidative stress by oral N-acetyl-L-cysteine treatment decreases plasma soluble vascular cell adhesion molecule-1 concentrations in non-obese, non-dyslipidaemic, normotensive, patients with non-insulin-dependent diabetes. Diabetologia Nov 1998; 41(11): 1392–6.

[75] Pelle E, Ingrassia M, Mammone T, *et al.* Protection against cigarette smoke-induced damage to intact transformed rabbit corneal cells by N-acetyl-L-cysteine. Cell Biol Toxicol Aug 1998; 14(4): 253–9.

[76] Bernard GR. N-acetylcysteine in experimental and clinical acute lung injury. Am J Med 1991; 91(3C): 545–95.

[77] Thies JC, Teklote J, Clauer U, *et al.* The efficacy of N-acetylcysteine as a hepatoprotective agent in liver transplantation. Transpl Int 1998; 11(Suppl. 1): S390–2.

[78] Roederer M *et al.* Cytokine-stimulated human immunodeficiency virus replication is inhibited by N-acetyl-L-cysteine. Proc Natl Acad Sci 1990; 87: 4884–8.

[79] Robinson MK *et al.* Glutathione deficiency and HIV infection. Lancet 1992; 339: 1603–4.

[80] De Flora S *et al.* Attenuation of influenza like symptomatology and improvement of cell mediated immunity with long-term N-acetylcysteine treatment. Eur Respir J 1997; 10: 1535–41.

[81] International Programme on Chemical Safety; Poisons Information Monograph 396: Paracetamol. Medical Toxicology Unit, Guy's and St. Thomas's Trust: London, 1996.

[82] Smith AR, Visioli F, Hagen TM. Vitamin C matters: increased oxidative stress in cultured human aortic endothelial cells without supplemental ascorbic acid. FASEB J 2002; 16(9): 1102–4.

[83] Jenner AM, Ruiz JE, Dunster C, Halliwell B, Mann GE, Siow RC. Vitamin C protects against hypochlorous acid-induced glutathione depletion and DNA base and protein damage in human vascular smooth muscle cells. Arterioscler Thromb Vasc Biol 2002; 22(4): 574–80.

[84] Tauler P, Aguilo A, Fuentespina E, Tur JA, Pons A. Diet supplementation with vitamin E, vitamin C and beta-carotene cocktail enhances basal neutrophil antioxidant enzymes in athletes. Pflugers Arch 2002; 443(5–6): 791–7.

[85] Guaiquil VH, Vera JC, Golde DW. Mechanism of vitamin C inhibition of cell death induced by oxidative stress in glutathione-depleted HL-60 cells. J Biol Chem 2001; 276(44): 40955–61.

[86] May JM, Qu Z, Li X. Requirement for GSH in recycling of ascorbic acid in endothelial cells. Biochem Pharmacol 2001; 62(7): 873–81.

[87] Nardini M, Finkelstein EI, Reddy S *et al.* Acrolein-induced cytotoxicity in cultured human bronchial epithelial cells. Modulation by alpha-tocopherol and ascorbic acid. Toxicology 2002; 170(3): 173–85.

[88] De la Fuente M, Victor VM. Ascorbic acid and N-acetylcysteine improve in vitro the function of lymphocytes from mice with endotoxin-induced oxidative stress. Free Radic Res 2001; 35(1): 73–84.

[89] Victor VV, Guayerbas N, Puerto M, Medina S, De la Fuente M. Ascorbic acid modulates in vitro the function of macrophages from mice with endotoxic shock. Immunopharmacology 2000; 46(1): 89–101.

[90] Cadenas S, Rojas C, Barja G. Endotoxin increases oxidative injury to proteins in guinea pig liver: protection by dietary vitamin C. Pharmacol Toxicol 1998; 82(1): 11–18.

[91] Packer L, Witt EH, Tritschler HJ. Alpha-lipoic acid as a biological antioxidant. Free Radic Biol Med 1995; 19: 227–50.

[92] Tirosh O, Sen CK, Roy S *et al.* Neuroprotective effects of alpha-lipoic acid and its positively charged amide analogue. Free Radic Biol Med (United States) 1999; 26(11–12): 1418–26.

[93] Bayer M, Fox Chase Cancer Center, Philadelphia, PA. Personal communication to Dr Paul Farber, 3 January 1995.

[94] Buckley HR, Temple University School of Medicine, Department of Microbiology and Immunology. Personal communication to Dr Paul Farber, 2 February 1995.

[95] Burgdorfer W, Schwan TG, National Institutes of Health, Rocky Mountain Laboratories, US Department of Health and Human Services. Personal communication to Dr Paul Farber, 13 January 1995.

[96] Henderson EE, Temple University School of Medicine, Department of Microbiology and Immunology. Personal communication to Dr Paul Farber, 2 February 1995.

[97] Becker RO. The effect of electrically generated silver ions on human cells. First International Conference on Gold and Silver in Medicine, Bethesda, MD, 13–14 May 1987.

[98] Eichhom GL, Shin YA, Butzow JJ, Clark P, Tarien E. Interaction of metal ions with biological systems, with special reference to silver and gold. First International Conference on Gold and Silver in Medicine, Bethesda, MD, 13–14 May 1987.

[99] Flick AB. Clinical application of electrical silver iontophoresis. First International Conference on Gold and Silver in Medicine, Bethesda, MD, 13–14 May 1987.

[100] Lee JV, Hibberd ML, Stanley SC. A Comparison of the Biocidal Properties of Silver Ions and Chloride against Legionella Species; PHLS Centre for Applied Microbiology and Research: Porton Down, DD3/2 AGREPORT, 1989.

[101] Thurman RB, Gerba CP. The molecular mechanisms of copper and silver ion disinfection of bacteria and viruses. CRC Crit Rev Environ Control 1989; 18(4).

[102] Henderson DA *et al.* Smallpox as a biological weapon (Consensus Statement). J Am Med Assoc 1999; 281(22): 2127–37.

[103] Fauci AS *et al.* Harrison's Principles of Internal Medicine, 14th edn. McGraw-Hill: New York, 1998.

[104] De Clercq E *et al.* Vaccinia virus inhibitors as a paradigm for the chemotherapy of poxvirus infections. Clin Microbiol Rev 2001; 14(2): 382–97.

[105] Taylor EW. Selenium and viral diseases: facts and hypotheses. J Orthomol Med 1997; 12–1: 227–39.

[106] Taylor EW, Ramanathan CS, Jalluri RK, Nadimpalli RG. A basis for new approaches to the chemotherapy of AIDS: novel genes in HIV-1 potentially encode selenoproteins expressed by ribosomal frameshifting and termination suppression. J Med Chem 1994; 37: 2637–54.

[107] Beck MA, Shi Q, Morris VC, Levander OA. Rapid genomic evolution of a non-virulent Cox-sackievirus B3 in selenium-deficient mice results in selection of identical virulent isolates. Nature Med 1995; 1: 433–6.

[108] Taylor EW, Ramanathan CS, Nadimpalli RG, Schinazi RF. Do some viruses encode selenoproteins? Assessment of the theory in the light of current theoretical, experimental and clinical data. Antiviral Res 1995; 26: A271, #86.

[109] Yu SY, Li WG, Zhu YJ *et al.* Chemoprevention trial of human hepatitis with selenium supplementation in China. Biol Trace Element Res 1989; 20: 15–22.

[110] Beck MA, Kolbeck PC, Rohr LH *et al.* Benign human enterovirus becomes virulent in selenium-deficient mice. J Med Virol 1994; 43: 166–70.

[111] Taylor EW, Ramanathan CS. Theoretical evidence that the Ebola virus Zaire strain may be selenium dependent: a factor in pathogenesis and viral outbreaks? J Orthomol Med 1995; 10: 131–8.

[112] Ramanathan CS, Taylor EW. Computational genomic analysis of hemorrhagic fever viruses: viral selenoproteins as a potential factor in pathogenesis. Biol Trace Element Res 1997; 56: 93–106.

[113] Hou JC. Inhibitory effect of selenite and other antioxidants on complement-mediated tissue injury in patients with epidemic hemorrhagic fever. Biol Trace Element Res 1997; 56: 125–30.

[114] Senkevich TG, Bugert JJ, Sisler JR *et al.* Genome sequence of a human tumorigenic poxvirus: prediction of specific host response-evasion genes. Science 1996; 273: 813–16.

[115] Cowgill UM. The distribution of selenium and mortality owing to acquired immune deficiency syndrome in the continental United States. Biol Trace Element Res 1997; 56: 43–61.

[116] Renis HE. In vitro anti viral activity of calcium elenolate. Antimicrob Agents Chemother 1969; 9: 167–72.

[117] Fleming H, Walter W *et al.* Antimicrobial properties of oleuropein and products of its hydrolysis from green olives. Microbiology 1973; 26(5): 777–82.

[118] Renis HE. Inactivation of myxoviruses by calcium elenolate. Antimicrob Agents Chemother 1975; 8(2): 194–9.

[119] Heinze J, Hale AH, Carl P. Specificity of the anti viral agent calcium elenolate. Antimicrob Agents Chemother 1975; 8(4): 421–5.

[120] Kaij-a-Kamb M, Amoros M, Girre L. Search for new antiviral agents of plant origin. Pharma-Acta-Helv 1992; 67(5–6): 130–47.

[121] Visioli F, Bellosta S, Galli C. Oleuropein, the bitter principle of olives, enhances nitric oxide production by mouse macrophages. Life Sci 1998; 62(6): 541–6.

[122] Ma SC, He ZD, Deng XL *et al.* In vitro evaluation of secoiridoid glucosides from the fruits of *Ligustrum lucidum* as antiviral agents. Chem Pharm Bull (Tokyo) 2001; 49(11): 1471–3.

[123] Walker M. Antimicrobial attributes of olive leaf extract. Townsend Letter for Doctors and Patients 1996; July: 80–5, #156.

[124] Kabara JJ, Swieczkowski DM, Conley AJ, Truant JP. Fatty acids and derivatives as antimicrobial agents. Antimicrob Agents Chemother 1972; 2(1): 23–8.

[125] Conley AJ, Kabara JJ. Antimicrobial action of esters of polyhydric alcohols. Antimicrob Agents Chemother 1973; 4: 501–6.

[126] Kabara JJ, Vrable R, Lie Ken Jie MSF. Antimicrobial lipids: natural and synthetic fatty acids and monoglycerides. Lipids 1977; 12: 753–9.

[127] Kabara JJ. Lipids as host resistance factors of human milk. Nutr Rev 1980; 38: 65–73.

[128] Kabara JJ. Medium-chain fatty acids and esters as antimicrobial agents. In: Kabara JJ (ed.) Cosmetic and Drug Presentation: Principles and Practice. Marcel Dekker: New York, 1984.

[129] Hierholzer JC, Kabara JJ. In vitro effects of monolaurin compounds on enveloped RNA and DNA viruses. J Food Safety 1982; 4: 1–12.

[130] Kabara JJ, Ohkawa M, Ikekawa T, Katori T, Nishikawa Y. Examinations on antitumor immunological, and plant-growth inhibitory effects of monoglycerides of caprylic, capric, and lauric acids and related compounds. In: Kabara JJ (ed.) The Pharmacological Effect of Lipids II. American Oil Chemists' Society: Champaign, IL, 1985.

[131] Flournoy DJ, Kabara JJ. The role of lauricidin® as an antimicrobial agent. Drugs of Today 1985; 21(8): 373–7.

[132] Crouch AA, Seow WK, Whitman LM, Thong YH. Effect of human milk and infant milk formulae on adherence of *Giardia intestinalis*. Trans R Soc Trop Med Hyg 1991; 85: 617–19.

[133] Dodge JA, Sagher FA. Antiviral and antibacterial lipids in human milk and infant formula. Arch Dis Child 1991; 66: 272–3.

[134] Enig MG. Lauric oils as antimicrobial agents: theory of effect, scientific rationale, and dietary applications as adjunct nutritional support for HIV-infected individuals. In: Watson RR (ed.) Nutrients and Foods in AIDS. CRC Press: Boca Raton, 1998.

[135] Epstein SE, Speir E, Zhou YF, Guetta E, Leon M, Finkel T. The role of infection in restenosis and atherosclerosis: focus on cytomegalovirus. Lancet 1996; 348(Suppl. 1): S13–17.

[136] Isaacs CE, Thormar H. Membrane-disruptive effect of human milk: inactivation of enveloped viruses. J Infect Dis 1986; 154: 966–71.

[137] Isaacs CE, Schneidman K. Enveloped viruses in human and bovine milk are inactivated by added fatty acids (FAs) and monoglycerides (MGs). FASEB J 1991; 5: A1288 (Abstract 5325).
[138] Witcher KJ, Novick RP, Schlievert PM. Modulation of immune cell proliferation by glycerol monolaurate. Clin Diag Lab Immunol 1996; 3: 10–13.
[139] van Rossum TG, Vulto AG, de Man RA, Brouwer JT, Schalm SW. Review article: Glycyrrhizin as a potential treatment for chronic hepatitis C. Department of Hepatogastroenterology, Erasmus University Hospital: Rotterdam (PubMed; PMID: 9570253).
[140] Shibayama Y. Prevention of hepatotoxic responses to chemicals by glycyrrhizin in rats. Exp Mol Pathol 1989; 51(1): 48–55.
[141] Vithoulkas G. Science of Homeopathy. ASOHM: Athens, 1978.
[142] Jonas WB. Do homeopathic nosodes protect against infection? Altern Ther Health Med 1999; 5(5): 36–40.
[143] Sankaran P. Prophylactics in homeopathy. Elements of Homeopathy. Homeopathic Medical Publishers: Bombay. (Originally published in British Journal of Homeopathy, c. 1960.)
[144] VanDenBerghe S. Anthracinum in splenic fever. Br J Homeop 1911; 460–5.

[3]

GLOBALIZATION MEETS FRANKENSTEIN? REFLECTIONS ON TERRORISM, NUCLEARITY, AND GLOBAL TECHNOPOLITICAL DISCOURSE

GABRIELLE HECHT*

Department of History, University of Michigan, Ann Arbor, MI 48109, USA

Post 9/11 discourse has important origins in Cold War technopolitical hierarchies that equated "nuclear" with colonizing nations and "non-nuclear" with colonized peoples. This paper gives examples of such equations in order to illuminate the place of nuclearity in current global technopolitics.

Keywords: Nuclear; Technopolitics; Cold War; Third World; Colonialism; Postcolonial

For those of us working in science and technology studies, the immediate media reaction to September 11, 2001 provided countless distressing examples of those deterministic, ahistorical ideologies about technological development we have sought to challenge. In commenting on the bitter irony of passenger airliners becoming weapons, for example, pundits asserted that the appropriation of technologies for something other than their intended purpose represented the *new* nature of violence in the 21st century. Most descriptions of the technological dimensions of the attacks invoked polarities taken straight from colonial-evolutionist discourse: "play the system right, and Neolithic technology can be leveraged to bring on nuclear-like devastation," said one journalist in the *New York Times*, presumably situating box-cutters in the Neolithic era. He continued: "it was not just planes that were hijacked but *technology*, to be used jujitsu style against its inventors."[1] As if the very "founding fathers" of America (learning, it must be said, from the Indians they displaced) hadn't used British guns in new ways in order to defeat the redcoats.[2] As if "technology" had fixed meanings, stable uses. Meanwhile, US president George W. Bush spluttered that the US would bomb Afghanistan "back into the Stone Age." The cry of protest from the left? "But Afghanistan already is in the Stone Age!"

In subsequent weeks, the complexities of the technopolitical networks undergirding the attacks became visible, and a few more sophisticated interpretations of the tragedy emerged. The attacks exploited weaknesses inherent in at least two complex technological systems (air travel and skyscrapers) that Americans themselves built. The attackers learned to fly in American flight schools. They learned terrorism in camps that the US instituted during the Soviet Union's war in Afghanistan. (A few even pointed out that Afghanistan was actually in

---

* E-mail: hechtg@umich.edu

the Rubble Age.) Pulling back for a macro view, some left-wing commentators found the roots of the crisis in the US's insatiable thirst for oil and the techno-geopolitical compromises made to quench it. Others suggested that the vast gulf between the promises and realities of "globalization" might provide reasons for many around the world to resent the US and the dominance of Western multinational corporations. A summary of these interpretations might be: globalization meets Frankenstein and his monster, that venerable archetype of unintended sociotechnical consequences.

Such observations were not popular in the American media, however, and they did not supplant cruder perspectives on the role of modernity and technology's relation to society. "The genius of the terrorists was to turn the artifacts of modernity into weapons against modernity,"[3] said one writer just a few weeks before the US launched a new Afghan war. He continued: "Odd and indeed disgusting as it is to find oneself writing that there is no alternative to war . . ., I find myself nonetheless with nothing else to suggest. Modernity, newly vulnerable, is, for all its faults, infinitely preferable to fascism." As if modernity hadn't always been fragile; as if Hitler hadn't shown that modernity and fascism were eminently compatible.[4]

As we know, these jumbled, false dichotomies (such as modernity vs fascism) and the historical ruptures they invoke are nothing new in public discourse about technology. The Cold War alone offers plenty of antecedents of what I call technopolitical rupture-talk[5]— namely, the rhetorical invocation of technological inventions to declare the arrival of a new era or a new division in the world. Most notorious in the Cold War, of course, were repeated political proclamations that nuclear weapons had produced a new world order. (More on this shortly.) Indeed, the Cold War itself figures as a significant trope for our present fearless leaders after September 11. In a fit of nostalgia for global Manichean struggle, Dick Cheney explained that the war against terrorism would resemble the Cold War, hinting darkly that— just as in those good old days—much of the current struggle would be invisible. And who didn't flash to Reagan's "evil empire" speech after Bush's puzzling pronouncement concerning the "axis of evil" allegedly formed by Iran, Iraq, and North Korea? Colin Powell took another tack, proclaiming the start of a new era—the post-post-Cold War—thereby suggesting the power of new alliances, and hinting at an ill-defined historical rupture. Clearly, whatever degree of post-ness we now find ourselves in with respect to the Cold War, the era looms large in our fantasies.

What leaders and media pundits generally fail to note, however, are the implications of Cold War infrastructure and discourse for our current crisis. Although such ahistoricism may not be surprising, its consequences become ever more severe as the US simultaneously reviews its own posture on the use of nuclear weapons and uses the potential nuclearity of "rogue states" to justify military action. In the remainder of this paper, I will consider some of the Cold War antecedents for the technopolitical rupture-talk of the early 21st century.

Since the onset of the Cold War, both the politics and the scholarship of the "nuclear age" has been all about rupture and dichotomy. The nuclear world has been portrayed as a polarized one, split into nuclear and non-nuclear states, nuclear and conventional technologies, nuclear and non-nuclear dangers, pro- and anti-nuclear politics. What it means to call something a "nuclear weapon" has seemed self-evident. Those weapons in turn have served as the basis for "nuclear diplomacy," which has also appeared to constitute a clearly defined set of practices. And so on. The dichotomies have appeared clear-cut, and they in turn have appeared to signal a profound historical rupture—especially in the mouths of Western political leaders, for whom "The Bomb" seemed to replace imperialism as the foundation for global power. Here the alleged rupture of nuclearity met the fundamental dichotomy posited by 19th and 20th century European imperialism: the opposition of "civilized" to "primitive." Premised on a correspondence between industrialization and human evolution, this dichotomy legitimated colonial practices and states. For former imperial states (especially France and Britain), the rupture of nuclearity could palliate the rupture threatened by the prospect of decolonization.

Such assertions of rupture and the polarities they invoked masked a more complex reality—an obvious point, perhaps, but nonetheless worth unpacking. The history of uranium mining, for example, shows that colonial practices and structures were appropriated—*not* overthrown—by the nuclear age, and proved central to its technopolitical success. Hiroshima uranium came from the Belgian Congo. After the war, Britain's colonial ties to uranium-supplying regions in Africa and Australia helped maintain nuclear relations with the US. South Africa's eagerness to place its vast uranium reserves at the disposal of the West led the US and Britain to gloss over the emerging apartheid regime.[6] France could pursue an independent nuclear program because it had access to uranium not just on metropolitan soil, but also in its African colonies.[7] Internal colonialism figured too: in the US, the richest uranium regions proved to be on Native American lands on the Colorado Plateau, while Australians found much of their uranium on Aboriginal lands in the Northern Territory. I could continue to enumerate examples: the Soviet Union mined uranium in East Germany and Czechoslovakia; South Africa mined uranium in (present-day) Namibia; Canada on native lands, India on tribal lands. And on and on. And the same for nuclear testing, as the US tested its weapons on the Marshall islands, France in Algeria and Polynesia, and Britain on Aboriginal lands.

Nuclear rupture-talk masked such local, regional, and national complexities while repeatedly invoking colonialism, decolonization, or post-coloniality in order to produce a vision of the world in which particular kinds of nuclear technopolitics served as the final arbiter of global status and power. This process operated in several ways. Let me offer a few rough sketches.

Perhaps most obviously, nuclearity appeared to provide imperial states with a geopolitical solution to the loss of status threatened by decolonization. With growing challenges to the legitimacy of colonial rule after World War II, Britain and France increasingly saw nuclear weapons as a means of retaining some measure of geopolitical power and glory. But it wasn't just that atom bombs could *replace* colonial states as an instrument of global power.[8] Atom bombs would also *prevent* these imperial states from *themselves* becoming reduced to the status of colonized subjects. Consider this remark by Churchill's chief scientific advisor, Lord Cherwell, in 1951: "If we have to rely entirely on the United States army for this vital weapon, we shall sink to the rank of a second-class nation, only permitted to supply auxiliary troops, like the native levies who were allowed small arms but no artillery."[9] And listen to French parliamentary deputy (and future prime minister) Félix Gaillard, also in 1951: "those nations which [do] not follow a clear path of atomic development [will] be, 25 years hence, as backward relative to the nuclear nations of that time as the primitive peoples of Africa [are] to the industrialized nations of today."[10]

These are but two examples of a rich discourse, which functioned by dialectically mapping two sets of bimodal geopolitical subject positions onto each other. Nuclear = (former) colonizer. Non-nuclear = colonized. Over the course of the Cold War this bimodal positioning shifted in complex ways, particularly as the language of colonialism mutated into the language of "development" and the category of "Third World" became a staple of international politics.[11] Thus, for example, international discourse on non-proliferation made it particularly inappropriate—morally, technologically, politically—for a "Third World" nation to go nuclear.

But several "Third World" nations did not accept the dictates of the international non-proliferation regime, viewing it instead as a neo-colonial effort on the part of the "developed" nations to preserve geopolitical dominance.[12] If Charles de Gaulle could declare that "a state does not count if it does not bring something to the world that contributes to the technological progress of the world,"[13] then why shouldn't Saddam Hussein assert that "nations and people are measured and influenced by the extent of their scientific and technological progress"[14]? For both leaders, the ultimate measure of technopolitical might was possession of atomic weaponry—and indeed, France played a major role in Iraqi nuclear development.[15] Geopolitical status could be measured by technological achievement—but not just any old technology would do. Of course, while Iraqi nuclear capability may have appeared manageable and desirable in the 1970s, in subsequent decades it has become one of France's Frankenstinian monsters. The US, meanwhile, has developed a special label for such Frankenstinian creations: the rogue state.[16] Not all challengers to nuclear non-proliferation regime are designated as rogues, however. Israel certainly isn't, and India and Pakistan were merely "prospective rogues."[17]

As a formerly colonized nation, India found special resonance in the complex discursive links between nuclearity and coloniality. Itty Abraham and George Perkovich have shown that nuclear development was central to India's construction of itself as a *post*-colonial state. In the 1950s and 60s, Indian scientists and technologists believed that nuclear development would shape their nation's post-coloniality with what Abraham calls a distinctive hybrid of "science, modernity, and indigeneity."[18] The precise nature of that hybridity was up for debate. Some elites thought that India should distinguish itself from the West by taking the moral high ground, *renouncing* military nuclear capability. Others thought that India *required* the military atom to attain a level of prestige commensurate with its size. Proclaimed to be a "peaceful nuclear explosion," the 1974 test was clothed as a tenuous compromise. But Indian relations with Pakistan continued to heat up, and by the 1980s (if not sooner) a full-scale nuclear arms race was underway in south Asia, culminating in the decidedly non-peaceful 1998 tests.

Perkovich argues that the Indian state legitimated its nuclear weapons in part by framing "the US-led non-proliferation regime as a racist, colonial project to deny India the fruits of its own labor."[19] In global technopolitical discourse, nuclearity had indeed replaced colonialism—uncomfortably, dialectically, and not at all the way the superpowers had anticipated. Perhaps predictably, many Western observers ignored the complex national and regional technopolitics involved in these weapons developments, casting the problem instead in terms of cosmic global conflict. What should the world do in the face of a "Hindu bomb"? An "Islamic bomb"? Did the tests mean that India and Pakistan had become full-fledged "rogues"? As tensions in the subcontinent heated up in early 2002, such questions gained particular salience.

The problem of what constituted appropriate nuclear behavior and how that was linked to "Third World"/post-colonial geopolitics was not limited to atomic weapons development. Consider Gabon, a central African nation that gained independence from French Equatorial Africa in 1960. Just 3 years earlier, in 1957, French geologists had found a major uranium deposit there. Fearing the possible consequences of looming decolonization for any operation run by the colonial or metropolitan state, the French atomic energy commission created a private corporation, the COMUF, to operate the uranium mine. This arrangement would make uranium mining politically viable in post-colonial Gabon, since anything run by the French state would have been suspect, and possibly subject to appropriation by the new government. As the Gabonese state grew stronger, it demanded a part of the action. In 1974, Gabon augmented the COMUF's capitalization by 760 million FCFA,[20] thereby acquiring a 25% share in the company.[21] Frenchmen continued as managers and engineers, and expected the Gabonese state to remain a silent partner. After all, what expertise could Gabonese officials possibly have in matters nuclear? So company managers were shocked to learn in 1975 that President Omar Bongo had agreed to sell 800 tons of uranium to Iran. The shock must have been even greater to their metropolitan bosses, since France had been secretly supplying reactor technology to Iran's biggest rival, Iraq. Bongo's "rogue" uranium diplomacy—of which this was not the only example—left the COMUF scrambling to figure out how to satisfy Bongo without undermining French nuclear diplomacy, all while staying solvent.[22]

The Iran deal collapsed at the last minute with the fall of the Shah, but Bongo had made his point: uranium could serve as a means for challenging the order of things in which atomic diplomacy was the prerogative of former colonizers-turned-nuclear-weapons-states. Nuclear rupture-talk assumes an all or nothing approach to nuclear diplomacy that has (or had) a peculiar kind of rigidity. Either you have the bomb (or are trying to get it) and can therefore practice some form of nuclear diplomacy or blackmail. Or you don't (and aren't trying), and are therefore ultimately powerless. This technopolitically rigid view of what it means to be a nuclear state ignores the real ambiguities inherent in nuclear technologies. The example of Bongo's Gabon is just one among many that show that it's never been a matter of all or nothing: there are dozens of intermediary steps between finding uranium in the ground and exploding it in a fission bomb. Each of those steps has its own technopolitics. The specter of radioactively laced "conventional" weapons should make that all too clear.

● ● ●

What do we get by juxtaposing these various examples? For one thing, they all illustrate the dialectical relationships between nuclear technopolitics and colonialism and its corollaries. Questions about geopolitical legitimacy lie at the heart of the ways that nuclear and post-colonial rupture-talk interact. In the first couple of decades of the Cold War, the "international community" (a phrase I'm highly suspicious of, but I use it here for convenience) increasingly condemned colonialism as an illegitimate means of ordering geopolitical relations. At the same time, metropoles and superpowers embraced nuclear technopolitics as a legitimate practice of global power—a practice that continued to depend on colonial networks. Yet nuclear technopolitics by their very nature had multiple meanings; their range of action was by no means limited to that defined by their early users. They could be used to redefine French radiance or British glory in an era of decolonization, and they could also serve to assert the post-coloniality of the Indian state.

At various moments, Western nuclear powers have censured India, Pakistan, North Korea, South Africa, Iran, Iraq, and Israel for their efforts to acquire nuclear weaponry. Bush's "axis of evil" phrase is only the most recent version of a longstanding discourse in which nuclearity was defined as appropriate for some nations but not for others. In return, these inappropriately nuclear nations have condemned the NPT and IAEA safeguards as neo-colonial. Thus the nuclear and the post-colonial both confront and depend on each other repeatedly in a battle for geopolitical legitimacy. The regimes of discourse produced in these confrontations shape the possibilities for action. Insistence on the illegitimacy of "third" or "second" world nuclear aspirations means, in effect, that attempts to persuade these nations *not* to develop nuclear weapons are decried as neo-colonial, and are therefore themselves illegitimate. Because the dichotomies of nuclear rupture-talk tend to erase national or regional political complexities and insist on a rupture from colonial relations, they have become—somewhat paradoxically—worse than useless in non-proliferation efforts.

On another front, consider the US's latest anti-ballistic missile defense fantasies. These descend directly from unrequited Cold War lusts embodied in systems such as SAGE and SDI. These systems never worked to fulfill their stated purpose of automatically tracking and shooting down incoming bombers (in the case of SAGE) or missiles from space (in the case of SDI)—though they did work in other, political and economic ways.[23] There's ample evidence that the latest version of a protective shield won't work either: its detection systems can't tell the most basic differences between a decoy and a warhead.[24] There's also good reason to think it won't work politically.[25] These problems don't seem to bother most

6   G. HECHT

lawmakers in Capitol Hill or the White House, however. Insisting on the "post-ness" of the post-Cold War world, ABM proponents argue that these systems will defend America from "rogue states," despite bloody evidence that "states" aren't necessarily our worst enemy, and that you don't in fact need a nuclear missile (or even biological or chemical weaponry) to terrify a superpower. No matter: the fantasists have apparently persuaded the nation to cling bravely to the conviction that technopolitical power can be circumscribed and fully specified; that despite the "diabolical" cleverness of turning box-cutters and airplanes into extraordinarily effective weapons, the true threat comes from those good old Cold War technologies: missiles and weapons of mass destruction.

Here the "axis of evil" slogan helps the fantasist cause mightily, since it defines states that could—if they were stupid and insane enough—manage to lob a missile over to US territory. Of course, since even the fantasists must admit that missile defense doesn't *currently* work, Bush and his Dr Strangeloves have several new plans allegedly aimed at foiling such scenarios. Plan A: attack Iraq. The justifications for such an attack oscillate. Some days Iraq's potential possession of nuclear weapons gets trotted out. When the imminence of Iraqi nuclearity is contested, the need for a "regime change" is invoked. At this writing, the fate of Plan A is very much up in the air. And debates about it have deflected attention from Plan B, which is in some ways bigger, more sweeping, and likely to keep the military-industrial complex happy for years to come: the 2002 Nuclear Posture Review (NPR). In this latest manifestation of nuclear rupture-talk, the US would develop tactical nuclear weapons to burrow into underground bunkers in which the "axis of evil" might be confectioning nuclear, chemical, or biological weapons. (This is not the only aim of the NPR, but I'll limit myself to this for this paper.) Plan B seemed to surprise observers, but as recently as October 2001 congressman Steven Buyer eerily presaged elements of the NPR when he advocated plugging up Afghan caves with tactical nuclear weapons—an idea also favored by several other Republican representatives. Plan B has been both decried and praised as a post- (or post-post-?) Cold War plan: either way, observers view the NPR as technopolitical rupture. Its opponents claim that this is the first time the US has contemplated using nuclear weapons against non-nuclear states; they forget Korea and Vietnam. Proponents claim that September 11 signaled the death-knell of traditional nuclear deterrence; in the era of suicide bombers, nuclear retaliation is no longer a protective threat. They further insist that such mini-nukes (a cutesy designation to soften the blow?), aimed at burrowing deep underground, wouldn't cause widespread radioactive devastation—this in the face of clear evidence that such weapons could never go deep enough to be significantly contained.

Like its predecessors, this latest manifestation of nuclear rupture-talk is aimed at soothing and/or terrifying its audience. And like its predecessors, what it decidedly does not do is leave room for complexities. The portion of the NPR aimed at "rogue states" leapfrogs over the deterrent posed by the doctrine of mutually assured destruction because these states don't have arsenals the size of Russia's. In initial public discussions of the NPR there was—weirdly, given September 11—no sense that other forms of retaliation might be possible. No sense that states subjected to nuclear attack might have angry friends. Certainly no admission of the ways in which imperial power regimes remain embedded in our own technopolitical systems. And ongoing total incomprehension of why and how former empires might want to strike back.

Just as the stark dichotomies posited by the Cold War world got fuzzier the closer you examined them, so too for today's dichotomies. Consider my personal favorite: the line between nuclear and non-nuclear. I've argued that even during the Cold War it was not in fact all that clear what was nuclear diplomacy and what wasn't. But in those good old days, you knew what nuclear weapons were (or at least you thought you did). Now, it's not so apparent. Do munitions loaded up with depleted uranium count as "nuclear"? Not if you're NATO or the US, using them in the Balkans or the Gulf War. But if you're a terrorist contemplating packing a bomb with radioactive material purchased on the black market, you've violated a fundamental taboo. By crossing the nuclear/non-nuclear divide, you've committed an act of pollution: you've made a "dirty bomb." (One does wonder which bombs are the clean ones.) What qualifies such bombs as "dirty" is not so much the *technical* infraction of mixing the "nuclear" with the "conventional," but rather the *technopolitics* of who's doing the mixing, how, and to what ends. The stubborn persistence of global technopolitical hierarchies figures here in important ways, most interestingly in the "how" part: calling these bombs "dirty" signals not just moral outrage at technological pollution, but also disdain for the inability of the bomb builders to produce a "real" nuclear weapon.

My point, of course, is *not* that it should be acceptable for terrorists to make radioactive weapons of any kind, or that Saddam Hussein should be allowed to develop weapons of mass destruction. Rather, it's that the current shape of global technopolitics has deep roots in the dialectics between nuclear and post-colonial rupture-talk, between nuclear and post-colonial technopolitics. These dialectics have defined the parameters for global power relations, and shaped geopolitical subjectivities in multiple registers and in ways whose significance we have barely begun to grasp. If we are indeed in a "post-" or a "post-post-" Cold War world, then it's the same kind of "post-ness" that we find in the "post-colonial." The infrastructures and discourses of Cold War technopolitics continue to shape the parameters of global and local action, just as the infrastructures and discourses of colonialism do. We ignore those roots—and the contradictions they produce—at our peril.

NOTES

1. George Johnson, "Order of Magnitude: The Toll and the Technology," *New York Times*, 16 September 2001: Wk 3, my emphasis.
2. Patrick M. Malone, *The Skulking Way of War: Technology and Tactics among the New England Indians* (Baltimore: Johns Hopkins University Press, 1993). For a more contemporary example, see the discussion of the Vietcong in Paul Edwards, *The Closed World: Computers and the Politics of Discourse in Cold War America* (Cambridge, MA: MIT Press, 1996).
3. David Rieff, "There is no alternative to war," http://www.salon.com/news/feature/2001/09/25/modernity/index.html?
4. Michael Allen, "The Puzzle of Nazi Modernism: Modern Technology and Ideological Consensus in an SS Factory in Auschwitz," *Technology and Culture* (1996), 37: 527–571.
5. Gabrielle Hecht, "Rupture-talk in the Nuclear Age: Conjugating Colonial Power in Africa," *Social Studies of Science* (December 2002): forthcoming.
6. Thomas Borstelmann, *Apartheid's Reluctant Uncle: The United States and Southern Africa in the Early Cold War* (New York: Oxford University Press, 1993).
7. Hecht, op. cit.
8. Gabrielle Hecht, *The Radiance of France: Nuclear Power and National Identity after World War II (Inside Technology)* (Cambridge, MA: MIT Press, 1998); Brian Cathcart, *Test of Greatness: Britain's Struggle for the Atom Bomb* (London: Murray, 1994); Margaret Gowing, *Independence and Deterrence: Britain and Atomic Energy, 1945–1952* (London: Macmillan Press, 1974).
9. Alice Cawte, *Atomic Australia, 1944–1990* (Kensington: New South Wales University Press, 1992), p. 41.
10. Quoted in Hecht, op. cit., p. 62.
11. Arturo Escobar, *Encountering Development: The Making and Unmaking of the Third World* (Princeton, NJ: Princeton University Press, 1995).
12. Richard Falk, "The Illegitimacy of the Non-Proliferation Regime," *The Brown Journal of World Affairs* (1997), Vol. IV No. 1, 73–82.
13. Quoted in Hecht, *Radiance*, op. cit., p. 93.
14. Quoted in Ahmed Hashim, "Iraq: Profile of a Nuclear Addict," *The Brown Journal of World Affairs* (1997), Vol. IV No. 1, 103–126, p. 116.
15. Pierre Péan, *Les Deux Bombes: Comment la France a "donné" la bombe à Israel et à l'Irak* (Paris: Fayard, 1982).
16. Michael T. Klare, *Rogue States and Nuclear Outlaws: America's Search for a New Foreign Policy*, 1st ed. (New York: Hill and Wang, 1995).
17. Ibid., p. 134.

18. Itty Abraham, *The Making of the Indian Atomic Bomb: Science, Secrecy and the Postcolonial State* (London, New York: Zed Books, St. Martin's Press, 1998), p. 156.
19. G. Perkovich, *India's Nuclear Bomb: The Impact on Global Proliferation* (Berkeley: University of California Press, 1999), p. 7.
20. Francs of the African Financial Community; this currency was tied to the French Franc.
21. COMUF, "Plan Quinquennal 1975," 31 May 1974. GH: plans quinquennaux, 1975–79. COMUF archives.
22. "Entretien avec M. Ampana, 28–29 November 1975"; "Compte-rendu des négociations entre le Gouvernement Gabonais—COMUF—et l'Organisation Iranienne de l'Energie Atomique," 1976 and associated memos; Edouard Alexis M'Bouy-Boutzit, "Confidentiel-Secret Note à la haute attention de Monsieur le Président de la République," 6 January 1976; correspondence between H. Basset and Edouard Alexis M'Bouy-Boutzit, 1976–1977; "Agreement between the Compagnie des Mines d'Uranium de Franceville 'COMUF' (Gabon) and Atomic Energy Organization of Iran," (draft, probably September 1976); misc. telex correspondence 1976–1978. GH: Iran contract (COMUF archives).
23. Edwards, op. cit.
24. See Gary Taubes, "Postol vs. the Pentagon: Missile Defense," *Technology Review* (April 2002). See also Andrew M. Sessler *et al. Countermeasures: A Technical Evaluation of the Operational Effectiveness of the Planned U.S. National Missile Defense System* (UCS, 2000). See also the web site of the Union of Concerned Scientists: http://www.ucsusa.org/security/sec-home.html
25. For an exceptionally clear argument about the political dangers of implementing National Missile Defense, see Steven Weinberg, "Can Missile Defense Work," *NYRB* (XLIX) 2, 14 February 2002: 41–47.

[4]

Challenges associated with creating a pharmaceutical stockpile to respond to a terrorist event

R. Havlak, S. E. Gorman and S. A. Adams

Centers for Disease Control and Prevention, National Pharmaceutical Stockpile Program, Atlanta, Georgia, USA

The Centers for Disease Control and Prevention (CDC) was called into action to develop a National Pharmaceutical Stockpile (NPS). The NPS was created to respond to terrorism events involving blast, chemical and biological agents. There are many challenges associated with creating, managing and using such an asset. This paper provides a helpful background for clinicians and those planning to develop pharmaceutical and/or medical materiel stockpiles for national use. It also describes major challenges and offers suggestions for meeting those challenges.

Keywords Stockpile, terrorism, emergency, pharmaceuticals

Clin Microbiol Infect 2002; 8: 529–533

INTRODUCTION

The attack on the USA on 11 September 2001, and the anthrax attacks in October 2001, marked the debut of the US approach to addressing challenges associated with the mass use of antimicrobial agents in a terrorist event. The National Pharmaceutical Stockpile (NPS) Program, of the Centers for Disease Control and Prevention (CDC), was called into action to respond to these attacks.

On 11 September 2001, the State of New York requested that the CDC send an NPS Program 12-h Push Package to help in treating casualties with trauma-related injuries who were expected to overwhelm the hospital system in New York City. A 12-h Push Package was built mainly for response to biological and chemical terrorism. It is used when the type of threat that an area is facing is unclear. It is a 50-ton package of approximately 100 specialized cargo containers that include antimicrobials and chemical antidotes as well as medical/surgical supplies, airway management equipment, fluids, and intravenous administration

Corresponding author and reprint requests: S. Gorman, Centers for Disease Control and Prevention, 1600 Clifton Road, MS D-08, Atlanta, GA 30333, USA
Tel: +404 639 0459
Fax: +404 639 1527
E-mail: spg4@cdc.gov

supplies. All of the medical supplies were expected to be of use in New York City.

Even though all air traffic and ground movement had been suspended, under a previously negotiated special agreement with the Federal Aviation Administration, the CDC deployed a 12-h Push Package, which arrived by a combination of ground and air transport within 7 h of the official request. A police escort ensured the smooth transport of assets being moved by ground.

The CDC also responded to the anthrax attacks that emerged in early October 2001. The NPS Program delivered oral antimicrobials for post-exposure prophylaxis to exposed mail handlers, employees in Congressional office buildings, and personnel from affected media organizations. These antimicrobials came not from the NPS Program 12-h Push Package, but from its Vendor Managed Inventory (VMI), the second part of the NPS Program. The VMI is a large inventory of NPS product lines that can be tailored to the emergent needs of an affected area. It is used for dealing with an identified, known threat agent. The NPS Program filled at least 80 VMI requests for antimicrobials across the USA and delivered them in an average of 5 h from receipt of the request.

The concept of an NPS Program has made apparent the many challenges associated with the mass use of antimicrobial agents in a terrorist event. We describe here the development of the

530   *Clinical Microbiology and Infection*, Volume 8 Number 8, 2002

NPS Program to address these challenges, and how it has worked and been adapted in actual terrorist attack conditions. This information may be useful for other nations considering their own response mechanisms.

CHALLENGES 1 AND 2: ENLISTING POLITICAL AND FISCAL SUPPORT FOR A STOCKPILE

The concept of a stockpile of antimicrobials and other medical materiel requires substantial political and fiscal support. In the USA, political support for the NPS Program manifested in 1999 through an authorization by the US Congress. Several Members of Congress who were committed to the idea of an NPS Program obtained an appropriation of $50 million to begin the program at the CDC. Appropriations remained level at $52 million annually for fiscal years 2000 and 2001. NPS Program funding proposals for fiscal year 2002 have exceeded $600 million. Political support was strong from the beginning. US officials had had a resolute appreciation of the terrorist threat for several years before it materialized, and recognized that an NPS would be a national security asset that would become particularly important if and when a threat materialized.

CHALLENGE 3: CENTRALIZED VERSUS DECENTRALIZED STOCKPILES

One challenge was deciding whether to have a centralized stockpile, decentralized stockpiles, or some combination of both. US preparedness for biological and chemical terrorism included the promotion of both types of stockpile, but emphasized centralization. Support for decentralized stockpiles, or those maintained in localities, has been limited to small quantities of antidote for chemical and nerve agent weapons. This is consistent with the reality that saving lives after an attack of chemicals or nerve agents requires having antidote immediately available for administration. The NPS Program decided that the NPS would be a stockpile of antimicrobials and antidotes (for ongoing care of patients) that is centrally operated as a resource to be made available promptly to any locality in need. This provides economies of scale in procurement, and efficiencies in oversight, while removing the burden from

each state or locality of creating and maintaining this asset. The NPS Program thus became a partnership enterprise in which each state, in exchange for access to the centrally operated stockpile, develops plans and prepares to effectively manage and use this asset if it ever needs to be deployed there.

CHALLENGE 4: ESTABLISHING STOCKPILE REQUIREMENTS

Another challenge was to determine stockpile 'requirements' or the target number of persons for which therapy and post-exposure prophylaxis should be amassed. Requirements were determined by the maximum numbers of persons expected to be casualties in a particular type of terrorist event [1]. This translated into the scope and amounts of medical materiel that the stockpile should contain for treating and preventing infections or other symptoms resulting from the most likely threat agents. Equally important was the determination of the ratio of intravenous versus oral medications to be included in the stockpile [2]. The NPS Program's approach to setting requirements was to consult with panels of experts on the subject of biological and chemical terrorism.

NPS Program antimicrobials and antidotes were determined largely by published treatment recommendations for the threat agents deemed to have priority on the basis of their lethality, capacity for weaponization, and ease of delivery [3–8]. Once the priority threat agents were identified and the projected casualties were predicted, these figures became the initial requirements for the NPS Program and formed its procurement objectives. Next, the NPS Program delegated decision-making to subject matter experts for certain ancillary products for the stockpile. These included: medical and surgical items; supplies for intravenous administration and airway management, and other emergency medications, as well as equipment for product cooling, oral drug repackaging, and containerization of the stockpile itself.

CHALLENGE 5: DECIDING ON THE ORGANIZATION OF THE STOCKPILE

A further challenge in creating a pharmaceutical stockpile designed for response to a terrorist attack is the way in which the assets should be structured in relation to likely terrorism scenarios. An initial response to an attack would need a follow-on response that adjusts for the scope and type of attack as the realities of the attack become clear. An initial response must also be prepared to deal with simultaneous attacks that may occur some distance apart. The CDC addressed this problem by designing the NPS around two tiers of response, the 12-h Push Package and the VMI.

The initial response is called the 12-h Push Package: 'Push', because an area needs only to request help and the CDC will send a 50-ton shipment of more than 100 specialized cargo containers that house a portion of each line item in the NPS inventory. The CDC has built 12 of these 12-h Push Packages and located them in 10 strategic storage sites across the USA. This enables the CDC to respond to simultaneous terrorist events, regardless of their distance from one another. Products are rotated in and out of the Push Packages in order to ensure that in-date, fresh product is available at all times.

The VMI is the second tier of the NPS. It consists of a larger supply of most product lines in the 12-h Push Packages. The manufacturers of the VMI store these products for the NPS Program, and rotate the items to maintain the longest possible period of freshness. The VMI is designed for a tailored response to a terrorist event, which could range from providing huge quantities of a particular product in follow-on, to an event large enough to call for a 12-h Push Package or, as in the response to recent US anthrax attacks, to an event too small to justify Push Package deployment. This structure has proven to be flexible and has served the NPS Program well.

CHALLENGE 6: DETERMINING A PROCUREMENT PARTNER

Because the CDC is a public-health agency that does not routinely engage in procuring antimicrobials, antidotes, and other medical materiel (except for childhood vaccines), the CDC had only limited experience and presence in the marketplace from which to negotiate favorable costs for product. To resolve these issues, the CDC partnered for procurement with the National Acquisition Center (NAC) of the US Department of Veterans' Affairs. The NAC annually purchases more than $3 billion in medicines and medical materiel for the health-

care system for US veterans of military service. This gives the NAC a solid relationship with manufacturers and distributors and a powerful marketplace position from which to negotiate such issues as price, manufacturing priority, delivery arrangements, and maximum product shelf life. The fee that the CDC pays to the NAC for each procurement is more than offset by cost savings and the convenience of having procurement conducted by an organization that specializes in the field. Any organization managing a stockpile is advised to seek a similar arrangement if it does not possess a presence in the marketplace.

CHALLENGE 7: DETERMINING A PRODUCT MANAGEMENT PARTNER

One of the most serious challenges for management of a pharmaceutical stockpile is product expiration date. This applies less often to medical supplies than to pharmaceuticals, but these products tend to be the most costly and critical items in a stockpile. The CDC partnered with the NAC's prime pharmaceutical distributor to rotate the potency-dated products in the NPS. Products are flagged for rotation approximately 12 months before their expiration, traded for fresh product, and sold to the distributor's commercial customers. The NPS pays a restocking fee for this service that is far below the cost of replacing the expiring product. Certain chemical antidotes and military-specific pharmaceutical devices are tested for potency as they near their expiration date. If these products pass a battery of tests, the US Food and Drug Administration (FDA) may extend the products' shelf life under a special program administered by the FDA. The manager of a pharmaceutical stockpile is advised to seek both types of arrangement.

CHALLENGE 8: DETERMINING STORAGE SITES/PARTNERS

A number of challenges exist in determining appropriate storage for a stockpile. Storage sites must be secured to prevent unauthorized access; they must be protected from the elements (e.g. water damage, rodent infestation); and they must be environmentally controlled so that product will not be exposed to temperature extremes. The CDC also chose storage sites for its NPS Program 12-h

Push Packages on the basis of transport considerations. The CDC believed that it was important to select sites from which its air and ground transport partners could smoothly move these large packages to points across the country within 12 hours of a federal decision to deploy the assets. Both civilian and military storage locations can be considered when determining storage partners.

CHALLENGE 9: DETERMINING TRANSPORT PARTNERS

A centrally operated stockpile must be able to move rapidly from its storage locations to any affected site(s) in the country. This requires cargo transport that has both dependable cargo handling and reliable response times. The CDC partnered with commercial transportation companies, with the US military as a back-up. Although the military may appear to be the preferred choice from the standpoint of dependability, security, and transportation of assets, its availability for performing civilian functions during a war situation could pose a problem. Defending the country in a time of war is the primary mission of the US military, and a terrorist act is considered an act of war. The military could never give absolute deference to the NPS Program, because a directive from the National Command Authority could change its mission.

The CDC partnered with two private cargo transporters. These partnerships allow for transportation by either air or ground. In selecting transportation partners, other countries should consider the transportation assets of their military force and the extent to which these assets could be firmly committed to transporting the stockpile during a major threat to the health and safety of its people. Where this cannot be ensured, the use of commercial transportation partners as the primary source may be prudent to consider.

CHALLENGE 10: DEVISING A STRATEGY FOR PREPARING UNIT-OF-USE ORAL PROPHYLAXIS

The consensus of experts is that the vast majority of persons exposed in a biological terrorist attack will require post-exposure prophylaxis rather than therapeutic treatment for symptomatic disease. Unit-of-use packaging is common in many parts of the world but is still a novelty in the USA. Bulk bottles of 100 or 500 tablets of various antimicrobials are the most marketable versions of these products in the USA, but the antimicrobials must be converted to unit-of-use form before they can be dispensed to individuals. The CDC has acquired tools for repackaging bulk tablets, including the use of industrial packaging machines, pill-counting machines, and volumetric devices for filling prescriptions by hand. To rapidly distribute antimicrobials to affected individuals, the CDC recently turned to advance repackaging of bulk product into unit-of-use form (i.e. 10-day or 25-day regimens) through firms licensed by the FDA to repackage antimicrobials under conditions that allow them to retain their original expiration dates. This keeps maximum product shelf life while saving time in distributing antimicrobials to individuals. It also emphasizes the need for local-level planning to move oral prophylaxis to points of distribution and the need for efficient operation of those points of distribution.

CHALLENGE 11: ENSURING EFFECTIVE MANAGEMENT AND USE IN A DEPLOYMENT

A challenge for any stockpile program, especially one that is operated centrally, is ensuring that its assets will be effectively managed and used when they are needed. A centrally operated stockpile could be designed to deploy with enough personnel to repackage, move and distribute antimicrobials and antidotes to the exposed population. This could be a function of how public health is administered and whether a local infrastructure exists upon which to build a process for response. Because public health in the USA is a shared responsibility, the CDC is developing partnerships with all states to help them plan and prepare to effectively manage and use the NPS in the event that the NPS is deployed to their states. The CDC NPS Program has engaged in an active campaign of education and technical assistance to develop such plans and preparations. In the event of deployment of the NPS, NPS Program staff will meet the shipment, and help state and local public-health and emergency response workers to rapidly set up and transport NPS Program assets to their intended locations. Regardless of the national infrastructure for moving and distributing a deployed pharmaceutical stockpile, having these components in place is as vital as

Havlak *et al* Pharmaceutical stockpile to respond to a terrorist event 533

having fresh antimicrobials for mass prophylaxis or treatment.

CONCLUSION: EXPECTING THE UNEXPECTED

In conclusion, there are many challenges associated with the creation and use of a pharmaceutical stockpile. This paper has attempted to present the major challenges encountered in this process. One final challenge for a stockpile program is the need to prepare for the unexpected. For this reason, the CDC has built redundancy into many aspects of the NPS Program. Examples include creation of multiple 12-h Push Packages, using multiple manufacturers of product wherever possible, having multiple transport partners, and having multiple methods of supplying unit-of-use antimicrobials. It is prudent for stockpile designers and operators to build in redundancy wherever possible. This is particularly important with mission-critical components, so as not to compromise readiness when a terrorist event occurs.

REFERENCES

1. US Department of Health and Human Services. *Operating plan for anti-bioterrorism initiative, Fiscal Year 1999.* Washington DC: US Department of Health and Human Services, 1999.
2. Barcyen OV, Blascović D, Evang K, Huisman L, Humphrey JH *et al. Health aspects of chemical and biological weapons. Report of a WHO Group of Consultants.* Geneva: World Health Organization, 1970: 98–9.
3. Inglesby TV, Henderson DA, Bartlett JG *et al.* Anthrax as a biological weapon. *JAMA* 1999; 281: 1735–45.
4. Friedlander AM, Welkos SL, Pitt MLM *et al.* Postexposure prophylaxis against experimental inhalational anthrax. *J Infect Dis* 1993; 167: 1239–42.
5. Inglesby TV, Dennis DT, Henderson DA *et al.* Plague as a biological weapon. *JAMA* 2000; 283: 2281–90.
6. Arnon SS, Schechter R, Inglesby TV *et al.* Botulinum toxin as a biological weapon. *JAMA* 2001; 285: 1059–70.
7. Dennis DT, Inglesby TV, Henderson DA *et al.* Tularemia as a biological weapon. *JAMA* 2001; 285: 2763–73.
8. Office of the Surgeon General. *Textbook of military medicine Part 1: Chemical and biological warfare.* Falls Church, VA, United States Army, 1997.

[5]

Biological weapons and bioterrorism preparedness: importance of public-health awareness and international cooperation

R. Roffey[1], K. Lantorp[2], A. Tegnell[3] and F. Elgh[1,3,4]

[1]Swedish Defence Research Agency, Division of NBC-Defense, Umeå, [2]Department of Infectious Disease Control, Jönköping, [3]Center for Microbiological Preparedness, Swedish Institute for Infectious Disease Control (SMI), Solna and [4]Department of Virology, Umeå University, Umeå, Sweden

Biological weapons and biological terrorism have recently come into focus due to the deliberate release of *Bacillus anthracis* via mail delivered in the USA. Since the 1930s, biological weapons have been developed in a number of countries. In 1975, the Biological and Toxin Weapons Convention entered into force; this prohibits the use of these weapons and has been signed by a large majority of countries (144). Unfortunately, several countries failed to respect this treaty. The Soviet Union continued and expanded its biological weapons program, and after the Gulf War it was revealed that Iraq also had an extensive biological weapons program. Large-scale deliberate release of, *Bacillus anthracis*, for example, or an epidemic following a release of smallpox virus, would have a devastating effect. This has motivated the world community to strengthen the Biological and Toxin Weapons Convention with a control mechanism which has, as yet, not been successful. Sweden, like other countries, is enhancing its preparedness with regard to stocks of antibiotics and vaccines, related to these improving the diagnostics these and similar agents, and is setting up an epidemiologic task force that can be used in infectious disease emergencies such as the deliberate release of biological warfare agents. International cooperation in this area has to be enhanced, not least in the European Union.

Keywords Bioterrorism, biological weapons, preparedness

Clin Microbiol Infect 2002; 8: 522–528

BIOLOGICAL WARFARE

Biological weapons are microorganisms, in particular bacteria, virus and fungi, but also other organisms, that can be deliberately dispersed to incapacitate or cause disease and death to humans, animals or plants. Biological warfare agents can be natural or genetically modified. Genetic modification of microorganisms is common and is worrisome if the technique is misused, as the progress in cell and molecular biology technology has opened new and dangerous possibilities. Here, we define bioterrorism as either the threat of use or deliberate use of biological agents to cause harm or disease by criminals, including terrorists, individuals or groups with political, economic, religious, ecological or other ideological motivations.

Microorganisms, and also toxins, have been used for such purposes for a long time. This misuse has its background in the fact that many of these pathogens are inexpensive and relatively easy to produce if one has basic microbiological training. Only small quantities are required to cause large and terrifying effects. Another important factor is that the effects of these types of biological warfare agents are not immediate; as there is an incubation period, there will be a short or long time delay, which makes it simple to carry out a covert attack. There could also be dangerous secondary effects, due to the dramatic overburdening of the healthcare system, demands on other community services, and the risk of further epidemic spread of the disease.

Corresponding author and reprint requests: F. Elgh, Center for Microbiological Preparedness, Swedish Institute for Infectious Disease Control, SE-171 82 Umeå, Sweden
Tel: +46 70 669 2540
Fax: +46 8 307 957
E-mail: fredrik.elgh@foi.se

The idea of using microorganisms as warfare agents has a very long history. An early example of this was the contamination of water wells with dead corpses of humans or animals to prevent the enemy from obtaining fresh drinking water. It is believed that the plague (the black death) in the Middle Ages started in Europe when that affliction spread among the Mongolian tartars besieging the Genoese city of Caffa on the Crimea in 1346. When the city could not be taken, the attackers catapulted corpses of their soldiers who had died of plague over the city walls. In this way, an epidemic was initiated which then spread via those with devastating effects those who fled by ship from the Crimea to the Mediterranean region and further up throughout Europe. Another important example is the fact that British military forces in eastern North America gave hostile Native Americans blankets previously used by people who had died of smallpox as presents, in order to spread the disease. This resulted in an epidemic among the Native Americans, who had no protection against the disease [1].

Microbiological science made big advances in the first half of the 20th century. In some circles, ideas were being developed concerning how these scientific developments could be used for military purposes. It was during the 1930s and 1940s that this resulted in the expansion and development of biological weapons programs. Such programs were initiated in Canada, France, the UK, Poland, the Soviet Union, the USA, and several other countries [1]. The Japanese also developed biological weapons during this period; they tested them on large numbers of prisoners of war, and used them against civilians in China. The Allies developed biological weapons because intelligence information had indicated that Germany and Japan already had such weapons. During World War II, the USA, the UK and Canada worked primarily with *Bacillus anthracis* as a biological warfare agent. The US program on offensive biological weapons continued until it was finally terminated during the Nixon administration in 1969, in order to make possible an international agreement to ban biological weapons. A treaty prohibiting the acquisition, development, storage and production of biological and toxin weapons was completed in 1972; however, all references to control procedures had been deleted from the text, as they were not be accepted by the Soviet Union. Most countries, numbering 144 at present, have

signed and ratified the Biological and Toxin Weapons Convention (BTWC), which entered into force in 1975. Countries that have not yet done so include some in the Middle East. Many countries believed, when the Convention was signed, that biological weapons no longer constituted a problem, and several states drastically cut down on their biological defense research. In retrospect, it has been shown that the Soviet Union, in spite of its ratification of the Convention, initiated a dramatic expansion of its biological weapons program [1,2].

Biological weapons have not so far been used on a large scale during warfare between states. One reason for this is that the military authorities have no experience of their use, and have found it difficult to calculate the effects in advance of use. Furthermore, they have believed that reprisals from the enemy would be too severe. Today's rogue states or terrorist organizations do not, perhaps, see the same limitations.

BIOLOGICAL WARFARE AGENTS

Many pathogens or toxins could be used for warfare or terrorism. Examples of pathogens are the smallpox, Venezuelan equine encephalitis, yellow fever, Ebola and Marburg viruses, and the bacteria *B. anthracis*, *Yersinia pestis*, and *Francisella tularensis*. Biological warfare agents would ideally be spread as an aerosol to maximize the effects. Other ways could be via food or water. Biological warfare agents could be spread using equipment for producing aerosols, such as spray devices, or via bombs or missiles. They could also be dispersed from aeroplanes, ships, or vehicles, or, as we have recently seen, via letters. In producing this type of agent, it is important that it is stable enough to survive environmental stress during dissemination. The particle size is also important, and should be $1–10\,\mu m$ to allow good penetration into the lungs of humans [2].

In the Soviet Union, there were more than 60 000 people involved in research on, and development and production of, biological weapons in several organizations, including the Ministry of Defense, the Ministry of Agriculture, and the so-called Biopreparat [3]. Large amounts of microorganisms were tested and produced for use as weapons, such as *B. anthracis*, *Y. pestis*, *F. tularensis*, and smallpox (variola), Venezuelan equine encephalitis and hemorrhagic fever viruses [4].

524 *Clinical Microbiology and Infection*, Volume 8 Number 8, 2002

Especially worrisome is that large amounts of smallpox virus, many thousands of kilos, were produced for use weapons, use as because this virus and disease had been eradicated during the 1970s, and vaccinations are no longer done [5]. There is also an international agreement through the WHO that the remaining virus stocks should be stored in only two official laboratories, one in the USA and one in Russia. Discussions are in progress at the WHO, to the effect that the remaining stocks should be destroyed after a certain period, during which essential research could be performed under WHO control. Another problem is that there are suspicions that more countries or groups could still have small quantities of smallpox virus.

It is well known that Iraq, since the 1970s, has had a well developed biological weapons program, including bombs and SCUD missiles filled with anthrax bacteria, botulinum toxin and aflatoxin [6]. This was of major concern during and after the Gulf War. Following the war, the United Nations Special Commission (UNSCOM), under its chairman, the Swedish ambassador Rolf Ekéus, made great efforts worked hard to identify and destroy facilities used for producing biological weapons. Iraq refused further UN inspections in 1998 as a result of US and UK bombing of Baghdad. The new United Nations Commission (UNMOVIC), under its chairman Hans Blix, has so far been unable to resume inspections. Of the Iraqi biological weapons program consisted/consists. As far as is known, based on Iraqi declarations, of agents such as *B. anthracis*, botulinum toxin, ricin and aflatoxin. The extent of the program is still not today. There are indications that as many as ten countries, as well as Russia and Iraq, are trying to acquire or have a program for research and development of biological weapons.

The proliferation of knowledge or technology that can be misused to develop biological weapons is today a serious problem. Internationally, work is therefore in progress to strengthen the BTWC a control regime, and by including to strengthen the existing export control arrangement, according to the Australia Group, which excludes microorganisms or equipment that can be misused. It is important to limit the proliferation of knowledge from the former Soviet biological weapons program: Western economic support to Soviet scientists may prevent them from making their knowledge available to rogue states that are trying

to acquire biological weapons. In Sweden, the questions connected with biological weapons have recently been highlighted in the latest Defense Bills and by the Parliamentary Defense Commission's reports.

BIOTERRORISM

The list of possible biological warfare agents that could be used by potential terrorists or disturbed individuals is long, and the threat of use is still very real and serious [3,7–13]. In 1984, a religious sect in Oregon in the western USA spread *Salmonella typhimurium* bacteria in a number of salad bars in order to cause disease; it is theorized that this was doue so that members of the sect might win win a local election. This deliberate release resulted in 751 cases of disease [13,14]. Another organization with religious/political motives, the Japanese Aum Shinrikyo, which dispersed the chemical nerve gas sarin in Tokyo's underground railway in 1995, causing 12 deaths and hundreds of injured individuals, also had a biological weapons program. Anthrax bacteria were spread from a building in Tokyo, but without success, as it was shown later that the bacterial strain used was not virulent [14]. The sect also tried to acquire of Ebola virus during the epidemic in Kikwit, Zaire in 1995, but this was not accomplished.

Since September and October 2001, when letters containing *B. anthracis* were sent within the USA, the situation has changed. In total, 22 persons have been diagnosed with *B. anthracis* infection, either cutaneous or pulmonary, So far, five of 11 patients with confirmed pulmonary anthrax infection have died [15]. Anthrax bacteria have been further spread via the postal distribution system in the Washington area, and this has resulted in contamination in a number of localities, for example, the US State Department, the Pentagon, and news media such as ABC, NBC and the New York Times. At the same time, a large number of letters, apporoximately 12 000, with suspected contents were discovered and had to be analyzed. Most of these contained some type of powder, but no anthrax. The situation in the Washington area became very difficult when large quantities of mail and a number of facilities had been contaminated. The same situation, with large numbers of suspect letters, has occurred in many countries, including Sweden, where more than 400 suspect letters have been identified and analyzed.

The recent events in the USA prove that there are people or organizations prepared to use virulent microorganisms to cause disease and death. Before these events, this was a possible scenario, but the situation is now an actuality [3]. Although the US anthrax incident has caused five deaths and accounts for a great economic loss, the direct effects are limited. This can be compared to the mass destruction that *B. anthracis* would cause if dispersed on a large scale as an aerosol in a city, in the ventilation system of a large building, or in a metro system. The casualties would then amount to thousands or even more. The hospital system would be overwhelmed, and large stocks of antibiotics would be necessary to limit the consequences. These consequences would be even worse if smallpox virus was used. It should be noted that the technical problems when producing smallpox virus are greater than those when producing bacteria such as *B. anthracis* or *Y. pestis*. On the other hand, very small quantities of smallpox virus could initiate an epidemic in today's world, where the population at large is not vaccinated and limited amounts of vaccines are available [5].

SWEDISH PREPAREDNESS

Swedish preparedness is based on the same principals as those applicable when combating natural epidemics [3]. It is probable that the first signs of a bioterrorist attack will appear in the same way as when new or changed patterns of infectious disease are identified. General practitioners and/or infectious disease physicians in hospitals will probably be the first to notice a new pattern of disease. These doctors will have noticed unusual cases or an unusual number of cases with the same symptoms. They will notify the County Medical Officer in charge of infectious disease control, who will investigate these cases, not least by a detailed epidemiologic analysis. Meanwhile, this information will also be forwarded to the Swedish Institute of Infectious Disease Control. If the information gained does not fit the usual pattern, further investigations will be done by national and county authorities. Necessary countermeasures will primarily be the responsibility of the County Medical Officer, with assistance from the national authorities when necessary. Today, with these new threats, it is even more important for the emergency ward staff and general practitioners to quickly respond to unusual incidences or

increased numbers of unusual cases and rapidly report them to the County Medical Officer, in order to enable a further investigation when needed.

The recent management in Sweden of a large number of suspect letters containing some kind of powder, suspected to be anthrax, has shown that Sweden has a fairly good capacity to handle this kind of biological threat. It has also been a good opportunity to evaluate our preparedness, both its strong and weak points. The new maximum containment laboratory at the Swedish Institute for Infectious Disease Control was used during this time, and proved to be an important resource. A review of the organization and capacity of the regional clinical laboratories in Sweden with respect to their preparedness for a larger bioterrorist incident is now needed.

In Sweden, every county (population approximately 400 000) has an infectious disease clinic with containment facilities. In order to treat patients with highly contagious serious infectious diseases, Sweden has a special containment unit at the university hospitals in Linköping and Stockholm. Sweden also has a special field epidemiologic group that can be called upon to investigate outbreaks of disease of different types, on both a national and an international level. In Sweden, the storage of antibiotics and vaccines has recently been reviewed and upgraded, and there is a well developed network linking all organizations involved in handling a biological threat.

The Swedish Defence Research Agency Division of NBC Defense analyzes the international developments and threats concerning biological weapons and bioterrorism. The research is, among other things, focused on the development of methods and technology for detection/identification of and protection against biological warfare agents. The Swedish Defence Research Agency cooperates with the Swedish Institute for Infectious Disease Control with regard to identification of specific biological warfare agents.

INTERNATIONAL MEASURES

In order to counter threats of biological warfare or bioterrorism, there is a need for more intensive international cooperation for threat assessment and planning, and also to enhance society's awareness. It is also important to limit the proliferation of this type of knowledge to organizations/states that have an interest in acquiring an arsenal of biological warfare agents and weapons.

In this context, it is important to bear in mind the Soviet program for biological weapons, with about 10 000 highly qualified scientists. After the fall of the Soviet Union, the economic resources for this type of research in Russia were dramatically cut, leaving many scientists unable to support, and many have, in one way or another, found their way to countries outside Russia. There is a themselves, temptation for these scientists to immigrate to countries that want to acquire biological weapons. In order to meet this threat, several initiatives have been taken by the world community. An example of this the Department of Defense Cooperative Threat Reduction Program (DOD CTR) in the USA, as well as other US agencies. Economic support is also given through the International Science and Technology Center (ISTC) in Moscow and the Science and Technology Center Ukraine (STCU) in Kiev, which are financed by the USA, the European Union (EU), Japan, and others. In June 1999, the EU agreed on a common strategy for Russia, which includes measures to limit the proliferation of weapons of mass destruction and promote disarmament, support weapons control, implement international treaties, and support export controls. In Sweden, the Ministry for Foreign Affairs has supported research cooperation between the Swedish Defense Research Agency (FOI), the Swedish Institute for Disease Control (SMI) and the Scientific Research Institute Vector in Novosibirsk, Russia in the areas of biosafety and diagnostics.

Since the BTWC entered into force in 1975, work, not least by Sweden, has been carried out in order to strengthen the Convention with a control regime. In 1994, it was agreed to start negotiations on such a control system, and during the spring of 2001 the chairman presented a compromise final text which should be the basis for termination of the negotiations. This proposal consisted of, among other things, an obligation to submit annual declarations of specific biotechnology activities, and the carrying out of 50–100 random visits to such facilities in order to varify their declarations. Another possibility was to carry out challenge inspections in cases of suspicions of a breech of the Convention [16]. All states except the USA agreed to continue work on the chairman's text. At the final session of the negotiations in July 2001, the USA would not agree on a final

report of the negotiations to be forwarded to the 5th Review Conference of the BTWC, to be held in Geneva in November 2001. This meant that the negotiations collapsed. At the Review Conference, the USA stated that it could not continue work on a control regime based on the chairman's text and that the approach of the negotiations since 1994 had been wrong. The USA presented new proposals, which gained limited support. There was no agreement at the conference after three weeks of negotiations, and the conference had to be postponed until November 2002. At present, it is not possible to say when or if agreement on a control mechanism for biological weapons will be possible. This is most unsatisfactory, as the threat from biological weapons is more real than ever, and the USA has been at the forefront in raising awareness of this threat.

Many countries have initiated plans for handling a bioterrorism attack. In the USA, more than 120 major cities now have special teams that, 24 h per day, can react to a suspected biological attack. Stores of antibiotics and vaccines have been built up, and recently the USA decided to acquire smallpox vaccine for its entire population. In a recent bill to Congress, three billion dollars were requested to improve preparedness against bioterrorism. In the EU, work has now been initiated, and discussions are underway concerning the need to better coordinate preparedness against bioterrorism [3]. At the EU Gent Summit of heads of state in October 2001, a program was proposed to improve preparedness against biological terrorism, which is now being developed, and includes initiatives on research and public-health measures.

DISCUSSION

Comparing Europe with other parts of the world, it can be argued that the Middle East or the USA are more likely to be targets for bioterrorism. Our preparedness in Sweden and the rest of Europe should be based on a realistic threat assessment that will result in balanced countermeasures. Strengthening the public-health and infectious disease infrastructure is probably one of the most effective steps towards averting the suffering that could be wrought by terrorist use of biological agents. International cooperation, not least in the EU, must be enhanced. Effective disease surveillance is an essential first step and is important in helping infectious disease control personnel and law enforcement officials to react swiftly. In Europe, there is a need to improve the surveillance system as well as improve the central coordination [17]. Adequate epidemiologic and laboratory capacity nationwide are prerequisites for effective surveillance systems. Preparations must also include plans for the rapid identification and characterization of the agents involved. There is also a need to further improve the network of qualified laboratories on a European level, as no single laboratory or country can have specialists on all of the exotic diseases that can possibly be used as biological warfare agents. The presence of a number of maximum biosafety (P4) laboratories in different countries is important in the battle against bioterrorism, since rapid diagnosis/identification of all possible microorganisms is necessary. Examples of recently opened European facilities are the Laboratoire P4 Jean Meureiux in Lyon, France, and the Containment laboratories at the Swedish Institute of Infectious Disease Control in Stockholm, Sweden. Bioterrorism poses a formidable new challenge to the clinical microbiology laboratory. Many of these do not possess the capacity or expertise to detect and accurately identify those biological agents classified as high priority, like those causing anthrax, tularemia, botulism, plague or smallpox [18]. Planning is also required for emergency distribution of medical supplies, especially antibiotics and vaccines. For example, in the case of smallpox, it is essential to rapidly identify those who might have been infected and to vaccinate them as well as all who might have come into contact with them. At present, the stocks of vaccine in many countries are very limited.

Coordination and communication also need to be strengthened, to minimize response times. If a bioterrorist event is suspected, established communication must be among hospital personnel, local and central healthcare departments, specialized laboratories, central and regional authorities for disease surveillance, and police and rescue services. A biological attack will also require of preservation evidence (at the scene of a crime), a unified command system, and the need to protect emergency responders against possible secondary devices intentionally placed to maim or injure them [19,20].

The management of the disease might not follow normal procedures, since diagnostic laboratory confirmation might take too long. Instead, it will be necessary to initiate a response based on the recognition of high-risk syndromes. Epidemiologic principles must be used to assess whether a patient's presentation is typical of an endemic disease or is an unusual event that should raise concern [21]. There should also be specialist teams on standby that can rapidly analyze any potential threat and give recommendations to responsible authorities. After an incident, there might be a need for decontamination of the affected area, depending on the type of agent and the quantity released; this is also an area for international cooperation, as expertise is not always available in the country under attack. From a European perspective, it can be questioned whether each country can afford or be motivated to set up qualified rapid response teams that could, at short notice, be deployed to the scene of a bioterrorist attack. Perhaps this could be one area for cooperation between countries. What could be a realistic goal for such teams in a European context? In the area of research and development, to enhance our knowledge of agents of concern and to develop rapid methods for identification and detection of agents, international cooperation is vital, given today's scarce economic resources. Another area for cooperation across borders is the training of personnel in handling situations involving the threat or use of biological warfare agents.

Legislation has a central role in countermeasures, such as national legislation in line with the BTWC. All countries that have not yet passed domestic legislation making the treaty prohibitions binding on their citizens and businesses should be strongly pressured to do so as soon as possible. It is also essential to break the recent deadlock in the negotiations to strengthen the BTWC with a control mechanism, and here the scientific community has a responsibility to put pressure on governments to create legislation concerning control and further prolifecation as well as storage, handling, transfers of highly pathogenic microorganisms. There is a proposal to instate legislation that could impose liability on anyone who publishes recipes for producing chemical or biological agents [22]. There has also been a proposal to make the possession of biological weapons a crime under international law, which could facilitate the prosecution of those who possess biological warfare agents and the means to deliver them [23]. Steps could be taken in order to curb terrorism activities by agreeing to initiate negotia-

528   *Clinical Microbiology and Infection*, Volume 8 Number 8, 2002

tions on a multilateral convention banning biological and chemical terrorism.

REFERENCES

1. Geissler E, van Courtland Moon JE. *Biological and toxin weapons research. Development and use from the Middle Ages to 1945*. SIPRI (Stockholm International Peace Research Insitute) Chemical & Biological Warfare Studies no. 18. Oxford: Oxford University Press, 1999.
2. Norlander L, Norqvist A, Roffey R, Sandström G, Sjöstedt A. *A briefing book on biological weapons*. Umeå: Swedish Defense Research Agency, 1995.
3. Roffey R. Bioterrorism, a Swedish view, is the threat overstated? In: *Proceedings of the 7th International Symposium on Protection Against Chemical and Biological Agents, Stockholm, Sweden*. Umeå: Swedish Defence Research Agency, 2001.
4. Alibek K, Handelman S. *Biohazard. The chilling true story of the largest covert biological weapons program in the world*. New York: Random House, 1999.
5. Henderson DA, Inglesby TV, Bartlett JG et al. Smallpox as a biological weapon. *JAMA* 1999; 281: 2127–37.
6. Zilinskas RA. Iraq's biological weapons. The past as future? *JAMA* 1997; 278: 418–24.
7. CDC. Investigation of bioterrorism-related anthrax and interim guidelines for exposure management and antimicrobial therapy. *MMWR Morb Mortal Wkly Rep* 2001; 50: 910–19.
8. CDC. Investigation of bioterrorism-related anthrax and adverse events from antimicrobial prophylaxis. *MMWR Morb Mortal Wkly Rep* 2001; 50: 973–6.
9. Inglesby TV, Henderson DA, Bartlett JG et al. Anthrax as a biological weapon. *JAMA* 1999; 281: 1735–45.
10. Inglesby TV, Dennis DT, Henderson DA et al. Plague as a biological weapon. *JAMA* 2000; 283: 2281–90.
11. Arnon SS, Schechter R, Inglesby TV et al. Botulinum toxin as a biological weapon. *JAMA* 2001; 285: 1059–70.
12. Dennis DT, Inglesby TV, Henderson DA et al. Tularemia as a biological weapon. *JAMA* 2001; 285: 2763–73.
13. Tucker J. *Assessing terrorist use of chemical and biological weapons*. BCSIA Studies in International Security. Cambridge, Massachusetts: MIT Press, 2000.
14. Miller J, Engelberg S, Broad W. *Germs the ultimate weapon*. New York: Simon & Schuster, 2001.
15. Jernigan JA, Stephens DS, Ashford DA et al. Bioterrorism-related anthrax: the first 10 cases reported in the United States. *Emerg Infect Dis* 2001; 7: 933–44.
16. Roffey R. Implications of the Protocol to the BTWC for the control and verification of BW. In: *Proceedings of the 7th International Symposium on Protection Against Chemical and Biological Agents, Stockholm, Sweden*. Umeå: Swedish Defence Research Agency, 2001.
17. Petersen LR, Catchpole M. Surveillance for infectious diseases in the European Union. *BMJ* 2001; 323: 818–19.
18. Snyder JW. Responding to bioterrorism: the role of the microbiology laboratory. *ASM News* 1999; 65: 524–5.
19. Socher MM. NBC Delta: special training beyond HAZMAT in the USA. *Resuscitation* 1999; 42: 151–3.
20. Editorial. How would you handle a terrorist act involving weapons of mass destruction? *ED Management* 1999; 11: 121–7.
21. APIC/CDC. Bioterrorism Readiness Plan. A template for health care facilities. *ED Management* 1999; 11: 1–14.
22. Bailey KC. Policy options for combatting chemical/biological terrorism. *Politics Life Sci* 1996; 15: 185–7.
23. Meselson MS, Perry Robinson JP. Criminalizing BW. *Chem Convention Bull* 1996; 31: 1.

[6]

Terrorists, WMD, and the US Army Reserve

CHARLES L. MERCIER, JR.

"The United States shall give the highest priority to developing capabilities to . . . manage the consequences of nuclear, biological or chemical materials or weapons use by terrorists."[1]

The dissolution of the Soviet Union and the end of the Cold War greatly reduced the risk of a global war. At the same time, leadership—whether among allies or friends—and control—whether of surrogates or beneficiaries—tended to dissipate along with the imminent threat of war. Violent political groups previously held in check by their Cold War masters became free to operate on their own, and ethnic, militia, and nationalist organizations began to attract notice.

Civilian and military organizations are equally interested in identifying likely antagonists, such as states that have declared their opposition to the West, and to the United States in particular; rogue states; nonstate criminal organizations, and terrorist groups. The latter have been around for centuries, advancing the interests of clients and their own organizations.[2] Sponsors often used them during the Cold War as surrogates to reduce the risk of direct confrontation between the superpowers. Client restrictions, including limitations on the types of weapons they would provide, were designed to prevent terrorist activities from escalating out of control.

It should come as no surprise, therefore, that once freed from other Cold War constraints, these groups would also reject limitations on the ways and means appropriate to their strategic ends. The emerging weapons of choice for terrorists appear to be those that can be manufactured readily from commonly available chemicals and contagious pathogens in ordinary surroundings and at low cost, especially compared to the cost of a standing force capable of inflicting comparable damage on state institutions. And because these weapons do not require a sophisticated manufacturing infrastructure, production facilities readily avoid the satellite's gaze. The same applies to delivery means; weapons can be carried to targets by individual terrorists operating anonymously across increasingly open borders. The methods have been identified during the continuing search in Iraq for chemical and biological manufacturing facilities and stockpiles. The model is the suicide bombers who have plagued Israel in recent years.

Knowing that there are those who wish us significant harm and that they have both the ability and the will use weapons of mass destruction to cause that harm, we clearly have a problem. Weapons of mass destruction have been within the technological grasp of terrorist groups for some time; they were not employed until a Japanese religious cult crossed that invisible barrier in March 1995.[3] While the cult's target—the Tokyo subway system—was what a terrorist might call "appropriate," Tokyo was fortunate that the cult's agent was impure and dissemination techniques were primitive. Unfortunately, fanaticism is not synonymous with stupidity, so we can expect the next attack with a weapon of mass destruction to be considerably more deadly.

Can we "jump-start" preparations to deal effectively with the threat and the consequences of such an attack? We can if we take advantage of existing experts and proven techniques; the US military is both equipped and organized to meet that threat outside the country.[4] Consequently, the Department of Defense has been given the task of adapting battlefield force protection and recovery techniques for nuclear, chemical, or biological attacks to procedures that will work domestically. Within the Department of Defense, the Army has been identified as the lead service for planning domestic defense against and recovery from terrorist use of a weapon of mass destruction. Within the Army, the Chemical Corps is the proponent for these plans.

This article describes the danger posed to America by terrorists using weapons of mass destruction, the capabilities of the Army Reserve to mitigate that danger, some inhibitors to the efforts of the Army Reserve, and ways they might be overcome.

Threat Motives and Organizations

Anti-Americanism remains a strong motive for certain groups and organizations to contemplate the use of weapons of mass destruction (WMD)

Colonel Charles L. Mercier, Jr. USAR, has served in both the National Guard and the Army Reserve, and as an infantry and a chemical officer. A major at the time, he commanded the first Army Reserve chemical unit to deploy to Saudi Arabia during Desert Shield and Desert Storm. His unit, the 907th Chemical Detachment, supported both the 593d Area Support Group and the Prince Abdul Rachman al Saud Light Infantry Brigade. He subsequently commanded the 490th Chemical Battalion and served as S3 of the 415th Chemical Brigade. In 1997 he became Deputy Chief of Staff, Logistics, for the 81st Regional Support Command. A graduate of the Army Command and General Staff College and the Army War College, Colonel Mercier holds an M.S. degree in nuclear physics from the University of Alabama.

against the United States and its allies. Retired Ambassador Morris Busby, former Counterterrorism Coordinator for the US government, warned that rogue states and subnational groups may now be more inclined than previously to "punish" us with weapons of mass destruction simply for being who we are.[5] Some believe that the use of chemical, biological, or nuclear weapons on American soil is a not matter of "if" but when it will happen. As one Senator bluntly observed, "Americans have every reason to expect a nuclear, biological, or chemical attack before the decade is over."[6]

One source defines terrorists as groups or individuals that conduct "premeditated, politically motivated violence . . . against noncombatant targets . . . usually intended to influence an audience."[7] A month rarely goes by without hearing about a terrorist attack somewhere in the world; after the World Trade Center, Oklahoma City, and the Atlanta Olympics, that world seems to be getting smaller. And as one of member of the Hezbollah noted, "We are not fighting so that the enemy recognizes us and offers us something. We are fighting to wipe out the enemy."[8]

The most successful terrorists have state sponsors who provide resources and a degree of sanctuary. Of the seven nations designated by the United States as state sponsors of terrorism (Cuba, Iran, Iraq, Libya, North Korea, Sudan, and Syria), Iran remains the most active. But whether terrorists have state sponsorship or not, they generally share two characteristics that should concern us. One is the human aspect of their behavior, involving their motivation and psychology; the other is the technological aspect, involving the destructive means at their disposal.

Although certainly helpful to terrorists, state sponsorship is not essential, and as demonstrated by the Aum Shinrikyo and Timothy McVeigh, terrorism is by no means confined to the Middle East. Narco-terrorists threaten South America in the name of greed while the Armed Islamic Group threatens Algeria in the name of religion. America's right-wing "militias" advocate reducing, if not eliminating, the federal government, while Germany's right-wing neo-Nazis still seek racial purity. Peru has its left-wing Sendero Luminoso (Maoist) and Tupac Amaru Revolutionary Movement (Marxist-Leninist). Russia, once seemingly immune to terrorist violence, has recently encountered ethnic terrorism in its conflict with Chechen separatists.

Diverse though terrorist groups may be, it is possible, based on evidence to date, to draw some distinctions among them based on the relationship between their motivation and their preferred weapons. "Politically motivated terrorist groups have generally not sought to use [chemical or biological] weapons in the past because they are unpredictable, indiscriminate, hard to handle, and might alienate supporters."[9] Conversely, weapons of mass destruction perhaps have more appeal to groups such as Aum Shinrikyo, generally considered to be "religious fanatics," than to political terrorists. True believers in religious groups seem satisfied that their values and motives are derived from their devotion to their deity, leader, or doctrine rather than from aberrant behavior generally classified as "fanaticism." Such beliefs render irrelevant the opinions and moral values of others; while political terrorists like the Red Brigade might hesitate to kill great numbers of civilians for fear of alienating support, those who believe they are fighting for their god will not shrink from killing as many "unbelievers" as possible. By their standards, unbelievers are doomed anyway.

Other terrorists, motivated by ethnic concerns, may fear genocide or may themselves desire to destroy their opponents; either way, they operate with fervor. As with religious terrorists, ethno-terrorists show no hesitation to inflict mass casualties; indeed, it seems often that the greater the death toll in one of their assaults, the higher their achievement. Unfortunately, "there is more ethnic conflict now than ten years ago,"[10] and such conflict seldom respects state boundaries, as fighting in Africa, the Balkans, and the Caucasus has demonstrated. Depending on the venue, it can also manifest itself as political terrorism; attacks by Algerian terrorists in France and by Kurdish factions in Germany attest to this pernicious aspect of ethnic strife.

Threat Technologies

All three classes of weapons of mass destruction—nuclear, biological, and chemical—are currently within the technological reach of terrorists. Without state sponsorship, nuclear weapons (fission or fusion type) are probably the least likely of the three to be used. Conversely, both biological and chemical agents can readily be developed by terrorists; each requires a college-level knowledge of biology or chemistry, less than $20,000 in supplies, and the forged documents or accomplices needed to obtain "seed" bacteria or precursor chemicals. Each of these means possesses its own special characteristics and threat; each is appropriate in varying degrees to the ends and ways of the group using it.

Nuclear Weapons

With the possible exception of the simplest "gun-type" fission device, considerable technology, infrastructure, and scientific knowledge are required to construct even a primitive nuclear weapon. Furthermore, for obvious reasons, practical tests to determine the reliability of nuclear weapons cannot be conducted clandestinely. Consequently, devices that can disperse radioactive materials over a wide area are much more likely to appeal to terrorists. These devices, usually consisting of a conventional explosive to spread radioactive materials (which need not be of weapons grade) would not necessarily destroy property. Their intent is to kill people and to contaminate terrain for indeterminate periods. In late 1995, a Chechen military commander planted a radiation dispersal device in Moscow's Izmailovsky Park and arranged for its discovery by a Russian news team.[11] It was a statement of capability that sent a loud and clear message to the Kremlin.

Biological Weapons

In a 1966 experiment that proved the ease with which terrorists could contaminate portions of the American populace, government personnel clandestinely released "harmless bacteria" into the New York subway system.[12] The contamination was distributed throughout major portions of the subway system by air turbulence created by the trains themselves. This experiment preceded the Aum Shinrikyo attack on Tokyo's subways by almost 30 years.

The technology for producing biological weapons is available to terrorists now: a US neo-Nazi group (the Order of the Rising Sun) produced 80 pounds of typhoid bacillus in 1972, and in 1984 Paris police raided an apartment rented by the Baader Meinhof gang and found flasks of *Clostridium botulinum* culture.[13] More recently, Japanese police found 160 barrels of peptone (a growth media for bacteria) along with *Clostridium botulinum* when they raided an Aum Shinrikyo compound near Mount Fuji.[14] Tricothecene mycotoxins (e.g., "yellow rain") can be produced simply using a corn meal slurry and the appropriate strain of fungus.

Getting started isn't too difficult. Pathogenic microorganisms can be acquired with relative ease with forged documentation and then cultured in makeshift laboratories into larger quantities; state-sponsored laboratories and production facilities are not necessary for success.[15] Terrorists do not need to match the large-scale production capabilities of state-operated facilities; very small amounts of biological agent would be adequate for a terrorist's purposes. As little as eight grams of *Bacillus anthracis* spores (the anthrax bacillus), properly milled, mixed with dispersal compounds to add volume and prevent clumping, and then optimally dispensed, could inflict heavy casualties over a one square mile area.[16] In fact, without effective medical intervention, inhalation of approximately 8000 spores of *Bacillus anthracis* is fatal in nearly all occurrences.[17] *Bacillus anthracis* has an incubation period of two to seven days; usually its victims show symptoms within 48 hours. Vaccination after the fact (without concurrent antibiotic prophylaxis) is of limited value in cases where incubation has begun.[18] It should be noted, however, that rapid intervention with the appropriate antibiotics can have positive results even if some symptoms have already appeared.[19]

Bacillus anthracis represents an almost ideal pathogenic microorganism for terrorists. It is a bacteria, and therefore is cultivated more easily than a virus such as Ebola. Furthermore, it forms spores possessing incredible durability in the soil, which creates the possibility of long-term contamination of an area. Its incubation period is long enough to allow terrorists to escape undetected, but short enough to prevent effective vaccination of victims already infected. The World Health Organization and the US Congressional

Office of Technological Assessment have determined in separate studies that, effectively dispensed, 30 to 50 kilograms of *Bacillus anthracis* could kill up to 100,000 people.[20]

Chemical Weapons

A chemical agent is "a chemical substance that is intended for use in military operations to kill, seriously injure, or incapacitate people through its physiological effects."[21] Fatal at about .01 milligrams per kilogram of human weight, sarin is extremely potent;[22] if a fatal dose is absorbed, death occurs within about 15 minutes. Although it can be absorbed through the skin, its primary source of entry is inhalation. The death toll in the 1995 Tokyo attack was low because the Aum Shinrikyo scientists made some mistakes in preparing the sarin gas and then did not disseminate it so as to maximize its effects.[23]

A much more deadly means of spreading a volatile chemical agent would be to break glass jars of the substance on the intake vents of a high-rise office building. The intake fans would vaporize the agent and distribute it to the floors supplied by the vents, essentially to a captive group of victims. Air turnover in office buildings is deliberately controlled to reduce energy loss, thus making large complexes inviting targets for terrorist organizations. This is especially true in large buildings with sealed windows; their only source of air is the vents.

Threat Summary

Each type weapon of mass destruction described above can cause casualties that would overwhelm established emergency care capabilities of civilian agencies. If contamination is present, such as from fission, fusion, or dispersion of nuclear materials, things only get worse. Although only persistent chemical agents result in contamination by military definitions, even minute residual amounts of non-vaporized nerve agent are outside acceptable bounds for civilians. Few biological agents cause contamination lasting for more than a few days to a few weeks. *Bacillus anthracis*, however, is a significant exception due to the bacteria's spore-forming characteristic. Contamination will have to be eliminated (chemical decontamination, physical removal, or aging) before civilians will feel safe to resume their normal occupation of the area. Decontamination will have to be significantly more thorough than that required for military operations.

Remembering that terrorists do not have the same high-volume delivery capacity seen in the military, maximum casualties could be inflicted with either chemical or biological agents by two methods. First, at night in a city or its suburbs, *Bacillus anthracis* or sarin could easily be spread over a wide area from a passenger van containing an electric motor crop duster. Such a simple dispersion method could be devastating, since "tests suggest that there is no effective filtration of the aerosol during passage of the air through the walls of a building."[24] Due to the clandestine nature of the dispersion, only the onset of consequences would indicate that we had suffered an attack. The second method is that alluded to above, in which high-density office buildings could be attacked by inserting the sarin gas or *Bacillus anthracis* spores directly into the buildings' air intake vents.

The first type of attack would ensure widespread casualties and, with *Bacillus anthracis*, possible long-term contamination of portions of the city along the route of pathogen dispersal. The second type of attack would insure high casualty rates (with sarin) or high infection rates (with *Bacillus anthracis*). The accompanying mortality rate for anthrax could possibly be moderated, but only with timely administration of antibiotics.

Consequences and Responses

Civilians who survive a terrorist attack with nuclear, biological, or chemical weapons will have the same general needs as survivors of any disaster: medical assistance and search and rescue activities. In addition to those needs, a domestic attack involving weapons of mass destruction will likely require someone to identify and restrict access to hazardous areas; as necessary and where possible, decontamination will be required to rid the area of weapon residue.

Medical Assistance

The first things a civilian population would require in the aftermath of a WMD attack would be medical assistance and information about where to obtain it.[25] The mix of that assistance between immediate and long term will be determined by the type of attack and the weapon used. A well-planned program of medical triage and treatment is therefore the first line of defense in dealing with the threat. Unfortunately, the first indication we may get that there has been a WMD attack is reports of massive casualties.

Chemical attacks would yield almost immediate casualties and probably would not involve persistent agents. Here the appearance of casualties would be something of an immediate "spike," leaving medical personnel with a tremendous overload but without the specter of additional casualties. There would be no structural damage hindering casualty location and recovery. Medical requirements would be immediate and massive in nature. The probable agent of choice would be non-persistent nerve gas, with immediate casualty management consisting of the administration of atropine and pralidoxime chloride. If neurologic involvement is severe, diazepam may be necessary to reduce convulsions and brain damage; ventilation and suction of airways may also be required.[26]

Due to their lack of equipment and training, civilian targets are much more susceptible to chemical attacks than are their military counterparts. Planning to deal with the consequences should include provision of at least rudimentary training to fire and police departments in how to assist victims of certain kinds of attacks. Inhalation, the most probable route of entry for a nerve agent to a civilian population, requires removal of the victim from the contaminated air and administration of an antidote such as atropine. Liquid contamination, a less probable occurrence than vapor but still possible, requires immediate removal of the agent from the victim's skin and then chemical decontamination if possible. Something as simple as applying flour, wiping it off with wet tissue paper, and then scrubbing the area with soapy water can be effective.[27] Speed of response may well determine success or failure in such cases.

Fission or fusion attacks would be spectacular and accompanied by massive structural damage, making the location and recovery of casualties extremely difficult and dangerous. Common knowledge of the effects of such attacks, and their low probability as a weapon of choice by terrorists, will allow us to confine discussion of nuclear materials to dispersion-type weapons.

Structural damage from a radiation dispersion device would be limited by the size of the conventional explosive, and residual radiation would be the real danger. The downwind hazard zone would fortunately be less than from a fission or fusion device since the radioactive material would not be propelled high into the atmosphere. A special risk is that unless authorities were expecting a radiation dispersal device to be employed, they might think it was a normal conventional explosive until large numbers of civilians began to appear with symptoms of radiation sickness. This delayed awareness would increase casualties since unsuspecting civilians would remain in the contaminated area much longer than if they had known of the danger. Medical requirements would be intensive and long term.

Biological attacks have a potential for producing very large numbers of casualties, in the range of 90-100 percent as a function of the type of pathogen and medical treatment available. The casualty stream seen by medical personnel would be zero from the time of attack until the end of the incubation period for the first victim, depending on the pathogen and, to a degree, on the victim. It would then climb rapidly and peak within a few days for anthrax to perhaps two months for brucellosis.[28] Medical requirements consequently could be overwhelming; they would peak rapidly if the pathogen is not particularly contagious. By the time casualties appeared and we learned there had been a biological weapon attack, it would be too late for vaccination to be effective for victims of the primary exposure. Vaccination would be required, however, if the pathogen was contagious, in order to prevent secondary infection. Furthermore, unless the individual had been vaccinated prior to cessation of antibiotics, spores such as *Bacillus anthracis* could remain dormant during the period of treatment with prophylactics and emerge much later to cause infection.[29] The incubation period of contagious pathogens, coupled with this country's mobile population, could, under severe circumstances, create pandemic conditions.

Search and Rescue

The only WMD incident that would cause severe structural damage would be a fission or fusion device. National Guard troops would usually be appropriate for search and rescue missions since they can be immediately called into state active duty status by the governor. Furthermore, Army National Guard units are trained to prevent riots, looting, and entry into prohibited areas. A significant problem, however, would be the coincident radiation hazard that would be present in, around, and downwind of a blast or dispersion area. Identification of radioactive areas, the severity of the radiation, determination of operational exposure guidance, and maintenance of radiation exposure records would be absolutely essential in such an incident to reduce the likelihood that rescue personnel would themselves become casualties. A difficult decision might be necessary: prohibition of search and rescue in certain highly contaminated areas to allow would-be rescuers to spend their time on activities of greater benefit to the majority of the affected population.

Hazardous Area Identification and Restriction

As far as possible, hazardous area identification and restriction should occur coincident with, if not prior to, search and rescue efforts. Without proper identification and containment, rescuers might not use adequate protective equipment or the risk of spreading contamination could be increased. Nothing is simple, of course, and just as nuclear, biological, and chemical weapons have different effects and different methods of treatment, so do they each require different means of detection.

A special problem is associated with contamination in urban areas: contamination would tend to settle in basements and other low areas, rubble piles, and similar collections of debris. This concentration would extend the period of lethality of chemical and biological agents.[30]

Decontamination

Decontaminating civilians would pose some unusual situations. It is unlikely that terrorists would use persistent chemical agents such as VX, since non-persistent agents such as sarin can cause more widespread casualties. So decontamination of chemical agents, for example, over extensive parts of an urban zone, might be unnecessary. Any contamination resulting from "pooling" of non-persistent agents should be quite localized and consequently fairly easy to decontaminate, both physically and logistically. "Unlikely," however, is not the same as impossible; the possibility of persistent agents in an attack must always be considered during decontamination planning.

Pathogens, with the exception of *Bacillus anthracis*, generally die fairly quickly after dissemination, and would likely no longer be threatening by the time serious decontamination efforts could be organized. Conducting thorough decontamination of an entire area containing *Bacillus anthracis* spores is very difficult, but fortunately is not impossible.

Radioactive residue cannot be decontaminated in the same sense that chemicals and pathogens can. It must be removed, buried, or simply allowed to age until it naturally decays. The latter option is probably not realistic due to the long half-life most potential contaminants possess; plutonium's half-life, for instance, is about 24,000 years. But if radiation can't be neutralized, at least it can be detected more easily than chemicals and much easier than pathogens.

The Army Reserve: Capabilities and Drawbacks

The Department of Defense, and specifically the Army, have been assigned responsibility for responding to terrorist use of weapons of mass destruction in the United States. The term "consequence management" is becoming a shorthand notation for that response. As part of its mission, the military has specifically been tasked to "develop and maintain at least one domestic terrorism rapid response team composed of members of the armed forces and employees of the Department of Defense who are capable of aiding federal, state, and local officials in the detection, neutralization, containment, disassembly, and disposal of weapons of mass destruction containing chemical, biological, or related material."[31] Part of the general and specific responsibilities accruing to the military can be carried out by the US Army Reserve. The following is a preliminary assessment of what that mission entails.

The Army trains to fight and win in an environment that includes the prospects of attacks by chemical and biological weapons. Consequently, the Army is one of the organizations best prepared to assist victims of attacks involving weapons of mass destruction. Army Reserve units have the organization, the training, and some of the equipment to provide such support, and the Army Reserve has the mission, implied if not yet actually stated.

But Army Reserve organizations are neither trained nor equipped to deploy within hours; even some active-duty units lack that capability. The Army Reserve doesn't train and prepare to respond to civil emergencies; in each state, National Guard units have the responsibility to respond to the orders of the governor or the President in a crisis. And although the Army Reserve has some equipment, it does not have the substantial stores of decontaminants, antibiotics, or atropine sure to be needed in such a crisis. Perhaps most significantly, the Reserve's mission focus is warfighting, not disaster recovery or support to local and state domestic authorities.

The Army Reserve nonetheless has a disaster recovery mission—in this specific case, consequence management. Even if it were not formally given to the Reserve, members of the Reserve would be accountable to their fellow citizens should they fail to provide aid when needed. So what can Reservists do to prepare themselves, and what resources does the Reserve need to do it?

The Total Army's chemical warfare organizations include soldiers who are specifically organized, equipped, and trained to respond to nuclear, chemical, and biological attacks on the battlefield. The active Army presently has three chemical battalion headquarters, one of which is in Korea, and a variety of other organizations with comparable missions.[32] However, in order to have space for maneuvers, most such units are located on military posts that generally are not near major cities. A high level of expertise is available in the Army's Technical Escort Unit, which is trained to identify and contain incidents involving weapons of mass destruction. The unit is small, however, and frequently has elements deployed over a wide area.

Similarly, the Marine Corps has a battalion-sized unit that was activated in April 1996 and trained in time to support the Atlanta Olympic Games. This unit, referred to as the Chemical-Biological Incident Response Force (CBIRF), can provide rapid assistance in a disaster involving certain kinds of contaminants. It augmented Olympics security in Atlanta and is capable of performing command and control, reconnaissance, decontamination, and medical assistance missions. It furnishes its own security and service support.[33] However, with the exception of security, each element in the USMC unit is small—about a squad for reconnaissance in specially designed and equipped vehicles and about a platoon for decontamination.[34] Though it offers an excellent model for rapid response to emergencies involving chemical or biological materials, the CBIRF is intended primarily for response to incidents involving State Department and Navy installations; it may also be sent overseas in response to threats to other US installations.[35]

National Guard units are located in cities and towns across each state and are each governor's primary military asset; they are commanded by each governor until they are federalized by executive order. National Guard personnel would be essential for maintaining order in the aftermath of a disaster, but chemical warfare units are located primarily within National Guard division organizations. The Guard has only two decontamination companies (at echelons above division) and its only battalion and brigade chemical headquarters units are scheduled to be inactivated. Once they are gone, there will be no chemical branch headquarters within the National Guard for command and control of specialized chemical units.[36]

The Army Reserve has eight battalion and three brigade headquarters, as well as 33 chemical companies capable of providing support to military units. Of that number, some 26 companies will be capable of performing decontamination missions after completion of the current modernization program and thus can provide a response to chemical weapon attacks by terrorists within the United States.[37]

To deal with a terrorist attack on the United States, resources would have to be provided by active, National Guard, and Reserve units of all the services. The first response would likely be from active units, such as the Army's Technical Escort Unit or the Marine's CBIRF battalion. However, based on available chemical assets and their proximity to population centers, the Army Reserve is in the best position to respond to a terrorist WMD attack on US territory with substantial numbers of personnel and equipment.

Rapid Response

Recognizing that time is the most critical factor in responding to a terrorist attack involving nuclear, biological, or chemical (NBC) weapons, the Department of Defense plans to establish a Chemical and Biological Quick Response Force (of about 500 soldiers) and place it under the Chemical and Biological Defense Command. This force is designed to respond rapidly to a WMD incident and, when deployed, will take orders from the Response Task Force of either First Army or Fifth Army, depending upon the location of the incident.[38]

Response time is important because effects from high concentrations of nerve agent continue to progress with exposure (maximum effects are usually reached within minutes after the exposure stops). Small amounts of liquid contamination, if not removed, can result in delayed effects up to 18 hours later,[39] making it unwise to completely ignore the possibility of contamination. To be most effective, atropine and pralidoxime chloride should be administered immediately after exposure, with diazepam given to reduce brain damage due to seizures.

With planning and training, significant Army Reserve chemical support could be available in affected areas within a few hours of an attack, ready to begin the search for additional casualties and identification of any contamination. If the agent was disseminated as an aerosol, there could be no residual contamination for the units to deal with.

Because Army Reserve units are spread throughout the United States, at least some chemical and medical units are within a few hours' driving distance of most major cities. There are two notable exceptions to this statement—the Midwest and the Pacific Coast regions. The closest chemical units to California (above the division level) are in Washington and Texas.[40] Under current staffing and planning guidelines, it is unrealistic to expect an entire Reserve unit to be able to assemble and move to an affected area in a few hours. It is not unreasonable, however, to expect a unit to send essential supplies (atropine, ciprofloxacin, etc.) within one or two hours, a small operations cell and perhaps a composite platoon within two or three hours, and the remainder of the unit in less than 24 hours.

Rapid response of personnel when dealing with the consequences of a terrorist attack is absolutely essential, but units cannot respond without planning and preparation. They need to know what is expected of them, where they will probably do it, and must always know who is available to do it with. Furthermore, basic equipment must be packed modularly and vehicles must be kept at a high level of maintenance. The National Strike Teams maintained and operated by the US Coast Guard provide an excellent model of preparedness for rapid deployment.[41] Given current funding and staffing restrictions, not every Army Reserve unit could operate at the tempo of our Force Support Package (FSP) units. To get started, perhaps we should initially focus on those types of units; recovery from a WMD attack is closely related to the wartime mission activities for which they habitually train. More units could be prepared for rapid response if provided the requisite funding and personnel allocations.

A Reserve unit's ability to respond to an emergency cannot be measured exclusively by time. The Army Reserve belongs to the federal government, not to the state; consequently it is constrained by the provisions of the Stafford Act concerning the services it can provide in support of civil authority. It is obvious, nonetheless, that if terrorists use weapons of mass destruction, the response cannot wait for normal procedures to be followed. Fortunately, an exception has been provided: "Under 42 U.S.C. 5170b reference (f) . . . the President may authorize the Secretary of Defense to use DOD resources for performing . . . emergency work that may ultimately qualify for assistance . . . which is essential for the preservation of life and property." In other words, based on the situation, "all military commanders are authorized to respond to requests from the civil sector to save lives, prevent human suffering, or limit property damage."[42] This is not a blank check, for commanders must notify in the most expeditious manner the DOD Executive Agent of their action; further, DOD emergency work cannot exceed 10 days without specific authorization. These constraints will have to be examined, however, for we are no longer discussing flood relief or controlling forest fires.

Command and Control

Command and control elements should be deployed to the affected area before or at least concurrent with the line units. Designated chemical battalion or chemical brigade control cells could deploy straight to planned control sites, with the senior officer on site taking command until relieved.

Unity of command is essential in any operation. In military support of civilian authority, the military chain of command runs from the Secretary of the Army (as executive agent) to the Director of Military Support (DOMS) in the Army staff, to the regional commanders in chief, to their component commanders, to the defense coordinating officer (DCO) located in the disaster field office. Coordination among state and federal agencies and the military occurs at two levels. The upper level includes the state governor, the Director of the Federal Emergency Management Agency, and the Director of Military Support. At the lower level it takes place at the disaster field office among the DCO, the federal coordinating officer (FCO), and the state coordinating officer (SCO).[43] Direct coordination must occur between Army Reserve commanders and their federal, state, National Guard, and local counterparts;[44] all should plan to provide liaison officers[45] to their counterparts involved in the relief effort. Successes and failures in the 1992 Los Angeles riots and the 1996 Atlanta Olympics demonstrate the importance of planning and continuous coordination in support of civil authorities, particularly law enforcement organizations.

Medical Assistance

A terrorist attack employing a radiation dispersal device would require immediate action, much as in response to a chemical attack. Medical personnel would need to deploy to the area, along with chemical units. There are no prophylactics or vaccinations for radiation, but symptoms of radiation sickness as well as the trauma effects from blast can be treated.

It is unlikely for economic reasons that major hospitals in our largest cities would stock large quantities of the drugs necessary for treatment of nerve agent poisoning. However, if some war stocks of nerve agent antidote kits and diazepam were divided among strategically located chemical or medical units, the military would have war supplies available and, if an emergency required it, the drugs would be available for civilian use. Of course, stocks would have to be rotated and diazepam (a controlled substance) would have to be adequately protected.

Severely affected nerve agent casualties, if they survived, would require lengthy and probably intensive hospital care, to include ventilation. Army Reserve hospital units could be activated and immediately deployed to safe zones around the affected area. Only units from outside the affected city or region should be called upon. To do otherwise could remove from the affected area medical personnel whose presence would be required at the local hospitals and clinics where they work in peacetime.

Search and Rescue

Army Reserve medical units should not be involved in search and rescue operations, and chemical units are no better trained than are the medics for such work. Army National Guard engineer and some combat units appear to be more likely candidates for this mission. Army Reserve chemical units can, however, identify hazardous chemical or radiological areas and are probably more capable than most units of protecting themselves from these hazards. Such units can be tasked to identify likely locations of victims as they conduct their survey of hazardous areas.

Hazardous Area Identification and Restriction

Some units are equipped with chemical and radiological monitoring equipment and should be able to survey an area attacked with nuclear dispersal, chemical, or biological weapons and determine whether or not contamination exits and if so, the extent of it. Results could be obtained quickly, except in the event of biological contamination; here samples would have to be submitted to a laboratory for analysis and positive identification (tests for "presumptive" identification of certain pathogens are possible in the field). Chemical detection reconnaissance vehicles were designed for much of this work, but are not at this writing available to Reserve units. Presently, and for the immediate future, decontamination and nuclear, biological, and chemical reconnaissance units would have to use vehicles and techniques that, although adequate, are far below the capabilities of current technology.

For years the military has trained many of its personnel to detect chemical and radiological hazards, and the required materiel is routinely available to most units. These units could be expected to help in conducting surveys and identifying contaminated areas. Biological hazards are different, however, for they pose far different detection problems. Presently only one company-size unit has the appropriate biological equipment. And even if the equipment were widely available, detection is based on air samples; once the airborne biological agent has settled to earth, the equipment's effectiveness is considerably reduced.

Decontamination

In normal combat operations, chemical units do not perform area decontamination; maneuver units are trained to avoid contaminated areas or to leave them as quickly as possible. Sometimes, however, seaports, airfields, or road junctions cannot be abandoned and chemical units may be called upon to perform decontamination operations over a wide area. Decontamination of urban areas will be a labor- and resource-intensive operation, made all the more difficult when current decontamination companies have been reorganized and no longer possess the heavy equipment useful in decontaminating terrain. An additional problem is the large amount of decontaminant needed to do terrain decontamination. Fortunately, commercially available substitutes, such as swimming pool chlorine, can be obtained in quantity as they are needed.

In all probability, large-scale decontamination of chemical agents would not be necessary. Decontamination of the persistent *Bacillus anthracis* spores, on the other hand, could be a significant challenge since the spores are not easily detected on building surfaces or in topsoil. Decontamination is possible, however, and saturation with formaldehyde is a decontamination technique used effectively on Gruinard Island.[46]

Training

Reserve chemical and medical units will need to be assigned an area of responsibility and then charged with developing and coordinating contingency plans for responding to a terrorist WMD attack in their assigned areas. Unit training for this new support mission will have to be integrated into training for existing combat missions; the new mission will be urban, we won't be under hostile fire, and our logistics tail will be short.

Units will need to maintain a current roster of where key personnel are (perhaps utilizing pagers) for the purpose of quickly calling up small command and control cells to manage a situation as it develops. Units will also need to be sure they can operate with "composite" sub-elements, as they will not have the luxury of waiting until the entire force arrives before sending assistance to the stricken area.

Medical groups, police and fire departments, and civil defense organizations could benefit from periodic training on NBC operations from Reserve units and, ideally, participate in joint practical exercises. The Army (as part of the Department of Defense), in conjunction with five other federal agencies, recently began a training program to assist cities in planning for WMD consequence management. By tailoring requirements to a city's specific needs, this integrated training team expects to assist 120 major US cities over the next three years.[47] The Army Reserve, not presently participating in planning or conducting this training, has divisions dedicated to both individual training and the conduct of exercises. These divisions have skills that could be useful in compressing the time required for reaching the 120 cities.

There are significant potential benefits of applying the Army's concept of wargaming—board games first, then more sophisticated automated versions—to the challenges inherent in protecting American citizens from the effects of WMD attacks on the nation. The benefits these gaming processes have provided to the military can be realized in work with civil authorities as well. In fact, the interagency training team conducted an exercise for Denver, the first city to receive this training, in June 1997.[48]

Conclusion

President Eisenhower said that in preparing for battle, "plans are nothing; planning is everything." Plans must be in place before we can respond appropriately to contingencies, but without the will to review and exercise them, the plans will eventually lose their relevance. It is the process of updating assumptions and planning factors, identifying changes to what had been agreed—sometimes painfully—in earlier discussions, and getting to know new or replacement personnel that creates the basis for success of the mission. Consequently, the following actions are among the essential prerequisites to engaging Army Reserve personnel in managing the consequences of a terrorist attack involving weapons of mass destruction:

● *Identify and resolve legal and other obstacles to rapid response in a crisis.* Hours are important in consequence management. Even though most Army Reserve units can do no more than begin deployment of a portion of their unit with a few hours' notice, the arrival of even a small advance party in the affected area could make a real difference to victims. Commanders must know that they are free to deploy their units and that their soldiers (or survivors) will have adequate protection or compensation for their operations in a hazardous environment. Issues such as authorization and notification procedures must be settled, as must such prosaic matters as the authority of designated unit commanders to respond to direct appeals from local authorities and activate unit assembly and movement plans.

• *Establish a chain of command for consequence management that is clear and unambiguous.* WMD consequence management will involve federal, state, and local jurisdictions working simultaneously with civilians, public servants, and the military. Matters such as the place of the Army Reserve in the response hierarchy need to be examined, as well as command and control arrangements for the period immediately after an attack when perhaps only local police and rescue, National Guard, and Reserve personnel will be on the scene.

• *Provide clear and executable missions to every unit assigned responsibilities for consequence management.* At least at the operational level, Army Reserve units have not been assigned the mission of consequence management in the aftermath of WMD use on American soil. Decisions on this issue should not be deferred. Introduction of an additional mission may not bring with it more time to train, but it will force the issue of limited resources and produce either compromises or the additional resources needed to respond satisfactorily to new tasks. Mission planning for responding to multiple simultaneous attacks will stress resources to an even greater extent.

• *Establish and maintain close working relationships with all responsible state and local authorities.* The Los Angeles riots demonstrated that if trust does not exist between civilian and military commanders before a catastrophe, efforts to develop it quickly under the pressure of events may not lead to success. Mutually developed plans, frequently updated, coordinated, and periodically rehearsed, are required if there is to be a seamless response to a disaster.

• *Prepare and conduct training.* For the most part, WMD consequence management, as seen from the chemical unit level, will not differ significantly from the type of activities already required in preparation for conflict. One could expect greater emphasis on operations in an urban environment, and planning processes will have to include local civil authorities. Exercises of the plans and technical training must by definition include civilian organizations. Good material well presented to local and state medical, police, and fire organizations will help establish confidence and trust in the military's capabilities.

• *Develop the capability to "surge" medical support to an affected area to ensure both immediate and long-term care.* Initial support from reserve component military medical units in the aftermath of an attack with weapons of mass destruction should be drawn from units outside the affected area. Coordination of medical response to the consequences of an attack will almost invariably involve several regions of the country and could conceivably extend into Canada and Mexico. Contingencies to be examined include responses to multiple simultaneous attacks. Caution must also be exercised in this regard; a common terrorist technique is to launch a second attack against those who rush to help victims of the first one.

• *Relocate existing chemical units or activate new ones to improve coverage of population centers.* Chemical units of all the services and components are significantly concentrated east of the Mississippi, away from populated areas of California and the Midwest. Decontamination companies in Washington State and Texas are too far from California's large population centers to be responsive in a crisis or readily accessible for the development, coordination, exercise, and rehearsal of essential contingency plans.

 • *Evaluate the costs and prospective benefits of deploying modified versions of third-generation technology to selected metropolitan centers.* Modified detection devices could be permanently installed in hospitals, police departments, or other locations that are continuously occupied by skilled personnel. Early detection of biological attacks, including pathogen identification, could significantly reduce civilian casualties. Recent work by the Centers for Disease Control indicates that a biological attack affecting 100,000 people would be so costly that as much as $250 million could be spent per year per potential attack area on early detection and intervention measures and still be fiscally responsible. These estimates are over and above sums presently being spent in those areas for police, fire, and rescue organizations, and for military units capable of responding in a crisis.

 • *Identify, set aside, and maintain supplies and equipment necessary for consequence management.* Prophylactic substances should be properly identified, packaged, secured, and rotated. This would ensure that war stocks were current; it would also improve access to initial supplies for metropolitan areas. Planning would also take into account emergency measures for replacing stocks as they were depleted.

The mission identified and described in this article is in some respects an extension of survival and force protection on the battlefield. It differs significantly from those functions, however, in that success will be determined by the quality of the partnerships we develop with civil authorities in every region where we envision a requirement for military support to those authorities. From those partnerships will grow the mutual trust and confidence needed to respond rapidly and effectively to any contingencies that threaten to overwhelm the capacity of local authorities to respond effectively.

Preparing for this mission will not excuse Army Reserve units from wartime missions, but prepare for it we must. If terrorists attack this country with weapons of mass destruction, we will have one chance to respond correctly.

NOTES

1. Chemical-Biological Incident Response Force, general officer's brief (photocopy), 17 December 1996, quoting Presidential Decision Directive 39, dated 21 June 1995.

2. One of the most successful terrorist groups was the "Assassins," an Islamic sect of the late 11th to 13th centuries, sworn to exterminate its enemies. Rafiq Zakaria, *The Struggle Within Islam* (London: Penguin Books, 1988), p. 145.

3. *Executive Seminar on Special Material Smuggling* (Carlisle Barracks, Pa.: Center for Strategic Leadership, 13 September 1996), p. 58. While the Tokyo attack gets all the press, the Aum Shinrikyo actually tested its sarin agent in June 1994. At that time members of the group sprayed an apartment complex in Matsumoto, Japan, in an effort to kill three judges. Although the judges did not die, seven other residents did and another 500 were injured.

4. "Testimony of The Honorable Morris D. Busby," US Senate, Permanent Subcommittee on Investigations, Committee on Governmental Affairs, 27 March 1996, accessed on the Internet on 23 November 1996 at

http://counterterrorism.com/busby.htm. The US military is prepared to fight on a nuclear, chemical, or biological battlefield and carries protective equipment and prophylactics to support that fight. What must be remembered is that the military addresses "militarily significant" amounts of chemical agents, biological pathogens or toxins, or residual radiation; decontamination is the minimum necessary for mission accomplishment and contaminated terrain is vacated as soon as possible. Civilians do not carry protective equipment nor are they willing to abandon their homes and businesses and so they expect thorough decontamination, which may not even be possible.

5. Ibid.

6. Senator Richard Lugar, quoted in William C. Mann, "Terrorists With Doomsday Weapons a Growing Threat, Experts Warn," *The Atlanta Constitution*, 1 November 1995, p. A6.

7. Barbara K. Bodine (Acting Coordinator for Counterterrorism, US Department of State), *Patterns of Global Terrorism: 1993* (Washington: GPO, 1994), p. iv.

8. Marvin J. Cetron and Owen Davies, "The Future Face of Terrorism," *Futurist*, 28 (November 1994), 12. The authors point out that religious and ethnically motivated terrorists are more willing than most to use whatever means necessary to accomplish their aims. They consequently will not shrink from mass murder, for they believe they are struggling against "the forces of darkness."

9. *Executive Seminar on Special Material Smuggling*, p. 28.

10. Robert L. Pfaltzgraff, Jr., and Richard H. Shultz, Jr., eds., *Ethnic Conflict and Regional Instability: Implications for US Policy and Army Roles and Missions* (Washington: GPO, circa 1994), p. 40.

11. *Executive Seminar on Special Material Smuggling*, p. 25. Weapons grade $_{94}Pu^{239}$ or $_{92}U^{235}$ are not required for a radiation dispersal device. Combining conventional explosives with Cesium-137, Cobalt-60, Strontium-90, or plutonium oxide can contaminate a wide area for years to centuries.

12. Robert Harris and Jeremy Paxman, *A Higher Form of Killing* (New York: Hill and Wang, 1982), p. 158.

13. Edward M. Spiers, *Chemical and Biological Weapons—A Study of Proliferation* (New York: St. Martin's Press, 1994), p. 170. The FBI has found cyanide held by the Revolutionary Action Movement (1967) and the Covenant Sword in the Arm of the Lord (1985), typhoid cultures held by the Order of the Rising Sun (1972), and nerve agent on an assassin planning to kill the president in Washington (1974). Terrorists can get agents, toxins, or pathogens from sponsor states or through theft or fraud from legitimate laboratories or supply firms.

14. Andrew Pollack, "Japanese Police Say They Found Germ-War Material at Cult Site," *The New York Times International*, 29 March 1995, p. A10.

15. Joseph D. Douglass and Neil C. Livingston, *America the Vulnerable* (Lexington, Mass.: Lexington Books, 1987), p. 24.

16. Bruce W. Nelan, "The Price of Fanaticism," *Time*, 3 April 1995, p. 40.

17. US Congress, Senate, Committee on Governmental Affairs, Permanent Subcommittee on Investigations, *Global Spread of Chemical and Biological Weapons*, Hearings, 101st Cong., 1st sess. (Washington: GPO, 1989), p. 32.

18. Abram S. Beneson, ed., US Army Field Manual FM 8-33, *Control of Communicable Diseases in Man* (Washington: US Dept. of the Army, 31 May 1991), p. 18. An official report of the American Public Health Association, this FM provides information such as mode of transmission, incubation period, fatality rate, and methods of control of a large number of diseases.

19. Interview with Arnold F. Kaufmann, D.V.M., and Martin I Meltzer, Ph.D., on the topic of "The Economic Impact of a Bioterrorist Attack," 16 January 1997, Centers for Disease Control and Prevention, Atlanta, Ga. Dr. Kaufmann and Dr. Meltzer have addressed the threat of a terrorist biological attack from a novel and useful point of view. Doctrinally sound delivery methods were coupled with a high-sided LD_{50} and a very conservative casualty rate, all designed to determine an economically conservative range of intervention costs that were actuarially equated to annual premiums. Essentially, this study determines the amount of money the country could spend on preparing for a biological attack from an economic viewpoint. This analysis determined that the overriding factor in minimizing the effects of a biological attack is the rapid initiation of a prophylaxis. The recommended treatment for anthrax is 28 days of doxycycline or ciprofloxacin coupled with vaccination. Effective intervention requires planning, training, and propositioned supplies.

20. Jon H. Moilanen, "Engagement and Disarmament: A US National Security Strategy for Biological Weapons of Mass Destruction," photocopy, Carlisle Barracks, Pa., US Army War College, p. 10. Biologic agents may be used to attack people, animals, or crops. Inhalation anthrax is fatal in extremely small doses. Vaccinations after infection are essentially useless (unless the bacillus remains in spore form for an extended period) due to the time required to develop antibodies.

21. US Department of the Army, Field Manual FM 3-9, *Potential Military Chemical/Biological Agents and Compounds* (Washington: US Dept. of the Army, 12 December 1990), p. 107.

22. Andrew Bilski and Sudvendrini Kakuchi, "Tokyo Terror," *Maclean's*, 3 April 1995, p. 29. Sarin is fatal to humans at a ratio of one to 100 million parts by weight.

23. William C. Mann, "Terrorists With Doomsday Weapons a Growing Threat, Experts Warn," *The Atlanta Constitution*, 1 November 1995, p. A6.

24. G. A. Cristy and C. V. Chester, *Emergency Protection from Aerosols* (Oak Ridge, Tenn.: US National Laboratory, July 1981), p. 23. This study was commissioned by the Department of Energy to determine the most effective means of protecting families inside their homes from a toxic aerosol passing over their dwelling. *Bacillus globegii* spores (average diameter of 2 microns) were used as the aerosol agent. Findings indicated that for an aerosol threat-duration longer than the structure's air exchange rate, protection factors of only about 3 were obtained. For aerosols of short threat-duration (where structures were opened and ventilated after cloud passage) protection factors of 10-200 were obtainable. If filtration devices and positive pressure systems are placed on the houses (accomplished with a simple vacuum cleaner) and the houses are ventilated after cloud passage, protection factors of as much as 7000 can be obtained. Interestingly, of five experiméntal arrangements of vacuum cleaner filtration set-ups, the most effective was a dirty bag with three months' accumulation of debris. (It is obviously essential to know the aerosol cloud is coming and when it has passed.)

25. Telephone interview with Arnold F. Kaufmann, D.V.M., on topics of intervention requirements of victims and the contamination effects of *Bacillus anthracis*, 7 February 1997, Centers for Disease Control and Prevention, Atlanta, Ga. Computer models run by Dr. Kaufmann indicate that *Bacillus anthracis* disseminated as an aerosol will deposit the heavier particles (those poorly milled or aerosolized) within 700-1000 meters of the line of dissemination. Once deposited on the ground, the threat of re-aerosolization is negligible. This relatively narrow band of contamination assumes the pathogen was spread from a vehicle with optimal atmospheric conditions (particle deposition depends on such factors as height of dissemination and wind speed). Lighter particles (those of neutral buoyancy) will stay aloft almost indefinitely—at least until the spores have been killed (by ultraviolet light, etc.). Even before complete destruction, pathogens can incur a loss in both viability (being alive) and virulence (ability to produce disease) during their downwind drift. Dr. Kaufmann's studies indicate intensive and early intervention after a biologic attack can significantly reduce fatalities and improve victim recovery. For example, inhalation anthrax had a mortality of perhaps 95 percent or more in the pre-antibiotic era; intensive modern treatment begun after symptoms have appeared can reduce mortality to 70-95 percent. Treatment begun before the appearance of symptoms can bring mortality significantly below 70 percent. Due to the short incubation period of some pathogens (i.e., *Bacillus anthracis*) it will be essential for civilians in the area of attack to be informed quickly where they should go to receive treatment. Successful intervention involves adequate antibiotic prophylaxis and vaccination availability, informing citizens where to obtain treatment, and personnel to prevent or control population panic.

26. US Army Medical Research Institute of Chemical Defense, *Medical Management of Chemical Casualties—Handbook* (Aberdeen Proving Ground, Md.: Dept. of the Army, September 1995), pp. 17, 30-32. This is an extraordinary handbook discussing such things as symptoms, decontamination, immediate management, and triage; it is written in plain language and is useful to the nonspecialist.

27. Ralph Trapp, "The Detoxification and Natural Degradation of Chemical Warfare Agents," Stockholm International Peace Research Institute (London: Taylor and Francis, 1985), p. 90. This SIPRI document lists various detoxicants and comments on their effects on chemical agents. It is particularly interesting in that it discusses ground decontamination using chemicals that are not military standard, as well as STB.

28. Beneson, p. 67.

29. Kaufmann and Meltzer interview.

30. US Department of the Army, Field Manual 3-19, *NBC Reconnaissance* (Washington: Dept. of the Army, 19 November 1993), p. A-2.

31. US Congress, House of Representatives, Conference Report on H.R. 3230, National Defense Authorization Act for Fiscal Year 1997, *Title XIV—Defense Against Weapons of Mass Destruction* (Washington: GPO, 1996), p. 3.

32. Telephone interview with Major Bill Van Nuys, FORSCOM Plans, Chemical Organizational Integrator, and briefing presentation on US Army Chemical Units (photocopy), 14 January 1997. The Total Army has 43 chemical companies at echelons above division, four brigade headquarters, and 12 battalion headquarters. The last National Guard Chemical Brigade Headquarters (404th) and Battalion Headquarters (44th) are scheduled to deactivate in the near future.

33. Chemical-Biological Incident Response Force, general officer's brief (photocopy), 17 December 1996, prepared for Generals Friel, Broderick, and Berndt. The CBIRF is mission ready. It consists of command, reconnaissance, decontamination, medical, security, and service support elements. Also associated with the CBIRF is a distinguished civilian advisory group and a mobile laboratory capable of detecting and identifying biological agents. See also Captain Chris Seiple, USMC, "Confronting the Domestic Consequences of WMD," in this issue of *Parameters*, 27 (Autumn 1997), 119-34.

34. Sergeant Lance M. Bacon, USMC, "Incident Response Force," *Surface Warfare*, 21 (November-December 1996), 19. The CBIRF's medical team, although small (six medical officers and 17 corpsmen) is trained in treating all types of chemical and biological casualties. It would be an excellent element to supervise the work of medical staffs less skilled in these areas.

35. Major Joseph Osterman, USMC, "Who Will Answer the Chemical/Bio Call?" *Proceedings*, 122 (December 1996), 40. Timeliness and coordination are the most important aspects of a response to biological or

chemical incidents. Coordination of a response is really a function of FEMA, but DOD has a greater capability to handle large-scale activities (e.g., Hurricane Andrew). The US Atlantic Command has been given the task of providing DOD support for the 48 contiguous states, Puerto Rico, and the Virgin Islands. To accomplish this mission, incident response units must be able to deploy rapidly, provide a nucleus for expansion, be technologically current, have a command structure able to influence decisions at the flag level, maintain security, conduct triage, and treat casualties. "Pick-up" response teams will clearly be less effective than integrated units whose members have trained together. No organization currently exists that can fill these requirements by itself.

36. Telephone interview with Major Bill Van Nuys and briefing presentation on US Army chemical units (photocopy), 14 January 1997.

37. Ibid. There are one BIDS, two reconnaissance, four mechanized smoke, 17 motor smoke, and nine decontamination companies in the USAR.

38. Telephone interview with Lieutenant Colonel John Ontiveros, Chemical and Biological Defense Command, 18 June 1997. The Department of Defense will never control operations, even when responding to an incident. The Chemical and Biological Defense Command office serving as the Army's lead agent in planning the training for and response to incidents of domestic WMD terrorism will for the first time be assigned representatives from the National Guard and Army Reserve not later than July 1997.

39. US Army Medical Research Institute of Chemical Defense, *Medical Management of Chemical Casualties—Handbook*, p. 27.

40. Telephone interview with Major Bill Van Nuys and briefing presentation on US Army chemical units (photocopy), 14 January 1997.

41. Telephone interview with Lieutenant Commander Denise L. Matthews, USCG, on the topic of "US Coast Guard National Strike Force Mission," 9 January 1997. Coast Guard Strike Force units respond to oil and hazardous chemical incidents. Although there are only three of these units, they are well situated to respond to emergencies (Atlantic Strike Team, Fort Dix, N.J.; Gulf Strike Team, Mobile, Ala.; Pacific Strike Team, Novato, Calif.). The National Strike Force Coordination Center controls each of these 38-member teams. All response equipment is palletized, loaded, and ready for immediate deployment by air or ground. Each team is able to dispatch two members immediately, four within two hours, and 12 within six hours.

42. US Department of Defense, Manual DOD 3025.1-M, *Manual for Civil Emergencies* (Washington: US Dept. of Defense, June 1994), pp. 2-11.

43. Ibid. The DOD response structure parallels the state and FEMA structures. The real key to success is the coordination that takes place between the SCO, the FCO, and the DCO.

44. Christopher M. Schnaubelt, "Lessons in Command and Control from the Los Angeles Riots," *Parameters*, 27 (Summer 1997), 88-109. Author identifies where military operations worked well during the riots and where they did not. When mid-level law enforcement leaders and the military units supporting them took the initiative to talk together, operations went smoothly. The civil disturbance was a non-linear "battlefield" and consequently many prepared plans, when they existed, just didn't apply, so support operations had to be negotiated in the field.

45. Major General William P. Bland, TAG, GAANG, report, "After Action, OPERATION CENTENNIAL GUARD, 1 June - 25 August 1996," 20 December 1996, p. 13. Active-duty and National Guard soldiers supported security operations at the 1996 Olympics in Atlanta. A total of 13,968 Guard Members from 47 states and territories, all under the command and control of the Adjutant General of Georgia, worked with ACOG security and state and local law enforcement. Liaison operations were essential to facilitate information flow between the Georgia National Guard TF G-2 and the numerous intelligence groups supporting the Olympics.

46. R. J. Manachee, et al., "Out of Gruinard Island," in *Proceedings of the International Workshop on Anthrax*, held in Winchester, England, 11-13 April 1989, ed. Peter C. B. Turnbull (Wiltshier, Eng.: Salisbury Medical Society, 1989), p. 17. During World War II, the British conducted tests to determine the viability of explosively disseminated *Bacillus anthracis* spores as a biological weapon. The tests were a success, but annual checks for more than 20 years after the war showed that large numbers of virulent spores persisted in the soil. The entire island was not contaminated, however—only 3.7 hectares in the test area. After analysis indicated that the spores would not decay to undetectable quantities until around 2050, the Ministry of Defense directed that the area be decontaminated with the intent of returning the island to civilian use. Tests of various biocides conclusively indicated that formaldehyde was most effective. Not only did it have a high sporicidal activity and persistence in peat, but it denatured living organic matter into fertilizer-like properties. An application of 50 liters per square meter of five percent formaldehyde was used to sterilize the soil to a depth of 15 cm (with greater concentrations of formaldehyde injected in areas of heavier contamination). Testing for residual contamination was done and some retreatment was necessary, but in October 1987 no more *Bacillus anthracis* was found.

47. "US DOD: Background briefing—Domestic Preparedness," M2 Press, Wire, 1 April 1997, p. 3, accessed on the Internet on 18 June 1997 at http://www.elibrary.com. The agencies involved in this training program are the Department of Defense, Federal Emergency Management Agency, Federal Bureau of Investigation, Department of Energy, Environmental Protection Agency, and the Public Health Service.

48. Ontiveros interview, 18 June 1997.

[7]
Defusing Nuclear Terror

by Jeffrey Richelson

O n October 16, 1994, the Federal Bureau of Investigation (FBI) received word that one of its informants was being held hostage by a domestic terrorist group, the Patriots for National Unity, in a New Orleans safe house. The next morning, after overhearing plans to kill the hostage, a raid by the FBI's hostage rescue team freed the informant. During a debriefing, the rescued informant revealed that members of the terrorist group were looking to obtain nuclear material and assemble several nuclear devices. The bureau also determined that one of the group's members may have leased a boat. In response to a possible nuclear threat, the FBI alerted a number of other federal agencies, including the Nuclear Emergency Search Team (NEST)—a special unit under the control of the Energy Department's Nevada Operations Office.

Fortunately, this entire scenario is fictional, just like the many incidents of nuclear terror portrayed in films and novels over the last 40 years: from Spectre's threat in the 1961 James Bond thriller *Thunderball* to employ stolen nuclear bombs against U.S. or British cities; to the Libyan-backed threat of atomic devastation in Larry Collins's *The Fifth Horseman* (1980); to the destruction caused by a terrorist nuclear device in Tom Clancy's *The Sum of All Fears* (1991); to the attempt by an aggrieved Serbian to incinerate the United Nations in the 1997 film *The Peacemaker* starring George Clooney and Nicole Kidman.

In the scenario described above, NEST was participating, along with the FBI, Federal Emergency Management Agency (FEMA), and several other organizations, in a "full-field exercise" designated "Mirage Gold." The purpose of the exercise was to test how successfully the agencies would respond to a nuclear terrorist threat—and if they could work together effectively.

Origins

The possible need to track down lost, stolen, smuggled, or "improvised" nuclear devices has concerned national security agencies for at least as long as novelists have been spinning fictional scenarios. A 1963 national intelligence estimate, *The Clandestine Introduction of Weapons of Mass Destruction into the U.S.,* addressed the question of whether the Soviet Union was likely to attempt to smuggle biological, chemical, or nuclear weapons into the United States. The intelligence community concluded that "the Soviets almost certainly would not contemplate the use of clandestinely delivered nuclear weapons except as a supplement to other weapons in the context of general war," and that "the Soviets probably recognize that it would be impracticable for them to mount a clandestine nuclear attack on a sufficient number of [U.S. delivery vehicles] to reduce substantially the weight of a U.S. strike."

There was also, in the 1960s, concern about the possible consequences

"If they were counting on us to save the good folk of Boston . . . well, it was bye-bye Boston."

of a crash of nuclear-armed aircraft. According to Duane C. Sewell, commonly referred to as the "father of NEST," this led to the creation of a team based at Lawrence Livermore National Laboratory that could send qualified people to pick up the remains of the aircraft, detect the pres-

Jeffrey T. Richelson is a senior fellow with the National Security Archive, Washington, D.C., and the author of The Wizards of Langley: Inside the CIA's Directorate of Science and Technology *(2001).*

ence of a nuclear device, determine the area at risk, remove the bomb, and minimize the physical and political damage. When a B-52 carrying four thermonuclear bombs crashed near Thule, Greenland, in 1968, the value of such a capability was demonstrated. "Project Crested Ice" involved transporting two technicians and an instrument for detecting plutonium, suitably winterized to operate at temperatures of minus 60 degrees Fahrenheit, to the accident scene. Within 24 hours of arrival, they were able to locate the area contaminated with plutonium.

Then, in the summer of 1972, the terrorist group Black September seized, and ultimately murdered, nine members of the Israeli Olympic team. Among those who became seriously concerned over the prospect of nuclear terrorism was James Schlesinger, then chairman of the Atomic Energy Commission (AEC). He held a series of meetings exploring whether terrorists could steal plutonium and make a bomb with it, whether they could steal a bomb, and whether the United States would be able to locate it. In 1974, while those issues were being considered and investigated, the FBI received a note demanding that $200,000 be left at a particular location in Boston or a nuclear device would be detonated somewhere in the city. This note was not part of an exercise, but the real thing (*New York Times Magazine,* December 14, 1980).

William Chambers, a Los Alamos nuclear physicist who was studying the detection issue, was instructed by the AEC and FBI to assemble the best team he could and head for Boston to search the city. The operation reflected its ad hoc origins. The group rented a fleet of mail vans to carry concealed equipment that could detect the emissions of a plutonium or uranium weapon. But the

team found that they did not have the necessary drills to install the detectors in the vans. NEST field director Jerry Doyle recalled, "If they were counting on us to save the good folk of Boston . . . well, it was bye-bye Boston." Fortunately, it was all a hoax—FBI agents waited, but no one showed up to claim the bag of phony bills they left at the designated location.

The threat to Boston resulted in a secret November 18, 1974 memo from Gen. Ernest Graves, the AEC's assistant general manager for military applications, to Mahlon E. Gates, manager of the commission's Nevada Operations Office. Titled "Responsibility for Search and Detection Operations," it authorized Gates to assume responsibility for the planning and execution of AEC operations to search for and identify "lost or stolen nuclear weapons and special nuclear materials, nuclear bomb threats, and radiation dispersal threats." Before the end of 1975, the NEST team was established to prepare for and manage such activities.

Capabilities

If necessary, NEST can deploy approximately 600 individuals to the scene of a terrorist threat, although actual deployments have rarely involved more than 45 people. According to a Nevada Operations Office briefing, deployed personnel come from a pool of about 750 individuals, most of whom work for Energy or its private contractors in other primary capacities. In addition to NEST members based at the team's Las Vegas headquarters, personnel are pulled from three Energy Department labs (Lawrence Livermore, Los Alamos, and Sandia), and from three contractors (Reynolds Electrical & Engineering, Raytheon Services of Nevada, and EG&G).

NEST personnel also have a wide variety of specialties. NEST briefing slides list 17 different categories of personnel, including four types of physicists (nuclear, infrared, atmospheric, and health), engineers, chemists, and mathematicians, as well as specialists in communications, logistics, management, and public information. As a result, the organization chart for a full NEST field deployment contains a multitude of divisions and subdivisions—what one might expect at a large government agency.

If a nuclear terrorist threat is received, the NEST team first assesses the threat's technical and psychological validity. To determine if the technical details are accurate and indicate some knowledge of building nuclear devices (or were simply lifted from a Tom Clancy novel), NEST maintains a comprehensive computer database of nuclear weapon design information—from reports in scientific journals to passages from spy novels. Meanwhile, psychologists and psychiatrists examine the letter writer's choice of words and sentence structure to try to assess the writer's state of mind and the region from which he or she originates.

If NEST were to move into the field, it would not travel lightly. Along with the ability to deploy about 600 people, it also has about 150 tons of equipment at its disposal. NEST's air force consists of four helicopters equipped with radiological search systems, and three airplanes (a King Air B-200, a Citation-II, and a Convair 580T) modified for remote sensing missions. It can deploy vans with equipment capable of detecting the emissions from nuclear material. And by applying appropriate artwork to the sides of vehicles, its graphics department can help undercover vans blend into the flood of commercial vans on the road. When asked if the artwork would be the same as a legitimate company's or be imaginary—possibly allowing a terrorist armed with the Yellow Pages to determine that the van was a phony—a NEST spokesperson remarked that the search team seeks to insure that it does not "raise the sus-

Two West German police helicopters used in the Black September hostage crisis at the 1972 Munich Olympics—the one in the foreground was destroyed by a terrorist grenade during a rescue attempt. The event raised concerns about nuclear terrorism.

picions of the terrorists."

NEST also has an arsenal of hand-held nuclear detectors that can be concealed in any one of many attaché cases, briefcases, lunch packs, and suitcases. The detectors can silently let a NEST member know that a radiation source has been detected by transmitting a signal to the member's concealed earphone.

In addition to equipment for detecting nuclear material, NEST also has diagnostic, disablement, and damage-limitation devices. Its diagnostic capability includes portable X-ray machines to peer under a bomb's outer shell as well as a hand-held device that looks like a Dustbuster and can pick up emissions to better estimate a threat. To disable a bomb, NEST might detonate explosives around it, or it could use a 30-millimeter cannon to blast the bomb into small pieces. The team can construct a nylon tent, 35 feet high and 50 feet in diameter, into which 30,000 cubic feet of thick foam can be pumped, which can mitigate the spread of radiation from a radiation dispersal device. According to a NEST team member, however, the foam is primarily intended to limit

the damage from a non-nuclear detonation used to disable a nuclear weapon.

Deployments

Since NEST's creation, about 100 threats involving alleged nuclear devices or radioactivity have come to its attention. At least a dozen, and possibly more than twice that number, have resulted in deployment of NEST personnel. NEST, in general, will not confirm or deny when or whether it has deployed to a particular city or region. However, it has been reported that between 1975 and 1981 NEST personnel were sent to investigate threats in Boston, Los Angeles, Spokane, Pittsburgh, New York, Sacramento, Tennessee, and Reno (*Time,* January 8, 1996; *Washington Post,* June 21, 1983).

The threat to New York came in July 1975 when terrorists claimed, "We have successfully designed and built an atomic bomb. It is somewhere on Manhattan Island. We refer you to the accompanying drawing in one-eighth scale. We have enough plutonium and explosives for the bomb to function. The device will be used at 6:00 p.m. July 10 unless our demands are met." As reported in the *New York Times Magazine,* the key demand involved $30 million in small bills.

NEST was impressed by the drawing. According to one account, it was

NEST's deployment to Washington, D.C. during the bicentennial may be the type of precaution that becomes more common after the September II attacks.

sophisticated, precise, and "made by someone with more than a passing acquaintance with nuclear physics." But that did not lead the United States to part with real money. A dummy ransom package was left at the drop site in Northampton, Massachusetts, and FBI agents waited for someone to claim it. Nobody showed up and there was no further communication from the extortionists.

That same year, Fred L. Hartley, chairman of the Los Angeles-based Union Oil Company of California, received a note claiming that there was a nuclear device on one of the company's properties. The extortionist wanted $1 million; otherwise, the bomb would be detonated. Such a threat, away from the natural radiation of an urban area—where radiation can be emitted by freshly paved streets or Vermont granite in an office building—made it easier to use NEST vans in the search for a nuclear device.

"The guys were out there in their trucks listening to their earpieces," former NEST official Jerry Doyle told Larry Collins, the author of the first major article on the search team. "Suddenly one got an intensive read-

ing, looked up and there, about 50 yards away, was a big bulky, unidentified wooden crate resting by a refinery fence. There was a moment of real panic," Doyle recalled. Fortunately, it was just a box left by some repairmen, and the signal came from natural radioactivity in the soil. The FBI managed to capture a suspect, who was tried and convicted, but was released after six months in prison.

NEST's deployment to Washington, D.C. during the bicentennial summer of 1976 may be the type of precautionary deployment that becomes more common after the September 11 attacks. Vans circled the streets and drove around federal buildings near the Mall, checking radiation levels. The FBI worried that a terrorist group might be tempted by the bicentennial's significance to threaten to explode or release nuclear material, but the summer passed without a threat.

Not all of NEST's deployments have involved nuclear terrorism. For three months in 1978, about 120 NEST personnel helped the Canadian government locate the remains of the Soviet Cosmos 954 ocean surveillance satellite that crashed into northern Canada. The following year, NEST equipment was used to monitor radiation in the vicinity of the Three Mile Island nuclear accident.

Mirage Gold

Returning to the Mirage Gold exercise, an intensive evaluation of NEST and the nature of the exercise revealed several problems.

By early morning on October 18, 1994, the first NEST search and support personnel had arrived in Louisiana and, along with FEMA and Defense Department personnel,

established command posts in an unused industrial complex across the Intercoastal Waterway from the New Orleans Naval Air Station. Communications equipment—including secure voice, data, and video display systems for the exercise—had been installed in September. That afternoon, "a maritime target was located (anchored at Lake Michoud) and put under surveillance," according to the Nevada Operations Office after-action report.

"Additional information," according to the report, directed NEST personnel to a small flying service at an airstrip near Magazine Road in Belle Chase (the Naval Air Station). During a drive-by, the team's radiation detectors registered a "hit" which led them to a mock nuclear device hidden in an airport shed. Following orders from the FBI, NEST waited until noon the next day when the three Patriots for National Unity members drove away from the airport. While NEST kept the terrorists under surveillance, the FBI proceeded to secure the airport. When the shed was searched, an improvised nuclear device was found, along with information indicating that it was armed and set to explode on Thursday at noon.

NEST personnel constructed a 35-foot cone around the shed and pumped in thick foam to limit blast effects and absorb radioactive particles. One part of the Nevada Operations Office after-action report asserts that the plan to disable the device "was successfully carried out before the deadline without the release of any radioactivity," although other parts are consistent with an account given by Andrew and Leslie Cockburn in their book *One Point Safe* (1997). According to the Cockburns, someone had failed to obtain permission to detonate explosive charges to disable the simulated bomb. As a result, the search team was left with a mound of foam that made it impossible to determine if the bomb had been properly disabled, and forensic experts were unable to search the crime scene.

But according to a scathing memo sent to the manager of the Nevada Operations Office by Adm. Charles J. Beers, then the Energy Department's deputy assistant secretary for military applications and stockpile support, problems with Mirage Gold went far beyond such mistakes and involved the very integrity of the exercise. The Beers memo "requested" a general assessment of NEST that would address a number of concerns regarding the exercise. These included the failure to employ a realistic estimate of the time the operation would require, the negative impact of the large NEST structure on rapid decision-making, the leaking to NEST personnel of key information, including the location of the device, and the deployment of communications systems before the FBI had requested assistance from NEST. The consequences of such actions were "optimistic and unrealistic results."

The Beers memo was also less than complimentary to the leadership of NEST. He wrote, "It is quite possible that we have allowed a management regime to be established that does not serve the NEST program as well as it should. . . . Perceptions of poor integration of assets, improper flow of information to players during exercises, and implications that an unrealistic time line has been advertised are not issues that can be solved by budget reallocations, but reflect on leadership and management of the program."

NEST management reacted swiftly, commissioning an outside review group, headed by Duane Sewell, to examine the entire program. The group conducted more than 120 hours of interviews and produced an 80-page report, which noted that a deteriorating relationship with Energy had lowered both the morale and effectiveness of NEST. In addition, the review group found a number of well-known but unspecified "technical constraints which limit the ability of NEST to respond effectively to the full range of nuclear devices which might be developed by a terrorist organization." Energy Department managers had not yet made a decision, according to the Sewell panel, as to whether they would continue to accept those limitations or seek the funding necessary for the research required to eliminate or reduce them.

A 1996 assessment of NEST, conducted by minority counsel to the Senate Governmental Affairs Committee, was relatively optimistic. NEST "is clearly a national asset which could not be duplicated by other organizations because of the unique scientific capabilities and field operational experience of the nuclear weapons laboratories that directly support it with volunteers and R&D." The assessment noted that since the Sewell report, NEST had "successfully conducted its first truly no-notice full-field exercises overseas." In addition, "in exercises since Mirage Gold, the NEST team had also deployed all of its resources within established time lines." The search team had conducted 16 major command post and full-field exercises. But the report also cited continuing technical constraints, again unspecified, that senior management at the Energy Department needed to address.

Outlook

The catalyst for NEST's creation in the mid-1970s was the attempt to enlist nuclear terror in the service of extortion. And some NEST exercises still employ a nuclear extortion scenario, according to a current team member. But the premise for Mirage Gold was different, and consistent with today's greatest fear— that terrorists may not be interested in money or changing government policy. They may simply want to detonate a nuclear weapon.

It is also a premise that puts a much greater premium on intelligence. Nuclear extortionists have to threaten a particular city or area and give the threatened party time to react, giving NEST time to deploy and attempt to locate any bomb that might be in place. But terrorists could strike anywhere, and would give no warning. A NEST spokesperson acknowledged that without advance intelligence, the team would have nowhere to go. Exceptions may include deployments at high-profile events, such as the Salt Lake City Olympics, which would be obvious potential targets for terrorists. But to prevent detonation of a terrorist nuclear device in other circumstances would require warning from the FBI, Central Intelligence Agency, National Security Agency, or an allied intelligence service.

Of course, even advance warning is no guarantee of success, given the difficulty of locating a hidden nuclear device and the limited time that may be available. A comment in the Nevada Operations Office's after-

> Today's terrorists may not be interested in money or changing government policy. They may simply want to detonate a nuclear weapon.

action report on Mirage Gold is chilling, not as a criticism of NEST members, with their diverse talents and dedication, but as an acknowledgment of a harsh reality. The report notes that it would be "a drastic mistake to assume that NEST technology and procedures will always succeed, resulting in zero nuclear yield." ❋

[8]

Keeping Track of Anthrax:
The Case for a Biosecurity Convention

by Michael Barletta, Amy Sands & Jonathan B. Tucker

L AST FALL, FIVE LETTE\S CONTAINING A highly lethal preparation of powdered anthrax spores were sent through the U.S. postal system, killing five people, sickening 18 others, and forcing tens of thousands to take powerful antibiotics. The anthrax mailings provoked worldwide anxiety when post offices and federal buildings were shut down, causing billions of dollars in damage. Today, the perpetrator(s) remain at large—perhaps capable of further attacks.

As bad as it was, the fallout from the anthrax letters only hints at the devastation that could result from a large-scale bioterrorist attack. In light of September 11, such a possibility must be taken seriously. Because bioterrorism poses a clear and present danger to international security, the United States and its allies must take concerted action to stop terrorists from getting hold of deadly pathogens and toxins. To this end, the Bush administration should take an international leadership role: first, by pursuing enhanced national regulations that control and secure these dangerous materials; and second, by launching the negotiation of a new "biosecurity convention."

Controlling access to germs

Although biological agents can be obtained from natural sources, such as soil or diseased animals, the collection of agents demands expertise in microbiology and a fair degree of luck. Effectively weaponizing anthrax is also tricky. Technical hurdles prevented the Japanese doomsday cult Aum Shinrikyo, for example, from perpetrating large-scale bioterrorist attacks in the early 1990s. Aum Shinrikyo scientists unwittingly obtained a natural strain of anthrax bacteria that turned out to be "avirulent"—incapable of causing disease. So although the cult successfully mass-produced and released anthrax spores in central Tokyo on several occasions, the attacks caused no known casualties. It would be far easier, and provide a greater chance of success, for would-be bioterrorists to buy or steal cultures of dangerous pathogens from academic, industrial, or commercial labs.

Whether or not the anthrax mailings were "made in America," as some now believe, the Federal Bureau of Investigation's difficulty identifying the source of the anthrax spores shows that the U.S. government does not effectively monitor culture collections within its own

Michael Barletta is senior research associate at the Center for Nonproliferation Studies (CNS) at the Monterey Institute of International Studies and the editor of After 9/11: Preventing Mass-Destruction Terrorism and Weapons Proliferation. *Amy Sands is deputy director of CNS and served as an assistant director of the U.S. Arms Control and Disarmament Agency from 1994–1996. Jonathan B. Tucker is director of the Chemical and Biological Weapons Nonproliferation Program at CNS and the author of* Scourge: The Once and Future Threat of Smallpox *(2001).*

borders, let alone in other countries. The number of U.S. labs that possess cultures of anthrax bacteria is thought to be in the hundreds and includes universities, private institutes, hospitals, veterinary clinics, and public health agencies. Simply banning laboratory stocks of these microbes is not a practical option; the pathogens must be available for legitimate scientific research and the development of new medical therapies.

Restricting access to legitimate scientists will be impossible until federal agencies develop a comprehensive inventory of the stocks of disease agents and toxins held by U.S. academic and industrial labs, research institutes, and commercial suppliers.

In 1996, following revelations that a leading biological-supply house had sold cultures of bubonic plague bacteria to an Ohio lab technician with links to the Aryan Nations (a violent white-supremacist organization), Congress passed anti-terrorism legislation tightening controls on transfers of dangerous pathogens

Congress tightened controls after Larry Wayne Harris (center, in 1998) illegally obtained bubonic plague cultures.

within the United States. Regulations introduced in 1997 require anyone intending to ship or receive agents on a list of 36 pathogens and toxins to register with the federal Centers for Disease Control and Prevention (CDC) and demonstrate a legitimate medical or scientific use for the material. Violations are punishable by prison terms and fines of up to $500,000.

Put it on the fast track

The Bush administration should signal its determination to craft a biosecurity convention to help prevent bioterrorism by pressing the U.S. Senate to grant the White House "fast-track" negotiating authority. By conferring such authority, the Senate would commit to an up-or-down floor vote by a two-thirds majority on whether to ratify the new treaty without attaching amendments or reservations of any kind, and with committee review and floor debate limited to a set time period. The fast-track approach was developed under President Richard M. Nixon for international trade agreements and has been used most often by his Re-

publican successors. Congress has also adopted streamlined procedures to ensure the timely and disciplined consideration of national security legislation, like the 1990 Defense Base Closure and Realignment Act, in cases when Congress has needed political cover.

In requesting fast-track authority, the Bush administration would outline its negotiating objectives in consultations with Senate leaders of both parties and with representatives of the U.S. biotechnology and pharmaceutical industries. The administration might also agree to inform and consult with the Senate by submitting quarterly reports on the status of negotiations.

Unfortunately, this law contains a major loophole: Labs that simply hold or work with dangerous cultures, but do not transfer them across state lines, are not required to register with the CDC. In the aftermath of September 11, Congress has moved to close the loophole by extending the law to regulate possession as well as transfers.

Perhaps more troubling is that U.S. efforts to combat bioweapons may have created unaccountable sources of dangerous pathogens. Recent rev-elations indicate that the U.S. biodefense program secretly produced weapons-grade anthrax powder for the purpose of testing detection equipment at Dugway Proving Ground in Utah. Given suspicions that the perpetrator of the anthrax mailings could be a biodefense program insider, the need for effective controls and oversight on work with dangerous pathogens has become all the more acute. Otherwise, expanding biodefense work (as the Bush administration wants to do) could have the paradoxical effect of increasing the availability of deadly germs to terrorists.

Germ trade

Even if the United States can put its own house in order, the international scope of the problem still looms large.

Hundreds of companies and labs around the world work with dangerous pathogens, but regulations on access vary widely. According to the World Federation for Culture Collections (WFCC), a loose association of 472 repositories of living microbial specimens in 61 countries, there are 46 germ banks—in countries as diverse as Germany, India, and Iran—that stock anthrax cultures. Although the federation recently urged its members to tighten access to dangerous microbes, it lacks the authority to force compliance. Moreover, more than 1,000 germ banks worldwide do not belong to the federation, and few of their culture collections are adequately secured or regulated.

Controls on "germ commerce," or trade in microbial cultures, are also far from universal. The United States and 32 other like-minded governments belong to an informal forum known as the Australia Group,

Aum Shinrikyo attempted both biological and chemical weapons attacks in Japan. Here, Tokyo inspectors check for nerve gas, April 1995.

A commitment to fast-track negotiating authority by the Senate's Democratic leadership would demonstrate bipartisan problem-solving and provide reassurance that the U.S. government is working to protect Americans. Although granting fast-track authority would curtail the leadership's prerogative to control committee and floor deliberations, Senate Democrats would gain influence over the negotiating goals and strategies of the Republican administration.

Granting fast-track authority now would shield senators from special-interest pressures later on. Moreover, barring filibusters and requiring a simple up/down floor vote would prevent a single powerful senator from delaying consideration of the treaty, as has occurred in recent years. Fast-track authority would also prevent a re-peat of the 1997 Senate debate over ratification of the Chemical Weapons Convention, when treaty opponents attached unilateral waivers and exemptions to the Resolution of Ratification, seriously weakening the accord by creating loopholes that proliferators could exploit.

Finally, granting the White House fast-track authority to negotiate the biosecurity convention would help reshape international expectations about what must be done to combat bioterrorism. Senate approval of fast-track would reflect the urgency of the issue and underscore the need for all countries to put aside "business as usual" when confronting the grave threat that biological weapons pose to international peace and security.

M. B., A. S. & J. T.

which serves to coordinate national controls over exports of dangerous pathogens and certain sensitive dual-use biotechnology equipment. Member states pledge not to undercut other suppliers by selling to countries that have already been denied access to sensitive goods. But states that seek bioweapons can evade Australia Group controls by using transshipment points and shell companies or by trading with countries that are not members of the group.

The most accessible source of biowarfare materials and equipment is foreign commercial suppliers. Unauthorized access to dangerous pathogens from these suppliers poses both an international and domestic threat. An international campaign to

October 31, 2001: After a recent anthrax attack, a mail carrier wears a protective mask and gloves.

regulate exports and imports of these materials and to harmonize the uneven patchwork of national regulations would significantly hinder would-be bioterrorists.

A new approach

Over the past year, international efforts to deal with state acquisition and use of biological weapons have come to a standstill. Although the 1972 Biological and Toxin Weapons Convention (BWC) bans the development, production, stockpiling, and transfer of microbial disease agents and natural poisons (toxins) as weapons, it lacks any formal measures to ensure treaty compliance. This lack of teeth has rendered the BWC incapable of dealing with a series of alleged violations.

In early 1995, a group of BWC member states began to negotiate a legally binding protocol to "strengthen the effectiveness and improve the implementation" of the treaty by establishing a system of mandatory declarations and on-site inspections of dual-use facilities like vaccine plants (which can be easily diverted to bioweapons production). These measures would have been backed up with the right to request "challenge" inspections of suspected undeclared facilities and field investigations of alleged bioweapons use or suspicious outbreaks of disease.

In July 2001, the Bush administration rejected the draft protocol to the bioweapons treaty and abruptly withdrew from the negotiations after more than six years of effort. Bush officials argued that the proposed inspection measures were ineffective and would allow a determined proliferator to

conceal an offensive biowarfare program with little risk of detection. At the same time, officials said, on-site inspections would jeopardize the trade secrets of American pharmaceutical and biotech companies.

In the wake of the U.S. rejection of the BWC protocol, several governments and non-governmental organizations are looking for a way to enforce treaty compliance. Although President Bush said in November that the United States remains committed to the bioweapons treaty, his administration has done little to prove it. During the Fifth Review Conference of the BWC last November and December, the United States proposed a package of nine alternative measures to strengthen the treaty. Most of the suggestions were based on domestic legislation and other voluntary actions. Some of these ideas have merit, such as urging treaty members to criminalize the possession and use of bioweapons and to facilitate extradition. But others are questionable (such as the proposal for states to accept international inspections of suspicious disease outbreaks and alleged bioweapons use on a politically, not legally, binding basis), or merely in the realm of good intentions (such as devising a code of bioethics for scientists).

Late on the conference's last day, the United States shocked attendees by proposing to do away with the forum that had negotiated the BWC protocol. When other countries objected, the conference came dangerously close to collapse before the chairman suspended the meeting for one year. During this "time out" it will be important for treaty members to find a way out of the current impasse. [See "Bioweapons: U.S. Vetoes Verification," by Susan Wright, March/April 2002 *Bulletin*.]

The manifest threat of bioterrorism dwarfs U.S. efforts to prevent it. In the wake of September 11, the United States and other countries have begun to address domestic bioterrorism problems. But these efforts must be expanded. If the United States were to promote a realistic agenda, a coordinated and multilateral international response to bioterrorism could be developed.

The biosecurity convention

U.S. officials should work with like-minded countries to develop domestic legislation to prevent unauthorized access to pathogens and to regulate germ commerce. Basing these laws on the strengthened U.S. legislation recently adopted by Congress would help to create more uniform regulations over labs that work with or transfer dangerous pathogens.

Parallel to these efforts, the United States should promote an international biosecurity convention, which would be distinct from the bioweapons treaty but would complement it by primarily addressing the threat of bioterrorism. In addition, the biosecurity convention should build on the ongoing implementation of the 1992 Biological Diversity Convention and its 2000 Cartagena Protocol on Biosafety, which includes provisions for the safe handling, transfer, and use of genetically modified organisms. By focusing on the safety and security of dangerous pathogens, the biosecurity convention would depart from the facility-inspection approach that was the basis of the rejected BWC protocol.

In many respects, the biosecurity convention could follow the model of the 1994 Nuclear Safety Convention, which set international benchmarks for the safe operation of civilian nuclear power plants. As an "incentive instrument," the Nuclear Safety Convention does not enforce compliance through adversarial inspec-

October 19, 2001: Hazardous material workers conduct tests in the Ewing Township, New Jersey, post office where an employee was believed to have been exposed to anthrax spores.

tions, but rather through a common interest in better nuclear plant safety. Political pressure and the need for the appearance of responsibility provide additional incentives for countries to participate.

Like the Nuclear Safety Convention, the biosecurity convention should not specify highly detailed rules because standards developed today may be rendered obsolete by technological advances. Instead, countries should agree on a set of basic obligations and guidelines, which would be implemented in detail by each member-state through its national legislative process.

The biosecurity convention should include three basic elements: a legal commitment by the contracting parties; agreed principles for developing progressively higher standards with respect to regulation and licensing of microbial culture collections; and mechanisms for oversight and progressive refinement of standards through periodic conferences.

The convention would:

● Require member countries to identify microbial and toxin agents of potential concern for biowarfare and terrorism and to establish national registers of culture collections containing these agents, as well as genetically modified strains and engineered agents containing virulence factors and toxin genes transferred from the listed microorganisms;

● Establish uniform international standards to account for and secure listed pathogens and toxins, whether they are stored, transferred, imported, or exported;

● Mandate the passage of domestic legislation to establish licensing and import/export controls over listed pathogens and toxins, and the creation of regulatory bodies to implement this system;

● Establish cooperative procedures to assist member-states in implementing the agreed safety and security standards and in establishing regulatory bodies;

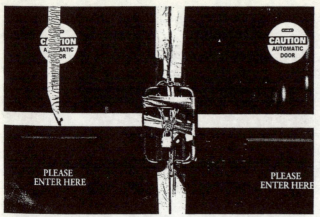

The Hart Senate Office Building was closed for 95 days for anthrax decontamination. It reopened on January 22.

⚖ Require member states to comply fully with the convention's safety and security standards within five years of joining;

⚖ Call for regular conferences where member states report on the development and implementation of their domestic regulatory systems and answer other countries' questions regarding their compliance;

⚖ Create a small secretariat staff in the Department of Disarmament Affairs at the United Nations to organize the review conferences and to facilitate implementation; and

⚖ Require member-states to terminate all commerce and scientific exchanges in the field of biotechnology with any state that does not join the convention within five years of its entry into force.

Needed: a negotiating forum

For several years, some members of the Nonaligned Movement (NAM)— including China, India, Pakistan, and Iran—have sought to link compliance with the bioweapons treaty to greater access to dual-use biotechnology equipment and materials for developing countries. These countries have also wanted to disband the Australia Group, which aims to prevent trans-

fers of such technologies to countries suspected of pursuing chemical or biological weapons. During the development of a biosecurity convention, the NAM states might try to link their acceptance of the new treaty to the elimination of export-control arrangements, as they did during BWC protocol negotiations. Such a quid pro quo would be unacceptable to the United States and other Australia Group members.

This problem could be avoided if the Western group of industrialized states negotiated the biosecurity convention, and then opened it to accession by other states. The drawback, of course, is that states like Brazil, China, Indonesia, Iran, Mexico, and Russia have pathogen collections that would not be covered, at least initially, and bioterrorists could simply focus their procurement efforts on those countries.

A second approach would be for the Western industrialized states to agree on a narrow negotiating mandate and then open the negotiation on an ad hoc basis to any state willing to accept it, while resisting efforts to link the biosecurity convention to other sensitive issues. This model would be similar to the negotiation of the 1997 Ottawa Convention on Landmines.

Enhanced domestic and international security through a new biosecurity convention will require U.S. presidential leadership. In the early 1970s, President Richard M. Nixon earned worldwide respect for his decision to terminate the U.S. offensive biological warfare program and to negotiate the BWC. Leading a global campaign to prevent bioterrorism would garner President Bush similar acclaim, to the benefit of the nation and the world. ⚖

[9]
Confronting Nuclear, Biological and Chemical Terrorism

Richard A. Falkenrath

The level of security and prosperity enjoyed by today's advanced democracies is virtually unprecedented in history. Internally, the basic political order of these states is not seriously contested. There are only a handful of external military threats, none truly global in reach. The world's many civil wars and internal conflicts are largely confined to specific regions, and their effects can be prevented from spilling over into the protected nations of the West. There are of course many serious long-term foreign-policy challenges – China's rise, Russia's decline, the stability of the Persian Gulf, energy depletion, environmental problems and widening economic inequality, for example – but the advanced democracies face few mortal vulnerabilities.

All modern societies, however, are vulnerable to massive loss of life from an attack involving a weapon of mass destruction (WMD) – nuclear, biological or chemical (NBC). This vulnerability has existed for many years: it is a function of accessible weapons, porous borders, free and open societies, and high population densities in cities. Yet while national-security leaders have generally recognised the military threat posed by NBC weapons, they have tended to downplay or disregard the possibility that these weapons might be used by a non-state or transnational actor in a campaign of mass-destruction terrorism. The threat of NBC terrorism had always had its adherents, and remains an inspiration for novelists and scriptwriters, but policy-makers have traditionally had more pressing concerns.

Something of a shift now appears under way, evident particularly in the United States since the early 1990s. Senior US officials, Congressional leaders and non-governmental experts now routinely call attention to the threat of WMD terrorism – particularly biological weapons – and rank it among the most serious challenges to US security.[1] Literally dozens of US federal, state and local government agencies have created new programmes, or augmented

Richard A. Falkenrath is a faculty member of the John F. Kennedy School of Government, Harvard University, Cambridge, MA. His latest book is co-authored with Robert D. Newman and Bradley Thayer, *America's Achilles Heel: Nuclear, Biological, and Chemical Terrorism and Covert Attack* (Cambridge, MA: Massachusetts Institute of Technology Press, 1998).

44 **Richard A. Falkenrath**

existing ones, against the threat. The media have produced countless stories on the subject, often with a sensationalist spin.

This article addresses one basic question: how serious is the threat of NBC terrorism to the national security of modern liberal democracies? More specifically, where should the responsibility for combating the threat of NBC terrorism lie within a country's national-security priorities as it allocates resources for new capabilities, organises its existing capabilities and declares its policies and threat assessments to the public? To help answer this question, I make four arguments.

First, increased concern with the possibility of NBC terrorism is justified. In many discussions of this threat, the basic distinction between national security and personal safety is often forgotten. If an individual were to rank the likely causes of death in terms of probability, it is unlikely that death from an act of NBC terrorism would be in the top 100. He or she would be more concerned with cancer and car accidents, even murder and natural disasters. However, if national leaders were to rank the single, purposeful events that could kill thousands or tens of thousands of their citizens, a terrorist NBC attack would be in the top three. The focus of this article is on the societal threat, not individual safety or well-being. Societal vulnerability to NBC terrorism is high, and no state has the civil-defence capabilities that would allow it to claim to be 'prepared' in any meaningful sense. In this sense, NBC terrorism poses one of the most serious national-security challenges of the modern era.

Second, NBC terrorism is a low-probability, high-consequence threat. Many assessments of this threat fix on either of these characteristics, resulting in polarised conclusions. The principal reason to be concerned with this threat is that even a single act of NBC terrorism could have devastating effects on the targeted society. This concern, however, must be tempered with a sober appreciation that NBC terrorism has been rare in the past, and that there are good reasons to believe that it will remain so in the future.

Third, the harm caused by even one successful act of NBC terrorism in a major city would be profound – and not only in terms of lives lost. Hundreds of thousands of people could be killed or injured in a single attack. These casualties, however, would only be the first in a series of consequences that could result from such an attack. Panic, economic damage and environmental contamination could follow in the near term. Over the longer term, the nation could be confronted with deep social-psychological questions about the standards of internal security it is willing to live with, and the costs – in terms of curtailed civil liberties or foreign commitments – it is willing to bear to maintain these standards. The conventional, low-technology terrorism of the past has exercised a social and political impact far out of proportion with the casualties it has caused. The massive, indiscriminate destruction caused by an act of NBC terrorism would have similarly disproportionate social, political, economic and strategic effects.

Fourth, the likelihood of acts of NBC terrorism in the future is low, but it is not zero, and it is rising. Future acts of NBC terrorism are by no means inevitable. However, there is no logical reason to believe that future acts are any less likely than other forms of NBC attack, such as a ballistic-missile strike. Given the severity of the potential consequences, future acts of NBC terrorism should be regarded as likely enough to place this threat among the most serious national-security challenges faced by modern liberal democracies.

Weapons Characteristics and Accessibility

NBC weapons are largely unfamiliar devices. Few people have ever seen – much less built – one, and a comparably small number have witnessed their effects on human beings. A basic understanding of the three weapon types is important for understanding the threat of NBC terrorism, and for fashioning an appropriate strategy against it.

Nuclear Weapons

Nuclear weapons release vast amounts of energy through one of two types of nuclear reaction – fission and fusion.[2] Fusion weapons are far more destructive than fission weapons, but they can only be produced by technologically advanced states, at great cost. Fission weapons are less powerful than fusion weapons, but are considerably less complex. A first-generation fission weapon – like those used on Hiroshima and Nagasaki – would have an explosive yield of around 10,000 tonnes of trinitrotoluene (TNT). In comparison, the Oklahoma City bomb of April 1995 was equal to about two tonnes of TNT – about 5,000 times less powerful than a small nuclear weapon. Depending on population density, weapon yield and the severity of subsequent fires, a nuclear-fission detonation in a city could kill over 100,000 people and devastate an area extending a kilometre or more from the epicentre. Unless the weapon can be found and disabled, evacuation is the only real possibility for damage limitation prior to the detonation of a nuclear weapon.

The main technical barrier to nuclear-weapons acquisition is access to a sufficient quantity of fissile material, either plutonium or highly enriched uranium (HEU).[3] If this obstacle were removed through the theft or purchase of fissile material, almost any state with a reasonable technical and industrial infrastructure could fabricate an improvised nuclear weapon. Some exceptionally capable non-state actors could also design and build a nuclear weapon, particularly if they had access to a substantial quantity of HEU metal, which allows an inefficient but simple weapon design to be used.[4] The collapse of the Soviet Union, which has exposed large stockpiles of fissile material to an unprecedented risk of theft and diversion, has significantly heightened the risk of nuclear-weapons acquisition by non-state actors and states without an indigenous fissile-material production capability.[5]

Biological Weapons

Biological weapons disseminate pathogenic organisms or biologically produced toxins to cause illness or death in human, animal or plant populations. Whereas normal diseases begin in small pockets and spread through natural processes of contagion, a typical biological weapon would release a large quantity of infectious organisms against a target population. The result is a massive, largely simultaneous outbreak of disease after an incubation period of a few days, depending on the agent used and the dose inhaled. Because of their ability to multiply inside the host, pathogenic micro-organisms can be lethal in minute quantities: an invisible speck of disease-causing microbes can kill or incapacitate an adult; a few kilograms of effectively disseminated concentrated agent could cause tens to hundreds of thousands of casualties. Biological-warfare agents without a system for aerosol dissemination cannot easily cause casualties on this scale, and should therefore be considered potentially dangerous contaminants, rather than WMD.

Toxin weapons disseminate poisonous substances produced by living organisms, and are therefore commonly classified as biological weapons. Like biological agents, toxins generally need to be delivered as an aerosol to be effective as anything more than a contaminant or an assassination weapon. Toxins differ from microbial biological-warfare agents, such as bacteria, in that they are non-living, like man-made chemical poisons. Gram for gram, toxins are less deadly than certain living pathogens, since the latter reproduce themselves in the victim. Toxins are not contagious, and thus cannot spread beyond the exposed population.

Aerosols of toxins and pathogenic micro-organisms in low concentrations are generally odourless, tasteless and invisible. Unless the agent-dissemination device (such as an aerosol sprayer) is noticed and identified, it is possible that a terrorist biological-weapon attack could go undetected until the infected population begins to show symptoms of disease or poisoning. Once a surreptitious biological attack is identified, it may be too late to limit its geographic extent or control its medical consequences. In addition, dispersal devices could have disappeared, perpetrators could be nowhere near the scene, and responsibility could be difficult to attribute. This combination of factors makes biological weapons especially suitable for terrorist use. Also, depending on the type of agent used and the nature of the disease outbreak, a surreptitious biological attack on a civilian population could initially be mistaken for a natural epidemic. Detection time will, therefore, depend on the nature of the attack and the quality of the public health system.

Biological weapons are regarded with opprobrium by the international community. Despite the minimal technical obstacles to their acquisition, their use has been rare. The US officially ended its offensive biological-weapons programme in 1969, and they are formally banned by the 1972 Biological Weapons Convention, an agreement ratified by 140 nations but lacking verification provisions. However, it is now known that both the Soviet Union and Iraq had large-scale illegal biological-weapons programmes, the former continued for some time (possibly to this day) by Russia. The US government and outside experts further suspect another eight countries – China, Egypt, Israel, Iran, Libya, North Korea, Taiwan and Syria – of possessing some form of offensive biological-weapons programme.[6]

Confronting Nuclear, Biological and Chemical Terrorism 47

Many states and moderately sophisticated non-state actors could construct improvised but effective biological weapons, as information on the necessary science and technology is openly available. Culturing the required micro-organisms, or growing and purifying toxins, is inexpensive and could be accomplished by someone with university-level training in biology and sound laboratory technique. Acquiring the seed stocks for pathogenic micro-organisms is also not particularly difficult, but the easiest acquisition option – placing an order with a biological supply service – has been made somewhat harder by improved national and international regulation. The most significant technical challenge in fabricating a biological weapon is effectively disseminating bulk biological agent as a respirable aerosol. The most efficient aerosolisation systems, which could reliably produce high casualties over wide areas, would require considerable technological sophistication, and remain beyond the reach of most states and most conceivable non-state actors. However, less efficient aerosolisation techniques are available, and could be mastered by many states and some highly capable non-state actors. The effects of biological attacks could vary greatly, but a single biological weapon could kill or incapacitate thousands of people even with an inefficient delivery system, especially if directed against large indoor populations.

Chemical Weapons

Chemical weapons are extremely lethal man-made poisons that can be disseminated as gases, liquids or aerosols. There are four basic types of chemical weapons: choking agents, such as chlorine and phosgene, which damage lung tissue; blood gases, such as hydrogen cyanide, which block the transport or use of oxygen; vesicants, such as mustard gas, which cause burns and tissue damage to the skin, inside the lungs and to tissues throughout the body; and nerve agents, such as *tabun*, *sarin* and VX, which kill by disabling crucial enzymes in the nervous system. Chemical-warfare agents are highly toxic, but must be delivered in large doses to affect large open areas. For open-air targets, the required amount of even highly toxic agents, such as *sarin*, rapidly reaches hundreds to thousands of kilograms per square kilometre, depending on weather conditions. This is true even if the agent is efficiently dispersed. A simple outdoor attack, involving no more planning and execution than a large truck-bomb, is thus likely to kill at most several hundred people even at high population densities. An attack on a crowded indoor area might kill several thousand people. Some chemical-warfare agents are persistent, and could render large areas uninhabitable for extended periods of time.

Chemical weapons have been used or stockpiled by many militaries for most of this century, beginning with their first large-scale use in the First World War. Immense quantities of chemical weapons were produced by the US and the Soviet Union during the Second World War and Cold War; these stockpiles are now being destroyed.[7] Most other major states with chemical-weapons arsenals have also pledged to destroy these stocks under the Chemical

48 **Richard A. Falkenrath**

Weapons Convention (CWC), but several states have either boycotted the Convention or are suspected of harbouring clandestine chemical-warfare programmes. No non-state actor is known to possess chemical weapons, although the Japanese cult Aum Shinrikyo manufactured significant quantities of the nerve gas *sarin* in 1994–95.

Chemical weapons suitable for mass-casualty attacks can be acquired by virtually all states and by non-state actors with moderate technical skills. Certain deadly chemical-warfare agents can be manufactured in a kitchen or basement in quantities sufficient for mass-casualty attacks. Production procedures for some agents are simple, are accurately described in publicly available sources and require only common laboratory glassware, good ventilation and commercially available precursor chemicals. Greater expertise and some specialised equipment are required to fabricate the most toxic chemical-warfare agents, but the acquisition of quantities sufficient for mass-casualty attacks would still be within the reach of some technically capable non-state actors. The use of a highly toxic chemical agent as a WMD is not especially difficult in principle.

Consequences of a Terrorist NBC Attack

The defining element of a terrorist NBC attack is that the weapon is delivered in a manner that cannot be readily distinguished from the normal background of traffic and activity. A wide variety of terrorist NBC delivery methods are available, ranging from the simple to the sophisticated. Any potential aggressors competent enough to acquire a WMD in the first place would be able to deliver it covertly against high-value targets in open societies with a high chance of success.

The consequences of a major NBC attack would come in waves, played out over a period of months or years. The first impact would be immediate physical damage, but terrorist NBC attacks would also have broad repercussions for the economy, for the nation's strategic position in world affairs and perhaps even for its ability to sustain itself as a strong democracy. These effects could be compounded by an organised campaign of multiple attacks, or if a range of different weapon types – including conventional weapons – were used in conjunction. At least seven general consequences are likely.

- *Massive casualties.* The first and most obvious effect of an NBC attack would be its destruction of human life. The March 1995 Tokyo subway attack killed 12 and injured about 5,000. If Aum Shinrikyo had been more proficient in its delivery of the nerve gas, fatalities would have climbed into the thousands. Biological-weapons effects are even more variable, but fatalities in the low tens of thousands are feasible even with unsophisticated weapons, while a more advanced biological weapon could kill or injure hundreds of thousands of people. A single nuclear weapon could easily kill over 100,000 people if detonated in a densely populated urban area. Only wars and plagues have produced casualties on such a scale in the past.

Confronting Nuclear, Biological and Chemical Terrorism *49*

• *Contamination.* An NBC attack could contaminate a large area. Depending on the type of weapon used, the area immediately affected by the attack could be rendered uninhabitable for extended periods of time, requiring a costly and perhaps dangerous clean-up operation. A nuclear weapon would also send radioactive waste into the atmosphere, affecting people downwind for years to come. NBC contamination could raise the disease rates and reduce the quality of life for a much larger population than that which suffered the immediate effects of the weapon.

• *Panic.* An NBC attack against a civilian population would, in all likelihood, trigger a panic incommensurate with the real effects of the weapons. After the World Trade Center bombing in February 1993, many more people reported to hospitals claiming ill effects than were injured in the incident. In a chemical or biological attack, hospitals are likely to be overwhelmed by people fearing contamination or infection. A nuclear attack – or even a limited radiological incident – is likely to stimulate uncontrolled movement away from the affected area, given the public's deep-seated fear of all things radioactive.

• *Degraded response capabilities.* The government personnel needed to conduct an effective operational response to a real NBC threat may themselves be unable to carry out their responsibilities, compounding the effects of an attack. Active-duty military personnel will generally have the training and discipline to conduct operations in a hazardous environment. But without appropriate equipment and training, emergency-response personnel such as police officers, fire-fighters and paramedics may be among the first casualties of an NBC incident. Those who arrive at the scene later might decide that the risks to themselves are too high. Congested roads and airspace will also complicate whatever operational response the government can mount.

• *Economic damage.* An NBC attack could cause major economic damage to the affected area. A large attack or series of attacks could affect the national economy, perhaps even precipitating a recession. Likely effects include death of and injury to workers, the destruction of physical plant and the contamination of workplaces. An attack could also trigger a run on international financial markets, especially if the target has economic significance. The loss of plant and productivity from even a single, moderately damaging NBC attack could amount to millions or billions of dollars.

• *Loss of strategic position.* An NBC attack or campaign of attacks could do great damage to the strategic position of the target state. The US, for example, could be deterred from entering a regional crisis in which its national interests were threatened. Key institutions and political leaders might be attacked directly, or military forces and force-projection capabilities might be damaged, in an effort to prevent an effective military response. An international military coalition might collapse, or an essential ally might request the withdrawal of

50 **Richard A. Falkenrath**

foreign forces from its territory, under threat of NBC attack. The precise nature of these strategic effects is impossible to predict, but they could seriously complicate efforts to deal with a foreign adversary or crisis.

• *Social-psychological damage and political change.* Actual mass-casualty attacks, and the prospect of their continuance, could have a profound psychological effect on the target population, and an equally profound impact on the nation's politics and law. Public terror in the aftermath of an NBC incident would likely be at least as intense as the abstract Cold War fear of nuclear war. Powerful, conflicting forces – including paranoia, xenophobia, isolationism and vengeful fury – would struggle for control of foreign policy. Domestically, the inability to prevent terrorist NBC attacks, or to respond to them effectively, could cause the population to lose confidence in its government, and initiate a chain of political and legal reactions leading to a shift in the relationship between citizen and state. A society that comes to fear massively destructive terrorist attacks is likely to demand action from its government. The response would probably involve curtailing the civil liberties that form the basis of democratic society.

The Likelihood of NBC Terrorism in the Future
Only one non-state actor has successfully acquired and used a WMD: the Japanese cult Aum Shinrikyo. In June 1994, it carried out a nerve-gas attack in Matsumoto, Japan, killing four people and injuring 150, but which went unnoticed by Western intelligence. Its second attack in the Tokyo subway killed 12 and injured over 5,000.

If threat assessment were a simple extrapolation of past trends, analysts would probably conclude that modern societies have little to fear from terrorist NBC aggression. But threat assessment must also consider the changing capabilities, motives and strategic options of potential adversaries, as well as the scope and character of their own vulnerabilities. The capacity to conduct terrorist NBC attacks is growing among states and non-state actors alike. It also appears that the motivation to conduct attacks of this kind is increasing.

A specific threat of NBC terrorism arises when a group emerges that falls into three categories simultaneously: capable of NBC weapons acquisition and use; interested in causing mass casualties; and wanting to use NBC weapons for this end. The threat of NBC terrorism is growing more serious because the number of non-state actors that are simultaneously NBC-capable and interested in causing mass casualties is growing. At a minimum, these two trends suggest that conventional non-state violence is likely to become more deadly; at the other extreme, however, these two trends suggest that an increasing number of violent non-state actors are moving into position for more frequent and more effective forays into the largely uncharted territory of NBC terrorism.

NBC Terrorism is Historically Rare, and Likely to Remain So
A review of the history of non-state actor involvement with WMD yields several empirical conclusions. First, with the important exception of Aum Shinrikyo, no non-state actor has conducted, or attempted to conduct, an

Confronting Nuclear, Biological and Chemical Terrorism *51*

effective, widespread attack with a functional NBC weapon. There is little evidence that any established terrorist organisation is or has been interested in acquiring, much less using, WMD. There are virtually no reports, much less solid evidence, linking established terrorist groups – the Irish Republican Army (IRA), *Hizbollah*, Jewish extremists, the Italian Red Brigade, the many different Latin American terrorist and revolutionary groups, the Japanese United Red Army, or various Turkish, Armenian or Palestinian terrorist organisations – to any serious interest in WMD. A possible exception is West Germany's Red Army Faction, which may have tried to produce botulinum toxin in Paris in the early 1980s, but it is not certain that the Faction had a clear delivery concept in mind, much less the determination to use it.[8]

Dozens of cases have been documented in which a non-state actor is known to have used, or attempted to use, lethal chemicals or harmful biological agents in indiscriminate poisonings. And there have been countless more individual assassinations and assassination attempts involving poisons. These incidents should not, however, be confused with an attack involving biological or chemical WMD, which require effective means for wide-area airborne dissemination and generally far more lethal agents. Murdering a few people with poison is a relatively simple matter, but there are logistical limits to the number of people who can be killed through product tampering.[9]

Similarly, many cases have been reported – including several in the mid-1990s – in which ostensibly hostile non-state actors have been caught in possession of lethal chemicals, dangerous biological agents or radioactive material. In April 1993, for example, Canadian border police confiscated 130g of ricin from Thomas Lewis Lavy, an Arkansas resident with reported links to survivalist groups, as he tried to enter Canada from Alaska. After a two-year investigation by the Federal Bureau of Investigation (FBI), Lavy was arrested and charged under the 1989 US Biological Weapons Anti-Terrorism Act with possession of a biological toxin with intent to kill. He was never tried because he hanged himself in his cell shortly after arraignment. In August 1994, Douglas Allen Baker and Leroy Charles Wheeler – both associated with the Minnesota Patriots Council, a right-wing militia group – were arrested for possession of ricin and planning to murder law-enforcement personnel. Their planned delivery technique was to smear the toxin on the doorknobs of their intended victims' homes.[10] In 1995, Larry Wayne Harris, an individual with some scientific training and right-wing affiliations, was arrested for mail fraud after ordering three vials of freeze-dried bubonic plague bacteria from American Type Culture Collection. These are not the only cases in which non-state actors have acquired some quantity of biological-warfare agents, but they are representative of the larger stock of cases. Although these cases indicate a worrying fascination with chemical and biological agents among some disaffected Americans, all have lacked evidence of serious intent or technical capacity to use the agent as an effective WMD.

There are at least four reasons why capable non-state actors have not conducted more mass-destruction attacks with NBC weapons. First and most important, inflicting massive human casualties generally does not serve the

objectives of terrorist groups and other hostile non-state actors. The fundamental purpose of acquiring WMD is to kill large numbers of people. Yet
terrorist attacks that seek to cause mass casualties are, in fact, quite rare (see
Table 1).

Table 1 Twentieth-Century Terrorist Attacks Incurring 100-Plus Casualties

Year	Event	Location	Deaths
1995	Bombing of federal building	*Oklahoma City, OK*	168
1993	Bombings (10 bombs in under 3 hours)	*Bombay*	235
1989	Bombing of Colombian Avianca aircraft	*Bogota*	107
1989	Bombing of French UTA airliner	*Niger*	171
1988	Bombing of Pan Am Flight 103	*Lockerbie, Scotland*	278
1987	Car bomb in bus station	*Sri Lanka*	113
1987	Bombing of South Korean airliner	*Thai–Burmese border*	117
1985	Bombing of Air India passenger airliner	*Irish Sea*	328
1983	Bombing of US Marine barracks	*Lebanon*	241
1979	Arson attack on cinema	*Abadan, Iran*	477
1946	Nakam poisoning of German POWs	*Nuremberg, Germany*	100s (?)
1925	Bombing of cathedral	*Sofia, Bulgaria*	160

Note: This table includes only conventional terrorist attacks. It does not include large-scale
massacres carried out by militaries or guerrilla groups using guns, machetes or other small arms;
or acts by guerrilla groups animated by a particular ethnic hatred or extreme ideology, such as
the Bosnian Serbs, Algerian Islamic radicals, Rwandan militias and the Vietcong.

Undoubtedly, other terrorist attempts to inflict mass casualties have been made
– the World Trade Center bombing and Aum Shinrikyo are examples – but the
available data strongly suggest that there has been a general aversion to mass
casualties among most violent non-state actors. This aversion has not resulted
from a technical incapacity or lack of opportunity to kill large numbers of
people; instead, terrorist organisations have made conscious decisions to kill
fewer people than they could. The reasons for this general aversion have been
that mass casualties undermine political support; they raise the risk of
unfettered government reprisal; and they do not make easier the terrorists'
efforts to achieve their aims through violence.

The second reason for the rarity of NBC terrorism is that mass destruction,
to the extent it is desired, is possible without WMD. The overwhelming
majority of organised violence undertaken by terrorist groups has involved
only conventional weapons – chemical explosives, guns and knives. Chemical
explosives – ranging from the simplest, such as ammonium nitrate mixed with
fuel oil, to the most advanced military high explosives, such as C4 and Semtex
– can be used to kill up to several hundred people.

Third, the acquisition and use of NBC weapons would entail additional risks
and challenges to a terrorist group beyond those associated with conventional
weapons. Holding other factors constant, a rational attacker will employ the

Confronting Nuclear, Biological and Chemical Terrorism 53

simplest, least costly, and most reliable means of attack available to it. There are of course costs, risks and challenges associated with acquiring conventional weapons as well, but these are less severe than those associated with WMD. With respect to acquisition, NBC weapons are clearly more technologically challenging than conventional weapons, and also generally more expensive. Moreover, work on WMD inevitably involves a heightened hazard to health. Attempts to acquire NBC weapons raise the risk that the group would be found out and crushed by the authorities, especially if individuals with special expertise must be recruited for the NBC-acquisition effort. With respect to the actual use of the device, NBC weapons again present risks and challenges beyond those of their conventional counterparts. Terrorists in particular prefer predictable and reliable forms of attack. The immediate and long-term effects of an NBC weapon will generally be less predictable than a conventional one. NBC weapons may also have a harmful physical or psychological effect on the human operatives charged with handling or delivering them.

The final and most controversial explanation for lack of interest in NBC weapons among groups capable of acquiring and using them is that group leaders and members may hold moral objections.[11] This may seem counter-intuitive, given the willingness of most terrorist groups and many states to kill innocent people in order to achieve their political goals. NBC weapons, how-ever, have a special stigma. This norm against NBC use probably is strongest in the case of biological weapons. While it will never be possible to separate the causal impact of self-interest (including group preservation) from that of morality on decisions not to launch NBC weapons attacks, the idea should not be ignored.

Explaining the capability constraints on groups 'interested' in mass-casualty terrorism is more difficult than explaining the lack of interest of NBC 'capable' groups. It is virtually impossible to untangle technical inability from genuine lack of motive. Nonetheless, the known cases suggest that most non-state actors with an interest in NBC weapons or materials would have trouble acquiring or using them successfully. Two reasons appear to explain this. The first is that the psychological make-up of an individual or group that wishes to cause human casualties on a massive scale is often incompatible with the technical and organisational requirements for acquiring and using NBC weapons. This argument applies most obviously to deranged individuals who are motivated to kill not by a clear, rational purpose, but by mental illness. A second possible explanation applies only to state-sponsored terrorist groups. In the unlikely event that such a group decided to obtain or use WMD, it is likely that the state sponsor would actively oppose its efforts because of the extreme risks involved.

Many of the factors described above that have discouraged NBC terrorism in the past will continue to obtain. However, some of these factors are operating with diminishing force. In particular, it is certain that more and more non-state actors will become capable of NBC acquisition and use. Moreover, a growing body of evidence suggests that increasing numbers of terrorist groups are motivated to cause mass casualties.

54 **Richard A. Falkenrath**

Latent NBC Potential of Non-State Actors is Rising

Non-state actors in all modern societies are becoming more capable of mastering the challenges associated with NBC attack. This gradual increase is a by-product of economic, educational and technological progress. It also results from the fact that, in most modern societies, the ability of the state to monitor and counter illegal or threatening activities is being outpaced by the increasing efficiency, complexity, technological sophistication and geographic span of the activities – legal and illegal – of non-state actors.

- *The impact of economic, educational and technological progress.* The technological and scientific challenges associated with covert NBC acquisition and use are significant, but they are no more difficult than they were 40–50 years ago. Meanwhile, non-state actors are growing steadily more capable, and thus better able to surmount the technical hurdles to NBC acquisition and use. Since the fundamental cause is social progress, this expansion of latent non-state actor NBC potential is inexorable, and is not reversible by governments.

How and why is the underlying capacity of non-state actors to master the technical challenges of NBC acquisition and use increasing? The first reason is that the basic science behind these weapons is being learned by more people, better than ever before. In the US alone, the number of people receiving degrees in science and engineering fields more than doubled between 1966 and 1994.[12] Education data on other countries suggest similar trends. An even more important gauge of the ability of non-state actors to build and use WMD, however, is the increasing level of knowledge available in school science courses, as well as the sophistication of laboratory and analytical tools – from computers to laboratory-scale fermentation equipment – that are now available. The new physics that the Manhattan Project scientists had to discover to make nuclear weapons possible is now standard textbook fare for young physicists and engineers.

Nowhere is this phenomenon more pronounced than in biology. The advance of the biological sciences is creating a situation in which a sophis-ticated programme can produce advanced biological weapons with heightened resistance to prophylaxis or treatment, increased virulence, controllable incubation periods and agent longevity, and conceivably even a selectivity that targets groups of people according to their genetic make-up.[13] The biotech-nology revolution is also increasing the number of people with the knowledge to use such agents. Similarly, the biotechnology industry's growth has made available a wide range of tools and supplies – such as efficient fermenters for producing large amounts of bacteria in small facilities, and increasingly sophisticated tools for measuring aerosols – that would ease a basic biological weapons procurement effort.

Finally, apart from rising education levels and growing familiarity with relevant technologies, the latent NBC potential of non-state actors is increasing because the ability to acquire information is growing. The internet contains a vast amount of information relevant to planning and executing complex violent

Confronting Nuclear, Biological and Chemical Terrorism 55

acts – including information on specific targets, detailed accounts of previous incidents and tactics, and basic technical information for making NBC weapons. The basic technical descriptions of NBC weapons that are available on the internet generally do not amount to the detailed, step-by-step instructions that might allow a novice to fabricate an improvised NBC weapon from scratch. Even so, today's terrorists, if they can conduct even a modest computer search for information, are able to start substantially higher on the terrorist learning curve compared to their predecessors of even a decade ago.

• *Non-state efficiency and flexibility is outpacing that of the state.* A complex, illegal activity like clandestine NBC weapons acquisition has several different constituent parts, any of which may be vulnerable to law-enforcement surveillance. A team of like-minded, appropriately skilled individuals must be assembled; places must be found for them to work; they must be able to communicate with one another, possibly over great distances; information, materials and equipment must be gathered, perhaps from abroad; and a dangerous weapon must be assembled and delivered without error. This is a challenging list of tasks, and would entail risks of detection in any state able to provide for its internal security. The rapid development of increasingly pervasive communications and transport systems makes several of these tasks easier, however, while the growth of legitimate uses of such systems makes criminal use harder to spot.

Whereas non-state actors once had access to little more than analogue phone lines and the postal system, today they can communicate by facsimile, cellular or satellite telephone, teleconference, alpha-numeric pagers, e-mail, computer modem and computer bulletin boards. They can quickly transport weapons and supplies via numerous shipping services. Telecommunications traffic has increased dramatically in both volume and variety over the last decades, easily outpacing the state's ability to track it all.[14] The communications systems available to non-state actors can also be more secure than ever. Strong encryption systems were once exclusive to governments, but virtually unbreakable encryption software is now readily available on the global market, and easily downloaded from the internet.[15] The benefits to legitimate users are considerable, but the implications of this trend on the ability of law enforcement to cope are profound. According to FBI Director Louis Freeh:

> Law enforcement is in unanimous agreement that the widespread use of robust unbreakable encryption ultimately will devastate our ability to fight crime and prevent terrorism. Unbreakable encryption will allow drug lords, spies, terrorists and even violent gangs to communicate about their crimes and their conspiracies with impunity. We will lose one of the few remaining vulnerabilities for the worst criminals and terrorists upon which law enforcement depends to successfully investigate and prevent the worst crimes.[16]

Before the information age, state agencies technologically dominated their non-state challengers, in areas ranging from eavesdropping equipment to

56 **Richard A. Falkenrath**

advanced surveillance cameras. Law enforcement and intelligence-gathering continue to benefit from improving technology, but cannot increase their effectiveness at detecting hidden illegal activities at the same rate as individuals because of the constraints of law, manpower, financial resources and technology. As one study put it, 'power is migrating to actors who are skilled at developing networks, and at operating in a world of networks'.[17] In this competition between a centralised process – the state seeking the needle of criminal activity in the haystack of an increasingly complex society – and decentralised criminal processes – where effectiveness is limited by human competence, resources and technology – the state is clearly at a disadvantage.

Terrorists' Propensity Towards Mass-Casualty Violence Appears to be Rising

This is a relatively new development, and it remains poorly understood. The classic conceptual model of a terrorist group – with limited political aims, a strategy of controlled violence for achieving them, and an interest in self-preservation – appears to be breaking down. New groups are emerging with hazier objectives, shorter life-spans and a more direct interest in violence for its own sake, often for religious or political reasons. The ascendance of Western culture and US power in the post-Cold War international system is making the US and its allies increasingly attractive targets for terrorism. In short, terrorism is changing in a way that points towards an expanding range of groups that are simultaneously NBC-capable and interested in inflicting human casualties at levels well beyond the norms of previous decades.

What evidence supports this claim of rising lethality? According to the US State Department, 'while the incidence of international terrorism has dropped sharply in the last decade, the overall threat of terrorism remains very serious. The death toll from acts of international terrorism rose from 163 in 1995 to 311 in 1996, as the trend continued toward more ruthless attacks on mass civilian targets and the use of more powerful bombs'.[18] The 1995 FBI report on terrorism noted that 'large-scale attacks designed to inflict mass casualties appear to be a new terrorist method in the United States'.[19] Based on the most detailed database of terrorism incidents in the public domain – the RAND–St Andrews Chronology of International Terrorist Incidents – Bruce Hoffman similarly concluded that 'while terrorists were becoming less active, they were also becoming more lethal'.[20] As Table 1 shows, most of the mass-casualty terrorist attacks in history have occurred since 1979.

Four trends, often tightly interrelated, suggest that the past disincentives to mass-casualty attacks will have diminishing force in the future. First, violence and terrorism motivated by religion are becoming more common and more lethal. Religious terrorism has undergone a renaissance in the last two decades, as the number of known terrorist groups believed to be motivated primarily by religious causes has grown.[21] Many of the reasons why secular terrorists have tended to refrain from causing mass casualties apply with limited force or not at all to terrorists motivated by religious beliefs.[22] Most secular terrorists have

Confronting Nuclear, Biological and Chemical Terrorism *57*

been politically motivated, and have sought either to extract specific concessions from a state, or to foment or block social and political change – purposes not often served by causing mass casualties. Religious violence follows a
different logic. For religious terrorists, violence can become a sacramental act,
dictated and legitimised by theology. The primary purpose of violent acts is not
to extract particular concessions, but to fulfil a spiritual requirement.[23] Loss of
popular support is of little concern to the religious terrorist, since the act is
done for God, or God's clerical proxy, not public opinion.[24] Group cohesion is
threatened less by practical matters – such as disagreements over the tactically
and morally appropriate level of violence – than by the possibility of appearing
unfaithful to the belief system that binds the group together. Harsh countermeasures by secular authorities are expected, but the deterrent effects of this
prospect are relatively modest for religious terrorists: in their own minds,
zealots are already locked in a life-and-death struggle with their opponents,
and heightened oppression serves mainly to reinforce the teachings of fanatical
spiritual leaders. For all these reasons, as religiously inspired terrorism
becomes more prevalent, terrorism in general will become more lethal.

Second, local opposition to foreign influence and military presence appears
to be intensifying in the moderate, pro-Western sheikdoms of the Persian Gulf,
resulting in increasingly frequent and damaging anti-military terrorist attacks.
Religious and political motives for terrorism clearly reinforce one another in the
Middle East, especially the Persian Gulf, and they do so in a way that suggests
that this is the region where the risks of mass-casualty terrorism against US and
other Western targets are growing most rapidly. This risk has become visible as
a result of two major bombings in Saudi Arabia: the first at the offices of the US
Program Manager for Security Assistance with the Saudi Arabia National
Guard in Riyadh on 13 November 1995, killing seven and wounding 40; and
the second at the Khobar Towers housing complex for US Air Force personnel
in Dhahran on 25 June 1996, killing 19 Americans and injuring more than 500.[25]
Exactly who was responsible for the two bombings remains a mystery, but the
rationale behind the attacks is clear. Certain strands of Islam, particularly some
elements of radical Shi'ism, are profoundly hostile to what they perceive as the
dominance of Muslim lands by foreign powers, especially the US. Radicalised
by a long colonial history, the Arab–Israeli conflict and the 1991 Gulf War,
many Muslims see the US regional presence and influence as fundamentally
incompatible with Islamic faith, primarily because the US abets secular
governance and transmits a Western culture some Muslims consider depraved.
In the Gulf region, this religious hostility is magnified by the *realpolitik* of Iran
and Iraq, whose aspirations towards regional hegemony are blocked by the
forward US presence, and by the anti-Americanism of many ordinary Arabs
and Muslims, some of whom hold Washington responsible for their poverty
and political powerlessness. Because of this combination of religious, geopolitical and social factors, the risk of mass-casualty terrorist attacks against
Western interests in the Persian Gulf appears to be rising, jeopardising the
political foundations on which the US presence in the region rests.

Third, right-wing terrorism appears to be growing both more prevalent and more lethal. In England, Germany, France, Israel and Russia, and several other former Soviet states, this has been manifested in racially motivated attacks on foreign residents.[26] Right-wing violence is chauvinistic and hateful. Opponents are seen not just as politically or ideologically mistaken, but as inferior, usually for reasons of race, religion or sexual orientation.[27] Far-right groups are by no means uniformly dangerous or effective. A handful have well-developed organisations, considerable resources and an active membership, but others are little more than a single extremist with a photocopier and a mailing list. In both organisation and ideology, the radical right is exceptionally fluid and eclectic – groups form and disband frequently, and individuals move from group to group often and with ease. There is rising concern among US law-enforcement officials that right-wing American extremists may seek to carry out mass-casualty attacks in the future, and may use exotic weapons in doing so. This US concern stems both from the precedent set by the Oklahoma City bombing and from the handful of incidents in the 1990s involving right-wing individuals caught in possession of biological-warfare agents.

Fourth, it now appears that more and more non-state violence is committed by *ad hoc* collections of like-minded individuals who come together for specific purposes, sometimes to commit a single attack. While these terrorists probably have a lower capacity to carry out mass-casualty attacks, the motivational restraints on their ability to do so are also likely to be lower. Unlike traditional terrorist organisations, 'amateur' terrorist groups have no political organisation to worry about, and form only to commit a limited number of violent acts. Amateur groups, especially those pursuing a goal they believe is ordained by God, or motivated by a political ideology that is more a justification for violence than a political blueprint, are likely to be less averse to causing mass casualties since they have a lower stake in group preservation.[28]

How Governments Should Respond

Arguing that the threat of NBC terrorism should be treated as a first-order national-security challenge raises questions about what can, and should, be done about it. To protect all potential targets all the time is impossible, and should not be attempted. But a purely passive, reactive posture is equally unsatisfactory. The governments of the world's leading democracies should instead institute a package of measures to make NBC terrorist threats less likely to emerge, and should create operational capabilities that give them a reasonable chance of detecting, defeating and minimising the consequences of terrorist NBC threats. These measures should be viewed as a prudent invest-ment in the long-term security of their citizens and national interests, not as an emergency campaign.

No two countries will respond identically to the threat of NBC terrorism, as the deficiencies in their policies, governmental organisation and operational capabilities vary.[29] Nonetheless, five key prescriptive concepts should guide the policy responses of any government.

Confronting Nuclear, Biological and Chemical Terrorism *59*

First, concerned policy-makers and legislators should not over-react – and in particular, should take no action that might compromise personal liberties and freedoms. The threat of NBC terrorism straddles the traditional domains of law enforcement and national security, and any discussion of how to respond to the terrorist NBC threat will almost inevitably raise questions about the relationship between the state and its citizens.[30] Many of the measures that could be taken to combat terrorist threats would increase the power of the state at the expense of the freedom and privacy of individuals or groups. An unprepared society's vulnerability to NBC terrorism can be significantly reduced through policy changes, improved government organisation and focused investments in new operational capabilities without undermining essential civil liberties. The threat of NBC terrorism is a serious challenge, but it is not so imminent that governments should pre-emptively begin to change the societies that they have been charged to protect.[31]

Second, before starting new programmes and initiatives, the government should have a comprehensive national strategy for addressing the problem, and should instigate a system for effective inter-agency coordination and long-range planning. This is a particularly marked deficiency in the US, which has an abundance of disparate policies and operational capabilities directed against the NBC terrorism threat – some quite formidable, others wholly inadequate. Although the Clinton administration has expressed concern over the threat of high-technology terrorism, it has not established a coherent national 'blueprint' for long-term capability building, and most new initiatives have been driven either by activist legislators or individual federal agencies.[32]

Third, intelligence is the first and most important line of defence. Specific conspiracies are relatively easy to defeat if the authorities discover their existence with adequate lead time and in sufficient detail to investigate and take action. Most intelligence services already look at the issue of NBC weapons proliferation, but specific enhancements are needed in their ability to acquire early warning of emerging NBC threats, especially by watching for the most likely signatures of small-scale, improvised NBC acquisition programmes, abroad and at home; to improve the use of public-health capabilities – particularly epidemiological surveillance – to detect medical evidence of NBC weapons programmes and biological-weapons attacks; to identify those responsible for NBC attacks after the incident has occurred; and to cooperate internationally against shared transnational threats. In the US, shortcomings in these areas are symptomatic both of the difficulty the US intelligence community has had in adapting to post-Cold War security challenges, and of its failure to make use of state-of-the-art information-processing technology. Since the Soviet threat disappeared, the shortcomings of US intelligence have been commented upon and studied at length, but the pace of reform is slow.

Fourth, the single best possible insurance policy against the risk of nuclear terrorism is to ensure that all stockpiles of fissile (especially HEU) and nuclear weapons themselves are properly accounted for and guarded. Nuclear terrorism is not a serious threat when all stockpiles of direct-use fissile material are held under secure conditions. However, the degradation of the Soviet nuclear custodial system has heightened the risk by rendering vast quantities of fissile material more accessible than at any time in history. The US government has been active in attempting to address this issue, but its European and Asian allies have largely ignored it, making only minuscule investments in the training and assistance programmes needed in Russia. The problem is so large that it will require sustained international effort for many years.

Finally, national governments should improve their operational capacity to detect and reduce the consequences of chemical- and biological-weapons attacks at home and, for states with external security commitments, abroad. This should be done not by establishing new stand-alone assets, but by strategically augmenting certain existing capabilities, most of which are independently valuable and worthy targets for further investment.[33] In preparing for biological terrorism, the most important area is the public-health sector, which already has systems in place to detect, contain and treat natural disease outbreaks.[34] Most biological weapons do not cause immediate ill effects, and the symptoms of many biological-warfare diseases initially resemble a cough or influenza, so acts of biological terrorism may be detected first by existing epidemiological-surveillance systems. Since the effective medical treatment of most biological-warfare diseases depends on early detection, states should invest in improving the speed and accuracy with which their epidemiological-surveillance systems can detect unseen biological-weapon attacks. Likewise, most states will have to enhance their emergency medical systems so that they are capable of mounting an effective, no-notice medical response in a major biological-weapons incident – an exceptionally demanding contingency that would require stockpiles of key medicines and vaccines, trained personnel to deliver them and a high-readiness mobilisation system.

Unlike biological weapons, chemical-warfare agents generally have prompt, noticeable effects on humans, and the chemical incident is likely to occur over a matter of hours rather than days. For this reason, the most important operational capability for mitigating the effects of a chemical terrorist act is the 'first-responder' community – the local police force, fire departments, hazardous-material specialists, emergency medical personnel and public-health and disaster-relief officials. In a no-notice chemical-weapon attack, there will be no time to bring in far-flung specialists to manage the incident, so this task will fall to municipal and state officials, the vast majority of whom have no special knowledge, training or equipment for dealing with WMD. Not all potential emergency staff in a large country can have a deep understanding of how to respond to this threat, but it is possible to create a layered system of preparedness, which would start with broad-based awareness training, specialised training and equipment for local specialists (for example, HAZMAT – hazardous-materials – teams, bomb squads, police special weapons and tactics teams and emergency-management officials), and specialised medical units for large-scale chemical or biological attacks at the regional level. These response capabilities should be regularly tested and examined through full-field

Confronting Nuclear, Biological and Chemical Terrorism *61*

exercises against realistic, challenging WMD simulations, with the participation of relevant agencies at all levels of government administration.

The military should be tightly integrated into any such national-preparedness plan, since the armed forces will generally contain most of a state's technical and operational capacity to counter specific NBC threats, including most of its capacity to operate in a chemically or biologically contaminated environment; to decontaminate casualties, equipment and facilities; and to treat large numbers of chemical- and biological-warfare victims. The capabilities needed to manage the consequence of domestic NBC-weapons attacks overlap substantially with those needed to fulfil the more traditional mission of protecting military forces on the battlefield and in rear areas against chemical and biological attacks. As the US and its allies work to enhance their armed forces' overall capacity to fight against NBC-armed regional adversaries, they should ensure that they also improve their society's capacity to cope with domestic NBC attacks.

Conclusion

WMD terrorism is a serious, often underestimated but not apocalyptic threat to the national security of advanced democracies. Liberal, urbanised nations are vulnerable to terrorist attack with NBC weapons, and the probability of such an attack is higher than commonly assumed – and growing. This situation merits broad programmes of action both to reduce national vulnerability and to make the emergence of future threats less likely. Such efforts would essentially be a hedge against a low-probability, high-consequence event – an act of prudence, not unlike an insurance policy on one's home. Many of the steps required, however, do not resemble traditional national-security programmes, and will encounter financial, institutional and conceptual obstacles.

These obstacles would disappear after a major domestic NBC attack. In the atmosphere of national emergency that would follow a successful NBC attack, or even a credible threat of NBC use, the political will and funding necessary to implement a vigorous response to the terrorist NBC threat would become considerably easier to generate, but there would also be a real risk of political overreaction. Unwise and wasteful measures – both offensive and defensive – might be taken reflexively, with costs measured not only in money, but in liberties, lives and strategic position. After a mass-destruction attack, the national leaders who were disinterested in hedging against an uncertain threat might find themselves accountable for the nation's failed preventive efforts and low level of preparedness. The excuses given for not having done more beforehand will ring hollow. The best action policy-makers can take to avoid having to make these excuses is to focus on the threat before it reaches emergency proportions, and to begin implementing a balanced programme of preventive and preparedness measures.

62 **Richard A. Falkenrath**

Notes

[1] Several studies have drawn attention to different aspects of the problem. They include Brad Roberts (ed.), *Terrorism with Chemical and Biological Weapons: Calibrating Risks and Responses* (Alexandria, VA: Chemical and Biological Arms Control Institute, 1997); Jonathan Tucker, 'Chemical/Biological Terrorism: Coping with a New Threat', *Politics and the Life Sciences*, vol. 15, no. 2, September 1996, pp. 167–83; and Defense Science Board, *Report of the 1997 DSB Summer Study on DoD Responses to Transnational Threats*, vol. 1 (Washington DC: Office of the Under-secretary of Defense for Acquisition and Technology, December 1997). For possible insight into the argument of a classified US study of the subject, see Joseph S. Nye, Jr. and R. James Woolsey, 'Defend Against the Stealth Enemy', *Los Angeles Times*, 1 June 1997, p. 4.

[2] Radiological weapons disperse radioactive substances but do not produce a nuclear yield. The simplest radiological weapon would consist of a conventional explosive surrounded by a quantity of any radioactive material. In its immediate physical effects, a radiological weapon is unlikely to produce mass casualties. In most cases, large quantities of highly radioactive material would be needed to produce strong effects over even a moderate area, and obtaining and working with large amounts of such materials would be challenging because of the high radiation levels involved. A radiological attack might, however, trigger panic out of proportion with its destructiveness.

[3] For more on the technical issues associated with nuclear weapons acquisition, see US Congress, Office of Technology Assessment (OTA), *Nuclear Proliferation and Safeguards* (New York: Praeger, 1977), pp. 139–44; Robert Serber, *The Los Alamos Primer* (Berkeley, CA: University of California Press,

1992); and J. Carson Mark, Theodore Taylor, Eugene Eyster, William Maraman and Jacob Wechsler, 'Can Terrorists Build Nuclear Weapons?', in Paul Leventhal and Yonah Alexander (eds), *Preventing Nuclear Terrorism: The Report and Papers of the International Task Force on Prevention of Nuclear Terrorism* (Lexington, MA: Lexington Books, 1987), pp. 59–60.

[4] The term 'non-state actors' includes traditional, familiar terrorist organisations; paramilitary guerrilla groups fighting for control of territory; cults and other religious organisations; militias or other geographically fixed paramilitary groups; organised-crime syndicates; mercenary groups; breakaway units of a state's military, intelligence or security services; corrupt multinational corporations; and lone individuals.

[5] See Graham T. Allison, Owen R. Coté, Jr., Richard A. Falkenrath and Steven E. Miller, *Avoiding Nuclear Anarchy: Containing the Threat of Loose Russian Nuclear Weapons and Fissile Material* (Cambridge, MA: Massachusetts Institute of Technology Press, 1996).

[6] US Congress, OTA, *Proliferation of Weapons of Mass Destruction: Assessing the Risks* (Washington DC: US Government Printing Office, August 1993), p. 83.

[7] The US stockpiled some 30,000 tonnes of chemical agent, which it is now incinerating at eight sites in the US and on Johnston Atoll in the Pacific Ocean. Russia has declared a chemical-weapons stockpile of 40,000t, but some estimates of its true size range as high as 200,000t. Russia has pledged to destroy the chemical-weapons stockpile it inherited from the Soviet Union, but this programme has been delayed by financial difficulties.

[8] See 'W. German Terrorists Said to Test Bacteria', *International Herald Tribune*, 8–9 November 1980, p. 2.

Confronting Nuclear, Biological and Chemical Terrorism *63*

[9] Apart from the Nazi gas chambers, the most lethal chemical poisoning ever appears to be the arsenic poisoning of several thousand captive German SS soldiers outside Nuremberg in April 1946 by the Jewish reprisal organisation 'Nakam'. Members of the group infiltrated the bakery that supplied bread to the camp, spreading an arsenic-based poison on the loaves before they were delivered. Despite being forced to flee before they had finished, the group is estimated to have killed hundreds of prisoners and sickened thousands. See Michael Bar-Zohar, *The Avengers*, translated by Len Ortzen (London: Arthur Barker, 1968), pp. 43–58.

[10] The pair had 0.7g of ricin in their possession. In February 1995, they were convicted under the US Biological Weapons Antiterrorism Act of 1989.

[11] See Brian Jenkins, 'Understanding the Link between Motives and Methods', in Roberts (ed.), *Terrorism with Chemical and Biological Weapons*, p. 46. Bruce Hoffman argues that this observation applies mainly to 'secular political' terrorists, not 'religious political' ones. See Hoffman, 'The Contrasting Ethical Foundations of Terrorism in the 1980s', *Terrorism and Political Violence*, vol. 1, no. 3, July 1989, p. 363.

[12] National Science Foundation, *Science and Engineering Degrees: 1966–94* (Arlington, VA: National Science Foundation, 1996), Table 1, p. 35.

[13] See Erhard Geissler, 'Implications of Genetic Engineering for Chemical and Biological Warfare', in Stockholm International Peace Research Institute (SIPRI), *World Armaments and Disarmament: SIPRI Yearbook 1984* (London: Taylor & Francis, 1984), pp. 421–51; Malcolm Dando, '"Discriminating" Bio-Weapons Could Target Ethnic Groups', *Jane's International Defense Review*, March 1997, pp. 77–78; and US Department of Defense, *Advances in Biotechnology and*

Genetic Engineering: Implications for the Development of New Biological Warfare Agents (Washington DC: US Department of Defense, June 1996), available at www.acq.osd.mil/cp/biotech96.htm.

[14] Likewise, with respect to physical traffic, 'huge increases in the volume of goods and people crossing borders and competitive pressures to speed the flow of trade by easing inspections and reducing paperwork make it easier to hide contraband'. See Jessica T. Matthews, 'Power Shift', *Foreign Affairs*, vol. 76, no. 1, January–February 1997, pp. 50–66.

[15] See National Research Council, *Cryptography's Role in Securing the Information Society* (Washington DC: National Research Council, 1996).

[16] Louis J. Freeh, 'The Impact of Encryption on Public Safety', statement before the Permanent Select Committee on Intelligence, US House of Representatives, Washington DC, 9 September 1997, available at www.fbi.gov/congress.

[17] John Arquilla and David Ronfeldt, *The Advent of Netwar* (Santa Monica, CA: RAND, 1996), pp. 15–16, 43, 81–82.

[18] US Department of State, *Patterns of Global Terrorism 1996* (Washington DC: US Department of State, April 1997), p. 1, available at www.state.gov/www/global/terrorism. The overall drop in the incidence of terrorism noted by the State Department results from the post-Cold War decline in left-wing, ideologically motivated terrorism and a marked drop in state-sponsored international terrorism.

[19] US Department of Justice, Federal Bureau of Investigation, *Terror in the United States 1995* (Washington DC: FBI, 1996), available at www.fbi.gov.

[20] Bruce Hoffman, 'Terrorism and WMD: Some Preliminary Hypotheses', *Nonproliferation Review*, vol. 4, no. 3, Spring–Summer 1997, p. 47.

[21] In 1968, none of the 11 identified

64 **Richard A. Falkenrath**

international terrorist groups was religiously motivated; in 1980, two of 64 were; in 1992, 11 of approximately 50. Data from the RAND–St Andrews University Chronology of International Terrorist Incidents, Centre for the Study of Terrorism, St Andrews University, Scotland.

22 See Bruce Hoffman, *'Holy Terror': The Implications of Terrorism Motivated by a Religious Imperative* (Santa Monica, CA: RAND, 1993) pp. 11–14.

23 This thesis is developed and applied to Sikh religious violence in Mark Juergensmeyer, 'The Logic of Religious Violence', in David Rapoport (ed.), *Inside Terrorist Organizations* (New York: Columbia University Press, 1988), pp. 185–90.

24 See Hoffman, 'Terrorism and WMD', pp. 48–49; Hoffman, 'The Contrasting Ethical Foundations', pp. 361–77; and Jenkins, 'Understanding the Link between Motives and Methods', p. 48.

25 On the Khobar bombing, see US Department of State, Bureau of Diplomatic Security, *Significant Incidents of Political Violence against Americans 1996* (Washington DC: US Department of State, July 1997); US Congress, *Bomb Attack in Saudi Arabia*, Hearings before the Committee on Armed Services, US Senate (Washington DC: US GPO, 1997); and US Congress, *Terrorist Attack against United States Military Forces in Dhahran, Saudi Arabia*, hearings before the. Committee on National Security, US House of Representatives (Washington DC: US GPO, 1997).

26 See Stan Taylor, 'The Radical Right in Britain', in Peter H. Merkl and Leonard Weinberg (eds), *Encounters with the Contemporary Radical Right* (Boulder, CO: Westview Press, 1993), pp. 165–84; Ekkart Zimmermann and Thomas Saalfeld, 'The Three Waves of West German Right-Wing Extremism', in *ibid.*, pp. 50–74; William Safran, 'The National Front in France: From Lunatic Fringe to

Limited Respectability', in *ibid.*, pp. 19–49; Ehud Sprinzak, 'The Israeli Radical Right: History, Culture, and Politics', in *ibid.*, pp. 132–61; Vladislav Krasnov, 'Pamiat: Russian Right-Wing Radicalism', in *ibid.*, pp. 111–31; and Paul Wilkinson, 'Violence and Terror and the Extreme Right', *Terrorism and Political Violence*, vol. 7, no. 4, Winter 1995, pp. 82–93.

27 See *ibid.*, p. 83; and Ehud Sprinzak, 'Right Wing Terrorism in a Comparative Perspective: The Case of Split Delegitimization', *ibid.*, vol. 7, no. 1, Spring 1995, pp. 17–43.

28 See Martha Crenshaw, 'An Organizational Approach to the Analysis of Political Terrorism', *Orbis*, vol. 29, no. 3, Autumn 1985, pp. 473–87.

29 For a detailed set of recommendations directed at the US government, see Richard A. Falkenrath, Robert D. Newman and Bradley Thayer, *America's Achilles' Heel: Nuclear, Biological and Chemical Terrorism and Covert Attack* (Cambridge, MA: Massachusetts Institute of Technology Press), pp. 261–336.

30 For an excellent study of these issues, see Philip B. Heymann, *Terrorism and America: A Commonsense Strategy for a Democratic Society* (Cambridge, MA: Massachusetts Institute of Technology Press, 1998).

31 As a corollary to this, states should also not begin to retreat pre-emptively from their international commitments, even if these are sometimes the source of heightened terrorist risk, as some analysts, such as Richard K. Betts, have suggested. See Betts, 'The New Threat of Mass Destruction', *Foreign Affairs*, vol. 77, no. 1, January–February 1998, pp. 26–41.

32 On the US concern, see President Bill Clinton's 'Commencement Address', the US Naval Academy, Annapolis, MD, 22 May 1998. The text of this speech is available at www.pub.whitehouse.gov/

Confronting Nuclear, Biological and Chemical Terrorism *65*

uri-res/I2R?urn:pdi://oma.eop.gov.us/ 1998/5/26/18.text.1.

[33] For an excellent analysis of initial US efforts in this area, see Jonathan B. Tucker, 'National Health and Medical Services Response to Incidents of Chemical and Biological Terrorism', *Journal of the American Medical Association*, vol. 278, no. 5, August 1997, pp. 362–68.

[34] Many national and international epidemiological-surveillance systems were allowed to decline in the 1980s, a period of misplaced optimism in the ability to manage infectious-disease threats. In the 1990s, these systems have struggled to cope with the emergence of new infectious diseases (such as Ebola, AIDS, Lyme disease, Legionnaires' disease and the hanta virus), the massive resurgence of familiar diseases (such as cholera, malaria, yellow fever, diphtheria and tuberculosis), and increasing bacterial resistance to antibiotics. See National Science and Technology Council, Committee on International Science, Engineering, and Technology (CISET), Working Group on Emerging and Re-emerging Infectious Diseases, *Global Microbial Threats in the 1990s* (Washington DC: The White House, 1996), available at www.whitehouse.gov/WH/EOP/ OSTP/CISET/html/ciset.html.

[10]

Biological Terrorism and Public Health

Christopher F. Chyba

Deterrence through the threat of retaliation remains the central strategy for preventing attacks using weapons of mass destruction against the United States or its forces and allies overseas. But biological terrorism challenges three requirements for successful deterrence. First, it may prove difficult to identify the perpetrators of certain biological attacks, especially since some diseases incubate for as much as a week before symptoms are manifest. Second, a terrorist group might hope that its attack would remain altogether unrecognised by government officials. History suggests that the origin of some disease outbreaks may remain ambiguous, or only be clarified as natural or intentional after some time. Finally, as with any form of terrorism, some apocalyptic or other non-state groups may not be concerned about punishment. In the face of these challenges, the United States and its allies must supplement deterrence against biological terrorism with an appropriate defence strategy.

An appropriate defence has to be based on improved public health surveillance and response. Because disease agents have lengthy incubation periods, biological terrorism may well bypass the traditional first-responders and quick-response teams that could be critical to coping with other types of attacks.[1] The 'first responders' for a biological attack would likely be doctors, pathologists and other health-care workers, and the speed of a response will depend on their rapid recognition that certain illnesses appear out of the ordinary. Regardless of whether the origin of a disease outbreak is intentional, a public-health response will be necessary to detect and contain it. Moreover, such a response will benefit the public whether or not a mass biological attack ever occurs.

In all these respects, preparing for biological terrorism has more in common with confronting the threat of emerging infectious diseases than with preparing for chemical or nuclear attacks. Defence against bioterrorism, like protection against emerging diseases, must instead rely on disease surveillance.[2] To be

Christopher F. Chyba is Co-Director of the Center for International Security and Cooperation at Stanford University, and holds the Carl Sagan Chair for the Study of Life in the Universe at the SETI Institute. He was formerly Director for International Environmental Affairs on the staff of the US National Security Council.

effective, this strategy must have strong domestic and international components. But the domestic component in the United States and most other nations remains far too weak, and the international component, despite new initiatives by the World Health Organisation (WHO), is gravely underfunded.[3]

Growing Threat or Growing Hype?

There is a commonplace set of reasons now used to argue that the bioterrorist threat has grown over the past decade.[4] The World Trade Center bombing in 1993, the Oklahoma City bombing of 1995, and *Aum Shinrikyo's* sarin gas attack in Tokyo in 1995 could suggest that terrorism has crossed a grim threshold and that the adage that terrorists prefer a lot of people watching to a lot of people dead may no longer always apply.[5] With the end of the Cold War, human and technological microbiological capacity may be spreading from the former Soviet Union, despite Western attempts to provide alternative opportunities to former Soviet biological weapons scientists. The overwhelming military strength of the United States may lead some nations or non-state groups to adopt weapons of mass destruction as a means of asymmetric warfare to counterbalance US power. Finally, and above all, *Aum Shinrikyo* conducted at least four attacks in Tokyo with *Bacillus anthracis*, the sporulating bacterium that causes anthrax, in June–July 1993. Attempted indiscriminate attacks on civilian urban populations are no longer in the realm of the fantastic.

Aum Shinrikyo dispersed anthrax from the top of a building in Tokyo and off the back of a truck driving through Tokyo streets.[6] These attacks were conducted for apocalyptic religious reasons, and remained unannounced. They had a mass civilian target, yet there were no recognised casualties. The attacks became widely known only years later, following the arrest of *Aum* members subsequent to the more effective sarin attack. It appears that *Aum* scientists failed both to culture the right anthrax strain and to aerosolise the agent into particles of a size appropriate to cause mass casualties.[7] Perhaps a successful mass urban attack is more difficult than some analysts had suggested, but we must also worry that next time the world will not be as lucky.[8]

There is a danger that the public attention and hype devoted to the threat of bioterrorism will do more to encourage hoaxes than to prepare for real attacks. Indeed, most 'attacks' so far have been hoaxes intended to intimidate or terrorise their targets. The goal of the United States and its allies should be to fashion a response that will be useful not only across the spectrum of possible scenarios, but even in the event that no such attack ever occurs. Only by including a strong public health component can these objectives be satisfied.

We cannot reliably forecast the form that future biological terrorist attacks might take, or indeed if they will occur at all. An attack could be overt and announced; it could be covert and insidious; or it could be used to cause economic damage and social panic by following covert releases with credible announcements and threats. The range of possible attacks against which the United States must prepare is illustrated better by historical examples than by doomsday scenarios.

Biological Terrorism and Public Health *95*

Scenarios Real and Fictitious

In 1947, an American businessman infected with smallpox arrived in New York City from Mexico. Despite headache, fever and rash, he spent several days sightseeing. Nine days later, he died. In the interim, he infected at least twelve people, two of whom also died. Public health officials viewed the possibility of further transmission to be so grave that over six million people in New York were vaccinated within a month.[9]

Desirable characteristics for military biological agents have traditionally been thought to include minimal contagiousness (as with anthrax) to ensure that the disease cannot boomerang against the attacker's forces or population.[10] This expectation has been called into question by reports from the former Soviet Union that the USSR weaponised smallpox, despite its extreme contagiousness.[11] The New York vaccinations in 1947 were carried out even though Americans at that time were still being routinely vaccinated against smallpox. This has not been the case since 1980. The current US inventory of smallpox vaccine stands at over 12m doses.[12]

In 1972, a pilgrim returned to Yugoslavia from Iraq infected with smallpox. To contain the resulting outbreak, over 20m people were vaccinated in less than two weeks, and more than ten thousand people were quarantined.[13] It is not difficult to imagine an intentional attack involving smallpox (or plague, which has a 2–3 day incubation period) that takes advantage of the incubation time and business travellers or tourists to spread the disease.[14] And it remains unclear whether clandestine samples of smallpox continue to be held.[15]

Since the variola virus that causes smallpox officially no longer exists outside of two laboratories – the Center for Disease Control and Prevention (CDC) in the United States and the State Centre of Virology and Biotechnology (VECTOR) in Russia – any smallpox outbreak would be viewed with extreme suspicion.[16] But a more recent outbreak of a different virus illustrates how difficult it may be in some cases to distinguish a natural outbreak from a terrorist attack. In late summer 1999, an outbreak of West Nile Fever led to 53 known infections and seven deaths in the New York City area. Effective action was taken beginning a month after the first physician notified the city health department that an unusual neurological illness was striking patients. This information had in turn been passed quickly to the State Department of Health and the CDC. The recognition that an unusual disease (which also turned out to be West Nile) was killing birds in the New York area played an important role in the diagnosis. West Nile had never previously occurred in the western hemisphere.[17]

There were two reasons for concern that the West Nile outbreak might be the result of bioterrorism. In April 1999, an Iraqi defector had claimed that Saddam Hussein had stated his intention to weaponise the West Nile virus.[18] The virus seemed an unlikely choice for this purpose, but only months later, an outbreak was occurring in a major US urban centre. Moreover, a decade earlier, a sample of the West Nile virus had been sent from the United States to Iraq for diagnostic purposes. However, the strain of West Nile in the New York outbreak does not match that sent to Iraq, and there is no evidence that the outbreak was anything other than natural, possibly carried by a mosquito or an infected traveller from the Middle East. [19]

West Nile is an example of a natural outbreak with some of the characteristics one might expect of an intentional attack. In 1984, by contrast, the United States experienced an intentional attack that was misidentified as a natural outbreak. In September 1984, followers of the Baghwan Shree Rajneesh introduced salmonella into restaurants in the town of The Dalles, Oregon, as a kind of dry-run for suppressing voter turnout in an upcoming election. Seven hundred and fifty people fell ill, and 45 were hospitalised. The possibility of an intentional attack was initially rejected, in part because there had been no terrorist announcement of the attack. The outbreak was proved to be intentional only over a year later, through informants and the discovery by authorities of the same bacterial strain within a laboratory in the Rajneeshi compound. [20]

A Public Health Response

The early symptoms of a biological warfare agent most likely will resemble those of the flu. [21] Sufficiently covert or widely dispersed attacks could, at least initially, be difficult to distinguish from the sort of naturally occurring outbreaks just considered. These examples suggest that recognition of and response to a biological attack may strongly depend on the sensitivity and connectivity of the national and international public health system.

Sensitivity refers to the likelihood that a physician, pathologist, or other health-care worker will recognise that a given illness represents something out of the ordinary. *Connectivity* refers to how quickly and accurately this and other relevant information gets passed 'vertically' from the clinical level to the city, state, national, or international level, and 'horizontally' within these levels. [22] Additionally, the West Nile example illustrates the importance of improving communication among physicians, epidemiologists and veterinarians. [23] Both national and international sensitivity and connectivity must be improved.

Many biological agents have incubation periods that are long compared to national and international travel times – the latter now less than 36 hours by air between virtually any two cities in the world. The United States receives over 47m visitors per year. [24] While high-volume, rapid, reliable and inexpensive screening for disease agents may some day be made available through advances in biotechnology, the United States and most other nations cannot currently hope to stop disease outbreaks at their borders.

The US also imports 30 billion dollars of food annually, less than 1% of which is inspected at all. [25] As agricultural markets become increasingly global, the vulnerability of nations to natural or intentional food-borne disease can only increase.

It will never be sufficient to monitor for human- or food-borne illnesses at ports of entry. Both forms of monitoring are important, should be strengthened, and should make use of advances in biotechnology, but many cases will inevitably elude this screening. Illnesses carried into the country by travellers or imported food may appear in a number of cities simultaneously, where they likely would become known first to medical professionals. There is no alternative to a defence in depth, with improved public health surveillance at all levels, from the local to the international. Detecting and stopping outbreaks quickly in their early stages while still abroad will both alleviate human suffering and help prevent disease from reaching other nations' shores or borders. National and international strategies of public health surveillance are needed, essentially identical to those which are needed for emerging, re-emerging and other infectious diseases.

Emerging Disease Surveillance

Diseases emerge from some natural reservoir into the human population for many, sometimes poorly understood, reasons.[26] The ebola virus lives in an unidentified animal or insect host and only occasionally jumps into the human population, for reasons that remain largely unknown.[27] The hantavirus outbreak in the American south-west in 1993 was due to an explosion of the deer mouse population because of local climate change: food sources became unusually abundant that year due to record precipitation.[28] Some diseases such as tuberculosis had a resurgence because of increased antibiotic resistance.[29] Diphtheria returned to Eastern Europe as vaccination programmes weakened, infected travellers spread the disease, and the number of immunologically compromised people in major cities expanded.[30] It is still not clear why HIV/AIDS emerged, but 22m are already dead, 36m are infected, 5m more are infected every year, and there is no end yet in sight.[31] The average life expectancy in 2010 for many sub-Saharan nations is expected to be less than one to three decades what it would have been in the absence of AIDS.[32]

Two examples from the mid-1990s illustrate the current range of response to disease outbreaks. The US hantavirus outbreak was recognised as unusual by the Indian Health Service after just a few cases (although it was subsequently realised that there had been occasional case of the disease since at least the 1970s). Racial tensions spurred by the outbreak were not altogether avoided, but the rapid national response helped limit such reactions.[33] This speedy response contrasts with the slow reaction to the ebola outbreak from December 1994–May 1995 in what was then Zaire. During that entire time the epidemic remained unknown to the outside world, allowing the disease to run through twenty generations of human hosts. Once the disease became known, the US Center for Disease Control and Prevention (CDC) had a team in the country within days.[34] But international disease surveillance had badly failed in the interim.

Within the United States, surveillance for infectious diseases relies largely on the reporting requirements each state sets for its physicians, hospitals, and other health care providers. Local or state health authorities are to be notified if a patient is diagnosed with a disease declared reportable by that state. Nationally, states voluntarily report weekly to the CDC on the incidence of some fifty diseases, including many of potential interest to bioterrorists such as smallpox, anthrax, brucellosis and plague. Reporting is mandatory for a small number of contagious diseases requiring quarantine. In addition, the CDC gathers data voluntarily provided to it by about 200 hospitals across the United States on the incidence of infections acquired while a patient is hospitalised. Finally, the CDC has ongoing pilot sentinel projects with individual physicians, cities, or states to gather additional data.[35]

One such pilot project is yielding striking results. Initial research suggests that 14% of deaths among previously healthy people one to 49 years of age in hospitals and emergency rooms in four US states appear to be due to infectious causes which remain unidentified.[36] Some of these could represent fatal infections by altogether new pathogens. From the point of view of improving surveillance for biological terrorism, it is striking that we cannot currently recognise what is causing the deaths of many Americans from infectious diseases. Some of these deaths could be due to altogether novel pathogens. Public health surveillance for bioterrorism must currently take place against the background of this reservoir of ambiguity.

Successes and Failures of Imagination

Too often, thinking about biological terrorism has mimicked that about chemical terrorism, as though the two involved different versions of the same weapon. The common shorthand reference to 'CBW' defence encourages this confusion, and reinforces an emphasis on the wrong approaches in preparing to counter the threat of biological terrorism.

In fiscal year 2000, the United States budgeted some $8.4bn to combat terrorism. Within this overall budget, $618m was dedicated to preparing the nation for and responding to terrorism employing weapons of mass destruction. Of this, $40m, or about 6%, was devoted to improving disease surveillance.[37] This amount does not represent an adequate allocation of resources.

Nevertheless, the $40m is important because it shows that in recent years Washington has begun to draw the right conclusions. Beginning in fiscal year 1999, the Bioterrorism Preparedness and Response Program was created within the CDC. In fiscal year 2000, the overall budget of this programme was $118m, including the $40m for improved surveillance, with the rest going to increasing the US pharmaceutical stockpile and to other public-health preparations.[38] Raising the sensitivity and connectivity of disease surveillance in all 50 states to appropriate levels will require substantially greater resources.

The CDC's explicit entry into preparations for bioterrorist attack marks an important step forward in better coordination among public health, law enforcement, and intelligence agencies. Coordination has been inhibited because of the conflicting demands created by the transparency required for public-health agencies to operate freely in the United States or abroad, and the requirements of law enforcement or intelligence gathering. Imagine, for example, a hospital experiencing an unexplained disease outbreak. Hospital

Biological Terrorism and Public Health *99*

personnel may exchange information freely with government doctors and epidemiologists investigating the outbreak for public health reasons, but be much less forthcoming if they perceive those investigators as surrogates for law enforcement agencies which could pursue possible prosecutions.

Internationally, the situation is even more delicate. For example, after the 1995 plague outbreak in Surat, India, the CDC's desire to send epidemiologists was described as suspicious by the Indian news magazine *The Week*. This magazine explicitly accused the US of being responsible for the outbreak and identified by name the members of the CDC team who had arrived in India to study it.[39] Both civilian and military agencies conducting international public health or epidemiological missions are reluctant to risk compromising their ability to operate overseas by appearing to have ties with intelligence gathering or covert activities. But despite these impediments, the logic of such cooperation is leading to better communication and coordination.

Improvements in global public-health surveillance have been very slow in coming. The broad capacities that are needed are clear: Trained health-care workers and epidemiologists to improve the sensitivity of disease recognition; teachers for additional local training; regional laboratories with reliable diagnostic equipment so that diagnoses can be made rapidly and proximately; good communications to ensure connectivity; and the ability to call on teams of experts when needed. The WHO is the obvious choice for a multilateral solution, but its international disease surveillance system is chronically underfunded and has too many geographical holes. (This is not difficult to understand when one considers that the WHO's budget totalled $1.8bn for the biennium 1999–2000).[40] The WHO's Collaborating Centres, which are established on the condition that the centres may report outbreaks directly to the WHO without the intervention of the host government, are critical to the international monitoring that does exist. Still, the centres have insufficient global coverage.[41] New approaches, such as the Global Public Health Information Network (GPHIN) have gone some way towards improving the situation. Created by Canada's Laboratory Centre for Disease Control with WHO participation, GPHIN monitors the Internet continuously for news of infectious disease outbreaks throughout the world.[42] But this electronic monitoring does nothing to improve local capacity, and will miss outbreaks that do not find their way to the net.

What is needed is the creation of a regional network of a dozen sentinel laboratories that can detect and diagnose disease outbreaks, be they natural or intentional. Costs for such a network should be minimised by building as much as possible directly upon the best existing laboratories and personnel. Annual expenses of tens of millions of dollars appear sufficient to make this network a reality.[43] Yet the funding has not been found.

Terrorists and Hoaxers

Any proposed response to the threat of biological terrorism must weigh the benefits of the preparations against their potential for damage. Published

100 **Christopher F. Chyba**

analyses of possible attack scenarios risk providing 'how-to' advice to terrorists. High-profile publicity for the threat may inspire unstable individuals to action. Even if some information is readily available in print or on the Internet, non-professional actors might not have the inclination or dedication to research such attacks without a media trigger.

Perhaps just as important is the danger of inspiring hoaxes. In 1997, the FBI recorded one anthrax hoax; in 1998, as media attention to bioterrorism grew, that number swelled to 150.[44] In more than 80 anthrax hoax incidents in 1999, over one-third were directed at women's or other health clinics, often in the form of an envelope delivered with a letter claiming to have enclosed the powdered agent.[45] The publicity given to biological terrorism, coupled with the small quantities required for a true anthrax powder to pose a credible threat, has given a new and easy weapon to terrorists operating by hoax. These hoaxes take a substantial toll on municipal and national budgets, as well as Americans' civil rights. Perhaps just as significant is the danger that such hoaxes may inspire the conclusion that the threat is merely hype, and lead to complacency.

A public-health response avoids or minimises many of these pitfalls. The improvement of domestic and international public-health infrastructure lacks the glamour or photo opportunities likely to engender substantial media hype or even attention. A public health response represents a kind of civil-defence programme that concretely benefits society even if no attack ever occurs. In this sense, civil defence for biological weapons differs substantially from civil defence against nuclear weapons.

Heightened sensitivity and connectivity in the public health system is the only effective strategy against a suite of possible biological attacks or failed attacks. By improving the baseline of disease statistics, increased public health surveillance improves the chances of detecting, at the earliest possible stage, the intentional use or inadvertent release of a biological agent. Moreover, there are natural outbreaks every year of many of the organisms used as biological warfare agents, so that baseline measurements will help set a threshold against which future outbreaks may be viewed if there are suspicions they may be artificial.[46] There seem to have been no casualties or perhaps even human illnesses due to *Aum Shinrikyo's* repeated releases of anthrax in Tokyo. The goal of the United States' public-health system should be to detect and properly diagnose even a small number of casualties from such a failed attack. This is less likely to be possible as long as 14% of deaths possibly due to infections remain undiagnosed.

While important to the detection of covert attacks, failed attacks, or inadvertent releases, public-health surveillance could also be crucial to minimising casualties and economic damage in the event of an unannounced but successfully executed mass urban attack. In such a case, the rapid implementation of a post-attack programme of antibiotics or vaccinations is the most important means of reducing human casualties and economic losses. For example, paper studies (fortunately the only kind of studies so far possible) by the US CDC show that deaths in a major anthrax attack can be reduced by a factor of three if post-attack intervention begins within one rather than four days of the attack. Deaths due to brucellosis (with an incubation time of three days to several weeks) in an urban attack involving an aerosol release would be cut by a factor of three if post-attack intervention began within two rather than eight weeks.[47] In the absence of a terrorist announcement, the sensitivity and connectivity of the public health system could be crucial to the earliest possible recognition of and response to even a major attack.

It is sobering that many of these conclusions are reiterations of arguments first made decades ago. In 1950, soon after the onset of the Korean War, the United States recognised that little could be done to stop a biological weapons attack within its borders. However, if early detection could be achieved, a quick response could be mounted. To this end, the Epidemic Intelligence Service (EIS) was formed within the CDC; medical officers were trained in field epidemiology and assigned to the CDC, state health departments, and universities.[48] In the absence of a terrorist attack, EIS members would maintain their expertise and improve American public health by analysing natural disease outbreaks. The resulting baseline assessments would aid the recognition of possible future attacks, since they would help determine whether infrequent occurrences of disease exceeded normal background levels. But public-health networks within the United States, to say nothing of the developing world, have remained inadequate to the task.

Biological terrorism may turn out to be a quintessential example of a high-consequences but low-probability event. Even so, a public-health response strategy remains exactly on target. Citizens will enjoy its benefits even if no attack ever occurs.

In for the Long Term

An effective approach to countering the threat of bioterrorism must emphasise domestic and international improvements in public-health surveillance. Domestic surveillance within the United States remains inadequate, but the establishment of the Bioterrorism Preparedness and Response Program within the CDC demonstrates that the right lessons have begun to be learned. The international disease-surveillance network is in dire need of attention. The funding necessary to upgrade this network radically must be found. Opportunities within the framework of the Biological Weapons Convention (BWC) should be explored. In particular, the right to epidemiological challenge inspections in the event of a suspicious outbreak should be secured.[49] However, a public-health response should not be hostage to progress within the BWC protocol negotiations. Finally, even if the will is found to improve the global health network, it is unclear how disease surveillance in strife-torn regions such as the Democratic Republic of Congo or southern Sudan can be sustained. Yet such regions are among the 'hot spots' where outbreaks may be most likely and monitoring the most important.

Once the necessary international public-health infrastructure is built, the annual operating costs must continue to be met. This will require the developed world, and the United States in particular, to view sustainable public-health practices throughout the developing world as being closely allied with its own self-interest. This vision will need to be maintained in the long-term: the threat of emerging diseases or biological terrorism is unlikely to diminish through the coming century.

Such long-term resolve will not be easy, given the difficulty of demonstrating the success of a prevention strategy. No level of preparedness can be proved responsible for the absence of an undesired or catastrophic outcome. Yet, given the importance of prevention, the United States and its allies must adopt a less direct measure of success: one of improved capabilities, rather than demonstrated response. But this measure is, after all, a familiar one in the national security realm – as familiar as the Cold War strategy of deterrence.

Notes

1 Incubation times for many potential biological agents are given in D.R. Franz et al., 'Clinical recognition and management of patients exposed to biological warfare agents', *Journal of the American Medical Association*, vol. 278, 1997, pp. 399–411.

2 C.F. Chyba, *Biological Terrorism, Emerging Diseases, and National Security*, (New York: Rockefeller Brothers Fund Project on World Security, 1998), http://206.135.15.24/pws/Chyba_Bioterrorism.pdf.

3 Institute of Medicine, *Emerging Infections: Microbial Threats to Health in the United States* (Washington DC: National Academy of Sciences, 1992); Centers for Disease Control and Prevention, *Addressing Emerging Infectious Disease Threats: A Prevention Strategy for the United States* (Atlanta, GA: CDC, 1994); Committee on International Science, Engineering, and Technology, National Science and Technology Council, *Infectious Disease – A Global Health Threat* (Washington DC: US Government Printing Office 1995); J.R. Davis and J. Lederberg (eds.), *Public Health Systems and Emerging Infections*, Institute of Medicine (Washington DC: National Academy Press, 2000); National Intelligence Estimate, *The Global Infectious Disease Threat and its Implications for the United States*, NIE 99-17D, January 2000, http://www.odci.gov/cia/publications/nie/report/nie99-17d.html. The most important new WHO activities are those of its Communicable Disease Surveillance and Response (CSR), http://www.who.int/emc.

4 W. Laqueur, 'Postmodern Terrorism', *Foreign Affairs*, vol. 75, no. 5, 1996, pp. 24–36; J.F. Sopko, 'The Changing Proliferation Threat', *Foreign Policy*, vol. 105, Winter 1996–1997, pp. 3–20; R. Betts, 'The New Threat of Mass Destruction', *Foreign Affairs*, vol. 77,

no. 1, 1998, pp. 26–41; A. Carter, J. Deutch, and P. Zelikow, 'Catastrophic Terrorism: Tackling the New Danger', *Foreign Affairs*, vol. 77, no. 6, pp. 80–94; R.A. Falkenrath, R.D. Newman, and B.A. Thayer, *America's Achilles' Heel: Nuclear, Biological, and Chemical Terrorism and Covert Attack* (Cambridge, MA: Belfer Center for Science and International Affairs, 1998); S. Simon and D. Benjamin, 'America and the New Terrorism', *Survival*, vol. 42, no. 1, Spring 2000, pp. 59–75; O. Roy, B. Hoffman, R. Paz, S. Simon and D. Benjamin, 'America and the New Terrorism: An Exchange', *Survival*, vol. 42, no. 2, Summer 2000, pp. 156–172.

5 'Terrorists want a lot of people watching and a lot of people listening, and not a lot of people dead.' B.M. Jenkins, 'International Terrorism: A New Mode of Conflict', in *International Terrorism and World Security*, D. Carlton and C. Schaerf (eds.), (London: Croom Helm, 1975), p. 15. See also B. Hoffman, *Inside Terrorism* (New York: Columbia University Press, 1998).

6 A carefully documented account of the *Aum*'s biological and other attacks is given by D.E. Kaplan, 'Aum Shinrikyo (1995)', in J.B. Tucker, ed., *Toxic Terror: Assessing Terrorist Use of Chemical and Biological Weapons*, MIT Press, Cambridge, MA, 2000, pp. 207–226. See also M. Leitenberg, 'The Experience of the Japanese Aum Shinrikyo Group and Biological Agents', in B. Roberts (ed.), *Hype or Reality: The 'New Terrorism' and Mass Casualty Attacks* (Alexandria, VA: CBACI, 2000) pp. 159–172.

7 W.J. Broad, S. Wu Dunn, and J. Miller, 'How Japan Germ Terror Alerted World', *New York Times*, 26 May 1998, p. A1.

8 The initial exaggeration of *Aum*'s biological-weapons capabilities has

104 **Christopher F. Chyba**

been emphasised by M. Leitenberg, 'The Experience of the Japanese Aum Shinrikyo Group and Biological Agents', in B. Roberts (ed.), *Hype or Reality: The 'New Terrorism' and Mass Casualty Attacks* (Alexandria, VA: CBACI, 2000), pp. 159–172; see also A.E. Smithson and L. Levy, *Ataxia: The Chemical and Biological Terrorism Threat and the US Response*, Stimson Center Report no. 35, pp. 75–80, http://www.stimson.org/cwc/ataxia.htm.

9   For a near-contemporary account, see T. Rosebury, *Peace or Pestilence: Biological Warfare and How to Avoid it* (New York: McGraw-Hill, 1949).

10 Office of Technology Assessment, *Technologies Underlying Weapons of Mass Destruction*, OTA-BP-ISC-115, December 1993 (Washington DC: US Government Printing Office, 1993).

11 K. Alibek, *Biohazard: The Chilling True Story of the Largest Covert Biological Weapons Program in the World – Told from Inside by the Man Who Ran It*, (New York: Random House, 1999); A.E. Smithson, *Toxic Archipelago: Preventing Proliferation from the Former Soviet Chemical and Biological Weapons Complexes*, Stimson Center Report no. 32, http://www.stimson.org/cwc/toxic.htm.

12 D. McClain, 'Smallpox', in *Textbook of Military Medicine, Part I: Medical Aspects of Chemical and Biological Warfare*, Office of the Surgeon General, Department of the Army, 1997, pp. 539–559. The CDC awarded a contract in 2000 to Ora Vax of Cambridge, Massachussetts, to produce smallpox vaccine; approximately 40 million doses will be produced initially with anticipated delivery of the first full -scale production lots in 2004. The contract allows for increased production of the vaccine should the need arise. See J. Koplan, 'CDC's Strategic Plan for Bioterrorism', presentation to

'Bioterrorism: Public Health Emergency and National Security Threat', Washington DC, November 28–29, 2000, http://www.hopkins-biodefense.org/sympcast/transcripts/trans_kopl.html.

13 L.K. Altman, 'Protection Urged for Possible Smallpox Attack', *New York Times*, 11 March 1998, p. A16.

14 The Soviet defector Ken Alibek envisions this type of attack in his article, 'Russia's Deadly Expertise', *New York Times*, 27 March 1998, p. A19.

15 J.J. Fialka, 'CIA Says North Korea Appears Active in Biological, Nuclear Arms', *Wall Street Journal*, 25 February 1993, p.16; D.R. Franz et al., 'Clinical recognition and management of patients exposed to biological warfare agents', *Journal of the American Medical Association*, vol. 278, 1997, pp. 399–411; R.F. Knouss, 'The Federal Role in Protection and Response', in S.D. Drell, A.D. Sofaer, and G.D. Wilson, eds., *The New Terror: Facing the Threat of Biological and Chemical Weapons*, (Stanford: Hoover Institution Press, 1999), pp. 348–359.

16 *Assessment of Future Scientific Needs for Live Variola Virus*, Institute of Medicine (Washington DC: National Academy Press, 1999).

17 A thorough summary of the West Nile outbreak in New York is given by M. Schock-Spana, 'A West Nile Virus Post-Mortem', *Biodefense Quarterly*, vol. 1, no. 3, December 1999, http://www.hopkins-biodefense.org/pages/news/quarter1_3.html#Anchor-cdc.

18 R. Preston, 'West Nile Mystery', *New Yorker*, October 18 and 25, 1999, pp. 90–108.

19 J. Steinhauer and J. Miller, 'In New York Outbreak, Glimpse of Gaps in Biological Defence', *New York Times*, 11 October 1999, p. A1; L.K. Altman, 'Officials Working to Contain West Nile Virus', *New York Times*, 26 April

2000.

20 T.J. Török et al., 'A Large Community Outbreak of Salmonellosis Caused by Intentional Contamination of Restaurant Salad Bars', *Journal of the American Medical Association*, vol. 278, no. 5, 1997, pp. 389–395; W.S. Carus, 'The Rajneeshees (1984)', in J.B. Tucker (ed.), *Toxic Terror: Assessing Terrorist Use of Chemical and Biological Weapons* (Cambridge, MA: MIT Press, 2000), pp. 115–138.

21 D.R. Franz et al., 'Clinical recognition and management of patients exposed to biological warfare agents', *Journal of the American Medical Association*, vol. 278, 1997, pp. 399–411; F.R. Sidell, E.T. Takafuji, and D.R. Franz (eds), *Medical Aspects of Chemical and Biological Warfare* (Washington DC: Office of the Surgeon General, 1997).

22 C.F. Chyba, *Biological Terrorism, Emerging Diseases, and National Security*, Rockefeller Brothers Fund Project on World Security, New York, 1998, http://206.135.15.24/pws/Chyba_Bioterrorism.pdf.

23 Birds had been dying from the West Nile virus for at least a month prior to the first recognised human cases. The connection between the bird deaths and a threat to humans was not made until after human illnesses began. See M. Schock-Spana, 'A West Nile Virus Post-Mortem', *Biodefense Quarterly*, vol. 1, no. 3, December 1999, http://www.hopkins-biodefense.org/pages/news/quarter1_3.html#Anchor-cdc; and J. Steinhauer and J. Miller, 'In New York Outbreak, Glimpse of Gaps in Biological Defenses', *New York Times*, 11 October 1999, p. A1.

24 *Time Almanac 2001*, (Boston: Family Education Company, 2000), p. 213.

25 J. Gerth and T. Weiner, 'Imports Swamp US Food-Safety Efforts,' *New York Times*, 29 September 1997, p. A1; R.L. Berkelman et al., 'Infectious Disease Surveillance: A Crumbling Foundation', *Science* 264, 1994, pp.

368–370.

26 R.M. Krause, 'The Origin of Plagues: Old and New', *Science* 257, 1992, pp. 1073–1078; S.S. Morse, 'Factors in the Emergence of Infectious Diseases', *Emerging Infectious Diseases*, vol. 1, no. 1, 1995, pp. 7–15.

27 D. R. Burton and P.H.I. Parren, 'Fighting the Ebola Virus', *Science* 408, 2000, pp. 527–528.

28 S. Sternberg, 'Tracking a Mysterious Killer Virus in the Southwest', *Washington Post Health*, 14 June 1994, p.10–13.

29 Institute of Medicine, *Emerging Infections: Microbial Threats to Health in the United States* (Washington DC: National Academy of Sciences, 1992).

30 J. Maurice, 'Russian Chaos Breeds Diphtheria Outbreak', *Science* 267, pp. 1416–1417.

31 See UNAIDS, 'AIDS Epidemic Update: December 2000', http://www.unaids.org/wac/2000/wad00/files/WAD_epidemic_report.htm.

32 National Intelligence Estimate, *The Global Infectious Disease Threat and its Implications for the United States*, NIE 99-17D, January 2000, http://www.odci.gov/cia/publications/nie/report/nie99-17d.html.

33 The outbreak initially struck members of the Navajo nation, leading some officials and media to dub the illness 'Navajo flu', and contributing to some anti-Indian reactions. S. Sternberg, 'Tracking a Mysterious Killer Virus in the Southwest', *Washington Post Health*, 14 June 1994, pp.10–13; L. Garrett, *The Coming Plague: Newly Emerging Diseases in a World Out of Balance* (New York: Farrar, Straus and Giroux, 1994), pp. 528–549.

34 A succinct history of the 1995 ebola outbreak in Zaire is given in the report by the Committee on International Science, Engineering, and Technology, National Science and Technology Council, *Infectious Disease – A Global Health Threat* (Washington

106 **Christopher F. Chyba**

DC: US Government Printing Office, 1995).

[35] An overview of infectious disease monitoring in the United States may be found in J. Lederberg, R.E. Shope, and S.C. Oaks, eds., *Emerging Infections: Microbial Threats to Health in the United States*, Institute of Medicine (Washington DC: National Academy Press, 1992), Chapter 3.

[36] B.A. Perkins et al., 'Unexplained Deaths Due to Possibly Infectious Causes in the United States: Defining the Problem and Designing Surveillance and Laboratory Approaches', *Emerging Infectious Diseases*, vol. 2, no. 1, 1996, pp. 47–53.

[37] A.E. Smithson and L. Levy, *Ataxia: The Chemical and Biological Terrorism Threat and the US Response*, Stimson Center Report no. 35, pp. 122–132, http://www.stimson.org/cwc/ataxia.htm.

[38] *CDC FY2000 Budget Summary*, http://cdc.gov/2000bdg/cdcbud/pdf

[39] R. Prasannan, 'Military Microbe', *The Week*, 23 July 1995, pp. 30–37.

[40] WHO Budget, http://www.who.int/aboutwho/en/qa6.htm.

[41] The WHO's international health surveillance networks and their geographic coverage is described in 'EMC Annual Report 1997', World Health Organisation, http://www.who.int/emc-documents/emc/docs/whoemc982.pdf.

[42] GPHIN is described at http://www.hc-sc.gc.ca/hpb/transitn/gphin_e.pdf.

[43] S.S. Morse et al., 'Controlling Emerging Infectious Diseases', 1997, http://www.fas.org/promed/papers/morse.htm; B.H. Rosenberg and J. Woodall, 'Sentinel Centres for Global Health Security', *The Lancet*, vol. 349, 1997; Centers for Disease Control and Prevention, *Addressing Emerging Infectious Disease Threats: A Prevention Strategy for the United States* (Atlanta, GA: CDC, 1994).

[44] J.B. Tucker, 'Introduction', in *Toxic Terror: Assessing Terrorist Use of Chemical and Biological Weapons*, (Cambridge, MA: MIT Press, 2000), pp. 1–14.

[45] G. Cameron, J. Pate, D. McCauley, and L. DeFazio, '1999 WMD Terrorism Chronology: Incidents Involving Sub-National Actors and Chemical, Biological, Radiological, and Nuclear Materials', *The Nonproliferation Review*, vol. 7, no. 2, Summer 2000, pp. 157–174.

[46] For example, in 2000 there were reports of outbreaks of anthrax in Ethiopia and tularemia in Kosovo. See the WHO's 'Disease Outbreak News' at http://www.who.int/disease-outbreak-news/.

[47] A.F. Kaufmann et al., 'The Economic Impact of a Bioterrorist Attack: Are Prevention and Postattack Intervention Programs Justifiable?', *Emerging Infectious Diseases* 3, 1997, pp. 83–94.

[48] D.A. Henderson, 'Surveillance Systems and Intergovernmental Cooperation', in S.S. Morse (ed.), *Emerging Viruses*, (Oxford: Oxford University Press, 1993) pp. 283–289.

[49] R.P. Kadlec, et al., 'Biological Weapons Control: Prospects and Implications for the Future', *Journal of the American Medical Association*, vol. 278, 1997, pp. 351–356; J.B. Tucker (ed.), *Procedures for Investigating Suspicious Outbreaks of Infectious Disease in a Noncooperative Environment* (Springfield, VA: National Technical Information Service, 1998); M Wheelis, 'Investigating Disease Outbreaks under a Protocol to the Biological and Toxic Weapons Convention', *Emerging Infectious Diseases* 6, 2000, pp. 595–600.

[11]

Smallpox: a potential agent of bioterrorism

Richard J. Whitley*

*Department of Pediatrics, Microbiology and Medicine Children's Hospital, The University of Alabama at Birmingham,
ACC 616, 1600 7th Avenue South, Birmingham, AL 35233, USA*

Received 20 May 2002; accepted 5 August 2002

Abstract

The events of 11 September 2001, in New York City, and subsequent identification of anthrax in the United States Postal System, have generated a new sense of awareness for the potential of biological terrorism, if not warfare. Among those agents identified by the Centers for Disease Control and Prevention as 'Class A Bioterrorist Threats', smallpox is among the most dangerous. The ease of transmission of this agent, the lack of immunity in the population at large to this agent, and rapidity of its spread, if released, all generate significant concern for its deployment. A vaccine directed against smallpox is available but it is also associated with significant adverse events—some of which are life-threatening. Further, no antiviral drug has proven efficacious for therapy of human disease, although one licensed drug, cidofovir, does have in vitro activity. Regardless, heightened awareness should lead to the development of a vaccine without significant adverse events and safe and efficacious antiviral drugs. The availability of a vaccine and antiviral drugs that are safe would significantly remove any major threat of smallpox deployment by a terrorist.

Keywords: Smallpox; Bioterrorism; Vaccination

1. Introduction

Smallpox is one of the oldest recorded infections of mankind. Likely, this agent, also known as *variola*, evolved by adaptation to humans from a rodent cowpox-like virus through an intermediate host, such as cattle. The earliest descriptions of smallpox date to 10,0000 B.C. in Asia and India. Subsequently, the spread of infection can be traced to Pacific Rim countries in the East and Europe and North Africa in the West. By the 17th century, smallpox was introduced into North America from Europe. At its peak, namely when the World Health Organization (WHO) decided to initiate an eradication program, 10–15 million cases occurred annually, as reviewed (Fenner, 2002).

Smallpox resulted in one of the first effective preventive measures for an infectious disease, namely immunization. Interesting, as early as 1000 A.D., dried smallpox scab material was utilized in China for intranasal inhalation in order to develop protective immunity. In India, the same material was used to generate pustules to cause variolation, result-ing in disease protection. Importantly, and surprisingly, the mortality following vaccination by such procedures, even if the material contained live virus, was approximately 2% rather than the customary 30%. Prevention by vaccination, however, was not introduced as a standard procedure until the late 18th century when it was recognized by Edward Jenner that milkmaids who acquired cowpox were resistant to smallpox. By the middle to late 19th century, utilization of vaccinia for the prevention of smallpox was routine. By the 1950s most industrialized countries had eliminated endemic smallpox by the use of vaccine prepared on the skin of either cattle or sheep and suspended in bactericidal concentrations of glycerol.

As early as 1958, the possibility of global eradication was suggested. Eradication was accomplished in only a few developing countries by 1965; however, in 1967, WHO launched an 'Intensified Eradication Program'. Utilizing the unique epidemiologic intervention principle of Foege and colleagues, known as 'ring vaccination', cases gradually decreased in West Africa. Henderson and colleagues facilitated the WHO program leading to global eradication with the last case occurring in Somalia in October of 1977 (World Health Organization, 1980; Fenner et al., 1988). Routine smallpox vaccination of civilians was discontinued in the United States in 1982.

* Tel.: +1-205-939-9594; fax: +1-205-934-8559.
E-mail address: rwhitley@peds.uab.edu (R.J. Whitley).

8   *R.J. Whitley/Antiviral Research 57 (2003) 7–12*

With the worldwide eradication of smallpox, the WHO launched an effort to destroy the remaining stocks of virus known to exist at the Centers for Disease Control and Prevention in the United States and in Koltsovo at the State Center of Virology and Biotechnology (Vector). As the issues of destruction of smallpox were publicly debated, societies of the western world developed an increasing concern that stocks of smallpox existed in the hands of individuals for its clandestine use in an offensive biowarfare program, particularly in individuals and countries as Iraq, Korea, Iran, and Libya. Polar positions existed in the United States regarding the destruction of the smallpox samples. Ultimately, however, following an Institute of Medicine Advisory Committee, (Institute of Medicine, 1999) a recommendation to maintain the stocks for purposes of antiviral and vaccine development was put forward by then President Clinton and supported by the Department of Defense and the United States Congress. This recommendation receives continued support from the Department of Health and Human Service and the Department of Defense.

Initially, scientists believed that the possibility of the reappearance of smallpox was miniscule; however, the safety of the population at large changed dramatically after the events of 11 September 2001, with the destruction of the World Trade Centers in New York City, United States. Further, the subsequent deaths related to anthrax in postal workers and community members heightened the possibility of the deployment of microbes for bioterrorism, particularly in developed societies. Because of waning immunity to smallpox, this agent becomes one of the most likely for consideration as a microbe of bioterrorism. Its pathogenicity is so virulent that only 50–100 cases could lead to massive outbreaks of disease (Meltzer et al., 2001). The epidemiology, natural history, and its use as an agent of bioterrorism will be described.

2. Epidemiology

At the beginning of the 20th century, smallpox existed worldwide; however, its distribution was not uniform as areas of endemicity existed. Two principle forms of the disease exist: variola major and the much milder form variola minor (or alastrim), as reviewed (Dixon, 1948; Marsden, 1948; Mack, 1972; Fenner et al., 1988; Henderson et al., 1999; Fenner, 2002). In 1970, 1300 new cases occurred in 1000 villages in Southwest India and in 1973, 10,000 new cases occurred in India.

Smallpox is a viral disease that is unique to humans; no known animal reservoirs exist. In order to sustain itself, virus must be transmitted from person-to-person. The mechanism of spread is by droplet, aerosol or direct person-to-person contact. Typically, an infected individual will cough or sneeze and virus is transmitted to the oral mucosa of a susceptible host. Direct contact is also a route of transmission, including contact with contaminated clothing or bed linens. The disease is characterized by a seasonal distribution with spread occurring during the late winter and early spring; a time when chickenpox is prevalent in most communities. However, it can be transmitted in any climate and in any part of the world. As would be predicted, transmission within families is increased by overcrowding during rainy periods. On the other hand, transmission between communities was increased by the greater mobility of individuals during dry periods. The transmission of smallpox among populations is slower than that of chickenpox or measles. As noted, spread was primarily to family members and friends but not among classroom contacts. The reason for this latter observation is based on the fact that transmission did not occur until the onset of rash. Since disease onset was abrupt with fever and malaise, confinement occurred early in the course of illness.

After the early descriptions of smallpox, the distinction between variola major and variola minor was defined on epidemiologic grounds. In Asia, for example, variola major was associated with a mortality of 30% or higher. In contrast, in South America and sub-Saharan Africa, a similar clinical entity resulted in a mortality of 1% or less, and was designated variola minor. Importantly, through the end of the 19th century, variola major predominated throughout the world. However, at the turn of the century, variola minor was detected at the very southern extremes of Africa and, subsequently, Florida. The distinction between these two strains relates to genetic and growth characteristics of the causative viruses in vitro.

Smallpox was typically a disease of children as nearly one third of case occurred under the age of 5 years and nearly three quarters in individuals less than 14 years. However, in rural communities where vaccination and natural infection were less common, disease incidence paralleled the age distribution. Both sexes are equally affected. The incidence of smallpox was higher in lower socioeconomic groups, presumably secondary to overcrowding.

Patients suffering from smallpox are most infectious during the early stages of illness, namely the first 7–10 days after the onset of lesions but, not before. Transmission occurs most frequently 4–6 days after the onset of cutaneous lesions. At that time, the skin lesions are in a papulovesicular stage. However, as scabs formed, infectivity waned rapidly. Patients were considered infectious until all the crusts separated.

3. Clinical manifestations

Issues relevant to clinical variola are summarized in Table 1. Infection is initiated by viral replication on the respiratory mucosa. Primary viremia leads to seeding of the reticuloendothelial system (Dixon, 1948; Marsden, 1948; Mack, 1972; Mack et al., 1972; Henderson et al., 1999). Secondary viremia results in clinical disease associated with fever, malaise and myalgia. Virus localizes in small blood vessels of the dermis. The incubation period for smallpox is characteristically 12 days. The first clinical sign of infection

Table 1
Smallpox

Clinical features	Flu-like symptoms with 2–4 day prodrome of fever and myalgia Rash prominent on face and extremities including palms and soles Rash scabs over in 1–2 weeks Rash onset is synchronous
Mode of transmission	Person-to-person
Incubation period	1 day–8 weeks (average 5 days)
Communicability	Contagious at onset of rash and remains infectious until scabs separate (about 3 weeks)
Infection control practices	Contact and airborne precautions N95 respirator Private room or cohort Discharge when noninfectious
Prevention	Live-virus intradermal vaccine that does not confer lifelong immunity Contact CDC Previously vaccinated person should be considered susceptible
Supply assessment	Number of airborne precautions rooms available Number of N95 respirators available Vaccine availability
Postexposure prophylaxis	Smallpox vaccine only within 3 days of exposure If greater than 3 days, vaccine and vaccinia immune-globulin (VIG) Instruct exposed individuals to monitor self for flu-like symptoms or rash for 7–17 days
Treatment	There is no licensed antiviral for smallpox (cidofovir is experimental) Supportive care

is a prodromal illness which last 2–4 days, characterized by malaise, headache, high fever, vomiting, and delirium. Likely, prodrome coincides with the phase of secondary viremia. As prodrome progresses to the third or fourth day, buccal and pharyngeal lesions begin to appear. Rash begins on the face and spreads to the forearms and hands and, then, to the lower limbs and trunk. Lesions were always more numerous on the face than other areas of the body. Lesions begin as macules and quickly evolve to papules and, subsequently, to vesicles by about the fifth day of illness. Pustules appear about the eighth day of illness. The pustules are usually round and tense and deeply embedded in the dermis. Pustules are followed by scabs and, ultimately, scars.

Hemorrhagic smallpox does occur, being the most serious form of disease and usually fatal. As would be anticipated, hemorrhages into the skin or mucous membranes characterize this clinical presentation. Secondary bacterial infection was not common. Death usually occurred during the second week and was attributed to immune complex mediated shock.

The illness associated with variola minor is less severe with few constitutional symptoms and a less pronounced rash.

The disease most commonly confused with smallpox is chickenpox (described later). During the first 2–3 days of rash, it may be difficult to distinguish these two entities. Chickenpox is characterized by the development of a rash that involves lesions in all stages of development—maculopapules, vesicles, pustules and scabs. Nevertheless, smallpox lesions do not demonstrate all stages of evolution simultaneously. The lesions of chickenpox tend to involve the extremities to a greater extent than the trunk.

4. Diagnosis

The identification of a single suspected case of smallpox should be treated as an international health emergency and brought immediately to the attention of national officials through local and state health departments. As discussed above, the clinical findings resemble those encountered with chickenpox. Laboratory confirmation of the diagnosis in a smallpox outbreak is important. Specimens should only be collected by someone who has been recently vaccinated. Vesicular/pustular fluid should be harvested and transmitted immediately to state or local health department laboratories for confirmation. Laboratory examination requires high containment (BL-4) facilities and should only be undertaken by experienced personnel. Typical approaches to the identification to the agent include electronmicroscopy, polymerase chain reaction, and isolation in cell culture. Differentiation from chickenpox can be accomplished by staining of scraped skin lesions with monoclonal antibodies directed against varicella zoster virus (Meltzer et al., 2001). A potentially confusing diagnosis, and one which occurs in a period of global travel, is that of monkeypox which would be identified in typical diagnostic assays (Centers for Disease Control and Prevention, 1998). From 1970 to 1986, there were 400 cases worldwide with recent outbreaks in sub-Saharan Africa. This disease more closely resembles chickenpox but has a 5–10% mortality. Monkeypox is indistinguishable from smallpox with the exception of the enlargement of cervical and inguinal lymph nodes. Also, monkeypox resolves more promptly.

5. Vaccination

In the United States, vaccination against smallpox was discontinued in 1982 (Centers for Disease Control and Prevention, 1990). Thus, a significant portion of the American population is susceptible to smallpox. Persistence of detectable antibodies as detected by ELISA, particularly for older individuals, is approximately 5–10 years (El-Ad et al., 1990). However, persistence of neutralizing antibody has been documented in a few individuals >10 years after

10   *R.J. Whitley / Antiviral Research 57 (2003) 7–12*

Table 2
Complications of Smallpox Vaccination in the United States for 1968 (Henderson et al., 1999)

Vaccination status age (years)	Estimated number of vaccinations	Number of cases						
		Postvaccinial encephalitis[a]	Progressive vaccinia[a]	Eczema vaccinatum[a]	Generalized vaccinia	Accidental infection	Other	Total
Primary vaccination[b]	5,594,000	16 (4)	5 (2)	58	131	142	66	418
Revaccination	8,574,000	0	6 (2)	8	10	7	9	40
Contacts	...[c]	0	0	60 (1)	2	44	8	114
Total	14,168,000	16 (4)	11 (4)	126 (1)	143	193	83	572

Adapted from JAMA 1999, 281, 2127–2137.
[a] Data in parentheses indicate number of deaths attributable to vaccination.
[b] Data include 31 patients with unknown vaccination status.
[c] Ellipses indicate contacts were not vaccinated.

vaccination. Regardless, the following can be concluded. First, immunity is not life long (Kempe, 1960). Second, some persistence of immunity has been documented in a limited number of individuals. In studies performed in Scandinavia, individuals exposed to smallpox but immunized as children had a lower mortality upon exposure to variola major than those not vaccinated. The implications for these findings are unclear.

Vaccination consists of the administration of vaccinia virus grown on scarified scabs of calves. Vaccine production is, likely, the crudest of all vaccines available. After purification, virus is freeze dried in rubber-stopped vials that contain sufficient vaccine for at least 50 doses. Vaccine is administered with a bifurcated needle (Henderson et al., 1972). Vaccine should be stored at −20 °C. Currently, there are approximately 90–100 million doses of vaccine available for administration in the United States.

Vaccination is not without complications. First, and most importantly, no immunocompromised host should be vaccinated, as illustrated by an immunocompromised military recruit inadvertently vaccinated (Redfield et al., 1987). Second, the rate of postvaccine encephalitis is approximately 2.3–2.9 cases per one million vaccinations with an associated 25% mortality (Lane et al., 1969; Goldstein et al., 1975). In addition, vaccinia gangrenosum occurs in approximately 2.6 per one million vaccinations and is associated with a high mortality. Generalized vaccinia is usually not fatal but occurs in as many as 290 individuals per one million vaccinations. Vaccine complications are summarized in Table 2 (Henderson et al., 1999).

6. Postexposure treatment

At the present time, no antiviral drug has been shown to be effective in the prevention or treatment of smallpox. However, cidofovir, a licensed phosphonate analog has demonstrated in vitro activity against monkeypox, vaccinia and variola (Neyts and De Clercq, 1993; Lalezari et al., 1997; Bray et al., 2000; Smee et al., 2001a,b). Furthermore, it has activity against other pox viruses as well (Meadows

et al., 1997; Davies et al., 1999; Zabawski and Cockerell, 1999; Ibarra et al., 2000; Toro et al., 2000; Geerinck et al., 2001). While this drug is active in vitro, cidofovir does have significant nephrotoxicity. In addition, lipid prodrugs of cidofovir that are orally bioavailable are under investigations (Neyts and De Clercq, 2001; Huggins et al., 2002; Kern et al., 2002; Smee et al., 2002). Cidofovir administration should be by physicians experienced with its use. In the opinion of this author, cidofovir is a logical current choice as a treatment. With the availability of vaccinia immunoglobulin, smallpox, at least, would at least be ameliorated if an outbreak occurred (Sharp and Fletcher, 1973).

7. Development of new vaccines

The original smallpox eradication campaigns used vaccines that were derived from many vaccinia virus strains, including the New York calf lymph virus, a New York City chorioallantoic membrane strain, EM-63 (USSR) and Temple of Heaven (China). By the late 1960s, over 70 produces used 15 principal strains of vaccinia virus for the development of vaccines. However, one strain, the 'Lister' or 'Elestree' derived from sheep in the United Kingdom, became the most prevalent used throughout the world. Historically, most of these vaccines were produced in live animals. More recently, the use of primary cell substrates, particularly embryonated chicken egg-produced smallpox vaccine, would help avoid some of the potential problems associated with vaccine production in animals. These problems include: harvesting, contamination, adventitious agents, allogenicity, and accompanying animal proteins. In addition, the Food and Drug Administration (FDA) has licensed live-virus vaccines that have been produced in diploid cell substrates (e.g. MRC-5, WI-38). The MRC-5 cell line was used for the preparation of a vaccine evaluated in a Phase I clinical trial (McClain et al., 1997). Likely, the FDA will consider acceptable the production of live smallpox vaccines produced in these diploid cell substrates.

Alternatively, the continuous cell line Vero has been used to prepare inactivated virus vaccines, particularly the inacti-

R.J. Whitley/Antiviral Research 57 (2003) 7–12 11

vated polio vaccine. While the FDA has not yet licensed this substrate for live-virus production, international experience suggests that it may be a suitable substrate for a smallpox vaccine. The selection of cell substrates of vaccine production in Vero cells has recently been addressed in an FDA letter (http://www.fda.gov/cber/letters.htm).

Strains selected for vaccine production warrants note. The LC16m8, an attenuated vaccinia virus strain was developed in Japan for primary vaccination in 1975. It was derived by passing the Lister strain 36 times through primary rabbit kidney cells at low temperature. Initial studies indicated lower reactive genicity with acceptable immunogenicity. Of note, there was lower neurovirulence in a monkey assay (Hirayama, 1975). The most highly attenuated vaccinia strain is the Ankara. It has been passaged over 570 times in chicken embryo fibroblasts. This virus is host restricted, being unable to replicate in human and other mammalian cells. Thus, for all intense purposes it behaves like an inactivated virus being acceptable in high-risk individuals. It has been safely used in over 100,000 persons in Turkey and Germany; however, its effectiveness in its prevention of smallpox is unknown.

Each of these constructs, as well as genetically engineered viruses is under consideration for use in humans. Of note, the recent availability of vaccinia pools at the Adventis laboratories in Swiftwater, PA, USA of classic vaccine stocks, remove some of the intense pressure for the immediate development of new constructs.

8. Bioterrorist use

Likely, smallpox was first initially deployed as a biological weapon during the French and Indian Wars (1754–1767) by British forces in North America. Apparently, blankets contaminated with smallpox virus (obtained from infected patients) were distributed to American Indians. The resulting epidemics led to a mortality of greater than 50% in the effected tribes, as reviewed (Henderson et al., 1999).

More recently, the potential spread of smallpox, if used as a biological weapon, was illustrated by two European smallpox outbreaks in the 1970s. These outbreaks were not thought to be intentional. The first occurred in Mashede, Germany in 1970 when aerosol deployment led to a widespread outbreak, even when low doses of smallpox were released.

The second outbreak occurred in Yugoslavia in 1972. In spite of routine immunization, a single case led to a logarithmic increase in the number of transmissions from person-to-person. From these two European studies, it would be anticipated that exposure of a limited number of individuals would result in an expansion factor of 10- to 20-fold. Inactivation of aerosol virus takes place over a period of approximately 48 h, as reviewed (Fenner, 2002).

9. Management of a smallpox outbreak

As soon as a diagnosis of smallpox is entertained, suspected infected individuals should be isolated and all household contacts vaccinated, if vaccine is available. Because of the potential of aerosol transmission, if feasible, patients should be managed in the home environment as it may prevent person-to-person spread. Vaccination administered within the first few days after exposure (up to 4 days) may prevent or significantly ameliorate subsequent illness. Currently, vaccine deployment, namely 'ring vaccination' versus universal, is under discussion to prevent the appearance of new cases.

Because of aerosol transmission, smallpox transmission within the hospital environment has been recognized as a problem for some time. As a consequence, many health care providers established two facilities for the delivery of health-related services during epidemics of smallpox. Standby hospitals dealt only with patients having smallpox.

10. Summary

The potential use of smallpox has ominous implications, particularly given its rapidity of spread amongst susceptible individuals. As we have learned from the deployment of anthrax in North America during the fall of 2001 and early 2002, aerosol release of a potentially life-threatening agent is both feasible and devastating. The terror engendered by such a series of events is such that it provides an agent with apt capability of serving the purposes of generating fear. With the recognition that improved vaccines will take time to develop and the lack of immediate antiviral therapy, research efforts to develop treatments and improve vaccines should be of high priority to the United Stated Research Establishment. As reported in *Emerging Infectious Diseases* in July of 2002, all of the above suggestions are being investigated by a team of investigators from the CDC (LeDuc et al., 2002).

Acknowledgements

Studies performed by the author and herein reported were initiated and supported under a contract (NO1-AI-65306, NO1-AI-15113, and NO1-AI-62554) with the Development and Applications Branch of the National Institute of Allergy and Infectious Diseases (NIAID), a Program Project Grant (PO1 AI 24009), by grants from the General Clinical Research Center Program (RR-032) and the State of Alabama.

References

Bray, M., Martinez, M., Smee, D.F., Kefauver, D., Thompson, E., Huggins, J.W., 2000. Cidofovir protects mice against lethal aerosol or intranasal cowpox virus challenge. J. Infect. Dis. 181, 1019.

12 *R.J. Whitley/Antiviral Research 57 (2003) 7–12*

Centers for Disease Control and Prevention, 1990. Vaccinia (smallpox) vaccine recommendations of the immunization practices advisory committee. MMWR 40 (RR-14), 445–448.

Centers for Disease Control and Prevention, 1998. Human monkeypox–Kasai Oriental, Democratic Republic of Congo, February 1996–October 1997. JAMA 279, 189–192.

Davies, E.G., Thrasher, A., Lacey, K., Harper, J., 1999. Topical cidofovir for severe molluscum contagiosum. Lancet 353, 20442.

Dixon, C.W., 1948. Smallpox in Tripolitania, 1946: an epidemiological and clinical study of 500 cases, including trials of penicillin treatment. J. Hyg. 46, 351–377.

El-Ad, R., Roth, Y., Winder, A., 1990. The persistence of neutralizing antibodies after revaccination against smallpox. J. Infect. Dis. 161, 446–448.

Fenner, F., 2002. In: Richmond, D.D., Whitley, R.J. Hayden, F.G. (Eds.), Clinical Virology, 2nd ed. ASM Press, Washington, DC, pp. 359–374.

Fenner, F., Henderson, D.A., Arita, I., Jezek, Z., Ladnyi, I.D., 1988. Smallpox and Its Eradication, vol. 1460. World Health Organization, Geneva, Switzerland.

Geerinck, K., Lukito, G., Snoeck, R., DeVos, R., De Clercq, E., Vanrenterghem, Y., Degreef, H., Maes, B., 2001. A case of human art in an immunocompromised patient treated successfully with cidofovir cream. J. Med. Virol. 64, 543–549.

Goldstein, J.A., Neff, J.M., Lane, J.M., Koplan, J.P., 1975. Smallpox vaccination reactions, prophylaxis and therapy of complications. Pediatrics 55, 342–3347.

Henderson, D.A., Arita, I., Shafa, E., 1972. Studies of the bifurcated needle and recommendations for its use. WHO Smallpox Eradications Paper SE/72.5, Geneva, Switzerland.

Henderson, D.A., Inglesby, T.V., Gartlett, J.G., Ascher, M.S., Eitzen, E., Jahrling, P.B., Hauer, J., Layton, M., McDade, J., Osterholm, M.T., O'Toole, T., Parker, G., Perl, T., Russell, P.K., Tonat, K., and the Working Group on Civilian Biodefense, 1999. Smallpox as a biological weapon. JAMA 281, 2127–2137.

Hirayama, M., 1975. The Vaccination: Theory and Practice. International Medical Foundation of Japan, pp. 113–122.

Huggins, J.W., Baker, R.O., Beadle, J.R., Hostetler, K.Y., 2002. Orally active ether lipid prodrugs of cidofovir for the treatment of smallpox. Antivir. Res. 53, A66.

Ibarra, V., Blanco, J.R., Oteo, J.A., Rosel, L., 2000. Efficacy of cidofovir in the treatment of recalcitrant molluscum contagiosum in an AIDS patient. Acta Derm. Venereol. 80, 315–316.

Institute of Medicine, 1999. Assessment of Future Scientific Need for Live Variola Virus. National Academy Press, Washington, DC.

Kempe, C.H., 1960. Studies on smallpox and complications of smallpox vaccination. Pediatrics 26, 176–189.

Kern, E.R., Hartline, C., Harden, E., Keith, K., Rodriguez, N., Beadle, J.R., Hostetler, K.Y., 2002. Enhanced inhibition of orthopoxvirus replication in vitro by alkoxyalklyl esters of cidofovir and cyclic cidofovir. Antimicrob. Agents Chemother. 46, 991–995.

Lalezari, J.P., Staagg, R.J., Kuppermann, B.D., Holland, G.N., Kramer, F., Ives, D.V., Youle, M., Robinson, M.R., Drew, W.L., Jaffee, H.S., 1997. Intravenous cidofovir for peripheral cytomegalovirus retinitis in patients with AIDS: a randomized, controlled trial. Ann. Intern. Med. 126, 257–263.

Lane, J.M., Ruben, F.L., Neff, J.M., Millar, J.D., 1969. Complications of smallpox vaccination, 1968: national surveillance in the United States. N. Engl. J. Med. 281, 1201–1208.

LeDuc, J.W., Damon, I., Relman, D.A., Huggins, J., Jahrling, P.B., 2002. Smallpox research activities: U.S. Interagency Collaboration, 2001. Emerg. Infect. Dis. 8, 743–745.

Mack, T.M., 1972. Smallpox in Europe 1950–71. J. Infect. Dis. 125, 161–169.

Mack, T.M., Thomas, D.B., Khan, M.M., 1972. Epidemiology of smallpox in West Pakistan, II: determinants of intravillage spread other than acquired immunity. Am. J. Epidemiol. 95, 157–168.

Marsden, J.P., 1948. Variola minor: a personal analysis of 13,686 cases. Bull. Hyg. 23, 735–746.

McClain, D.J., Harrison, S., Yeager, C.L., Cruz, J., Ennis, F.A., Gibbs, P., 1997. Immunologic responses to vaccinia vaccines administered by different pare routes. J. Infect. Dis. 175, 756–763.

Meadows, K.P., Tyring, S.K., Pavia, A.T., Rallis, T.M., 1997. Resolution of recalcitrant molluscum contagiosum. Arch. Dermatol. 133, 987–990.

Meltzer, M.I., Damon, I., LeDuc, J.W., Millar, J.D., 2001. Modeling potential responses to smallpox as a bioterrorist weapon. Emerg. Infect. Dis. 7, 959–969.

Neyts, J., De Clercq, E., 1993. Efficacy of (S)-1-(3-hydroxy-2-phosphonylmethoxypropyl) cytosine for the treatment of lethal vaccinia virus infections in severe combined immune deficiency. J. Med. Virol. 41, 242–246.

Neyts, J., De Clercq, E., 2001. Efficacy of 2-amino-7-(1,3-dihydroxy-2-propoxymethyl) purine for treatment of vaccinia virus (orthopoxvirus) infections in mice. Antimicrob. Agents Chemother. 45, 84–87.

Redfield, R.R., Wright, C.D., James, W.D., Jones, S.T., Brown, C., Burke, D., 1987. Disseminated vaccinia in a military recruit with human immunodeficiency virus (HIV). N. Engl. J. Med. 316, 673–676.

Sharp, J.C.M., Fletcher, W.P., 1973. Experience of antivaccinia immunoglobulin in the United Kingdom. Lancet 1, 656–659.

Smee, D.F., Bailey, K.W., Sidwell, R.W., 2001a. Treatment of lethal vaccinia virus respiratory infections in mice with cidofovir. Antivir. Chem. Chemother. 12, 71–76.

Smee, D.F., Bailey, K.W., Sidwell, R.W., 2002. Treatment of lethal cowpox virus respiratory infections in mice with 2-amino-7-((1,3-dihydroxy-2-propoxy)methyl) purine esters or cidofovir and cyclic ester prodrug. Antivir. Res. 54, 113–120.

Smee, D.F., Bailey, K.W., Wong, M.H., Sidwell, R.W., 2001b. Effects of cidofovir on the pathogenesis of a lethal vaccinia virus respiratory infection in mice. Antivir. Res. 52, 55–62.

Toro, J.R., Wood, L.V., Patel, N.K., Turner, M.L., 2000. Topical cidofovir: a novel treatment for recalcitrant molluscum contagiosum in children infected with human immunodeficiency virus 1. Arch. Dermatol. 136, 983–985.

World Health Organization, 1980. The Global Eradication of Smallpox: Final Report of the Global Commission for the Certification of Smallpox Eradication. World Health Organization, Geneva, Switzerland.

Zabawski Jr, E.J., Cockerell, C.J., 1999. Topical cidofovir for molluscum contaglosum in children. Pediatr. Dermatol. 16, 414–415.

[12]

The Prospect of Nuclear and Biological Terrorism

Joseph W. Foxell, Jr.*

This paper contends that the current dangers posed by terrorism will become much more severe in the short- to mid-term future, due to increasing terrorist access to a wide range of materials and technological expertise for manufacturing biological and nuclear weapons. To cope with these growing threats to survival, agencies must immediately set-up and carry-out changes in national and international policies to reduce the risks posed by new, virulent forms of terrorism. This article proposes several such specific measures.

The Escalating Threat of Nuclear Terrorism

The Risk of Nuclear Terrorism

Weak access-control safeguards for nuclear bomb-making resources in many areas throughout the territories of the former Soviet Union may have already allowed the diversion of fissionable material necessary for building an atomic bomb to nations sponsoring rogue-state terrorism. The actualization factor for this risk potential is high, a conjecture underlined by Central Intelligence Agency estimates that at least 3 per cent of Russia's tactical nuclear arsenal of land mines and artillery shells remains unaccounted. If this has already happened, it now exposes American cities to a dual-sided, malignant danger. The first peril is that such material could build an Iranian, Iraqi, Sudanese, Syrian, Lebanese, Afghan or Libyan nuclear weapon, which its possessor might pass on to terror-group surrogates who would then threaten its use to cantilever changes in US foreign or domestic policies. A second hazard is the possibility that such terrorist subordinates can now deliver this atomic bomb to urban-core heartlands via small boat, glider, van or truck (Stern, 1996).

Technical advances in fabricating processes for the miniaturization of nuclear weapons have made such an event increasingly probable. Here, the United States and Israel are most at risk due to the volatility of political flashpoints throughout the Middle-East, where, during episodes of crisis-induced tension, such rogue-state nuclear, chemical or biological terrorism could receive wide-scale public and regime support. This particularly endangers Israel as more than 50 per cent of its citizens live within a twenty-five-kilometre radius of Tel Aviv. Unclaimed nuclear attack by such hidden adversaries would leave the victim without an obviously responsible nation to target for retaliation, rendering Washington's and Jerusalem's interdiction nuclear strike forces tactically impotent. Because extremism is an inherent element in both religious-fanatic and rogue-state terrorism, extrapolating that the detonation of a primitive nuclear weapon, or the use of a radiological-contamination device (a 'dirty bomb' that spreads nuclear radiation without exploding), represents a continuation of past behaviour, not a radical departure, is logical. Furthermore, the threatened spectre of a nuclear holocaust would be a powerful sword in the arsenals of terrorists as they up the ante when trying to gain the freedom of imprisoned or encircled comrades. It could prove decisive when used as an end-game tactic in a major terrorist operation, particularly if this forced a mortifying conclusion and consequent loss of political credibility on a publicly-humiliated opponent.

Iran May Spread Nuclear Materials to Terrorists

Iran's lengthy history of support for several surrogate-terror organizations poses an acute danger that rogue-state terrorists will eventually attain nuclear capabilities. Tehran's agreement with Moscow to resume construction on the long-delayed, eight-million-dollar project to build a large-scale, thirteen-hundred megawatt pressurized-water nuclear reactor, Bushehr I, at Halileh on Iran's Gulf coast, intensifies the likelihood of this threat (*New York Times*, 1995b; *Jordan Times*, 21 April, 1996). Adding further to these concerns, China has agreed with Tehran to build two, three-hundred megawatt reactors near Iran's border with Pakistan (Foreign Report, 1995a: 3). Although Tehran has accepted

International Atomic Energy Agency (IAEA) non-proliferation safeguards, the lessons learned from disclosures concerning North Korea's and Iraq's evasions of such controls teach us that rogue states (that is, nations with histories of using surrogate-group terrorism) will resort to all possible means of deception to further their covert nuclear weapons' acquisition programs. The plutonium that Tehran could obtain from secretly bypassing non-proliferation safeguards at these proposed nuclear plants would boost its atomic munitions' production capability substantially, offering tangible prospect for exponential growth in the lethality of Iranian-sponsored terrorism (Milivojevic, 1995; Schmemann, 1995). US Under Secretary of State for International Security Affairs, Lynn Davis, has accused Iran of trying to obtain nuclear arms by stealing the materials and technology needed to construct atomic weapons: 'We have reasons to believe that the Iranians are looking to see whether they can find means to augment the development of their own capabilities. If they succeed in stealing it, they can reduce the time needed for developing a weapon dramatically' (*Muslim News*, 1996: 13). Most worryingly, there are reports that Iran may have purchased an intact nuclear weapon — or more likely, all such a bomb's hardware except the nuclear-core material itself — from Kazakhstan in the earliest days of the confusion resulting from the USSR's breakup in 1991 (*Intelligence Digest*, 1996: 3). Such an event would be extremely worrisome because of hints that Iran may again resort to a major rogue-state-terrorist, anti-US offensive to disrupt the ongoing Middle-Eastern peace process, and, thus, distract attention from Tehran's current domestic economic and political crises. These fears have substance, as Iran had traceable links to three significant terror attacks in 1994–1995: the bomb blast outside a Jewish-owned building in Buenos Aires in July 1994 that killed ninety-six; the sabotage destruction of an airliner carrying mostly Jewish passengers in Panama that same month killing twenty-one; and the failed attempt to car-bomb the Israeli Embassy in Bangkok in March 1995 (*Foreign Report*, 1995b: 2, Hoffman and Hoffman, 1995: 210–211).

The CIA's prediction that Iran could probably build a nuclear bomb within five years, while using only presently extant facilities, compounds this dilemma (Milivojevic, 1995: 14).

Since Iran has aggressively sought to build-up its dominance capabilities in and around the Persian Gulf over the past three years, the prospect of a surreptitious atomic attack by Tehran's terror surrogates on a US aircraft-carrier-led flotilla patrolling the region's waterways, has prospectively blunted not only US guarantees of freedom of passage for commercial maritime traffic — including economically strategic oil tankers — through the Straits of Hormuz, but also the effectiveness of a proposed American-Israeli mutual security pact. Compounding these difficulties, an Iranian-inspired nuclear, chemical or biological attack against Israeli territory or US military brigade encampments in Saudi Arabia, Oman, Qatar, Bahrain or Kuwait could pose weighty dilemmas in Washington, due to the ambiguity that the possible role of Tehran's terror surrogates in such an attack would introduce when setting about to the task of definitively identifying Iran as the assailant.

Where Will Terrorists Get Nuclear Weapons?

Louis Freeh, Director of the Federal Bureau of Investigation, has identified the smuggling of nuclear materials as 'the greatest long-term threat to the security of the United States' (*Kansas City Star*, 1994:A4). Although other states (for example, Egypt, Taiwan, Pakistan, Saudi Arabia, Indonesia, Singapore, the United Arab Emirates, Argentina or Turkey — to name only a few) might willingly participate in such trafficking, the chief buyers of illicit nuclear contraband are rogue states that have covert nuclear weapons' acquisition programs (Klare, 1995: 26). In 1994, Stella Rimington, then director of the UK's MI5, estimated that 'some two dozen governments are currently trying to obtain such [that is, nuclear] technology. A number of these countries sponsor or even practice terrorism and we cannot rule out the possibility that these weapons could be used for that purpose' (Cameron, 1996: 424). Obtaining such fissile materials would spare about ten years of development time from proliferations-control-evading nuclear-weapons-acquisitions programs, while improving the chances of keeping such plans hidden (Cameron, 1996: 423). This circle includes Libya, Syria, Iraq, and Iran, but excludes North Korea, as most arms control experts rate Pyongyang as nuclear capable (*Jane's Intelligence Review*, 1996: 7). If any of these 'pariahs' (that is, rogue states censured by international bodies for unlawful efforts to develop weapons of mass destruction) achieve success in getting the bomb, this would seriously escalate the risk that some form of nuclear terrorism, involving at least thousands of casualties, will occur sometime within the next decade.

One avenue that could bestow nuclear capability on terrorists has been too little examined — high-level radioactive-hazardous-waste facilities. Because of the scant attention this area has received, it is imperative that nuclear security programs develop new methodologies to ensure that contraband raw materials deriving from nuclear-medical technology waste products, scrapped tactical or strategic nuclear weapons, or expended atomic-power-generation fuel rods do not supply terrorists with sufficient fissile matter to build a bomb. Additionally, since enterprising terrorists can presently mine on their own for secondary-source atomic-bomb-making elements at nuclear-research institutes, we must also provide these inadequately-protected radiological-substances repositories with more effective anti-pilferage safeguards. This risk is particularly acute at those sites in Russia that have had documented nuclear-material thefts, including the Orel branch of the Moscow Instrument-Making Institute, the All-Russia Research Institute of Experimental Physics, the Scientific Research Institute of Technical Physics in Snezhinsk, the All-Union Isotope Association, and the Kurchatov Research Center (Williams and Woessner, 1995: 213, Woessner, 1995). Also at significant risk are several atomic-power plants and nuclear-related facilities in those Commonwealth of Independent States' (CIS) areas currently experiencing significant intervals of social or political disorder, such as the Center for Applied Research at Georgia's Institute of Physics (Gordon, 1997: A1) and Armenia's recently-restarted nuclear-power plant that sits astride a geological fault line (Specter, 1997: A1), as well as others in Ukraine, Moldova, and the Central Asian republics. Also, Chechen or Tajik separatist terrorists could raid such facilities to gain nuclear capability, or even blow them up as part of their war with Russia — a possibility that becomes more likely as Russian forces become increasingly bogged down in the conflicts in Chechnya and Tajikistan.

Because more-recent technology, nuclear power-generation spent fuel-rods contain mostly plutonium-240, rather than plutonium-239, their use by terrorists in assembling a bomb would make the weight of that device heavier than one using plutonium-239 — and, therefore, harder to transport, conceal or deliver than the plutonium-239-based weapon [plutonium-239 is ideal raw material for building a bomb] (Sidhu, 1996a: 171). Moreover, since the International Atomic Energy Agency's (IAEA) safeguards-standards' committee might notice the diversion of a nuclear-power-generation facility's reactor to producing bomb-grade fissionable materials when it reduced the electricity available within the national power-grid, rogue states have an additional reason to gamble that a comparable clandestine switch of purpose in a nuclear-research reactor, whose output is not so closely monitored, could more easily escape observation. Thus, using atomic bomb-making materials deriving from a nuclear research centre's reactor that has been clandestinely

dedicated to plutonium-239 production, would be preferable to reprocessing or employing expended fuel-cycle rods containing plutonium-240 when rogue-states engage in creating nuclear feedstocks destined for surrogate-terrorist end-users. Therefore, research reactors often serve as quiet incubators for covert nuclear weapons' acquisition projects of proliferation-safeguards-evading countries. For example, since 1985, India has used its Dhruva research reactor at the Bhabha Atomic Research Center, whose official role is the 'production of isotopes and development of power-reactor technology' to produce twenty kilograms of un-safeguarded weapons-grade plutonium per year (Sidhu, 1996a: 171). This forms a prime danger that chauvinistic 'super patriots' may divert shrinkage-type inventory losses to terror surrogates. Additionally, such covert acquisition programs are subject to extortionate blackmail by terrorists, who might threaten to publicize details of these clandestine nuclear capabilities, unless the possessors shared such materials with them. The thus-threatened government might decide to hand over some nuclear substance upon receiving assurances that terrorists would target any devices built with it elsewhere (Schelling, 1982: 62).

To provide a gauge for understanding how quickly a rogue state can create nuclear feedstocks for possible terrorist use by employing a dedicated research institute's reactor, consider that the CIA estimates that North Korea's five megawatt research reactor at Yongbyon has manufactured between four and seven kilograms of plutonium per annum since 1985 — its first year of operation — theoretically yielding enough material for the construction of at least seven atomic bombs (Croddy, 1966: 273; *Jane's Intelligence Review*, 1996: 7; Gordon, 1997: A1). In this regard, noting that the atomic material used to build the bomb exploded in India's 1974 nuclear test derived from the Canadian-built CIRUS forty megawatt Indian research reactor is important (Sidhu, 1996a: 171).

On the other hand, technologically-inexperienced terror-group fabricators might forgo the size advantages of a plutonium-derived bomb and try to obtain highly enriched uranium for constructing their first atomic device, as this type of weapon requires a gun-barrel type, bomb-trigger mechanism that is much easier to build than the more complicated implosion detonator demanded by plutonium-based weapons (Sidhu, 1996b: 280). Several seizures of highly-enriched uranium by successful German and Russian intelligence 'sting operations' suggest this material is available on the nuclear-substances black market in quantities sufficient to build a terrorist micro-bomb.

The Inevitability of Nuclear Terrorism

Several counter-terrorism experts and arms-control specialists consider that prospective acts of nuclear terrorism are inevitable due to the widening porosity of international nuclear-reagent, anti-smuggling controls, as unfortunately, raw weapons materials are only too-readily available for sale via a spent-nuclear-fuel-rod causeway presently running west through the territories of the former Soviet Union and its satellites into Central Europe. It is one of many, as former CIA director John Deutch, in testimony before Congress on 20 March 1996, highlighted a second transhipment path through southern Russia and Afghanistan as 'a particular source of concern' to US counter-terrorism security planners (Cameron, 1996: 423). The following history illustrates the dangers posed by such trafficking. On 9 April 1992, the police in Miskolc, in northeastern Hungary, reported arresting two Hungarians after seizing a 5.7 pound cache of fuel-cycle uranium found in the trunk of their automobile (US Department of State, 1992a: 1). Thieves had taken this material from power-generating plants in Ukraine. Further investigation determined that this material came from a power-generating plant in Ukraine. On 3 June 1992, confiscation by an Austrian counter-terrorism task force of several partial nuclear-fuel-cycle rods stolen from an atomic-power plant in the Czech and Slovak Federal Republic revealed an even more disconcerting customs-control lapse (US Department of State, 1992b: 1). According to the Austrian Counter-Espionage Intelligence Service, East European organized criminals had offered this material to an unnamed Middle-Eastern country (Indian intelligence sources assert that Pakistan was the attempted purchaser) (Sidhu, 1996a). In August 1994, German police arrested a Colombian and two Spaniards in Munich for illicit possession of plutonium-239, enriched to a level of 87 per cent. Though the amount was small (three-hundred and sixty-three grams, as well as two-hundred and one grams of lithium-6) this event illustrates the widening diversity of the nuclear-substances black market (Williams and Woessner, 1995). It is gravely worrying because plutonium-239 and lithium-6 are the chief components of thermonuclear bombs. Most probably, the sellers offered these materials as samples of a larger consignment for later delivery. These fissionable substances originated in Russia — very likely deriving from the Russian Tomsk-7 nuclear plant — but could also have been produced by a dedicated weapons' grade plutonium-production research

reactor (Atkinson, 1994). Former Soviet military stockpiles are equally vulnerable. For example, in January 1996, military prosecutors in Belarus tried three men *in absentia* for the theft of eight kilograms of plutonium taken from the former twenty-fifth arsenal of the Soviet Strategic Rocket Forces (Foreign Report, 1996a: 8). According to Freeh, 'the traffickers and middlemen handling [such] materials have included internationally organized gangs and smugglers, as well as individual businessmen and con men' (Williams and Woessner, 1995: 215).

Most alarmingly, although the plutonium which rogue-state terrorists could obtain from re-processing even the largest number of spent fuel-rods so far reportedly recovered due to undercover nuclear substances' anti-smuggling operations, is beneath CIA low-end estimates for atomic-bomb-making requirements, these confiscated materials would suffice to construct a low-level, irradiation-style radiological contamination device. Although lacking the devastating power of a nuclear blast, this type of weapon could kill thousands, while transforming a large urban area into an environmentally devastated wasteland.

In fact, terror-group atomic capabilities may be fast approaching the threshold limits for building an exploitable device, as, despite International Atomic Energy Agency (IAEA) assumptions that terrorist fabricators need eight kilograms of plutonium or twenty-five kilograms of highly-enriched uranium to construct a one-kiloton fission bomb, less than three kilograms of the former or six kilograms of the latter may be all that knowledgeable experts require. Thomas B. Cochran, senior scientist at the National Resources Defense Council, a private nuclear research group, estimates that 'a technically-competent scientific team could use twelve pounds of highly-enriched uranium to fabricate a weapon with a yield of a kiloton' (Gordon, 1997: A6). Some analysts have speculated that little more than a kilogram of plutonium could be sufficient to build a low-yield, miniature bomb.

When terrorists, eventually, obtain enough nuclear material to satisfy a detonable bomb's fissionable requisites, the first device they can probably assemble and explode would be an atomic demolition munition (ADM) — in essence, a nuclear land-mine. Such devices are similar to conventional land-mines, but have greater range of destructive capability. While qualifying as a 'device' — the label given a nuclear bomb that has an unpredictable yield — rather than a 'weapon' — where the force of the bomb's explosion falls within a pre-determined range — the ADM would, if detonated in any heavily populated urban area, devastate that city, rendering it uninhabitable for decades.

Adding to the likelihood of this transpiring,

stolen nuclear materials keep turning-up with frightening frequency — as evidenced by the discovery during early 1995 of seventeen hundred and sixty grams of Radium-226 in Kiisa, Estonia (*Foreign Report*, 1995b). There, several townspeople suffered lethal exposure levels after having secreted these radioactive bars on their person while transporting them to covert market places. Posing a more crucial problem, the former Soviet Union's abandoned nuclear submarine base at Paldiski, Estonia, offers rich off-shore troves of easy-to-retrieve nuclear materials. The Russian military ordered these radioactive elements hastily dumped in shallow waters, despite the otherwise leisurely pace of Russia's 1991 military withdrawal from the three newly-independent Baltic States republics, as Moscow chose to discard nuclear wastes *in situ* rather than provide for their adequate, but more costly, transport to, and disposal in, the Russian Federation. Indeed, the USSR's training reactors in Estonia were themselves only shipped to Russia's main nuclear-waste storage depot at Chelyabinsk in 1994, as it was not until then that the TUK-18 spent-fuel casks needed for their transport by rail could be spared from other nuclear-fuel-rod salvage operations (Handler, 1995: 140). Also of concern are the three-thousand tons of radioactive waste products at Sillamae (Marx, 1994: 566). Several more sites within the Commonwealth of Independent States (CIS) and in Russia's former East European satellites, where similar nuclear substances were left dangerously unsecured for several months after the loss of atomic energy administrative controls due to the then-occurring disintegration of the Union of Soviet Socialist Republics, now present counter-terrorism planners with the complex task of devising strategies to limit similar risk exposure dangers (Gordon, 1997). The danger revealed by the theft at the Ingnalina power plant in Lithuania, where over six-hundred pounds of uranium and strontium disappeared in 1993, is but one example of the staggering dimensions of the perils directly stemming from this chaotic period (Williams and Woessner, 1995: 213).

Additionally, the lack of secure high-level radioactive-waste storage facilities and adequate disposal procedures has created many malignant risks in today's Russia, including the possible theft or diversion of atomic bomb-making resources — posing the danger that such materials may, eventually, find their way into the hands of terrorists, if this has not happened already (Williams and Woessner, 1995: 213). The most critical of these hazards are at two of Russia's Pacific Fleet's land-based facilities for storing, handling and transhipping radioactive waste and spent-nuclear fuel sited in Shkotovo and Kamchatka. Here, thousands of spent-nuclear-fuel assemblies, dozens of damaged submarine reactor compartments resulting from severe reactor accidents in 1979–1985, and tons of radioactive wastes 'pose serious environmental consequences' of staggering proportions (Harder, 1995: 140). Also, several hardware components from Russian nuclear missiles have been found in Iraq, signaling the potential widespread dispersion of atomic bomb-related equipment to rogue states (Stern, 1996). Collectively, these events jeopardize the prognosis for the integrity of global nuclear controls.

Since successful anti-terrorist operations reveal only terrorist failures, no corresponding way exists of knowing when terrorists have silently contravened nuclear safeguards. Prudently, national security planners should acknowledge that some atomic substances most probably have already fallen into the hands of radical terror groups, as in reality, if nuclear-security anti-smuggling measures succeed at a 98 per cent rate — which is a much higher reliability ratio than most counter-terrorism experts and law enforcement officials consider obtainable — this would still leave a 2 per cent lacuna in the efficacy of non-proliferation control regimens (Perlez, 1995: A3). A more pessimistic assessment contends 'that at least a third of the nuclear material stolen and traded illegally escapes detection and seizure' (Williams and Woessner, 1995: 208). In this light, it is not surprising that a full-fledged incident of nuclear terrorism has already occurred, as happened in Moscow during late 1995, when Chechen separatist leader Shamil Basayev, brazenly told Russian television reporters where to unearth a thirty-pound box containing radioactive cesium that was then found buried under the snow near the entrance to Izmailovsky Park, one of Moscow's most popular recreation areas (Specter, 1995). This package emitted three-hundred times the normal background radiation, marking the first documented use of a radiological-contamination device by terrorists (Cameron, 1996: 425).

How Terrorists Can Get Atomic-Bomb Source Material

Besides these occurrences, several potential breaches in the matrix of international anti-smuggling customs controls and nuclear non-proliferation safeguards increase the likelihood that atomic bomb-making materials may fall into the hands of terrorists. The operations of Iranian-backed terror surrogate groups — whose anti-American zealotry underpins Tehran's cynical campaign to exploit the Islamic revitalist religious and cultural renaissance to drive American business, commerce and investment from traditionally observant Moslem countries — are spreading across the Maghreb. If such efforts lead to an Iranian-backed satrapy in either Niger, Algeria or Mali, this could allow the diversion of some uranium produced there to religious-fanatic or rogue-state terror groups. Analogous Muslim unrest in uranium mining areas in western China poses comparable opportunities for further erosion of international nuclear weapons' non-proliferation protocols. Worse, Kazakhstan has agreed to sell enriched uranium — possibly bomb-grade — to Libya as reactor fuel. It is not clear if Tripoli will use this material to make nuclear weapons or pass it along to its surrogate-terror groups, but Libya, an oil exporting country, has no nuclear reactors (*New York Times*, 1995a). Adding to these concerns, if the currently besieged government in Algeria falls to a vehemently anti-Western Islamic fundamentalist regime, willing to co-operate with rogue-state terror-group sponsors, such as Iran, Libya, Iraq, North Korea, Syria or Sudan, this could permit the re-opening of the former French Army nuclear detonation test site at Reggany, in the southern Sahara, as an international terror consortium's atomic weapons' proving ground.

Russian 'Soft' Support for Terrorists

Western intelligence agencies have amply documented the former Soviet Union's longstanding patronage for Iraqi, Libyan, Cuban and Syrian rogue-state terrorism. Yet, Bonn's 1991 release of German Democratic Republic State Security and Intelligence (STASI) dossiers on the Middle-East, shocked many counter-terrorism experts by revealing the enormous extent of the USSR's lesser-known financial, political and logistical support for Tehran's surrogate group espionage, sabotage and terrorism directed against the West. As part of this shadowy war, Russia's covert nuclear co-operation with Iran continues into the present, despite interruptions in 1979–1982 and again in 1989–1993. Such secret aid enabled Iran's Nuclear Research Center to get critical assembly capability at its five-million kilowatt reactor in 1990 (Milivojevic, 1995). This reactor may now be producing weapons' grade plutonium in quantities sufficient to allow Iran to explode a prototype nuclear device before the turn of the century. More worryingly, many counter-terrorism analysts warn that Tehran has strong incentives to forgo the status that a successful demonstration test would confer and directly turn such a weapon over to its terror-group protégés. Factionalism within Iran's current leadership at the time of a liberalizing governmental transition/succession could lead to unilateral dispersal of any hoarded nuclear

substances to militants or terror surrogates, who would be committed to carrying out radical goals no longer pursued by a more moderate regime.

Providing assistance in nuclear development to the enemies of the United States whenever Washington opposes Moscow's goals is, progressively, developing into a major tactic within the context of Russia's contemporary foreign policy, as evidenced by the Kremlin's previously mentioned agreement to help Tehran in building a large-scale nuclear reactor at Halileh. This action underlined Moscow's umbrage at American endorsement of NATO's expansion plan to incorporate four of the USSR's former satellites — Poland, the Czech republic, Slovakia and Hungary — into what Russia's military leadership still perceives as an anti-Russian alliance (Greenhouse, 1995). Indeed, the technical assistance that Moscow provided to Iranian nuclear engineers in starting their fledgling research reactor in 1990 may have been a tit-for-tat response to Washington's covert aid to Afghan Mujahideen insurgents stalwartly challenging Russia's then-loosening grip on Afghanistan. According to *Segodnya*, a hard-line nationalist Russian newspaper, Moscow would threaten to sell nuclear weapons to Iran and Iraq, if NATO invites Estonia, Latvia or Lithuania to join — an event that *Segodnya's* editorial writers claimed would be as threatening to Russia as the presence of Soviet missiles in Cuba was to the United States during Kennedy's presidency (*Foreign Report*, 1995a). The decision by Russia's Nuclear Energy Ministry to aid Cuba in resuming construction on the long-mothballed nuclear power plant in Juragua, is further evidence that Moscow has, primarily, designed its bilateral nuclear cooperation policy to threaten geopolitical adversaries, as its announcement came at a time of heightened US/Cuban and US/Russian tensions (Rohter, 1996). Similarly, Russian foot dragging in helping resolve the critical issue posed by several large caches of inadequately-safeguarded nuclear materials in Georgia, Kazakhstan, and Uzbekistan that terrorists or organized criminals could easily steal, may similarly have stemmed from Moscow's desire to pressure Washington to delete Slovakia from the list of first-round invitees to NATO membership.

Biological Weapons

A Fast-Growing Threat

Biological terrorism is based on using microorganisms, (that is, viruses, bacteria, fungi, rickettsiae, and protozoa) or toxins (poisonous chemicals from organic matter) as weapons (Smith 1991: 483). This class of weapons present a significant risk that a potently-incremented terrorist capability will soon threaten world order and global stability. A failure to solve the problems posed by the palpable lack of effectively-implemented controls on trafficking in biological pathogens makes the realization of this hazard even more likely (Latter, 1994: 93). Due to a want of tightly-administered restrictions on purchasing and transhipping such materials, terror groups can easily obtain feedstock starter batches of many different bacteria, including yersinia pestis, bacillus anthracis, vibrio cholera, salmonella typhi and clostridium botulinum. The prognosis for controlling the proliferation of this menace is poor, as the processes for manufacturing biological weapons are not only well known but also much less complicated than those for making nuclear or chemical bombs — and the needed materials are cheap and readily available. For instance, twenty-five kilograms of anthrax, botulism, alfatoxins, or other deadly viral or bacterial agents will suffice to build a biological-toxin dispersion device (or a more conventional pathogenic-substance explosive bomb) that can devastate a several-miles-wide region for decades. Compounding the difficulty of devising adequate countermeasures, the physical site requirements for biological-weapons assembly plants are small and the location of this type of facility lacks a telltale signature, thus rendering the use of satellite imagery futile. This leaves law-enforcement officials without effective discovery mechanisms to alert them to the existence of a terrorist biological-bomb factory that could be operating right under their noses (Baily, 1995: 385). Because many microorganisms are sensitive to ultraviolet light, terrorist use of such a weapon would most probably be at night (Smith, 1991: 486).

Worse, from a terrorism control standpoint, a handful of lay people can produce biological-agent bomb-sized payloads, some of which can be prepared in as little as a few days. Moreover, these weapons do not require sophisticated storage arrangements and cost only a few thousand dollars to produce (Bailey, 1995: 386). The former Director of the Central Intelligence Agency, John Deutch, has observed that 'any modern pharmaceutical facility can produce biological warfare agents as easily as vaccines or antibiotics' (Weiner, 1996:A8). In contrast to a nuclear device, that must weigh at least two hundred and fifty pounds, the light weight — as much as 80 per cent less — of biological munition reduces the bomb's physical dimensions to suitcase-sized devices that urban terrorists, riding municipal subway trains, can deliver. In the self-encapsulated environments of subway tunnel labyrinths, underground ventilation ducts connected to street-level air

exchange towers, would widely propagate a biological toxin released by such a weapon throughout a city. Tossed from a moving train by terrorists or sprayed as droplets in the air using aerosol-dispersing devices, these next-generation terror weapons could kill tens of thousands, while paralyzing government, commerce and industry within a major urban area. The resulting contamination could take years to clean-up.[1]

Therefore, it is hardly unexpected that several terrorist incidents involving biological agents have already taken place. During the 1970s, a mind-control-cult religious group, in Oregon, used salmonella bacteria to infect residents in a nearby town (Cameron, 1996: 425). In 1980, Parisian police raided an apartment occupied by several members of a German terrorist group, the Red Army Faction, and found lethal bacteriological pathogens. The December 1995 arrest of an Arkansas man with connections to the Minnesota Patriots Council, a right-wing survivalist terror organization, for attempting to smuggle one hundred and thirty grams of ricin, a virulent, hard-to-detect poison, into the United States further underscores the dangers that biological terrorism now presents. Nine months previously, a federal court had convicted two members of this group of planning to use ricin to murder Federal law enforcement officials (Kifner, 1995).

Additionally, terrorist-wielded bacteriological bombs present a rapidly-spiraling menace to global security, as they offer rogue states easy venues for creating an international crisis or waging covert warfare. Currently, Libya, Iran, Syria and North Korea possess domestically-manufactured biological weapons and, also, the ability to deliver them via terror-group surrogates.

New Technology Potentiates this Risk

Tehran's growing expertise in fabricating remotely-piloted reconnaissance drone aircraft introduces an equally worrisome hazard. These television guided, self-propelled vehicles can aerosol-spray biological toxins over municipal water supplies, air-drop biological bombs or deliver infective agents by crash-impact (Bailey, 1995: 383). Such capabilities make these drones ideal clandestine bomb-delivery systems for a wide-ranging variety of rogue-state terror-surrogate groups' weapons of mass destruction including nuclear and chemical weapons. On 20 February 1996, one of these devices also assaulted Israel when Hizb Allah terrorist/guerrillas launched an ultra-light aircraft from the Bani Hayyam/Markaba salient in Lebanon toward Galilee. Luckily, this pilotless drone hit a high-tension wire and the mission failed (*Foreign*

Report, 1996d). An analogous device may have attacked US soldiers during the Gulf War when a remote-controlled MIG-21, equipped with spray-nozzle foggers, for air-dispersion of biological reagents was destroyed by a US cruise missile. Additional intelligence data on Baghdad's use of this type of weaponry may, eventually, account for some perplexing cases of American soldiers complaining of yet unexplained symptoms of pathological toxin infection after returning home from Operation Desert Shield/Storm. Remotely-piloted aircraft represent a new class of technologically-advanced terror weapons, requiring immediate efforts to develop successful counter-measures.

Development of 'Designer' Biological Weapons

Breakthroughs in genetic research may soon enable terrorists to develop racially-based biological weapons that target specific ethnic groups (*Foreign Report*, 1996c). Created through modern gene-splicing techniques, such designer infective agents, potentially allow rogue-state terror sponsors to annihilate their ethnically-distinct enemies directly by fusing lethal viruses, bacteria and fungi to genetic markers for racial characteristics revealed through the Human Genome Mapping Project's research and analysis. Such current medical scourges as Lhasa hemorrhagic fever, Ebola virus, West African river blindness and drug-resistant strains of malaria and tuberculosis may become vectors of a silent ethnic cleansing that could devastate legions of unsuspecting victims whose military, health care and governmental protectors would be impotent to defend them.

The World Health Organization has estimated that if anthrax was aerosol-sprayed over a city of five million residents, the epidemic that followed would most probably kill one-hundred-thousand, while incapacitating another one-hundred-fifty thousand. If emergency rescue squads effectively carried out immediate counter-measures and emergency-care prphylaxis, they could halve casualties. However, if adequate medical and sanitary infrastructures were lacking, emergency treatment could only reduce such casualties by 5 per cent (Smith, 1991: 483). Unlike ordinary injuries, terrorist-cause biological wounding results in a further peril to those attempting to provide emergency medical care to the injured, as, if the medical personnel do not protect themselves, they will also become infected. The need for decontamination and isolation of the injured add to the psychological horror of this type of terrorism — and thus further potentiates the efficacy of the terrorists' actions. Furthermore, through modifying the genomic or protein structure of an organism or toxin, terrorists may create drug-resistant strains of

viruses and bacteria that will defy current antibiotic treatment. Such genetic engineering of bacterial and viral diseases also presents an impediment to counter-measure efforts to develop effective vaccines against the threat of biological terrorism, as production of efficacious vaccines requires knowledge of the strain of the organism beforehand (Baker, 1993: 44).

Policy Issues

The Need for International Co-operation

As of this moment, the segmental pieces that media reportage has revealed of various German, American, British, Japanese and Israeli standalone national policies to contain terrorism, appear to have been individually well crafted. However, evaluation of the multilateral coordination provided for most international terrorist-event incident management, often discovers it to be inconsistent and/or limited in scope with, seemingly, little more to offer than a hodgepodge of overlapping national bureaucracies embroiled in jurisdictional disputes or blame-avoidance fingerpointing. In view of this, a critical need exists for immediate development of a comprehensive set of multilateral convenants and policies to integrate more fully the considerable expertise and experiential wisdom gained by European, Middle-Eastern, Asian and American anti-terrorist organizations in their three-decades-long struggle to contain the threats presented by terrorism. This requires the development of several multi-disciplinary approaches to replace the existing autonomous segmental systems upon which international anti-terrorism control efforts are now predicated, in order to deny terrorists the opportunity to act or enjoy the fruits of their labors, while, simultaneously, ensuring that they pay the price for their actions. To realize this, that is, *nullum crimen sine poena* (no crime without a punishment), trans-governmental response to acts of terror, through use of deterrent-inducing measures, should be universal, swift, appropriate and effective.

Thus, the road to the solution is many tracked, but, none the less, clearly discernible. Those states finding themselves in the cross-hairs of terrorist gun-sights must improve their anti-terrorism intelligence capabilities, develop their own full-fledged counter-terrorism programs and field effectively trained intervention forces, combat-ready on a 24-hour standby basis. Steps to accomplish these goals include: the creation of nation-state-level, commando-style, hostage-rescue Special Weapons and Tactics (SWAT) teams; establishment of terrorist-crisis command and control centres; identification of effective mechanisms for more efficient use of the

INTERPOL's data-exchange capabilities; and the signing of reciprocal aid agreements with primary topical area counter-terrorism security services. Because prospective acts of terror now span a spectrum of nuclear, chemical and biological threats, the war against terrorism needs better-integrated administrative procedures. To meet these new dangers, imperiled governments have to establish more effective communication among appropriate topical anti-terrorist centres in cooperatively-allied foreign ministries, defense departments, nuclear regulatory agencies, disease control centres, drug-trafficking and money-laundering programs, law enforcement divisions and border and customs control bureaus. Besides fostering enhanced cooperation between individual thematically-specialized national agencies, this will also help use extradition laws more energetically to reinforce border controls so as to be better able to detect forged passports, visas, bills of landing fraudulently-altered, export control licenses, sensitive technology transfer authorizations and other materials' travel documents. If taken, these measures will significantly reduce terrorists' ability to obtain or traffic in nuclear, chemical and bacteriological weapons-related materials. Additionally, each vulnerable nation must establish programs for training local police in anti-terrorist tactics, interrupt international fund raising activities inside their borders by terrorist organizations and join their voices with others to convince states harboring terror groups' publicly accessible local, regional and international headquarters to shut these offices. Major airports, shipping terminals, container ports, rail depots and parcel delivery and postal services in threatened countries have to obtain modern anti-terrorist technology. This includes advanced vapor and radiation detection devices, X-ray imaging systems, robotics for handling suspected bombs and the latest radar and thermal sensors for identifying dynamite, plastic explosives and nuclear materials (Schmemann, 1996). We must undertake defensive measures against biological terrorism, including vaccination and distribution of masks and antidotes. This is essential, if medical remedies are to be applied effectively. Nations must also develop a new generation of weapons from the panoply of promising anti-terrorist strategies encompassed within the many non-lethal biological and chemical weapons currently undergoing tests at laboratories in the US, the UK, France, Japan, Israel and Russia. One such strategy uses bio-deterioration agents, that is, genetically-engineered bacteria, to eat a variety of infrastructure materials, such as rubber, concrete and metal. Another stratagem — derived from technologies developed to fight oil spills — destroys the lubricating ability of oil or fouls fuel quality through release of microbic metabolic

products. A different, but promising, approach consists of spraying terrorists with insect pheromone to attract stinging or biting insects. Chemical, non-lethal anti-terrorist deterrents include slippery sprays, instantly-bonding adhesives, super-corrosives and super-caustics. Disabling gases can also be useful — including hydrogen sulphide that causes nausea and dimethyl sulfoxide which acts as a sedative (Kier and Mercer, 1996).

Elected officials and leaders in the private sector must correlate their efforts to defeat terrorists, protect civil liberties and ensure the welfare of the public. Consequently, democratic government should stimulate the collation of a public/private consortiums to design terrorist event-handling policy guidelines, incident management plans and educational programs to make the public aware of the virulent dangers posed by terror groups' activities. When an actual terrorist attack occurs, such bodies can inform the public of the scope of the problem, while authorities are devising reactive and proactive solutions and carrying out effective countermeasures. One should couple these endeavours with innovative approaches to foster deterrent and prophylactic measures, including reinvigorated efforts at economic development and job creation in vulnerable countries to deter frustrated job seekers from succumbing to the lure of various terror groups' simplistic-solution 'social-justice' rhetoric and thus turning to terrorism.

Policy Recommendations

The following steps, if taken, will reduce the dangers posed by the threats of biological and nuclear terrorism. First, imperiled nations must cultivate greater intelligence penetration of terrorist groups. Former United States Defense Secretary Perry calls this 'the key to success in fighting terrorism' (Erlanger, 1996: A9). 'Real-time' HUMIT intelligence (that is, gathered by *in situ* agents) is an indispensable tool in helping democratic governments maintain the psychological 'upper hand' in their fight against all forms of terrorism. Secondly, national leaders must foster the public's realization that many lives will be lost if nations do not thwart terrorists armed with weapons of mass destruction and that they, therefore, must take stalwart measures to foil these terrorists from perpetrating large-scale human rights violations through acts of such savage depravity. Thirdly, one must avoid state-led dirty war tactics (regime terrorism) that would undermine the legitimacy of those governments laid siege by terrorists, as this would transform the contest into a struggle for dominance between equally unworthy adversaries. Fourthly, agencies must lead the public to understand that they may, occasionally, have to abridge individual constitutional guarantees to prevent terrorists from permanently abrogating democratic freedoms for everyone. Most democracies are extremely resilient and many have survived the temporary restrictions placed on their societies' constitutional guarantees during protracted anti-terrorism campaigns. Examples of similar present-tense transient abridgements include the ability to conduct searches of suspected terrorists and any residential and non-residential areas they occupy without judicial writs, to cordon-off designated anti-terrorist 'security' areas for lengthy periods and to impose temporary or permanent visa entrance, exit, or transit bans without legislative consent (*New York Times*, 1996:A9). Fifthly, government leaders have to remember that terrorism is a political, economic and social phenomena that must be understood within that context. Governmental spokespersons and print, voice and visual media representatives should work to develop protocols for reporting terrorist events to prevent terror groups from manipulating elected officials, government agencies, the media and the public in an attempt to achieve increased gain of their goals. Finally, avoiding a legislative or executive over-response that compromises, or even abrogates, the very system of constitutional government that the terrorists are attempting to overthrow is important. One must tightly circumscribe the extraordinary, statutory authority conferred on governmental bodies through passage of special anti-terrorist legislation and delimit the powers of counter-terrorist bureaucracies to prevent such anti-violence safeguards from infringing on the civil liberties of the general population or their misuse by being applied for non-terrorism control purposes. This is a crucial point, as without public support, agencies cannot effectively carry out anti-terrorism control measures. On the other hand, one should grant the fight against terrorism the same exemption from restrictions that other anti-crime investigations receive. Thus, exceptions made to wiretap authorization for other types of emergency exclusions — for example, such as often occur in cases of organized criminal involvement — should also apply to counter-terrorist operations. Agencies should maintain the strict quarantine of military intervention in domestic law enforcement activities. However, it makes no sense to prohibit military assistance to civilian law enforcement officials in cases of biological or chemical weapons' threat. Here, the inordinate dangers that possible terrorist uses of weapons of mass destruction present serves to justify the weakening of the strictures against the use of military forces as a tool of governmental administration within civilian society.

The war against terrorism will, at times, be a real 'gutter contest' and the United States must seek to persevere while trying to remain as faithful to its democratic ideals as the tactics used by terrorists will allow. The moral and intellectual leaders of this nation have to awaken all levels of society to the exceedingly dangerous threats that nuclear and biological terrorism will present in the future. US rulers must exercise persuasive moral leadership to alert their constituents that such terrorist violence poses a dire menace to their well-being and freedom of action, as it ultimately threatens to undermine the existence of democracy and the continuity of multi-party, pluralistic governance.

Note

1 Counter-terrorism analysts in Jerusalem are particularly concerned that Syrian terror surrogates might use water-born bacteriological agents to poison the main Israeli watershed in the north, the Sea of Galilee (Smith, 1991: 486). Egypt also has extensive biological-weapons capability that could fall into the hands of terrorists if a radical, terror-supporting regime was to come to power there.

References

Atkinson, R. (1994), 'A Nuclear Nightmare', *Washington Post National News Weekly Edition*, 5–11 September, p. 6.

Bellona Foundation Report (1996), *The Russian Northern Fleet: Sources of Radioactive Contamination*, Moscow.

Beres, L.R. (1996), 'Intelligence and Nuclear Terrorism: Preventing "Pain" into Power', *International Journal of Intelligence and Counter-Intelligence*, Volume 9, Number 2.

Croddy, E. (1996), 'Chuche: The Political Economy of the Democratic People's Republic of Korea', *Jane's Intelligence Weekly*, Volume 8, Number 6, June, p. 273.

Erlanger, S. (1996), 'An Israeli Peace Team Flies Home, Clinton Calls a Special Meeting', *New York Times*, 5 March, p. A9.

Foreign Report (1996a), 'The Biggest Fast-Breeder Reactor', Number 2402, 6 June, p. 7.

Foreign Report (1996b), Number 2396, 25 April, p.8.

Foreign Report (1996c), 'Genetic Weapons', Number 2391, 14 March, p. 1.

Foreign Report (1996d), 'Hizbullah's Air Force', Number 2389, 29 February, p. 2.

Foreign Report (1995a), 'Russia's Secret Plans', Number 2378, 30 November, p. 7.

Foreign Report (1995b), Number 2362, 3 August, p.8.

Foreign Report (1995c), 'Iran's Silence Explained', Number 2350, 11 May, p. 2.

Greenhouse, S. (1995), 'Russia Insists Reactor Sale to Iran is Firm', *New York Times*, 25 February, p. A5.

Hoffman, B. and Hoffman, D.K (1995), 'The RAND-St Andrews Chronology of International Terrorism, 1994', *Terrorism and Political Violence*, Volume 7, Number 4, Winter, pp. 210–211.

Jordan Times (1996), 'Russia May Train Iran Nuclear Experts', 21 April, p. 1.

Kansas City Star (1994), 'Nuclear Smuggling Called a Grave Threat', 13 August, p. A4.

Kier, E. and Mercer, J. (1996), 'Setting Precedents in Anarchy: Military Intervention and Weapons of Mass Destruction', *International Security*, Volume 20, Number 4, Spring, pp. 100–101.

Kifner, J. (1995), 'Antiterrorism Law Used in Poison Smuggling Case — Man Had Enough Powder for Mass Killing', *New York Times*, 23 December, p. A7.

Klare, M. (1995), *Rogue States and Nuclear Outlaws: America's Search for a New Foreign Policy*, Hill and Wang, New York.

Milivojevic, M. (1995), 'Russia and Iran: Nuclear Deal', *Middle East International*, Number 492, 20 January, p. 14.

Mathews, R.J. and McCormack, T.L.H. (1995), 'Entry into Force of the CWC: National Requirements and Prospective Timetable', *Security Dialogue*, Volume 26, Number 1, March, pp. 93–107.

Muslim News (1996), 'US Worries: Iran Wants to Steal Nuclear Capability', March 7–17, p. 13.

New York Times (1996), 'Britain Widens Powers of Police in Terrorism', *New York Times*, 3 April, p. A9.

New York Times (1995a), 'Iran Nuclear Contract with Russia is Due', 8 August, p. A8.

New York Times (1995b), 'Libya to Buy Uranium from Kazakhstan', 10 January, p. 5.

Perlez, J. (1995), 'Tracing a Nuclear Risk: Stolen Enriched Uranium', *New York Times*, 15 February, p. A3.

Potter, W. (1995), Director of the Center for Non-Proliferation Studies, Monteray Institute of International Studies, Personal Communication, 3 August.

Rohter, L. (1996), 'Cuba's Nuclear Plant Project Worries Washington', *New York Times*, 25 February, p. A3.

Saribrahimoglu, L. (1996), 'Dev-Sol Kills Three Executives', *Jane's Intelligence Review — Pointer*, Volume 3, Number 5, May, p. 8.

Schmemann, S (1996), 'Clinton in Israel: Stresses Support for Peace Effort', *New York Times*, 15 March, p. A1.

Schmemann, S (1995), 'Peres Says Israel, With Regional Pact, Would End Atom Effort', *New York Times*, 23 December, p. A5.

Sidhu, W.P.S. (1996a), 'Pakistan's Bomb: A Quest for Credibility', *Jane's Intelligence Review*, Volume 8, Number 6, June, p. 280.

Sidhu, W.P.S. (1996b), 'India's Nuclear Tests', *Jane's Intelligence Review*, Volume 8, Number 4, April, p. 171.

Specter, M. (1995), 'Russians Assert Radioactive Box Found in Park Posed No Danger', *New York Times*, 25 November, p. A7.

Stern, J. (1996), 'Preventing Portable Nukes', *New York Times*, 10 April, p. A19.

Tagliabue, J. (1996), 'Italy Opens Inquiry Into Jail Escape by Achille Lauro Gunman', *New York Times*, 5 March, p. A10.

US Department of State (1992), *Country Contact Data Report*, 8 October, p. 1.

Weiner, T. (1996), 'Huge Chemical Arms Plant Near Completion in Libya, US Says', *New York Times*, 25 February, p. A8.

Williams, P. and Woessner, P. (1995), 'Nuclear Material Trafficking: An Interim Assessment', *Transnational Organized Crime*, Volume 1, Number 2, Summer, pp. 207.

Woessner, P. (1995), 'Chronology of Nuclear Smuggling Incidents: July 1991–May 1995', *Transnational Organized Crime*, Volume 1, Number 2, Summer, pp. 288–329.

[13]

Report of the CIMERC*/Drexel University Emergency Department Terrorism Preparedness Consensus Panel

Michael I. Greenberg, MD, MPH, Robert G. Hendrickson, MD

Abstract

This report describes the consensus recommendations of an expert panel convened to develop recommendations for a hospital-based emergency department (ED) to attain a minimal level of preparedness necessary to respond to mass casualty events derived from the use of weapons of mass destruction. The recommendations were created for use by hospital-based EDs of a variety of sizes and locations (urban, suburban, or rural). The disasters that were considered included those that are biological, chemical, or radiological. The panel focused on preparation for a single disaster that could generate 250–500 total patients in 24–48 hours. This number included asymptomatic, exposed, and symptomatic patients. The panel chose not to address circumstances where a small number of patients with an infectious disease are seen in one or a few hospitals. In addition, the panel believed that preparation of a single hospital for an overwhelming mass casualty situation (e.g., 10,000 patients) would not be broadly applicable and would not be required for an individual ED to "minimally prepared." Prior to the convening of this consensus panel, in June 2002, a search of all relevant agencies found no comprehensive, published, validated recommendations for preparedness for individual EDs. Although several agencies had released information on disaster management, clinical diagnosis and treatment tools, and training, no agency had produced a comprehensive list of items and issues that individual EDs must consider when preparing for a terrorist attack. The current report attempts to fill this void in information regarding ED preparedness. **Key words:** emergency departments; disaster preparedness; terrorism; mass casualty incidents; weapons of mass destruction; recommendations. ACADEMIC EMERGENCY MEDICINE 2003; 10:783–788.

Since the September 11, 2001, attacks on New York City, Pennsylvania, and the U.S. Pentagon, the medical community has been widely focused on assessing and upgrading the nation's ability to respond to a terrorist attack. While efforts to augment out-of-hospital resources and public health assets have progressed, relatively little attention has been focused on the preparedness of hospital-based emergency department (ED) services with regard to their ability to treat casualties resulting from terrorist attack.[1,2] A review of past terrorist events reveals several patterns that stress the need for EDs to be prepared for such an event:

From the Department of Emergency Medicine, Division of Medical Toxicology, Drexel University College of Medicine, Philadelphia, PA (MIG); the Department of Emergency Medicine, Temple University School of Medicine, Philadelphia, PA (MIG); the Department of Emergency Medicine, Oregon Health & Science University, Portland, OR (RGH); and the Oregon Poison Center, Portland, OR (RGH).
Received September 17, 2002; revisions received January 2, 2003, and January 20, 2003; accepted January 22, 2003.
Supported under a contract with the U.S. Army Research and Material Command, Fort Detrick, MD 21702-5012: U.S. Army Medical Research Acquisition Activity; Cooperative Agreement DAMD17-99-2-9012. The content of the information does not necessarily reflect the position or policy of the U.S. government or the US Army and no official endorsement should be inferred.
Address for correspondence and reprints: Michael I. Greenberg, MD, MPH, Department of Emergency Medicine, Medical College of Pennsylvania Hospital, 3300 Henry Avenue, Philadelphia, PA 19129. e-mail: michael.greenberg@drexel.edu.
*CIMERC = the National Bioterrorism Civilian Response Center.

1. The majority of patients after a chemical, biological, or explosive terrorist attack are seen by hospital EDs, not by out-of-hospital personnel.[3–5]
2. Most patients leave the scene of an explosive or chemical terrorist act quickly[3] and visit local EDs in the first six hours.[4–6]
3. A decontamination facility may not be erected at the site of a chemical or radiological attack before many victims have already left the scene.[3]
4. Most patients arrive to EDs by foot, taxi, or private vehicle, not by ambulance.[3–6]
5. The majority of patients seeking emergency care in EDs are asymptomatic people who have been exposed to a chemical, radiological, or biological agent, or victims seeking prophylactic medications. These patients are likely to overwhelm hospital resources.[7]

This report describes the consensus panel's recommendations for a hospital-based emergency service to attain a minimal level of preparedness necessary to respond to mass casualty events due to weapons of mass destruction. The recommendations were created for use by hospital-based EDs of a variety of sizes and locations (urban, suburban, or rural). The disasters that were considered included those that are biological, chemical, or radiological. The discussion focused on preparation for a single disaster that could generate 250–500 total patients in 24–48 hours. This number included asymptomatic, exposed, and symptomatic patients. The panel chose not to address circumstances where a small number of patients with an infectious disease are seen in one or a few hospitals. In addition, the panel believed that preparation of a single hospital for an overwhelming mass casualty situation (e.g., 10,000 patients) would not be broadly applicable and would not be required for an individual ED to "minimally prepared."

Although several reports on ED preparedness have been published,[8–13] this report is the first that we are aware of to formulate its recommendations through panel consensus and to incorporate lessons learned from the September 11, 2001, and anthrax attacks.

Prior to the convening of this consensus panel, in June 2002, a search of all relevant agencies found no comprehensive, published, validated recommendations for preparedness for individual EDs. Although several agencies had released information on disaster management,[14] clinical diagnosis and treatment tools,[15] and training,[16] no agency had produced a comprehensive list of items and issues that individual EDs must consider when preparing for a terrorist attack. In this regard, we searched the websites of, or contacted by telephone, the following agencies: Society for Academic Emergency Medicine, American College of Emergency Physicians, American Academy of Emergency Medicine, World Health Organization, American Hospital Association, American Public Health Association, American Medical Association, Johns Hopkins Center for Civilian Biodefense Strategies, Center for Disease Control and Prevention (CDC), Joint Commission on Accreditation of Healthcare Organizations (JCAHO), and Center for Medicare and Medicaid Services.

The charge for the consensus panel was to determine, by consensus, minimal requirements for a hospital-based ED to evaluate and treat victims of a domestic terrorist attack.

CONSENSUS METHODS

Members of this consensus panel were selected from the Department of Defense Domestic Preparedness Program and from recommendations of a core group of experts in emergency medicine. Physicians were chosen from both academic and community hospitals and from urban and suburban communities. In addition to physicians, the consensus panel contained members of fire departments, police departments, and disaster management teams (DMATs), representatives from nursing and emergency medicine residencies, and physician's assistants. Several of the panel members had extensive on-site experience in both World Trade Center disasters. Panel members and their affiliations are listed in Appendix A.

Prior to convening of the panel, panel members were asked to provide a list of at least five but not more than 25 issues and items that they believe are essential for a generic hospital-based ED to be prepared to

evaluate and treat civilian victims of a terrorist attack. Panel members considered hospitals of all sizes and locations (urban, suburban, and rural) and disasters involving chemical, radiological, and biological weapons. The lists obtained from the panel members were collated and duplicate items were eliminated. The list of issues and items were then grouped into four topic headings as follows: Training, Planning/Policy, Equipment, and Antidotes/Medications.

Panel members met over a two-day period and debated all items on the collated list until consensus was obtained. Prior to convening the panel, "consensus" was defined as representing at least agreement of the majority. However, the final conclusions were agreed upon unanimously and there were no dissenting opinions.

PANEL CONCLUSIONS

Baseline Assumptions. The panel proposed, and agreed by consensus, that certain specific underlying assumptions should form the foundation for the establishment of minimal ED preparedness. These baseline assumptions are listed in Table 1. In addition to the baseline assumptions, the panel defined specific items and issues that were believed to be necessary for a minimal level of preparedness. One of the most pressing issues that the panel recommended as a "baseline" is the concept that the hospital ED is not the appropriate venue for the distribution of prophylactic antibiotics, medications, and/or vaccines to asymptomatic patients. Rather, community-based emergency planning and public health initiatives should provide for alternate sites for the evaluation of patients for the receipt of, and record keeping related to, prophylaxis. These alternative sites may be within the hospital, but should be distinct from the ED, as distribution of prophylactic medication may quickly overwhelm the ED's resources and detract from the care of symptomatic patients. In addition, the panel recommended that pre-incident education efforts be put into place so that the media and public

TABLE 1. Baseline Assumptions for All Emergency Departments (EDs)

1. Every ED should be in compliance with JCAHO* (or equivalent organization) requirements for disaster emergency management, including a hazard vulnerability analysis, the development of a disaster plan, and practice drills.

2. Each hospital should be included in a regional plan for dispensing of prophylactic antibiotics, medications, and vaccines for asymptomatic, potentially exposed patients that is distinct and removed from the ED.

3. A community-wide plan for emergency management, including federal, state, and local plans, already exists around each hospital.

*JCAHO = Joint Committee on Accreditation of Healthcare Organizations.

ACAD EMERG MED • July 2003, Vol. 10, No. 7 • www.aemj.org

may be rapidly instructed on where to obtain prophylaxis.

The panel included in its baseline assumptions that hospitals are in compliance with JCAHO or equivalent agency requirements. This ensures that each hospital has conducted a hazard vulnerability analysis and developed a disaster management plan.[17] In that plan, the hospital must provide for the evacuation of the hospital or areas of the hospital and must conduct emergency drills regularly.[18] The panel believed that these requirements are essential to the management of a disaster and are basic assumptions when preparing for a threat that is specific to domestic terrorism.

Training. Table 2 lists the training issues defined by the consensus panel. The panel agreed that every hospital employee needs some level of training or education regarding weapons of mass destruction, specific to his or her role in the emergency management plan. This includes every person who is assigned to, or works in, the hospital ED. Specifically, all physicians and nurses who work in the ED should have initial as well as ongoing training and education. Training and education may be aimed at specifying individual roles during a disaster. However, it was the panel consensus that this training should be flexible and fashioned to meet the needs of each specific hospital facility recognizing that levels of service and capabilities may vary widely from institution to institution.

The panel also recommended that all hospitals have on staff, or have access to, a core group of consultants and/or experts with specific knowledge for both reference and training. These individuals should have special expertise in the medical aspects of the weapons that terrorists might use, including radio-logical, biological, and chemical weapons. This core group should include individuals with expertise in decontamination of casualties, infectious diseases, medical toxicology, radiological exposures, and training of other physicians and nurses in related issues. The panel recognized that it is not possible for all hospitals to employ these experts, so the recommendation stresses that these experts should be available and contact numbers easily accessible in case of emergency as well as for training.

The panel recommended that all ED staff whose role in a disaster requires personal protective equipment, be trained in its use. This may range from barrier precautions for most employees to higher levels of protection for those responsible for decontamination. Because there may be a need for the rapid expansion of personnel to assist in the ED in the event of a terrorist attack, the emergency management plan should consider the ability to rapidly educate and train volunteers and non-ED personnel in issues of personal protection and tasks they may be required to perform. In addition, since EDs may get inundated with health care personnel wanting to volunteer,[4,7] the panel recommended a plan to rapidly train and utilize volunteer health care workers and to pre-define training-appropriate roles. This could include rapid training on site in such areas as stretcher-bearers, patient transports, family support, and other logistical assistance.

Planning/Policy. The issues and items recommended by the consensus panel with regard to planning and policy are listed in Table 3. The panel noted that the establishment of a plan to control access to the hospital ED is critical in order to prevent disruption of ED activities as well as to prevent potential contamination of the ED and the hospital facility itself. The panel recommended the development of policies and

TABLE 2. Panel Recommendations Concerning Training

1. Every hospital employee needs some level of training or education regarding weapons of mass destruction (WMD) specific to his or her role in the emergency management plan.

2. Each hospital emergency department (ED) should have access to a core group of consultants/experts with specific knowledge for both reference and training.

3. Emergency department personnel require specialized training in the medical care of victims of WMD. This training should be flexible and fashioned to meet the needs of each specific hospital facility recognizing that levels of service and capabilities may vary widely from institution to institution.

4. Training should exist for ED staff in the proper use of personal protection equipment (PPE) specific to their roles in decontamination and patient treatment according to the hospital and regional emergency disaster plan.

5. Emergency management plan should incorporate rapid, on-site training of volunteers and non-ED personnel.

TABLE 3. Panel Recommendations Concerning Planning and Policy

1. Plans to control access to the hospital and the emergency department (ED).

2. A plan to identify, mobilize, train, and utilize hospital staff and volunteers in an organized, scheduled fashion.

3. A plan for prophylactic antibiotics or immunization of hospital staff and their families to ensure staff safety, prevent exposure of worker families, and allow for the continuing function of the ED.

4. Stress management for staff during and after the disaster.

5. Policy and procedures for contacting appropriate agencies that delineates who and when to call in the event of a terrorist or suspected terrorist act.

6. Rapid access to treatment algorithms in the ED.

7. A plan to evacuate and protect existing ED patients.

8. A decontamination plan that does not interfere with normal ED operations (physicians should not decontaminate).

procedures, based on local issues, for contacting appropriate agencies that delineates whom and when to call in the event of a terrorist, or suspected terrorist act. In addition, the panel recommended that a plan for distribution of prophylactic antibiotics or immunization of hospital staff and their families be addressed. The purpose of this is to ensure staff safety, to prevent exposure of worker families, and to allow for the continuing function of the ED. The panel recommended the development and implementation of stress management programs for staff both during and after the disaster.

The panel recommended that there be ready access to treatment algorithms in the ED for those weapons that might be used by terrorists. The panel recommended that a plan to evacuate and protect those patients who were in the ED at the time the incident occurred. Finally, a decontamination plan that does not interfere with normal ED operations was recommended. Specifically, the panel recommended that the emergency physician on duty should not be responsible to decontaminate patients, as the community is best served with physicians treating patients in the ED and avoiding contamination.[19] In addition, the duties and roles of decontaminators should be predetermined and practiced. Finally, the panel recommended that an area for asymptomatic or exposed individuals be pre-established and physically removed from the ED.

Equipment. With regard to equipment issues, the panel made only two recommendations (Table 4). The first recommendation is that the ED have the ability to decontaminate victims prior to their admission to the inside of the ED. The decontamination system should be hospital-based and rapidly deployable. The panel noted that the ED should not depend on mutual agreements with other, community-based organizations (fire, police, emergency services, hazardous materials [hazmat] providers) to provide for the equipment and manpower needed to provide patient decontamination. The panel thought that community-based resources would be occupied in other tasks and activities during the early stages of a terrorist attack. Consequently, these resources would not be available to the ED. In addition, the panel recommended that visual reminders (charts, diagrams, flow sheets) be available in the ED to assist clinicians in the

recognition and management of various clinical aspects of terrorism threats: smallpox, anthrax, chemical agents, etc.

Antidotes/Medications. The panel based its determination of antidote/medication stocking on several principles. That most hospitals stock enough antibiotics to treat a small number of casualties (1–5 patients); that it will not be possible for every hospital to stock enough medications to treat thousands of symptomatic patients within hours; and that, in the event of a national emergency, the CDC will release antibiotics, medications, and vaccines and the CDC estimates that those medications may be available to a hospital in approximately 12 hours.[20] Since training exercises suggest that significant logistical barriers may occur in this distribution, a more realistic estimate may be 24–48 hours. With this in mind, the panel attempted to determine what additional stocking was needed to prepare a hospital ED to treat patients from a single chemical, biological, or radiological attack in a 24–48-hour period.

Given that many of the biological agents may have delayed, rather than immediate health effects, the panel's recommendations with regard to the stocking of antibiotics are limited. Panel recommendations concerning antidotes and medications are listed in Table 5. The panel realized that a single release of a biological agent would most likely produce casualties over a longer period of time than a chemical or radiological attack.[21] The consensus of the panel was that hospitals generally have adequate amounts of antibiotics on hand to be able to meet immediate needs and that public health resources may provide adequate backup.[20-23] Otherwise, the panel did not believe that distribution of prophylactic antibiotics to the public at large is an appropriate role for a hospital ED and should be addressed by public health planning. Similar recommendations apply for drugs that might be used to provide prophylaxis in the event of the use of a nuclear dispersion device or other nuclear weapon.

The panel did recognize that during the initial stages of a biological threat, a significant amount of intravenous antibiotics might be utilized. Again, however, public health and federal stockpiles should be adequate to supplement the hospital approximately 24 hours after identification of the agent.[20] The panel felt that most hospitals need no additional stocking to be minimally prepared for a biological agent. Hospitals should consider, however, stocking

TABLE 4. Panel Recommendations Concerning Equipment

1. Ability to decontaminate victims prior to their admission to the inside of the emergency department (ED). The decontamination system should be hospital-based and rapidly deployable. The ED should not depend on mutual agreements with other organizations for decontamination.

2. Visual reminders for clinical aspects of terrorism threats: smallpox, anthrax, chemical agents, etc.

TABLE 5. Panel Recommendations Concerning Antidotes/Medications

1. Atropine
2. Pralidoxime chloride
3. Oral prophylactic antibiotics and potassium iodide for staff and their families

ACAD EMERG MED • July 2003, Vol. 10, No. 7 • www.aemj.org 787

intravenous antibiotics to treat patients for up to 24 hours based on their hazard analysis.

One method of stocking was specifically noted by the panel and involved a change in ordering habits of hospital pharmacies. Hospital pharmacies generally order additional antibiotics when their supply is low ("just in time" ordering). A change to pre-ordering an amount that the hospital typically uses in a two-to-four-week period may allow additional antibiotics, particularly doxycycline, gentamicin, and ciprofloxacin, to be available. These antibiotics could then be cycled into the hospital's normal distribution system after one month. This method may allow hospitals to be minimally prepared while not requiring hospitals to stockpile antibiotics that may expire and incur a significant cost. Although this process has not yet been studied or validated, the panel felt this method might allow for minimal preparedness for a 24-hour period without the need to purchase and store a cache of antibiotics. As stated above, individual hospitals must assess their risks via a hazard analysis and determine whether antibiotic stocking is possible or necessary. In addition, hospitals may choose to stock oral antibiotics for distribution to health care and hospital workers and their families.

The panel does recommend the specific stocking of atropine as well as pralidoxime chloride. These drugs form the basis for the treatment needed for victims of nerve agent exposure. Since these agents produce toxicity immediately, the majority of patients will be seen within the first six hours after an event.[6] This period of time is too short to rely on public health or federal stockpiles for antidotes.[20] In addition, significant quantities of both atropine and pralidoxime may be required to treat patients of a nerve agent attack.[6]

The panel noted that the lyophilized form of the drug atropine is available, has an extended shelf life, and can easily be reconstituted to treat large numbers of causalities should the need arise. In addition, shortly after the panel meeting evidence that parenteral atropine remains potent for at least 12 years was published.[24] Therefore, atropine in vials or pre-packaged injectors may possibly be stocked without concern of expiration provided they are appropriately stored. Further studies will clarify this issue.

As noted above, pralidoxime chloride may be needed in cases of severe nerve poisoning. Unfortunately, due to relatively small-scale production of the agent and use of the agent by the armed forces and disaster management teams, it is most likely not available for stockpiling by all hospital pharmacies at this time. Production may increase in the future and allow significant stocking in hospitals.

While the panel noted the potential utility of other antidotes in various situations, the consensus was to not provide overburdening recommendations and to limit cost expenditures as hospitals strive to become better prepared. This consensus panel sought to determine minimal preparedness for hospitals of all sizes. Individual hospitals wishing to be better prepared may certainly decide to stock other antidotes, including naloxone, physostigmine, potassium iodide, thiosulfate, and British anti-Lewisite (BAL). Hospitals in close proximity to particular hazards may require stocking of antidotes that are specific to individual threats, such as particular industrial chemicals (e.g., cyanide).

The panel chose not to specify individual items for stocking (e.g., ventilators, Morgan lenses, and endotracheal tubes) as these items should be included in the disaster management plan and the treatment of any mass casualty situation.

CONCLUSIONS

Since September 11, 2001, the probability of and concern about domestic terrorist attacks have heightened. While much money and training have gone into the out-of-hospital arena, little attention has been given to the preparedness of hospital emergency departments for such an attack. A review of previous terrorist-related disasters reveals, while emergency services personnel may be prepared and able to decontaminate and treat patients in the field, the vast majority of patients arrive to the ED for care.[6,25]

Until now, no comprehensive, consensus recommendation for ED preparedness has been published. The CIMERC/Drexel University Emergency Department Terrorism Preparedness Consensus Panel attempted to outline what individual EDs must accomplish in order to have a minimal level of preparedness for a mass casualty situation involving weapons that may be used by terrorists.

References

1. Greenberg MI, Jurgens SM, Gracely EJ. Emergency department preparedness for the evaluation and treatment of victims of biological or chemical terrorist attack. J Emerg Med. 2002; 22:273–8.
2. Treat KN, Williams JM, Furbee PM, Manley WG, Russell FK, Stamper CD Jr. Hospital preparedness for weapons of mass destruction incidents: an initial assessment. Ann Emerg Med. 2001; 38:562–5.
3. Okumura T, Suzuki K, Fukuda A, et al. The Tokyo subway sarin attack: disaster management, part 1: community emergency response. Acad Emerg Med. 1998; 5:613–7.
4. Hogan DE, Waeckerle JF, Dire DJ, Lillibridge SR. Emergency department impact of the Oklahoma City terrorist bombing. Ann Emerg Med. 1999; 34:160–7.
5. Rapid assessment of injuries among survivors of the terrorist attack on the World Trade Center—New York City, September, 2001. MMWR. 2002; 51(1):1–5.
6. Okumura T, Suzuki K, Fukuda A, et al. The Tokyo subway sarin attack: disaster management, part 2: hospital response. Acad Emerg Med. 1998; 5:618–24.
7. Okumura T, Takasu N, Ishimatsu S, et al. Report on 640 victims of the Tokyo subway sarin attack. Ann Emerg Med. 1996; 28:129–35.
8. Macintyre AG, Christopher GW, Eitzen E, et al. Weapons of mass destruction events with contaminated casualties. Effective planning for health care facilities. JAMA. 2000; 283:242–9.

9. Brennan RJ, Waeckerle JF, Sharp TW, Lillibridge SR. Chemical warfare agents: emergency medical and emergency public health issues. Ann Emerg Med. 1999; 34:191–204.

10. Burgess JL, Kirk M, Borron SW, Cisek J. Emergency department hazardous materials protocol for contaminated patients. Ann Emerg Med. 1999; 34:205–12.

11. Richards CF, Burstein JL, Waeckerle JF, Hutson HR. Emergency physicians and biological terrorism. Ann Emerg Med. 1999; 34:183–90.

12. Keim M, Kaufmann AF. Principles for emergency response to bioterrorism. Ann Emerg Med. 1999; 34:177–82.

13. Schultz CH, Mothershead JL, Field M. Bioterrorism preparedness 1: the emergency department and hospital. Emerg Med Clin North Am. 2002; 20:437–55.

14. American College of Emergency Physicians. Disaster Response and Biological/Chemical Terrorism Information Packet. Dallas, TX: ACEP, Oct 2001.

15. Inglesby TV, Henderson DA, Bartlett JG, et al. Anthrax as a biological weapon. Medical and public health management. JAMA. 1999; 281:1735–45.

16. Joint Commission on the Accreditation of Healthcare Organizations. Document EC.1.4 (The organization has an emergency management plan). Oakbrook Terrace, IL: JCAHO, Jan 2002.

17. Joint Commission on the Accreditation of Healthcare Organizations. Document EC.2.9.2 (Drills are conducted regularly to test emergency management). Oakbrook Terrace, IL: JCAHO, Jan 2002.

18. Nozaki H, Hori S, Shinozawa Y, et al. Secondary exposure of medical staff to sarin vapor in the emergency room. Intensive Care Med. 1995; 21:1032–5.

19. Waeckerle JF, Seamans S, Whiteside M, et al. Executive summary: Developing objectives, content, and competencies for the training of emergency medical technicians, emergency physicians, and emergency nurses to care for casualties resulting from nuclear, biological, or chemical (NBC) incidents. Ann Emerg Med. 2001; 37:587–601.

20. Centers for Disease Control and Prevention/National Center for Environmental Health, National Pharmaceutical Stockpile website: www.cdc.gov/nceh/nps/synopses.htm. Accessed September 2002.

21. Meselson M, Guillemin J, Hugh-Jones M, et al. The Sverdlosk anthrax outbreak of 1979. Science. 1994; 266:1202–8.

22. Tucker JB. National health and medical response to incidents of chemical and biological terrorism. JAMA. 1997; 278:362–72.

23. Sharp TW, Brennan RJ, Keim M. Medical preparedness for a terrorist incident involving chemical or biological agents during the 1996 Atlanta Olympic Games. Ann Emerg Med. 1998; 32:214–23.

24. Schier JG, Mehta R, Mercurio-Zappala M, Nelson LS, Howland MA, Hoffman RS. Preparing for chemical terrorism: stability of expired atropine. J Toxicol Clin Toxicol. 2002; 40:625–6.

25. Okudera H, Morita H, Iwashita T, et al. Unexpected nerve gas exposure in the city of Matsumoto: report of rescue activity in the first sarin gas terrorism. Am J Emerg Med. 1997; 15:527–8.

•

APPENDIX A. CONSENSUS PANEL MEMBERS

Principal Investigator:

Michael I. Greenberg, MD, MPH, Professor of Emergency Medicine, Professor of Public Health

Medical Toxicologist, Drexel University College of Medicine, Philadelphia, PA.

Co-investigator:

Robert G. Hendrickson, MD, Assistant Professor, Department of Emergency Medicine, Oregon Health & Science University, Medical Toxicologist, Oregon Poison Center, Portland, OR.

General Members:

Robert MacNamara, MD, Professor of Emergency Medicine, Chair, Department of Emergency Medicine, Temple University School of Medicine, Philadelphia, PA.

Howard Levitin, MD, Emergency Physician, Indianapolis, IN, Clinical Assistant Professor of Medicine at Indiana University School of Medicine, Disaster Planning International.

Fred Henretig, MD, Professor of Pediatrics, Children's Hospital of Philadelphia, Philadelphia, PA, Medical Toxicologist, Medical Director, The Poison Center, Philadelphia, PA.

Thomas Rahilly, PhD, Emergency Department Administrator, North Shore University Hospital, Manhasset, NY, Instructor, National Fire Academy – Emergency Response to Terrorism.

Thomas Row, RN, Nurse, Emergency Department, St. Charles Hospital, Police Officer, New York City Police Department, Emergency Services Unit, New York DMAT team.

David Kao, PA, New York DMAT team, New York FEMA team, Physician's Assistant, Winthrop University Hospital, Mineola, NY, New York Police Department, Emergency Services Unit, Hazardous Material Response Team, New York, NY.

Timothy Farrell, New York City Police Department, Counter Terrorism Division, New York, NY, Former Hazardous Materials Coordinator, New York City Police Department, Emergency Services Unit, New York, NY, Department of Justice, Center for Domestic Preparedness.

Scott Phillips, MD, Medical Toxicologist, Associate Clinical Professor, University of Colorado School of Medicine, Denver, CO.

Anthony Morocco, MD, Emergency Physician, Medical Toxicologist, Department of Emergency Medicine, Guam Memorial Hospital, Tamuning, Guam.

Jason Stillwagon, MD, Senior Resident, Department of Emergency Medicine, Drexel University College of Medicine, Philadelphia, PA.

Polly Dole, MD, Senior Resident, Department of Emergency Medicine, Drexel University College of Medicine, Philadelphia, PA.

[14]

Trends in Bio-Terrorism: Two Generations of Potential Weapons

Joseph W. Foxell, Jr.

Introduction

As more effective countermeasures begin to be deployed to limit the lethality and destructiveness of large-scale bombings, coupled with better executive protection services in countries where terror group kidnappings are endemic (for example, Mexico and Colombia), the hazard increases that terrorists may turn to biological weapons. There are some undercutting factors to this line of argument, however. The obvious lapses in perimeter security, as well as the failure to follow risk assessment guidelines and audit recommendations after prior embassy bombings, that resulted in the carnage at Dar es Salaam and Nairobi, suggest that this may not happen immediately. Moreover, to date, there has been very little bio-terrorism – due mainly to the long standing taboo on the use of such infective substances, even in wartime, as well as the inherent difficulties and dangers in handling and deploying such materials.

It is important that society be prepared to deal with the threat of biological terrorism – whenever the threat will be offered. To accomplish this, society must gain a better understanding of what it encompasses. There is no single form for such biological terror devices. Rather, there are many very different possible ones. Indeed, the effort to build defences against such unconventional threats has not kept pace with the rapid rate of development of new kinds of biological mass casualty weapons. While the most likely threats of the future are the use of anthrax and botulinum based weapons, countermeasures to blunt the effectiveness of such devices may prove relatively easy to implement, thereby driving terrorists to consider other biological infective vectors.

This article discusses the nature of more than three dozen potential biological terror agents; describes how they work; identifies some of the possessors of such weapons; examines a broad range of plausible delivery systems; identifies a seldom considered category of risk posed by the creation of new classes of biological agents

(for example, genetically engineered infective agents); summarizes the vulnerability of several Russian biological weapons production centres; explains why biological weapons have rarely been used even in combat; and offers an assessment of several logical countermeasures.

The Nature of Biological Terror Agents

Unlike other mass casualty munitions (for example, nuclear and chemical devices, ammonium-nitrate/fuel-oil (ANFO) bombs and semtex based plastic explosives), biological weapons are powered by organic agents. Biological terrorism encompasses the use of toxins (that is, poisonous chemical compounds produced by organic matter) and diseases – ordinarily highly infectious – caused by other lethal micro-organisms (for example, fungi, protozoa, viruses, bacteria, *pasturella pestis* and rickettsias) against non-combatant populations, crops or livestock. Biological terrorists thus have a wealth of source materials to choose from in constructing their weapons – especially since the vector (that is, the mode of contagion (for example, tainted water, infected persons or animals, or fleas) that spreads such pestilence from one victim to the next) varies with the specific agent. Fungi are plants of the sub-kingdom *Thallophyta* and lack chlorophyll. They include yeasts (various uni-cellular fungi capable of fermenting carbohydrates), blasts (a plant disease that results in failure of flowers to open or fruit or seeds to mature), moulds (growths producing disintegration of organic matter), rusts (an affliction characterized by reddish or brownish spots on a plant's leaves) and smuts (the formation of black, powdery masses of spores on the plant's infected parts). Protozoa are single celled, usually microscopic, organisms that include the most primitive forms of animal life. Rickettsias are micro-organisms carried as parasites by fleas, ticks and lice. Toxins are cellular by-products and, as such, do not replicate. They are very close to chemical agents in both character and use, but their origin is biological. Bacteria are single celled organisms that cause disease or produce toxins. Viruses are tiny organisms that invade and take over cells by injecting their genes into them. *Pasturella pestis* is a bacterium that causes buboes swelling in lymph nodes, especially in the groin. Many of these pathogens occur spontaneously or are naturally present in our environment (for example, anthrax spores are often found in sheep manure). Specific potential agents for biological terror weapons include the following: fungi (for example, *Nocardia asteroidea* that causes pneumonia and tumors); toxins (for example, *Clostridium botulinum* that, in sufficient quantities, can engender muscular paralysis resulting in death, tricothecine mycotoxins that affect multiple organ systems in the body simultaneously – the resultant trauma being catastrophic, or aflatoxin infection that results in liver cancer); viruses (for example, *Equine encephalomyelitis* that produces deadly convulsions, or rotavirus infection that often leads to a virulent, fatal form of diarrhoea); bacterial infections (for example, *E. coli 0157:H7* that frequently leads to kidney failure); rickettsias (for example, *Bacillus anthracis* that causes carbuncles, swelling and death); and *Pasturella pestis* (for example, the Bubonic plague, a highly contagious airborne bacterial organism, which, known as the Black Death, killed one-in-three people, or almost twenty-five million individuals, in Western Europe during a three-year period (1348–1350) in the mid-fourteenth century) (Broad and Miller, 1998a).

A particular species of a toxic pathogen can have hundreds of varieties and sub-varieties. These variations, called strains, produce dissimilar amounts of the pathogen's toxin or different sized clusters of its micro-organisms' colonies. For example, *Clostridium botulinum*, type-A (the so-called Hall strain), is the most deadly form of this toxic microbe, *variola major* is the most virulent form of smallpox, and Vollum 1B is the deadliest of the dozens of highly lethal stains of *Bacillus anthracis*, while *E. Coli 0157:H7*, unlike most instigators of infectious food poisoning that require consumption of ten-thousand micro-organisms, can make a person deathly ill through ingestion of only ten micro-organisms. According to William C. Patrick, III, one of the foremost US experts on biological weapons development programmes, 'the greatest hurdle for would-be biological terrorists is getting the most infectious and virulent culture for their seed stock' (Broad, 1998b: A4). Therefore, the task for such terrorists is to find the most deadly strain and, then, to propagate it from a small starter sample to quantities sufficient for use in a germ warfare-style terror weapon (Broad and Miller, 1998b).

There is another important division in the realm of biological pathogens, analogous to the difference between the effects of biological and of chemical agents. Chemical weapons materials, although extremely deadly, have only direct exposure effects (that is, they cause damage in proportion to the amount inhaled or splashed on the skin). Thus, they harm solely those who have immediate contact with them. Biological agents are divided into two groups – those that are contagious and those that are not. The non-contagious types (for example, toxins such as *Bacillus anthracis*) behave primarily like chemical poisons. The contagious kinds (for example, viruses, such as pneumonic plague, viral meningitis, or hepatitis, type-A) enter the victim's body, multiply and, then, days or weeks later as the disease progresses, are discharged as infectious sputum, mucous, or other bodily excretions that can infect others.

The six main types of biological agents that terrorists might exploit to fashion a weapon are shown in Table 1. Those agents with medium-to-low lethality ratings are considered incapacitating, rather than killing, instruments.

Because of their availability, uncomplicated use and high degree of lethality, *Bacillus anthracis* and *Clostridium botulinum* are the agents most likely to be used in any biological weapons terror attack that might take place within the short term (that is, the next five years). Since both of these pathogens are fatal upon direct exposure to high concentrations, and are also quite durable, the delivery systems for these bio-toxins can be relatively easily improvised (that is, jerry-rigged by amateurs). Weapons based on many of the other potential agents described in Table 1 – some of which could have much more catastrophic impact – are far less likely to be employed, at least in the near term, because they would be enormously more difficult to construct and deploy. However, the eventual use of these other agents in the long term (that is, in the next ten to fifteen years) – once countermeasures to anthrax and botulism-type weapons have been devised and implemented, thus limiting the effectiveness of such devices – could pose an even more serious threat.

How Biological Terror Agents Work

Biological materials have to be carefully prepared (that is, propagated), packaged and delivered if they are to accomplish the terrorists' goal of fatally infecting as many victims as possible. Several counter-terrorism experts predict that some bio-terrorists will try to achieve this effect by attempting to weaponize such materials (Wiener, 1991: 130). This process (that is, weaponization) is called microencapsulation. It occurs through impregnating a culturing medium with a specific biological pathogen, adding a rough surfaced crystalline thickener that will augment the poison's ability to stick to lung tissue and, then, granulating the product. This can best be accomplished through use of commercial, sterile-isolation, freeze-drying lockers, centrifuges and milling machines. The result is a powdered substance, which can be reduced to a fine dust consistency that is not perceptible to human senses (that is, is odorless, colourless and tasteless). Terrorist operatives could release this powder opportunistically from vistas positioned at a slight elevation over their designated target, most likely a congested urban area. The qualities obtained through weaponization would allow the biological-contamination-dispersal weapon's particles to be inhaled deeply into the victims' lungs, penetrate their blood streams and begin the cycle of infection that will end in killing the hosts (that is, the victims) and, if the pathogen produces contagious discharges (sputum or other bodily fluids), spread the infection to others (Preston, 1998). In other circumstances, liquid fluorocarbons (for example, Freon) could be used as aerosol propellents for such micro-encapsulated pathogenic substances. Since biological weapons quickly degrade in sunlight, an attack involving their use would most probably take place at night, early dawn, or on a dank, misty (but not rainy) day.

Who Are the Possessors of Such Weapons?

Many countries have, or have had, biological weapons development programmes (see Table 2). Some have been driven by political motives, others by security concerns. For example, many candidate states seeking bio-weapons capabilities are unhappy with regional order, believe they are targets of great power intervention or confront nuclear armed states.

According to information provided by several Soviet biological weapons experts who have defected to the West, some terror sponsoring states (including Iran, Iraq, North Korea and, seemingly, Syria, Cuba and Libya) have smallpox-based biological weapons arsenals (Preston, 1998). If these reports are true, the startup feedstock for these smallpox weapons may have been provided sometime during the Cold War by the USSR, East Germany, Czechoslovakia or China, or might even have been collected directly by the rogue state's epidemiologists sent to underdeveloped third world countries to provide medical assistance during isolated outbreaks of this disease that periodically occurred in the1960s or 1970s

(Bermudez, 1998). If employed in the format of granulated powders (that is, as weaponized bio-pathogens as previously described), these currently untreatable illnesses would strike without notice, until the many victims seeking medical care eventually alerted emergency services personnel as to the true character of the epidemic they were confronting. In any event, unless medical authorities were either forewarned or extremely lucky, it is most likely that, for the first few days, or perhaps weeks, the cause of the outbreak would be mis-diagnosed. James M. Hughes, director of the US National Center for Infectious Diseases, has observed that 'because none of the biological agents considered most likely to be used as mass casualty weapons currently cause national public health problems, we have limited capacity to diagnose them, either at the local, state, or federal level' (Miller, 1998a: A14). Smallpox, for instance, is an extremely contagious, highly lethal virus that would spread rapidly – possibly killing hundreds of thousands before the nature of the outbreak could be identified and civil defense emergency procedures initiated. Moreover, since most countries stopped inoculating their citizens for smallpox in the 1970s, and because the vaccine wears off after twenty years, the disease probably would progress quickly throughout any such nation so attacked, due to a lack of antibody inhibitors within the general population.

Implementation and Deployment of Biological Terror Weapons

Biological devices in the hands of terrorists may very well be the quintessential terror weapons, as they are quite suited to silent attack on extended civilian populations, many of whom could become fatally infected long before the onset of symptoms would reveal the nature of the onslaught against them. Such an event would have a potent psychological impact on the nation attacked, and it would doubtless shatter its citizens' perceptions of their personal, as well as collective, security. Shortly after such an attack, the victimized locality's ability to provide emergency medical services could become severely eroded due to the sheer numbers of casualties the incident would generate. The overwhelming demands placed upon these resources by the scope of the disaster thus created could stretch even regional acute health care systems past the breaking point. Furthermore, emergency room facilities and personnel may be secondary casualties of the attack, as, if these biological agents were to be used in combination with chemical weapons such as lewisite, mustard gas or sarin, the former's

Table 1: *Potential Biological Terror Agents*

Pathogen	Symptoms	Days to Effect	Lethality	Vector
BACTERIA				
• *E. coli 0157:H7*	E. coli bacteria are normal inhabitants of the digestive system. Only a few strains can cause illness. This strain produces a toxin that results in severe cramping, abdominal pain, watery or bloody diarrhoea, vomiting, or fever. It can also cause renal failure that is fatal in about 30 per cent of all cases.	1–5	Medium.	Undercooked meat, unpasteurized fruit juices, vegetables grown in fields fertilized by cow manure, or contaminated water from wells, lakes, water parks and swimming pools.
TOXINS				
• *Pfiesteria piscicida*	Impaired memory, disorientation and learning and reasoning difficulties.	1–7	Low. Begins to fade away after three months.	Contaminated seawater.
• *Tricothecene mycotoxins*	Systemic toxicity is manifested by weakness, prostration, dizziness, ataxia (uncoordination of the gait), tachycardia (rapid heartbeat), hypothermia (low-body temperature) and hypotension (low-blood pressure). Death may occur in minutes, hours, or days.	1–4	High.	These toxins are more effective as particles on the skin than as respiratory inhalations.
• *Ricin*	Shortness of breath. Death usually occurs within two hours.	Hours to days.	Very high.	Ricin can be injected into the skin (as it was to kill Gregorii Markov, in a famous KGB assassination). As a terror weapon it would most likely be dispersed as an aerosol cloud.
• *Clostridium botulinum*	Fatigue, vomiting, constipation, sweating, giddiness, convulsions, respiratory paralysis, haemorrhagic conjunctivitis that causes extreme pain, temporary blindness and, in high doses, death.	1–6	65 per cent fatal without an antitoxin. Vaccine is available.	Tainted food or water.
• *Staphylococcus enterotoxins*	Violent vomiting and diarrhoea.	1	Medium. Antiserum and vaccine available.	Tainted food, water, or human carriers.
FUNGI				
• *Histoplasma capsulatum*	Skin or mucous membrane lesions.	5–18	Medium.	Tainted dust.
• *Coccidiodes immitis*	Disabling respiratory infection and, abscesses.	10–21	Medium.	Tainted dust, vegetation, or soil.
• *Nocardia asteroidea*	Pneumonia, tumors and headache.	?	High.	Tainted soil.

Table 1: Continued

Pathogen	Symptoms	Days to Effect	Lethality	Vector
RICKETTSIA				
● *Coxiella burnetii* (Q fever)	Sudden fever, chills, headache, weakness and profuse sweating.	14–26	Medium.	Ticks.
● *Bacterium tularense* (Deer fly fever)	Chills, fever and prostration.	1–10	Medium.	Infected animals, ticks, or tainted water.
● *Shigella dysentariae*	Fever and diarrhoea.	1–7	Medium to low.	Infected food or drink, or flies.
● *Vibrio cholera 01* (cholera)	Nausea, vomiting and diarrhoea.	1–5	Medium.	Infected foodstuffs, water, or flies.
● *Rickettsia prowazeki*	Headache, fever, generalized pains and skin rash.	6–15	Medium.	Lice.
● *Rickettsia mooseri*	Headache, fever, generalized pains and skin rash.	6–14	Medium to low.	Rat fleas.
● *Rickettsia tsutsugamushi*	Headache, fever, generalized pains and skin rash.	7–10	Medium to low.	Rodent mites.
● *Rickettsia rickettsii* (Rocky Mountain Spotted fever)	Skin rash, fever and generalized pains.	3–10	Medium to low.	Ticks.
● *Brucella Group* (Brucellosis – Undulant fever)	Irregular fever and pain in joints and muscles.	6–60	Medium to low.	Infected foodstuffs, or untreated dairy products.
● *Corynebacterium diptheriae* (Diphtheria)	Slight sore throat and fever.	2–5	Medium to low.	Droplet infection.
● *Bacillus anthracis* (Anthrax)	High fever, laboured breathing, rapid pulse, carbuncles, coughing, swelling and shock, leading to death in most cases.	1–7	Fatal without treatment with penicillin before signs of the disease appear.	Animal products.
VIRUSES				
● *Dengue fever*	Fever, intense headache and skin rash.	3–15	Medium. No suitable vaccine. No suitable chemo-thera-py	Mosquitos.
● *Hepatitis A*	Fever, nausea, headache and jaundice.	15–40	Medium.	Nasal and intestinal discharges from infected persons.
● *Hepatitis B*	Fever, nausea, headache and jaundice.	40–150	Medium.	Blood, serum, or plasma from infected persons.
● *Venezuelan Equine encephalomyelitis*	Fever, drowsiness and muscular paralysis often resulting in death.	7–21	High. No suitable vaccine.	Bloodsucking insects.

Table 1: Continued

Pathogen	Symptoms	Days to Effect	Lethality	Vector
• Psittacosis	Pulmonary infection, headache, backache and constipation.	6–15	Medium.	Infected birds.
• Japanese Encephalitis	Headache, confusion and delirium.	2–15	High. 20 per cent chance of permanent mental impairment	Mosquitos and ticks.
• Tick-borne Encephalitis	Headache, drowsiness, delirium, neck pain and convulsions.	2–15	High. 40 per cent chance of permanent limb impairment	Ticks.
• Chikungunga	Severe joint and spine pains, the victim is immobilized for 1 to 6 days.	1–4	Medium to low. No suitable vaccine.	Mosquitos.
• Yellow fever	Fever, aches, jaundice and severe gastrointestinal symptoms.	3–6	10 per cent fatal with fluid treatment. Vaccine available.	Mosquitos.
• Rift Valley Fever	Sudden fever, nausea, vomiting, headaches, muscle pain and dizziness.	1–2	Medium.	Mosquitos.
• Ebola virus	One of the most pathogenic viruses known to science, causing death in 90 per cent of all cases.	2–21	High.	Transmitted through direct contact with the blood, secretions, organs, or semen of infected persons, or chimpanzees.
• Variola (Smallpox)	Severe fever and blisters.	7–21	60-80 per cent fatal without antibiotic therapy.	Infected persons.
PASTURELLA PESTIS				
• Mycobacterium tuberculosis	Coughing, fever, fatigue and weight loss.	30–45	Medium.	Human carriers.
• Salmonella typhimurium (Salmonella food poisoning)	Headache, chills and abdominal pains.	1–2	Medium.	Rodents or human carriers.
• Salmonella typhi (Typhoid)	Fever, enlargement of the spleen and spots on the skin.	3–38	50 per cent fatal without treatment.	Tainted water, shellfish, or human carriers.
• Malleomyces mallei (Glanders)	Lesions of skin, mucous membranes and viscera.	3–5	Low.	Infected horses, mules, or asses.

Table 1: Continued

Pathogen	Symptoms	Days to Effect	Lethality	Vector
• *Malleomyces pseudomallei* (Whitmore's Disease)	High fever, vomiting and weakness.	A few days.	High.	Rodents.
• *Septicaemic plague*	High fever and extreme weakness.	1–7	Fatal without antibiotic therapy.	Via wounds or skin abrasions.
• *Bubonic plague*	High fever and extreme weakness.	4–7	Fatal without antibiotic therapy.	Rodent fleas and ticks.
• *Pneumonic plague*	High fever and extreme weakness.	1–7	Fatal without antibiotic therapy.	Droplet inhalation.
• *Sylvatic plague*	High fever and extreme weakness.	1–7	Fatal without antibiotic therapy.	Rodent fleas.

presence might not be detected, and the required prophylaxis would not be observed, until the infection had spread throughout the medical centers treating the wounded, with devastating effect on the care givers, their hospitals and the surrounding communities. In cases where treatment with antibiotics before the onset of symptoms is required (for example, anthrax infection), such confusion could prove fatal to most of those so infected. A variant of this scenario would have terrorists mix a quantity of carcinogenic aflatoxin into the batch of chemical agents. Many of the survivors of the 'chemo-terror' attack would be put through a second nightmare several years later when they were struck down by the development of liver cancer.

The most immediate danger stems from the simplicity of the tasks required for manufacturing a biological terror, mass casualty weapon based on either *Bacillus anthracis* or *Clostridium botulinum*, as preparing such devices calls for exponentially lower levels of skills, resources and expertise in comparison to those needed for making chemical or nuclear terror devices – and the materials are much more readily available. Many everyday items, even such innocuous devices as paint-spraying machines, can serve as impromptu biological-pathogen contamination dispersal mechanisms. For example, terrorists can install such spraying apparatuses beneath cars, vans, or trucks, or under the wings of light aeroplanes, helicopters or pilotless drones to fashion mobile aerosol-type dispensers (Purdum, 1998). If *Bacillus anthracis*, type-Vollum 1B, were to be so dispersed as an airborne mist at or near

ground level within a densely populated urban-core area, tens of thousands could die (untreated pulmonary anthrax is 90 per cent lethal to those it infects) (Probst, 1991: 235). Complicating the prognosis for their recovery, the effectiveness of antibiotics against exposure to massive quantities of anthrax aerosols is uncertain. Similarly, twenty-five kilograms of *Clostridium botulinum*, the Hall strain, spread at an altitude of five-hundred feet over the non-chlorinated water supply reservoirs for a city of two-hundred-fifty-thousand would probably infect one out of two inhabitants. If the terrorists used *E. coli 0157:H7*, the most deadly strain of this bacterium, perhaps one out of three would perish in similar circumstances (Brody, 1998). Although such victims can be successfully treated with massive doses of antibiotics, as with anthrax infection, treatment must begin immediately after exposure – otherwise, it will be too late to save most of them. Counter-terrorism planners should be prepared for the possibility that terrorists may use pre-positioned, timing device controlled, aerosol containers to spray not only anthrax or botulism, but other biological pathogens as well (for example, tricothecene mycotoxins, diphtheria, meningitis or pneumonic plague) in heavily trafficked public places to cause mass epidemics. Alternatively, and on a smaller scale, terrorists could attack tourists leaving such politically volatile, terrorism plagued areas as the Middle-East, the Balkans or the Caucasus by spraying biological infectives in the cabin of a homeward-bound aeroplane, causing an epidemic that would start to spread

Table 2: *National Biological Weapons Programmes*

Country	Status	Technical Level Other Comments
Canada	Abandoned Programme.	
China	Suspected.	Operational Quantities.
Egypt	Suspected.	
France	Abandoned Programme.	Dismantled arsenals in 1972.
Libya	Under Development.	Operational Quantities?
Iran	Suspected.	Operational Quantities.
Iraq	Known.	Before the Gulf War, Iraq had extensive capabilities, including biological weapons mounted on missiles. Iraq may still have several missiles armed with biological warheads, as well as agent seed stocks, weaponized agent and biological weapons production capabilities.
Israel	Suspected.	Advanced capabilities?
Japan	Abandoned Programme.	
North Korea	Suspected.	Operational Quantities.
Russia	Suspected. Renounced Programme in 1972. Ran Secret Programme from 1972 to 1992. Again Renounced Programme. Some elements of the programme may still exist.	Advanced Capabilities.
South Africa	Abandoned Programme.	
Syria	Suspected.	Operational Quantities.
Taiwan	Suspected.	Operational Quantities.
United Kingdom	Abandoned Programme.	
United States	Abandoned Programme.	Renounced programmes (but continued research into defensive measures) in 1969. Destroyed its last stocks of biological agents in 1975.
Vietnam	Suspected.	

one to four days later. The terrorists, who would presumably either be inoculated against whatever strain of the pathogens they were using or else willing to accept martyrdom for their cause, could smugly ride the same aeroplane as their potential victims. If they used vaporizers, individual air-cleaners, or portable oxygen tanks, ostensibly for relieving symptoms of asthma, emphysema or other lung disease, they could spread these infectious agents in a deadly banana-shaped cloud, an effect that would be enhanced if they were to change seats several times during the flight. The terrorists would likely escape undetected, as the effect of such bio-pathogen dispersals would not be immediately obvious. Terrorists could also release disease laden *Aedes* mosquitos that carry yellow-fever, *Anopheles* mosquitos, the carriers of malaria, or *Acarnia Ixodidae*, bearing tick-borne encephalitis to cause a different type of silent epidemic that would be indistinguishable from a naturally occurring outbreak of disease. Unless the terrorists chose to 'take credit' for the incident, the resulting illnesses would likely be diagnosed as an international-air-travel-related sickness, that is, an 'airport epidemic.'

Genetically-Engineered Biological Terror Weapons

The risk that increasing widespread familiarization with chromosome-level, gene-manipulating, genetic-engineering techniques will enable scientists affiliated with terrorists to produce hybrid strains (for example, drug-therapy-resistant variants) of several biological agents, exponentially raises the jeopardy posed by this whole issue. This could occur through modifying the genomic structure or protein coat of an organism or toxin. Pyongyang, for example, is rumored to be engaged in attempting to re-engineer a strain of influenza (supposedly A/Japan/305/57) in this fashion for

Table 3: Russian Biological Institute Vulnerabilities To Recruitment

Location – Facility Name	Speciality	Present Task Environment	Known Recruiting Effort Made by Rogue State, Terror Group or Organized Criminal Enterprise
MOSCOW			
Shemyakin and Ovchinnikov Institute	Genetically-altered biological toxins and vaccines.		
Institute of Molecular Biology	Virology.		Teheran has successfully recruited several senior researchers who are now working or teaching in Iran.
All-Russian Institute of Phytopathology (located in Golitsino, just west of Moscow)	Pathogens for killing crops (agricultural terror-warfare).	Pesticide research; production of transgenic plants, whose genes have been manipulated to resist certain herbicides, insects and diseases.	Teheran Medical Sciences University – Pharmacology Department.
Institute of Medical Biotechnology	Genetically-altered viruses and vaccines.		
LENINGRAD			
Institute of Ultra-Pure Bio-Preparations	Vaccine research; Weapons production.		Several senior scientists have defected to a variety of Middle Eastern countries.
KOLTSOVO			
The State Research Centre of Virology and Biotechnology	Production of bio-weapons materials.		
MOLDOVA			
Institute of Biological Protection	Animal and human experimentation.		Teheran has recruited a few junior researchers who are now working or teaching in Iran.
OBOLENSK			
State Research Centre for Applied Microbiology	The nearby VECTOR germ bank has more than 110 'highly lethal' pathogens that 'could cause a catastrophe' if stolen or diverted to terrorists. Stocks include antibiotic resistant strains of Yersinia Pestis, variola major, Ebolapox and Veepox (Venezuelan Equine Encephalitis and smallpox combined).	Active participant in the International Science and Technology Centre's (Moscow) programme of finding peaceful work for former weapons scientists.	Iranian recruitment efforts stymied by cooperation with US-financed alternative venues programme.
KAZAKHSTAN			
Stepnogorsk Biological Weapons Manufacturing Plant	Design and construction of weapons using bacillus anthracis.		
UZBEKISTAN			
Institute for Plant Disease Research	Plant viruses, moulds, toxins and so on.	The US Department of Agriculture, at the Pentagon's request, purchased the Institute's entire stock of plant germs. This will help in tracking strains and creating antidotes.	

use as a biological weapons agent. Influenza is highly attractive for such purposes because of its ease of transmission (that is, it spreads via airborne droplets); short incubation period (3–7 days); and high level of susceptibility (that is, as a new influenza sub-type, everyone is at risk) (Bermudez, 1998). Such a task could be accomplished by altering the protective antigen that helps the microbe's toxins penetrate the walls of the cells that they are attacking. This new variety of protective antigen would be more difficult for the usual antibiotic treatment of choice to interrupt. Once released into the environment, these modified organisms would swiftly engender a multifaceted public health calamity, as such genetically engineered variants of what are now routinely treated and well controlled bacterial and viral diseases would introduce a severe impediment to counter-measure efforts aimed at developing effective medical treatments. This is so because pro-duction of efficacious vaccines and antibiotics requires knowledge of the strain of the organism beforehand (Foxell, 1997). As a case in point, Russian scientists, supposedly, have genetically engineered a new form of *Bacillus anthracis* by blending four different strains of the anthrax organism to beget a fully virulent strain for which current vaccines may be ineffective (Demicheli, Rivetti and Pratt, 1998). Moreover, Dr. Vladimir Pasechnik, formerly the director of the Institute of Ultra-pure Bio-preparations in Leningrad, who defected to Great Britain in 1989, stated in his debriefing that scientists at the Soviet Union's State Research Centre for Applied Microbiology at Obolensk, south of Moscow, had succeeded in developing a strain of *Yersinia pestis* that is immune to existing antibiotic treatment. Since *Yersinia pestis* (a form of the plague) is spread from one person to another by airborne droplets from coughs and sneezes, an aggressive, drug-resistant strain could rapidly sweep through community after community until a nationwide pandemic had been generated. Dr. Ken Alibek (formerly known as Kanatjan Alibekov), another biological weapons expert of the former USSR who defected to the US, in his case after the collapse of the Soviet Union, reports that Russian biological-weapons researchers have also developed genetically altered, antibiotic resistant strains of tularaemia – a bacterium that causes a virulent form of pneumonia – as well as glanders (that is, *Malleomyces mallei* – a contagious, chronic, occasionally fatal disease caused by the bacillus *Actinobacillus mallei*, marked by purulent nasal discharge and ulcers in the lungs, respiratory tract and skin).[2] Alibek (1988) adds that his former colleagues are now working on propagating a strain of anthrax that will

overwhelm the immune system by attacking blood cells.

These abilities are no longer confined to the government supported research arena. Dr. Peter Jahrling, chief scientist at the US Army Medical Research Institute located in Ft. Detrick, Maryland, states: 'I think genetic engineering has been reduced to simple enough principles so that any reasonably equipped group of reasonably good scientists would be able to construct a credible threat using genetic engineering' (Preston, 1998: 64).

Table 3 illustrates the risk that biological weapons materials may be sold to rogue states or fall into the hands of terrorists as a result of the dissolution of the former USSR's bacteriological-warfare programme, known as Biopreparat, or 'The System'. At its height in the late 1980s, 'The System' employed more than thirty-eight-thousand scientists and professional staff. The chart also suggests the complexity of the tasks involved in preventing the dispersal of Russia's stable of experts to states seeking to acquire such weapons. Alibek estimates that several senior-level researchers and even larger numbers of their junior colleagues have accepted employment offers from Iraq, Syria, Libya, China, Iran and India. Other nations, for example, Taiwan, Egypt and Israel, have also sought these scientists. The bio-weapons facilities at Sergiyev Posad, Kirov, Yekaterinburg (Sverdlovsk) and Strizhi are not depicted in this chart due to the lack of reliable information available about them.

The possibility that terrorists will obtain biological materials, manufacturing equipment or scientific expertise from Russian bio-weapons development programmes is not the only source of concern. Many other countries have such programmes that could provide these items. North Korea, for example, is not only attempting to re-engineer a strain of influenza for use as a biological weapon's agent, but is also studying the use of *E. coli 0-157:H7* – a highly-lethal bacteriological agent – as a bio-warfare pathogen (Bermudez, 1998: 28). If terror groups or rogue states need technological expertise, many Iraqi and South African bio-weapons scientists and engineers are available on the job market. In 1994, Libya was thwarted in its attempt to hire Dr. Woutor Basson, the director of the Union of South Africa's covert biological weapons development programme, when the post-apartheid successor government moved to dissolve such clandestine projects (Broad and Miller, 1998c). However, this did not stymie Libya's drive to obtain bio-weapons expertise, as UNSCOM's inspectors in Iraq reported that Libya had hired Dr. Amir Medidi, a leading figure in Baghdad's germ warfare programme – and may have even let him continue to work for his old employers while in Libya (Broad and Miller, 1998c).

Additionally, any of several rogue states' scientific establishments, or those of other nations locked in near-genocidal, terrorist incident fuelled, cross-border conflict (for example, Indo-Pakistani skirmishes over Kashmir or Iranian-Afghan frictions over the execution of eight Iranian diplomats during the siege of Mazar-i-Sherif) could breed a horrifying batch of new pathogens. For example, the release of a new type of syphilis spirochete that was immune to penicillin, the standard treatment for this venereal infection, would reinvigorate a disease that has seemingly been tamed (Wade, 1998c). To defeat this new breed of mass casualty terrorists, defensive strategies for fighting such bio-weapons terrorist incident scenarios must, in large part, be kept secret. For, if a rogue-state backer of terrorism could identify the specific antibiotic prophylaxis that their opponent's health care system was planning on using to combat a biological-agent terror attack, their scientists could, eventually, genetically engineer a new strain immune to this treatment regimen. A case example. In the face of a possible Iraqi state sponsored, mass casualty terrorist assault using anthrax bombs, artillery shells, or SCUD missile warheads during the period of Gulf War tensions that occurred in late-1997, the Israeli government distributed Doxycycline, without a prescription, to all its citizens. American and Israeli military experts are now concerned that Iran, Iraq, Syria, Libya, or any other terrorist-sponsoring country capable of producing biological weapons, will develop an anthrax strain that is immune to Doxycycline. According to several biomedical experts, this is a fairly-straightforward task that could be accomplished within a year and a half of such a programme's inception (*Foreign Report*, 1998).

There are many facets to this risk. Terror group recruited, laboratory trained, biomedical scientists could attach respiratory-illness bacterial genes to an existing virus, such as *herpes simplex*, thus creating a new, potentially catastrophic health threat. Or, bio-terrorists could combine two or more viruses to produce a super virulent pathogen. This scenario is not farfetched, as there are credible reports that Russian scientists have succeeded in making DNA copies of the disease causing mechanisms of the Ebola virus, which they then grafted onto *variola major*, creating a mega threat that they have labelled 'blackpox' (Preston, 1998: 63). If this has occurred – and there are doubters (Pringle, 1998) – this new illness, the haemorrhagic ; form of smallpox, would be extremely contagious and persistently fatal. If wielded by terrorists, it might wipe out millions before effective medical counter-measures could

be devised. In a separate development, other Russian scientists reputedly have contrived a new anthrax germ containing two non-anthrax genes that alter the way in which the organism causes disease (Broad, 1998a). This was achieved by inserting toxin-making genes from a closely related and usually harmless microbe, *Bacillus cereus*, into *Bacillus anthracis* (Wade, 1998b). According to Col. Arthur Friedlander, chief of the bacteriology division of the US Army's Medical Research Institute of Infectious Diseases at Fort Detrick in Frederick, Maryland, the Army's anthrax vaccine 'would not be effective against this genetically engineered organism that is not really anthrax anymore' (Riechmann, 1998).

Alternatively, terrorist biological engineers might concoct new diseases by fusing mammalian viruses, bacteria and fungi to human DNA and RNA, thus enabling the resulting infectious agents to break the species barrier. This could convert several currently non-communicable-to-mankind sicknesses into pandemic level human afflictions. For example, biological terrorists could use cutting edge gene-manipulating techniques to alter the DNA instruction set for the monkeypox virus – a simian type of smallpox – so that it would become communicable to humans, thus producing a new health threat for which no vaccine exists. Or, terrorist bio-engineers might find a way to propagate syphilis in animal hosts (currently, the bacterium has none), thus creating a potential veterinary public health nightmare and setting the stage for possible transmission of the disease to humans through animal bites. Although biological terrorists could alter any mammalian illness, those affecting mice, rabbits, cattle, horses, cats, dogs, deer, racoons and monkeys would probably be the easiest, and deadliest, to use, not only because most biomedical scientists are likely to have had extensive experience working with such materials and their associated techniques during their laboratory training, but also considering these animals routine close contact or kinship with humans.

Using a different tack, biological terrorists could attach traditional 'human scourge' diseases (for example, muscle or organ tumors, bone cancer, leukemia or Hodgkin's disease) to markers for racial characteristics, or to 'disease genes' (Fisher, 1998) affecting specific ethnic groups as revealed through the Human Genome Mapping Project's research. This process would be speeded if the rich trove of information and innovative laboratory techniques were to be integrated with data drawn from the gene-pool analysis conducted by the Human Genome Diversity Project, which is structured around an effort to survey humankind by studying blood samples from hundreds of ethnic groups (Wade, 1998a). The proposal for this had first been advanced by a Swedish scientist, C.A. Larsen, in a 1970 article published in the US Army's *Military Review* (Larsen, 1970; Beckwith, 1972). Five years later, an American military manual noted the possibility of such a scenario's enactment – although for chemical, not biological, agents (US Army Mobility Equipment Research and Development Center, 1975). If eventually perfected, such weapons could kill or cripple countless thousands selectively by race and ethnicity. Here, certain types of cancers could ultimately become vectors of a silent ethnic cleansing that could devastate legions of unsuspecting, genetically vulnerable victims whose military, health care and governmental protectors would be impotent to defend them. Given the past decade's exponential increases in ethnic group inter-communal violence, which have spawned several ethnic cleansing terror campaigns, coupled with the propensity of religious fanatic terror groups to resort to acts of atrocity fuelled barbarism that, in toto, compute as mass casualty terrorism, the issue of the propagation of such designer illnesses has serious implications for international public health planning bodies.

A change in the vector (that is, the way a particular disease is spread) would enhance the potential of a wide variety of pathogens as terror weapons agents. In principal, if scientists could develop new vectors for specific categories of existing pathogens, this would overcome the biggest obstacle to employing myriad fungi, rickettsias, viruses and toxins now considered too vulnerable to weather conditions, heat or sunlight for use in aerosol-dispersed mass-casualty weapons targeted against civilian populations. If, for example, Enterovirus-71, which causes hand, foot and mouth disease and sometimes leads to life-threatening complications (for example, viral meningitis, encephalitis or a poliomyelitis-like paralysis), were to be transformed from a mildly contagious disease spread only by direct contact with nose, throat and anal secretions of those infected into a mosquito or tick-borne disease, the results could be catastrophic. Conversely, similar perils would result if Dengue fever, which is spread by mosquitos, were to be recast as a highly contagious, airborne droplet spread disease. Here, it is not the change of vectors, *per se*, but the introduction of a contagious, lethal illness into a new ecological or climatological niche, that constitutes the dimension of the heightened risk.

Biological terrorists could also exhume the bodies of victims of long ago pandemics (for example, the influenza virus that killed at least twenty-million people in 1918) to obtain still viable samples of the virus for propagation

(Kolata, 1998). This would be an exceptionally difficult task, which would require a team of pathologists, virologists, molecular biologists, geologists and medical archeologists. Once this cadre of biomedical scientists was assembled, they could begin to search above the permafrost line for mass graves of the epidemic's victims. Using a technique known as needle biopsy, these researchers might, eventually, retrieve tissue samples from the victims' livers, intestines, spleens and lungs containing traces of genetic material of this now forgotten killer virus, plus antibodies or serums produced in the acute phase of the disease, or even bacteria from complicating corollary infections, which the permafrost's dry cold had preserved. The team could then use polymerase chain reaction, or PCR, to recover the virus from these tissue samples and to identify it as the 1918 influenza virus. Next, these scientists could attempt to correlate the identified virus isolates from several different cadavers by use of a phylogenetic tree – a diagram that scientists make by comparing the chemical letters of genetic materials from different viruses. If the virus isolates were all identical (that is, all of the victims had died of the same virus), there would be no branches on the phylogenetic tree. Once they were to recover such viral DNA and RNA, these immunological terrorists undoubtedly would seek to propagate the dormant virus until they had produced quantities sufficient for making a biological-contamination-dispersal device. Or, the terrorists might decide to intensify the nature of their threat. Under this scenario, they would attempt to insert genes from the 1918 influenza virus into other, more common viruses, even non-respiratory ones. This could be accomplished once they had determined the specific structure and composition of the virus by mapping its DNA. The terror group's biomedical scientists could then focus on the character and composition of the exterior surfaces of the virus' protein coat to learn more about how the virus attaches itself to the lining of the lungs and the upper-respiratory tract (Wilford, 1998a). This would involve decoding the sequence of genetic units composing two important genes – the hemagglutinin gene and the neuraminidase gene. The former directs the production of proteins that enable the influenza virus to attach itself to cells in the respiratory system. The latter allow this virus to penetrate individual cells, then use these new homes parasitically as bases for making more virus particles that continue to spread the infection by invading more cells (Wilford, 1998b). An understanding of the genetic structure of these two genes would enable a terror group's scientists to turn on such capabilities in other, more common, respiratory viruses, thus creating a grievous public-health crisis. The modalities for doing this lie within the present capabilities of contemporary epidemiology and molecular biology. Dr. Yoshihro Kawaoka and Dr. Hideo Goto, both researchers at the University of Wisconsin's School of Veterinary Medicine, have made preliminary breakthroughs in this area by identifying a molecular mechanism involving neuraminidase that jump-starts hemagglutinin replication (Wilford, 1998b). According to these researchers, this could be 'the means by which influenza viruses, and perhaps other viruses as well, could become highly pathogenic in humans' (Wilford, 1998b: F3).

Indeed, a somewhat different circumstance involving biological agents that had been confiscated through Allied intelligence agents discovery of German biological warfare terrorist activities during World War I and, subsequently, stored for eighty years without any special precautions, illustrates the practicality of such an effort at resuscitation of long-dormant pathogens. In this instance, scientists working in June 1998 were able to culture and propagate a few surviving organisms of anthrax bacilli found in a piece of sugar taken from the luggage of Baron Otto von Rosen, who was detained by a British counter-intelligence team in Karasjok, Norway, in January 1917, on suspicion of espionage and sabotage (Broad, 1998c).

Countermeasures

The scope and significance of the dangers society will some day face pose extraordinary challenges to those charged with devising appropriate, effective safeguards against these contingencies. Any deficiency in the design or construction of such countermeasures may lead to enormous civilian casualty tolls. When dealing with bio-terrorists, what appears as obvious at first inspection, often does not hold true in retrospect, as even well-thought-out, finely crafted strategies sometimes have Achilles heels. William C. Patrick, III, an American expert on biological weapons development strategies, warns that many precautions (for example, prophylactic use of serums, vaccines and antibiotics) can be easily countered by terrorists. 'It is a hell of a problem. Defensive measures are much more difficult that offensive ones' (Broad and Miller, 1998a: A10). Even a pre-announced attack could prove infeasible to prevent, as the task of interdicting a biological terror assault predicated upon silent aerosol dispersion of biotoxins is exceedingly difficult. Developing effective countermeasures for other deployment modalities is similarly challenging. Despite more stringent rules recently promulgated by the Federal Centers for Disease Control and

Prevention for regulating the shipment of forty of the most deadly biological organisms, many identity-verification and purchaser-authorization grey areas and loopholes remain. Though these regulations require that prospective recipients of such substances have affiliation with reputable laboratories, Amy E. Smithson, an expert on chemical and biological weapons at the Henry L. Stimson Center, a Washington-based group that studies weapons-of-mass-destruction arms-control and non-proliferation issues, estimates that determined terrorists can bypass, outwit or bluff their way through these safeguards and get all the necessary makings for a biological-contamination-dispersal device (that is, a germ-warfare bomb) (Revkin, 1998). The size of the task involved in preventing an act of biological terrorism from occurring is brought into a clearer focus when one realizes that biological pathogens are easily fabricated, readily transported and very hard to detect. This raises doubts about the achievability of the international community's counter-terrorism, biological weapons containment programme's non-proliferation goals. Thus, it is not surprising that, up to this point, many governments have focused more on plugging the most obvious security holes than on proactively combatting biological mass casualty terrorists. Moreover, important portions of current international contingency planning guidelines for coping with biological-terrorist incidents have been extrapolated from pre-existing emergency-management plans for other terrorist emergencies and several crisis-handling components were derived by retrofitting nuclear and chemical weapons crisis and consequence management techniques. Many counter-terrorism analysts believe that building a network of protective safeguards specifically designed for containing biological terrorism from the ground up is the only way to provide an adequate level of security coordination among the various associated international organizations responsible for handling a bio-pathogens mass casualty attack.

In this regard, the current situation regarding biological materials international anti-terrorism coordination is analogous to the chaos that reigned during the period of unfettered free trade in bio-pathogens that existed before the imposition of primary-user identity controls. Those earlier circumstances had enabled several Iraqi pharmaceutical companies, while fronting for that nation's defense ministry's biological weapons acquisition programme, to purchase pathogens' feedstock from American and European biological materials repositories during the late 1980s. This security breach served as a wake-up call for instituting tougher industrial and commercial mailorder sales purchaser-verification requirements. Pioneering work in this area occurred when the 'Australia Group', an informal body of twenty industrialized nations that share intelligence on arms control issues, requested that its members ban exports of toxic microbes to several 'high-risk' rogue states (including Iran, Iraq, Syria and Libya) (Revkin, 1998). However, these wholly voluntary restrictions did nothing to ban the shipment of deadly pathogens to individual terrorists living elsewhere. Additional work needs to be done in this area. Similarly, more effort must be expended on international anti-terrorism collab-oration in the area of bio-toxin anti-pilferage inventory controls used for managing pharma-ceutical companies' and research institutes' central stockpiles of hazardous microbes. World-wide, internal security accounting procedures for these bio-pathogens have often been haphazard or inadequate. The need for such regulation is readily apparent, but even the occurrence of a major biological terrorist incident does not always ensure that reforms will be enacted. For example, despite *Aum Shriniko's* attempted biological-terror attacks on the Diet, the Imperial Palace, the city of Tokyo, Narita airport, the US Naval Installation at Yokohama and the American naval base at Yokosuka, which is headquarters for the US Navy's Seventh Fleet, Tokyo, to date, has not set-up domestic anti-terrorism biological materials controls.[3] Here, Japan's reluctance to take a tough stance against potential biological mass casualty terrorists stems from fears that such measures would impede legitimate biomedical research, as well as stifle cutting-edge pharmaceuticals production capabilities.

The critical need for a fully internationalized set of biological materials controls is under-scored by the operation of over fifteen-hundred toxic microbe research banks, situated all over the globe, that currently store more than a million strains of micro-organisms, many of them highly lethal. These repositories supply govern-ment laboratories, university and corporate experimental centres, biomedical research institutes and local and regional hospitals with samples of human pathogens for a wide variety of purposes (for example, as benchmarks for assessing the proficiency of diagnostic pro-cedures, testing machines and infection-control protocols; providing feedstock for pharma-ceuticals production; supplying cultures for double-blind efficacy tests for serums, vaccines and medicines; and as a source for therapeutic stocks of *Clostridium botulinum*, which is commonly used as a wrinkle relaxer by thousands of dermatologists). One of these central repositories, the World Federation for Culture Collections, has over four-hundred international affiliates in more than fifty countries, including Pakistan, Bulgaria and Iran

– three countries that, reputedly, have violated the Biological Weapons Convention to further clandestine bio-weapons development pro-grammes or facilitate illicit pharmaceutical materials trafficking operations (Bonner, 1998). Another, the notoriously-porous American Type Culture Collection in Rockville, Maryland, sold toxic microbes to Iraq before Baghdad's invasion of Kuwait.

Controls, however, have finite limits. In the early 1990s, *Aum Shriniko's* biomedical scientists were able to locate naturally occurring feedstock of *Clostridium botulinum* for their bio-terror weapons on the northern island of Hokkaido, near the Tokachi River wilderness area (Bonner, 1998). They also sent field teams to what was then Zaire to bring back samples of the Ebola virus. Additionally, the cult imported feedstock for propagating Q fever (an infectious disease caused by the rickettsia, *Coxiella burnetii*, marked by fever, weakness, muscle pains and coughing) from *Aum Shriniko's* vast livestock ranches in Australia. In these three incidents, even the most stringent international controls would not have prevented the terror group from obtaining the biological pathogens it was seeking due to the free-form nature of the open hunt techniques used.

The prognosis for winning the fight against biological terrorists is not totally inauspicious, however. There are several drawbacks to biological weapons, chief among them the danger of the 'boomerang' effect, also known as 'blowback' (that is, self-contamination). During World War II, this unexpected repercussion forced the Japanese Army to abandon its use of the biological agents that the Empire's biochemists had developed as terror weapons, after several brigades of their own infantry fell victim to the infectious diseases that the Imperial air force had deployed against a dozen Chinese civilian population centers (Miller, 1998b). Once scattered to the winds, biological infectious agents spread unpredict-ably. For this reason, germ weapons are often considered useful only when used far from the terrorists' operating areas or homeland. Moreover, for all its fearsomeness, biological terrorism has many inherent weaknesses that judiciously contrived countermeasures can effectively exploit. For instance, the lengthy incubation periods of many bio-weapons pathogens allow a window of opportunity for the treatment of the victims with medical palliatives and stopgaps that, if the interval were long enough, might provide a hedge until the appropriate vaccines, medicines and serums, as well as medical specialists trained in biological-weapons containment techniques, could arrive in precincts near the contaminated area. Furthermore, many biotoxins are fragile organisms that quickly perish when exposed to sunlight, heat or air pollution. Likewise, when used as an airborne anti-personnel weapon, aerosol dispersed biotoxins rapidly dissipate to non lethal concentrations through dilution with fresh air. Here, the 'downwind' concentration of such an airborne infective agent depends on the mass of the agent released, the size of the particles, the height of the release and the initial size of the aerosol cloud, as well as the stability of the atmosphere, wind speed, mixing height and temperature (Fetter, 1991: 19). Particle size is important. Large particles (that is, those more than ten microns in diameter) fall more quickly to the earth than do smaller ones. While they may severely contaminate a narrowly defined area, they usually do not pose a grave threat unless that space is heavily trafficked. Small particles, particularly those less than five microns wide, continue to swirl in the air longer, spreading a cigar-shaped bandwidth of infection over a much larger expanse, for a longer period, requiring more elaborate quarantine and infection-control measures.

A brief discussion of prophylaxis and treatment will help clarify a looming debate over countermeasures' strategy. There is a significant difference in the way vaccines and antibiotics work that has major implications for the countermeasures we are examining. Vaccines are proactive (that is, preventive) in nature and scope, while antibiotics, for the most part, are reactive (that is, after-the-fact damage control). Composed of 'live' (that is, weakened) or 'dead' (that is, deactivated) germs, vaccines stimulate the body's immunological system to produce disease specific antibodies that, then, help the patient's immune system fight off the disease. Conversely, antibiotic therapy, when followed as a treatment regimen, makes direct chemical attack on the invading cells of viruses, bacteria, or other pathogens. Because they are not disease specific in the manner of vaccines, antibiotics are more flexible tools for treating germ infected terror victims. However, unlike vaccines, antibiotics do not kill viruses. This represents a serious shortcoming (Broad and Miller, 1998a). While preventing outbreaks of disease with vaccines is universally preferential to having to attempt to suppress an epidemic with antibiotics, future technologically adept terror groups will probably knowingly select either viral agents that are outside the mainstream of predictable candidates or genetically altered hybrid strains of the more common ones to circumvent vaccine based defensive strategies. This ensues because production of vaccines requires knowledge of the strain of the organism beforehand. In the final analysis, both vaccines and antibiotics are co-equal subsets of a nexus of survival strategies that must be deployed in unison, when and

where possible, to provide adequate protection during a biological terrorist incident.

A word on countermeasures to cope with possible terrorist use of the influenza virus as a bio-weapon. There is a promising new class of medicines (a tablet, *GS4104*, and a nasal spray, *Zanamivir*) that may help in this fight. These drugs appear to offer not only reductions in the duration and severity of symptoms of both the 'A' and 'B' strains of the influenza virus, but, if taken daily during the first five days of such an incident, appear to provide immunity from catching the illness (*New York Times*, 1998). While not substitutes for vaccines, these medications could serve as a secondary-level countermeasure's strategy for blunting the impact of a deliberately propagated influenza epidemic, if used immediately upon the discovery of such a scheme.

Conclusion

If terrorist use of biological weapons occurs within the next few years, it will likely be of the simplest kind (that is, un-weaponized, non-genetically-altered, 'wet' anthrax or botulinum toxins delivered via conventional explosives powered devices, resulting in the release of a cloud of infected air into a crowded, public place, or pollution of a municipality's water mains) for which already enunciated, preset countermeasures can most likely be rapidly and effectively deployed. Such an attack would probably be fatal to perhaps no more than several-hundred individuals, and the ultimate outcome painful, but not catastrophic, to society. Such an incident would, however, most likely create a groundswell of political support for the implementation of a comprehensive countermeasures strategy, which before the event's occurrence would have been considered too costly. At that time, preparations against the contingent deployment of the inventory of biological infectives, as surveyed herein, would likely be demanded by the general public as an urgent response to a clearly demonstrated danger. Likewise, the government might decide to press making it a crime to publicly encourage political violence, as well as proscribe membership in organizations that are linked to the terrorists' cause, even though such groups are careful to deny espousing violence. Neither of these actions is currently prohibited under present anti-terrorism laws. Such suspension of basic freedoms, guaranteed in the US, under the Bill of Rights, could only occur if the need for such a step were readily apparent due to dire jeopardy posed by, for example, an imminent biological terrorist attack in which thousands were to be incapacitated or killed.

The necessity for a resource intensive, broad-scale preventive programme against such a wide array of potential biological weapons threats is based on a simple calculation: while the probability of terrorists resorting to the more esoteric and terrifying agents described throughout this study is slim, the potential impact on society of a successful attack is so horrendous that prevention virtually at all costs becomes imperative. To assure that such a prophylactic strategy can be developed and promptly implemented when required, awareness of, and continued research on the whole range of such agents is warranted and necessary.

Notes

1. Adapted from Smith (1991).
2. Dr. Alibek reports that when he was director of the Soviet Union's biological weapons manufacturing plant at Omutninsk, he learned that wild rodents living outside the weapons complex had become chronically infected with an antibiotic-resistant form of tularaemia. This was gravely worrisome as rodents can transmit the disease to humans. If this happenstance, which was caused by a leaking drain pipe, were to be replicated elsewhere and be exploited as a terror tactic, the results could be devastating.
3. For all of their scientific expertise and accomplishments, *Aum Shriniko's* quest for biological weapons capabilities was undone by their own ill-fated designs for aerosol-dispersion devices. After clogged sprayers, weak mist-production capabilities and inexact dispersal techniques, as well as poor quality control in preparing batches of pathogenic substances, severally caused all nine of their biological terror assaults to fail, the cult's leader ordered that the organization's huge investment of time, money, and effort spent for the development of biological-pathogen terror weapons be abandoned. *Aum Shriniko* then switched to poison gas (that is, sarin) as the active ingredient in its terror devices. Despite the significant casualties caused by the Tokyo subway incidents, Japanese society would have ultimately suffered exponentially larger losses, if the cult's leadership had persisted with its bio-weapons development scheme until its scientists had mastered the techniques necessary for germ warfare terrorism. Here, the cult's technological short-sightedness, ineptitude and bungling, rather than international controls, frustrated the full-blown maturation of an otherwise pernicious threat.

References

Alibek, K. (1998), 'Russia's Deadly Expertise', *New York Times*, 27 March, p. A19.
Beckwith, J. (1972), 'Science for the People', *Annals of the New York Academy of Sciences*, Volume 196, June.
Bermudez, Jr., J.S. (1998), 'Exposing the North Korean BW Arsenal', *Jane's Intelligence Review*, Volume 10, Number 8, August, pp. 28–29.
Bonner, R. (1998), 'Bulgaria Becomes a Weapons Bazaar,' *New York Times*, 3 August, p. A3.
Broad, W.J. (1998a), 'Gene-Engineered Anthrax: Is It a Weapon?', *New York Times*, 14 February, p. A4.
Broad, W.J. (1998b), 'How Japanese Cult's Failed Germ War Succeeded in Alerting the World', *New York Times*, 26 May, p. A10
Broad, W.J. (1998c), 'Norway's 1918 Lump of Sugar Yields Clues on Anthrax in War', *New York Times*, 25 June, p. A11.
Broad, W.J. and Miller, J. (1998a), 'Iraq's Deadliest Arms: Puzzles Breed Fears', *New York Times*, 26 February, p. A10.
Broad, W.J. and Miller, J. (1998b), 'Once He Devised Germ Weapons; Now He Defends Against Them', *New York Times*, 3 November, p. F1.
Broad, W.J. and Miller, J. (1998c), 'The Threat of Germ Weapons Is Rising. Fear Too', *New York Times*, 27 December, Section 4, p. 1.
Brody, J.E. (1998), 'Shift in Cow Feed May Make Beef Safer', *New York Times*, 11 September, p. A14.
Demicheli, V., Rivetti, D. and Pratt, M. (1998), 'The Effectiveness and Safety of Vaccines Against Human Anthrax: A Systematic Review', *Vaccine*, Volume 16, Numbers 9 and 10, May, pp. 880–890.
Fetter, S. (1991), 'Ballistic Missiles and Weapons of Mass Destruction: What is the Threat? What Should Be Done?', *International Security*, Volume 16, Number 1, Summer, pp. 5–42.
Fisher, L.M. (1998), 'Smoother Road from Lab to Sales: DNA Technique Aims to Predict Whom a Drug Will Benefit', *New York Times*, 25 February, p. D1.
Foreign Report (1998), 'Biological Blunder', *Jane's Information Group Ltd.*, Number 2485, 26 February, p. 3.
Foxell, Jr., J.W. (1997), 'The Prospect of Nuclear and Biological Terrorism', *Journal of Contingencies and Crisis Management*, Volume 5, Number 2, June, p. 105.
Kolata, G. (1998), 'Lethal Virus Comes Out of Hiding', *New York Times*, 24 February, p. F1.
Larsen, C.A. (1970), 'Ethnic Weapons', *Military Review*, Volume 50, Number 11, November, pp. 20–32.
Miller, J. (1998a), 'US Unprepared for Bioterrorism, Experts Say', *New York Times*, 3 June, p. A14.
Miller, J. (1998b), 'Biological Weapons, Literally Older Than Methuselah', *New York Times*, 29 September, p. A1.
New York Times (1998), 'Pill Offers Hope of Flu Relief, Researchers Say', 26 September, p. A16.
Preston, R. (1998), 'The Bioweaponeers', *The New Yorker*, 9 March, pp. 59–60.
Pringle, P. (1998), 'Bioterrorism: America's Newest War Game', *The Nation*, 9 November, pp. 11–17.
Probst, P. (1991), 'Future Trends: Some Observations', *Terrorism*, Volume 14, Number 4, October-December, pp. 233–236.
Purdum, T.S. (1998), 'Two Men Accused of Possessing a Biological Toxin in Nevada', *New York Times*, 20 February, p. A15.
Revkin, A.C. (1998), 'Arrests Reveal Threat of

Biological Weapons', *New York Times*, 21 February, p. A7.

Riechmann, D. (1998), 'Pentagon Preparing Troops for Anthrax', *Staten Island Advance*, (AP), 4 March, p. A10.

Smith, J. (1991), 'Biological Warfare Developments', *Jane's Intelligence Review*, Volume 3, Number 11, November, p. 485.

US Army Mobility Equipment Research and Development Centre (1975), *Decontamination of Water Containing Chemical Warfare Agent*, Fort Belvoir, Virginia.

Wade, N. (1998a), 'The Struggle to Decipher Human Genes', *New York Times*, 10 March, p. F1.

Wade, N. (1998b), 'Tests With Anthrax Raise Fears That American Vaccine Can Be Defeated', *New York Times*, 26 March, p. A24.

Wade, N. (1998c), 'Genetic Map of Syphilis is Decoded: Hope for Vaccine Is Raised', *New York Times*, 17 July, p. A12.

Wiener, S. L. (1991), 'Terrorist Use of Biological Weapons', *Terrorism*, Volume 14, Number 2, April-June, pp. 129–133.

Wilford, J.N. (1998a), 'In the Norwegian Permafrost, a New Hunt for the Deadly 1918 Flu Virus', *New York Times*, 21 August, p. A6.

Wilford, J.N. (1998b), 'Quest for Frozen Pandemic Virus Yields Mixed Results', *New York Times*, 8 September, p. F3.

[15]

Audience and Message:
Assessing Terrorist WMD Potential

DANIEL S. GRESSANG IV

One of the more debated aspects of the study of terrorism over the last few years has been the likelihood of terrorists using weapons of mass destruction (WMD).[1] The immediacy of the question has been brought home by a rash of terrorist spectaculars, pushing as never before the possibility of WMD use by non-state actors into the spotlight. The February 1993 bombing of the World Trade Center in New York City forced Americans to realize committed adversaries could strike in the United States as easily as they could abroad. Aum Shinrikyo's sarin gas attack on the Tokyo subway in March 1995 represnted the first large-scale use of mass-casualty weapons by a non-state actor for the express purpose of causing large numbers of deaths and injuries. Only weeks later, the bombing of the Alfred P. Murrah Federal Building in Oklahoma City underscored for Americans the potential for large-scale attacks by domestic groups or individuals. The attacks on Khobar Towers in Saudi Arabia and on the United States Embassies in Kenya and Tanzania likewise demonstrated the sophistication, coordination and dedication expected of today's terrorists.

These attacks make the question of potential WMD use by terrorists an important and timely one, especially when considered in light of the explosion in information availability and growing concerns over proliferation and material control issues. The possible level of physical destruction, injury and loss of life from these weapons is so great in and of itself that the potential for terrorist acquisition and use warrants serious consideration. Jessica Stern, Walter Laqueur, and others have presented chilling scenarios for terrorist WMD use,[2] directing our attention to the unparalleled devastation which *could* result. Such 'what if' visions provide a valuable service in directing inquiry both to the critical necessity of effective prevention and deterrence and to the attendant consequences should those efforts fail.

By the same token, the specter of WMD use, or the credible threat of use, conjures deeply held fears and insecurities. With the exception of

The views expressed in this article are those of the author and do not reflect the official policy or position of the Department of Defense or the US Government

84   TERRORISM AND POLITICAL VIOLENCE

Tokyo, the application of chemical, biological or radiological weapons has been generally limited to either state actions or to relatively isolated and limited applications against specific individuals, or select groups, or within limited locales.[3] Offensive nuclear weapons use, similarly, has been limited to state application for over 50 years. The limited use of these weapons suggests there is a widely shared reluctance to use them, so much so that serious large-scale application against a general population is seen as beyond the pale of tolerable behavior. A decision to use these weapons might then indicate the existence of an actor with little or no regard for the larger social structure such that the range of potential acts they might initiate would truly be unpredictable.

Adding to these perceptions are the present realities of access and proliferation concerns. The breakup of the Soviet Union, particularly in light of press reports of alarming degradation of security associated with WMD stocks, raises concern over terrorist access to either complete weapons or component materials. Persistent media reporting of proliferation concerns, echoed by the intelligence community,[4] heightens emphasis on the possibility of easier acquisition by terrorists. We seem to see relatively lax security, greater availability of arms and component materials, and a relaxation of effective state control over those materials and weapons and we wonder how hard it would be for a terrorist group to put those weapons to use. We see a tremendous growth in dual use technologies and quite naturally wonder how difficult it would be to divert those technologies for illicit application. That ambiguity is mirrored in considerations of weapons use, particularly with respect to biological weapons: How do we know, for example, that an outbreak of cholera or anthrax is not a natural outbreak? How do we identify transgressors, assign blame and seek retribution? By the same token, how would we determine the credibility of simple threats to unleash such weapons?

Recent publications tend to agree that the expected consequences demand serious consideration of the potential for WMD use by terrorists. Identifying and accurately addressing the threat potential have become important components of planning, prevention, and consequence management efforts.[5] Yet many of those same assessments seem either to treat all terrorist organizations and motives as essentially equivalent or to seek to differentiate terrorist groups by sometimes tenuous ideological or theological categorizations. As a result, competing assessments of terrorist WMD potential often appear to address different topics. In one sense, many of these competing assessments speak past each other, rather than addressing the same fundamental issue. In much the same way that Thomas Kuhn addressed the inability of proponents of competing paradigms to effectively speak to and understand each other,[6] proponents of different visions of the terrorist WMD potential appear to have reached something of a stalemate in the ongoing dialogue.

This article broadly outlines the competing themes in the debate, demonstrating in the process the dialogic disconnect, then offers a preliminary model for reassessing the terrorist WMD potential. The model seeks to incorporate salient features of each perspective while addressing underlying motivational factors and the dynamic interaction between terrorist and society. A fundamental tenet adopted in this effort is the belief that all terrorists are alike in at least one important way: they seek to acquire and maintain some degree of influence over an identifiable audience. While that audience may vary widely, the desire to have and exercise influence is seen as the most basic driving motivation of terrorists, regardless of additional motivational, ideological or theological imperatives.

Nature and Source of the Threat

In the literature on terrorism, the question of potential for WMD use has generated considerable attention and disagreement. Through a series of arguments, rejoinders, rebuttals, and alternatives, two principal orientations to the question have emerged. On the one hand, some analysts maintain that terrorist use of mass-casualty weapons is unavoidable. One interpretation of the Aum Shinrikyo case suggests that now the barrier between conventional and non-conventional weapons has been broken, further consideration of the question becomes a matter of assessing when, where, and by whom the next attack will come. An alternative interpretation is that Aum Shinrikyo was an aberration, a unique example unlikely to be repeated. Given the outcry and reaction to Aum's acts, this interpretation suggests, other terrorists are likely to learn valuable lessons about the weight of disproportional response and revise their own plans and aspirations accordingly. Others suggest that the terrorist will understand that WMD has never offered sufficient tactical or strategic advantage, even for states,[7] and will likely moderate actions to reflect a rather sophisticated understanding of cost–benefit assessment with respect to weapons selection. The possibility of WMD use by terrorists then becomes a mostly moot question.

Given the wide divergence between these two perspectives, it may be instructive to highlight several of the major sub-themes operative in each. Belief that terrorists will likely use mass-casualty weapons, on a large scale, frequently leads to considerations of the ideological motivations of the terrorist. Often, the motivational imperative tied to expectations of WMD potential revolves around religious themes or orientations. A common view is that religious imperatives or motives, particularly when associated with apocalyptic beliefs or visions, makes the group or individual more prone to accept violence as an acceptable mechanism for action.[8] Here, terrorists' guiding philosophies are seen informing their judgments in several important ways. For some, the religious outlook determines degrees of guilt and appropriate levels of retribution. The terrorist may see himself as God's instrument, carrying out divinely inspired or demanded punishment for real or perceived infractions. Since the attack and resulting destruction are directed or expected by the Deity, the terrorist effectively shifts blame, at least in his mind, to the Deity. By the same token, apocalyptic orientations may direct the terrorist toward believing that the end times are at hand, and attacks will either reflect the Deity's desires or will serve to hasten the coming apocalypse and subsequent establishment of God's kingdom on earth, or similar envisioned paradise. Other religious traditions are seen, from this perspective, as having similar visions, interpretations and imperatives which loosely parallel or presage those from a Christian orientation.

Other observers see a distinctly secular motivation in the terrorist. One major argument stems from the growth of information availability,[9] suggesting that the more widely knowledge has been disseminated the more easily radical groups have found the information they would need to develop and implement their own WMD capability. Knowledge, from this perspective, is power and when that power is coupled with materials accessibility, the likelihood of terrorists gaining and employing mass-casualty weapons rises. Also, terrorists are held to have many more opportunities to gain access to previously denied weapons and weapons components. Then-Director of Central Intelligence John Deutch raised this possibility,[10] although neither he nor others have claimed that this would be the sole reason for the greater threat.

A third major sub-theme envisions a greater likelihood of terrorist WMD rooted in frustration and desperation that build until mass-casualty weapons are seen as a preferable alternative.[11] In this assessment, the terrorist sees himself facing insurmountable odds, with no other options available. In such a case, the terrorist would lash out as a last act of desperation with any and all means available to him, including mass-casualty weapons. Others have suggested that desperation may play a part, but that the decision would be less emotional and more methodically reached.[12] One common argument holds American military superiority on the battlefield to be so overwhelming that terrorists could quite naturally come to see weapons of mass destruction as strategic and tactical equalizers.

But not all observers are convinced that terrorist use of mass-casualty weapons is likely or even possible. The most frequently cited deterrent to terrorist use of WMD is the sheer weight of technical demands and material needs required of such an undertaking. Nuclear weapons development and manufacture would likely require significant outlays of capital, significant high technology machining equipment and facilities infrastructures, and spatial presence. Each of these, in turn, imposes considerable limitations on a non-state group. Similarly, the suggestion that a rogue state might provide a nuclear device is often dismissed with the suggestion that a state which takes the time and energy to construct its own weapon is not likely to offer it to a group over which it may not have absolute control. The likelihood of the sponsoring state becoming the target, aside from the possibility of retaliation by the terrorists' victim, is seen as offering a significant deterrent. By the same token, the threat of retaliation for chemical, biological or radiological use is judged high enough to discourage state sponsorship of WMD terrorism. Like the technical and physical difficulties presented by nuclear devices, radiological weapons offer significant hazards for terrorists unable to contain radiation until employment; biological agents are not as easily weaponized as often imagined nor are they as predictable as the terrorist might desire; and chemical weapons are relatively difficult to apply on a large scale, without advantage of a confined space.

Others have suggested that deep-running psychological barriers are likely to prevent most groups from ever seriously considering large-scale WMD use. From this perspective, the terrorist wants a lot of people watching, as Jenkins indicated,[13] not a lot of people dead. The dead audience can do little for the terrorist, particularly if the intent is to compel some specified action, and going beyond the limits of toleration destroys any good will and support previously gained and limits his ability to act. Additionally, some contend that terrorists are not great weapons innovators and tend to use tried and true methods. The image then emerges of terrorists much more comfortable with known, proven and predictable weapons.

Building on the notion of rationality, Rapoport added another level of consideration in arguing that terrorists are quite capable of realistic cost–benefit calculations.[14] In this view, terrorists understand quite well the limits of WMD, even when those weapons have been employed by state militaries in the course of conventional warfare. Arguing that even the most egregious application of mass-casualty weapons have proven to be relatively ineffective in bringing about the desired tactical or strategic advantage, Rapoport notes that such lessons are not likely lost on today's terrorists. If terrorists do, indeed, understand the relationship between the costs of acquisition and employment of such weapons, the limited effectiveness of even large-scale use and the likelihood of state response would lead the terrorist to conclude that the attendant risks of WMD use are simply too high to accept.

We are left, then, with two competing perspectives, each of which offer compelling arguments for or against the likelihood of terrorists employing mass-casualty weapons. Accepting the contention that WMD use is likely, however, leads to questions about how assessments are subsequently framed. The notion that a religious imperative offers a greater propensity for violence and a greater likelihood of WMD use is problematic, since religious motivation explanations may not explore the dynamic in sufficient depth. The resulting danger lies in the potential to overgeneralize and stereotype motivations. Emphasizing the religious imperative could also lead to the unintended incorporation of biases against differing religious orientations. We assume the worst, in such instances, based more on our interpretation of the group's core beliefs than their motives and outcome expectations. But denying the potential for terrorist WMD-use outright seems equally problematic in that such assessments would either discount existing evidence or assume a degree of rationality which might not, in fact, be present. Assuming the rational terrorist might lead to an assessment based more on observer notions of rationality and less on the perspectives and cognitive processes of the terrorists themselves.

The reality may fall somewhere between the two competing perspectives, with the potential for terrorist use of mass-casualty weapons existent, but unlikely for most groups. Not all terrorist groups are likely WMD candidates, as the religious imperative argument holds, but the determining factor may be something subtler than gross ideology. To suggest that the Irish Republican Army, the Basque ETA, or the Red Army Faction would be unlikely to seriously consider WMD use strikes us as intuitively acceptable. The suggestion that groups such as Hamas, Hizballah, Palestinian Islamic Jihad, various Christian Identity groups in the USA, or Osama bin Laden's al-Qa'ida would seriously consider WMD use strikes many as equally acceptable intuitively. Some may see advantage for these groups in using mass-casualty weapons, either in ideology or desperation, but the more important issue lies in determining those for which such a choice is realistic. All groups could be considered candidates, but we would waste considerable time and energy assessing many organizations which would not see value in WMD use.

The challenge, then, is to move beyond simple considerations of access and capabilities. The degree of sophistication and depth of ability may vary considerably from group to group, but from the victim's standpoint there is little to distinguish a crude, but functioning, device from a sophisticated one. We must also move beyond surface considerations of ideological or theological imperatives so as to avoid stereotyping, overgeneralization, and unintended biases.

How might we do this? Motives drive terrorists. Each terrorist who takes up arms has a reason. To observers, the reasoning may seem just or unjust, sensical or nonsensical, reasonable or unreasonable, rational or irrational.

But the reason nevertheless exists and the words and the deeds of the terrorist are likely to reveal what those reasons are, at least at the organizational level.[15] The words and deeds of the terrorist offer a unique glimpse into his cognitive decision-making.

Elevating the perspectives of the terrorist to prominence is the first step. First is the identification of the terrorists' audience. Here, however, we must continually bear in mind *that the terrorists' perspective is preeminent*, directing analysis toward considering the terrorist's own understanding of audience. Determining who the apparent audience of the act of terror is, from this analytic standpoint, is not as germane as asking who the terrorist believes his message is directed towards. The two may not be the same. Terrorists 'speak' through their acts, a point acknowledged and driven home by anarchists' 'propaganda of the deed' in the late nineteenth century. By the same token, terrorists speak to multiple audiences beyond their immediate victim, both internal and external to the group, and the message may differ for each,[16] even in the context of a single act.[17] At the same time, the content and context of the terrorist's message to his primary audience is a critical component for understanding the linkage between motive and action. Since the terrorist exists and functions within the larger society, the way in which the terrorist interacts – *and sees himself and his organization interacting* – with society speaks to the role the terrorist sees for himself and his organization.

Underlying Framework

Inherent in this approach to the assessment of terrorist WMD potential are several assumptions. First among these is that terrorists are, in their own fashion, rational actors. By this, terrorists are seen as having a specified and identifiable set of preferences which can be ordered from most preferable to least preferable. This preference order is seen as driving cost–benefit calculations such that the terrorist acts in ways generally in accordance with his established preference order. Terrorists are likely to be preference maximizers, acting in ways expected to lead to realization of the highest preference possible given existing circumstances. That is not to say that terrorists are expected to adhere rigidly and blindly to that preference order, but that given the choice and the opportunity to seek satisfaction of a preference, the natural choice would be the preference cognitively assigned the greatest worth. Preference orders and their associated weights are not static, but are expected to change as the prevailing situation changes and as the terrorist's understanding of his alternatives and options changes. As long as the terrorist acts to the extent possible in accordance with *his* particular preference set and preference order, his behavior can be considered rational.

A second assumption is that the terrorist has both motivation and outcome expectation. Something is wanted, and actions are taken in pursuit of that goal. The relative realism of the goal is not, however, nearly as important as the existence of the goal itself and the desire to bring that goal to fruition. These goals shape, in turn, the terrorist's perspective and it is from that perspective that the terrorist acts. Despite the multiplicity of goals which might be identified, terrorists share an outcome expectation – gaining and exercising influence. Whether the more tangible outcomes expected are political, social, or religious, all terrorists seek to influence an audience. Their efforts may center around persuasion, in which the target audience is asked to accept and adopt the terrorist's vision of the future, or coercion, in which the terrorist seeks to compel desired actions by force or threat. Influence bridges the gap between persuasive efforts and coercive efforts to affect, in one way or another, a given outcome.

To gain and exercise that influence, the terrorist must also direct his message, whether in words or deeds, to an appropriate audience. The dead among the terrorist's victims are not the core audience, since their death eliminates their ability to act in accordance with the terrorist's wishes. The terrorist's core, or primary, audience is that group or entity *which the terrorist believes* he is 'speaking' to. Osama bin Laden might, for example, refer to Allah's will and the need to liberate holy Muslim lands from occupation by infidels in justifying an attack on American facilities. While it is easy to think his audience is Allah, bin Laden is addressing the US government and the American people, telling the former to leave Saudi Arabia and telling the latter to pressure the government into compliance. More important, however, is bin Laden's effort to reach the Islamic community and to persuade them the 'crusaders' can be expelled.[18] In a single act and statement, bin Laden reaches three audiences.

A Preliminary Model

Consideration of ideology and its role in shaping and directing terrorists actions often seems inadequate. It is easy and convenient to lump together a number of groups into loosely-defined and organized conceptual conglomerates. Consequently, terrorist groups within a common ideological framework are treated as almost interchangeable units, suggesting that the basic content of the ideology sufficiently defines the perspective and motivations of distinct organizations. That summary understanding of the groups' operative ideological framework, in turn, colors observer perceptions by obviating the need to delve further into the specifics of those ideological roots. Yet a more detailed and context-sensitive examination seems almost intuitively warranted, since there are frequently vast differences between ideological kin. The depth, strength and source of religious beliefs, for example, speaks volumes of the degree of tolerance for violence, the shape and context of violence acceptance, and the overall willingness to consider violence as inherently justified.[19] Rapoport's note on the role of religion in terrorism is instructive in reminding us that not all religious traditions are alike, offering an incredible variety of belief and outlook, each with implications for violence. There is reason to believe the same types of cognitive and perceptual differences similarly affect the secular terrorist.

In the end, terrorist actions are purposive acts, designed to produce, directly or indirectly, expected outcomes. Terrorist attacks are not random and senseless acts of brutality designed for no overt purpose. Each act serves a purpose, whether the audience understands that purpose or not. The purpose may be quite obvious or more subtle, ranging from the assassination of a hated adversary in order to eliminate a real or perceived threat, to a wave of attacks exhibiting no easily discernible pattern, designed to sow fear and uncertainty in the target population.

Emphasizing the purposive aspect of each terrorist act, and consolidating that understanding across the range of attacks and non-violent communications, allows for the development of a more sophisticated understanding of the terrorist's decision-making calculus. To begin that development, three aspects of the communicative dynamic between terrorist and audience are posited as critical facets for analysis and successful assessment of terrorists' WMD potential.

Audience Identification

The first aspect suggested is a determination of the terrorist's core audience. Verbal and written communications are offered by terrorists to explain and justify their actions and existence,[20] with imagery and phraseology designed to attract and engage a particularly oriented audience, whether religious or secular. They typically seek to cast themselves as saviors, leaders, or martyrs for some noble cause, be it liberation from an oppressor, heralding a newer and more equitable social and political order, or attainment of some religious condition. These messages offer an understanding of how the terrorist sees his actions as contributing to a greater good while also persuading the audience that the terrorists' goals are, in fact, desirable. Such claims often fall on deaf ears, since the rhetoric can be dense and the logic convoluted. Nevertheless, such communications are the concrete manifestation of the group's efforts to force by proclamation its ideology and objectives onto center stage in public attention.

By the same token, the terrorist's actions, particularly violent actions, serve as an important adjunct to written and verbal communications. The means by which the target was selected, the weapons chosen for the attack,[21] the identity of the victim of violence, and the location of the attack all speak of the motives and the desires of the terrorists. The bombing of the World Trade Center, for example, by followers of Sheikh Abdul Rakhman, reflects his earlier calls for destruction of the 'twin pillars' of western decadence. The symbolic nature of the victims, or of attack timing, offers additional insight into the terrorist's objectives by highlighting critical aspects of the terrorist's message.

The actual and symbolic nature of the message suggests that audience identification can be quite subtle. Looking beyond the immediate victim to identify the terrorist's core audience is not a new notion; it forms a significant basis for much terrorism-related analysis of the last several decades. Rather than consider a single audience beyond immediate victims, however, greater insight may be possible by asking what message and action, in combination, say about primary and secondary intended audiences. The core audience is the single most important recipient of the message, and it is the attempt to reach this audience that remains the single most important driving force for the terrorist. When we assess from our observer's standpoint, we too often assign meaning to terrorist acts based on our interpretation of the event rather than on what the terrorist attempts to say. To better understand the terrorist's intentions and primary audience identification, considerations of motive, audience, *and* expectation are necessary. The bombing of the Khobar Towers complex in Saudi Arabia, for example, is often blamed on Osama bin Laden. Many observers immediately took the United States to be the intended recipient of the message the bombers sought to send. It seemed clearly to say 'leave'. Observers also suggested that the message, taken a step further, was telling the Saudi regime to expel the Americans.

If bin Laden was responsible, that interpretation would overlook his primary intended audience, especially when his 'Declaration of War' is also considered.[22] In that declaration, bin Laden makes clear his core audience is the Islamic community, whom he expects to lead to a return to the purity and sanctity he envisions in a united Islamic community free of corrupt and corrupted Arab regimes, like the Saudis, and free of occupation by infidels. Khobar Towers could be seen as an act directed at influencing the Islamic community, first and foremost, in promoting a particular brand of belief and in promoting a particular view of the righteousness and efficacy of violent action against unwanted invaders. A secondary message would be to the United States, demanding withdrawal or suffer the continuance of violent and costly opposition. The Saudi regime would, by the same token, be bin Laden's tertiary audience for a message warning of continued retribution on behalf of the faithful as long as foreign occupation and corruption are tolerated.

We might, then, consider the identification of a terrorist's audience largely in terms of their expectations, rather than our observations. But some terrorists have a target audience rather difficult to grasp. For those groups which seem to address a deity rather than a worldly audience, the determination can become problematic with respect to separating intent of the group from observer interpretation. Rhetoric which promotes a religious imperative adds to this problem in making the intent of the group difficult to isolate. Was the Khobar Towers bombing truly a political act, or was it a religious act, as bin Laden's declaration might have us think? Does the suicide bomber in Israel act for political or religious reasons? How are we to distinguish between the two, separating the rhetoric from the message? By incorporating the ideological writings and pronouncements, then coupling them with an assessment of the act and history of those responsible, we might begin to make such a determination. When combined, the religious motivation tends to give way to an underlying political or social motivation. Similarly, it is equally important to distinguish between the motivations of the individual and of the group itself, for it is the group which provides the overall direction and delineates the ultimate objectives for action. In short, it is necessary to look beyond the motives of the suicide bomber, who may very well act individually because of religious beliefs, and examine the group itself, which may be motivated by more prosaic and secular motives.

By keeping the motivational assessment at the group level we can posit a simple dichotomy in intended core audiences. Since it is from this audience that the group expects to gain satisfaction of demands, positively or negatively, or gain additional support and sympathy, this audience plays a critical role in determining the degree and scope of violence tolerable. If the terrorist's principal purpose was to garner support and sympathy, or at least passive neutrality, there would be a level of violence and destructiveness beyond which the terrorist likely understands that actions would prove counterproductive. This human audience is tangible and reacts in physically manifested ways to the messages and acts of the terrorist. In most cases, the human audience is worldly, identifiable, concrete, and generally secular, although it does not necessarily have to be the latter.

A human audience can be a religious audience. The terrorist may have religious goals and motives, and may seek to persuade a community of believers or co-religionists, for theological reasons. Neither the selection criteria employed by the terrorist, nor system of shared belief between terrorist and audience, is as important as the nature of the terrorist's expected primary correspondent. Most of the groups usually labeled 'religious' terrorists are animated by belief, at least in part, and their interpretation of theology informs and shapes the way in which they act. Yet almost all of these groups maintain a primary dialogue with a human audience often to persuade or convert, even when that audience is defined and selected or limited by religious criteria. The terrorist who truly holds a deity as his primary audience is rare, with the Thugs perhaps the last well-known group fitting that category. The ethereal is hard to pin down, since any understanding or expectation of message acceptance and acknowledgment is predicated on the belief of the human communicant. Whereas the human audiences' receipt of the terrorist's message can be seen and measured, the ethereal audience's acceptance of a message can not. Distinguishing at the most basic level between those terrorists who believe they are addressing a human audience and those who believe they are addressing an ethereal audience, is a first step.

Addressing a human audience suggests that the terrorist seeks to promote change. He may want a change in policy, to compel a certain action or set of actions, to delay or prevent implementation of policy, to generate support or sympathy, to persuade someone to behave in certain ways, or to paralyze them into inaction. Messages to a human audience carry an expectation of physically manifest outcomes, whether positive, neutral, or negative. The terrorist addressing a human audience has a positivist outlook in that he expects his message to be heard, understood, and acted upon. For this, he needs interaction.

Terrorists addressing an ethereal audience, on the other hand, may be quite acceptant of one-way communications since it would be the ethereal 'recipient' that decides if and when, and by what means, to respond. The resulting communication with the deity would likely be a form of praise, a request for acknowledgment and later reward for acts undertaken in the physical world. The emphasis in messages to an ethereal audience is less concrete, more nebulous, extolling the virtues, needs, or desires of a deity or belief set. Response might be desired, but not necessarily required, given that the response sought may be available only in an afterlife or next incarnation. Worldly concerns are of lesser consequence and importance than the philosophical and theological.

Given such a dichotomy, and the associated levels of importance to worldly and other-worldly matters, those groups which actively seek to address an ethereal audience may be more prone to accept greater levels of violence and, perhaps, see considerable utility in the use of mass casualty-weapons.[23] A greater emphasis on a deity may suggest a greater propensity to mass casualties, but does not guarantee use of such weapons. There may be, however, fewer cognitive barriers to creating mass casualties since an ethereal primary audience allows the terrorist to rationalize and justify exceeding existing behavioral and social barriers by citing divine will or other unverifiable criterion. Those groups which, on the other hand, seek to establish a dialogue with a human audience are more likely to accept self-imposed limits to the level of violence used to further their ends. The existence of such limits has been a hard lesson to learn, but remains one which has helped determine the ultimate effectiveness and longevity of more than one group.[24] For these, the defining limits on casualties and weapons lies in the reaction and tolerance levels of the human audience. Cognitive barriers to WMD-use are tied to public reactions, and to expected reactions, limiting the terrorist's perceived range of available choices.

Message Content

A second aspect for determining the likelihood of terrorist use of mass-casualty weapons lies in the content of the message the terrorist group seeks to bring forward through words and deeds. The message directed towards the group's primary audience holds the greatest importance. The content of this message needs to be taken as a combination of rhetorical communications and attack 'content' in order to afford a clearer, more nuanced understanding. The content of the terrorist's message, however, is often taken to be the surface rhetoric and overt rationalization without considering the underlying reasoning. But the underlying core message is critical, since it addresses most accurately the objectives and motivations of the group. The rhetorical window-dressing serves a purpose, but this purpose lies more in making the act of violence more palatable to a general audience.[25] By explaining its actions in terms expected to have emotional relevance to the general public, the group heightens the chances that the overall message will be received, understood and acknowledged in a favorable manner. The act of violence itself also sends a message, reinforced by the rhetorical. Through target selection,[26] weapon selection and timing, the act of violence demonstrates in very real and concrete ways the objectives and determination of the terrorist.

Given the rhetorical and symbolic messages transmitted, it is possible to draw distinctions between the content of the messages. Assessing specific references and demands of distinct groups, however, can easily result in very narrowly defined, group and event-specific analyses. Despite the specific set of objectives and motives each group holds, the generalized claims and demands fit well in broad terms with those of other groups. Maintaining this broader perspective allows for a division of message content into a generalized dichotomy, based on the essential direction and scope, or theme, of the message transmitted.

Most terrorists advocate social or political change, a new form of government, perhaps, or a reordering of social institutions. They may want power, to be the government, to set the rules of social and political interaction. They could demand adherence to certain policy guidelines, abandonment of others, a shift in policy or the adoption of a new set of policies. They may demand justice, social equity, greater governmental emphasis on basic human needs such as education, fair wages, lifting the yoke of oppression. They might call for class struggle, calling on the oppressed to rise up and overthrow the oppressors. Or they may demand self-determination and independence. All these carry with them a common theme – that of political or social change. The target of change may be governments or people, policies or institutions, relationships or methods, structures or conditions of existence, but each seeks some form of reordering political or social relationships.

Alternatively, some terrorists call for the destruction of their enemy, for the elimination of a people, a nation or a state. Such calls frequently focus on destruction without specifying envisioned outcomes. Early Palestinian calls for the destruction of Israel[27] have been taken by some at face value, yet the message directed to the Palestinian people was not so much Israel's destruction as it was the need to liberate Palestinian lands. The message to the secondary Israeli stressed destruction, but the primary message of liberating Palestine was directed more toward stirring the aspirations of the Palestinian people. In this light, the original PLO charter was directed more toward cultivating Palestinian aspirations for statehood and, consequently, can be taken as more of a call for change. Determining which messages are true calls for destruction may be more difficult, but when actions and words are combined with a sensitivity to primary audiences being addressed, the distinctions between calls for change and calls for destruction becomes evident.

A dichotomy of message content can be one of change versus destruction. Those terrorists seeking change want a reordering of social and political structures rather than destruction. To affect change, there must be something surviving the violence, something, in effect, to change. Because the outcome expectations of those seeking change rest on a foundation of what already exists and on the need for some degree of social continuity, the change-demanding terrorist would seem less likely to consider seriously the large-scale use of weapons of mass destruction. Terrorists seeking destruction without precondition, on the other hand, would be unmoved by considerations of social survivability. For this terrorist, destruction is the end, the objective, the goal, and it would not matter whether any element of social structure – including the people – survives a WMD attack. Eliminating the possibility of social continuance is the goal for these terrorists and those seeking to convey a message of destruction, without consideration or exception, may well be predisposed to use mass-casualty weapons.

ASSESSING WMD TERROR 97

Social Interaction

The third aspect for considering the likelihood of mass casualty weapons use revolves around the group's perceptions and understanding of its interactions with the larger society within which it operates. For groups seeking political or social objectives, interaction with other members of society is a necessity. It is this larger social structure which is either the primary audience, contains the primary audience, or offers the transformational object. Regardless of specific group goals, society forms an important message-recipient for the terrorist since it is the principal entity to which the message of violence is delivered. There is, consequently, an expectation of reciprocity in which the terrorist communicates his desires, expectations, demands and goal identification and then anticipates in return some form of popular response.

Expected responses, like the terrorist's message, can be positive or negative. Terrorists seeking to promote an idea which they consider a public good may seek acceptance, support and sympathy. They work to promote themselves and their cause as beneficial, just, desirable or needed. Liberation, freedom from oppression and self-determination are expected to receive positive public response. Terrorist's expectations can also emphasize and promote the negative, generating in turn a negative response from the public. Messages of ethnic, religious or racial intolerance and hatred, vows to eliminate or destroy a specified group, and calls for retribution for some real or perceived wrong are examples of negative messages, considered from the perspective of those targeted. Faced with a call for its destruction, that audience would quite naturally react negatively even if secondary and tertiary audiences are more tolerant and supportive of the message.

In either case, the series of interactions between terrorist and society constitute a 'dialogue'. Often bloody, this 'dialogue' nevertheless forms the underlying basis for what the terrorist seeks to do or say. Violence is undertaken purposively in order to bring about an expected response or to create a necessary precondition for the realization of expectations. The nature and focus of the attack, then, reflects the terrorist's expectation of response. Those promoting self-determination or freedom from oppression, for example, would be more likely to direct their violence against the agents or symbols of oppression and subjugation than against the individuals, institutions or symbols of the people on whose behalf they claim to operate. Groups espousing extreme hatred or other negatively oriented messages, in contrast, would be more likely to stage seemingly indiscriminate and unrestrained acts of violence.

In sharp contrast to most terrorists, who maintain some form of reciprocal relationship with the society around them, some may act to avoid any meaningful and lasting relationship with society. Fringe religious cults sometimes practice extreme self-isolation, but a religious imperative is neither a necessary nor sufficient condition for engaging in violent acts. Nevertheless, the examples set by the Branch Davidians, Heaven's Gate, the Solar Temple, and other religious groups which chose relative isolation and which largely severed ties to society, have been used in popular debate to illustrate the presumed danger posed by religious isolationists. Terrorists who act similarly could be said to have an inapposite, or non-existent, relationship with society. Reality, however, often intrudes on desires and demands minimal interactions. The purchase of food or crop seeds, needed equipment or weapons, acquisition of other goods and services the group can not produce internally yet need nevertheless, as well as recruiting new members, offer clear examples of necessary, if unwanted, interactions. With an understanding of minimal necessities in mind, an inapposite relationship can be taken as the predominate desire to eliminate all non-essential interactions with society. The group seeking to affect an inapposite relationship with society does not strive to influence society and does not care, in return, what the members of society think of it.

Given the dichotomy between reciprocal and inapposite relationships, groups can be categorized by the extent to which their actions and statements reflect a desire for and degree of severance and isolation from society. The likelihood of WMD-use would logically be greatest for those most committed to the inapposite relationship. Most terrorists, though, want a live audience paying attention to their message and this observation is no less applicable today than it was 30 years ago. Most terrorists maintain a reciprocal relationship, positive or negative, with society and are much less likely to seriously consider WMD-use due to that relationship. A terrorist indifferent to public reaction would be less psychologically or cognitively inhibited in weapons selection and targeting. The lack of social inhibitions may allow those seeking to disconnect from society a greater propensity for serious WMD consideration. But like the audience and message aspects, a greater likelihood or potential based on expected societal relationships does not necessarily translate into action.

Synthesis

Combining audience, message, and social relationship offers an opportunity to distinguish between terrorist groups which are most likely to consider the large-scale use of mass-casualty weapons and those which are not. These do not offer an avenue for definitively determining if, when, or under what conditions a group would in fact resort to the use of mass-casualty weapons, nor is it intended to. It is, rather, a framework for narrowing the range of possibilities such that further observation, study and emphasis can be directed where it would be most appropriate.

For a terrorist group to seriously consider WMD use for the purpose of killing or injuring hundreds or thousands in a single act, the greatest likelihood conditions associated with each aspect would need to be met simultaneously. Groups can fluctuate between extremes, meeting all three likelihood criteria during their organizational lifetime, but it is only when all three reach the critical stage together that the threat would become real. Failure to meet any one of the criteria would suggest significant barriers to implementing any existing desire for WMD use. Lacking sufficiency in any single area also suggests the group would place enough importance on maintaining organizational viability and continuity while simultaneously preserving avenues for message transmittal. The terrorist's cost-benefit calculations would result, in these instances, in more limited activities.

To influence a human audience, some sensitivity to audience perceptions and reactions is necessary. Successfully relaying a message requires that the audience receive the message, understand it, be capable of weighing its options, consider potential outcomes of each response and make a choice of response. Crossing the bounds of acceptable action, whatever society defines that to be, serves to alienate that audience. Germany's Red Army Faction (RAF) and 2 June Movement, and Iran's Mojahedin-e Khalq, for example, failed to incorporate their audience's needs and expectations and, consequently, lost or failed to garner significant support from the very groups which they claimed to represent. For the RAF and the 2 June Movement, indiscriminate violence which had little obvious relationship to existing social, economic, or political concerns of the German people, or with little apparent connection to the groups' claimed social and political agendas limited meaningful dialogue between the groups and their intended audiences. Even the fundamental constituency of the RAF and 2 June Movement, radical students in the German universities, abandoned the groups as the clear criminality of attacks outweighed political objectives.[28] While indiscriminate criminal acts were the ultimate downfall of the German groups, the Iranian Mojahedin failed to consider the sensitivities of its primary audience, the Iranian people, by siding with Saddam Hussein and Iraq during the Iran–Iraq war. Rather than crossing unacceptable limits associated with proportionality and appropriateness, the Mojahedin demonstrated their disdain for Iranian public opinion by assisting Iran's chief enemy during open hostilities. Such insensitivity seems astonishing given the extent of support the Mojahedin enjoyed immediately after the Shah's fall from power.[29] Similarly, the more active American extreme right organizations appear to alienate most of their intended audience in part through the unending viciousness and naked hatred of their exclusionary message.[30]

Combining relationship characteristics, audience identification, and message content (Figure 1) allows one to visualize a confluence of factors

FIGURE 1
CONVERGENCE OF ASPECTS

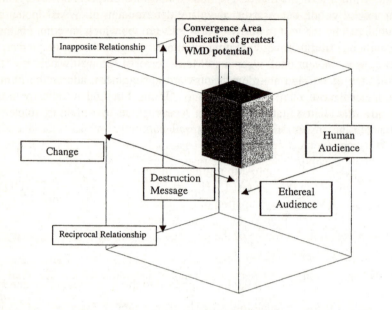

indicative of a potentially greater disposition for serious WMD consideration. Groups which see themselves speaking to a human, rather than ethereal audience seek the observable reaction found in human audiences rather than being content to rely on a belief that the message was successfully received. Where there is a human audience, there is an expectation of tangible reciprocity. Groups maintaining a reciprocal relationship with society seek to coerce, intimidate or otherwise influence and have little reason to resort to mass-casualty weapons. The survival and prosperity of the group depends on its continued ability not only to recruit new members, but to exert a degree of influence. At the opposite extreme, groups which maintain an inapposite relationship with society, who seek to address only an ethereal audience, and whose message is focused on destruction, can more easily envision a purposive utility in realizing their objectives through WMD use. For these groups, the 'biggest bang for the buck' may hold the greatest ideological and operative relevance.

The 'New' Terrorist?

Much recent debate on potential WMD use has emphasized that groups with a religious imperative are more prone to a propensity for lethality.31 These arguments have considerable merit, particularly when it is understood that

ASSESSING WMD TERROR 101

the only group which has, to date, used such weapons on a large scale – Aum Shinrikyo – fits that description. A religious purpose, however, is not an exclusive or necessarily adequate determinant of WMD potential, evidenced by the vast majority of religious groups which have not engaged in violence, and the overwhelming number of religiously-inspired terrorists who use conventional weapons. Many terrorist groups which use the language of religion are, despite outward appearances, addressing human audiences more than an ethereal one. Osama bin Laden calls for *jihad* against the United States and corrupt Arab regimes, but in doing so clearly indicates he is speaking to the Muslim *umma*:

> The latest and the greatest of these aggressions [of the USA, Israel, the UN and corrupt Arab regimes] incurred by the Muslims since the death of the Prophet (ALLAH'S BLESSINGS AND SALUTATIONS ON HIM) is the occupation of the land of the two Holy Places [Saudi Arabia], the foundation of the house of Islam, the place of the revelation, the source of the message ... by the armies of the American Crusaders and their allies ...
>
> From here, today we begin the work, talking and discussing the ways of correcting what had happened to the Islamic world in general, and the Land of the two Holy Places in particular. We wish to study the means that we could follow to return the situation to its normal path. And to return to the people their own rights, particularly after the large damages and the great aggression on the life and the religion of the people. And injustice that had affected every section and the groups of the people ...[32]

Similarly, Hizballah's message is directed at the Palestinians displaced and/or oppressed by the Israelis, calling for the liberation of Palestine so that an Islamic state, governed by God's law, can be established.[33] Even in the language of Islam, the goal of political and national liberation remains clear, as is the understanding that this is a goal of the Palestinian people:

> The Islamic Resistance Movement is a distinguished Palestinian movement, whose allegiance is to Allah, and whose way of life is Islam. It strives to raise the banner of Allah over every inch of Palestine, for under the wing of Islam followers of all religions can coexist in security and safety where their lives, possessions and rights are concerned. In the absence of Islam, strife will be rife, oppression spreads, evil prevails and schisms and wars will break out.[34]

Other groups, most notably Aum Shinrikyo, call for complete destruction as a necessary precondition for achieving objectives. For Aum, salvation lay in reincarnation in the next world. Yet the philosophy of Aum is clearly distinct from other violent groups motivated by religion. For Aum and its leader, Shoko Asahara, death was a welcomed and sought-after avenue to a higher state of being. Destruction of the world was, consequently, necessary in order to bring about the next stage in the cycle of death and rebirth.[35] Death, for Asahara, is inevitable but the enlightened, those who followed his path, could 'completely surpass death'. In that case, the enlightened need not worry about death, with Asahara asking the faithful 'if we have a goal close to ourselves and attain it, if we could completely surpass death by it, don't you think that the coming of World War III would be a great thing for us?'[36]

Do such distinctions explain an inclination, a propensity, a likelihood for the use of mass-casualty weapons? Perhaps not as much as we would like, since the question begs for a more complete and assured answer than we are able to give. Psychological studies suggest the disaffected, the alienated and the lonely may accept or seek entry into a terrorist group and, once there, become even more susceptible to complete subordination of personal interests and inhibitions to those of the group. The organization replaces family, with the subsequent development of strong bonds between the individual and his or her comrades, shaping and directing the behavior of the individual in altogether different directions than might otherwise be expected.[37] By much the same token, students of religious cults have offered convincing arguments suggesting psychological processes and intra-group dynamics help determine the way in which religious belief might be directed. Belief may manifest itself passively or violently, inwardly or outwardly, as proselytizing or as meditation, as witnessing to the masses or as violence, as suicidal tendencies or as homicidal tendencies.[38] Addressing the psychological and organizational characteristics offer part of the answer to the nagging questions of whether or not a sub-state group will again use mass-casualty weapons for political, social, or religious purposes and, if so, when.

It may be possible to offer more useful insights, and offer greater understanding, if the conventional wisdom was more rigorously challenged and, where appropriate, addressed under new analytic frameworks.[39] We may do that by asking if we might better address the likelihood of terrorist use of mass-casualty weapons by shifting focus from questions of ideological underpinnings or access and capabilities toward the dynamics of the dialogue between terrorist and audience. Emphasizing that dynamic may offer a subtler and more utilitarian approach unencumbered by emotion and rhetoric of claim and counterclaim by terrorist and their opponents. Terror does not take place in a vacuum. It seeks to levy demands and, in return, seeks to generate a response. That on-going dynamic colors and shapes the actions and reactions of both sides, offering a continuing cycle of give and take, call and response dynamic that limits analytic and predictive opportunities.

ASSESSING WMD TERROR   103

The model outlined here is incomplete and without limitation. More work is needed, including empirical testing. But it may offer a starting point, one that can stimulate new research and testing which could ultimately lead to a greater capacity to predict, and prevent, terrorist spectaculars. Will terrorists again use mass casualty weapons on a large scale? No one knows. At best we can guess, and hope that those guesses are based on reasonable and appropriate criteria. We hope we ask the right questions, generate the right data, and interpret those data accurately. Proof, in a sense, is the non-event, for if we can understand the dynamic well enough to predict and prevent, we have succeeded.

ACKNOWLEDGEMENTS

The author gratefully acknowledges the helpful comments and criticisms from David C. Rapoport, Gavin Cameron, Mark Kauppi, Sean Lynn-Jones, and anonymous reviewers.

NOTES

1. For the purposes of this article, 'weapons of mass destruction' (WMD) and 'mass-casualty weapons' are used to denote the same class of weapons. In each, the terms are taken to mean chemical, biological, radiological, or nuclear weapons which are intended to create hundreds or thousands of casualties in a single event or application. They are weapons of immediacy, with death and destruction at or shortly following weapon use.
2. See, for example, Jessica Stern, *The Ultimate Terrorists* (Cambridge: Harvard University Press 1999) pp.1–2; Walter Laqueur, *The New Terrorist: Fanaticism and the Arms of Mass Destruction* (New York: Oxford University Press 1999) pp.49–53, where he outlines several published fictional scenarios; and Joseph W. Foxell, Jr., 'The Debate on the Potential for Mass-Casualty Terrorism: The Challenge to US Security', *Terrorism and Political Violence* 11/1 (Spring 1999) pp.100–104.
3. Excellent compendia can be found in Jonathan B. Tucker (ed.), *Toxic Terror: Assessing Terrorist Use of Chemical and Biological Weapons* (Cambridge: MIT Press 2000) and Lt.Col. George W. Christopher (USAF) et al., 'Biological Warfare: A Historical Perspective', *JAMA* 278/5 (6 Aug. 1997) pp.412–17.
4. Examples available on the Internet include John M. Deutch, 'Speech Presented at the Conference on Nuclear, Biological, Chemical Weapons Proliferation and Terrorism, 23 May 1996', <http://www.cia.gov/cia/public affairs/speeches/archives/1996/dci speech 052396 .html>; Deutch, 'Fighting Foreign Terrorism', <http://www.cia.gov/cia/public affairs/ speeches/archives/1996/dci speech 090596.html>; John A. Lauder, 'Statement by Special Assistant to the DCI for Non-Proliferation John Lauder on the Worldwide Biological Warfare Threat to the House Permanent Select Committee on Intelligence as prepared for delivery on 3 March 1999', <http://www.cia.gov/cia/public affairs/speeches/lauder speech 030399.html>; and Lauder, 'Unclassified statement for the record on Worldwide WMD Threat to the Commission to Assess the Proliferation of Weapons of Mass Destruction as prepared for delivery on 29 April 1999', <http://www.cia.gov/cia/public affairs/speeches/ lauder speech 042999.html>.
5. An overview of US government initiative can be found in Government Accounting Office (GAO) publications *Combating Terrorism: Federal Agencies' Efforts to Implement National*

104   TERRORISM AND POLITICAL VIOLENCE

Policy and Strategy, report GAO/NSIAD-97-254 (1997); *Combating Terrorism: Threat and Risk Assessments can Help Prioritize and Target Program Investments*, report GAO/NSIAD-98-74 (1998); *Combating Terrorism: Observations on Crosscutting Issues*, report GAO/TNSIAD-98-164 (1998); and *Combating Terrorism: Issues to Resolve to Improve Counterterrorism Operations*, report GAO/NSIAD-99-135 (1998); and Deputy Chief, DCI Counterterrorism Center, 'International Terrorism: Challenge and Response', http://www.ia.gov/cia/di/speeches/ intlterr.html. Non-government contributions include Gavin Cameron, 'The Likelihood of Nuclear Terrorism', *Journal of Conflict Studies* 18/2 (Fall 1998) pp.5–28; Foxell (note 2); and Ian Lesser et al., *Countering the New Terrorism* (Santa Monica: RAND 1999) pp.34–35, 74–80, and 85–144.

6. Thomas S. Kuhn, *The Structure of Scientific Revolutions*, 3rd ed., (Chicago: University of Chicago Press 1996) pp.148–52.

7. David C. Rapoport, 'Terrorism and Weapons of the Apocalypse', *National Security Studies Quarterly* 5/3 (Summer 1999) pp.49–67 and Ehud Sprinzak, 'The Great Superterrorism Scare', *Foreign Policy* 112 (Fall 1998) pp.110–24.

8. Bruce Hoffman's argument in '"Holy Terror": The Implications of Terror Motivated by a Religious Imperative', *Studies in Conflict and Terrorism* 18/4 (Oct.–Dec. 1995) pp.273, is one of the most widely cited references. Examples which incorporate Hoffman's argument include Cameron (note 5) pp.19, 23; Joel Dyer, *Harvest of Rage: Why Oklahoma City is Only the Beginning* (Boulder: Westview Press 1998) pp.75–106; Hoffman, 'Enter the New Terrorist, Mute and Bloodthirsty', *The Baltimore Sun* (18 Aug. 1998) pp.9A; and Foxell (note 2) p.97.

9. See, for example, Stern (note 2) pp.138–9, 151–4; Lauder, March and April 1999 speeches (note 4).

10. Deutch, May and September 1996 speeches (note 4).

11. Dyer (note 8) pp.27–71, provides an extensive argument on this point.

12. Richard K. Betts, 'The New Threat of Mass Destruction', *Foreign Affairs* 77/1 (Jan.–Feb. 1998) pp.27–9 and Ashton Carter, John Deutch, and Philip Zelikow, 'Catastrophic Terrorism: Tackling the New Danger', *Foreign Affairs* 77/6 (Nov.–Dec. 1998) pp.81–94.

13. Brian Jenkins, 'Will Terrorists Go Nuclear?', *Orbis* 29/3 (Fall 1985) p.511.

14. Rapoport, 'Weapons of the Apocalypse' (note 7).

15. See C.J.M. Drake, 'The Role of Ideology in Terrorists' Target Selection', *Terrorism and Political Violence* 10/2 (Summer 1998) pp.53–85 and Drake, *Terrorists' Target Selection* (London: MacMillan 1998).

16. See, for example, David C. Rapoport, 'The Politics of Atrocity', in Yonah Alexander and Seymour Maxwell Finger (eds.), *Terrorism: Interdisciplinary Perspectives* (New York: John Jay Press 1977) pp.46–61, especially pp.51–3 and Joanne Wright, *Terrorist Propaganda: The Red Army Faction and the Provisional IRA, 1968–86* (New York: St Martin's Press 1991) pp.4–7, 35–7.

17. Message effect on multiple audiences parallels the terrorist's effort to solve his collective action problem. For a detailed discussion of efforts and efficacy in addressing those audiences, see Mark I. Lichbach, *The Rebel's Dilemma* (Ann Arbor: University of Michigan Press 1995) especially pp.111–27.

18. Osama bin Laden, 'Expel the Mushrikeen from the Arabian Peninsula' (1996), <http://www.webstorage.com/~azzam/html/declaration_of_war.html> and as 'MSANEWS: The Lebanese Epistle: Declaration of War, parts I through III', <http://msanews.mynet.net/ MSANEWS/199610/19961012.3.html>.

19. David C. Rapoport, 'Fear and Trembling: Terrorism in Three Religious Traditions', *American Political Science Review* 78/3 (Sept. 1984) p.674.

20. Bonnie Cordes, 'When Terrorists do the Talking: Reflections on Terrorist Literature', *The Journal of Strategic Studies* 10/4 (Dec. 1987) pp.150–51.

21. Drake (note 15).

22. bin Laden (note 18).

23. Hoffman, 'Holy Terror' (note 8); Bruce Hoffman, 'Terrorism and WMD: Some Preliminary

ASSESSING WMD TERROR   105

Hypotheses', *The Nonproliferation Review* 4/3 (Spring–Summer 1997) p.48; Hoffman, *Inside Terrorism* (note 8) pp.94–5, 201; Hoffman, 'Enter the New Terrorist' (note 8); James K. Campbell, *Weapons of Mass Destruction Terrorism* (Seminole: Interpact Press 1997) pp.5, 143–4; and Foxell (note 2) p.97 are noteworthy examples in which religious imperative is linked to propensity for violence.

24. See, for example, National Council of Resistance of Iran web pages, <http://www.iran-e-azad.org/english/ncri.html>.

25. Cordes (note 20).

26. Drake (note 15).

27. Palestinian Liberation Organization, 'The Palestinian National Charter', Resolution of the Palestine National Council (July 1–17, 1968). Those portions of the charter specifically calling for Israel's destruction have since been amended.

28. Michael Baumann, *Terror or Love? Bommi Baumann's Own Story of his Life as a West German Urban Guerrilla* (New York: Grove Press 1977) pp.86, 106–10; Jillian Becker, *Hitler's Children: The Story of the Baader-Meinhof Terrorist Gang* (Philadelphia: Lippincott Co. 1977) pp.12, 260–61, 268–71; and RAF, 'The Urban Guerrilla is History... Final Communiqué of the Red Army Faction' (March 1998).

29. See, for example, John D. Stempel, *Inside the Iranian Revolution* (Bloomington: Indiana University Press 1981) pp.300, 320; Gary Sick, *All Fall Down: America's Tragic Encounter with Iran* (New York: Penguin Books 1985) pp.232–8; and Ervand Abrahamian, *The Iranian Mojahedin* (New Haven: Yale University Press 1989) pp.187–9, 198, 206–23.

30. See, among others, Lyman Tower Sargent (ed.), *Extremism in America: A Reader* (New York: New York University Press 1995) pp.137–59, 176–90; Jeffrey Kaplan, 'Right-Wing Violence in North America', in Tore Bjørgo (ed.), *Terror from the Extreme Right* (London: Frank Cass 1995) pp.44–95, especially quotes; Rafael S. Ezekiel, *The Racist Mind: Portraits of American Neo-Nazis and Klansmen* (New York: Viking Books 1995) pp.184, 310–19 for example; Andrew MacDonald [pseud. William Pierce], *The Turner Diaries* (New York: Barricade Books 1996); and Thomas E. Nelson, Rosalee A. Clawson, and Zoe M. Oxley, 'Media Framing of a Civil Liberties Conflict and its Effects on Tolerance', *American Political Science Review* 91/3 (Sept. 1997) pp.567–83.

31. Betts (note 12) pp.29, 39–41; Cameron (note 5) pp.19–23; and Hoffman 'Holy Terror' (note 8) p.273 are examples.

32. bin Laden, 'Mushrikeen' (note 18).

33. Khalid Mish'al, 'Interview: Occupation should not feel like stability', *Palestinian Times* (Sept. 1997), <http://members.tripod.co.uk/alquds/ptimes_mishal.htm>.

34. Islamic Resistance Movement (Hamas), 'The Covenant of the Islamic Resistance Movement' (1988), article six. Posted to newsgroup 'talk.politics.mideast', 21 Dec. 1992.

35. Shoko Asahara, 'Rebirth in a Higher World', <http://www.aum-shinrikyo.com/english/teaching/rebirth.htm>; Asahara, 'How to Live during the Time of Radical Change', <http://www.aum-shinrikyo.com/english/teaching/changes.htm>; and Asahara, 'World War IIIis Coming Soon! The Control of Plasma', <http://www.aum-shinrikyo.com/english/teaching/ plasma.htm>. See also Manabu Watanabe, 'Religion and Violence in Japan Today: A Chronology and Doctrinal Analysis of Aum Shinrikyo', *Terrorism and Political Violence* 10/4 (Winter 1998) pp.84–7.

36. Asahara, 'Plasma' (note 35).

37. Jerrold Post, 'Prospects for Nuclear Terrorism: Psychological Motivations and Constraints', in Paul Leventhal and Yonah Alexander (eds.), *Preventing Nuclear Terrorism: The Report and Papers of the International Task Force on Prevention of Nuclear Terrorism* (Lexington: Lexington Books 1987) p.93.

38. See, for example, Charles B. Strozier, *Apocalypse: On the Psychology of Fundamentalism in America* (Boston: Beacon Books 1994) pp.89–92; Michael Barkun, 'Millenarians and Violence: The Case of the Christian Identity Movement', in Thomas Robbins and Susan J. Palmer (eds.), *Millenium, Messiahs, and Mayhem: Contemporary Apocalyptic Movements* (New York: Routledge 1997) pp.247–60; Dick Anthony and Thomas Robbins, 'Religious

Totalism, Exemplary Dualism, and the Waco Tragedy', in Robbins and Palmer (eds.) pp.261–84; John R. Hall and Philip Schuyler, 'The Mystical Apocalypse of the Solar Temple', in Robbins and Palmer (eds.) pp.285–311; Mark R. Mullins, 'Aum Shinrikyo as an Apocalyptic Movement', in Robbins and Palmer (eds.) pp.313–24; and Dyer (note 8) pp.211–13.

39. David C. Rapoport, 'To Claim or not to Claim: That is the Question – Always!' *Terrorism and Political Violence* 9/1 (Spring 1997) p.12 and Martha Crenshaw, 'The Psychology of Terrorism: An Agenda for the 21st Century', *Political Psychology* 21/2 (June 2000) pp.405–20.

[16]

Responding to Chemical, Biological, or Nuclear Terrorism: The Indirect and Long-Term Health Effects May Present the Greatest Challenge

Kenneth C. Hyams
Frances M. Murphy
Department of Veterans Affairs

Simon Wessely
Guy's, King's and St. Thomas' School of Medicine
and Institute of Psychiatry, London

Abstract   The possibility of terrorists employing chemical, biological, or nuclear/radiological (CBN) materials has been a concern since 1995 when sarin gas was dispersed in a Tokyo subway. Contingency planning almost exclusively involved detection, containment, and emergency health care for mass casualties. However, it is clear that even small-scale CBN incidents—like the recent spread of anthrax spores through the mail—can cause widespread confusion, fear, and psychological stress that have lasting effects on the health of affected communities and on a nation's sense of well-being. More emphasis therefore needs to be placed on indirect effects and on the medical, social, economic, and legal consequences that follow months to years afterward. To respond effectively to CBN attacks, a comprehensive strategy needs to be developed that includes not only emergency response, but also long-term health care, risk communication, research, and economic assistance. Organizing an effective response challenges government institutions because the issues involved—eligibility for health care, the effects of low-level exposure to toxic agents, stress-related illnesses, unlicensed therapeutics, financial compensation—are complex and controversial.

Now that a deadly biological weapon, anthrax spores, has been spread through the mail, attention has focused on the possibility that future terrorism using chemical, biological, or nuclear/radiological (CBN) mate-

The following article was written over one year prior to the September 2001 terrorist attacks on the World Trade Center and the Pentagon and the mailing of anthrax spores to news organizations and political leaders. Sadly, some of the concerns raised in the original manuscript about the acute health effects of a terrorist attack have come to pass. What we underestimated in our original analysis was the impact that a terrorist attack would have on every segment of society, not just the targeted community but also the general population and its leaders. As a consequence, we have revised the original manuscript to reflect these recent developments.

274   Journal of Health Politics, Policy and Law

rials could cause mass numbers of casualties (Falkenrath 1998; Franz et al. 1997). For example, it has been estimated that 100,000 deaths could result from an airborne release of anthrax spores over a large urban area (Inglesby et al. 1999). As a consequence, considerable funding, resources, and training are being devoted to the rapid detection and containment of a CBN attack and to the provision of emergency health care (Brennan et al. 1999; *New York Times* 2001).

Although a catastrophic attack is conceivable, it is more likely that limited casualties would result from direct exposure to CBN agents because of technical difficulties in using these weapons against civilian populations (Betts 1998). Nevertheless, the confusion, fear, and long-term health consequences still may be severe. As demonstrated by recent events involving letters containing anthrax spores, even a small-scale incident with CBN materials can have a profound impact on the health of a community and a nation's sense of well-being (Guillemin 1999:245; Okie 2001) and lead to protracted social and economic problems (Falkenrath 1998).Why are terrorist attacks using CBN materials so devastating? Mainly because terrorism already is frightful, but the use of unconventional weapons is even more so. CBN agents are terrifying because they cause injury and death in strange and prolonged ways (Franz et al. 1997). In addition, we feel more vulnerable to these weapons than conventional explosives because they can harm large numbers of ordinary citizens in places generally considered safe, such as in the workplace and residential neighborhoods.

Other characteristics of CBN weapons place them in the category of health hazards that are likely to cause both public fear and heightened anxiety (Renn 1997). A large body of research has indicated that the following features of a health threat are associated with prolonged effects: (1) involuntary threats that occur without warning (as opposed to personal choices like cigarette smoking), (2) manufactured threats versus natural disasters ("acts of God"), (3) unfamiliar threats with unknown health effects, and (4) threats that pose a danger to children and future generations (Bennett 1999a; Smith et al. 1986). It is clear that CBN weapons fulfill all of the criteria for creating a major catastrophe. Not only are these weapons intended to cause death and terror, but a CBN incident also has the characteristics of disasters that induce lingering medical, psychological, and social reactions.

In order to combat acts of mass terror, contingency planning has to involve more than just emergency response. An effective strategy will have to consider a broader array of immediate and long-term consequences, which will arise regardless of the type of toxic exposure or number of casualties (Holloway et al. 1997; Institute of Medicine 1999).

Immediate Harm

The first casualties of a terrorist attack result from the direct effects of the CBN agent. Emergency response training is ongoing for this eventuality. This aspect of medical care may appear clear cut but could cause immediate controversy. Prophylactic measures that have been used to protect against biological and chemical warfare agents—like the anthrax vaccine and pyridostigmine bromide pills—have been postulated to cause chronic medical problems (Presidential Advisory Committee 1996:114, 117; Institute of Medicine 2000). Attempts to use these problematic drugs and vaccines fuel controversy and add to a traumatized community's health concerns (Rosen 2000; Weiss 2001).

In addition to direct harm from a CBN agent, the impact on those not exposed may be almost as traumatic, as amply demonstrated since the terrorist attacks on the World Trade Center and Pentagon. In the immediate aftermath of a large-scale CBN attack, there is fear and bewilderment (Holloway et al. 1997). Everyone involved worries about his or her family and friends. Accidents can occur from people fleeing the disaster area (Erikson 1990). Essential hospital employees may be incapacitated by secondary exposure to the CBN agent or leave work out of personal concerns (Guillemin 1999:54). The normal reaction to an unfamiliar, life-threatening event—fear, confusion, and flight—could cause greater damage than the attack itself (Bleich et al. 1991).

Until the nature of the CBN exposure is clearly determined, uncertainty and fear will be present even among skilled rescue and medical personnel (Holloway et al. 1997). Although prophylactic drugs and vaccines and the use of gas masks and protective clothing help alleviate anxiety among "first responders," dramatic and hurried activities of rescue workers frighten residents of the disaster area (Barker and Selvey 1992). The perceptions of a much larger population can be affected by television and newspaper reports of emergency medical care and decontamination efforts (Jones et al. 2000). Media images of spacesuit-clad investigators unsettled a worldwide audience during recent anthrax scares (Dobbs 2001). With uncertainty about the identity of the perpetrators and the extent of anthrax contamination, no person is certain that he or she will not be involved in a terrorist attack.

Following reports of a CBN attack, health care facilities can become quickly overrun by both medical and psychological casualties and concerned citizens (Falkenrath 1998). For example, after recent anthrax deaths, it has not been possible to satisfy public demand for ciprofloxacin, an antibiotic approved for the treatment of anthrax; patients have inundated emergency rooms seeking reassurance; and, the public health system has been stretched to the limit trying to screen populations that may have been exposed to contaminated letters (Firestone 2001; Prial 2001). For another example, after the incident in Goiânia, Brazil, in which accidental exposure to a medical radiation source led to several hundred casualties and four deaths, 10 percent of the population (more than 100,000 people) sought medical checks (Collins and Carvalho 1993; Petterson 1988).

Urgent questions can be expected about the causes of common physical (somatic) complaints because nonspecific symptoms are often the first manifestation of injury from CBN agents (Bleich et al. 1992; Rosen 2000). However, somatic symptoms are frequently reported in healthy populations of adults and become even more prominent under stressful circumstances (Barsky and Borus 1999; Schwartz, White, and Hughes 1985). There already have been reports of increased complaints of pain, sleeplessness, headaches, palpitations, and other somatic symptoms since the 11 September 2001 terrorist attacks in the United States (Morin 2001; Goldstein 2001). Common flu-like symptoms, such as cough and fever, are particularly frightening after an attack with anthrax spores. Symptoms that arise from normal fear and uncertainty in a chaotic emergency, like headaches and difficulty concentrating, are indistinguishable from the early effects of nerve gas exposure (Bleich et al. 1991). The nonspecificity of these symptoms and the resulting difficulty in rapidly determining their causes can misdirect and deplete emergency medical care and containment resources.

Even though there has been acknowledgment that the indirect consequences of a CBN incident will be substantial (Falkenrath 1998), official planning may nevertheless underestimate the potential scale of the response. With uncertainty about who was exposed and whether further exposures were occurring, large numbers of both endangered and unaffected residents will present to medical care providers with health concerns, as occurred after the release of sarin in a Tokyo subway (Woodall 1997) and more recently following potential exposure to anthrax spores (Prial 2001). Additionally, stress, fear, worry, and grief can exacerbate existing medical and psychological problems in the entire community.

As one example of indirect outcomes, a widely reported CBN incident could act as a powerful trigger for outbreaks of "mass sociogenic illness" (DiGiovanni 1999). In fact, several outbreaks have occurred in the aftermath of recent terrorist attacks (Wessely, Hyams, and Bartholomew 2001). These episodes of physical symptoms suggestive of acute injury, which have been misleadingly called mass hysteria, can be set off by toxic exposures, unusual odors, or even rumors of contamination (Boss 1997). The immediate response to multiple casualties, such as the arrival of emergency workers wearing decontamination clothing and television cameras, accelerates the spread of this illness (Krug 1992; Selden 1989). It is important to realize that, given the appropriate circumstances of stress, fear, and confusion (Boss 1997), mass sociogenic illness can affect any population. Because there is limited understanding of this phenomenon, symptoms of mass sociogenic illness frequently are medicalized rather than treated with education and reassurance, which subsequently leads to protracted controversy in affected communities.

In addition to increased demands for health care after a CBN attack, immediate changes in reproductive behavior may occur. Following the Chernobyl radiation disaster there was a decrease in the birth rate across Western Europe and an increase in induced abortions (Bertollini et al. 1990; Knudsen 1991). More recently, abortions and delayed pregnancy became an issue in the Balkans during aerial bombing of chemical plants (Fineman 1999). Similar fears about birth defects were expressed by victims of the 1995 Tokyo sarin attack (Watts 1999). Whether recent terrorist attacks will affect reproductive behavior is not yet known, but numerous anthrax hoaxes were perpetrated against abortion clinics in the United States immediately following reports that anthrax spores were being spread through the mail (Booth 2001).

For the emergency response to a major CBN event, planning therefore has to take into account two different health care scenarios. The first relates to managing the deaths and injuries caused directly by the attack. The second involves dealing with the fears, health concerns, and psychological reactions that normally arise in disasters. Because enormous numbers of people will feel at risk before the extent of exposure can be determined, these indirect consequences may pose the greater challenge to authority, acute health care, and public confidence. After the emergency response, many of these initial health problems may have prolonged consequences.

Long-Term Consequences

As natural and manufactured disasters have shown, the long-term effects can be substantial. Experience indicates that following a CBN attack there would be four major health concerns: (1) chronic injuries and diseases directly caused by the toxic agent, (2) questions about adverse reproductive outcomes, (3) psychological effects, and (4) increased levels of somatic symptoms (David and Wessely 1995; Schwartz, White, and Hughes 1985; Nakajima et al. 1999). Acute injuries caused by a particular CBN exposure are manageable because they can be identified and treated according to established guidelines.

As during the emergency response, more difficulties may result over the longer term from harder to prove or disprove health outcomes. For instance, cancer, birth defects, and various neurological, rheumatic, and immunological diseases are increasingly being attributed to diverse types of chemical and radiation exposures (Neutra, Lipscomb, and Satin 1991). There are many social, historical, and cultural reasons why these health concerns would be prevalent after a CBN attack. Everyone has been sensitized by the AIDS epidemic, mad cow disease, and numerous environmental tragedies. The scientific debate over the health effects of pesticides, genetically modified food, electrical power lines, and cellular telephones also has influenced public perceptions. The result is a heightened sensitivity over environmental exposures. A terrorist attack not only would create new fears but would surely amplify existing concerns about the safety of our food, water, and air. For instance, residents downwind of an anthrax-contaminated building in Florida were concerned about the possibility of infection (Firestone 2001).

The current scientific uncertainty over the chronic health effects of low-level exposure to toxic agents will further increase anxiety in the affected communities (Brown and Brix 1998). Because health officials cannot give blanket assurances that no harm will result from brief or non-symptom-producing exposure to chemical, biological, or radiological materials (Institute of Medicine 2000), distrust of medical experts and government officials may result (Birchard 1999). Furthermore, unconfirmed and controversial hypotheses about the health effects of exposure to CBN materials can become contentious scientific and legal issues (Birchard 1998).

One contemporary example demonstrates the potential long-term impact of environmental concerns. Residents in a market town in the west of England have blamed a variety of health problems on "germ warfare experiments" that involved aerial spraying of bacteria thirty years ago during the Cold War (Townsend 1997). What is noteworthy is the wide range of conditions attributed to the experiments: cancers, cerebral palsy, Down syndrome, miscarriages, learning difficulties, autism, and skin ulcers, to name a few. The result has been "an entire Dorset village torn apart." Similar health fears can be anticipated on a larger scale following recent deaths from exposure to anthrax-contaminated letters.

The long-term psychological consequences of a CBN incident also can be substantial. Posttraumatic stress disorder (PTSD), which is characterized by reexperience of traumatic events, affects victims, witnesses, and rescue workers most directly involved in the initial exposure (Holloway et al. 1997). Recent estimates are that one-third of those who were most closely involved with the World Trade Center tragedy may suffer from the condition. However, PTSD will be only one of the mental health problems facing a community, as demonstrated in Japan following two terrorist attacks with the chemical nerve agent sarin (Ohbu et al. 1997; Watts 1999). And as we have recently witnessed, routine activities that once felt familiar and safe, like visiting the post office, can now seem threatening and strange (Whoriskey and Jenkins 2001). The general level of fear and anxiety can remain high for years, exacerbating preexisting psychiatric disorders and posing a challenge to the entire public mental health system. In the case of the recent World Trade Center events, thousands of children were left without a parent or orphaned, and even more more witnessed the tragedy both directly and on television (Davidson, Baum, and Collins 1982; Prince-Embury and Rooney 1988; Stepp 2001).

Although we have considerable information about high background levels of physical symptoms in adult populations (Hannay 1978; Mayou 1991), there is less understanding of the causes of more complex symptoms and of the factors that affect the experience and reporting of distress (Roht et al. 1985; Shusterman et al. 1991). As a consequence, when clusters of unexplained symptoms have been observed following toxic exposures (Hyams, Wignall, and Roswell 1996; Reuters 1999), there is often heated debate over the role of psychological stress in causing or contributing to reported health problems (Joseph et al. 1998; Stiehm 1992; Presidential Advisory Committee 1996:123–125). These controversies are difficult to resolve because stress is an inevitable aspect of any life-threatening experience. A population exposed to a terrorist attack experiences both direct injuries and numerous physical symptoms due to prolonged stress, muscular tension, and sleep deprivation (Bravo et al. 1990; Nakano 1995).

As noted in the discussion of emergency medical care, public concern can arise from well-intended health care decisions. The nonstandard, off-label, and even investigational drugs and vaccines that may help save lives in a CBN attack can become protracted health and legal issues. In particular, therapeutic agents that have not received official approval, like licensing from the U.S. Food and Drug Administration (FDA), are distrusted (Berezuk and McCarty 1992). Increased symptoms and illnesses reported long after a terrorist attack may be attributed to side effects of medical interventions (Institute of Medicine 2000).

It has been difficult to obtain FDA approval for many potentially useful therapeutic and prophylactic measures because CBN materials are too toxic to expose human volunteers in required efficacy studies (Institute of Medicine 1999:110–164). To address this problem, the FDA is considering a different standard—the use of animal studies—for the approval of new vaccines and pharmaceutical products to counter chemical and biological warfare agents (Zoon 1999). These rule changes will directly impact the development of a new generation of vaccines for anthrax and smallpox because it is not ethically feasible to expose study subjects to these deadly diseases in order to demonstrate protection.

Controversy over the health effects of hazardous exposures and therapeutic interventions may impede other aspects of the recovery effort. As in any disaster, government assistance will be required to rebuild communities and restore the local economy. However, the issue of compensation for personal injuries could have a damaging effect on public faith in government (David and Wessely 1995). The reason is that many health claims will be hard to prove or to relate to the CBN incident (Huber 1992:92–110). The fear of cover-up may surface, and litigation will lead to an adversarial relationship between the public and the government. Assigning blame and legal liability could become the focus of acrimonious public and political debate, which hinders public health efforts.

The nature of the particular terrorist weapon also has a consequential impact on recovery efforts. For example, chemical nerve agents dissipate rapidly and do not pose a long-term health risk (Institute of Medicine 1999:174–183). In contrast, anthrax spores and radiological material can persist in the environment for decades; this would make decontamination efforts problematic and lead to persistent health concerns.

The demographic and cultural characteristics of an affected community, as well as the availability of public transportation and medical and social services, further influence recovery efforts (Nakano 1995). Less well-off communities need greater medical, social, and economic assistance. In wealthy communities, however, it is difficult to monitor the health impact of the attack because residents have greater mobility and access to a diversity of health care services. The economy of a community may be permanently harmed because of fears that locally produced agricultural and manufacturing products may be contaminated with harmful CBN agents (Petterson 1988). For the same reason, the value of individual homes and commercial property could drop precipitously, which will engender feelings of hopelessness in the community (ibid.).

Recommendations

A community attacked with a CBN weapon will need both emergency intervention and long-term health care, extensive medical and risk assessment information, and economic support. Also, multiple challenges to the credibility of governmental and scientific authority could hamper recovery efforts. The following recommendations are made for dealing with these consequences.

Health Care

Emergency response teams already train for acute medical care of mass casualties. What remains to be decided is how long health care should be provided and whether health care should be comprehensive or restricted to the probable toxic effects of the CBN agent. These are critical questions in countries like the United States, which does not have universal health care. In the event of a large-scale CBN attack, there are compelling reasons for offering comprehensive health care over an extended period of time. For one, readily available clinical care would ensure that an affected community's health care needs are met, which is arguably a prime responsibility of the government after a disaster. In addition, provision of medical care represents one of many tangible indications that the government is committed to recovery and as such helps restore confidence in public institutions (Watts 1999).

If health care is offered, who should provide the care? In the United States, health care would have to be furnished by private physicians and health maintenance organizations or by the two major federal health care systems in the Department of Veterans Affairs (VA), which maintains hospitals in every state, and the Department of Defense (DOD). The VA

282   Journal of Health Politics, Policy and Law

and DOD already are involved in the emergency response under the Federal Response Plan but would require appropriate authority and resources to provide health care for a longer period (Montello and Ames 1998).

Several arguments can be made for centralizing health care in local medical facilities. For one, this approach would ensure access to health care. Second, a smaller number of health care providers could be more intensively educated on relevant health issues and new scientific findings. Finally, a consistent set of providers would be more likely to detect the development of new or worsening health problems in the affected population.

The need for readily available health care and specially trained providers cannot be underestimated. The Gulf War syndrome controversy demonstrates how complex health issues can become after a possible CBN attack and how important it is for health care providers to have up-to-date information (Murphy et al. 1999). When a traumatized population cannot obtain answers to health questions from knowledgeable providers, misinformation fills the void and concerns multiply. Moreover, specially trained providers could maintain standardized medical records, which are important for scientific and medical-legal purposes.

Although it can be argued that freely available health care will foster the sick role and prolong disability, properly trained health care providers can help patients work through their health problems and grief, with restoration of function as the primary goal of treatment. Although offering mental health care after an act of mass terror is important, immediate grief counseling or psychological debriefing may not be the most effective approach (Raphael, Meldrum, and McFarlane 1995; Wessely, Bisson, and Rose 1999).

Risk Communication and Management

A concerted risk communication and management effort is critical after a CBN attack in order to keep the public informed and to promote recovery (Bennett, Coles, and McDonald 1999). In the immediate aftermath of a terrorist attack, the primary method for rapidly disseminating information is through the popular news media. Accordingly, public officials and scientific experts have to be as open, clear, and forthcoming as possible with the press and avoid the development of an adversarial relationship. After a community's sense of well-being has been shattered, there is a tendency for information and reassurance to be met with disbelief and anger (Brewin 1994; David and Wessely 1995). A frustrated press corps only makes communicating with the public harder.

To enlist the help of the press, health officials have to provide the press with the best available information. It is important for crisis managers to work cooperatively with the press to discourage the reporting of false rumors and inaccurate information, while at the same time not providing false reassurance (Modan et al. 1983). The press also has to educate itself about a new health threat in order to accurately report the news, as exemplified recently by early media reports that did not distinguish between anthrax exposure and infection. Over time, diverse methods have to be developed for communicating with the affected population (Neutra 1985). These include mass mailings, use of the Internet, and especially community meetings. Open meetings help disseminate useful information and involve the public in the recovery process, which speeds recovery and increases confidence in governmental actions (Holloway et al. 1997). Effective risk communication is a long-term process that requires a two-way exchange of information with the affected population. Public concerns should also be addressed by working closely with community leaders (Coote and Franklin 1999).

Maintaining credibility over the long term will be one of the most difficult challenges for government institutions. Precipitous decisions made in a crisis to care for casualties and to prevent further injury will be judged later in a deliberative manner using more complete and accurate information. Mistakes will be identified. The government should take responsibility for its mistakes and clearly explain the reasons for critical decisions in order to maintain trust.

As noted, unsupported health claims could become a problem. There will be nonorthodox views and hypotheses on events and scientific issues (Glassner 1999; Presidential Advisory Committee 1996:90–91). These ideas cannot be ignored, but public health policy and medical care cannot be based on unsubstantiated opinion. A successful risk communication strategy has to deal fairly and openly with unproven assertions and new hypotheses, not least because the existence of dissident views appeals to the popular media's commitment to balanced reporting (Singer and Endreny 1993).

For recovery to work, risk management efforts have to prevent demoralization and ensure that members of the affected population are ultimately characterized as survivors rather than as victims. A shift in thinking from vulnerability and dependency to pride in overcoming adversity will do more to overcome long-term health problems in both the targeted community and the nation at large than any other health measure (Giel 1991; Summerfield 2000). Even after a devastating disaster, communities display substantial resilience when not rendered helpless and passive in the recovery process (Bravo et al. 1990). Additionally, rapid financial assistance and the rebuilding of the community's economy provide substantial health benefits (Summerfield 1999).

Surveillance and Research

An extensive surveillance and research effort is important following a major CBN attack. The identification of persons injured or killed by a CBN weapon will be a priority during the emergency response. Accurate detection requires the establishment of a case definition of affected individuals (Brennan et al. 1999). This case definition should be based primarily on the objective characteristics of the injury caused by the particular CBN exposure (Franz et al. 1997; Pavlin 1999). Diagnostic criteria should not rely on nonspecific symptoms that become prominent in a highly stressful situation and may be related to mass sociogenic illness (Jones et al. 2000). Misclassification of unaffected communities as exposed to a deadly CBN agent will not only misdirect emergency efforts, but will also confuse the public and result in protracted scientific and legal disputes about who was injured. The recent confusion over who may have been exposed to anthrax spores from contact with contaminated mail could easily lead to prolonged controversy.

After a major CBN attack, longitudinal surveillance studies should be initiated. Evidence-based answers have to be available for questions that will arise after a toxic exposure about increased rates of various diseases, birth defects, physical and mental symptoms, and psychiatric disorders. Failure to conduct epidemiological surveillance is likely to lead to accusations of government insensitivity, incompetence, and cover-up (Schwartz, White, and Hughes 1985). Delaying sound research also opens the door to unsubstantiated claims and may eventually preclude the initiation of definitive research studies because accurate data become less accessible over time (Institute of Medicine 2000).

Although a concerted research effort may be misinterpreted as evidence of more widespread harm than officially acknowledged (Jones et al. 2000), it is better for the responsible authorities to initiate scientific investigations rather than to be pushed into them by public and media criticism (David and Wessely 1995). By being able to respond to the public's legitimate need for answers, fear and anxiety can be lessened and credibility of responsible authorities improved. Research is necessary, not only to answer pressing health questions but as part of the risk-management process itself.

To implement the preceding set of recommendations, a high degree of communication, coordination, and cooperation is required among governmental and social institutions. To organize an effective response is difficult given the many different groups involved, such as the civilian government agencies at the local, state, and national level; law enforcement; the military; emergency response teams; community health care providers; social services; local business interests; the court system; and the news media (Tucker 1997). Because most of these organizations are not accustomed to working together and have different priorities, conflicts arise. Therefore, clear lines of authority are essential to guide an effective response and recovery effort (Centers for Disease Control and Prevention 2000).

In the United States, lead responsibility for the initial operational response to acts of terrorism ("crisis management") has been assigned to the Federal Bureau of Investigation (PDD-39, 1995). The U.S. attorney general can subsequently transfer lead responsibility to the Federal Emergency Management Agency (FEMA) for "consequent management," that is, measures to protect public health and safety, restore essential government services, and provide emergency relief to governments, businesses, and individuals affected by the consequences of terrorism. The establishment in the United States of the new Office of Homeland Security should lead to greater coordination in the government's response to acts of terrorism (Pianin 2001).

Conclusion

Because of the success of recent terrorist attacks, concrete steps have to be taken now to better prepare for further threats. Along with efforts to prevent acts of mass terrorism and to mount an effective emergency response, greater discussion and awareness are needed about the potential for indirect and long-term consequences. Without a comprehensive plan of action that considers all eventualities, government agencies are more likely to respond ineffectually or to overreact, creating unnecessary panic and infringing on basic civil liberties (Stern 1999; Guillemin 1999:248; Lancaster 2001). Thorough preparedness could also aid deter-

286 Journal of Health Politics, Policy and Law

rence efforts. In the future, terrorists may be dissuaded from attempting to use these technically demanding and unpredictable agents if they think the responses will minimize widespread injury and fear.

Responding to an actual CBN attack is an even more daunting task because many of the issues involved—eligibility for health care, the effects of low-level chemical and radiation exposure, stress-related illnesses, unlicensed therapeutics, financial compensation—are complex and controversial. Only government institutions that maintain credibility with the public will be capable of dealing effectively with the broad range of problems that evolve after a terrorist attack.

A successful recovery effort must provide for long-term health care, risk communication, and surveillance. Although advanced technologies help in the emergency response, there is a greater need for a general plan of action, central coordination, and basic education (Pincus 1999; Sharp et al. 1998). Not just the medical community but government officials, the press, and the general public have to be more fully informed about the nature of this threat. Moreover, additional research is necessary concerning the best methods of risk management and communication (Bennett 1999b).

Future chemical, biological, or nuclear terrorism should be anticipated. In preparing for these attacks, we have to walk a fine line between lack of preparedness and creating undue fear in our daily lives (Shalala 1999). Terrorism is not simply about killing people; it is also about destroying our sense of well-being and trust in government. This outcome cannot be allowed to happen either before or after a terrorist attack.

References

Barker, P., and D. Selvey. 1992. Malathion-Induced Epidemic Hysteria in an Elementary School. *Veterinary and Human Toxicology* 34:156–160.

Barsky, A., and J. Borus. 1999. Functional Somatic Syndromes. *Annals of Internal Medicine* 130:910–921.

Bennett, P. 1999a. Understanding Responses to Risk: Some Basic Findings. In *Risk Communication and Public Health*, ed. P. Bennett and K. Calman. Oxford: Oxford University Press.

———. 1999b. Research Priorities. In *Risk Communication and Public Health*, ed. P. Bennett and K. Calman. Oxford: Oxford University Press.

Bennett, P., D. Coles, and A. McDonald. 1999. Risk Communication as a Decision Process. In *Risk Communication and Public Health*, ed. P. Bennett and K. Calman. Oxford: Oxford University Press.

Berezuk, G., and G. McCarty. 1992. Investigational Drugs and Vaccines Fielded in Support of Operation Desert Storm. *Military Medicine* 157:404–406.

Bertollini, R., D. DiLallo, P. Mastroiacovo, and C. Perucci. 1990. Reduction of Births in Italy after the Chernobyl Accident. *Scandinavian Journal of Work, Environment, and Health* 16:96–101.

Betts, R. 1998. The New Threat of Mass Destruction. *Foreign Affairs* 77:26–41.

Birchard, K. 1998. Does Iraq's Depleted Uranium Pose a Health Risk? *Lancet* 351:657.

———. 1999. Experts Still Arguing over Radiation Doses. *Lancet* 354:400.

Bleich, A., A. Dycian, M. Koslowsky, Z. Solomon, and M. Wiener. 1992. Psychiatric Implications of Missile Attacks on a Civilian Population: Israeli Lessons from the Persian Gulf War. *Journal of the American Medical Association* 268:613–615.

Bleich, A., S. Kron, C. Margalit, G. Inbar, Z. Kaplan, S. Cooper, and Z. Solomon. 1991. Israeli Psychological Casualties of the Persian Gulf War: Characteristics, Therapy, and Selected Issues. *Israel Journal of Medical Sciences* 27:673–676.

Booth, William. 2001. Bioterror Takes on Another Face. *Washington Post,* 21 October, A8.

Boss, L. 1997. Epidemic Hysteria: A Review of the Published Literature. *Epidemiologic Reviews* 19:233–243.

Bravo, M., M. Rubio-Stipec, G. Canino, M. Woodbury, and J. Ribera. 1990. The Psychological Sequelae of Disaster Stress Prospectively and Retrospectively Evaluated. *American Journal of Community Psychology* 18:661–680.

Brennan, R., J. Waeckerle, T. Sharp, and S. Lillibridge. 1999. Chemical Warfare Agents: Emergency Medical and Emergency Public Health Issues. *Annals of Emergency Medicine* 34:191–204.

Brewin, T. 1994. Chernobyl and the Media. *British Medical Journal* 309:208–209.

Brown, M., and K. Brix. 1998. Review of Health Consequences from High, Intermediate, and Low-Level Exposure to Organophosphorus Nerve Agents. *Journal of Applied Toxicology* 18:393–408.

Centers for Disease Control and Prevention. 2000. Biological and Chemical Terrorism: Strategic Plan for Preparedness and Response. *Morbidity and Mortality Weekly Report,* 12 April:1–14.

Collins, D., and Carvalho A. 1993. Chronic Stress from the Goiânia 137 Cs Radiation Accident. *Behavioral Medicine* 18:149–157.

Coote A., and J. Franklin. 1999. Negotiating Risks to Public Health—Models for Participation. In *Risk Communication and Public Health,* ed. P. Bennett and K. Calman. Oxford: Oxford University Press.

David, A., and S. Wessely. 1995. The Legend of Camelford: Medical Consequences of a Water Pollution Accident. *Journal of Psychosomatic Research* 39:1–10.

Davidson, L., A. Baum, and D. Collins. 1982. Stress and Control-Related Problems at Three-Mile Island. *Journal of Applied Social Psychology* 12:349–359.

DiGiovanni, C. 1999. Domestic Terrorism with Chemical or Biological Agents. *American Journal of Psychiatry* 156:1500–1505.

Dobbs, Michael. 2001. Anthrax Scare Spreads around the World. *Washington Post,* 18 October, A15.

288   Journal of Health Politics, Policy and Law

Erikson, K. 1990. Toxic Reckoning: Business. *Harvard Business Review,* January–February, 118–126.

Falkenrath, R. 1998. Confronting Nuclear, Biological, and Chemical Terrorism. *Survival* 40:43–65.

Fineman, M. 1999. Yugoslav City Battling Toxic Enemies. *Los Angeles Times*, 6 July, A1.

Firestone, David. 2001. In Florida, an Outbreak of Anthrax Turns the Air into a Terror Suspect. *New York Times*, 12 October, 9.

Franz, D., P. Jahrling, A. Friedlander, D. McClain, D. Hoover, and W. Bryne. 1997. Clinical Recognition and Management of Patients Exposed to Biological Warfare Agents. *Journal of the American Medicial Association* 278:399–411.

Giel, R. 1991. The Psychosocial Aftermath of Two Major Disasters in the Soviet Union. *Journal of Traumatic Stress* 4:381–393.

Glassner, B. 1999. *In the Culture of Fear: Why Americans Are Afraid of the Wrong Things.* New York: Basic Books.

Goldstein, Avram. 2001. Terrorism Tied to Jump in Pain Problems. *Washington Post,* 1 October, A1.

Guillemin, J. 1999. *Anthrax: The Investigation of a Deadly Outbreak.* Berkeley: University of California Press.

Hannay, D. 1978. Symptom Prevalence in the Community. *Journal of the Royal College of General Practitioners* 28:492–499.

Holloway, H., A. Norwood, C. Fullerton, C. Engel, and R. Ursano. 1997. The Threat of Biological Weapons: Prophylaxis and Mitigation of Psychological and Social Consequences. *Journal of the American Medical Association* 278:425–427.

Huber, P. 1992. *Galileo's Revenge: Junk Science in the Courtroom.* New York: Basic Books.

Hyams, K., F. Wignall, and R. Roswell. 1996. War Syndromes and Their Evaluation: From the U.S. Civil War to the Persian Gulf War. *Annals of Internal Medicine* 125:398–405.

Inglesby, T., D. Henderson, J. Barlett, M. Ascher, E. Eitzen, A. Friedlander, J. Hauer, J. McDade, M. Osterholm, T. O'Toole, G. Parker, T. Perl, P. Russell, K. Tonat, and the Working Group on Civilian Biodefense. 1999. Anthrax as a Biological Weapon: Medical and Public Health Management. *Journal of the American Medical Association* 281:1735–1745.

Institute of Medicine. 1999. *Chemical and Biological Terrorism: Research and Development to Improve Civilian Medical Response.* Washington, DC: National Academy Press.

———. 2000. *Gulf War and Health: Volume 1. Depleted Uranium, Sarin, Pyridostigmine Bromide, Vaccines.* Washington, DC: National Academy Press.

Jones, T., A. Craig, D. Hoy, E. Gunter, D. Ashley, D. Barr, J. Brock, and W. Schaffner. 2000. Mass Psychogenic Illness Attributed to Toxic Exposure at a High School. *New England Journal of Medicine* 342:96–100.

Joseph, S., K. Hyams, G. Gackstetter, E. Mathews, and R. Patterson. 1998. Persian Gulf War Health Issues. In *Environmental and Occupational Medicine*, 3d ed., ed. W. Rom. Philadelphia: Lippincott-Raven.

Knudsen, L. 1991 Legally-Induced Abortions in Denmark after Chernobyl. *Biomedicine and Pharmacotherapy* 45:229–232.

Krug, S. 1992. Mass Illness at an Intermediate School: Toxic Fumes or Epidemic Hysteria? *Pediatric Emergency Care* 8:280–282.

Lancaster, John. 2001. House Approves Terrorism Measure. *Washington Post,* 25 October, A1.

Mayou, R. 1991. Medically Unexplained Physical Symptoms. *British Medical Journal* 303:534–535.

Modan, B., M. Tirosh, E. Weissenberg, C. Costin, T. A. Swartz, A. Donagi, C. Acker, M. Revach, and G. Vettorazzi. 1983. The Arjenyattah Epidemic—A Mass Phenomenon: Spread and Triggering Factors. *Lancet* 2:1472–1475.

Montello, M., and T. Ames. 1998. The Federal Disaster Response Plan. *Federal Practitioner,* December, 48–50.

Morin, Richard. 2001. Poll: National Pride, Confidence Soar. *Washington Post,* 25 October, A7.

Murphy, F., R. Allen, H. Kang, S. Mather, N. Dalager, K. Kizer, and K. Lee. 1999. The Health Status of Gulf War Veterans: Lessons Learned from the Department of Veterans Affairs Health Registry. *Military Medicine* 164:327–331.

Nakajima, T., S. Ohta, Y. Fukushima, and N. Yanagisawa. 1999. Sequelae of Sarin Toxicity at One and Three Years after Exposure in Matsumoto, Japan. *Journal of Epidemiology* 9:337–343.

Nakano, K. 1995. The Tokyo Sarin Gas Attack: Victims' Isolation and Post-Traumatic Stress Disorders. *Cross-Cultural Psychology Bulletin* 29:12–15.

Neutra, R. 1985. Epidemiology for and with a Distrustful Community. *Environmental Health Perspectives* 62:393–397.

Neutra, R., J. Lipscomb, and K. Satin. 1991. Hypotheses to Explain the Higher Symptom Rates Observed around Hazardous Waste Sites. *Environmental Health Perspectives* 94:31–38.

New York Times. 2001. Editorial: Responding to the Anthrax Threat. *New York Times,* 25 October, 20.

Ohbu, S., A. Yamashina, N. Takasu, T. Yamaguchi, T. Murai, and K. Nakano. 1997. Sarin Poisoning on Tokyo Subway. *Southern Medical Journal* 90:587–593.

Okie, Susan. 2001. Use of Anti-Anxiety Drugs Jumps in U.S. *Washington Post,* 14 October, A8.

Pavlin, J. 1999. Epidemiology of Bioterrorism. *Emerging Infectious Diseases* 5:528–530.

Petterson, J. 1988. Perception versus Reality of Radiological Impact: The Goiânia Model. *Nuclear News,* November, 84–90.

Pianin, Eric. 2001. Ridge Assumes Security Post amid Potential for New Attacks. *Washington Post,* 9 October, A6.

Pincus, W. 1999. U.S. Preparedness Faulted: Weapons of Mass Destruction Concern Panel. *Washington Post,* 9 July, A2.

Presidential Advisory Committee on Gulf War Veterans' Illnesses. 1996. Final Report. December. Washington, DC: U.S. Government Printing Office.

Presidential Decision Directive 39 (PDD-39). 1995. United States Policy on Counterterrorism. Available on-line at http://www.fema.gov/r-n-r/frp/frpterr.htm.

Prial, Dunstan. 2001. Mayor: Earlier Letter to News Anchor Tom Brokaw Contained Anthrax That Infected His Assistant. Associated Press wire story, 13 October. Accessed on-line at www.nandotimes.com/healthscience/story/135560p-1375072c. html.

Prince-Embury, S., and J. Rooney. 1988. Psychological Symptoms of Residents in the Aftermath of the Three-Mile Island Nuclear Accident in the Aftermath of Technological Disaster. *Journal of Social Psychology* 128:779–790.

Raphael, B., L. Meldrum, and A. McFarlane. 1995. Does Debriefing after Psychological Trauma Work? *British Medical Journal* 310:1479–1480.

Renn, O. 1997. Mental Health, Stress, and Risk Perception: Insights from Psychological Research. In *Health Effects of Large Releases of Radionucleotides*, ed. G. Bock, G. Carden, and V. V. Lake. CIBA Foundation Symposium 203. New York: John Wiley.

Reuters. 1999. Dutch Crash Report Sees Health Link, Slams Government. Report broadcast on Cable Network News, 23 April.

Roht, L., S. Vernon, F. Weir, S. Pier, P. Sullivan, and L. Reed. 1985. Community Exposure to Hazardous Waste Disposal Sites: Assessing Reporting Bias. *American Journal of Epidemiology* 122:418–433.

Rosen, P. 2000. Coping with Bioterrorism: Is Difficult, but May Help Us Respond to New Epidemics. *British Medical Journal* 320:71–72.

Schwartz, S., P. White, and R. Hughes. 1985. Environmental Threats, Communities, and Hysteria. *Journal of Public Health Policy* 6:58–77.

Selden, B. 1989. Adolescent Epidemic Hysteria Presenting as a Mass Casualty, Toxic Exposure Incident. *Annals of Emergency Medicine* 18:892–895.

Shalala, D. 1999. Bioterrorism: How Prepared Are We? *Emerging Infectious Diseases* 5:492–493.

Sharp, T., R. Brennan, M. Keim, R. Williams, E. Eitzen, and S. Lillibridge. 1998. Medical Preparedness for a Terrorist Incident Involving Chemical or Biological Agents during the 1996 Atlanta Olympic Games. *Annals of Emergency Medicine* 32:214–223.

Shusterman, D., J. Lipscomb, R. Neutra, and K. Satin. 1991. Symptom Prevalence and Odor-Worry Interaction near Hazardous Waste Sites. *Environmental Health Perspectives* 94:25–30.

Singer, E., and P. Endreny. 1993. *Reporting on Risk*. New York: Russell Sage Foundation.

Smith, E., L. Robins, T. Przybeck, E. Goldring, and S. Solomon. 1986. Psychosocial Consequences of a Disaster. In *Disaster Stress Studies: New Methods and Findings*, ed. J. Shore. Washington, DC: American Psychiatric Press.

Stepp, L. S. 2001. Children's Worries Take New Shape. Artwork Reveals the Effects of September 11. *Washington Post,* 2 November, C1.

Stern, J. 1999. The Prospect of Domestic Bioterrorism. *Emerging Infectious Diseases* 5:517–522.

Stiehm, E. 1992. The Psychologic Fallout from Chernobyl. *American Journal of Diseases of Children* 146:761–762.

Summerfield, D. 1999. A Critique of Seven Assumptions behind Psychological

Trauma Programs in War-Affected Areas. *Social Science and Medicine* 48:1449–1462.

———. 2000. War and Mental Health: A Brief Overview. *British Medical Journal* 321:232–235.

Townsend, Mark. 1997. What Has Caused These Tragedies? *Western Morning News* [U.K.], 1 October, 16.

Tucker, J. 1997. National Health and Medical Services Response to Incidents of Chemical and Biological Terrorism. *Journal of the American Medical Association* 278:362–368.

Watts, J. 1999. Tokyo Terrorist Attack: Effects Still Felt 4 Years On. *Lancet* 353:569.

Wessely, S., J. Bisson, and S. Rose. 1999. A Systematic Review of Brief Psychological Interventions ("Debriefing") for the Treatment of Immediate Trauma Related Symptoms and the Prevention of Post Traumatic Stress Disorder. In *Depression, Anxiety and Neurosis Module of the Cochrane Database of Systematic Reviews, 1999*, ed. M. Oakley-Browne, R. Churchill, D. Gill, M. Trivedi, and S. Wessely. Oxford: Cochrane Collaboration, Issue 3, Update Software (updated quarterly).

Wessely, S., K. C. Hyams, and R. Bartholomew. 2001. Psychological Implications of Chemical and Biological Weapons. *British Medical Journal* 323:878–879.

Weiss, Rick. 2001. Demand Growing for Anthrax Vaccine. *Washington Post,* 29 September, A16.

Woodall, J. 1997. Tokyo Subway Gas Attack. *Lancet* 350:296.

Whoriskey, P., and C. L. Jenkins. 2001. Mailbox Trip Meets with Trepidation. *Washington Post,* 24 October, B1.

Zoon, K. 1999. Vaccines, Pharmaceutical Products, and Bioterrorism: Challenges for the U.S. Food and Drug Administration. *Emerging Infectious Diseases* 5:534–536.

[17]

Chemical Warfare and Chemical Terrorism: Psychological and Performance Outcomes

James A. Romano, Jr.

Commander
U.S. Army Medical Research Institute of Chemical Defense
Aberdeen Proving Ground, Maryland

James M. King

Deputy Director
Chemical and Biological Defense Information Analysis Center
Aberdeen Proving Ground, Maryland

The battlefields of the late 20th century have come to include a significant new health threat: the use of modern chemical weapons. The potential to cause large numbers of serious casualties among deployed and deploying military forces and among civilian populations provides a stark reminder to medical planners of the limits of military and civilian medicine. However, medical countermeasures to these chemical warfare agents (CWAs) have been, and continue to be, developed. These CWAs, their countermeasures, and their health care implications are described in the articles of this special issue. These articles suggest likely psychological, physiological, and neurological effects that will be encountered should these agents be employed against U.S. forces on the integrated battlefield or against homeland facilities. Also suggested are countermeasures that U.S. forces and medical teams may use to protect or treat our forces or citizens undergoing such CWA attacks. Knowledge of the behavioral effects of the CWAs and of their medical countermeasures is imperative to ensure that military and civilian medical and mental health organizations can deal with possible incidents involving weapons of mass destruction. This first study, in contrast to the remaining studies in this special issue, focuses on the psychological factors in chemical warfare and terrorism. It also serves as an overview of the remaining articles in this special issue.

This article is part of a special issue, "Chemical Warfare and Chemical Terrorism: Psychological and Performance Outcomes," of *Military Psychology*, 2002, *14*(2), 83–177.

Requests for reprints should be sent to Col. James A. Romano, Jr., U.S. Army Medical Research Institute of Chemical Defense, 3100 Ricketts Point Road, Aberdeen Proving Ground, MD 21010–5400.

The integrated battlefield of the late 20th century has come to include a significant new health threat: modern chemical weapons. Traditionally, U.S. armed forces have been concerned with four classes of chemical warfare agents (CWAs): (a) choking (e.g., phosgene [CG]), (b) blood (e.g., cyanide [CN]), (c) blister (e.g., sulfur mustard [HD]), and (d) nerve agents (e.g., sarin [GB]). These agents differ in terms of rapidity of action, lethality, and the requirement for prompt or sustained medical care. Table 1 provides a summary of the major CWAs of concern, including their historical mortality/morbidity, principal target tissue, and proposed countermeasures. Their potential to cause large numbers of serious casualties provides a stark reminder to medical planners of the limits of military and civilian medicine. The articles in this issue suggest likely psychological, physiological, or neurological effects that will be encountered should these agents be used on the integrated battlefield or against homeland facilities and personnel. This latter eventuality is clearly an emerging threat, both to our military (Chandler & Backschies, 1998; Chandler & Trees, 1996) and civilian

TABLE 1

Twentieth-Century Morbidity of Four Classes of Chemical Warfare Agents and Their Principal Targets and Medical Countermeasures

Class of Chemical Warfare Agents	Historic Lethality and Morbidity in Warfare	Principal Target Tissue	Medical Countermeasures
Choking (e.g., phosgene)	10%[a]	Airway	Nonspecific; symptomatic treatment
Blood (e.g., cyanide)	Unknown[b]	Cellular respiratory enzymes	Sodium nitrate, sodium thiosulfate
Blister and vesicant agents (e.g., "mustard gas")	2.2%[c]	Skin, airway	Nonspecific; symptomatic treatment
Nerve (e.g., sarin)	Unknown[d]	Central nervous system, neuromuscular transmission	Atropine, oxime, anticonvulsants

Note. From "Psychological Factors in Chemical Warfare and Terrorism" (pp. 398, 401), by J. Romano and J. King, in *Chemical Warfare Agents: Toxicity at Low Levels,* edited by S. Somani and J. Romano, 2001, Boca Raton, FL: CRC Press. Adapted with permission.

[a]World War I figures are estimates because phosgene was often mixed with chlorine. Total personnel injured directly attributed to phosgene = 6,834 directly attributed to phosgene; 66 fatalities. [b]No data from wartime use; however, wartime experiences suggest difficulty in achieving militarily effective concentrations unless confirmed to closed spaces. [c]World War I: 2%, with 27,711 U.S. personnel injured. Iran–Iraq War: 45,000 Iran/Iraqi personnel estimated injured. [d]No data from wartime use; however, on March 20, 1995, using a primitive method of dispersal, sarin was released on Tokyo subways, with 5,500 people seeking medical care. Approximately 1,500 had defined symptoms of exposure, and 12 casualties died. Less well known is the fact that, on June 27, 1994, sarin was released in Matsumoto, Japan, with an estimated 471 people exposed to sarin and 7 deaths.

(National Domestic Preparedness Office, 2001; The White House, 1998a, 1998b) populations and facilities.

During World War I (WWI), when choking and blood agents were used, the choking agent phosgene produced a large number of casualties requiring extensive hospitalization. Sciuto, Moran, Narula, Forster, and Romano (2001) indicated that the primary effects of phosgene on military performance are due to its capacity to produce deep lung injury. Sciuto et al. suggested that phosgene may produce a toxic encephalopathy in humans as phosgene decreases O_2 delivery to the central nervous system (CNS) and other body systems, with accompanying behavioral and functional deficits when continuous mental or physical performance is demanded. They also describe some of these behavioral effects as demonstrated in the psychological literature.

Blood agents appeared in WWI within weeks after the initial use of choking agents (often phosgene and chlorine were employed simultaneously) and produced lethal casualties more rapidly. Cyanide in particular is a biochemical poisoning with affinity for CNS tissue (S. Moore & Gates, 1946). Although highly toxic, gradients of CNS effects can be observed either after exposure to lower concentrations or exposure to lethal amounts via the oral or percutaneous routes (Baskin & Brewer, 1997). Baskin and Rockwood (2002/this issue), in their article, "Neurotoxicological and Behavioral Effects of Cyanide and Its Potential Therapies," report that initial signs of CNS excitement, including anxiety and agitation, may progress to signs of CNS depression, such as coma and dilated, unresponsive pupils. In fact, pathological studies from WWI and WWII indicate that residual cyanide lesions are significant only in the case of animals receiving a narrow range of exposures just below the lethal dose. Recovering animals show residual neurological damage, principally in cerebrum and cerebellum (S. Moore & Gates, 1946).

The most effective agent at producing casualties in WWI was so-called mustard gas, or HD. As Smith (2002/this issue) points out in his article, "Vesicant Agents and Antivesicant Medical Countermeasures: Clinical Toxicology and Psychological Implications," mustard produced hundreds of thousands of casualties, even more casualties than were seen with phosgene, who required extensive hospitalization. The pernicious nature of mustard was reinforced in the mid-1980s in the Iran–Iraq War, in which it produced an estimated additional 45,000 casualties from chemical exposure. The major clinical effects of exposure to HD are significant skin, eye, and pulmonary lesions, which are usually nonfatal. The length of hospitalization for these injuries was estimated to be 46 days per casualty during WWI (Joy, 1997) and up to 10 weeks during the Iran–Iraq War (Willems, 1989). Reports of neuropsychiatric effects, such as severe apathy, impaired concentration, and diminished libido, are given a balanced discussion by Smith.

Following WWI, work in Germany progressed on the development of organophosphorus insecticides, leading to identification of a new a class of compounds of extreme toxicity, the nerve agents. This toxicity, and their rapid action, led to their adoption as weapons of warfare. As highly active CNS agents, sublethal exposures to this type of CWA can be expected to produce prominent deficits in behavior and performance. McDonough's (2002/this issue) article, "Performance Impacts of Nerve Agents and Their Pharmacological Countermeasures," provides a review of the toxicological and neurobehavioral effects of exposure to nerve agents and their medical countermeasures, with an emphasis on human reports. A considerable body of literature exists on this topic, and the interested reader is encouraged to use McDonough's review as well as Longo (1966), Karczmar (1984), and Romano, McDonough, Sheridan, and Sidell (2001) as useful starting points. Somewhat less effort has been given to characterizing the effects of low-level exposures to nerve CWAs, perhaps due to the steepness of their toxicity curves (Romano, Penetar, & King, 1985) and the resultant difficulty in determining low-level dosages. Recent concern over the possible sublethal exposure of U.S. armed forces to the nerve agent sarin (GB) during operations following the Gulf War has led to a renewed study of this problem. The reader can identify pertinent ongoing studies and their annual abstract reports on the Internet at http://www.va.gov/resdev/pgrpt00.htm (*Annual Report to Congress: Federally Sponsored Research on Gulf War Veterans' Illnesses for 2000*, April 2001).

Pharmacological or medical countermeasures to these CWAs can produce CNS sequelae, which are discussed briefly in each of the articles in this issue, with due consideration given to demonstrated or potential psychological effects. Of course, those CWAs, like the nerve agents and the blood agents, which have high affinity to CNS tissue, require medical countermeasures that can be expected to produce significant CNS and performance effects. Two areas of interest are highlighted. First, Baskin and Rockwood (2002/this issue) discuss pretreatment for cyanide poisoning by methemoglobin formation, pointing out that it is estimated that methemoglobin levels of 5% to 7% will protect humans against up to 2 times the LD_{50} of cyanide. To put this in perspective, the level of methemoglobin in smokers' blood is 2%. The effects of a level of 5% to 7% of induced methemoglobin on performance need to be evaluated. Second, medical protection from the effects of nerve agents may involve pretreatment with the reversible acetylcholinesterase inhibitor, pyridostigmine, or with biological scavengers targeted at these compounds. The drug pyridostigmine bromide (PB), which is a reversible acetylcholinesterase inhibitor, has been given a considerable amount of scrutiny recently. This attention may stem from its having been used as a pretreatment to protect U.S. armed forces against the potential use of nerve agents by Iraqi forces during the 1991 Persian Gulf War. Its effects on military performance have been reviewed (Dunn, Hackley, & Sidell, 1997), and its potential health consequences in otherwise healthy U.S. forces are described. The reader is directed to http://www.va.gov/resdev/pgrpt00.htm or http://www.gulflink.osd.mil (Office of the Special Assistant for Gulf War Illnesses, 2001). This Web site provides summaries and abstract reports of research projects examining the health effects of PB either alone or due to its interaction with a variety of other compounds. A detailed consideration of the interactions of PB and stressors is available for interested readers (Somani, Husain, & Jagannathan, 2001).

Protection may also involve pretreatment with a biological scavenger. As Cerasoli and Lenz (2002/this issue) point out in their article, "Nerve Agent Bioscavengers: Protection With Reduced Behavioral Effects," this novel approach avoids the side effects associated with the current nerve agent antidotes. Furthermore, the animal data available, pretreatment with a biological scavenger, appears to prevent or significantly alleviate the neurobehavioral effects of the nerve agents. As a result, the level of protection from the neurobehavioral effects of nerve agents is greater than that seen following use of conventional therapy for nerve agents.

One final point about the response to chemical agents on the battlefield or in the homeland concerns the possible presence of stress casualties. These have been variously labeled as cases of "gas hysteria," "gas mania," or "gas neurosis." It is conceivable that widespread confusion leading to panic and the potential mental health disorder could result from fear or from actual use of CWAs. In a recent review in this journal, Stokes and Banderet (1997) reported that the official U.S. Army Medical Department history notes that two such cases occurred for each actual chemical injury. Their analysis suggested several origins for these cases: (a) conversion disorders, (b) mistaking normal physiological stress symptoms for exposure to CWA (despite significant efforts to train soldiers in proper recognition of signs of poisoning), (c) mistaking or magnifying the symptoms of minor illnesses, and (d) deliberate faking or malingering. One might add the possibility of an additional type of self-inflicted wound to this categorization (i.e., the inadvertent or misguided use of antidotal compounds, e.g., atropine and diazepam). Self-administration of two nerve agent antidote autoinjectors can produce headache, restlessness, and fatigue, symptoms that can be aggravated in a tired, dehydrated, or stressed individual.

Had this issue been compiled in the late 1980s, its application and focus would have generally been limited to the protection of deployed U.S. armed forces. We believe that the world has changed. The CWAs and the medical countermeasures discussed in this issue should be considered as threats to deployed and deploying forces, to fixed military installations either overseas or in the continental U.S., and to the American homeland and its population. Moreover, in the last decade the unthinkable has happened: CWAs have been employed against unprotected civilians by terrorists. These events have challenged the civilian medical and mental health systems, along with the associated first-response systems charged with protection of the population (Ohtomi, 1996; Romano & King, 2001). The magnitude and impact of this challenge to the military and civilian medical and mental health care systems is carefully delineated by Jones (1995), Sidell (1997), Stokes and Banderet (1997), and D. H. Moore and Alexander (2001). These works provide a detailed examination of the current approaches to management of CWA casualties and of plans for the public health response. The current world situation requires that we properly prepare for such CWA attacks by ensuring that accurate, up-to-date information on the behavioral, functional, and neurological impacts of the CWAs and their medical countermeasures is available.

This special issue was conceived to complement the work done by Gerald P. Krueger and Louis E. Banderet in 1997 in the special issue of *Military Psychology* on the "Effects of Chemical Protective Clothing on Military Performance." Their issue addresses the physiological and performance effects of protective clothing and is summarized in the preface (Krueger & Banderet, 1997b). Krueger and Banderet (1997a) also presented a short history on the use of chemical weaponry on the battlefield during the last century. The set of articles in this special issue illustrates the methodologies and results of many U.S. military medical research programs on the threats of the chemical agents to the human body, the research on antidotes to counteract those effects, and the resultant effects of both the threat agents and the antidotes on human psychology and behavior.

Because of the obvious medical and biological threats to humans, much of the research cited here was done by multidisciplinary scientists using animal models in studies designed to predict human bodily and behavioral responses to both CWA threats and to the challenges that accompany use of medical prophylactic countermeasures or treatment regimens.

ACKNOWLEDGMENTS

The opinions or assertions contained herein are the private views of the authors and are not to be construed as official or as reflecting the view of the U.S. Army or the U.S. Department of Defense. The authors thank Patricia D. Little for her skillful editorial assistance in preparation of this article. Her excellence in secretarial skills, assistance in compiling accurate tables, and methodical approach to presentation of the reference citations enabled the publication of this material.

REFERENCES

Annual report to Congress: Federally sponsored research on Gulf War veterans' illnesses for 2000. (2001, October). Washington, DC: Department of Veterans Affairs. Retrieved April 4, 2002, from http://www.va.gov/resdev/pgrpt00.htm

Baskin, S., & Brewer, T. (1997). Cyanide poisoning. In F. R. Sidell, E. T. Takafuji, & D. R. Franz (Eds.), *Medical aspects of chemical and biological warfare* (pp. 271–286). Washington, DC: Office of the Surgeon General.

Baskin, S. I., & Rockwood, G. A. (2002/this issue). Neurotoxicological and behavioral effects of cyanide and its potential therapies. *Military Psychology, 14,* 159–177.

Cerasoli, D. M., & Lenz, D. E. (2002/this issue). Nerve agent bioscavengers: Protection with reduced behavioral effects. *Military Psychology, 14,* 121–143.

Chandler, R. W., & Backschies, J. R. (1998). *The new face of war* (pp. 397–406). McLean, VA: AMCODA Press.

Chandler, R. W., & Trees, R. J. (1996). *Tomorrow's war, today's decisions* (pp. 165–204). McLean, VA: AMCODA Press.

Dunn, M. A., Hackley, B. E., & Sidell, F. R. (1997). Pretreatment for nerve agent exposure. In F. R. Sidell, E. T. Takafuji, & D. R. Franz (Eds.), *Medical aspects of chemical and biological warfare* (pp. 181–196). Washington, DC: Office of the Surgeon General.

Jones, F. D. (1995). Neuropsychiatric casualties of nuclear, biological, and chemical warfare. In F. D. Jones, L. R. Sparacino, V. L. Wilcox, J. M. Rothberg, & J. W. Stokes (Eds.), *War psychiatry* (pp. 85–111). Washington, DC: Office of the Surgeon General.

Joy, R. J. T. (1997). Historical aspects of medical defense against chemical warfare. In F. R. Sidell, E. T. Takafuji, & D. R. Franz (Eds.), *Medical aspects of chemical and biological warfare* (pp. 87–109). Washington, DC: Office of the Surgeon General.

Karczmar, A. G. (1984). Acute and long-lasting concentrations of organophosphorus agents. *Fundamental and Applied Toxicology, 44*(2), S1–S17.

Krueger, G. P., & Banderet, L. E. (1997a). Effects of chemical protective clothing on military performance: A review of the issues. *Military Psychology, 9,* 255–286.

Krueger, G. P., & Banderet, L. E. (1997b). Preface to the special issue. *Military Psychology, 9,* 251–253.

Longo, V. G. (1966). Behavioral and electroencephalographic effects of atropine and related compounds. *Pharmacology Review, 18,* 965–966.

McDonough, J. H. (2002/this issue). Performance impacts of nerve agents and their pharmacological countermeasures. *Military Psychology, 14,* 93–119.

Moore, D. H., & Alexander, S. M. (2001). Emergency response to a chemical warfare incident: Domestic preparedness, first response and public health considerations. In S. Somani & J. Romano (Eds.), *Chemical warfare agents: Toxicity at low levels* (pp. 409–435). Boca Raton, FL: CRC Press.

Moore, S., & Gates, M. (1946). Hydrogen cyanide and cyanogen chloride. In *Summary technical report of Division 9, National Defense Research Committee: Vol. 1. Chemical warfare agents and related chemical problems* (Pt. 1–2, pp. 7–16). Washington, DC: National Defense Research Committee.

National Domestic Preparedness Office. (2001). *Blueprint for the National Domestic Preparedness Office.* Washington, DC: Department of Justice, Federal Bureau of Investigation. Retrieved April 4, 2002, from http://www.ndpo.gov

Office of the Special Assistant for Gulf War Illnesses. (2001). Washington, DC: Department of Defense. Retrieved April 4, 2002, from http://www.gulflink.osd.mil

Ohtomi, S. (1996). Medical experience with sarin casualties in Japan. In J. M. King (Ed.), *1996 Medical Defense Bioscience Review Proceedings* (pp. 1182–1190). Aberdeen Proving Ground, MD: U.S. Army Medical Research Institute of Chemical Defense.

Romano, J., & King, J. (2001). Psychological factors in chemical warfare and terrorism. In S. Somani & J. Romano (Eds.), *Chemical warfare agents: Toxicity at low levels* (pp. 393–407). Boca Raton, FL: CRC Press.

Romano, J. A., McDonough, J. H., Sheridan, R., & Sidell, F. (2001). Health effects of low-level exposure to nerve agents. In S. Somani & J. A. Romano (Eds.), *Chemical warfare agents: Toxicity at low levels* (pp. 1–24). Boca Raton, FL: CRC Press.

Romano, J. A., Penetar, D. M., & King, J. M. (1985). A comparison of physostigmine and soman using taste aversion and nociception. *Neurobehavioral Toxicology and Teratology, 7,* 243–249.

Sciuto, A. M., Moran, T. S., Narula, A., Forster, J. S., & Romano, J. A., Jr. (2001). *Disruption of gas exchange following exposure to the chemical threat agent phosgene: Implications for human performance* (Rep. No. USAMRICD TR–01–06). Aberdeen Proving Ground, MD: U.S. Army Medical Research Institute of Chemical Defense.

Sidell, F. R. (1997). Nerve agents. In F. R. Sidell, E. T. Takafuji, & D. R. Franz (Eds.), *Medical aspects of chemical and biological warfare* (pp. 129–179). Washington, DC: Office of the Surgeon General.

Smith, W. J. (2002/this issue). Vesicant agents and antivesicant medical countermeasures: Clinical toxicology and psychological implications. *Military Psychology, 14,* 145–157.

Somani, S. M., Husain, K., & Jagannathan, R. (2001). Pharmacokinetics and pharmacodynamics of carbamates under physical stress. In S. Somani & J. Romano (Eds.), *Chemical warfare agents: Toxicity at low levels* (pp. 145–189). Boca Raton, FL: CRC Press.

Stokes, J. W., & Banderet, L. E. (1997). Psychological aspects of chemical defense and warfare. *Military Psychology, 9,* 395–415.

The White House. (1998a). *Combating terrorism: Presidential Decision Directive 62* [Fact sheet]. Washington, DC: Office of the Press Secretary.

The White House. (1998b). *Protecting American's critical infrastructures: Presidential Decision Directive 63* [Fact sheet]. Washington, DC: Office of the Press Secretary.

Willems, J. (1989). Clinical management of mustard gas casualties. *Annales Medicinal Militaris Belgicae, 3*(Suppl.), 1–6.

[18]

Redefining NATO's Mission: WMD Terrorism

Richard G. Lugar

Will the United States and Europe succeed in fashioning a common strategy for a global war on terrorism? This question is crucial for the future of the trans-Atlantic relationship. Will we stand shoulder to shoulder, just as we confronted the Soviet Union during the Cold War? Are political leaders on both sides of the Atlantic willing to make the political commitment necessary to hammer out common objectives and policies and to recast our institutions to meet this challenge? We must ask ourselves whether we as leaders are prepared to draw the right conclusions and do what we can to reduce this threat or whether it will take another, even deadlier, terrorist attack to force us into action.

In 1996 I made an unsuccessful bid for the presidency. Three of my campaign television ads depicted a mushroom cloud and warned of the threat posed by the growing danger of weapons of mass destruction (WMD) in the hands of terrorist groups. I argued that the next president should be selected on the basis of a perceived ability to meet that challenge.

At the time, those ads were widely criticized for being far-fetched and alarmist. Recently, national television networks have replayed the ads, which are now viewed from a different perspective. The terrorist attacks of last September on the United States have graphically demonstrated how vulnerable we are. The terrorists seek massive impact through the indiscriminate killing of people and the destruction of institutions, historical symbols, and the basic fabric of our societies. The next attack could just as easily be in London, Paris, or Berlin as in Washington, D.C.; Los Angeles; or New York City; and it could involve WMD.

Richard G. Lugar is the senior senator from Indiana and is a member of the Foreign Relations Committee and the Select Committee on Intelligence.

The U.S.-led war in Afghanistan has succeeded in destroying many members of Al Qaeda and the Taliban regime. President George W. Bush has made it clear that the United States will extend the military campaign to other countries and to other terrorist cells or governments that support terrorism. As the United States prosecutes this war, it should be mindful of the world from which it has emerged—the Cold War world with its residual instruments of mass destruction.

The sober reality is that the danger of Americans and Europeans being killed today at work or at home is perhaps greater than at any time in recent history. Indeed, the threat we face may be almost as existential as the one we faced during the Cold War, because it is increasingly likely to involve WMD use against our societies.

The Opportunity Ahead

Amid the current signs of crisis, we must not lose sight of the enormous opportunity we have to build a new trans-Atlantic relationship that can be a central pillar of the war on terrorism and the constructive prospects for peace that will follow. Unfortunately, neither side of the Atlantic has embraced this opportunity thus far.

> NATO should play the lead role in addressing the central security challenge of our time.

The opportunity we have is twofold. First, overcoming the division of Europe is within our grasp. NATO and the European Union (EU) will hold summits in Prague and Copenhagen in November and December, respectively, and make historic decisions on their individual memberships. Both institutions are considering launching rounds of enlargement that will encompass many, if not all, of the countries from the Baltic Sea to the Black Sea. Both NATO and the EU have also launched new initiatives to expand cooperation with Russia. If done properly, we should be able to say by the end of the decade that the job of securing a new peace in Europe is largely complete—a truly historic accomplishment.

We also have a second opportunity. September 11 showed, in an all too tragic fashion, that we still face existential threats to our societies and our security and that these threats largely come from beyond Europe. For a number of years, experts have been writing about the threats to our security posed by terrorism and the spread of WMD. Such threats seemed too theoretical and too abstract for many people.

A Clear Definition of Victory

We must define what is to be done and then look at what role NATO and our allies can play in helping to achieve success. We need a clear definition of victory in the war on terrorism if we are to sustain the support of the American people as well as that of our allies overseas.

Without oversimplifying the motivations of terrorists in the past, most acts of terror attempted to transform a regime or alter the governance or status of a community or state. Usually, targets were selected to create and increase pressure for change. In contrast, Al Qaeda planned its terrorist attacks on the United States to kill thousands of people indiscriminately. Osama bin Laden was filmed conversing happily about the results of the attack, which exceeded his predictions of destruction. He sought massive destruction of institutions, wealth, national morale, and innocent people. We can safely assume that those objectives have not changed.

We must realize, however, that the next attacks are likely to be different from those of September 11. Most threatening is the nexus between terrorists and WMD. Bin Laden or Al Qaeda doubtless would have used WMD had they possessed them, and the efforts they have made to obtain these weapons are becoming increasingly apparent. As horrible as September 11 was, the death, destruction, and disruption to U.S. society was minimal compared to what a weapon of mass destruction could have inflicted. We must therefore undertake the ambitious goal of comprehensively preventing WMD proliferation. The list of priorities for fighting the war on terrorism is endless. Although we must not relinquish any of these imperatives, we must find a way to organize our mission.

Two lists can provide a simple and clear definition of victory. The first list is of nation-states that house terrorist cells—voluntarily or involuntarily. Those states can be highlighted on a map to illustrate who and where they are. Our stated goal will be to shrink that list nation by nation. Through intelligence sharing, termination of illicit financial channels, support of first responders, diplomacy, and public information, a coalition of nations led by the United States can root out each cell in a comprehensive manner and maintain a public record of success that the world can observe.

The second list would contain all of the states that possess WMD or programs that support them. An international verification body for maintenance and compliance would hold each of these states accountable. Under the rules set forth by this body, the nations would secure weapons and materials from theft or proliferation using funds of that country and, if required, supplemented by international funds. The purpose of these two lists accomplishes the same end: victory comes when we keep the world's most dangerous technologies out of the hands of the world's most dangerous people.

Global Cooperative Threat Reduction

Today, we lack even minimal international confidence about the safety of many weapons systems around the world, not to mention the amounts of materials produced, the storage procedures employed, and the production or destruction programs utilized. Unfortunately, beyond Russia and other states of the former Soviet Union, cooperative threat reduction programs aimed at counterproliferation do not exist. Given the size of the problem, we must do something about it, but the resources needed to accomplish this task necessitate that we cannot do it alone.

Then-Senator Sam Nunn (D-Ga.) and I wrote the legislation creating the Nunn-Lugar Cooperative Threat Reduction (CTR) program in 1991. The program has expended about $400 million annually to destroy the Soviet detritus of the Cold War and has demonstrated that extraordinary international relationships are possible to improve controls over WMD.[1] Programs similar to Nunn-Lugar should be established in each of the antiterror coalition countries to work toward safe storage, accountability, and planned destruction of dangerous weapons and materials. Pakistan and India, for example, could be future partners in Nunn-Lugar–style threat reduction. Under the right conditions and with the requisite transparency, such programs would certainly advance U.S. national security interests and would give the administration the authority it needs to launch emergency operations to prevent a WMD threat from "going critical."

Precise replication of the Nunn-Lugar program will not be possible everywhere, but a satisfactory level of accountability, transparency, and safety can and must be established in every nation with a WMD program. When nations resist accountability or when governments make their territory available to terrorists who are seeking WMD, NATO nations should be prepared to apply their collective military, diplomatic, and economic power to ensure cooperation.

NATO's Role

To make a global CTR plan work, the United States will need the support of its allies. NATO should play the lead role in addressing the central security challenge of our time.

The United States needs the Europeans—their political support; police; intelligence cooperation; economic assistance; and, not least of all, military might. Americans do not want to carry the burden of this war alone, nor should they. When the attack was on its homeland, the United States was prepared to respond immediately and do most of the work itself, but a broader campaign requires a bigger team. NATO must and will become an effective organization in the war on terrorism by addressing those countries directly involved and by isolating those who continue to proliferate WMD.

Broadening NATO's focus will require it to change significantly. The alliance has shown its capacity to adapt to new challenges, particularly when the United States offers leadership. In 1993, after the collapse of communism and the Soviet Union, I was among the first to call for the expansion of the organization. I often said that the task we faced was to reorganize the West to deal with the East. I used the phrase that NATO had to go "out of area or out of business" to capture this shift in alliance responsibility. Many on both sides of the Atlantic said it could not be done, but President Bill Clinton and European leaders set a new strategic direction for NATO. Today, Europe and NATO are stronger and better as a result.

> **W**e are facing a 'vertex of evil'— an intersection of WMD and terrorism.

The time to take the next logical step is now. In a world in which terrorist attacks on our countries can be planned in Germany, financed in Asia, and carried out in the United States, old distinctions between "in" and "out of area" have become irrelevant. We have surpassed the old boundaries and other geographical distinctions that guided our thinking on NATO. If the United States and Europe—the most advanced Western democracies and the closest allies in the world—cannot organize ourselves to meet the new terrorist threat, we will have given the enemy a huge advantage. Those seeking to do us harm would like nothing more than to see the West divided over its own security.

The tragic events of September 11 did bring the United States and Europe closer together, and our cooperation to win this war has been unprecedented. Many Europeans recognize that the threat is real and that Europe is a target. Although unpublicized for security reasons, European support in terms of police cooperation and intelligence sharing is unprecedented and has been essential to our progress. In the earliest stages of the fighting, more Europeans than Americans were on the ground in Afghanistan. As we move into the reconstruction stage, Europe has paid much of the bill for rebuilding the nation.

Unfortunately, U.S. and European views diverge sharply on how to deal with Iraq and Iran. In part, Europeans are preoccupied with their efforts to come together within the EU in the midst of a recession. They worry about the United States going into unilateralist overdrive, citing Bush's "axis of evil" comments in his State of the Union address as evidence.

Some worry that the president went too far, but I would suggest that he did not go far enough. To continue the geometric metaphor, I believe we are facing a "vertex of evil"—an intersection of WMD and terrorism. The threat is greater and the response more sweeping than the debate surrounding the president's phrase. The United States and our allies must prepare to keep the lines of terror away from nuclear, chemical, and biological weapons, materials, and knowledge. We need partners for this effort, and there are no better candidates than our NATO allies.

November in Prague: No Time Like the Present

Our efforts in this war should be measured not by what we think is doable, but by what must be done. The questions of new missions and the war on terrorism must become the focal point of the Prague summit this year. Although NATO enlargement and deepened NATO-Russia cooperation will be central to the agenda, they must be complimented by making the campaign against terrorism a central NATO task.

> Terrorism must be front and center on NATO's agenda in Prague.

U.S. capabilities would be severely degraded if NATO cannot be redirected in this manner. Indeed, the current military nature of the campaign suggests that the Prague agenda ought to focus on developing a comprehensive plan for restructuring European military capabilities, a task which could extend to rethinking completely the current Defense Capabilities Initiative (DCI) that was formulated with Bosnia and Kosovo in mind. In its place should be substituted a "DCI-2"—a capabilities package born of the lessons of Afghanistan. A DCI designed to close the gap between the European allies and United States is no longer feasible, if it ever was. More important now is the redirection of the capabilities initiative so as to create and harmonize counterterrorism and counterproliferation capabilities to serve both U.S. and European interests.

Leaving NATO focused solely on defending the peace in Europe from old threats would reduce it to a housekeeping role. If we fail to defend our societies from a major terrorist attack involving WMD, the alliance will have failed in the most fundamental sense of defending our nations. This possibility is why terrorism must be front-and-center on NATO's agenda in Prague. We can launch the next round of NATO enlargement in Prague, as well as a new NATO-Russia relationship, and the alliance could still be failing—unless it transforms itself into a new force in the war on terrorism.

Redefining NATO's Mission: WMD Terrorism   13

The Leadership Challenge

Leadership by the president of the United States is crucial. Bush has declared the need to pursue NATO enlargement. His June 2001 speech in Warsaw that sketched a vision of NATO embracing new democracies was historic. He has also expressed the need to expand the NATO-Russia relationship and to invite Moscow to assume a central role in the war on terrorism. Accomplishing this task would send a clear message to friend and foe that he is prepared to lead a transformation of NATO to meet this new threat.

The president must also identify the critical components of a stronger alliance that, if properly articulated in Prague, can define the foundation for a new NATO. The administration must not be caught playing referee among competing interests as the European nations jockey for influence over the agenda. This summit must assume a grander scale, by identifying the key elements that will reinvigorate the trans-Atlantic alliance and sow the ashes of the World Trade Center and the Pentagon as the foundations of the second postwar order.

NATO has prevented war in Europe for more than 50 years. If the alliance does not address the most pressing security threat to our countries today, however, it will become increasingly marginalized. This outcome is not in any of our security interests. Allowing this opportunity to forge a new trans-Atlantic understanding slip away would be a historic mistake. All U.S. alliances will be reviewed and recast in light of this new challenge. If NATO is not up to the challenge of becoming effective in the new war against terrorism, then our political leaders will be inclined to search for something else that will answer this need.

Leaders on both sides of the Atlantic should focus at this moment on our rich heritage of cooperation and mutual sacrifice. The Prague summit is the place to establish a NATO that clearly defines the requirements of victory in the war on terrorism and organizes to win that victory.

Note

1. See http://www.senate.gov/~lugar/weapons.htm for more information on the CTR program.

[19]

The Threat of Biological Terrorism in the New Millennium

STEVEN KUHR
Strategic Emergency Group, Ltd.

JEROME M. HAUER
Science Applications International Corporation

The use of biological weapons in times of war has a long and detailed history in the 20th century. Today, analysts, law enforcement, and intelligence experts suggest that biological weapons may be used to cause mass illness and death by terrorists domestically and internationally. In fact, an incident of biological terrorism was perpetrated on the citizens of a rural Oregon community in 1984. Government agencies at the local, state, and federal levels must establish programs to detect natural or intentional epidemics early so as to afford the maximum protection for citizens by way of mass prophylaxis and mass medical care.

The use of biological weapons by terrorists has the potential to harm and kill thousands of people. With forethought and planning, local government agencies can develop programs that can detect an outbreak early in its progress and implement a response and that will reduce morbidity and mortality. This is critical as we enter the new millennium. We now face an ever growing threat of the use of bacterial and viral agents by terrorist groups, some of which may have ties to rogue nations known to manufacture and have in their arsenals products including agents that can cause diseases such as anthrax and tularemia.

HISTORY OF BIOLOGICAL WARFARE

Biological warfare agents made their way into the history books in the 20th century. As early as World War I, governments used biological agents against humans and animals to further their strategic and tactical objectives. World War I saw the use of *Burkholderia mallei* and *Bacillus anthracis* to cause glanders and anthrax, respectively, in military cattle and horses. Enemy forces were also accused of dropping "plague bombs" on allied targets (Iavarone, 2000; Sidell, Takafuji, & Franz, 1997).

By 1918, chemical and biological weapons development programs were flourishing on both sides of the Atlantic and Pacific Oceans. Governments recognized that these weapons had a great impact on enemy armies while incurring little expense. The toxin ricin appeared on the scene early as a battlefield weapon as work on biological weapons and chemical weapons continued (Sidell et al., 1997).

Governments recognized that biological agents were of great value as weapons on the battlefield, but they also realized that their effects were horrendous. In 1925, the *Protocol for the Prohibition of the Use in War of Asphyxiating, Poisonous or Other Gases, and of Bacteriological Methods of Warfare* was developed. This document, better known as the *Geneva Protocol*, prohibited the use of chemical and bacterial agents in times of war. The *Geneva Protocol* had little effect and was not worth the paper it was printed on. The use of chemical and biological agents in war continued, some would say, up to and beyond the 1990s (Roberts, 1993; *Protocol for the Prohibition*, 1925).

The Japanese are known to have used biological weapons in their war with the Chinese as well as during World War II against Chinese and American forces. It is well documented that the Japanese engaged in a large-scale biological weapons development and analysis program located at death camps that rivaled or surpassed those operated by the Nazis. One such camp, known as Unit 731, was the home of Japan's largest biological weapons development laboratory and testing facility. At this camp, atrocities such as vivisection and the testing of bacterial agents were conducted on Allied and Chinese prisoners of war. More than 3,000 deaths occurred at Unit 731, many of which were attributed to anthrax (Harris, 1994; Kristof, n.d.; Sidell et al., 1997; Tien-wei, n.d.).

Allied armies also dabbled in biological warfare. The British, in an effort to develop and test anthrax as a biological agent, bombed a small island off the coast of Scotland. The island, Gruinard, was considered contaminated until the early 1990s, when it was decontaminated with sea water and formaldehyde (Hornsby, 1996; Roberts, 1993; Sidell et al., 1997).

The United States also had a robust biological weapons program housed at what was then Camp Detrick in Maryland. This program, which started shortly after World War II, was credited with creating some of the most infective, "weapons-grade" products ever developed. Agents produced at Camp Detrick included *B. anthracis* and *Coxiella burnetii*, which causes Q fever. Under this program, a series of live agent tests were conducted in a number of American cities (using inert agents such as *Bacillus globigii* and *Bacillus subtillus*). Of note are the tests conducted in San Francisco, where the aerosolized release of simulated anthrax positively demonstrated an effective attack on an urban population center from a marine vessel, and the test in New York City, where the demonstration illustrated an effective attack on an underground subway system. The operation at Camp Detrick evolved away from an offensive weapons production program to the defensive program now known as the U.S. Army Medical Institute for Infectious Diseases (Patrick, 1998, personal communication, November 23, 1998).

In 1972, more than 100 nations ratified the *Convention on the Prohibition of Development, Production and Stockpiling of Bacteriological (Biological) and Toxin Weapons and on Their Destruction.* This document also proved to be somewhat useless in that the development of biological weapons continued until the 1990s (*Convention on the Prohibition*, 1972).

An incident during the spring of 1979 in the Russian city of Sverdlosk deserves special mention. Sverdlosk, which was later renamed Ekaterinburg, was the site of a major accidental release of a biological agent into a noncombatant population. The number of casualties resulting from this incident is said to be between 200 and 1,000. Investigators confirmed 66 deaths, 42 of which were verified by autopsy as having resulted from pulmonary disease consistent with the inhalation of aerosolized anthrax spores. For years after the incident, the Soviet government claimed that the illnesses and deaths occurred from the consumption of contaminated meat (Roberts, 1993; Sidell et al., 1997; U.S. Army Medical Research Institute of Infectious Diseases, 1998).

THE THREAT

Biological weapons are known to have been produced by rogue nations such as Iraq and are believed to be in the possession of other nations such as North Korea. Harmful pathogens can be produced with some very rudimentary skills in biology. The question is whether they can be produced by amateur biologists at or near the military specifications needed to cause mass illness and death. Biological agent development is also relatively inexpensive, making it an attractive choice for today's economy-minded terrorists. However, an individual or group of individuals with some basic laboratory skills and basic knowledge of biology can produce a biological agent in quantities large enough to sicken and even kill a large number of people. This point was clearly illustrated in 1984, when followers of the Rajneesh, the leader of a cult based in Oregon, placed *Salmonella typhimurium* bacteria on open salad bars in a number of restaurants throughout the city of The Dalles. About 750 people became ill, but no deaths are known to have occurred as a result of this incident (Cole, 1996; Torok et al., 1997; WBFF Staff, 1997; Wildavsky, 1999).

Biological agents are generally categorized as either bacterial, viral, or toxin agents. Table 1 briefly displays the agents believed to convey the greatest threat based on the history of their development and ease of production.

PREPARING FOR BIOLOGICAL TERRORISM

Early recognition of an event is the frontline defense against biological terrorism. Unlike chemical agents, which act quickly, biological agents take longer to produce effects due to their incubation period as well as other environmental

TABLE 1:   **Most Threatening Biological Agents Based on Development and Ease of Production**

Agent	Disease	Class	Incubation Period	Treatment	Early Signs and Symptoms
Bacilllus anthracis	Anthrax	Bacteria	1 to 5 days	Ciprofloxacin, doxycycline	Fever, malaise, fatigue, cough, chest discomfort with dyspnea, diaphoresis, stridor, cyanosis
Francisella tularensis	Tularemia	Bacteria	1 to 10 days	Streptomycin, doxycycline	Fever, chills, headache, malaise, substerbal discomfort, prostration
Coxiella burnetii	Q fever	Bacteria	14 to 26 days	Tetracycline, doxycycline	Fever, cough, pleuritic chest pain
Brucella species	Brucellosis	Bacteria	5 to 21 days	Streptomycin, tetracycline	Fever, headache, weakness, fatigue, chills, diaphoresis, arthralgias, myalgias
Yersinia pestis (contagious)	Plaque (pneumonic)	Bacteria	1 to 3 days	Ciprofloxacin, doxycycline	High fever, chills, headache, hemoptysis, dyspnea, stridor, cyanosis
Variola (contagious)	Smallpox	Virus	10 to 12 days	Supportive care	Acute onset with malaise, fever, rigors, vomiting, headache, backache followed by lesions in 2 to 3 days
Venezuelan equine encephalitis virus	Venezuelan equine encephalitis	Virus	1 to 6 days	Supportive care	General malaise, fever, rigors, severe headache, photophobia, myalgias
Staphylococcus enterotoxin (b)	Intoxication (aerosol exposure)	Toxin	1 to 6 hours	Supportive care	Sudden onset of fever, chills, headache, myalgia, nonproductive cough, possible chest pain and dyspnea, nausea, vomiting and diarrhea (if swallowed)

SOURCES: Slidell, Patrick, and Dashiell (1998), U.S. Army Medical Research Institute of Infectious Diseases (1998).

factors present during their release. These include meteorological factors such as wind speed and direction, time of day (sunlight contributes to the decay of biological agents), and temperature, which has an effect on inversion layers, affecting the ability of an agent to remain airborne. A narrow window of opportunity exists during which aggressive medical treatment, including prophylaxis (for bacterial agents), can positively affect the outcome of the disease.

To ensure that an outbreak is recognized early, hospital emergency departments, emergency medical service (EMS) personnel, and primary care physicians, the group most likely to observe an emerging disease incident (either natural or intentional), must be trained to recognize the signs and symptoms of the diseases considered to be biological terrorism threats. This will hopefully raise their suspicion when considering differential diagnosis surrounding an unusual infectious disease or fever of unknown etiology.

In addition to passive surveillance, whereby trained medical practitioners look for signs of an event through their patients, an active surveillance system is designed to identify an outbreak early by aggressively monitoring and analyzing health and medical indicators. One critical indicator in health data surveillance is EMS demand. EMS serves as a gateway to health care for many Americans, especially in densely populated, urban areas where economic conditions often bring people to public health care by EMS conveyance. Variations in EMS data are often associated with events that affect the population. These include summer and winter weather extremes and certainly unusual disease outbreaks. This makes EMS data an excellent barometer for assessing and analyzing the health of a given populace. Other data include hospital emergency department activity as well as death statistics from medical examiners and coroners. Once a baseline is established for a specified area, perhaps a metropolitan area or region (an analysis of at least 3 previous years is recommended), the daily evaluation of current indicators against the baseline is made simple.

Advanced surveillance can also be conducted by analyzing medical data in more specific terms. Considering that most diseases resulting from biological agents present as influenza-like illnesses, monitoring hospital and EMS data for the signs and symptoms of influenza, influenza-like illnesses, and even respiratory illnesses can aid in early detection.

REPORTING

Many local public health departments require physicians and other medical personnel to report unusual infectious and contagious diseases. The eight agents listed in Table 1 should be on every local list as reportable diseases. However, the requirement should also include that notification be made on encountering any unusual or suspicious disease. This will allow public health agencies to acquire information from multiple sources, which will alert them that an unusual outbreak is occurring. This has benefits far beyond monitoring for acts of terrorism: The system is simple yet robust enough to signal even naturally occurring outbreaks. Reporting emerging diseases must become routine; it is the responsibility of public health agencies to ensure that medical practitioners are instructed to make timely notifications. Conversely, public health agencies must notify medical practitioners of emerging disease events as they become aware of them. This will alert medical personnel and hopefully raise their awareness and suspicion.

RESPONDING TO BIOLOGICAL TERRORISM

Once an incident of biological terrorism is recognized, there is little time to put a response into operation. This is critically important when dealing with bacterial agents, especially anthrax, for which early prophylaxis and treatment can have a profound effect on the outcomes of those infected or possibly infected. Signs and symptoms of anthrax generally appear from 24 to 36 hours after inhalation of anthrax spores. Once clinical effects appear, even aggressive antibiotic therapy may not prevent serious illness and death.

Considering that an aerosolized release of a military-grade product in a populated, confined environment such as a theater or airport can infect hundreds or even thousands of individuals, the medical community and government agencies will find themselves faced with a rapidly evolving incident. As the situation unfolds, strong potential exists for events to become overwhelming very quickly. Two medical strategies will be needed at this point: mass prophylaxis and casualty management.

MASS PROPHYLAXIS

Two basic models exist for the distribution of mass quantities of medication to a large population: Deliver the medication to the people or bring the people to the medication. One caveat exists: There must be a stockpile of antibiotics large enough to provide to the population for at least the first dose regimen. For example, the recommended preliminary dose of ciprofloxacin required to treat anthrax is 500 milligrams taken twice daily for 4 weeks. Multiplied by the size of a given population, one gets an idea of the problem of designing a mass prophylaxis program.

In bringing antibiotics to the people, a large, organized, personnel commitment (perhaps the military or national guard) is needed for door-to-door delivery. When bringing people to antibiotics, less of a human resource commitment is needed. People are simply instructed, through a mass media campaign, to report to medication distribution centers, which can be set up in community-based facilities such as community centers and houses of worship.

CASUALTY MANAGEMENT

Hospitals and EMS agencies will become overwhelmed very quickly. Strategies to compensate for this should be developed in the planning stages, long before an incident occurs. Mutual aid agreements for the sharing of ambulance resources with surrounding municipalities and the identification, staffing, and equipping of alternate care facilities to offset the demand on hospitals should be determined well in advance of an incident. The integration of federal and state resources should be a part of the plan as well. The U.S. government has enacted programs to augment and support local medical activities during a disaster. These programs include Disaster Medical Assistance Teams (DMATs), which are essentially mobile hospitals, as well as DMATs specially trained and equipped to treat chemical and biological casualties, called National Medical Response Teams.

Fatality management is another critical undertaking. As the disease evolves, deaths will occur more and more frequently. To avoid an additional public health emergency and to ensure that appropriate dignity is offered to the deceased as well as the living, strategies for mass quantities of fatalities should be developed in advance of an incident. This would include alternate mortuary facilities, alternate means of storage and disposal, and plans to offer dignified, professional services to family and friends of the deceased.

MULTIJURISDICTIONAL RESPONSE

Biological terrorism knows no borders. Consider the release of a biological agent in an outbound commuter rail car. Depending on the agent, the disease may not manifest for many hours or even days. Once the disease emerges, cases will be scattered. Even if the disease is not contagious, like smallpox, people who were on the train will seek medical care throughout the region. Planning and preparedness must take a regional approach. This especially includes surveillance programs whereby data such as those mentioned above are monitored throughout a region and reported to a centralized location for analysis and action. Public health and emergency management agencies at the local, state, and federal levels must all be tied in. Mass prophylaxis and mass casualty planning should also be coordinated regionally. The demand for services and resources will not be localized; therefore, federal partnerships including the Federal Bureau of Investigation (the lead agency for crisis management), the Federal Emergency Management Agency (the lead agency for consequence management), and the U.S. Public Health Service (the lead agency for medical emergency management) should be an integral element on the planning team.

PROGRAM AGENDA

In an effort to bring it all together, a solid biological terrorism program agenda is needed. Table 2 presents a comprehensive agenda designed for local jurisdictions endeavoring to create an effective plan and response protocols to counter biological terrorism.

TABLE 2:   Agenda for Local Jurisdictions Endeavoring to Create an Effective Plan and Response Protocols to Counter Biological Terrorism

Planning Issue	Objective(s)	Agencies Needed
Threat/risk assessment	Identify actual threats as well as possible threats based on local politics, population density, economics, etc. Attempt to validate the planning process.	FBI, state and local law enforcement, public health, emergency management
Hazard analysis	Identify potential worst-case and other scenarios on which to base planning.	FBI, state and local law enforcement, public health, emergency management
Public safety agency capabilities	Assess and enhance local capabilities such as plans and materials for field biological hazmat operations, proper levels of personal protection and training, documentation and recording, testing, sample collection and analysis, and interagency participation.	Fire department, hazmat team, EMS, local law enforcement, public health, emergency management
Health surveillance	Assess local public health surveillance to identify whether it is sensitive enough signal a biological agent release. Develop and establish routine surveillance of local indicators such as EMS demand, hospital activity, and medical examiner volume.	Emergency management, EMS, public health, medical examiner/coroner, hospitals
Laboratory capabilities	Assess state and local public health lab capability to analyze biological samples. Enhance capabilities to rapidly identify biological agents locally.	State and local public health agencies, fire department, emergency management, FBI, local law enforcement
EMS capabilities	Assess capacity of local EMS system to manage a surge of calls for service. Develop regional mutual aid agreements. Train EMS personnel to recognize biological agent signs and symptoms. Provide personal protection when confronted with a contagious agent.	Regional EMS agencies, emergency management
Mass prophylaxis	Develop a mechanism to distribute medication/ antibiotics en masse using community-based distribution centers.	Emergency management, public health, EMS, law enforcement, national guard
Medical system capabilities	Assess the patient capacity at local hospitals. Identify on-hand and just-in-time stocks of antibiotics (ciprofloxacin, doxycycline, penicillin, tetracycline, streptomycin, gentamycin, and others as determined by public health). Identify regional quantities of ventilators (needed for many inhaled infectious agents (e.g., anthrax and tularemia). Develop capabilities to rapidly expand hospital internal and external patient care capabilities. Undertake initiatives to fill identified gaps.	EMS, hospitals, public health, emergency management, FEMA, U.S. Public Health Service, NDMS

(continued)

TABLE 2 Continued

Planning Issue	Objective(s)	Agencies Needed
Medical examiner capabilities	Assess capacity of regional mortuaries. Under take efforts to expand mortuary processing and storage capabilities. Train medical examiner personnel in personal protection.	Local and regional medical examiner/coroner, U.S. Public Health Service, NDMS
Emergency management capabilities	Assess emergency management agency capability to coordinate the response to a major, regionwide public health emergency. Assess capacity of the local emergency operations center and its technology. Coordinate the biological terrorism planning program.	Local and state emergency management agencies
Field incident (biological hazmat)	Assess and expand on local capability to operate at field biological incidents such as a package suspected to contain a biological agent (e.g., recent anthrax hoaxes).	Fire department, hazmat team, EMS, emergency management, FBI, local law enforcement, public health

NOTE: FBI = Federal Bureau of Investigation, hazmat = hazardous materials, EMS = emergency medical services, FEMA = Federal Emergency Management Agency, NDMS = National Disaster Medical System.

PREPARING FOR THE FUTURE

Improvements in our capabilities and systems will evolve as we learn more and more about recognizing and combating biological terrorism. Technology is needed for devices that can rapidly identify biological agents in the environment as well as in humans. Disease monitoring and information distribution systems using various forms of media and technological outlets must be refined for the rapid sharing of reports of outbreaks, and research and development must continue in the areas of vaccine development and mass production. We must also ensure that our political leadership is well versed in the topic to ensure a steady stream of funding for research and development, planning and preparedness, and major emergency response. Considering the threat and gravity of the release of a biological agent in a city, now is the time to plan and prepare. Continuous education of medical and health care professionals, private physicians, and EMS personnel and a strengthened public health infrastructure designed to recognize emerging diseases early will hopefully allow us to avert a catastrophe.

Kuhr, Hauer / BIOLOGICAL TERRORISM   1041

REFERENCES

Cole, L. A. (1996, December). The specter of biological weapons. *Scientific American*, *275*, 60-65.

Convention on the prohibition of development, production and stockpiling of bacteriological (bio-logical) and toxin weapons and on their destruction [Online]. (1972). Available: http://fletcher.tufts.edu/multi/texts/BH596.txt

Excerpts: F.B.I. report on domestic terrorism (domestic terrorism shifts to the right) [Online]. (1997, April 17). Available: http://www.usis-israel.org.il/publish/press/justice/archive/1997/april/jd10418.htm

Harris, S. H. (1994). *Factories of death: Japanese biological warfare, 1932-45, and the American cover-up*. London: Routledge.

Hornsby, M. (1996, July 22). Anthrax outbreak casts shadow over homes site. *The Times* [Online]. Available: http://www.cyber-dyne.com/~tom/anthrax.html

Iavarone, M. (2000). *Armory: Gas warfare* [Online]. Available: http://www.worldwar1.com/arm006.htm

Kristof, N. D. (ŋ.d.). Unlocking a deadly secret. *The New York Times* [Online]. Available: http://centurychina.com/wiihist/germwar/germwar.htm#killgirl

Patrick, W. (1998, July). *Lecture at Department of Defense biological weapons improved response program* [Online]. Available: http://dp.sbccom.army.mil/bwirp/index.html

Protocol for the prohibition of the use in war of asphyxiating, poisonous or other gases, and of bacteriological methods of warfare [Online]. (1925, June 17). Available: http://www.lib.byu.edu/~rdh/wwi/hague/hague13.html

Roberts, B. (Ed.). (1993). *Biological weapons: Weapons of the future?* Washington, DC: Center for Strategic and International Studies.

Sidell, F. R., Takafuji, E. T., & Franz, D. R. (1997). *Textbook of military medicine. Part 1, warfare, weaponry, and the casualty: Vol. 3. Medical aspects of chemical and biological warfare*. Falls Church, VA: Office of the Surgeon General, U.S. Army.

Sidell, F. R., Patrick, William C., III, & Dashiell, T. R. (1998). *Jane's chem-bio handbook*. Arlington, VA: Jane's Information Group.

Tien-wei, W. (n.d.). *A preliminary review of studies of Japanese biological warfare Unit 731 in the United States* [Online]. Available: http://www-users.cs.umn.edu/~dyue/wiihist/germwar/731rev.htm

Torok, T. J., Tauxe, R. V., Wise, R. P., Livengood, J. R., Sokolow, R., Mauvais, S., Birkness, K. A., Skeels, M. R., Horan, J. M., & Foster, L. R. (1997). A large community outbreak of salmonellosis caused by intentional contamination of restaurant salad bars. *Journal of the American Medical Association*, *278*, 389-395.

U.S. Army Medical Research Institute of Infectious Diseases. (1998, July). *Medical management of biological casualties: Handbook* [Online]. Fort Detrick, MD: Author. Available: http://www.vnh.org/BIOCASU/toc.html

WBFF Staff. (1997, August 10). *Food terrorism* [Online]. Baltimore, MD: WBFF. Available: http://www.wbff45.com/news/97/ft.htm

Wildavsky, R. (1999, January). Are we ready for bioterror? *Reader's Digest*, *154*, 84-91.

[20]

Bioethics after the Terror

Jonathan D. Moreno, University of Virginia

Bioethics as a field has been fortunate that its values and concerns have mirrored the values and concerns of society. In light of the September 11th attacks, it is possible that we are witnessing the beginning of a transition in American culture, one fraught with implications for bioethics. The emphasis on autonomy and individual rights may come to be tempered by greater concern over the collective good. Increased emphasis on solidarity over autonomy could greatly alter public response to research abuses aimed at defense from bioterrorism, to privacy of genetic information, and to control of private medical resources to protect the public health.

There is no more trivial nor fundamental observation about bioethics than that it is a child of the 1960s. Not only the civil rights movements, but also a generalized skepticism about establishment institutions, nourished a field that made the reevaluation of medical paternalism and the establishment of patient self-determination central to a critique of physician-patient relations, a critique unprecedented in its scope and eventual success. Like so much of the sensibility of the 1960s, bioethics itself has become part of the establishment, as have those who profess it.

It should not be surprising, therefore, if certain themes that are characteristic of bioethics should be caught up in historic shifts in cultural sensibilities. What if individual autonomy and patient self-determination were no longer self-evident primary values in our public discourse? What if efficiency concerns about resource allocation were thought more respectable as compared to individual access to healthcare than has generally been the case? What if the public and the courts were less sympathetic to claims from persons who believe themselves to have been victimized by careless or unscrupulous experimenters for the sake of the greater good, particularly if those experiments had a national security purpose?

It is too early to tell if the tragic events of 11 September 2001 presage a significant or enduring cultural shift in American attitudes toward the way that personal self-determination is factored into our civic life. Much will of course depend on the outcome of the current international crisis, as well as its longevity. In the meantime it is well to reflect on the favorable relationship mainstream bioethical constructs have enjoyed with mainstream cultural values. Put simply, up to now bioethics and those who espouse the study of moral values in the life sciences have been on the right side of history, for that history has been characterized by intensifying concern about human rights. As a result, bioethicists have been privileged to participate in a social agenda that has won widespread approbation, first in public media and finally even in the healthcare institutions that once resisted these "strangers at the bedside," in David Rothman's (1991) felicitous phrase.

In this essay I examine some potential implications for bioethics—understood as a body of moral theory as well as a set of social practices—that could create novel tensions for a field that has never experienced a fundamental shift in the priorities of its surrounding culture. Only one assumption need be made for this analysis to proceed: that no intellectual pursuit that keeps at least one eye fixed on public affairs can remain apart from the sort of sea change that we might now be witnessing.

All-Too-Human Experiments

One week before the attacks on the World Trade Center and the Pentagon, the United States government stated that the Defense Intelligence Agency was preparing to develop a new and more virulent strain of anthrax thought to be in Russia's possession. No contravention of the treaty permitting only defensive bioweapons research was admitted, for these projects were aimed at preventing a successful attack and, government officials reasoned, research aimed at defense could only be effective if undertaken in light of the potentialities of actual offensive devices. Simultaneously, the CIA was reported to have built a replica of a biological weapons dispersal device or bomblet developed by the former Soviet Union, again for purposes of defensive studies (NYTimes.com 2001).

I confess to being somewhat taken aback by

these revelations, not, I hope, out of any naivete about the need for continued biodefense work nor by the thin line between defensive and offensive research. Rather, I recalled the many questions I received while promoting a book on the history and ethics of national security experiments, when both sophisticated and simple-minded conspiracy theorists pressed me for my opinion about whether abusive secret experiments might still be going on (Moreno 2001). My response: Although I can't prove a negative, it seems quite unlikely that covert human experiments could continue today. Could I be so confident following the admission of research that stretched, if it did not break, the spirit of an international treaty obligation? Could I be so sure that secret human experiments were not now taking place under the sponsorship of U.S. national security entities?

After the attacks this story, like so many others, understandably took a back seat to the national emergency. Yet I have wondered whether the outrage that greeted revelations of human experiments conducted without adequate consent and under risky circumstances, especially those sponsored by national security agencies, might be tempered with the change in certain objective conditions. After all, the original scandals concerning the Central Intelligence Agency (CIA)'s MKULTRA program and the army's LSD experiments came in the wake of Vietnam and Watergate. Twenty years later the human radiation experiments controversy surfaced following a largely (for Americans) bloodless victory in the Persian Gulf and in the context of suspicious sequelae of service in the Gulf that again undermined confidence in our government's concern with its men and women in uniform.

Counterfactuals being what they are, it is impossible to be certain that the public outrage about abusive human experiments involving people in uniform, hospitalized patients, institutionalized children, prisoners, and others would have been lessened had the information not become available when it did. But it is hard to argue that, for example, any new revelations about secret state experiments designed to minimize the effects of a terrorist attack would excite quite the public reaction that they would have before 11 September. My confidence in this regard might of course be short-lived, depending, as I have said, on the course of the international conflict. Yet at least in the short-term I do not see how one can draw any other conclusion.

That having been said, what shall we expect if the United States and its allies are indeed engaged in a struggle against terrorism that is years in duration, as President George W. Bush and other leaders have indicated? Without suggesting that history will simply cycle back to a hands-off attitude with respect to covert government activity, it seems unlikely that a great deal of public energy would be expended on the kinds of investigations we have witnessed in the past, at least not with the same intensity. Would the American people today applaud spending tens of millions of dollars investigating Cold War human radiation experiments, for example, as was the case in the mid-1990s?

In the early 1970s, scandals about unethical human experiments by civilian organizations and a widespread loss of public sympathy for the military preceded the revelations of the army and CIA chemical weapons research. The country was prepared for outrages when they were discovered. What if, nearly 30 years later, the process was to reverse itself? A new preoccupation with "homeland defense" and a renewed respect for the professionals engaged in these efforts, including the granting of greater legal flexibility for espionage activities, could easily spill over into an enhanced image for civilian institutions whose mission is to protect our national survival. Medical organizations and healthcare professionals will play an important role in ameliorating the effects of a chemical or biological attack, and the public health system will be needed to identify an outbreak as well as to organize the response. The esteem in which the medical profession is held, so battered in recent years, could well be improved in the eyes of a jittery public through their identification with these initiatives.

Surely the tradition of civil libertarianism that has always influenced American political thinking will remain. But the strength of the rights orientation has waxed and waned, depending partly on perceptions of external threats. As we enter a new political and ideological framework the recent intense concern about the rights and welfare of human research subjects could be blunted. This could come about not only because the public's attention would be focused mainly on matters of larger national interest, with room to concentrate on a relatively small set of domestic problems, but also if continued scientific progress is given greater priority with increased momentum for the research imperative.

All this is not to assert, of course, that the international and domestic conventions governing ethical human experimentation will be erased or even explicitly disavowed. Rather, the energy and dynamism behind the identification of questionable research practices is likely to lessen if a besieged society views science as an important ally and therefore sees occasional ethical improprieties as lapses in judgment rather than indicators of a larger crisis of humanism in the pursuit of knowledge.

Autonomy and Solidarity in Clinical Ethics

Some writers have urged that a "principle of community" be incorporated into the pantheon of bioethical principles, particularly concerning research involving populations in underdeveloped countries. Whatever the merits of this proposal, there can be little argument that a principle of autonomy or self-determination has been virtually the philosophical flagship of modern bioethics. I have been among those who argue that the emergence of this principle in the discussion of physician-patient relations marks a qualitative distinction between traditional medical ethics and modern bioethics (Ahronheim, Moreno, and Zuckerman 2000). According to the standard analysis, individual rights in healthcare can only be trumped by a serious public health concern for which there is an available and effective intervention. The communitarian analysis that has been proposed would privilege public well-being to a far greater degree than the standard view.

Without resorting to communitarianism, it is surely plausible to imagine a future in which the press of recent events has stimulated a reevaluation of a strong autonomy presumption. Without knowing the precise content or result of such a reevaluation, we might simply refer to a sentiment of social solidarity. This sentiment might not qualify as a valorized "principle" of biomedical ethics, nor might it even appear in bioethics textbooks and journal articles per se. Yet it might be perceptible in the way cases in clinical ethics are analyzed, for example, especially if it is one of those sorts of cases in which an analysis modeled on self-determination has never been all that satisfactory.

To explain my point I need to note what is obvious even to the casual student of clinical bioethics. In cases of terminally ill "moral strangers"—those who lack capacity and whose prior wishes concerning end-of-life care are unknown to any reasonable degree—certain contortions must be performed in order to make an autonomy-based

analysis fit. Thus we apply a "best interests" or even "reasonable person" test. Yet as many have noted these are largely fictions intended to reproduce, *per impossibile*, the decisions that we imagine the gravely ill patient would have made himself or herself. The real purpose of these exercises often seems to be to reassure ourselves that we retain a coherent doctrine of autonomy-based medical ethics. And, besides, what's the alternative?

Thus when it is urged that the persistently vegetative patient whose individual wishes are wholly unknown must nonetheless continue to be artificially hydrated and indefinitely provided nutrients, what can our autonomy-based medical ethicist say? That the patient's best interests are being violated? But such people have no interests. That such a condition is an affront to human dignity? There is little agreement about what counts as dignity in these extreme cases. That resources are being wasted? Quite apart from its unpleasant implications, the appeal to resource allocation is not an autonomy-based position.

Among the few prominent ethicists who have argued on behalf of continued artificial feeding in such cases is Daniel Callahan (1987). His appeal to what sounds very much like a social solidarity view has been largely dismissed. Nonetheless, as autonomy has less of a hold on our imaginations, his position might well be up for reassessment. However persuaded we might be that, as the court in Cruzan stated, artificial feeding is more like a medical treatment than actual eating, a less individualistic society might feel more qualms about finding autonomy-based reasons to let moral strangers die.

A cultural shift of the kind about which I am speculating in light of the recent catastrophe and the impending "war" on terrorism might also sensitize us to the rationale underlying certain current practices that, again, are not comprehended by the regnant principles or modes of analysis. For instance, experienced clinical ethics consultants are familiar with situations in which a duly authorized healthcare agent is both aware of a terminally ill patient's wishes not to be sustained indefinitely and is in concert with healthcare professionals on the appropriate course. Yet this agent may ask for a reasonable amount of time, say one or two days, to bring the rest of the family along toward acceptance of this conclusion of their loved one's life. In my experience clinical ethicists would accept temporizing for this purpose, perhaps even in the case of a patient who is dead by neurologic criteria.

Yet what patient-centered criteria, either autonomy or beneficence-based, could contemplate such a position? The most obvious theoretical gambit, reference to the patient's likely wishes in favor of familial harmony, is the usual kind of stretch. Surely it would be more accurate to acknowledge that the death of this patient is an event that affects others than only the patient. Though this event obviously does not have the significance for the patient that it does for the family, it may still have enormous emotional consequences. The instinct to make this the best death possible for the family as well as the patient is not grounded in the patient's rights, interests, or even preferences, but rather in a latent sense of the importance of social solidarity in the face of death. Whatever one thinks of communitarianism, this fact about our social sensibilities is hard to deny and at best difficult to capture in standard bioethical theory.

Resource Allocation

Besides research and clinical ethics matters, other bioethical issues that have been rather frozen in the recent past may be shaken into a different mix by a lengthy crisis. In a recent MSNBC column Arthur Caplan (2001) observed that the families of those killed or injured on 11 September may lack adequate health insurance, in spite of the outpouring of giving intended to help them through the short term. A sense of social solidarity that this country has not experienced since the early 1950s and the advent of social security could alter the balance in favor of greater concern for equity in access to healthcare. The balance could well be altered in the face of a simmering worry about a threat of large-scale terrorism and its ensuing casualties. It would not be the first time that the ripples of a crisis in foreign affairs have advanced an item on the liberal social agenda. The modern civil rights movement was anticipated and, some would say, found its first great victory in President Truman's order to desegregate the military following World War II.

The societal obligations of managed-care organizations (MCOs) may well be up for reevaluation as well in light of the impetus to plan for biological terror attacks. As much as a decade ago a few epidemiologists raised questions about the ability of the public health system to coordinate with medical personnel who are employees of private entities with private interests. MCOs routinely consider their obligations as providers of healthcare to lie with their enrollees. Under what circumstances may their facilities and resources be commandeered by public health authorities? The

original discussions did not anticipate the kind of national security worries we are now facing, but stemmed from questions about naturally occurring epidemics. The new agenda could force a basic critique of the role of privately held clinics in dealing with critical incidents that threaten national security.

Genes at War

The confidentiality of genetic information, whether acquired through modern genetic testing or family histories, has been a matter of intense concern. Mainly this concern has expressed itself in the context of medical records that may be of interest to health insurers, life and disability insurers, current or potential employers, and educational institutions. All of these entities may wish to know if a certain individual is a "bad risk." Studies that seek to determine the prevalence and penetration of genetic alterations within certain groups, such as BRCA1 and BRCA2 in Jewish women of Eastern European descent, have raised worries about stigmatization. These concerns may extend to genotyping or haplotyping of national or ethnic groups for public health purposes. The recent project to develop a genetic database for Icelanders may provide a useful model for any ensuing discussion.

Now consider moving from genetic information unlinked to individuals and suitable for public health purposes to individually linked data justified for national security reasons. How might such a transition take place?

Although the United States is far from concluding, much less beginning, a national debate about standardized identification cards, if that sort of proposal is considered by federal officials, the role of genetic information will be on the table. To be sure, the idea of a national ID is the bane of civil libertarians and has never been seriously considered by elected representatives. Yet in the current climate it is not unreasonable to suppose that the concept will be revisited with all sorts of refinements. "Genetic fingerprinting" will surely be one option. Moreover, in an atmosphere in which the value of social solidarity is given enhanced weight, advocates will surely note the byproduct of improved public health surveillance.

A closely held, comprehensive genetic library of all Americans will also be attractive to those who worry about the most extreme scenario of biological warfare, one that targets human beings at the chromosomal level itself. Sudden and inexplicable changes in the genetic profiles of many

Americans could indicate the most insidious of all biowarfare campaigns, perhaps in the form of slow-acting variations that interfere with normal metabolic processes. That public officials could seriously consider this sort of scenario, much less a drastic response in the form of a genetic database for all Americans, seems like bizarre fiction. So did the events of 11 September the moment before they occurred.

A New Turn in Bioethics?

I want to be clear about what I am claiming here, and what I am not. I am not advocating any particular substantive view among those I have arrayed, only trying to anticipate some positions that may gain currency in light of recent events and a continuing sense that an important shift is occurring in American society. Nor am I asserting that the field of bioethics, either in its theory or practices, will need to undergo some basic shift in light of the 11 September tragedies, any more than constitutional interpretation or legal practices will have to be altered. I do not anticipate wholesale abandonment of previous theoretical work in bioethics, including a prominent role for autonomy-oriented analysis.

Yet, as in the law, great public events cause ripple effects in moral thinking, especially if the struggle against terrorism is protracted and if Americans in particular are forced to come to terms with a level of risk that seemed to apply only to others. A heightened sense of group vulnerability and patriotic unity has implications for the interpretation of underlying values. One need not be a Marxist to appreciate that even philosophy responds to altered facts on the ground. Indeed, that is how bioethics emerged when it did and why it "saved the life of philosophy," as Toulmin (1986) noted years ago.

Again, the effects we shall see are as yet underdetermined. For example, at some point attention will return to such relatively mundane issues as federal policy on the use of embryonic stem cells in research. Will a new societal mood turn toward a more aggressive posture in favor of scientific advancement, perhaps as a reaction to what might be perceived as religious fundamentalism? Or will the turn rather be in the direction of extending respect toward these clumps of cells as precursors of precious human life, its frailty so nauseatingly depicted for us all as the World Trade Center collapsed? Or will the course of future developments

in stem cell research be among the social issues that seem unaffected by what has transpired?

It is of course too early to tell, but I am inclined to think that the third possibility, that the recent catastrophe will have no effect at all, is the least likely. Historic crossroads do affect the interpretation and application of moral values if not their foundations (so far as we can distinguish them), and bioethics is nothing if not the interpretation and application of moral values. Even seemingly arcane and distant matters can fall within the web of change in a society's worldview.

In at least one respect our field can and should respond to the terrible events of 11 September. Western scholars in all humanistic disciplines now have an urgent responsibility to familiarize themselves with Islamic teachings and to integrate Muslim learning as never before. For all our sakes, legitimate Islamic scholarship must be supported, and non-Muslim thinkers must incorporate it into their work. As well, we should reach out to colleagues in Islamic studies both here and abroad. Even those of us trained mainly in secular bioethics are familiar with certain basic concepts in Jewish and Christian medical ethics, but we are woefully ignorant of Islamic law. This is a serious enough lapse in a country where there are more Muslims than there are Episcopalians; for bioethics after the terror, this is a lapse in urgent need of correction.

References

Ahronheim, J., Moreno, J. D., and Connie Zuckerman. 2000. *Ethics in clinical practice*, 2nd. ed. Gaithersburg: Aspen.

Callahan, D. 1987. *Setting limits: Medical goals in an aging society.* New York: Simon and Schuster.

Caplan, A. 2001. New world calls for new health care. 28 September. Available from: http://MSNBC.com.

Moreno, J. D. 2001. *Undue risk: Secret state experiments on humans.* New York: Routledge.

NYTimes.com. 2001. Pentagon plans to proceed with development of anthrax strain. 5 September. Available from: http://NYTimes.com.

Rothman, D. 1991. *Strangers at the bedside: A history of how law and ethics transformed medical decision making.* New York: Basic Books.

Toulmin, S. 1986. How medicine saved the life of ethics, in *New directions in ethics*, ed. J. P. DeMarco and R. M. Fox, 265–281. New York: Routledge and Kegan Paul.

Washington Post. 2001. U.S. seeks duplicate of Russian anthrax microbe to be used to check vaccine. 5 September, A16.

[21]

Dimensions of biological terrorism: to what must we mitigate and respond?

Henry W. Fischer III

The author

Henry W. Fischer III is Associate Professor of Sociology at Millersville University of Pennsylvania, Pennsylvania, USA.

Keywords

Disasters, Terrorism

Abstract

The emergence of biological weapons of mass destruction as likely terrorist means of reigning terror on domestic urban populations is outlined. The dimensions of such a possible future catastrophe are described. The lack of preparedness to mitigate and respond to such an event is noted and it is argued that the disaster research literature should be consulted as a guide to help develop effective mitigation and response plans.

Disaster Prevention and Management
Volume 8 · Number 1 · 1999 · pp. 27–32

New danger from weapons of mass destruction

In 1995 the Japanese Aum Shinrikyo cult released sarin nerve gas in Tokyo – several people died. Is it only a matter of time until a nuclear, biological, or chemical terrorist act is perpetrated on a metropolitan area within the USA? Some analysts believe that the 1993 World Trade Center bomb was laced with cyanide, but failed when it burned up in the explosion (Betts, 1998). Future terrorist attempts may be more successful in exposing their target population to their weapon of choice.

Legacy of the Cold War

With the end of the Cold War, the fear of mutual nuclear destruction through the unleashing of the nuclear arsenals of two superpowers has largely dissipated among the citizenry at large (Betts, 1998; Christopher *et al.*, 1997). While concern remains for the "loose nuke" problem, the USA has been actively trying to mitigate against it. Nuclear arms, however, are no longer the only concern. Chemical and biological weapons are probably more likely to be used as weapons of mass destruction (WMD). These are increasingly seen as more viable choices for weaker states or terrorist groups which find themselves as decidedly disadvantaged in contrast to US conventional weapons capability. US strategy during the Cold War era emphasized deterrence via conventional and nuclear capability. Chemical and biological WMD pose an increasingly more serious deterrence challenge. This is especially true when WMD are in the hands of terrorists (Betts, 1998).

Emerging domestic threat

During the last 30 years administrations of both main US political parties have taken steps to make it increasingly difficult for terrorists to attack US personnel and facilities overseas (Simon, 1997; Tucker, 1998). Terrorists launched 177 attacks on US diplomats, military personnel, and other US government officials in 1980. In 1995 ten such acts occurred. Americans have not ceased to be targeted by terrorists, greater overseas security measures have simply been implemented by the US government. Unfortunately, this success has probably been somewhat offset by the likelihood that disrupted terrorist attacks have probably deflected some attacks onto

Dimensions of biological terrorism
Henry W. Fischer III

Disaster Prevention and Management
Volume 8 · Number 1 · 1999 · 27–32

easier targets, such as US business people or other civilians. What about the US domestic population? How safe from terrorist attack are citizens living within US borders? The 1993 World Trade Center bombing, the 1995 release of sarin nerve gas in Tokyo, and the Oklahoma City bombing point to the need for heightened US awareness and mitigative activity. In June 1995, the White House issued Presidential Decision Directive 39 (PDD-39), "United States Policy on Counterterrorism". PDD-39 stipulated measures be taken to reduce the nation's vulnerability to terrorism, to deter and respond to terrorist acts, and to strengthen capabilities to prevent and manage the consequences of terrorist use of nuclear, biological, and chemical (NBC) weapons including weapons of mass destruction.

Since the Cold War has ended, the likely future weapon of choice for domestic terrorism is expected to shift from conventional explosives to NBC agents of mass destruction (Betts, 1998; Steinbruner, 1997; Zilinskas, 1997). While nuclear and chemical WMD continue to be of great concern, it is the menu of biological agents that may be more attractive to terrorists. How has this come to pass? During the Cold War, WMD were the centerpiece of US foreign policy. Nuclear deterrence theory suggested that aggression was deterred through the mutually assured destruction of the superpowers. With the breakup of the former Soviet Union and the reduction of nuclear stockpiles by both the USA and the former Soviet states, the risk of nuclear miscalculation has shifted from superpower nuclear warfare to the use of nuclear weapons by rogue governments or terrorist groups. The difficulty (and expense) of delivering nuclear WMD to a target, along with the likelihood that the perpetrator would have access to few such weapons, makes the use of this terrorist option possible, but less likely than other options.

Terrorist use of chemical WMD
Chemical weapons were employed by Iraq against Iranian troops in the 1980-88 Iran-Iraq War and against Kurdish civilians in 1988. Chemical weapons are far more widely available than nuclear weapons. The technology to produce them is simpler. Chemical weapons, however, are not as capable of inflicting a huge number of civilian casualties in a single strike as a nuclear weapon. This is

not to say that attempts to eradicate chemical weapons are misguided. It is merely argued that nuclear weapons are probably preferred to chemical by those seeking to inflict huge casualties quickly. However, there is another alternative likely to be preferable to both of these options.

Terrorist use of biological WMD
Biological WMD have the advantage of combining maximum destructiveness with easy availability. While nuclear arms have great killing capacity, they are difficult to obtain; while chemical weapons are easy to obtain, they lack great killing capacity. A 1993 Office of Technology Assessment study concluded that 100 kilograms of anthrax spores distributed by aerosol on a clear, calm night over Washington, DC, by an airplane could *kill between 1 and 3 million people* (Betts, 1998). Anthrax spores constitute the dormant phase of a bacillus that multiplies rapidly in the body, producing toxins and rapid hemorrhaging within days of exposure.

Bacteria, viruses, or toxins may be used as biological agents. Examples of likely biological agents include anthrax (*B anthracis*), botulinum toxin, plague (*Yersinia pestis*), staphylococcal enterotoxin B, viral encephalitis virus, brucellosis, Q fever, tularemia, smallpox and viral hemorrhagic fevers (Franz *et al.*, 1997). They can be dispersed in aerosols which may remain suspended for hours for inhalation by numerous potential victims. The aerosols may be delivered by simple industrial sprayers from an airplane or boat upwind of the potential target. Diseases produced by such agents could be disabling or lethal for many civilians. Some biological agents (e.g., anthrax) produce diseases not communicable between individuals, while other agents produce those which are.

Illustration
Anthrax is caused by *B anthracis*, a sporulating bacillus. Found naturally in the soil, the organism is found worldwide. Anthrax spores can remain viable for decades in adverse environmental conditions. Aerosol delivery would most likely be employed in a terrorist attack using this biological agent, resulting in inhalational anthrax. After being inhaled, the spores would be deposited in the lower respiratory tract, germinate into vegetative bacilli, and produce necrotizing hemorrhagic mediastinitis. Symptoms begin with fever, malaise,

Dimensions of biological terrorism	Disaster Prevention and Management
Henry W. Fischer III	Volume 8 · Number 1 · 1999 · 27–32

and fatigue. They may include a nonproductive cough and vague chest pains. There may appear to be improvement for two or three days, or the victim may progress directly into severe respiratory distress, meningitis, and death within 24 to 36 hours (Franz *et al.*, 1997).

The medical response differs depending on whether measures are initiated before exposure, after exposure but before symptoms appear, or after symptoms are present. Active immunization with antibiotics may prevent illness if administered before exposure – an unlikely possibility among the civilian population at large. After exposure, but before symptoms are present, active or passive immunization, as well as pretreatment with therapeutic antibiotics or antiviral drugs, may ameliorate disease symptoms – a viable medical response if the terrorist announces what was done, where and when and if medical supplies are available in sufficient quantities for a sufficient number of medical personnel to administer to a sufficiently responsive population (all this seems problematic). Once symptoms of inhalational anthrax appear, treatment is likely to be ineffective. Diagnosis of the disease and general supportive care remain the only viable options for health care providers (Franz *et al.*, 1997).

If future exposure is expected, the vaccine, an aluminum hydroxide, may be administered in doses at 0, 2, and 4 weeks, then again at 6, 12, 18 months, followed by annual boosters. After exposure penicillin has been the usual treatment for inhalational anthrax. Two million units given intravenously every two hours. Streptomycin has been found to provide additional benefit. It is apparent that in addition to the detrimental health effects on the target population, the health care system would be significantly impacted as unprecedented numbers of patients would inundate providers. Large quantities of medications and vaccines, which are not generally available in standard pharmaceutical stocks, would be needed. Health care and lab personnel may be exposed to biological hazards pursuant to interring the remains (Franz *et al.*, 1997).

So, what can we expect if a terrorist act employing a biological agent occurs? Protective equipment and vaccines are not currently readily available to civilian populations at large. If there is no prior knowledge of an attack, human victims will likely be the first detectors of a biological attack (Franz *et al.*, 1997). Most diseases caused by biological agents will present nonspecific symptoms, easily misinterpreted as natural occurrences. Epidemiological investigations of such a disease outbreak are not likely to occur rapidly enough to avoid undesirable results. While a compressed epidemic curve with a peak in a matter of days or hours would be a good indicator (in naturally occurring epidemics disease incidence gradually increases as people are progressively exposed; those exposed to a biological attack would come into contact with the agent at approximately the same time), a large number of fatalities would already be likely by the time an attack could be verified and the pathogen identified (Franz *et al.*, 1997).

Need for mitigation and response planning

A serious programme to blunt the effects of WMD should now be given the highest priority. Attempts during the Cold War to implement a civil defense programme were ultimately ignored by many and even opposed or ridiculed by some. Hindsight yields a clear understanding of the inadequacy of the "duck and cover" approach of the 1950s. Subsequent attempts at civil defense were often viewed as providing a false sense of security which may even contribute to miscalculation in the use of nuclear weapons. It should be easier to appreciate the value of effective contemporary measures which could be taken in the face of more limited attacks. A host of measures, which are actually far more inexpensive than attempts to provide a defensive umbrella to missile attack, are available to mitigate against greater death and suffering than need occur in a chemical or biological attack. Examples include stockpiling or distribution of masks, the distribution of equipment for decontamination, implementation of training programmes, the mass inoculation of vaccinations (or at least a standby programme to do so), creation of standby programmes for emergency treatment with antibiotics, and the implementation of public education efforts to enhance co-operation in evacuation, sheltering, and health care provision. Such attempts should limit death and injury, but probably not even approach eliminating them. It is better, however, to act in the face of the limitations of defense than fail to try.

Dimensions of biological terrorism
Henry W. Fischer III

Disaster Prevention and Management
Volume 8 · Number 1 · 1999 · 27–32

Preparation also needed for behavioural and organizational response challenges

Mitigation and response planning must also consider the behavioural and organization response problems likely to be encountered in such a catastrophic event (Holloway *et al.*, 1997). How will individual citizens respond? How will organizations function? All too often there is a tendency to overlook the sociological outcomes likely to confound responders. A discussion of the likely behavioural challenges must be undertaken in order to enhance mitigation and response planning for these WMD. The disaster research literature (for example, see Fischer, 1994) should be instructive in outlining the behavioural challenges a community or nation would face, the problematic as well as effective role the media would likely play, and the political, medical and emergency organization response challenges. NBC terrorist acts would likely result in challenges, albeit on a much larger scale, as found to occur in hazmat circumstances. Hence, researchers and practitioners should be able to draw from the knowledge base of 35 years of disaster research to help guide mitigation and response planning to possible terrorist use of NBC WMD on urban populations of civilians. Anecdotal evidence suggests that we are currently far from adequately prepared for such mitigation and response. We must enhance our efforts. Recent world events serve as a reminder that we have perhaps been remiss.

References

Betts, R.K. (1998), "The new threat of mass destruction", *Foreign Affairs*, Vol. 77 No. 1, pp. 26-41.

Christopher, G.W., Cieslak, T.J., Pavlin, J.A. and Eitzen, E.M. (1997), "Biological warfare: a historical perspective", *Journal of the American Medical Association*, Vol. 278 No. 5, pp. 412-7.

Fischer, H.W., III (1994), *Response to Disaster: Fact versus Fiction and Its Perpetuation*, University Press of America, Landam.

Franz, D.R., Jahrling, P.B., Friedlander, A.M., McClain, D.J., Hoover, D.L., Bryne, W.R., Pavlin, J.A., Christopher, G.W. and Eitzen, E.M. (1997), "Clinical recognition and management of patients exposed to biological warfare agents", *Journal of the American Medical Association*, Vol. 278 No. 5, pp. 399-411.

Holloway, H.C., Norwood, A.E., Fullerton, C.S., Engel, C.C. and Ursano, R.J. (1997), "The threat of biological weapons: prophylaxis and mitigation of psychological and social consequences", *Journal of the American Medical Association*, Vol. 278 No. 5, pp. 425-7.

Simon, J.D. (1997), "Biological terrorism: preparing to meet the threat", *Journal of the American Medical Association*, Vol. 278 No. 5, pp. 428-30.

Steinbruner, J.D. (1997), "Biological weapons: a plague upon all houses", *Foreign Policy*, Winter, pp. 85-96.

Tucker, D. (1998), "Responding to terrorism", *The Washington Quarterly*, Winter, pp. 103-17.

Zilinskas, R.A. (1997), "Iraq's biological weapons: the past as future?", *Journal of the American Medical Association*, Vol. 278 No. 5, pp. 418-27.

Further reading

Anderson, W.A. (1969), *Local Civil Defense in Natural Disaster: From Office to Organization*, Disaster Research Center, The Ohio State University, Columbus, OH.

Beres, L.R. (1997), "Preventing the ultimate nightmare: nuclear terrorism against the US", *International Journal of Intelligence and Counter-Intelligence*, Vol. 10 No. 3, pp. 333-42.

Bryan, J.L. (1982), "Human behavior in the MGM Grand Hotel fire", *Fire Journal*, Vol. 76, 2 March.

Chandessais, C.A. (1966), *The Feyzin Catastrophe*, Centre d'Etudes Psychosociologiques des Sinistres et de Leur Prevention, Paris.

Demerath, N.J. (1957), "Some general propositions: an interpretive summary", *Human Organization*, Vol. 16, Summer, pp. 28-9.

Drabek, T.E. (1968), *Disaster in Aisle 13*, College of Administrative Science, The Ohio State University, Columbus, OH.

Drabek, T.E. (1969), "Social processes in disaster: family evacuation", *Social Problems*, Vol. 16, Winter, pp. 336-49.

Drabek, T.E. (1986), *Human System Responses to Disaster: An Inventory of Sociological Findings*, Springer-Verlag, New York, NY.

Drabek, T.E. and Boggs, K. (1968), "Families in disaster: reactions and relatives", *Journal of Marriage and the Family*, Vol. 30, August, pp. 443-51.

Drabek, T.E. and Quarantelli, E.L. (1967), "Scapegoats, villains, and disasters", *Transaction*, Vol. 4, March, pp. 12-7.

Dynes, R.R. (1970), *Organized Behavior in Disaster*, Heath Lexington Books, Lexington, MA.

Dynes, R.R. and Quarantelli, E.L. (1975), *The Role of Local Civil Defense in Disaster Planning*, Disaster Research Center, The Ohio State University, Columbus, OH.

Dynes, R.R., Quarantelli, E.L. and Kreps, G.A. (1972), *A Perspective on Disaster Planning*, The Disaster Research Center, The Ohio State University, Columbus, OH.

Fischer, H.W. III (1988), *Disastrous Fantasizing in the Print Media: Differences in How Natural versus Technological Disasters Are Portrayed over a Forty-year Period*, Social Research Center, Mount Union College, Alliance, OH.

Dimensions of biological terrorism

Henry W. Fischer III

Disaster Prevention and Management

Volume 8 · Number 1 · 1999 · 27–32

Fischer, H.W., III (1989), *Hurricane Gilbert: The Media's Creation of the Storm of the Century during September 1988*, The Natural Hazards Research and Applications Information Center, The University of Colorado, Boulder, CO.

Fischer, H.W., III (1996), "What emergency management officials should know to enhance mitigation and effective disaster response", *Journal of Contingencies and Crisis Management*, Vol. 4 No. 4, pp. 208-17.

Fischer, H.W. III and Bischoff, B.B. (1988), "Technological disasters: as portrayed by the National Print Media, 1945-1985", paper presented at the annual meetings of the North Central Sociological Association, Pittsburgh, PA.

Fischer, H.W., III and Drain, E.M. (1993), "Local offices of emergency preparedness (LEMA) belief in disaster mythology: what has changed and why?", *International Journal of Disaster Prevention and Management*, Vol. 2 No. 3, pp. 58-69.

Fischer, H.W., III and McCullough, K.(1993), "The role of education in disaster mitigation adjustment", *International Journal of Disaster Management*, Vol. 5 No. 3, pp. 123-9.

Fischer, H.W. III and Trowbridge, M.L. (1992), "The limited role of disaster experience in mitigation adjustment", *The International Journal of Disaster Management*, Vol. 4 No. 2, pp. 131-7.

Fischer, H.W. III, Schaeffer, S. and Trowbridge, M.L. (1992), *The Impact of Media Blame Assignation on the EOC Response to Disaster: A Case Study of the Response to the 26 April 1991 Andover (Kansas) Tornado*, The Natural Hazards Research & Applications Information Center, The University of Colorado, Boulder, CO.

Fischer, H.W. III, Stine, G.F., Trowbridge, M.L. and Drain, E.M. (1995), "Evacuation behavior: why do some evacuate, while others do not?", *International Journal of Disaster Prevention and Management*, Vol. 4 No. 4, pp. 30-6.

Foster, H.D. (1980), *Disaster Planning: The Preservation of Life and Property*, Springer-Verlag, New York, NY.

Fritz, C.E. (1957), "Disasters compared in six American communities", *Human Organization*, Vol. 16, Summer, pp. 6-9.

Fritz, C.E. (1961), "Disasters", in Merton, R.K. and Nisbet, R.A. (Eds), *Contemporary Social Problems*, Harcourt, New York, NY, pp. 651-94.

Fritz, C.E. and Mathewson, J.H. (1957), *Convergence Behaviour in Disaster*, National Research Council Disaster Study 9, National Academy of Sciences, Washington, DC.

Goltz, J.D. (1984), "Are the news media responsible for the disaster myths? A content analysis of emergency response imagery", *International Journal of Mass Emergencies and Disasters*, Vol. 2 No. 3, November, pp. 345-68.

Gray, J. (1981), "Characteristic patterns of and variations in community response to acute chemical emergencies", *Journal of Hazardous Materials*, Vol. 4, pp. 357-65.

Haas, J.E., Cochrane, H.C. and Eddy, D.G. (1976), *The Consequences of Large-scale Evacuation Following Disaster: The Darwin Australia Cyclone Disaster of 25 December 1974*, Natural Hazards Research Working Paper No. 27, The University of Colorado, Boulder, CO.

Hodler, T.W. (1982), "Residents' preparedness and response to the Kalamazoo Tornado", *Disasters*, Vol. 6 No. 1, pp. 44-9.

Hultaker, O.E. and Trost, J.E. (1978), "The family and the shelters", *Disaster Studies*, No. 1, Uppsala University, Uppsala.

Janis, I.L. and Mann, L. (1977), "Emergency decision making: a theoretical analysis of responses to disaster warnings", *Journal of Human Stress*, Vol. 3, June, pp. 35-48.

Kreps, G.A. (1978), "The organization of disaster response: some fundamental theoretical issues", in Quarantelli, E.L. (Ed.), *Disasters: Theory and Research*, Sage, Beverly Hills, CA, pp. 65-85.

Mileti, D.S. (1975), *Natural Hazard Warning Systems in the United States: A Research Assessment*, Institute of Behavioral Science, The University of Colorado, Boulder, CO.

Mileti, D.S., Drabek, T.E. and Haas, J.E. (1975), *Human Systems in Extreme Environments*, Institute of Behavioral Science, The University of Colorado, Boulder, CO.

Moore, H.E., Bates, F.L., Layman, M.V. and Parenton, V.J. (1963), *Before the Wind: A Study of Response to Hurricane Carla*, National Research Council Disaster Study 19, National Academy of Sciences, Washington, DC.

Perry, R.W. (1985), *Comprehensive Emergency Management: Evacuating Threatened Populations*, JAI Press, Greenwich, CT.

Perry, R.W. and Greene, M.R. (1983), *Citizen Response to Volcanic Eruptions: The Case of Mount St Helens*, Irvington Publishers, New York, NY.

Perry, R.W., Lindell, M.K. and Greene, M.R. (1981), *Evacuation Planning in Emergency Management*, Lexington Books, Lexington, MA.

Presidential Decision Directive 39, PDD-39 (1995), *United States Policy on Counterterrorism*, The White House, Washington, DC.

President's Commission on the Accident at Three Mile Island (1979), *Report of the President's Commission on the Accident at Three Mile Island (The Need for Change: The Legacy of TMI)*, US Government Printing Office, Washington, DC.

Quarantelli, E.L. (1976), "Human response in stress situations", in Halpin, B.M. (Ed.), *Proceedings of the First Conference and Workshop on Fire Casualties*, Applied Physics Laboratory, Johns Hopkins University, Laurel, pp. 99-112.

Quarantelli, E.L. (1980), *Evacuation Behavior and Problems: Findings and Implications from the Research Literature*, Disaster Research Center, The Ohio State University, Columbus, OH.

Dimensions of biological terrorism

Henry W. Fischer III

Disaster Prevention and Management

Volume 8 · Number 1 · 1999 · 27–32

Quarantelli, E.L. (1984), *Organizational Behaviour in Disasters and Implications for Disaster Planning*, National Emergency Training Center, Federal Emergency Management Agency, Emmitsburg, MD.

Quarantelli E.L. and Dynes, R.R. (1972), "When disaster strikes (it isn't much like what you've heard and read about)", *Psychology Today*, Vol. 5 No. 9, pp. 66-70.

Sandman, P.M. and Paden, M. (1979), "At three mile island", *Columbia Journalism Review*, July/August, p. 43.

Scanlon, T.J. (1977), "Post-disaster rumor chains: a case study", *Mass Emergencies*, Vol. 2, pp. 121-6.

Scanlon, T.J., Dixon, K. and McClellan, S. (1982), *The Miramichi Earthquakes: The Media Respond to an Invisible Emergency*, Emergency Communications Research Unit, School of Journalism, Carleton University, Ottawa.

Scanlon, T.J., Luukko, R. and Morton, G. (1978), "Media coverage of crisis: better than reported, worse than necessary", *Journalism Quarterly*, Vol. 55, Spring, pp. 68-72.

Singer, T.J. (1982), "An introduction to disaster: some considerations of a psychological nature", *Aviation, Space, and Environmental Medicine*, Vol. 53, March, pp. 245-50.

Wenger, D.E. (1980), "A few empirical observations concerning the relationship between the mass media and disaster knowledge: a research report", in *Committee on Disasters and the Mass Media, Disasters and the Mass Media: Proceedings of the Committee on Disasters and the Mass Media Workshop*, National Academy of Sciences, Washington, DC, pp. 241-53.

Wenger, D.E., Dykes, J.D., Sebok, T.D. and Neff, J.L. (1975), "It's a matter of myths: an empirical examination of individual insight into disaster response", *Mass Emergencies*, Vol. 1, pp. 33-46.

Wenger, D.E., James, T.F. and Faupel, C.F. (1980), *Disaster Beliefs and Emergency Planning*, Disaster Research Project, University of Delaware, Newark, DE.

Williams, H.B. (1956), *Communications in Community Disasters*, Dissertation, University of North Carolina, Chapel Hill, NC.

[22]

Mitigation and response planning in a bio-terrorist attack

Henry W. Fischer III

The author

Henry W. Fischer III is Professor of Sociology at the Social Research Group, Millersville University of Pennsylvania, Millersville, Pennsylvania, USA.

Keywords

Terrorism, Disaster planning, Biological weapons

Abstract

With the emergence of biological weapons of mass destruction as potential tools of terrorism, Presidential Decision Directive 39 initiated US plans to enhance mitigation and response activity. Anecdotal information suggests many of the likely behavioral and organizational response challenges are not being addressed. The current paper applies the disaster research literature to identify the likely behavioral and organizational response challenges a community or nation would encounter in a bio-terrorist attack on a metropolitan area. Mitigation and response planning, it is argued, would be enhanced if these likely challenges were actually taken into account.

Disaster Prevention and Management
Volume 9 · Number 5 · 2000 · pp. 360–367

Is a domestic incident in our near future?

An apparent outbreak of flu has impacted a major US metropolitan area. Family medical practitioners are inundated with patient phone calls for appointments; medical centers and hospital emergency rooms are suddenly besieged with those experiencing severe symptoms. Initial diagnoses are made based upon the general flu-like symptoms and apparent appropriate remedies are prescribed. Within 24-36 hours, at least half of these patients are dead. Serious testing has begun to determine the precise medical culprit. Local political leaders and the media, almost simultaneously, become aware of what the medical practitioners are encountering. It is determined that perhaps tens of thousands have developed these symptoms in this metropolitan area alone (for example, see Betts, 1998). The local health care delivery system has become completely overwhelmed.

Rumor is rapidly spreading throughout not only the city, but also the nation and the world, as television networks pick up the story. Reporters speculate that there is either a problem in the food distribution system, or there has been an accident at a laboratory that has been covered up, or we may be under attack from a foreign or domestic enemy. Political leaders at various levels indicate that an investigation has begun, the Centers for Disease Control have begun their work, and all appropriate steps are being taken to control the problem – there is no need to panic. They admit, however, all they really know at this point is what they themselves are getting from the media.

Emergency response organizations begin to take steps to determine what they should do. Political leaders, law enforcement, and others discuss what steps they should take to prevent further exposure to whatever is causing the illness. The idea to quarantine emerges. The question is asked, "who and how large an area should we quarantine?" Others suggest an evacuation of the healthy to prevent further exposure to the causal agent. It is also noted that the point of release has yet to be identified. Attempts are made to project an air of confidence to the public. In the absence of hard information on what is occurring, leaders are actually freelancing what the appropriate action should be (much like federal and state leaders and agencies found

Mitigation and response planning in a bio-terrorist attack   Disaster Prevention and Management
Henry W. Fischer III   Volume 9 · Number 5 · 2000 · 360–367

themselves doing during the Three Mile Island incident).

It is eventually determined that the city has been exposed to anthrax spores. An act of terrorism is assumed. All appropriate federal agencies have become involved. Fear is widespread throughout the nation. Is this the first of numerous cities to be attacked? Will the country fall? A media feeding frenzy has ensued. Reporters demand to know from the President what is being done to prevent further deaths, who is responsible for this despicable act, and what retaliatory steps are to be taken? Broadcast media is giving constant coverage to the crisis. Some are suggesting retaliatory military strikes on those suspected of responsibility. Estimates indicate a million people have died from the disease in the last three days.

One year later. The city's final death toll was 2.5 million. Several rogue governments and terrorist groups are suspect, but the actual perpetrator is still not known. There is increasingly the realization that no one (individuals, cities, states or the nation) was prepared to mitigate or respond to something like this. Since biological agents are invisible, odorless, and tasteless, no one knew an attack was under way until it was too late for the victims (Simon, 1997). Political careers are in ruin. The civil rights of certain ethnic groups have been abridged as a direct result of suspicion that their compatriots are guilty. A crash program is underway to stockpile protective masks and decontamination equipment. Widespread training in decontamination procedures has begun. Mass vaccinations have been initiated, as well as standby programs for mass emergency treatment with antibiotics. Planning for appropriate emergency response procedures has been initiated. Public education programs are being created to teach citizens what to do should such an attack ever occur again.

Response to terrorism?

If a biological or chemical agent were to be deployed against a US urban population, what would the behavioral response be (see Beres, 1997)? What do political-decision makers, medical personnel, and emergency organization co-ordinators need to know about likely behavioral responses to enhance mitigation and to organize an effective response (Presidential Decision Directive 39, 1995)? The sociological findings describing

the behavioral response to other disaster agents will be applied to answer these two questions. We will first review these sociological findings; we will then apply them to outline the likely behavioral response to a chemical or biological terrorist act.

Applying sociological research findings to anticipate the likely behavioral response to biological terrorism

More than 50 years of research on the behavioral and organizational response to disaster has given us a rather clear understanding of how victims and survivors, organizations, and the media respond during the various time periods of a natural or technological disaster (for example, see Drabek, 1986; Fischer, 1998; Foster, 1980; Fritz, 1957; Quarantelli, 1984; Scanlon, 1977; Wenger *et al.*, 1975). If we extrapolate from these sociological research findings, the implications of the likely behavioral response to incidents of domestic terrorism come into focus. Anecdotal information from previous terrorist acts, e.g. the World Trade Center bombing and the Oklahoma City bombing, suggests the validity of such an application (for example, see Fischer, 1998). The reader should note, however, the writer is nevertheless making the assumption that findings in natural and technological disasters parallel likely responses to biological terrorist events. Researchers have fortunately not had the opportunity to conduct exhaustive research to absolutely confirm the accuracy of this assumption. In the absence of any reason to suggest the contrary, we will assume the veracity of such an application.

Pre-impact and impact time periods

If a biological or chemical agent is released without prior warning, the first victims will provide the first indication that an attack is underway (Betts, 1998; Christopher *et al.*, 1997). Of course, without prior warning, the first victims to fall ill will not know they had been exposed to a biological or chemical agent. Disease symptoms appear several days after exposure to the agent. Victims will assume they are "coming down with something" such as the flu. Many will simply take steps to treat themselves, others will contact their family physician, and still others will go to the emergency room of a hospital or

Mitigation and response planning in a bio-terrorist attack	Disaster Prevention and Management
Henry W. Fischer III	Volume 9 · Number 5 · 2000 · 360–367

medical center. Medical personnel are likely to initially view the symptoms as indicators of a common illness as well. Medical practitioners will suddenly suspect something is amiss when they are inundated with telephone calls and emergency-room patients. The media will become aware of the rash of patients overwhelming the health care system long before the outbreak of disease is confirmed to be the result of a terrorist attack. Normal programming will be interrupted to report on the sudden outbreak of disease. Not only the impacted area, but also the world will quickly learn of the existence of a severe medical problem. (If the terrorists decide to announce that an attack is about to be or has been unleashed, then the initial confusion over whether or not the symptoms are a result of natural events, a hazmat accident, or a terrorist attack will be eliminated. Hysteria, i.e. false belief among many that they have contracted such an illness, may overload the health care system even more quickly than if the attack had not been announced. Other behavioral response patterns would be expected to commence earlier as well – these will be outlined below. On the other hand, medical practitioners and emergency organizations may be able to initiate their response more quickly, thereby effecting greater mitigation.)

Immediate post-impact period

Initial behavioral response. The media will initially focus on reporting hard news (Fischer, 1989) describing the dramatic convergence of the ill on health care providers in the impacted metropolitan area. In the absence of more details, as well as media attempts to get at the story, rumor will increasingly be reported as fact. Media personnel, concerned relatives, and the curious will converge on the area. Many of those already there will converge on the medical centers. Telephone and electronic communications will converge on the area, overwhelming the communications system. If the agent is still viable, more potential victims run the risk of being exposed. If the disease developed by those previously exposed is communicable, more potential victims will result. Political decision makers will be scrambling for answers. Confusion will be a common experience for citizens, medical practitioners, media personnel, political leaders, and emergency organizations alike.

Massive death rates can be expected. Political decision makers and emergency personnel struggle to determine the appropriate organizational response to an event they do not yet fully understand. Is it a massive hazmat accident of some kind? Is it a terrorist attack? What is the exact causal agent? Their mitigative and response efforts are tied to the answers generated by these questions. Of course, the initial answers may or may not be correct; hence, the initial mitigation and response decisions may, or may not, be effective ones.

Evacuation behavior. If an evacuation is deemed appropriate to mitigate against further exposure, how will those who are apparently healthy respond (Fischer, 1998; Quarantelli, 1980)? Families will not want to leave as individuals, they will seek to determine where each family member is located (adding to the already overloaded local communications system) and to arrange a meeting time and place. They will not want to leave until they can leave together. Unfortunately, many (perhaps most) healthy citizens will not become aware of the evacuation order at first. Some will be asleep, others will simply not be accessing media outlets when the order is given. In fact, many will not even know the emergency exists. Many will refuse to evacuate for fear that they may actually become exposed to the agent by doing so. Many will refuse to leave for fear that their property may be looted. They will need to be convinced that their property will be safe, or at least be convinced that their lives are more important than any property. For all these reasons, a large percentage of the population to be evacuated will not evacuate when told to do so. The percentage that does evacuate (perhaps one third to one half of the affected population) will be larger than when a natural disaster event is pending (which is normally only 10 per cent of the affected population), but many will remain in the metropolitan area.

Some of those who do evacuate will follow the instructions provided, i.e. use of designated roads; many, however, will not. There is, of course, the expected gridlock as traffic converges along the exit routes. Those who decide to evacuate will not leave immediately, they will tend to straggle out over a period of hours. Those who have the ability to relocate to relatives or friends will do so. Those without other options will go to

Mitigation and response planning in a bio-terrorist attack
Henry W. Fischer III

Disaster Prevention and Management
Volume 9 · Number 5 · 2000 · 360–367

a designated evacuation center. While panic will be the outcome most feared and assumed by citizens, media personnel, and officials, there will be far less of it than the stereotyped image suggests. What will be mistakenly cast as panic will be the hurried, but purposeful exit by those leaving. Indeed, if the perception among those in the process of evacuating is that their opportunity for survival is diminishing rapidly, a panic response may then ensue. But only under such a circumstance would such a response be likely to occur. Too much attention will probably be given to the fear of a panic response by decision makers. In fact, decision makers may indeed make poor response decisions due to their exaggerated fear of panic. They may hesitate to order an evacuation for fear of causing panic. They may question whether they should even try to evacuate for fear of creating panic – not only an unethical and cynical response, but one not justified by previous disaster research findings (Fischer, 1998). Failing to call for an evacuation if one is justified would likely result in greater victimization rather than mitigating further exposure. The greatest challenge will actually be how to convince the healthy population to evacuate and to do so in a timely manner. Repeated efforts will be necessary to increase the percentage of those who will do so.

Those with critically ill family members will not want to leave. They will want to stay to provide aid and comfort. The challenge of getting these people to evacuate will be even more difficult. A convergence of an increasing number of telephone calls from outside and within the area will strain the communications system as relatives seek to determine the whereabouts and safety of their loved ones. Emergency responders and health care providers will seek to determine that their families are safe. Most will stay on the job but will be distracted until they know their loved ones are safe.

Quarantine behavior. If quarantine is determined to be the appropriate mitigation decision, several challenges will present themselves. First, many of the exposed may work in the city but live in the suburbs. By the time symptoms appear, they will already be outside of the city. Second, some will have spontaneously evacuated before decision makers announce the quarantine. Third, some will successfully avoid attempts to keep them within the quarantined area. Most will

probably co-operate without incident. Most will accept their fate with resignation, but there will be those who will feel and openly express resentment at such treatment.

Many will expect deviant behavior to emerge, e.g. looting, price gouging, even though such fears are not justified. Many will also fear that victims and their loved ones will become emotionally incapacitated and unable to cope. This behavior, however, is also unlikely to occur. During the first days of the crisis citizens will be very altruistic. They will help one another. They will rise to the occasion emotionally as well. As the crisis continues over time, it will become increasingly difficult for victims, survivors, and caregivers to meet all the challenges they face. If it becomes difficult to meet basic human needs during the crisis, citizens will take whatever action they deem appropriate to address those needs. For example, those in need of food and medical supplies may decide to take what they need from available sources. This will not be an incident of looting, but rather the operation of the collective will to meet basic needs by procuring necessities from available resources. Individuals will generally not go hungry while perishable food lies rotting in the grocery store. Emergent norms will develop to guide behavior to foster survival in the new circumstance within which the healthy and critically ill find themselves.

If residents are able to obtain food through the normal distribution process, the food supplies in these stores will rapidly be depleted – primarily because there will be a mass convergence of shoppers who fear additional supplies will not be available for some time to come (especially milk, bread, and other staples). Telephone calls into, out of, and within the area will continue to exceed the capacity of the communications system. Similarly, gasoline stations are likely to experience a convergence of such customers and the health care system will continue to be overwhelmed.

Media response. An audience rivaling any preceding it will turn to the print and broadcast media for information (Fischer, 1998). The various talking heads will result in a conflicting view of what is occurring and what is to be done. It is imperative that political decision makers and emergency organizations seek to distribute information through a highly-trained spokesperson. Information, instructions, and so forth,

Mitigation and response planning in a bio-terrorist attack	Disaster Prevention and Management
Henry W. Fischer III	Volume 9 · Number 5 · 2000 · 360–367

should be given repeatedly, clearly, specifying precisely what is being suggested to the audience. There will be a tendency to distrust political decision makers as rumor is reported as fact.

Local broadcasters will tend to relay information on evacuation or quarantine plans, medical distribution centers, and other helpful news for the victims and survivors. National broadcasters will tend to focus on broader issues of what happened, who did it, how people are responding (or believed to be responding, as the network reporting will be heavily laden with myth). Local and national news organizations will look to decision makers as the primary source of information. Failure to provide a steady diet of information will result in the feeding frenzy turning on decision makers, consuming them in the process.

Print and broadcast news personnel will converge from throughout the country and the world. The EOC, the site command post and the perimeter of the affected area will be the locations most targeted by the media. Again, the role of the press demands a steady diet of information. Information and answers must be provided – the alternative will be to find them turned loose to find their own story, which will undoubtedly not be helpful to the community or to the decision makers trying to cope with the crisis. The press tends to function as pack animals seeking to avoid being scooped rather then seeking a scoop. One need only look to the experience of O.J. Simpson, Princess Diana and Monica Lewinsky for illustrations.

Altruism and acting to help the victims will gradually give rise to the inevitable blame fixing (Fischer, 1998). Voices will increasingly be asking why more had not been done to prevent the attack. Some will charge that those responsible for mitigating against further exposure to the biological agent and for responding with aid were slow to meet their responsibilities. A desire for vengeance will emerge when the focus turns to seeking to capture, prosecute or retaliate against those believed responsible for unleashing the attack. Domestic ethnic populations who share a heritage with the perceived perpetrators will be in danger of citizen (or even official) retaliation akin to that experienced by Japanese-Americans after the bombing of Pearl Harbor.

Decision makers and emergency organizations A number of challenges face political decision

makers and emergency organizations. If the attack was not suspected or announced in advance, they will not even know one has occurred until mass symptoms and deaths become apparent. Even then, they will not know if it is a local hazmat accident, terrorism, or something else. It will take time to determine the location and type of agent that victims were exposed to and how to best respond, i.e. evacuate, quarantine, or what? Medical supplies and medical personnel will not be adequate in number to meet the need (not too dissimilar to the Hiroshima and Nagasaki experiences). The community will be unable to tend to its dead in any kind of normal fashion. The crisis will place demands on all organizations, e.g. health care providers, law enforcement, political decision makers, that far exceed their ability to effectively respond. An incidence of biological terrorism will obviously not be a normal emergency. Federal support, such as military transport and dissemination of needed medical and subsistence supplies, will take longer than what the public would imagine, for reasons obvious to most planners. A large percentage of the exposed will likely be dead before it is totally understood what has occurred and long before additional personnel and supplies are brought onsite. Expectations will always be unrealistic and blame fixing will begin early in the post-impact period. Training and stockpiling of relevant supplies within metropolitan areas is, of course, very important; it is also important to educate the public to the reality of the challenges facing victims and survivors, emergency organizations, and governments. Citizens need to be armed with accurate, factual information to enhance their chance of effectively responding at the individual and family level, thereby enhancing mitigation. Without an honest dialogue with the public, potential victims will have unrealistic expectations of their (local, state, and federal) officials. Greater deaths and injury are likely to occur. Decision makers and emergency personnel need to use their expertise to act in partnership with the less knowledgeable public. We must put aside the fear of scaring the public. Such a fear insults those who should be served, increases the likelihood of harm to potential victims, and casts such officials in the role of the all-knowing, yet ineffective Big Brother.

Slow citizen response. During an emergency event, citizens respond slowly to information and instructions (Fischer, 1998; Quarantelli,

Mitigation and response planning in a bio-terrorist attack	Disaster Prevention and Management
Henry W. Fischer III	Volume 9 · Number 5 · 2000 · 360–367

1980). Instructions for obtaining medical assistance and subsistence supplies, as well as instructions for an evacuation or quarantine, are more likely to be responded to if they are frequently repeated, articulated clearly and with specificity. All too often, emergency personnel assume that because the information was disseminated, the intended recipients have received it, understood it, and responded to it in the desired fashion. Nothing could be further from the truth. Many will not receive the information the first, second or even third, time it is provided. Many of those who do receive the information will not have a clear understanding of what is being communicated and will fail to respond. Many will interact with others to determine what is to be done. Rumor and fact will blur in the process. Even when the information is clearly understood, the recipient may still not follow the instructions for any number of reasons (e.g. disbelief, distrust, refusal to leave home, at least while awaiting other family members). As with natural disaster agents, the best time to begin educating citizens on how to respond to a biological or chemical terrorist attack is during normal time. They will be in a much better position to respond effectively if they have prior training. Decision makers may hesitate to engage the public in such a dialogue prior to an actual terrorist event, for fear of upsetting the public or contributing to a panic. Anecdotal evidence consistently supports the argument that the public can be trusted far more than decision makers think it can. Such decision makers should, perhaps, be reminded that they are, after all, public servants; it is their role to provide such information to the public, so that citizens can then be armed to be better able to act on their own behalf.

Conclusions: behavioral response to a biological terrorist attack

What can we conclude about the likely behavioral and organizational response to an act of biological terrorism (for example, see Fischer, 1998)? Victims and survivors are likely to act in ways that many in the media and emergency organizations will not expect. Individual citizens are likely to be altruistic, initiate search and rescue activities, offer whatever medical assistance they can, and generally behave very rationally. They will not behave in ways many of the untrained believe is typical. For example, almost no one will panic, almost no one will steal from another (though

they may appropriate property collectively defined as necessary for response to the event), will not become emotionally incapable of responding. Many will hesitate, or even fail, to evacuate even after being told to do so. Some will resist attempts to enforce quarantine.

The media will both help and hinder. Local media will assist in disseminating needed information to the public to facilitate an effective response to the attack. National media will be less helpful in that their self-perceived role will be to describe the unfolding story that will often be largely fiction. Their reporting will be governed by their belief in the disaster mythology. They will actually increase concern for panic, looting, price gouging, and incapacitating emotional shock. Rather than covering the story in such a way as to help ameliorate misplaced concern for these behavioral myths, they will facilitate their growth. Both the local and national media will converge on the area. Curious non-residents will also converge on the area, creating traffic control problems over the life cycle of the event.

Officials will also fear panic and believe in the likelihood of the largely mythical deviant behavior. As a result, many will hesitate to announce that an attack is underway. The greater concern should be with how to accurately, clearly and convincingly inform the public what is happening, what they need to do, how to do it, and when. For example, who, when, how, and where should people evacuate? Who, when, and where should they seek medical assistance? Chaos will mostly typify the initial organizational response. The lack of good information will drive the confusion. Medical and emergency organizations will find themselves outpaced by the scope of the event.

The opportunity for effective mitigation is tied, but not limited to, the following. The public must be honestly educated about the scope of the likely medical outcome and response problems. The public must be educated about how to prepare themselves for such an event. Citizens, who elect to, should receive appropriate inoculations. Appropriate equipment and medical supplies should be stockpiled in a manner that will lead to their effective use during the pre-impact and immediate post-impact time periods. Decision makers and emergency personnel should receive training in the actual rather than mythical behavioral and organizational

Mitigation and response planning in a bio-terrorist attack	Disaster Prevention and Management
Henry W. Fischer III	Volume 9 · Number 5 · 2000 · 360–367

response problems likely to be encountered. After doing our best we can still expect to experience a large number of casualties; this likely outcome does not deter the necessity of planning and acting in a manner likely to reduce that number. Appropriate national political and economic policies remain very important ingredients in mitigation against a terrorist attack. The USA will lessen its chances of being attacked, by reducing terrorist motivation to launch a biological attack on one or several metropolitan areas simultaneously.

References

Beres, L.R. (1997), "Preventing the ultimate nightmare: nuclear terrorism against the US," *International Journal of Intelligence and Counter-Intelligence*, Vol. 10 No. 3, pp. 333-42.

Betts, R.K. (1998), "The new threat of mass destruction", *Foreign Affairs*, Vol. 77, No. 1, pp. 26-41.

Christopher, G.W. and Cieslak, T.J., Pavlin, J.A. and Eitzen, E.M. (1997), "Biological warfare: a historical perspective", *Journal of the American Medical Association*, Vol. 278 No. 5, pp. 412-17.

Drabek, T.E. (1986), *Human System Responses to Disaster: An Inventory of Sociological Findings*, Springer-Verlag, New York, NY.

Fischer, H.W., III (1989), *Hurricane Gilbert: The Media's Creation of the Storm of the Century During September 1988*, The Natural Hazards Research and Applications Information Center, The University of Colorado, Boulder, CO.

Fischer, H.W., III (1998), *Response to Disaster: Fact Versus Fiction & Its Perpetuation*, 2nd ed., University Press of America, Landam, MD.

Foster, H.D. (1980), "Disaster planning: the preservation of life and property", Springer-Verlag, New York, NY.

Fritz, C.E. (1957), "Disasters compared in six American communities", *Human Organization*, Vol. 16, Summer, pp. 6-9.

Presidential Decision Directive 39, PDD-39 (1995), *United States Policy on Counterterrorism*, The White House, Washington, DC.

Quarantelli, E.L. (1980), *Evacuation Behavior and Problems: Findings and Implications from the Research Literature*, Disaster Research Center, The Ohio State University, Columbus, OH.

Quarantelli, E.L. (1984), *Organizational Behaviour in Disasters and Implications for Disaster Planning*, National Emergency Training Center, Federal Emergency Management Agency, Emmitsburg.

Scanlon, T.J. (1977), "Post-disaster rumor chains: a case study", *Mass Emergencies*, Vol. 2, pp. 121-6.

Simon, J.D. (1997), "Biological terrorism: preparing to meet the threat", *Journal of the American Medical Association*, Vol. 278 No. 5, pp. 428-30.

Wenger, D.E., Dykes, J.D., Sebok, T.D. and Neff, J.L. (1975), "It's a matter of myths: an empirical examination of individual insight into disaster response", *Mass Emergencies*, Vol. 1, pp. 33-46.

Further reading

Anderson, W.A. (1969), *Local Civil Defense in Natural Disaster: From Office to Organization*, Disaster Research Center, The Ohio State University, Columbus, OH.

Bryan, J.L. (1982), "Human behavior in the MGM Grand Hotel fire", *Fire Journal*, Vol. 76, March 2.

Chandessais, C.A. (1966), *The Feyzin Catastrophe*, Centre d'Etudes Psychosociologiques des Sinistres et le Leur Prevention, Paris.

Demerath, N.J. (1957), "Some general propositions: an interpretive summary", *Human Organization*, Vol. 16, Summer, pp. 28-9.

Drabek, T.E. (1968), *Disaster in Aisle 13*, College of Administrative Science, The Ohio State University, Columbus, OH.

Drabek, T.E. (1969), "Social processes in disaster: family evacuation", *Social Problems*, Vol. 16, Winter, pp. 336-49.

Drabek, T.E. and Boggs, K. (1968), "Families in disaster: reactions and relatives", *Journal of Marriage and the Family*, Vol. 30, August, pp. 443-51.

Drabek, T.E. and Quarantelli, E.L. (1967), "Scapegoats, villains, and disasters", *Transaction*, Vol. 4, March, pp. 12-17.

Dynes, R.R. (1970), *Organized Behavior in Disaster*, Heath Lexington Books, Lexington, MA.

Dynes, R.R. and Quarantelli, E.L. (1975), *The Role of Local Civil Defense in Disaster Planning*, Disaster Research Center, The Ohio State University, Columbus, OH.

Dynes, R.R., Quarantelli, E.L. and Kreps, G.A. (1972), *A Perspective on Disaster Planning*, The Disaster Research Center, The Ohio State University, Columbus, OH.

Fischer, H.W., III (1988), *Disastrous Fantasizing in the Print Media: Differences in How Natural versus Technological Disasters Are Portrayed over a Forty-year Period*, Social Research Center, Mount Union College, Alliance.

Fischer, H.W., III (1996), "What emergency management officials should know to enhance mitigation and effective disaster response", *Journal of Contingencies and Crisis Management*, Vol. 4 No. 4, pp. 208-17.

Fischer, H.W., III and Bischoff, B.B. (1988), "Technological disasters: as portrayed by the National Print Media, 1945-1985", paper presented at the annual meetings of the North Central Sociological Association, Pittsburgh, PA.

Fischer, H.W., III and Drain, E.M. (1993), "Local offices of emergency preparedness (LEMA) belief in disaster mythology: what has changed and why?", *International Journal of Disaster Prevention and Management*, Vol. 2 No. 3, pp. 58-69.

Fischer, H.W., III and McCullough, K. (1993), "The role of education in disaster mitigation adjustment", *International Journal of Disaster Management*, Vol. 5 No. 3, pp. 123-9.

Fischer, H.W., III, Stine, G.F., Trowbridge, M.L. and Drain, E.M. (1995), "Evacuation behavior: why do some evacuate, while others do not?", *International Journal of Disaster Prevention and Management*, Vol. 4 No. 4, pp. 30-6.

Mitigation and response planning in a bio-terrorist attack

Henry W. Fischer III

Disaster Prevention and Management

Volume 9 · Number 5 · 2000 · 360–367

Fischer, H.W., III and Trowbridge, M.L. (1992), "The limited role of disaster experience in mitigation adjustment", *The International Journal of Disaster Management*, Vol. 4 No. 2, pp. 131-7.

Fischer, H.W., III, Schaeffer, S. and Trowbridge, M.L. (1992), *The Impact of Media Blame Assignation on the EOC Response to Disaster: A Case Study of the Response to the 26 April 1991 Andover (Kansas) Tornado*, The Natural Hazards Research & Applications Information Center, The University of Colorado, Boulder, CO.

Franz, D.R., Jahrling, P.B., Friedlander, A.M., McClain, D.J., Hoover, D.L., Bryne, W.R., Pavlin, J.A., Christopher, G.W. and Eitzen, E.M. (1997), "Clinical recognition and management of patients exposed to biological warfare agents", *Journal of the American Medical Association*, Vol. 278 No. 5, pp. 399-411.

Fritz, C.E. (1961), "Disasters", in Merton, R.K. and Nisbet, R.A. (Eds), *Contemporary Social Problems*, Harcourt, New York, pp. 651-94.

Fritz, C.E. and Mathewson, J.H. (1957), *Convergence Behaviour in Disaster*, National Research Council Disaster Study 9, National Academy of Sciences, Washington, DC.

Goltz, J.D. (1984), "Are the news media responsible for the disaster myths? A content analysis of emergency response imagery", *International Journal of Mass Emergencies and Disasters*, Vol. 2 No. 3, November, pp. 345-68.

Gray, J. (1981), "Characteristic patterns of and variations in community response to acute chemical emergencies", *Journal of Hazardous Materials*, Vol. 4, pp. 357-65.

Haas, J.E., Cochrane, H.C. and Eddy, D.G. (1976), *The Consequences of Large-Scale Evacuation Following Disaster: The Darwin Australia Cyclone Disaster of 25 December 1974*, Natural Hazards Research Working Paper No. 27, The University of Colorado, Boulder, CO.

Hodler, T.W. (1982), "Residents' preparedness and response to the Kalamazoo tornado", *Disasters*, Vol. 6 No. 1, pp. 44-9.

Holloway, H.C., Norwood, A.E., Fullerton, C.S., Engel, C.C. and Ursano, R.J. (1997), "The threat of biological weapons: prophylaxis and mitigation of psychological and social consequences", *Journal of the American Medical Association*, Vol. 278 No. 5, pp. 425-7.

Hultaker, O.E. and Trost, J.E. (1978), "The family and the shelters", *Disaster Studies*, No. 1, Uppsala University, Uppsala.

Janis, I.L. and Mann, L. (1977), "Emergency decision making: a theoretical analysis of responses to disaster warnings", *Journal of Human Stress*, Vol. 3, June, pp. 35-48.

Kreps, G.A. (1978), "The organization of disaster response: some fundamental theoretical issues", in Quarantelli, E.L (Ed.), *Disasters: Theory and Research*, Sage, Beverly Hills, CA, pp. 65-85.

Mileti, D.S. (1975), *Natural Hazard Warning Systems in the United States: A Research Assessment*, Institute of Behavioral Science, The University of Colorado, Boulder, CO.

Mileti, D.S., Drabek, T.E. and Haas, J.E. (1975), *Human Systems in Extreme Environments*, Institute of

Behavioral Science, The University of Colorado, Boulder.

Moore, H.E., Bates, F.L., Layman, M.V. and Parenton, V.J. (1963), *Before the Wind: A Study of Response to Hurricane Carla*, National Research Council Disaster Study 19, National Academy of Sciences, Washington, DC.

Perry, R.W. (1985), *Comprehensive Emergency Management: Evacuating Threatened Populations*, JAI Press, Greenwich, CT.

Perry, R.W. and Greene, M.R. (1983), *Citizen Response to Volcanic Eruptions: The Case of Mount St Helens*, Irvington Publishers, New York, NY.

Perry, R.W., Lindell, M.K. and Greene, M.R. (1981), *Evacuation Planning in Emergency Management*, Lexington Books, Lexington, MA.

President's Commission on the Accident at Three Mile Island (1979), *Report of the President's Commission on the Accident at Three Mile Island (The Need For Change: The Legacy of TMI)*, US Government Printing Office, Washington, DC.

Quarantelli, E.L. (1976), "Human response in stress situations", in Halpin, B.M. (Ed.), *Proceedings of the First Conference and Workshop on Fire Casualties*, Applied Physics Laboratory, Johns Hopkins University, Laurel, MD, pp. 99-112.

Quarantelli E.L. and Dynes, R.R. (1972), "When disaster strikes (it isn't much like what you're heard and read about)", *Psychology Today*, Vol. 5 No. 9, pp. 66-70.

Sandman, P.M. and Paden, M. (1979), "At Three Mile Island", *Columbia Journalism Review*, July/August, p. 43.

Scanlon, T.J., Dixon, K. and McClellan, S. (1982), *The Miramichi Earthquakes: The Media Respond to an Invisible Emergency*, Emergency Communications Research Unit, School of Journalism, Carleton University, Ottawa, Ontario.

Scanlon, T.J., Luukko, R. and Morton, G. (1978), "Media coverage of crisis: better than reported, worse than necessary", *Journalism Quarterly*, Vol. 55, Spring, pp. 68-72.

Singer, T.J. (1982), "An introduction to disaster: some considerations of a psychological nature", *Aviation, Space, and Environmental Medicine*, Vol. 53, March, pp. 245-50.

Steinbruner, J.D. (1997), "Biological weapons: a plague upon all houses", *Foreign Policy*, Winter, pp. 85-96.

Tucker, D. (1998), "Responding to terrorism", *The Washington Quarterly*, Winter, pp. 103-17.

Wenger, D.E. (1980), "A few empirical observations concerning the relationship between the mass media and disaster knowledge: a research report", in Committee on Disasters and the Mass Media, *Disasters and the Mass Media: Proceedings of the Committee on Disasters and the Mass Media Workshop*, National Academy of Sciences, Washington, DC, pp. 241-253.

Wenger, D.E., James, T.F. and Faupel, C.F. (1980), *Disaster Beliefs and Emergency Planning*, Disaster Research Project, University of Delaware, Newark, NJ.

Williams, H.B. (1956), "Communications in community disasters", dissertation, University of North Carolina, Chapel Hill, NC.

Zilinskas, R.A. (1997), "Iraq's biological weapons: the past as future?", *Journal of the American Medical Association*, Vol. 278 No. 5, pp. 418-27.

[23]

WMD Terrorism: An Exchange

Karl-Heinz Kamp

How serious is the potential threat from terrorists wielding weapons of mass destruction (WMD)? In his article – 'Confronting Nuclear, Biological and Chemical Terrorism' (*Survival*, Autumn 1998, pp. 43–65) – Richard A. Falkenrath argued that a nuclear, biological or chemical (NBC) terrorist attack, although of 'low probability', could have 'devastating effects on the targeted society'. Falkenrath ranked the threat as 'among the most serious national-security challenges faced by modern liberal democracies'. Just after the article's publication, on 20 August 1998, the US launched a cruise-missile attack against a pharmaceutical plant in Sudan. The facility was said to be producing precursors for chemical weapons, and was allegedly linked to Osama bin Laden, who is accused of masterminding the bombings of US Embassies in Kenya and Tanzania, which also took place in August.

There is intense controversy about the US claims, and about its actions. There is also growing concern about the WMD terrorist threat. Against this background, *Survival* has invited three eminent experts in the field to comment on Falkenrath's article. His reply follows their responses.

Nuclear Terrorism Is Not the Core Problem
Karl-Heinz Kamp

Richard A. Falkenrath, one of the most thoughtful analysts in the field of non-proliferation, rightly calls attention to the menacing link between terrorism and WMD. Indeed, Western policy-makers come close to negligence in their passive response to the emerging threat posed by non-state actors with increasing access to weapons and devices that can inflict large numbers of casualties among civilian populations.

Nevertheless, I find myself in strong disagreement with Falkenrath's suggestion that nuclear terrorism should be included in his triad of existential and realistic threats to our societies. Admittedly, the scenario of terrorist groups forcing Western governments to their knees by depositing nuclear devices in New York or Berlin has not only provided the plot for Hollywood thrillers, but also raised concerns on the political level. In 1983, President Ronald Reagan brought up the issue as one of the justifications for his Strategic Defense Initiative (SDI). A decade later, President Bill Clinton pointed to the problem as one of the reasons for his concept of 'Counter-proliferation', a programme to tackle the dangers posed by the

Karl-Heinz Kamp is head of the Foreign and Security Policy Research Section, Konrad-Adenauer-Foundation, St Augustin, Germany.

spread of WMD. The combination of terrorism and nuclear weapons has a further dimension – the idea of combatting terrorist organisations with nuclear strikes. In August 1998, press reports cited a US Joint Chiefs of Staff document of February 1996 in which non-state actors were explicitly described as potential targets for American nuclear weapons.[1] Notwithstanding the fact that documents from the Joint Chiefs do not mirror official US nuclear policy since they are neither approved by the Office of the Secretary of Defense (OSD) nor by the President, the scenario of a counter-terrorism policy with nuclear weapons caused some public concern.

These anxieties aside, religious zealots or political extremists may present many dangers, but wielding nuclear bombs and killing hundreds of thousands of innocent people is not one of them. Not to be misunderstood: we are not talking about nuclear crime like the release of radioactive substances, or about acts of sabotage in nuclear-power plants. Dispersing radioactive waste by conventional explosives – as Falkenrath describes in a footnote (note 2, p. 62) – is almost always possible, but this is not nuclear terrorism in the strict and existential sense. Such an act would doubtless cause panic, but it would not kill thousands of people. The more dramatic scenario of a criminal organisation creating fear or terror through a credible threat or actual execution of a nuclear explosion is far-fetched.

This optimism is certainly not the result of a simple extrapolation from past trends. The fact that there has not been a single act of nuclear terrorism, despite the tens of thousands of nuclear weapons produced, transported, deployed and dismantled all over the world, may still not permit a hopeful prediction. Of course, nuclear blackmail by a non-state actor could happen tomorrow, but the simple fact that, up to now, terrorist groups apparently have not even seriously *attempted* to seize possession of nuclear weapons should tell us something. Over seven years after the break-up of the Soviet Union, Brian Jenkins' observation still holds true: 'Terrorists want a lot of people watching but not a lot of people dead'.[2]

What about Falkenrath's argument that the traditional model of a terrorist group – limited aims, a strategy of controlled violence and an interest in self-preservation – appears to be breaking down? Is it not true that, for instance, fanatical Muslim killers ready for suicide operations increasingly seem to regard it as a bonus if as many 'enemy' civilians as possible are killed? I fully agree with this argument, but those groups interested in mass-murder will almost certainly not use nuclear weapons. Falkenrath himself enumerated some of the reasons why.

- Notwithstanding the fact that any gifted student might be able to master the theoretical design of a crude nuclear weapon, actually building one is

---

[1] See, for example, 'USA Erwägen auch einen Nukleareinsatz', *Süddeutsche Zeitung*, 24 August 1998.
[2] Brian M. Jenkins, 'Will Terrorists Go Nuclear?', *Orbis*, vol. 29, no. 3, Autumn 1985, pp. 507–15.

extremely difficult. A number of countries with vast resources and expertise, such as Iraq, have struggled unsuccessfully to produce one. It is difficult
to imagine that a small terrorist group would find bomb-building any
easier.

- State-sponsored terrorism – that is, the support of non-state actors by 'rogue
  regimes' – is widespread in the non-nuclear field. However, the idea that
  any state, whether a 'rogue nation' or not, would hand over control of
  nuclear weapons to an organisation of criminals or religious zealots is hard
  to believe. The risk of these groups turning against their patrons would be
  far too great.
- Even the major problem of 'loose nukes' and vagabonding nuclear material
  in the former Soviet Union only slightly increases the likelihood of nuclear
  terrorism. Fortunately, and not least as a result of Western and in particular
  American support, up to now the Russian nuclear-weapons complex has
  proved to be more stable than initially feared. Even if a complete nuclear
  weapon were to fall into the hands of a nuclear terrorist group, technical
  built-in safeguards and self-destruct mechanisms would make the weapon's
  detonation very difficult. In addition, given their size and the transportation
  difficulties involved, most nuclear weapons are simply unsuitable for
  clandestine terrorist action. Hence, while uncontrolled proliferation of
  nuclear weapons and fissile material is indeed a serious danger, this holds
  true primarily with regard to nuclear threshold states, not non-state actors.
- Assuming that a terrorist group seriously tried to obtain or build a nuclear
  device, what could be their intention? If it were nuclear blackmail, the goal
  would have to be truly staggering, because less important aims, such as
  forcing the authorities to release jailed comrades, can be achieved without
  recourse to anything even approaching a nuclear threat. Any truly
  monumental demand – the withdrawal of a country from an occupied
  region for instance, can hardly be maintained over a long period. Once the
  terrorists are located and eliminated, all concessions made by blackmailed
  countries could always be revoked.

As a result, while nuclear terrorism cannot be entirely ruled out, it seems very
unlikely. If a terrorist organisation wanted to inflict mass casualties, it could
easily use biological or chemical weapons which, as Falkenrath lucidly describes,
are quite simple to acquire or produce. What is more, given the vulnerability of
modern industrial societies, terrorists could commit indiscriminate mass-murder
without recourse to *weapons* of mass destruction at all. They could, for example,
contaminate a large city's supply of drinking water.

Yet even if the risk of nuclear terrorism is exaggerated compared to that of
biological and chemical terrorism, why should it not be brought to people's
attention, thereby sharpening the public's sensitivity to the dangers of WMD?
Maybe overstating the risk is the only way to raise awareness in an era in which
any untoward development becomes a crisis, and the slightest departure from
the ordinary is immediately labelled 'historic'. However, with regard to nuclear
terrorism, such tactics will be counter-productive. Including nuclear weapons

in the emerging challenge of international terrorism is not only analytically inaccurate, it also devalues Falkenrath's first recommendation of how to respond to the threat: do not over-react. This is good advice, but will be difficult to sell to politicians if, at the same time, the scenario of nuclear terrorists causing 100,000 casualties is depicted as a realistic contingency. Merging the various threats posed by different types of WMD will almost certainly create the impression of 'problem overkill', thereby diverting politicians' attention from the true challenges – chemical and biological terrorism.

Apocalypse Now – or Never?
Joseph F. Pilat

Concern about NBC terrorism is rising. Although the policy community has been interested in NBC terrorism in the past (particularly nuclear terrorism), its interest soon faded as fears went unrealised and other issues came to the fore. Will this latest wave follow the same course?

Current attention was stimulated primarily by the March 1995 sarin nerve-gas attack on the Tokyo subway by the *Aum Shinrikyo* sect and, for the US, by the Oklahoma City bombing a month later (which did not involve NBC weapons, but raised the awareness of US vulnerabilities to terrorism). Recent reports about the interest of US white supremacists, terrorist supporter Osama bin Laden and others in NBC capabilities are likely to reinforce this attention. In this atmosphere, the emerging debate appears distinct from those of the past in terms of both the level of political attention the issue has received, and the creation of response programmes. The terms of the debate are not yet fully established. Yet there is a growing convergence of thinking on threat and response. The danger that the threat will be dismissed has faded, and some of the threat's worst exaggerations are no longer seen as credible.

Falkenrath's article reflects to some degree the convergence of views about threat and response, but also reveals the limitations of current thinking. While it should further the debate, his analysis also reflects several flawed assumptions and raises the prospect that the threat will be misunderstood. One is that the threat is defined by the technological possibilities open to terrorists and the theoretical vulnerabilities of Western societies. Second, it is assumed that an NBC terrorist attack will be so devastating that governments and societies could not withstand its effects. Finally, it is thought that, with sufficient resources, the problem can be resolved and that 'technical fixes' are possible. All of these assumptions are held to some degree by Falkenrath – and many other commentators. All are misleading, and need to be reexamined.

First, the assumption that threat assessments should be based on technological possibilities and abstract vulnerabilities implies cataclysmic scenarios, but has little value for understanding real threats. The world has yet to experience mass-destruction terrorism. Falkenrath recognises this point, but he also holds that mass destruction as a result of NBC terrorism is more likely now than ever before. The assessment that the propensity towards NBC

Joseph F. Pilat is a Research Associate at the IISS, London.

172 **Joseph F. Pilat**

terrorism is rising but is by no means inevitable is correct.[1] But it is not clear whether Falkenrath himself is fully convinced when he writes that the threat is 'often underestimated' and that 'the probability of such an attack is higher than commonly assumed – and growing'. Falkenrath's argument that this is a 'first-order national-security challenge' is in fact undermined by much of his analysis, which raises legitimate questions about that characterisation.

Falkenrath's arguments are muted; at times he seems to recognise the difficulties of terrorists achieving mass destruction. Nonetheless, he frequently exaggerates the technological ease of acquiring and using NBC weapons. For example, he states that 'deadly chemical-warfare agents can be manufactured in a kitchen or basement in quantities sufficient for mass-casualty attacks'. This is theoretically possible, but should be tempered by the *Aum Shinrikyo* experience, where a well-funded, technologically capable group was unable to produce high-purity sarin and was not, in Falkenrath's words, 'proficient in its delivery'.

Assessing vulnerabilities is another problem. Terrorists have long been aware of the weaknesses of technologically dependent Western industrial states and societies. However, most terrorists have not yet demonstrated that they can fully exploit these vulnerabilities, nor that they desire and are able to wield NBC instruments effectively. Vulnerabilities to NBC terrorism must be understood in this light and addressed on the basis of sober assessments and a prioritisation of risks. After the Tokyo attack, however, weaknesses are seen everywhere. Of course, a wide spectrum of vulnerabilities exists in the West and in the world, including not only NBC terrorist threats but also environmental degradation, disruption of critical infrastructures and the prospect of an asteroid striking the earth. But not all of these vulnerabilities can be addressed effectively – or, in some cases, at all.

Civilian vulnerabilities, particularly in the West, are at the forefront of political concern about NBC terrorism. Basing a response on all possible vulnerabilities, however implausible, is likely to be counter-productive as it would fuel public concerns without addressing them adequately. What could have been done to prevent *Aum Shinrikyo*'s attack? Clearly, without undermining the principles of democratic societies, there were significant limits on actions. But adequate intelligence, surveillance and possibly intervention by the Japanese authorities were possible and might have been effective.

Falkenrath attempts to bring patterns of terrorism into his analysis, but he does little to illuminate motivations. His judgements seem to exaggerate differences between past and present terrorist behaviour. Terrorists have been technically able to undertake some level of NBC terrorism for 30 years, but they have largely not chosen even to attempt mass destruction. Changing patterns of terrorism, including greater lethality and lesser constraints on behaviour are real and make NBC terrorism more likely, but neither probable nor inevitable. Falkenrath admits as much while exaggerating the likely impact of these

---

[1] Joseph F. Pilat, 'Prospects for NBC Terrorism After Tokyo', in Brad Roberts (ed.), *Terrorism with Chemical and Biological Weapons: Calibrating Risks and Responses* (Alexandria, VA: Chemical and Biological Arms Control Institute, 1997), pp. 4–15.

trends, along with those of technology diffusion – especially communications and transportation technologies – on NBC terrorism. Some of these trends have yet to be fully felt; others have been evident for over a decade, as in the case of growing terrorist lethality, and have not created unbounded NBC terrorism.

The increasing deadliness of terrorist acts is worrisome, but it is a great leap from death tolls in the low hundreds to mass casualties in the hundreds of thousands. As Falkenrath recognises, acts causing hundreds of casualties have occurred rarely (see Figure 1, p. 52). Have terrorists sought to kill more than people than actually died as a result of these acts? We do not always know what terrorists intend to achieve by their actions, but the bombing of New York's World Trade Center in 1993 was clearly meant to create mass destruction by bringing down one tower onto another, and there were reports – now largely discredited – of an attempt to generate cyanide gas in the explosion that would have poisoned even more people. Other than this act and the Tokyo gassing, there appear to be few clear and credible instances of terrorists attempting to create a massive number of casualties.

The caricature of religious terrorists as unconstrained mass killers, which Falkenrath also seems to hold, is not demonstrated. Even though terrorists with religious motivations are probably the most likely to engage in acts of mass destruction, an analysis of motivations that sought to demonstrate why these terrorists might turn to NBC means would have been useful.

The second questionable assumption is based upon the notion that NBC terrorism is a low-probability, high-consequence event. Falkenrath appears to have more confidence in the latter part of the equation. The worst cases imaginable can be construed in these terms, and this perspective has value in bounding the problem. However, our experience to date indicates the value of a different perspective on the threat.

The phenomena that will need to be addressed by governments are more likely to have a higher probability and a far lower impact. The most likely actions will be nuisance threats and hoaxes, or abortive or inconsequential incidents. There may be some attacks that produce casualties, like the Tokyo gassing, but these are more likely to fall into the range of casualties produced by conventional terrorism. But Falkenrath has a different view. His discussion of consequences suggests numbers of deaths well in excess of those previously suffered. He believes the effects of even one act would be 'devastating', creating panic, economic disruption, strategic effects, social and psychological damage and political change. These speculations are not convincingly argued.

The belief that NBC terrorist acts will have an impact disproportionate to their real physical damage because of public hysteria about WMD is not groundless, but it is exaggerated. Falkenrath himself recognises that NBC attacks are unlikely to be 'apocalyptic', but he does not follow his own logic to its conclusion. The belief that widespread panic or perhaps the collapse of public order would result from such attacks is speculative and ill-founded. The societal responses to accidents or natural disasters that produce massive destruction or disruption have been on the whole measured and reasonable: public order in Japan did not collapse in the wake of the Kobe earthquake in

174 **Joseph F. Pilat**

1995 or of the subway gassing in Tokyo. The strength and resilience of liberal-democratic societies in the face of such threats tend to be underestimated.

Falkenrath seems to believe that a strategy of terror would be successful against a powerful nation – if not by destroying it, by coercing it to change its strategies or its perceptions of its vital interests. But this view is highly questionable. In early 1998, UK and US authorities were reportedly preparing for a possible retaliatory chemical or biological terrorist attack by Iraq if they used military force in the crisis over UN weapons inspections. The fact that force was not ultimately used was not, however, due to this threat. This prospect did not deter either state from proposing air strikes; in fact, the WMD threat was seemingly used to strengthen public support for the British and American stand against Iraqi leader Saddam Hussein.

Turning to the third assumption, although Falkenrath does not stress technical solutions, his article oversells their potential effectiveness. It is important to develop reasonable response efforts. This should not be under-estimated. However, relying on unrealistic threat assessments based on abstract technological possibilities jeopardises appropriate and sustainable responses. As a result, responses may not target the real problem, or they may not do so effectively because, for example, they focused authorities' attention on the wrong groups, targets and the like. Exaggerating the threat may also increase dangers and inadvertently reveal to terrorists knowledge of how to proceed technologically (via NBC 'cookbooks' available on the internet, for example); uncover social vulnerabilities; make NBC actions seem inevitable; and create or widen the gulf between a declared threat and actual response capabilities.

Prudence dictates that governments should take reasonable steps to reduce the prospects for, and effects of, these acts. Falkenrath puts forward several widely discussed and appropriate guidelines, including warning against overreaction and highlighting the importance of intelligence and of protecting nuclear weapons and materials at source.[2] He makes an important point when arguing for a strategy to guide various response efforts and programmes, but he fails to follow it through. In thinking about what is to be done, it will probably be necessary to work to prevent, neutralise or mitigate the most likely kinds of attacks – probably lower-impact actions – rather than to attempt to prevent or defend against all possible terrorist scenarios. Even the best intelligence cannot guarantee 'actionable' information on all attempted attacks. In the current political and budgetary climate, it will not be possible to sustain a programme based wholly on unlikely worst-case scenarios.

Whatever the likelihood of NBC terrorism, it is a real possibility. After the Tokyo subway attack, improved responses are essential. In the event of a major act, governments will be judged on the basis of their preparations. Falkenrath recognises this but seems to contradict himself. He begins his analysis by

---

[2] Pilat, 'Prospects for NBC Terrorism After Tokyo', pp. 16–19.

noting increased attention to the issue and a host of new initiatives, but at the end of the piece he says that 'the excuses given for not having done more beforehand will ring hollow'. Assuming he is not merely confused, Falkenrath desires a more active policy response. If so, he should provide the outlines of a concrete action programme that aims to reduce the threat and minimise its consequences. The problem of the 'day after' – significant because the worst cases possible, however improbable, cannot be ruled out – is more likely to be aggravated by oversold responses that could not do what they advertised. A related and equally worrisome problem is the growing gap between threat rhetoric and available responses. If a massively destructive act does occur, this gap might create the impression of irresponsibility on the part of the authorities and might undermine governments and societies.

As this discussion demonstrates, many of the assumptions in Falkenrath's article and the emerging debate over NBC terrorism need to be questioned. The debate is being driven by a fear of events far worse than any yet experienced. It is quite possible that current speculations will focus policy-makers' and pundits' attention on the wrong issues, thereby worsening any dangers and reducing the prospects of a reasonable response. However, that does not mean that NBC threats can be dismissed. On the contrary, significant NBC terrorism is possible – but not probable, given the interests and objectives of most terrorist groups, the capabilities it would require and the difficulties and dangers it would present to the terrorists. If mass-destruction terrorism were to occur, it would more likely be chemical or biological than nuclear, with chemical terrorism perhaps the most likely prospect of all.

Any assessment is necessarily speculative, however, and it is sensible neither to dramatise the possibility nor to veil the threat. The difficulties of assessing and responding to emerging NBC terrorist threats should be clear. Despite real uncertainties about these threats – some of which are intrinsic to projections on terrorism in general, and some specific to these new, largely uncharacterised, phenomena – there is a widespread sense of their imminent and overwhelming danger that could have terrible, perhaps apocalyptic, consequences. Will societies crumble under such attacks? Could NBC attacks be orchestrated or exploited by terrorists or others? These possibilities cannot be ruled out. As noted above, though, Western societies are stronger and more resilient than their enemies imagine and their experiences during the twentieth century have created a revulsion against tyrannies. If adequate responses are to be developed, analysts will have to understand better both the phenomenon's parameters, and the groups and activities identified with mass-destruction and disruptive terrorism. Terrorists' motivations and likely choices among nuclear, biological and chemical weaponry are little understood, but understanding these elements of the threat is essential if we are to deal effectively with this problem. It will also be important to prioritise the most likely targets and tactics that may be used to help to build effective counter-terrorism strategies. Falkenrath's article, with its strengths and weaknesses, will no doubt contribute to this end.

176 Jessica Stern

Apocalypse Never, but the Threat Is Real

Jessica Stern

Until the *Aum Shinrikyo* attack in 1995, only a handful of scholars and policy-makers were thinking about NBC terrorism. Since the attack, the field has attracted attention from a wide range of analysts and journalists, especially in the US. Unfortunately, a great deal of reporting on the subject has been careless and exaggerated, creating a mood of political paranoia.

There are several reasons why attention to the threat of NBC terrorism has increased. First, law-enforcement officials are observing (and reporting) growing interest in NBC weapons from non-state actors. The US Federal Bureau of Investigation (FBI) opened more than 86 inquiries into the threatened or actual use of NBC materials in the US in the first nine months of 1998, a significant increase over previous years.[1] The US government has reported that Osama bin Laden, the wealthy backer of violent Islamic extremist groups, has been seeking nuclear and chemical weapons.[2] Second, and almost as worrying, politicians and journalists seem afflicted with NBC hysteria. This is dangerous: it is leading to overly dramatic and exaggerated reporting, which in turn generates more nervousness and, even worse, bad policy.

Richard Falkenrath's article is a welcome change from much of the recent reporting. It is refreshingly thoughtful, thorough and cautious in its conclusions. The article has four particular strengths. Falkenrath emphasises the possible social-psychological effects of an NBC attack, an issue that has been largely ignored in the literature on the subject. Second, he makes clear that NBC weapons are not necessarily mass-casualty ones. Moreover, terrorists would not need to acquire unconventional weapons if mass-murder were their aim, since strategically placed conventional weapons could achieve this goal. Third, Falkenrath describes three necessary conditions for terrorist groups to use NBC weapons successfully, and correctly observes that they are unlikely to be present. Finally, Falkenrath reassures anxious readers that mass-casualty attacks with WMD are unlikely. But if national leaders rank the dangers most likely to kill thousands of their citizens, NBC terrorism comes high on the list. As Falkenrath observes, the most likely form that an NBC attack would take would be the dissemination of chemical, biological or radiological agents in an enclosed space. Such attacks would not be apocalyptic, but they could still kill hundreds, even thousands, of people. Thus, governments need to be prepared to reduce the likelihood of NBC terrorism and to mitigate its consequences if it happens. But they must not make hasty decisions that they will later regret.

---

[1] Susan Ellis, 'Clarke Says US Will Revamp Anti-Terrorism Measures', *Washington File*, US Information Agency, 8 October 1998.
[2] Michael Grunwald, 'Bin Laden Effort to Obtain N-Weapons, Documents Reveal', *Buffalo News*, 26 September 1998, p. 2A.

Jessica Stern is a Fellow at the Council on Foreign Relations, Washington DC. She is the author of *The Ultimate Terrorists* (Cambridge, MA: Harvard University Press, forthcoming).

Falkenrath reminds readers of the lethal potential of conventional weapons, and the danger of focusing excessively on unconventional ones in setting counter-terrorism policies. Another danger that has largely been ignored is the prospect of terrorists using common industrial and agricultural chemicals, some of which are highly toxic. The leak of methyl isocyanate from Union Carbide's pesticide plant at Bhopal in India in December 1984 illustrates their deadly potential. Union Carbide concluded that a disgruntled employee caused the explosion that led to the leak by adding water to the contents of a storage tank.[3] Four months after the leak, the Indian government reported that 1,430 people had died. In 1991, New Delhi reported that the death-toll had risen to over 3,800 and some 11,000 disabled.[4] Whether or not the leak was caused deliberately, the incident shows that industrial chemicals can be extremely dangerous: more people were killed at Bhopal than in any single terrorist attack to date. It would make sense for governments and private industry to think carefully about how to minimise such threats. Many plants are designed to withstand accidents, but few are designed to withstand sabotage.

Falkenrath describes the obstacles that terrorists would have to overcome before they could use NBC weapons to create mass casualties. A specific threat of NBC terrorism arises, Falkenrath writes, when a group falls into three categories simultaneously: it must be capable of acquiring and using NBC weapons; it must be interested in mass-murder; and it must want to use NBC weapons to achieve it. But analysis of groups that have attempted to cause mass casualties (not necessarily with NBC weapons) shows that the obstacles to such attacks are not only technical, but also organisational.[5] Terrorist groups are not monolithic. Even if most members of a group are committed to an attack, a single defector can mean the difference between success and failure. For example, in April 1997 the FBI prevented four members of a Texas-based chapter of the Ku Klux Klan from blowing up a natural-gas refinery. The chapter's leader had misgivings about the plot and informed the FBI about his colleagues' plans.[6] Operatives can be struck with moral scruples at the critical moment, even if they were committed to carrying out an attack in advance. For example, an *Aum Shinrikyo* member reportedly did not arm a biological weapon because he suddenly felt that attacking innocent people was wrong.[7]

---

[3] Author's interviews with former and current Union Carbide officials, Aspen, CO, 6 July 1998, and by telephone, 13 October 1998.

[4] Jackson B. Browning, 'Union Carbide: Disaster at Bhopal', www.bhopal.com. Assessments of the number of deaths vary; see, for example, Peter Marsh and John Elliott, 'Bhopal Disaster "Sabotage" Says Company Report', *Financial Times*, 11 May 1998, p. 4.

[5] Jessica Stern, 'Terrorist Motivations and WMD', in Peter Lavoy, Scott Sagan and Jim Wirtz (eds), *Planning the Unthinkable*, forthcoming.

[6] David E. Kaplan and Mike Thrall, 'Terrorism Threats at Home', *US News and World Report*, 29 December 1997, pp. 22–27.

[7] David E. Kaplan and Andrew Marshall, *The Cult at the End of the World* (New York: Crown Publishers, 1996), pp. 235–36.

178 **Jessica Stern**

Operatives (including former members aware of plots) sometimes turn their colleagues over to the authorities in return for a promise of clemency. The 'Covenant, the Sword, and the Arm of the Lord', an American neo-Nazi group active in the mid-1980s, plotted to poison municipal water supplies in major US cities. But a number of participants, in exchange for leniency, became FBI informants after their arrest on unrelated charges.[8] Groups capable of carrying out mass-casualty attacks would have to be unusually organised, disciplined and ruthless to avoid being penetrated by law-enforcement and intelligence agencies. *Ad hoc* groups that come together to carry out a specific attack or a series of attacks are more likely to meet these organisational requirements than traditional terrorist organisations. A number of Middle Eastern groups are structured along these lines, as are some American anti-government ones. Governments should focus their efforts on learning how to penetrate such groups.

Scholars and policy-makers have indulged in extreme thinking about NBC terrorism. Until recently, the threat was entirely ignored; now, it is attracting too much frenzied attention and too little careful analysis, inspired by a widespread conviction that the *Aum Shinrikyo* case proves that NBC attacks resulting in hundreds of thousands of deaths are all but inevitable. Both attitudes are dangerous. The first has led to the underfunding of programmes designed to prevent or mitigate the threat. The second is leading to over-reaction and hasty decisions, some of which will harm international security. The US attack on a pharmaceutical plant in Sudan on 20 August 1998 is a case in point. The plant was suspected of producing chemical weapons for bin Laden. While preventive strikes against NBC facilities can be an important component of the fight against terrorism and proliferation, adequate intelligence is critical to ensure that the right facility is targeted. Perhaps more facts will come to light. However, based on what we currently know, the decision to strike seems to have been made on the basis of incomplete information. In defending the decision to attack the Al Shifa plant, the US government claimed that Empta, the precursor to the VX nerve agent found in the soil outside the facility, clearly demonstrated that the facility was producing VX. But a number of chemists have claimed that Empta or Empta-like compounds could be by-products of the breakdown of pesticides.[9] In addition, the Aldrich Chemical Company based in Milwaukee, WI, makes and sells Empta to research laboratories.[10] Most surprising, Secretary of Defense William Cohen admitted that policy-makers did not know until after the attack that the plant

---

[8] Jessica Stern, 'Cyanide and Armageddon: The Covenant, the Sword and the Arm of the Lord', in Jonathan Tucker (ed.), *Chemical and Biological Terrorism: Motivations and Patterns of Behavior* (Monterey, CA: Monterey Institute for International Studies, forthcoming).

[9] Chemists also claim that Fonofos, a pesticide produced in Africa, could look like Empta, if the soil sample is kept in less than ideal conditions. Steven Lee Myers and Tim Weiner, 'After the Attack: The Chemicals; Possible Benign Use is Seen for Chemical at Factory in Sudan', *New York Times*, 27 August 1998, p. 1.

was actually producing medicine.[11] Cohen also admitted that the financial connection between bin Laden and the plant was at most 'indirect', a modification of his statement on the night of the attack that bin Laden 'had contributed to this particular facility'.[12]

Whether or not the plant was producing VX for bin Laden, as the US government alleged, the desire to retaliate swiftly seems to have led policy-makers to lower their standards of evidence. The US government's inability (or refusal) to persuade the international community that it targeted the right facility suggests that policy-makers are not fully prepared for the threat of NBC terrorism – intellectually, militarily or politically. As Falkenrath makes clear, the risk of apocalypse is essentially nil, but the threat of terrorism with chemical, radiological and biological agents is real and growing. It demands better intelligence, careful analysis and a sober, steady and careful response – not hasty judgement.

---

[10] Author's telephone interview with Aldrich Chemical Corporation employee, 19 October 1998; Myers and Weiner, 'After the Attack'. While it is highly unlikely that Al Shifa was producing Empta for research or commercial purposes, official US statements after the missile strike suggest that the government was unaware of these alternative explanations for the apparent presence of Empta in the soil.
[11] Tim Weiner and Steven Lee Myers, 'US Notes Gaps in Data about Drug Plant but Defends Attack; Sudan Envoy is Angry', *New York Times*, 3 September 1998, p. 6.
[12] *Ibid.*

Unknowable Threats, Prudent Policies
Richard A. Falkenrath

Given the level of media and government interest in the subject of mass-destruction terrorism, a debate on the issue is entirely appropriate. I appreciate the responses that my article has provoked from Jessica Stern, Karl-Heinz Kamp and Joseph Pilat. Clearly, Jessica Stern and I are in substantial agreement about most issues within this debate. Indeed, I have benefited from her work on this subject in the past, and expect to continue to do so in the future. I agree that the obstacles to mass-casualty terrorism are organisational, as well as technical, in nature, and that factionalism within terrorist groups will tend both to reduce their ability to carry out complex operations, and to increase the risk of discovery by the authorities.

Our main disagreement is over an issue that my article did not address: the unilateral use of military force against terrorist threats, including those related to WMD. Stern criticises the US airstrikes against the pharmaceutical plant in Sudan. However, the intelligence behind the decision to attack is classified, and properly so. Likewise, the 'standards of evidence' applied by Clinton and his closest advisors are unknown, at least to me. It seems, therefore, that we simply do not know enough at this time to conclude that the airstrikes were

Richard A. Falkenrath is a faculty member of the John F. Kennedy School of Government, Harvard University, Cambridge, MA.

180 **Richard A. Falkenrath**

unwarranted or incompetently executed. They may well have been both, but so far only one side of the case has been publicly heard.

The more fundamental point, however, concerns the appropriateness of using military force unilaterally against terrorist threats. Taking military action against terrorists in a foreign country is not easily justified under current international law. But using force will still be the right thing to do under certain circumstances.

1. When there is high-quality intelligence on the location and activities of a serious non-state threat to a nation's vital interests.
2. When the military options available to deal with this threat offer a good chance of achieving operational objectives with minimal collateral damage.
3. When other available multilateral and/or non-military options have been exhausted.
4. When the diplomatic and legal repercussions of the action (including its possible failure) are manageable.

There is, of course, a risk that unilaterally using force will create new terrorist threats, even as old ones are stamped out. But more serious is the risk of creating an international environment in which violent, motivated individuals might think it possible to take up arms against the world's most powerful sovereign entities without putting themselves in extreme personal jeopardy. An unambiguous, credible threat of forceful retaliation is the essence of deterrence. A strategy to deter non-state aggression should include the ability and the willingness to use military force unilaterally and decisively.

Karl-Heinz Kamp endorses my analysis of the chemical- and biological-terrorism threat, but argues in his response and elsewhere that governments and analysts should not be alarmed by the possibility of nuclear terrorism. Our differences, although principally about threat assessment, have prescriptive implications. I emphasise in my article that threat assessment is a function of both assessed probability and assessed consequences, and that all forms of mass-destruction terrorism are low-probability, high-consequence threats. Kamp is silent about the severity of the consequences of a terrorist detonation of a nuclear weapon in an urban area, implying that he agrees with the widely held view that these potential consequences are extremely high.

Our disagreement, therefore, seems to turn on the question of likelihood. But even here, the difference between Kamp and myself is slight. Although Kamp dismisses scenarios involving nuclear terrorism as 'far-fetched', he also concludes that nuclear terrorism 'cannot be entirely ruled out', even if it 'seems very unlikely'. In my article, I write that the 'likelihood of acts of NBC terrorism in the future is low, but it is not zero, and it is rising'. The difference in these formulations is relatively minor, so it is difficult to see the source of Kamp's 'profound disagreement' with me. Indeed, we agree on the most fundamental point: that nuclear terrorism is possible, though unlikely. In any case, the reason to be concerned about nuclear terrorism starts – but does not end – with the severity of its potential consequences. My contention is that the threat is likely enough to cause serious concern, particularly since developments in the former Soviet Union have contributed to making nuclear terrorism more likely. It is here that the prescriptive implications of Kamp's difference with me are borne out. I argue that the risk of nuclear terrorism is rising principally because the Soviet nuclear-custodial system is degrading; Kamp argues that the Soviet Union's collapse 'only slightly increases the likelihood of nuclear terrorism'. I believe that Kamp's 'only slightly' qualifier is incorrect, but reasonable people can disagree on this point. However, I cannot understand Kamp's nonchalance about *any* increase in the likelihood of nuclear terrorism.

Given the severity of the potential consequences of nuclear terrorism, even slight increases in its likelihood should hold the attention of security analysts and officials. This point has important policy implications. As far as nuclear terrorism is concerned, my primary policy prescription is that Western governments should work with the states of the former Soviet Union (most importantly Russia) to ensure that all stockpiles of nuclear weapons and nuclear materials there are properly guarded and accounted for. Working to enhance nuclear security in the former Soviet Union is a moderate prescription. While in my judgment Kamp underestimates the importance of these on-going programmes in controlling the risk of nuclear terrorism and proliferation over the long term, he implicitly endorses them. His disagreement with me does not therefore appear to extend to my policy conclusions. I worry, however, that his contribution to the nuclear-terrorism debate has had the unfortunate side-effect of succouring those in the West who oppose nuclear-assistance efforts in the former Soviet Union. I would urge Kamp to spend less time criticising a nonexistent hysteria about nuclear terrorism, and more time arguing for more ambitious international efforts to improve the quality of fissile-material security and accounting in the former Soviet Union. Germany's programmes in this area could certainly be stronger.

Pilat's response to my article is the most puzzling of the three. His critique seems directed more at what he believes to be my underlying mindset, than at the article I wrote. Rather than address the arguments I make explicitly, he attacks a set of simplistic assumptions he claims that I hold. The trouble with this approach is that I hold none of the assumptions he ascribes to me. At the same time, he either openly agrees with the four basic arguments I make and the prescriptive agenda I outline, or offers no substantive arguments against them.

My first argument is that increased concern with the possibility of NBC terrorism is justified. Pilat writes: 'Whatever the likelihood of NBC terrorism, it is a real possibility. After the Tokyo subway attack, improved responses are essential.' Our reasoning may be different, but his conclusion is indistinct from mine.

My second argument is that NBC terrorism is a low-probability, high-consequence threat. Pilat seems to admit that this is the right way to think about the problem. He suggests only that I have less confidence in the formula's 'low probability' aspect than in its 'high consequence' one. This insinuation is not only incorrect but also logically unrelated to the validity of my characterisation of the threat.

My third argument is that 'the harm caused by even one successful act of NBC terrorism in a major city would be profound – and not just in terms of lives lost'. Here, Pilat may actually disagree with me, but it is difficult to be sure. He describes at some length how he believes that I have exaggerated NBC terrorism's potential consequences, particularly with respect to its implications for democratic governance and civil liberties. Pilat attacks a series of misrepresentations of what I actually say in the article.[1] But he never says that I am wrong in my basic point that the consequences of a major NBC terrorist incident would be high and would go beyond the immediate physical damage of the attack. Because he offers only vague and contradictory ruminations, rather than a distinct argument about the potential consequences of NBC terrorism, it is impossible to rebut what he says.

My article's fourth argument is that the probability of future acts of NBC terrorism is low, but not zero, and is rising. Pilat writes: 'Changing patterns of terrorism, including greater lethality and lesser constraints on behaviour, are real and make NBC terrorism more likely, but neither probable nor inevitable'. Since this assessment is indistinct from my own, Pilat's claim that I am exaggerating the impact of the apparent changing patterns of terrorism is perplexing.

I end my article with a compressed prescriptive agenda for responding to NBC terrorism. Pilat seems to agree with my recommendations, and offers no substantive objection to any of them. Instead, he says that I see the possibility of a technical 'fix' to a nation's vulnerability to NBC terrorism, and that I oversell the importance of technical solutions to the problem. Both charges are incorrect, and I believe a rereading of my section on 'How Governments Should Respond' (pp. 58–61) would make this clear. Indeed, I believe that advanced technology in general has a rather small role to play in a nation's overall preparedness for terrorism, including NBC terrorism, and that the most important measures involve careful improvements in how the nation organises its existing capabilities, institutions, equipment and technologies. I have never, for instance, identified a requirement for 'sensitive NBC sensors for use in satellite-based monitoring' of mass-destruction terrorist threats, as Pilat has.[2]

Pilat endorses my call for a comprehensive national strategy for domestic preparedness against terrorism, but notes that I fail to 'follow through' on this recommendation. It is true that for reasons of space I was unable to elaborate my ideas on this issue in this article. A few lines before my discussion of the national-strategy issue, however, I included a footnote to the prescriptive chapter of my recently published co-authored book, where these and other

---

[1] Nowhere do I suggest, for example, that 'governments and societies could not withstand' the effects of NBC terrorism, only that the physical, economic, social and political effects of a major NBC terrorist attack would be severe.

[2] Joseph Pilat, 'Prospects for NBC Terrorism After Tokyo', in Brad Roberts (ed.), *Terrorism with Chemical and Biological Weapons: Calibrating Risks and Responses* (Alexandria, VA: Chemical and Biological Arms Control Institute, 1997), p. 17.

ideas are discussed at length.[3] I would refer interested readers to that discussion.

Pilat's views fail adequately to challenge my argument or my conclusions. I have points of disagreement with Stern and Kamp, but their positions are substantive and crisply articulated. Pilat claims wide disagreement without establishing any significant differences with my conclusions. If his overarching message is that one should avoid exaggerated descriptions or hysterical responses to the threat of NBC terrorism, this is a view I share and, I believe, apply in my writing and speaking on this subject.

---

[3] Richard A. Falkenrath, Robert D. Newman and Bradley Thayer, *America's Achilles' Heel: Nuclear, Biological, and Chemical Terrorism and Covert Attack* (Cambridge, MA: Massachusetts Institute of Technology Press, 1998).

[24]

The threat of nuclear terrorism

JACK HARRIS, EDITOR

Cam, Gloucestershire, UK

Over the past couple of years two Pugwash researchers, Tom Milne and Henrietta Wilson, have been exploring the possibility of the Atomic Weapons Research Establishment (AWE) at Aldermaston undertaking more work in the general field of nuclear disarmament.[1] The main conclusion from the study is that the remit of AWE should indeed be expanded, to include research on verifying nuclear disarmament and other aspects of nuclear arms control. There are precedents in the USA for nuclear weapons laboratories allocating considerable resources to work on disarmament and verification, and in the UK the Chemical and Biological Defence Establishment at Porton Down is well known internationally for its research on chemical and biological arms control and disarmament. Indeed AWE itself in the past has carried out valuable work in the field of nuclear weapon test detection. It is not a new principle which is being recommended by Milne and Wilson, but an expansion in scale of effort, a radical revision of priorities.

A small steering group was appointed to oversee the Milne–Wilson investigation, consisting of Joseph Rotblat, Martin Rees, and myself. We provided a touch of the tiller here, a piece of advice there, and accompanied the two authors in discussions with the Ministry of Defence (MoD) and, at Aldermaston itself, with representatives of Hunting–BRAE, the organisation responsible for running the site. On an earlier occasion we visited Porton Down.

During the course of this study my own thinking has been very much influenced by our discussions with the MoD (*see* below), and by my attendance at an international workshop on disarmament in Moscow and Sarov (Arzamas-16), Russia's 'Los Alamos' and one of its 10 'secret cities'. (I should stress at this point that I am expressing in this Editorial my own views, and not necessarily those of Pugwash or my collaborators on the AWE project.) I have in fact become alarmed, almost to the point of hysteria, at the possibility of leakage of fissile material occurring from Russia and other states of the Former Soviet Union (FSU) into the hands of representatives of rogue states and terrorist groups. (By 'fissile material' in this context I refer to plutonium of almost any isotopic composition and to weapons grade highly enriched uranium (HEU) with isotopic composition $>90\%^{235}U$).

Leakage of fissile material from FSU

A significant leakage of nuclear material from the FSU would of course have far greater implications than simply affecting the security of the UK. It would allow such countries as Iran, Iraq, North Korea, and Libya to acquire nuclear weapons and this would in turn give an excuse for neighbouring countries, such as Turkey, Saudi Arabia, South Korea, Taiwan, and Japan, to take similar actions. It would certainly provoke the collapse of the Non-Proliferation Treaty, and on the whole cause global destabilisation.

Failure of MoD to take problem seriously

Returning to the Aldermaston exercise, when we had our discussions with the MoD I asked what steps were being taken to assist Russia make its fissile stockpiles more secure. We were told that in the early 1990s the MoD provided a number of 'supercontainers' for the transport of Russian warheads together with 20 heavy duty trucks, but that is all. As far as we could make out, currently they are doing *nothing* to assist Russia, though we noted that at the periphery BNFL is assisting the Mayak Reprocessing Plant with improvements to its fissile accounting system and the UK Atomic Energy Authority is assisting the Russians with dismantling nuclear facilities.

It appears that the MoD's nuclear budget is almost entirely spent on maintaining Trident, a defence system which seems completely irrelevant to what I would regard as the greatest danger to this country – a nuclear attack by terrorists. In fact it is hard to escape the conclusion that our security would be greatly enhanced if Trident were mothballed and its budget spent on assisting Russia's nuclear disarmament and decommissioning programme.

Public misconceptions

What is surprising is that the danger of nuclear attack by terrorists is not much more widely recognised. Perhaps Western society has lived for so long under the threat of a nuclear holocaust that it no longer fears it – familiarity has bred contentment. Many now believe that chemical or biological weapons in the hands of terrorists represent a greater threat than nuclear devices. Such misconceptions are due in part to the belief that fissile materials are so radioactive they would fatally harm anyone who stole them and assembled them into weapons. It is further believed that the manufacture of nuclear weapons is a highly complex process, quite beyond the ability of a subnational terrorist group.

In fact both weapons grade uranium and plutonium are only mildly radioactive and no more toxic in the solid form than say lead. The metals themselves can safely be held in the bare hands and only become hazardous if they are finely divided and ingested into the lungs. Both uranium and plutonium are extremely dense (approaching 20 g cm^{-3}), so critical masses occupy only small volumes (about grapefruit size for uranium and golf ball size for plutonium). These small volumes and low toxicities make stealing and smuggling near critical amounts of fissile material relatively uncomplicated operations.

Ease of manufacture of uranium bomb

The manufacture of a plutonium bomb, although not particularly hazardous, is actually quite complicated and would require the resources of a national body. In contrast, the production of an unsophisticated uranium bomb could be accomplished by a subnational terrorist group once it had obtained a supply of HEU. About 50 kg of HEU would be needed for a crude atomic bomb, which sounds a lot until it is realised that something like a million and a half kilograms of HEU exists in more than a hundred, often poorly guarded sites, all over Russia and other FSU countries. The acquisition of tens of kilograms of HEU does not seem beyond the bounds of possibility in the chaos that is Russia today.

To manufacture a uranium atom bomb, all that would be involved would be the firing of one subcritical mass of HEU into another (say placed at the other end of the barrel of a redundant artillery gun), thereby creating a critical mass. The presence of a neutron source would ensure that the outcome was a nuclear explosion with a yield equivalent to that of between ten and twenty thousand tons of TNT. Recalling the devastation caused by the detonation of a ton or two of high explosive in the City of London, Manchester, and London's Docklands in the UK, and at the World Trade Centre in New York and Oklahoma City's Federal Office in the USA, the devastation such a nuclear explosion would cause can readily be imagined.

Such a uranium bomb would not be very large; not inappropriately it would be about the size and dimensions of an adult coffin and hence it could readily be hidden in a small van (or a hearse!). It would only be very mildly radioactive and hence undetectable; nothing could stop it being driven into and parked in central London, and with the aid of a time switch detonated after the driver had escaped. Imagine such an occurrence, with an epicentre at Hyde Park Corner, at a time when the Queen and the Prince of Wales were entertaining other members of the Royal Family in Buckingham Palace, when both Houses of Parliament were full during important debates, when the Archbishop of Canterbury was at a crowded meeting in Church House and the Archbishop of Westminster was conducting a service in his cathedral, and when the Prime Minister was in Downing Street.

Consequences of explosion in central London

All these leading figures would be killed, together with up to a hundred thousand other people, and Buckingham Palace, Westminster Abbey and Cathedral, the Houses of Parliament, Downing Street, and all the major government offices would be obliterated. Piccadilly's Eros and the Albert Memorial would have melted and the Albert Hall collapsed, Nelson's Column would have fallen over, and the Queen's collection of art and the national collections in the National Gallery, the Tate, and the V&A would have been destroyed. A well organised group of terrorists might simultaneously explode another nuclear device half way between St Paul's and the British Museum, thereby destroying both buildings, and including in the devastation the British Library and the financial heart of the City, with the Bank of England, the Stock Exchange, and major merchant banks.

At a stroke the country would lose its titular head, its prime minister and most of its legislators, most of its senior civil servants, its central bank and financial institutions, the leader of its established church, and, incidentally, many of its most important cultural treasures. It would be a disaster of millennial proportions, and it is doubtful if the country could ever recover sufficiently to re-establish itself as a leading member of the community of nations. It is not likely to happen, but it is not impossible, and it would be worth spending some money to make it even less probable. Other capital cities of the world are of course equally defenceless: New York with its high population density and very tall buildings would be particularly vulnerable.

To mitigate, but not eliminate, the danger of leakage, the UK should join with other members of the European Union in augmenting the USA's considerable (and enlightened) programme of assistance to Russia in dismantling and making safe its nuclear arsenals. At the same time it should assist in Russia's economic recovery by paying particular attention to establishing high technology 'swords into ploughshares' programmes for the 10 secret cities created by the former USSR as part of its nuclear programme. These cities are now largely redundant and are close to economic collapse, yet contain nuclear experts of the highest calibre who are not being paid and could be tempted to take their expertise to rogue states. Also in these cities are inadequately protected stores of nuclear weapons and stockpiles of fissile materials. Such a 'Marshall Plan' programme would of course involve secondment of British and other European nuclear experts to Russia and reciprocal movement of Russian scientists to European laboratories.

A 'Marshall Plan' for FSU states?

The debt we owe to Russia, and the extent of the Russian people's suffering, especially during the Second World War, are sometimes forgotten. In a taxi into Moscow from the airport one passes a massive iron memorial which marks the nearest the invading German troops got to the centre of Moscow during their advance of late 1941. They had only 20 more miles to go – a close run thing. A new estimate of the number of

Our wartime debt to Russia

inhabitants of the USSR killed in that terrible conflict is 47 million, a number which exceeds the total population of Great Britain at that time.

Last year I arrived in Moscow on 13 July, the very day 55 years earlier that Hitler was forced to call off operation 'Citadel', the codename for the attack by his tanks on Red Army defences in the cornfields around Kursk, a small town south of Moscow. The battle, the greatest tank battle in history, had ended with a crushing defeat for Hitler's finest divisions and finest tanks. It represented a pivotal point in the war: had it ended differently the Allies might not have been victorious and this would have had unimaginable consequences. The aid supplied by the Allies to the Russians in convoys of ships along the Arctic route had been repaid a thousandfold. Our debt to mother Russia is incalculable and we should not balk at being generous now in her new crisis, for our own sakes as much as for hers.

Note

1. The project was made possible by a grant from the Joseph Rowntree Charitable Trust, and a report of its findings, entitled 'Verifying nuclear disarmament: a role for AWE Aldermaston', is available from Pugwash (63A Great Russell Street, London WC1B 3BJ, UK, email pugwash@qmw.ac.uk).

[25]

A Perspective: Risk Analysis as a Tool for Reducing the Risks of Terrorism

Paul F. Deisler, Jr.*

The destruction by terrorists of the twin towers of the World Trade Center and major damage wrought to the Pentagon on September 11, 2001, followed closely by the bioterrorist anthrax attacks via the mails raised the question of whether risk analysis might have a place in defending the United States against terrorist attacks. After first reviewing the multifaceted nature of terrorism and the reasons it is likely to become endemic in world society in the long term, just as other areas of crime are endemic, this article surveys several fields of risk analysis, finding possible short- and long-term uses of risk analysis. The areas chiefly considered are: risk communication and chemical, biological, and technological risk analysis. Broad policy and other uses are also considered. The author finds that risk analysis has already played some role, perhaps informally, but he sees the possibility for a much larger, formal one, a role that is centrally important for the present and future of the United States and the world.

KEY WORDS: Terrorism; attack; risk; analysis; communications; health; technological; defense

1. INTRODUCTION

On October 12, 2001, Elizabeth L. Anderson, Editor-in-Chief of *Risk Analysis: An International Journal*, invited the submission of written perspectives on the question: "To what extent can we use our risk analysis approaches and methods to address the challenging issues we face in bioterrorism?" Later, on October 24, 2001, the question was broadened to include "addressing terrorist's risk," a more general topic. This author has elected to write on the latter, broader subject of how risk analysis can aid in addressing terrorist's risk in general. While there are distinct issues associated with each type of terrorism, there are also commonalities to be addressed.

Because of continuing studies and intelligence gathering, much is known about terrorism, individual terrorists, and terrorist organizations. Still, the

horrendous attacks of September 11, 2001 on the World Trade Center and the Pentagon were neither foreseen nor prevented, the economic impacts on the United States following the attacks were high, and the acts continue to have effect. Foreseeing and preventing such acts lies in the area of intelligence gathering, an area that might possibly be improved by introducing risk analytical thinking of types familiar to members of the Society for Risk Analysis. However, intelligence gathering and the way intelligence and law enforcement agencies, at every level of government, do their work lie well outside this author's knowledge so that foreseeing, estimating the probability of and, thereby, being able to act to prevent terrorist acts will not be addressed here.

Many professionals in many activities weigh risks in one way or another. Throughout this article the term "risk analysis" will be used to mean the use of multiple risk analytical methods and types of thinking familiar to members of the Society for Risk Analysis. "Risk analysis" will be taken to include risk assessment, risk management, and risk communication.

*Address correspondence to Paul F. Deisler, Jr., 2001 Mountain View Road, Austin, TX 78703; sinprisa@earthlink.net.

The question addressed in this article is, then: Can the application of any forms of risk analysis help lessen the immediate, or longer term, impacts of future terrorist attacks? Before considering this question, a brief examination of the nature of terrorism, the threats it poses, its scope, and its possible duration will be made.

2. THE NATURE AND EXTENT OF TERRORISM AND ITS THREATS

Terrorism was not unknown within the United States before September 11, 2001 but the instances were few and far between compared to those in some other countries and they were almost all of domestic origin. They were seen as different from, say, the bombings by the Basque separatists in Spain or those of the Irish Republican Army in England, acts of terrorism clearly aimed at advancing local, political, nationalist agendas. Most instances of terrorism on U.S. soil in recent history, however horrible, were the isolated, uncoordinated acts of individuals or of fringe groups, with differing, unconnected motivations.

The first major act of terrorism by aliens on U.S. soil in recent times was the truck bombing of the World Trade Center in New York City in 1993. The conspirators were extremist Muslims from various mid-eastern countries headquartered in Jersey City, New Jersey. Whatever the experts may have known at the time, the public did not link this event to any broad conspiracy. It, too, seemed to be a terrorist attack by a small but determined group driven by faith in an extreme interpretation of Islam linked to political aims. The perpetrators were caught and, once the trials were over, the public feeling seemed to be that this, too, was a one of a kind event.

The next acts on U.S. soil by foreign terrorists were the suicidal, murderous destruction of the World Trade Center towers and the heavy damage done to the Pentagon and its employees on September 11, 2001. These events raised terrorism to new levels of harm, viciousness, and heartlessness and the linking of these acts to terrorist leader Osama Bin Laden's Al Qaeda organization, operating from Afghanistan, was not long in coming. The public quickly became aware that these acts were not the isolated events of yesteryear and that the United States is faced with a type of subtle, destructive, major warfare new to the United States in which individual U.S. citizens everywhere are, to some degree, at risk. These attacks were followed

almost immediately by the discovery that the mail was being used to disseminate anthrax in this country. This attack, while not linked definitely to a particular source or group as of this writing, raised the public's consciousness of its vulnerability still further.

The U.S. Department of State maintains surveillance of terrorist activities worldwide, publishing annual summaries of its findings. These reports paint a grim picture of the extent to which terrorism is used for many different ends throughout the world. Some of the information published in *Patterns of Global Terrorism—2000*[1] is summarized here to demonstrate the widespread nature of terrorism.

The report lists 29 groups currently designated as Foreign Terrorist Organizations pursuant to Section 219 of the Immigration and Nationality Act as amended by the Antiterrorism and Effective Death Penalty Act of 1996, which, among other things, forbids the provision of funds to such organizations. Over half of these 29 groups are Islamic. Of these, most are local to one nation or region. Several are international in their operations, however, having members and cells in a variety of countries including the United States. Some have links to Osama bin Laden's Al Qaeda organization and some have the apparent, if often tacit, support of individual nations, receiving funding and other assistance from such nations as well as from other sources. Many are anti-Western, especially anti-United States, and have among their chief goals the establishment of fundamentalist, Islamic states. In addition to these 29 groups, the report lists another 15 groups and goes on to state that there are others of too little scope to list. Among the listed groups, none is based in North America.

Al Qaeda, the largest terrorist organization with a membership that may be "several hundred thousand members," was established by Osama bin Laden in the 1980s. Its goal is stated to be to establish a pan-Islamic, worldwide Caliphate by working with allied Islamic extremist groups to overthrow regimes it deems non-Islamic. Al Qaeda aims to expel Westerners and non-Muslims from Muslim countries. In February 1998 it stated that it is the duty of all Muslims to kill U.S. citizens, civilian or military, and their allies everywhere as part of a "World Islamic Front for Jihad Against the Jews and Crusaders." Al Qaeda is extremely well funded and it provides training, financing, and logistic support to other terrorist groups who support these goals.

Al Qaeda has been involved in promoting many attacks in many countries throughout the world. These include bombings, shootings, and other types of attacks resulting in many individual deaths as well as mass murders, mostly but not entirely against U.S. facilities or citizens abroad. One planned attack that did not take place, for example, was to assassinate President Clinton during his visit to the Philippines in early 1995.

There are many differences in different groups' types of attacks. Some are car-bomb explosions that destroy small businesses, cafes, or small military posts, for example. Some are delivered through a medium that can enter any household, such as the mail; some of these have been in the form of letter bombs or, as now, envelopes containing anthrax. These attacks are aimed at generating fear by attempting to show that no one is safe, that attacks can happen at any time or place, and that no person, however exalted or humble, is safe. Such attacks also are intended to show the power and reach of the perpetrators by showing how easily vulnerable society is to them.

Many of the attacks sponsored by Osama bin Laden's Al Qaeda, however, have been high profile, outrageous attention-getters, whatever the cost in human life, including the lives of the direct perpetrators. These attacks have the same objectives as the smaller ones just mentioned but are intended to inspire such intense terror that they seriously interrupt many of the normal activities of the attacked society, causing panic to such an extent that people are inspired to take actions that are, in sum, against the national good. The concerns raised about traveling by air since the September 11 attack have apparently caused would-be travelers to cancel their plans, despite tighter security measures, while concerns about anthrax have caused others to hoard Cipro, thus decreasing the supply available to those who really need it. These are examples of behaviors much desired by the terrorists.

The September attacks and the homicidal and suicidal manner of their implementation have demonstrated clearly that this enemy, at least, has no conscience with regard to human life, no hesitation in committing its own people to striking suicidal blows, and recognizes no limits to the means it will employ to conduct an attack. The foot soldiers of terrorism, in this war, are as much in the thrall of blind, obsessive obedience to a perverted version of a major religion, to hatred, and to loyalty to the leaders, religious and secular, who preach it as were the Japanese kamikaze pilots of World War II, if not more so.

The zealotry and hatred that motivate these kinds of terrorists and evidently exist to some degree among fringe groups and individuals in many countries are not things that will die down in any short time. President George W. Bush has stressed that the war against terrorism that the United States is now engaged in will be a long one, though he has refrained from saying how long. Because of the religious-ideological nature of the known terrorists, their common hatred of Western culture (typified by the United States) and the dispersed nature of the components of the many cooperating organizations, it is quite likely that a successful capture and trial of Osama bin Laden will not end this particular war. Seymour Hersh, writing in the *New Yorker*[2] quotes a source as saying: "The war was declared by bin Laden, but there are thousands of bin Ladens." The kind of terrorism the United States now faces is not dependent for its continuation on the continued leadership of bin Laden.

In thinking about risk analysis and terrorism, then, terrorism must be considered as an ongoing phenomenon affecting the world's societies, as is the case with other crime. Like crime in general, once new weapons or means for committing terrorist acts are invented or introduced, they continue to be used and are superseded only when "better" methods and weapons arise. Moreover, the newer techniques are usually adopted by more and more groups. In thinking about the uses of risk analysis to abate the risks of terrorism, it is the author's opinion that it should be thought of in the context of terrorism, from one source or another, becoming as endemic to the societies of the world as are other forms of crime. The attacks will continue and may well mount in number and intensity.

Keeping in mind that the war on terrorism may not ever totally end, this article addresses four areas: risk communication, chemical and biological risk analysis, technological risk analysis, and preparations for new risk crises. Brief mention is made of other applications.

3. RISK COMMUNICATION

Immediately following the catastrophes of September 11, and the subsequent discovery of the anthrax attack, the United States demonstrated how ready its emergency services of all kinds and at all levels of government are to come forward promptly and deal with the situations, even in the case of so huge and unexpected a set of catastrophes. The United States, a large nation with many climatic, geographical, and geological zones, is continually subject to natural catastrophes of high magnitude such as floods, hurricanes, tornadoes, earthquakes, and urban, grassland, and forest fires; additionally, epidemics are a feature of life in the United States as elsewhere. Traditionally, the United States has taken care of its own catastrophes and has built an enormous and expert infrastructure from the grassroots level to the federal level to do so. While very decentralized, thus achieving quick response, the structure of agencies is nonetheless closely linked through communications and training. It was not surprising but very, very gratifying and reassuring to see such excellent performance of the emergency services following the recent attacks.

Not gratifying at all was the performance in the area of risk communication either in the case of the September 11 disaster or in the case of the bioterrorist anthrax attack. Statements by federal officials were slow to come on September 11. It was not until four hours after the south tower of the World Trade Center was hit that President Bush gave his initial message of assurance to the public, a statement that, by its very existence, gave assurance that he, the President, was safe and actively on the job. Other government spokespeople in subsequent days were often circumspect in tone but the message content was mixed or, later, obviously inaccurate. Little was said, at first, to help the average citizen know what, if anything, he or she could personally do. The divergent behavior of the two houses of Congress in the face of the anthrax threat served to confuse the message further: stay and keep on working in the face of terror or decamp as quickly as possible, bringing your work to a halt.

Since the terrorist act is designed to spread fear, preferably panic, as widely as possible among the public, it is very important to take immediate steps to reduce fear and avoid panic through sound communication. The longer the delay, the more fear and panic can grow.

Governmental leaders and spokespersons need to have an understanding of at least the rudiments of good risk communication. The knowledge is abundantly available. Many studies of terrorism, of emergency and crisis management and communication, a large literature on risk communications, and experts in these fields exist in the United States but

it was clear that none of this expertise was known to many of our leaders on September 11.

These problems did not escape notice. Erica Goode, writing recently in the *New York Times*[3] summarizes some simple principles for communicating about risks. According to her, good communication should include full disclosure about what is and is not known, delivery of the information in a nonpatronizing manner, avoiding speculation, never mixing facts with reassurance, a detailed account about what is being done to counter the threat, and specific steps that people may take to protect themselves. In this latter regard, the U.S. Post Office recently mass-mailed a very constructive card setting out seven things that should make a recipient suspicious of a piece of mail and four specific things a recipient can do to help deal with the risk.

One of the very best theoretical and practical sources of knowledge and understanding of risk communications, despite the fact that it was published as long ago as 1989, is a study carried out under the aegis of the National Research Council entitled "Improving Risk Communication."[4] This study offers much useful guidance. For example, it notes (p. 165) that a message should be related to an audience's perspective—in this case, that of the public encountering a terrible event with little prior understanding of its possibility—and it offers four guidelines setting out that a message should:

1. Emphasize information relevant to any practical actions that individuals can take.
2. Be couched in clear and plain language.
3. Respect the audience and its concerns.
4. Seek strictly to inform the recipient, unless conditions clearly warrant the use of influencing techniques.

In some ways these guidelines are subtler than the previous set, especially in the matter of knowing when and how to apply "influencing techniques."

Another principle is that a spokesperson must speak from the heart. Reading dully from a script will ruin the message, however excellent.

The press, experienced at reporting, did not distinguish itself in the first few days after the attacks or at the start of the anthrax attacks. Some members of the press apply better sense, now, but not all of them. Too many approached these two events as though they were normal "big" news, hyping that which did not need to be hyped. Too often phrases such as "the public is jittery," "public fear," or "public panic" appeared in stories, phrases that did not necessarily report what was happening or even necessarily reflect majority moods. This is a kind of editorializing while reporting that distorts the actual news itself, tending to create the atmosphere that leads to self-fulfilling prophesy. The news is needed, spin is not. In the United States, with its freedom of the press, it is highly undesirable to consider censoring the press, even slightly. The press itself must undertake to report clearly and, one would hope, with such simple principles or guidelines as those given above in mind.

One proactive step the Society for Risk Analysis might be able to take to improve the risk communication situation would be to hold a workshop with experts, members of government, and the press as participants and publicize the results widely in the public press itself.

The need for sound risk communication did not end after the first few days following the attacks. Ongoing risk communication needs to include risk education for the public to help people understand the long-term, continuing nature of the war against terrorism and to help them to adapt to that fact—just as the public has learned to adapt to other crime: taking the necessary precautions and going about its affairs normally. When the author first bought a house in Connecticut nearly 40 years ago he asked the seller for the front door key at the closing. There was no key. In fact, the author did not buy a key until he was going to sell the house in case the new owner wanted one. As times have changed, protection against burglary has become a standard thing; the author's current house in Austin, Texas, not a very high-crime city, has a burglar alarm and dead-bolt locks. It does not as yet have bars on its windows or doors as some do. This is not because of fear; it is a simple, prudent precaution. The author goes about his daily round without fear, knowing he has done what he reasonably can to reduce the risk of burglary. Risk education can help build this attitude of prudence combined with freedom from fear into the public's daily life.

Good, sound risk communication practices, applied early and continually, are essential to inform the public accurately of what is happening, what is being done about it, and what they can do themselves. Only this approach can serve to curb the development of panic, put the public in a constructive mood, and instill the understanding and courage needed to face and live with the events that occur in our world. If international terrorism does become an endemic form of crime, good risk communication practices must also become endemic.

4. CHEMICAL AND BIOLOGICAL RISK ANALYSIS

The United States has just suffered a deadly, terrorist, microbiological attack. Before this anthrax attack, the country suffered deliberate releases of microorganisms, none of which were launched to produce terror. Indeed, it was the intention of the perpetrators that the attacks remain secret. An excellent recent study, "Bioterrorism: A New Threat with Psychological Sequelae,"[5] includes a brief history of biological warfare and research conducted in many nations, including the United States, dating back to the German efforts during World War I.

Starting in 1951 and on into the 1960s, several cities in the United States were subjected to clandestine releases of Serratia marcenscens by personnel of American military facilities at Ft. Detrick, Maryland and Pine Bluff, Arkansas to test the dispersal of biological agents under realistic conditions. The microorganism was thought to be harmless though it may have been responsible for one death and several urinary tract infections in San Francisco. After *The Washington Post* reported on these tests in 1976, public outcry brought on congressional investigations and a halt to the program.

Another case was the bizarre attempt to influence the outcome of an election in Wasco County, Oregon, in 1984, by the followers of Guru Baghwan Rajneesh. Salmonella was introduced into salad bars in 10 restaurants in The Dalles in an effort to sicken enough voters to allow the cult members' votes to swing the election. Some 751 people contracted salmonellosis. Public health officials at first thought the outbreak was natural, which would have suited the perpetrators, but subsequent investigation soon showed that it was not and the perpetrators were caught. Thus, there was little actual, relevant experience to rely on for addressing an attack when the anthrax attack came.

The resources that are available to deal with actual cases of chemical or biological attack are enormous, however, and well organized as a result of having to meet the needs of the U.S. population for protection against diseases of all kinds and origins. Before discussing possible uses of risk analysis in combating chemo- and bioterrorism, it is desirable to obtain some sense of what the federal government already has in existence to help address these risks.

4.1. Government Institutional Approaches Chemo- and Bioterrorism

At the federal level, the chief organization is the Department of Health and Human Services (HHS). Within that department, three organizations in particular are of importance in dealing with the consequences of an attack or, indeed, in carrying out any necessary analyses of risk: the Centers for Disease Control and Prevention (CDC), the Agency for Toxic Substances and Disease Registry (ATS-DR), and the National Institutes of Health (NIH). These three organizations, taken together, have an enormous amount of organized information, the ability to educate and train, the ability to do relevant research, large laboratory capacity, the ability to detect disease, extensive emergency response capabilities, and many communications links with state and local health departments, health-care institutions, local poison centers, universities, and individual health professionals. The CDC has a specific role to provide nationwide, emergency response leadership in health emergencies, including those caused by bioterrorism. It maintains, among other things, a National Pharmaceutical Stockpile. (To learn more about the HHS and its suborganizations, go to the website, www.os.dhhs.gov).

The HHS has prepared a strategic plan, Emerging Infectious Diseases: A Strategy for the 21st Century,[6] which explicitly includes outbreaks that may result from bioterrorism. It also includes further development of its ability to communicate electronically with state and local health departments, U.S. quarantine stations, and health-care professionals, among others, and it stresses the desirability of having a strong and flexible public health infrastructure, such as now exists, and of continuing to build it. The importance of having a strong, flexible infrastructure, especially in the first stages of an outbreak, is that only such an infrastructure can yield prompt detection of outbreaks, which depends on the flow of reliable data from physicians, hospitals, clinical labs, and epidemiologists to state and local health departments and CDC, that is, from the front line.

The CDC has its own strategic plan for preparedness and response to biological and chemical terrorism.[7] In its report on this plan the CDC goes into great detail on types of attacks (overt and covert), the high vulnerability of the United States to attack (and the ease of making such attacks), and detailed plans covering many aspects of preparedness and response.

These are but some of the plans federal agencies have developed to cope with these kinds of attacks in their own spheres of responsibility. Clearly, the federal government has been concerning itself seriously with the possibility of such attacks for some time. Moreover, at the state, county, and city level, the kind of infrastructure needed exists and is mobilizing itself to meet further attacks.

4.2. Role of Human Health Risk Analysis

There are many common elements between human health risk analysis, as it is applied to chemicals in the environment on the one hand, and to microorganisms on the other hand. The risk analysis paradigms[8,9] developed for analyzing human health risks caused by exposures to chemicals have been applied successfully to analyzing health risks caused by exposure to microorganisms in setting regulatory standards in such diverse media as air, water, or food. Consideration of an FAO/WHO report, "Application of Risk Analyses to Food Standards Issues,"[10] shows that these same paradigms can be applied in various ways to reducing the risks of exposure caused by terrorist attacks. There are some differences in the application. For instance, quantitative dose-response data are often lacking for biological agents; the Dose Response Assessment step therefore cannot as often be used quantitatively for bioterrorist attacks as it can for chemicals. Instead, a step called Hazard Characterization is substituted, which gives a description of the actions of biological agents once exposure takes place—their severity and duration, for example. The Exposure Assessment step is more complex for biological agents. Although biological organisms can come into contact with humans by the same routes as chemical ones, unlike chemicals they can grow and multiply (or they can die and disappear), given the right conditions, thus increasing (or decreasing) the "dose." Also, infectious microorganisms can transfer from one person to another, directly or indirectly, adding to the exposure pathways. Moreover, some microorganisms can become dormant, sometimes for years, awaiting suitable conditions for reproduction. From the standpoint of risk reduction, an apparent disappearance of an outbreak can thus be misleading. All these kinds of factors, and others, must be taken into account in analyzing biological risks.

Much of what the HHS and CDC have undertaken already lies in three areas of risk analysis for biological agents: hazard identification, hazard characterization, and risk management (reducing the effects of an attack). Thus, in effect, some parts of risk analysis are already in action in chemo- and bioterrorism, even if not explicitly so named by those involved.

It would be well to involve risk analysis explicitly and by name, and to involve actual risk analysts, in the work of the public health organizations of the United States. The FAO/WHO report[10] already mentioned states: "The importance of risk assessment lies not only in its ability to estimate human risk, but also in *its use as a frame-work for organizing data as well as allocating responsibility for analysis*" (emphasis added). Thus, the risk analysts' mode of thinking itself would enhance efforts to protect the public. Smith *et al.*[5] note that "Congress has appropriated funds to assess the risks associated with specific agents and for development of coordinated federal, state and local response capabilities."

Some of the areas in which human health risk analysis would be especially involved are: defining areas where research is needed; helping to identify hazards more rapidly, including new ones (associated, for example, with genetically modified microorganisms); offering an organized approach to defining exposure pathways; helping to decide when a risk posed by a chemical or a microorganism has been sufficiently abated as to pose no further significant risk; helping to assess the vulnerability to chemical and biological attack of specific sites, activities, or areas (cities, manufacturing complexes, transportation systems, etc.) so as to enable the allocation of resources to reducing such vulnerabilities before attack and to dealing with the effects of attack if one should occur. Smith *et al.*[5] provide a table of what amounts to estimates of population risks of mortality and morbidity for a variety of hypothetical population exposure scenarios for some seven different microorganisms, including anthrax. The calculations were made for the release of 50 kg of each microorganism by aircraft along a 2-km line upwind of a population center of 500,000 inhabitants. This is the type of scenario-based study that can be useful in examining vulnerabilities, given adequate data, and in determining how much risk reduction might be achieved in a given case through different means proposed for reducing risk.

The work of reducing the risks of chemical and biological attacks after they occur and of reducing vulnerabilities to such attacks before they occur is fundamentally the work of risk analysis but not necessarily only of human health risk analysis. The reduction of risks at vulnerable sites will involve not only human health risk analysis but, also, technological risk analysis. The two fields and their practitioners will have to work together to reduce vulnerabilities.

5. TECHNOLOGICAL RISK ANALYSIS

Technological risk analysis took a great leap forward in 1974 with the introduction of the use of probabilistic risk analysis (PRA) by the well-known Rasmussen Report,[11] so-named for Dr. Norman C. Rasmussen of MIT who chaired the committee of the Nuclear Regulatory Commission (NRC) that generated the report. This is but one of the many methods now available for assessing technological and engineering risks and includes items such as fault trees, event trees, human factor analysis, and more.

The application of technological risk analytical tools to reduce risk from terrorist attacks of all kinds, from physical attacks such as those of September 11, 2001, bombs, fires, and so forth to those aimed directly at creating disease such as chemical and biological attacks, are numerous. These applications range from retrofitting current buildings, manufacturing facilities, transportation systems, or other kinds of facilities to the design of new ones. Highways are vulnerable to attack, for example, especially at the sites of bridges, tunnels, or freeway interchanges and alternate routes need to be provided so as not to interrupt the flow of traffic. The applications range from the installation of warning systems for specified areas to enable people to take protective action to methods for calling for help in fending off physical attack. They also include the identification of activities or facilities that have higher vulnerabilities than others and that, if attacked, might cause more overall harm than others. Buildings, manufacturing facilities, and facilities of all kinds need to be designed to incorporate fast-escape routes, emergency shelters, air filtration treatment, pressurization, or supply, and other means for protecting the populations in or near the affected facilities.

In every case, each risk reduction proposal can be tested for the degree of reduction of risk to be expected under different kinds of attacks using the tools of technological risk analysis, combined, in the case of chemical or biological attacks, with human health risk analysis. Thus, the best methods for risk reduction can be chosen. Just as in earthquake-prone states, building codes include design and construction requirements aimed at minimizing damage from earthquakes, so one can envision new, risk analysis-tested codes for use in the emerging age of terrorism.

A recent study, "Major Problems/Opportunities Facing Texas and the Chemical and Refining Industries in the 21st Century,"[12] discusses areas to which the State of Texas needs to give concerted attention if it is to prepare itself adequately for future growth and change. Although the report has a section on bioterrorism as a problem to be faced, the report is not aimed primarily at dealing with terrorism. Because Texas is a very varied state, having within its borders most of the activities whole nations often include, it offers a model for considering the problems of the nation as a whole.

The report emphasizes the amount of interdependence one activity has with others. This interdependence can lead terrorist organizations to find opportunities to do great damage to several economically important systems by harming only one, well-chosen system. This and the specific problems the report deals with (water supply, transportation, etc.) often suggest areas of new development where technological risk analysis should be applied.

One such new development is a proposal that the Texas Department of Transportation is considering: the possibility of creating multimodal transportation centers where different forms of transportation come together and the transfer of goods from one to another is facilitated, decreasing shipping times and, therefore, costs. Such a development is emerging now at the Alliance Airport at Dallas/Ft. Worth. Considerations of technological risk, combined with those of human risk, should clearly play a part in the furtherance of this kind of development. Whether such a multimodal center can be better defended against terrorist attacks or the consequences of such attacks than a more dispersed arrangement, including the costs of defense versus the costs of dispersal, human safety, and other factors, needs to be analyzed before the best arrangement is selected. The report contains many other ideas, each provocative of further possibilities for the effective use of risk analysis.

As in the case of human health risk analysis, the use of technological risk analysis cannot all be done centrally. The incorporation of capabilities for addressing technological risk problems must also exist, in adequate amounts, at the grass-roots level, public and private. This is a tall order; although the nation has an abundance of technically educated people, not all are well versed in the use of the tools of technological risk analysis. Clearly, a major effort is needed to bring the necessary resources to the task. If, as the author believes, terrorism is endemic, investments made now to bring the resources into being and full use will pay off not only now but in the future.

6. LEARNING FROM PAST DECISIONS, PREPARING FOR THE FUTURE

With or without formal risk analysis, risk decisions must nevertheless be made. However past decisions may have been made, risk analytical methods can assist in their analysis to aid in preparing for future, major decisions.

As an example, a case that it would be useful to analyze is the decision that was announced by the Federal Aviation Administration (FAA) to halt all flight operations at U.S. airports following the September 11 attacks. This decision was announced only 55 minutes after American Airlines Flight 11 was smashed into the north tower of the World Trade Center. The brief time delay between the event and the announcement did not allow for a deep weighing of risks or for risk analysis. It may be that the risks had already been weighed well before the attack as part of preparing the FAA to act during major emergencies. It may also have been a "best gut feel" decision, made at the time, aimed at ensuring the safety of travelers and crew while better security measures were instituted. However made, this decision gave *de facto* weight, correctly or not, to many risk factors of great importance, whether they were explicitly weighed or not, including those already mentioned. Some of these factors include: the impact on the airline industry and the many industries associated with it and airline travelers; the impact on the many employees who lost their jobs; the gift, to the terrorists, of a major economic impact of their actions; the message of fear sent to the public by the decision; and the risks associated with options other than an immediate and total shutdown for a period not at first announced. Such an analysis would at least provide knowledge of what kind of information is needed that might not then have been available (such as the ability of the terrorists to mount another, early attack) in similar situations. In any event, what is learned from such an analysis will make for more sure decisions in the wake of future attacks on what option to pursue to achieve the desired ends while posing fewer or lesser collateral risks. Emergency procedures now in place in many public and private organizations can be improved by similar, risk-analysis-based examinations.

This type of risk analysis will require the integration of information and knowledge from many fields, a process of integration well known to many risk analysts. It appears to the author that this is a fertile field for such broad risk analysis and that new, improved methods of risk analysis will surely evolve in it.

7. FINAL REFLECTIONS

It is clear that formal risk analysis and risk analytical thinking have major roles to play in defending against and mitigating the consequences of terrorist attacks of many kinds. The same may be said about risks not yet incurred: nuclear explosions, modified microorganisms, new chemicals, radioactive aerosols, ecoterrorism, or any of many other new threats that can be imagined in our science-fiction-come-true world.

One thing that the techniques and examples considered cannot do is assist in the development of that ultimate tool of risk management—the reduction to insignificance of the sources of threats. At the moment, the attack on the Taliban in Afghanistan and the effort, by armed force, to capture or neutralize Osama bin Laden and his Al Qaeda is the approach being undertaken not just to reduce but also to eliminate that particular source of threat.

In the future, supposing that the premise of a never-ending war on terrorism, parallel to that on other forms of crime, holds true, all kinds of policies involving such things as international diplomacy, negotiation, coalition-forming, political sensitivity, cultural and societal considerations, communications, military and quasi-military actions, or other options must be weighed and the comparative risks assessed. Intelligence gathering will play a major role in all of this type of activity. The kind of risk analysis needed to aid in decision making in this

broad area is, without doubt, one that is multidisciplinary and integrative in the extreme. Adding this type of risk analysis to the risk decision processes now used cannot help but make for better policy making, decision making, and option selection. At the same time the effort itself will engender new types and approaches to risk analysis, new paradigms, broadening the scope of risk analysis still further and making it more useful in further decision making in the area of the reduction or elimination of the sources of terrorist threats in the world.

REFERENCES

1. U.S. Department of State, Office of the Secretary of State. 2001. *Patterns of Global Terrorism—2000.* Washington, DC: Department of State Publication.
2. Hersh, S. M. 2001. Annals of National Security—King's Ransom. *The New Yorker* October 22, 35–49.
3. Goode, E. 2001. Anthrax Offers Lessons in How to Handle Bad News. *New York Times* October 23.
4. National Research Council, Committee on Risk Perception and Communication. 1989. *Improving Risk Communication.* National Academy Press, Washington, DC: National Academy Press.
5. Smith, C., Veenhuis, G., Philip, E., and MacCormack, J. N. 2000. Bioterrorism: A New Threat with Psychological and Social Sequelae. *North Carolina Medical Journal 61*(3): 150–165.
6. Centers for Disease Control and Prevention (CDC), Department of Health and Human Services. 1998. *Emerging Infectious Diseases: A Strategy for the 21st Century.* Atlanta, GA: CDC.
7. Centers for Disease Control and Prevention, U.S. Department of Health and Human Services. 2000. Biological and Chemical Terrorism: Strategic Plan for Preparedness and Response—Recommendations of the CDC Strategic Planning Workgroup. *Morbidity and Mortality Weekly Report 49* (RR-4): 1–14.
8. Committee on Institutional Means for Assessment of Risks to Public Health, National Research Council. 1983. *Risk Assessment in the Federal Government: Managing the Process.* Washington, DC: National Academy Press.
9. Committee on Risk Assessment of Hazardous Air Pollutants, Board on Environmental Studies and Toxicology, National Research Council. 1994. *Science and Judgment in Risk Assessment.* Washington, DC: National Academy Press.
10. Joint FAO/WHO Expert Commission. 1995. *World Health Organization—Application of Risk Analyses to Food Standards Issues, Report No. WHO/FNU/FOS/95.3.* New York: World Health Organization.
11. U.S. Nuclear Regulatory Commission (NRC). 1974. *Reactor Safety Study, Document No. WASH-1400.* Washington, DC: NRC.
12. Texas Institute for the Advancement of Chemical Technology (TIACT). 2000. Major Problems/Opportunities Facing Texas and the Chemical and Refining Industries in the 21st Century. *INSIGHTS 9*(2). (Copies may be requested of Dr. Charles D. Holland, President, TIACT, Texas A&M University, Mail Stop 3125, College Station, Texas 77843; see also http://www-chen.tamu.edu/TIACT/majproblemsinsights.pdf.).

[26]

Nuclear Terrorism and Warhead Control in Russia

Jon B. Wolfsthal and Tom Z. Collina

Since 11 September, there has been unprecedented concern that the next terrorist attack against the United States could involve a nuclear weapon or 'dirty' nuclear bomb. To respond to this threat, the Bush administration has placed radiation sensors at US borders, put an elite commando unit – the Delta Force – on high alert to seize control of nuclear materials and is actively considering the development of a new generation of small 'bunker busting' nuclear weapons. According to *The Washington Post*, after an October briefing by CIA director George Tenet on al-Qaeda's nuclear ambitions, President George W. Bush 'ordered his national security team to give nuclear terrorism priority over every other threat to the United States'.[1]

While the US assessment of the proliferation threat has changed since 11 September, the most likely source from which terrorists might acquire nuclear material, or a complete warhead, has not. Russia inherited a vast nuclear complex where hundreds of tonnes of 'fissile material' (plutonium and highly enriched uranium) exist under inadequate and even non-existent security measures. In January 2001, a bipartisan panel chaired by Howard Baker and Lloyd Cutler found that

> The most urgent unmet national security threat to the United States today is the danger that weapons of mass destruction or weapons-usable material in Russia could be stolen and sold to terrorists or hostile nation states and used against American troops abroad and citizens at home.[2]

More recently, the US intelligence community confirmed to Congress in February 2002 that 'weapons-grade and weapons-usable nuclear materials have been stolen from some Russian institutes. We assess that undetected smuggling has occurred, although we do not know the extent or magnitude of such thefts'.[3] According to Viktor Yerastov, chief of Minatom's Nuclear Materials Accounting and Control Department in Russia, 'quite sufficient material to produce an atomic bomb' was stolen from Chelyabinsk administrative region in 1998.[4] Commenting on that theft to *The Washington*

Jon B. Wolfsthal is an Associate with the Non-Proliferation Project with the Carnegie Endowment·for International Peace. **Tom Z. Collina** is Director of the Global Security Program at the Union of Concerned Scientists

72 **Jon B. Wolfsthal and Tom Z. Collina**

Post, an Amercian official said that 'given the known and suspected capabilities of the Russian mafia, its perfectly plausible that al-Qaeda would have access to such material'.[5]

A terrorist attack involving nuclear weapons could easily surpass the damage (literally and psychologically) of 11 September. To properly address this highest priority threat, one would expect that US policy toward Russia would place concerns about securing Russian nuclear weapons and materials above all others. But recent information about US policy on nuclear weapons indicates that this is not the case. The Bush administration's nuclear policy, reflected in the Nuclear Posture Review (NPR), actually exacerbates the threat of nuclear proliferation by leading Russia to keep a large reserve of nuclear warheads and materials and to maintain an artificially large nuclear complex. Given the dangerous state of this complex – and the fact that terrorists are known to be targeting it – US policy should instead be aimed at getting Russian nuclear warheads secured, dismantled and their nuclear materials securely and quickly eliminated.

To do so, the Bush administration will have to give up the notion that it needs to keep a reserve force of thousands of nuclear warheads for future use. There is no compelling justification for a reserve of this size, which could exceed twice the planned size of the 2,200 weapon deployed arsenal in 2012. Bush and Russian President Vladimir Putin should make a commitment at their May summit in Moscow for their governments to work out a verifiable warhead-elimination agreement and to work more actively to secure vulnerable parts of the Russian weapons complex.

The shell game

Last November, Presidents Putin and Bush announced that they would reduce their strategic operational nuclear forces from roughly 5,000 Russian and 7,000 US warheads today to between 1,700 and 2,200 weapons by 2012. Russian officials have expressed their expectations that these arsenal reductions will be binding, or irreversible, and that the warheads would be dismantled. Igor Sergeyev, Putin's military adviser, said on 19 February that 'real and irreversible liquidation of nuclear weapons will show the world community how reliable and serious the course for nuclear disarmament is'.[6]

Although previous arms-control agreements have not legally required the elimination of warheads or procedures to monitor their elimination, both countries had been moving in this direction. Since 1995, the United States and Russia have cooperated to develop technical means and procedures to help verify warhead dismantlement without revealing classified information. This work had made enough progress that by the 1997 Helsinki summit meeting between Presidents Bill Clinton and Boris Yeltsin the two could agree that the proposed START III treaty. would include measures relating to the transparency of strategic nuclear warhead inventories and the destruction of strategic nuclear warheads and any other jointly agreed technical and organisational measures, to promote the irreversibility of deep reductions including prevention of a rapid increase in the number of warheads. Such steps would not only have helped ensure that arms reductions could not be easily reversed, but would have aided efforts to securely dispose of much larger amounts of excess nuclear materials in Russia and the United States.

The Bush administration now plans to keep several thousand warheads to be offloaded from land and submarine based missiles as part of US 'reductions'. This reserve includes roughly 2,000 warheads in the so-called 'responsive force' that will be kept ready for rapid redeployment. According to Undersecretary of Defense for Policy Douglas J. Feith, the Pentagon believes it 'must retain these weapons to give the United States a responsive capability to adjust the number of operationally deployed nuclear weapons should the international security environment change and warrant such action'.[7] This stance has raised major objections from Russian officials, especially within the Ministry of Defence, who are concerned that the United States could quickly return its forces to START I levels, providing no long-term confidence in the irreversibility of the arms reduction process. This unpredictability, they argue, could lead to major instabilities and undercut international non-proliferation efforts which are predicated on the US pledge that it is 'unequivocally committed' to the elimination of nuclear weapons.

In response to the US position, Russian officials have indicated that they will be forced to adopt a worse-case assessment of the size of the US nuclear arsenal. Despite US intentions to deploy 2,200 strategic offensive weapons, Russian defence officials have indicated that they will use START I counting rules to assess the size and capability of the US arsenal. This means that, in Russian eyes, the US will retain the ability to launch some 6,000 warheads.

The administration's plan is, essentially, to move warheads from one place to another, with no guarantee that they won't go back. The catch is that if the US keeps thousands of warheads in storage, so likely will Russia. The whole point of binding arms control is to provide both sides with confidence that limits will be enforced and thus arsenals can safely be reduced, permanently. Preserving the US option to reverse the reductions later will encourage Moscow to do the same. 'By failing to destroy nuclear warheads', said Senator Carl Levin, chairman of the Committee of Armed Services, 'the [Bush administration] would increase the threat of proliferation at the very time when the al-Qaeda terrorist network is known to be pursuing nuclear weapons'.[8]

Less than secure: the Russian complex

The size of Russia's strategic forces will dramatically decline over the course of this decade. Most of the Russian strategic arsenal of missiles and submarines will reach the end of their service lives by 2007. Projections show that Russia could deploy as few as 300 missiles and perhaps 20 strategic bombers by the end of the decade, with no more than 1,350 strategic nuclear warheads.[9] This means that about 3,500 warheads in Russia, containing roughly 84,000 kilograms of fissile material, will be removed from deployment over the next decade.[10]

74 **Jon B. Wolfsthal and Tom Z. Collina**

The life cycle of Russian nuclear warheads differs in several key respects from that in the United States. Deployed warheads removed from service are sent to central storage locations. Next, warheads are shipped from storage sites to dismantlement facilities, where they are taken apart, and their nuclear cores (plutonium and highly enriched uranium) recycled and replaced, before being shipped back to active storage or deployment. Unneeded fissile materials removed from warheads are shipped for long-term storage or eventual disposal.

Russia's nuclear reductions are supported by a network of US-funded programmes designed to secure Russian nuclear warheads and materials. These programmes are also working to downsize the Russian complex, so that Russia's ability to reconstitute its nuclear arsenal is reduced. These programmes were needed because, after the collapse of the Soviet Union, the Russian system was inadequate to protect its nuclear weapons and materials in a modern threat environment. These vulnerabilities in accounting and physical protection created an enormous risk of proliferation of nuclear weapons and material. It was quickly recognised that proliferation risks could only be reduced by securing nuclear weapons and materials in the near term and achieving their eventual verified elimination.

While imperfect, US sponsored programmes have made progress in securing Russian nuclear materials, and establishing a set of incentives and facilities that would ensure that Russian warheads were securely stored, dismantled and their nuclear materials eliminated. After a year-long review, the Bush administration endorsed the programme of cooperative threat reduction and weapons material elimination, building upon the work of the previous administration. The decision to store and not dismantle US nuclear warheads, however, will directly undercut efforts to reduce the size and vulnerability of the Russian complex.

According to the US intelligence community, the Russian warhead security system 'was designed in the Soviet era to protect weapons primarily against a threat from outside the country and may not be sufficient to meet today's challenge of a knowledgeable insider collaborating with a criminal or terrorist group'. General-Colonel Igor Valynkin, head of the military organisation responsible for warhead storage in Russia (12th GUMO), announced in October 2001 that security had been heightened earlier in the year after 'Russian authorities had twice thwarted terrorist efforts to reconnoitre nuclear weapons storage sites', according to the National Intelligence Council (NIC).[11] Although the terrorists did not succeed in entering the storage sites, according to Valynkin, the fact they tried is cause for alarm.

Moreover, according to the NIC, the 12th GUMO has suffered from wage arrears and shortages of food and housing allowances. In 1997, one nuclear-weapons storage site was closed due to hunger strikes by the workers. Although wages are now paid regularly, they rarely exceed $70 a month and spouses cannot earn second incomes since storage sites are usually isolated from cities. Acknowledging the potential vulnerability of its nuclear security personnel, Valynkin has said that 'the greatest problem is the person who works with nuclear warheads. He knows the secrets, he has the access, he knows the security system'.[12]

Much is already being done to improve Russian nuclear security through programmes run by the US Departments of Defense and Energy. Overall, these programmes have helped the former Soviet states upgrade their accounting of nuclear weapons and materials and physical security at dozens of facilities. Even so, according to the intelligence community, 'Russia's nuclear [security] has been slowly improving over the last several years, but risks remain'.[13] By the Department of Energy's (DOE) own estimates, even the most basic security upgrades over Russia's nuclear materials will not be in place until 2006.

The Russian weapons cycle differs from that in the US in one important issue. The US system is highly secure, while the Russian complex contains glaring vulnerabilities at virtually every step that pose a significant threat of nuclear theft and proliferation. Each major step – weapons storage, weapons dismantlement and fissile material storage – represent unique security problems.

Weapons storage

The United States is working with the 12th GUMO to improve the security of central weapon storage sites. Fences, alarm systems and response kits have been provided for 123 nuclear weapon storage sites and cooperation with the Russian navy to secure warheads is ongoing. In addition, the United States is helping Russia create a modern accounting and warhead-tracking system.

These efforts, however, are still in process and have not yet resulted in a secure system for storing Russian nuclear warheads. More than half of Russian storage facilities may still lack basic modern security features. Valynkin was quoted in the NIC report as saying that he was 'troubled because only a third of the new equipment had been put into service due to funding shortages ... Even with the enhancements, security problems may still exist at the nuclear weapons storage sites'.[14] In August 2001, an anonymous military officer claimed in a Russian television interview that security was lax at 12th GUMO sites. The officer outlined a number of problems at the storage sites, including charges that there are personnel shortages and that alarms systems operate only 50% of the time.

The NIC report points out that there is much work to be done before the Russian weapons complex can reach even minimum security standards and reinforces the need to maintain a vigorous sustainability programme for all US provided security upgrades. It is also unclear if the upgrades being provided by the United States will be implemented soon enough, or at a large enough number of facilities to handle the coming glut of offloaded nuclear weapons.

Weapon dismantlement

Russian warhead maintenance poses other challenges for the Russian security complex. Unlike the US, Russia cannot store its active warheads indefinitely. Russian warheads were designed to be routinely remanufactured. The plutonium removed from these weapons is shipped to purification sites and

76 **Jon B. Wolfsthal and Tom Z. Collina**

re-used. Throughout the 1990s, US efforts to provide security enhancements to Russian nuclear facilities have been constrained by Russian concerns over controlling access by foreigners to sensitive facilities. As a result, while much security work has been completed at research and civilian sites, some of the most sensitive nuclear facilities in Russia have not benefited from US assistance. This is especially true in the case of the four Russian nuclear-weapon assembly and dismantlement sites. These large complexes contain many tens of tonnes of direct-use weapon materials, and are believed to contain massive security vulnerabilities, including poor perimeter and facilities security, accounting and overall nuclear material monitoring.

Thus, if Russia responds to US policies by maintaining a large number of warheads in reserve and reducing the amount of material slated for elimination, the result will be a greater amount of nuclear material in various stages of processing and in transport – the two most vulnerable points of the weapons complex to theft and diversion.

This facet of the problem is especially disturbing since the warhead production facilities remain potentially the weakest link in Russia's nuclear complex. Because of the sensitive nature of these facilities, security upgrades at these sites have been slow. US personnel have not been allowed to oversee or supervise the installation of equipment, and the overall nature of security at these sites is unknown. These sites – Sarov, Seversk, Trekgornyy and Zarechnyy – possess many tonnes of direct-use nuclear material.

Moscow currently plans to close two of these four warhead production sites, and Russia's Ministry of Atomic Energy is seeking help to convert some of its weapons plants to commercial uses. Concerns over the reversibility of US reductions may lead Russia to reconsider its plan to quickly close these vulnerable facilities.

To help reduce the security risks posed by nuclear materials released from nuclear weapons and no longer needed for defence purposes, the United States and Russia are nearing completion of the Mayak Fissile Material Storage Facility. The facility – due to open this year – was built at a cost to US taxpayers of $397 million to store nuclear materials from dismantled nuclear weapons. Up to 66 tonnes or 25,000 containers of nuclear material can be stored on-site, and a second, equally large facility is under consideration. To ensure that the materials will not be reused in weapons, however, the facility is not permitted to accept materials unless they are placed under international inspection and are then slated for elimination. If Russia holds back a larger stock of materials for possible future weapons production, then those 'hedge materials' could not be stored at Mayak. The extensive security benefits gained by Mayak may never be extended to tonnes of vulnerable Russian nuclear material.

Nuclear materials storage
The nuclear security situation is worse in the areas of nuclear materials than in active or stored warheads. There are two potential sources from which nuclear materials in Russia could be stolen: loose nuclear materials outside nuclear

Nuclear Terrorism and Warhead Control in Russia 77

weapons; and nuclear materials made vulnerable during the warhead remanufacture process.

The Soviet Union produced the world's largest stockpile of weapons-usable plutonium and highly enriched uranium and these vast amounts continue to pose an acute proliferation risk ten years after the Soviet Union's demise. According to the NIC report, 'Russian facilities housing weapons-usable nuclear material ... typically receive low funding, lack trained security personnel, and do not have sufficient equipment for securely storing such material'.[15] These direct-use nuclear materials are stored in many hundreds of buildings at over 50 facilities across the country. As noted above, Russian institutes are known to have have lost weapons-grade nuclear materials in thefts. The US has been engaged in efforts to provide quick security upgrades at all 53 facilities known to contain nuclear material. Even when completed, security at these sites will not reach the highest international standards for physical protection and accounting.

This situation will only be made worse as Russian warheads are retired and dismantled unless the systems of security improves more rapidly and room is made within secure storage sites. The Bush administration, to its credit, is working to accelerate security upgrades and has proposed funding levels for 2003 well above its initial budget requests. However, it must be recognised that the Russia complex has inherent security flaws that can only be addressed by the permanent disposal of excess nuclear materials.

This disposal requires the downblending of weapon-grade uranium into forms not directly usable in weapons (low enriched uranium) and the transformation of weapons-usable plutonium into forms that are no more attractive for use in weapons as the plutonium contained in irradiated commercial reactor fuel. Altering these direct-use weapons materials into forms less attractive for theft and diversion reduces the risk that Russia's Cold War legacy will become the tools for would-be nuclear terrorists, and reduces the costs and difficulty associated with the long-term storage of these materials.

One argument frequently made as a possible remedy to the risk posed by the storage and management of Russia's nuclear weapons is to keep them where they are likely to be most secure – in active deployment. This argument maintains that weapons in storage can also be highly secure, since warheads are easier to count than loose materials in various stages of storage and manipulation. These positions, however, ignore several important facts. As regards warheads in active deployment, these weapons are going to come off active launchers as the majority of Russian missiles and submarines are retired over the next decade. This means that for most Russian weapons, continued long-term deployment is not an option. Second, the Russian strategic early-warning system continues to deteriorate at an alarming rate. Major gaps in the Russian system already exist, leaving it blind to potential attack, and open to the possibility of false attack readings and mistaken launches. Lastly, while it is possible to store warheads securely, US efforts to help the Russians to date have failed, and warheads will remain very attractive targets for theft and

78 **Jon B. Wolfsthal and Tom Z. Collina**

diversion. Also, due to the sensitive nature of the items being guarded, US access and independent verification of security measuress at weapon-storage sites is limited.

It is true that warheads must pass through various processes on the path to elimination – processes that can increase the near-term risk of the fissile material being diverted. This increased risk, however, is necessary to achieve the long-term security benefits that come with verified nuclear warhead and material elimination. The cumulative risk over time will increase as long as unneeded weapons are stored, and will decline over time as warheads and materials are eliminated.

This response, however, ignores two central facts. First, the majority of Russian strategic launchers are rapidly reaching retirement age. This means that for most Russian weapons, continued long-term deployment is not an option. Second, the Russian strategic early-warning system continued to deteriorate at an alarming rate. Major gaps in Russia's system already exist, leaving it potentially blind to potential attack or, worse, open to the possibility of false attack readings and mistaken launches. These reasons alone mean that continued deployment is neither possible nor advisable. One way or another, the Russian nuclear complex is going to have to absorb several thousand nuclear weapons over the next decade. The choice of how securely and quickly this glut is managed is, in part, in US hands.

Ten years after the launch of US assistance programmes, glaring vulnerabilities within the Russian nuclear weapons and material storage complex remain. Security upgrades are in process, but will take at least 5–10 years to bring the entire Russian complex up to basic security standards – to say nothing of the highest international standards. The strains on this complex are enormous, even to handle the material and weapons now in storage. The coming glut of nuclear weapons and materials from retired Russian weapon systems must be handled quickly and securely if their presence is not going to exacerbate an already dire situation.

Security experts know that Russian nuclear security is fleeting, and the longer nuclear weapons or material are stored, the greater the risk of theft or diversion. The assistance provided by the United States was never intended to create permanent solutions, but only to mitigate the risks of nuclear assets being stolen while the nuclear dismantlement process went forward. Unless this approach changes, efforts need to be made now to continue moving Russian warheads through the dismantlement and disposition chain. Prolonged storage is simply not a long-term solution.

What is the point?

The Bush proposal to store large numbers of warheads is as unnecessary as it is counter-productive. The United States has no foreseeable need to use nuclear weapons for anything other than deterring nuclear attack against itself or its allies. It is the unchallenged global conventional superpower as demonstrated in Iraq, Yugoslavia and most recently in Afghanistan.

Nuclear Terrorism and Warhead Control in Russia 79

Conventional forces are capable of anything from destroying enemy armies to effecting regime change.

The NPR and administration officials contend that a large responsive force is needed, in the words of Undersecretary of State for Arms Control John Bolton, to guard against 'uncertainty'. In addition, the NPR argues that the growing use of hardened underground bunkers around the world may require the development of a new breed of smaller, earth-penetrating nuclear weapons for use in rooting out these strategic storage facilities. But it remains unclear what possible targets the Pentagon could have in mind when it talks about maintaining some 5,000 warheads deployed and in the responsive force. Even if nuclear weapons were required to hold such underground targets at risk, their numbers would be small.

The US plans to retain up to 2,200 operationally deployed strategic warheads by 2012 – or up to about 2,500 when warheads on submarines in overhaul are included. This is more than the nuclear arsenals of China, France, the United Kingdom, India and Pakistan combined. It is far and away more than enough to deter any conceivable adversary, including Russia.[16] According to the Pentagon's Douglas Feith,

> the NPR's responsive force is not being sized according to the dictates of a possible resurgence in the threat from Russia. Instead, our new responsive capability is being defined according to how it contributes to the four goals of dissuading potential adversaries, assuring allies, deterring aggression, and defeating enemies.[17]

But what enemies does he have in mind? According to the intelligence community, China's nuclear force will pale in comparison to America's, even if Beijing builds up to 100 warheads on long-range missiles as projected. North Korea, Iran and Iraq could acquire only a handful of nuclear weapons over the next decade, if any.[18]

The new policy recommendations in the NPR envisage using nuclear weapons not only to deter nuclear attack against the United States and its allies, but also to deter and respond to chemical or biological weapon attacks, and even conventional attacks that produce mass casualties. It is possible that using nuclear weapons for these other missions may deter some from using chemical or biological weapons in the near term, but such threats will only spur the further development of nuclear and other weapons of mass destruction in the long term to deter US threats. Such development undercuts the US conventional advantage and reduces US freedom of action overseas. Moreover, it remains to be seen what type of conventional attacks would warrant a nuclear response. Against whom in Afghanistan would the US have launched a nuclear strike in response to 11 September?

Moreover, there is no conclusive or reliable evidence that the evolving policy to threaten nuclear retaliation against chemical or biological weapons has slowed the pursuit of such weapons by potential US enemies. Iraq and North Korea have long faced veiled and even open nuclear threats from the United States, and both have continued their weapons development

80 **Jon B. Wolfsthal and Tom Z. Collina**

programmes. The possible US use of nuclear weapons against North Korea, as much as its own insecurity, is seen as the driving force behind Pyongyang's pursuit of nuclear weapons. US nuclear threats during the Korean War against China fuelled its development of nuclear weapons. It is not at all clear that the thinly veiled nuclear threat made against Saddam Hussein in the Gulf War deterred Iraq's use of chemical or biological weapons, but may have only hardened his desire to resist UN weapon inspectors and hold onto whatever remaining WMD capability he still possesses.

Supporters of this new, expanded deterrence policy claim that the US must keep all options on the table in order to dissuade states from pursuing weapons of mass destruction. Deterring the acquisition and use of such weapons should be a top defence priority, but reliance on nuclear weapons for this mission is simply not needed and not credible. Empty threats only weaken the overall nuclear deterrent of the United States, along with its broader international credibility – just as such threats did during the 1960s and 1970s in Europe, when the US tried to rely on the threat of quick nuclear escalation to deter Soviet conventional attacks in Europe.

It would appear that the authors of the NPR have failed to consider, or have ignored, the implications of their recommendations with regard to Russia's response. As discussed, it is the Russian nuclear complex that remains the greatest potential source of nuclear weapons and materials for would be nuclear terrorists. Instead of making this already dangerous state of affairs worse by preparing for undefined and ephemeral threats, the United States should rely on its conventional firepower to hold targets and even regimes at risk, and make reducing the nuclear proliferation risk from Russia its priority.

What is to be done?

The United States should work cooperatively and aggressively with Moscow to securely store, remove and dismantle nuclear warheads, and facilitate the secure storage and disposal of the released nuclear materials. Whether acquired from a stored nuclear weapon, or diverted from some other part of the insecure weapons complex, a viable terrorist nuclear threat against the United States or its allies would be a devastating blow not only to the war on terrorism, but to global security overall. To pursue the goal of downsizing the Russian nuclear arsenal without increasing the proliferation risks in the Russian complex, the two governments should resume discussions on establishing a monitored and secure warhead dismantlement regime. The basis of this agreement should be creating an effective 'chain of custody' from when weapons are removed from deployed systems until they enter the disposal programme.

A significant amount of cooperative research has been conducted between US and Russian experts on ways the two sides could monitor warhead elimination without revealing classified information. Examples of techniques include the tagging of warheads as soon as they are removed from missiles and planes, dismantling the warheads in a manner that could be observed by both sides (while protecting warhead design secrets), and disposing of the fissile material or otherwise making it unusable in weapons (for example, the weapons-grade uranium could be blended down for use in power reactors and the plutonium could be burned in power reactors or mixed with waste).

The key benefit to this approach is that American monitors could be involved every step of the way. In theory, the US could have as much control over the process as it is willing to give the Russians over its dismantlement process. But herein lies the problem. For Russia to give America some control over its retired warheads, Moscow will want a reciprocal role in the US system. This means that the Bush administration would have to agree to dismantle those warheads coming off of strategic launchers.

Don't ask, don't tell

The Bush policy on stored warheads is akin to 'don't ask, don't tell'. In order to maintain flexibility, the US is willing to sacrifice the possibility of tracking the Russian warheads from missile to grave. And what does it gain? How important is it to maintain the option to return thousands of warheads to service?

Asked to explain the administration's rationale for keeping so many warheads on hand, Feith testified that, in addition to hedging against unforeseen threats, the reserve could make up for an imbalance in US and Russian warhead production capacity. According to Feith, it is no big deal for the Russians to dismantle their warheads, since Moscow can produce large numbers of new warheads if needed. But, says Feith, 'the United States today is the only nuclear-weapon state that cannot remanufacture replacements or produce new nuclear weapons', and until it can the US must depend on stored weapons. Feith's statement contradicts the Bush administration's position that the US arsenal is no longer sized to counter the Russian threat. Moreover, it is misleading.

It is true that, since 1989, the United States has not operated facilities that can produce new nuclear weapon cores, known as plutonium 'pits'. But other warhead parts can still be produced at other sites in the US nuclear-weapons production complex. Moreover, US plutonium pits can last significantly longer that those in Russia – perhaps 50 years or more.[19] Thus, if the oldest warheads in the arsenal are now approaching 25 years (such as the W76 warhead on the *Trident* missile, the W78 warhead on the *Minuteman* III missile, and B61 bomb), their pits should last another 25 years or longer.

Also, according to John Gordon of the National Nuclear Security Administration in the Department of Energy, there are plans to have a large modern pit plant built in about 15 years. Until then, the DOE has the capacity to build 20 pits per year, with a surge capacity of 50 per year if needed. According to Gordon, the US could produce new pits in about seven years in small numbers, and in large numbers in 15 years, well before there is a 'pit crisis'. The $5 billion stockpile stewardship programme, which continues to certify the safety and reliability of US nuclear weapons without testing, is in place to detect any potential problems. In the event that new pits are needed sooner in an emergency, there are already large numbers of pits in storage that could be reused. According to Feith, 'To be very strictly [sic] and technical, it would be possible, at least theoretically to put together a weapon from older components in some sort of a mix and match fashion'.[20]

While a case can be made for keeping a fraction of the deployed arsenal in reserve for reliability testing and to replace warhead parts that are found to be defective, this line of thought cannot support keeping a reserve twice as large as the deployed force. Moreover, there is no need to have any of these warheads in the 'responsive' force, that is, ready for rapid redeployment.

Finally, while it is true that Russia continues to produce warheads, it does so to replace older warheads, not to increase the stockpile. Russian warheads simply do not last as long as American ones, and thus must be rebuilt. Moreover, the size of Russia's stockpile is constrained because most of its missiles are nearing retirement, and there is almost no money for replacing systems. Production of the only new Russian missile is proceeding at a rate of seven per year, a rate that will leave Russia with the ability to field about 100 inter-continental ballistic missiles (ICBMs) by the end of the decade. Russia may well end up placing multiple warheads on its SS-27 ICBMs, and has options to further MIRV other weapon systems, including some submarine-launched ballistic missiles (SLBMs). But, if the Bush administration is truly worried about Russia's warhead production capability, then it should work to reduce the size of Russia's production complex and negotiate a cap on the number of warheads that Russia could produce in a year or agree to limit strategic nuclear-delivery vehicles as part of the agreement under negotiation. It is not clear, however, why this should be an issue, since the administration claims that it is not sizing the US arsenal to the Russian arsenal.

Easy choice

The Bush administration must choose. It can work with Russia to prevent nuclear proliferation and terrorism by bilaterally monitoring the storage and dismantlement of excess nuclear warheads and tracking the fissile material until it is no longer usable in weapons. Or it can keep thousands of nuclear warheads that have no justifiable purpose. But it can't do both. And when one compares the probability of nuclear material theft in Russia to the probability that the US will need to double the size of its arsenal in the future, the choice should be easy.

Nuclear Terrorism and Warhead Control in Russia *83*

Notes

1   Barton Gellman, 'Fears Prompt US To Beef Up Nuclear Terror Detection', *Washington Post*, 3 March 2002, p. 1.
2   US Department of Energy, 'A Report Card on the Department of Energy's Non-Proliferation Programs with Russia', Secretary of Energy Advisory Board, 10 January 2001.
3   National Intelligence Council, Annual Report to Congress on the Safety and Security of Russian Nuclear facilities and Military Forces, February 2002, p. 2.
4   *ibid*
5   Barton Gellman, 'Fears Prompt US To Beef Up Nuclear Terror Detection', p. 1.
6   Sharon LaFraniere, 'US, Russia Divided Over Iran After Talks', *Washington Post*, 20 February 2002, p. 2.
7   Statement of the Honorable Douglas J. Feith, Undersecretary of Defense for Policy, Senate Armed Services Hearing on the Nuclear Posture Review, 14 February 2002, p. 9.
8   *ibid*
9   This projection assumes 200 SS-27s with three warheads each, seven *Delta IV* submarines with 112 SS-N-23 missiles with four warheads each, ten *Bear* and ten *Blackjack* bombers, with eight weapons apiece. See Jonathan Wolfsthal *et al*, *Nuclear Status Report: Nuclear Weapons, Fissile Material, and Export Control in the Former Soviet Union*, report published by the Carnegie Endowment for International Peace, Washington, and the Monterey Institute of International Studies, California, 2001, p. 35.
10 3,500 × 4kg plutonium + 20kg weapon-grade uranium
11 National Intelligence Council, Annual reort to Congress on the Safety and Security of Russian Nuclear Facilities and Military Forces, February 2002, p. 6.
12 *ibid*
13 *ibid*
14 *ibid*
15 *ibid*, p.2.
16 In fact, half this many would be enough to deter any potential adversary, even if they had 10 times as many weapons. See *Toward True Security: A Nuclear Posture for the Next Decade*, June 2001, produced by the Federation of American Scientists, the Natural Resources Defense Council and the Union of Concerned Scientists, available at www.ucsusa.org.
17 Statement of the Honorable Douglas J. Feith, Undersecretary of Defense for Policy, Senate Armed Services Hearing on the Nuclear Posture Review, 14 February 2002, p. 9.
18 Foreign Missile Developments and the Ballistic Missile Threat Through 2015, Unclassified Summary of a National Intelligence Estimate, Central Intelligence Agency, January 2002.
19 For example, the W89 warhead for the SRAM-II missile (cancelled by President George H. W. Bush in 1991) was designed to use pits from retired W68 *Poseidon* warheads. These pits were then at least 18 years old. Assuming the W89 was expected to have an average lifetime, we estimate that pits can last at least two warhead lifetimes, or about 50 years.
20 Hearing transcript on *Nuclear Posture Review*, 14 February 2002, Office of Congressional Affairs, National Nuclear Security Administration, DOE, p. 23.

[27]

A New Vigilance: Identifying and Reducing the Risks of Environmental Terrorism

*Elizabeth L. Chalecki**

Environmental terrorism is an old type of conflict with a new face. Large, costly wars between two or more states have become less prevalent over the past 50 years, and with the end of the Cold War and the demise of the Soviet Union, there has been no bipolar superpower standoff to suppress the many ethnic, religious, and multipolar political and cultural tensions that motivate terrorist actions. Even the very nature of terrorism itself is changing. Attacks are becoming lethal to a greater number of people, as the events of September 11, 2001 demonstrated to the world. Most recent discussions of terrorism have focused on the identity of the terrorists, their motivations, and the increasingly destructive potential of the "weapons" at their disposal. However, to date, there has been relatively little discussion about their choice of targets. Environmental security scholars know that a strong argument can be made for linking certain resource and environmental problems with the prospects for political tension, or even war and peace. History shows that access to resources has been a proximate cause of war, resources have been both tools and targets of war, and environmental degradation and disparity in the distribution of resources can cause major political controversy, tension, and violence.[1]

Terrorism experts have opined that, in the last decade, the nature of terrorism has changed from professional, politically-motivated acts to amateur acts motivated by any number of grievances: religious, social, political, or personal.[2] There are well-known ambiguities in defining "terrorism" and specifically "environmental terrorism." Yet there are also real risks facing governments and the public and an effort must be made to better understand these risks and appropriate responses. An examination of environmental terrorism adds a new dimension to these definitions, identifying the target as a natural resource or envi-

---

* My thanks to Gary Wolff for discussions on the possible costs of environmental terrorism, and to the Ploughshares Fund for its support.
1. See Gleick 1993 and 1998; Lee 1995; Wolf 1998; Lietzmann and Vest 1999; and Baechler 1999, among others.
2. Gilmore Commission 1999; Hoffman 1999; Chalk 2000; Laqueur 1996 and 1999; and Wilkinson 1996.

ronmental feature. At a time when populations all over the world are increasing, the existing resource base is being stretched to provide for more people, and is being consumed at a faster rate. As the value and vulnerability of these resources increase, so does their attractiveness as terrorist targets. The destruction of a natural resource can now cause more deaths, property damage, political chaos, and other adverse effects than would have been the case in any previous decade.

This paper will define environmental terrorism as distinct from eco-terrorism and from environmental warfare, discuss the risk of environmental terrorism as a function of consequence and probability, and examine various types of attacks that use the environment both as a target and a tool of terror. Finally, several ideas for reducing the risk of environmental terrorism will be discussed.

Defining Environmental Terrorism

There are as many definitions of terrorism as there are acts of terrorism. Like pornography, it seems to depend on the perceptions and politics of the viewer. Terrorism as a concept first appeared in the Oxford English Dictionary in 1795 as, "a government policy intended to strike with terror those against whom it is adopted." Over the course of the next two centuries, terrorism went from being defined as government-sponsored policy to being regarded as anti-government policy. The word "terrorism" began to have an exclusively negative connotation by the middle of the 20th century, so that terrorist groups wishing to avoid bad publicity began calling themselves "freedom fighters," and governments employing terrorist tactics against opponents began calling them "police actions." Today, the word "terrorism" brings to mind hijacked airliners, the World Trade Center, and the violent death of unsuspecting people.

The FBI definition of terrorism states that terrorism is "the unlawful use of force or violence against persons or property to intimidate or coerce a government, the civilian population, or any segment thereof, in furtherance of political or social objectives." Title 22, Section 2656 of the US Code states that terrorism "means premeditated, politically motivated violence perpetrated against non-combatant targets by subnational groups or clandestine agents, usually intended to influence an audience." Both of these definitions concern themselves primarily with the motive behind terrorist actions and not with the selection of target, other than defining it as "non-combatant persons or property."

Regardless of the actual definition employed, acts of terrorism have four essential components: motivation, means, target, and enemy. For example, Osama bin Laden's motivation in the New York and Washington attacks was political and religious, his means were four jet airliners, and his targets were the World Trade Center and the Pentagon. But he chose those targets because they represented his enemy, the United States. Terrorists, whether groups or individuals, have various motivations: religious, cultural, political, economic, psychological, or some combination of these. The means at their disposal are often explosives, guns, poisons, or other destructive agents, although, as the recent at-

48   •   A New Vigilance: Identifying and Reducing the Risks of Environmental Terrorism

tacks showed, they can employ more creative weapons. Their enemies are usually governments or political figures, but with the advent of eco-terrorism, we
see enemies such as commercial developers and biotechnology firms. And their
targets are often chosen because of what they represent for the terrorists.[3] These
targets may be skyscrapers, federal buildings, and—rivaling both of those for the
amount of long-term damage that can be inflicted upon a country—*environmental resources.* For the purposes of this paper, environmental terrorism can be
defined as the unlawful use of force against *in situ* environmental resources so as
to deprive populations of their benefit(s) and/or destroy other property.

Environmental Terrorism vs. Eco-Terrorism

Most readers, when they hear the term "environmental terrorism" are actually
thinking of eco-terrorism. Not to be confused with environmental terrorism,
eco-terrorism is the violent destruction of property perpetrated by the radical
fringes of environmental groups in the name of saving the environment from
further human encroachment and destruction.[4] Based in deep ecology theory,
the professed aim of eco-terrorists is to slow or halt exploitation of natural resources and to bring public attention to environmental issues such as unsustainable logging or wildlife habitat loss through development.

Earth First! is the organization that first brought eco-terrorism to the public debate. Founded in 1980, Earth First! is known for tree-spiking in the Pacific
Northwest (although they have since repudiated this tactic),[5] and protests
against activities such as old-growth logging, road building in wilderness areas,
and dam construction. Its furor wound down under pressure from law enforcement groups. In addition, when the environmentally friendly Clinton Administration took office, the group believed that its agenda would receive positive attention.[6] The modern inheritor of the eco-terrorist mantle is the Environment
Liberation Front (ELF), an Earth First! splinter group formed in 1993 in England. In an action purportedly aimed at saving lynx habitat, the American wing
of ELF burned down a ski lodge in Vail, Colorado in October 1998, resulting in
$12 million in property damage, an act ironically repudiated by Earth First! it-
self.[7] ELF made headlines in January 2001, when members set fire to newly built
homes on Long Island to protest what they view as humans' unceasing encroachment on nature, and again in March 2001, when they set fire to a ware-
house containing transgenic cotton seed[8] and a biogenetic research facility at
the University of Washington.[9] Because the group is decentralized and ideologi-

3. Drake 1998, 53.
4. *San Francisco Chronicle,* 1 July 2001, A10.
5. See Judi Bari, "The Secret History of Tree-Spiking," *EarthFirst! Journal,* 21 December 1994, as
   found at bari.iww.org/iul20/local/Judi11.html.
6. Zakin 1993, 442.
7. FACTNet, Inc., October 1998, as found at www.factnet.org/cults/earth_liberation_front/
   vail_fire.html; and *Associated Press,* 23 October 1998.
8. *San Francisco Chronicle,* 6 March 2001, A2.
9. *New York Times,* 23 May 2001.

cally motivated, and thus extremely difficult to catch, the FBI considers ELF its number one domestic terrorist threat.[10]

At first glance, the distinction between environmental terrorism and eco-terrorism might seem academic. However, operationally there is a significant difference. Environmental terrorism involves targeting natural resources. Eco-terrorism involves targeting built environment such as roads, buildings and trucks, ostensibly in defense of natural resources. Earth First!, ELF, and other eco-terrorists do not practice environmental terrorism *per se* if they do not choose environmental resources as their targets. ELF has targeted a ski resort, houses on Long Island, logging trucks and office buildings, but has damaged no resources and killed no one. (In fact, ELF claims to go out of its way to avoid human casualties.[11]) It could be argued that ELF did commit environmental terrorism by burning the transgenic cotton seed. However, the members would likely argue that genetically engineered plants are not "natural" and hence are not an environmental resource. Their stated aim remains to inflict economic damage to built facilities in defense of the environment, an important distinction to be made when considering the intersection of environmental issues and terrorism.

Environmental Terrorism vs. Environmental Warfare

The difference between environmental terrorism and more conventional environmental warfare is one that mirrors the larger difference between terrorism and warfare in general. The easy distinction, that warfare is conducted by states and terrorism by rebel groups, obscures the uncomfortable fact that unlawful acts against non-combatants are often carried out by states. Warfare is governed by two complementary criteria: *jus ad bellum* (war must be declared for a good reason) and *jus in bello* (war must be conducted in a just fashion). The first criterion states that the cause for war must be right and that legal, economic, diplomatic, and all other recourses must have been attempted. However, the government of a state fighting a civil war might "rightly" see rebel forces as threats to the existence of the state, whereas the same rebel forces might "rightly" see the government as an oppressing force. Because there is no universally accepted judgment as to what constitutes rightness of cause, applying this criterion to terrorism is problematic.

The second criterion contains several behavioral constraints on the part of the combatants, chief among them the principle of discrimination: non-combatants are not to be targeted in the conflict.[12] Terrorism clearly violates the *jus in bello* criterion, since targeting non-combatants lies at the very core of its strategy. That the target is environmental and not human does not blur the distinction between warfare and terrorism. Environmental warfare operates within the larger objective of war: to defeat the enemy's military forces or capacity. The

---

10. *Washington Post,* 13 January 2001, C13.
11. *New York Times,* 8 January 2001.
12. For a more comprehensive summary, see Beres 1995; or Stern 1999.

50 • A New Vigilance: Identifying and Reducing the Risks of Environmental Terrorism

jus in bello criterion, the guiding force behind the Geneva Conventions and the Environmental Modification Convention, indicates that while collateral environmental damage may occur, environmental resources are not to be intentionally targeted during war unless there is a direct military advantage to doing so. The objective of environmental terrorism, however, is to have a psychological effect on the target population, and just as terrorists do not apply the *jus in bello* criterion to human non-combatants, neither do they apply it to the environment.

Risk of Environmental Terrorism: Consequence vs. Probability

The United States is a signatory to eleven major multilateral conventions related to states' responsibilities for combating terrorism. Currently, almost every federal agency has some responsibility for terrorism planning and response. The State Department, the Environmental Protection Agency, the Department of Defense, the Federal Emergency Management Agency, the Justice Department, the FBI, and others are all spending millions of dollars to prepare for and respond to acts of terrorism. For the FBI alone, counter-terrorism spending and manpower have gone from $78.5 million and 550 agents in 1993 to $301.2 million and 1,393 agents in 1999.[13] In fiscal year 2001, $1.555 billion have been requested to protect against chemical, biological, radiological and nuclear attacks.[14] In September of 2001, the US Congress authorized a $20 billion emergency fund to assist the victims of the September 11 attack and punish the perpetrators.[15]

Environmental terrorism, however, can be more efficacious than either a standard conventional weapon attack on civil targets or "weapons of mass destruction" (WMD) attack involving chemical, biological, radiogenic, or nuclear weapons, the "worst-case" scenarios. This is because its risk profile is different. There are two components to measuring the risk of terrorism: severity of the attack, and the probability of a particular scenario actually occurring. This is where the approximately $7 billion[16] spent to analyze WMD attacks may be misspent: scenarios such as detonation of a nuclear device or deployment of a biological weapon in a populated area, while frightening, fall into the high-consequence/low-probability category. As risky are the common, low-consequence/high-probability scenarios such as bombings or kidnapping (low-consequence only in that the number of people directly affected is relatively small compared to a large-scale WMD incident). Environmental terrorism has the potential to combine the worst of both of these scenarios: it can have higher consequences than conventional civil terrorism because the potential damage from an environmental attack can be long-lasting and widespread, and it is

13. Freeh 1999.
14. Chalk 2001.
15. *Washington Post*, 13 September 2001, A3.
16. *Weekly Defense Monitor*, 1 October 1998, 2.

more likely than WMD terrorism because it can be carried out using conventional explosives or poisons.

WMDs are still extremely difficult to obtain and deploy successfully, and are consequently out of range for most amateur terrorist individuals or groups.[17] As a result, terrorists may increase their destructive potential by directing conventional methods against environmental targets, where they are likely to cause more human health and economic damage with less risk to themselves. Federal counter-terrorism spending priority ought to consider what is practical and likely, not just what is flashy or media-induced.[18] This is not a suggestion that federal agencies no longer consider the risks and consequences of WMD terrorism, but rather that additional attention be paid to environmental terrorism.

Environmental Terrorism and Popular Media

RAND terrorism expert Brian Jenkins has cautioned that assessment of possible terrorist threats of any kind is heavily influenced by popular culture. Entertainment often portrays terrorist threats for suspense value, and environmental terrorism has begun to rank among those threats. Various novels and movies such as *The Monkey Wrench Gang*,[19] *H.M.S. Unseen*[20] and Steven Seagal's *On Deadly Ground* have featured acts of environmental terrorism such as blowing up dams and oil platforms for political or environmental purposes. According to Jenkins, policy-makers read these books or see these movies and become convinced that such a situation might actually occur. They then spend time and resources analyzing these "threats" and this very process legitimizes a scenario that otherwise might never have occurred.[21] It seems that while this caveat may be founded in reality, Jenkins' advice is unclear: do we withdraw terrorist scenarios from popular entertainment? Do we keep serious analysis of these threats secret from public knowledge? Do we assume that if a particular scenario appears in a movie, it's too outlandish to actually happen? We know this is not true: the pilot episode of the "X-Files" spin-off show "The Lone Gunmen" features a hijacked airliner being flown from Boston into the World Trade Center! If popular writers, and even the author of this paper, can think up scenarios such as these, it seems safe to assume that more motivated individuals such as terrorists can do so as well.

Another media angle arises when we consider the relationship of terrorists and journalists. Terrorism scholar Walter Laqueur points out that the media's preoccupation with some countries and not others and with cities over countryside leads terrorist groups to change their tactics so as to garner maximum media exposure.[22] Certainly the 24-hour media coverage following the New York

17. *New York Times*, 26 October 2000, A20; and *Weekly Defense Monitor*, 1 October 1998, 2.
18. *RAND Review*, Fall 2000, 5.
19. Abbey 1975.
20. Robinson 1999.
21. *RAND Review*, Fall 2000, 5.
22. Laqueur 1999, 44–45.

52 • A New Vigilance: Identifying and Reducing the Risks of Environmental Terrorism

and Washington incidents was every terrorist's dream, and environmental terrorists may have to follow this example. As environmental awareness increases in both the media and the general public, environmental targets begin to look more and more attractive as their importance to society becomes clearer.

Resource-as-Tool Terrorism and Resource-as-Target Terrorism

There are various ways to define environmental terrorism further,[23] but this report will consider two types: resource-as-tool terrorism and resource-as-target terrorism. The former occurs when environmental resources such as crops, livestock, or water supplies are used as delivery vehicles to carry a destructive agent to a human population. For example, terrorists wishing to inflict damage using resource-as-tool terrorism on a town below a reservoir might poison the water supply. Conversely, the latter occurs when the environment or resources themselves are targeted for destruction or compromise, with the collateral damages being felt by the population the terrorists wish to impact. Using the same example, terrorists wishing to employ resource-as-target terrorism might blow up the dam and flood the town. While these types of attacks are atypical now, according to terrorism experts,[24] they appear to be becoming more prevalent as terrorists adopt more single-issue agendas, and as WMD technology remains difficult to obtain and deploy. Moreover, there is a long history of the use of resources as both targets and tools during war.[25] Following are numerous examples of both types of environmental terrorism; the applicable type depends upon the particular environmental resource being targeted.

Vulnerable Resources

Criteria to assess the likelihood of an environmental attack can be developed by attempting to identify the attributes of a resource or a particular site that render it vulnerable to some form of environmental terrorism. Physical attributes such as scarcity and prestige of the targeted resource, its physical location, its vulnerability to attack and capacity for regeneration are the key determinants. Resources that are relatively inaccessible or heavily guarded are less attractive to terrorists, since attacking such a target presents less chance of successful escape. Geopolitical considerations also play a role: international terrorists striking at another country might choose a resource close to the border rather than one deep inside national borders. Scarcity of the resource is important, since greater economic and even physical hardship can be inflicted by attacking a resource such as fresh water, for which there is no substitute. Redundancy of the resource

23. Schwartz 1998.
24. Chalk 2000.
25. For examples related to water resources, see the Pacific Institute's water conflict chronology developed by Gleick (1998), also available on-line at www.worldwater.org/conflictIntro.htm. This chronology includes details of acts of environmental terrorism.

is also a consideration: a country with few freshwater sources is likely to be more vulnerable than one with multiple sources.

Other non-physical attributes such as economic, political, and cultural factors also bear on terrorist selection of vulnerable resources. Greater economic value, often linked to physical scarcity, makes a resource very attractive. Resources with high cultural or social value can also become targets: giant panda bears, California redwood trees, koalas, bald eagles, and the Nile River are all cultural icons for their respective countries, and have significance far greater than their economic value. One example is the recent intentional attack on an environmental icon—Luna, the old-growth redwood tree occupied by environmental activist Julia "Butterfly" Hill.

Water Resource Sites

Sites involving water resources are vulnerable to environmental terrorist attacks in the form of explosives or the introduction of poison or disease-causing agents. The damage is done by rendering the water unusable and/or destroying the purification and supply infrastructure. Water resource sites have many vulnerable physical attributes that make them attractive to terrorists. Most water infrastructure, such as dams, reservoirs, and pipelines are easily accessible to the public at various points. Many dams such as Hoover or Glen Canyon are tourist attractions and offer tours to the public, while many reservoirs such as the Triadelphia outside Washington, DC are open to the public for recreational boating and swimming. A terrorist carrying a small but powerful explosive device would not necessarily be conspicuous among tourists, sport fishermen, or hikers.

Water resource sites are also attractive to environmental terrorists because water is a vitally necessary resource for which there is no substitute. Whether its lack is due to a physical supply interruption or not, a community of any size that lacks fresh water will suffer greatly. Furthermore, a community does not have to *lack* water to suffer. Too much water at the wrong time in the form of a flood can cause greater damage, and flooding towns and settlements is a time-tested tactic in warfare.

Finally, water itself is an attractive terrorist weapon. Not only can it cause great damage in large quantities, as mentioned above, but the ability of water to spread agents downstream makes it a perfect method of transporting poison or disease-causing agents such as *Cryptosporidium* bacteria. As an example of the economic and personal chaos this type of attack can cause, the April 1993 *Cryptosporidium* outbreak in Milwaukee killed more than a hundred people, affected the health of more than 400,000 more,[26] and cost $37 million in lost wages and productivity. The outbreak was thought to be due to a combination of an improperly functioning water treatment plant and illegal pollution dis-

26. MacKenzie et al. 1994, 161.

charges upstream from the water intake point,[27] and not from a terrorist attack, but a similar outbreak in a large city such as New York or Chicago might cost billions and kill thousands of people.

An example of a resource-as-tool type of attack on a water resource site might be as follows. A terrorist hikes to a publicly accessible city reservoir such as Los Vaqueros, serving suburban San Francisco, and drops a certain amount of concentrated water-soluble contaminant (chemical or biological) near the intake pipe. In the best-case scenario, the contaminant is detected as it enters the water treatment plant, and the plant is shut down while the contaminant is neutralized. This can result in interruption of potable water service to the city and a "boil-water" alert for city residents. In the worst-case scenario, the contaminant is undetected and people begin to get sick, panic ensues, and health and economic damages soar.

Such scenarios are not purely hypothetical. Environmental resource-as-tool terrorism directed at water sites has already occurred. In July 2000, workers at the Cellatex chemical plant in northern France dumped 790 gallons of sulfuric acid into the Meuse River when they were denied workers' benefits. Whether they were trying to kill wildlife, people, or both is unclear, but a French analyst pointed out that this was the first time "the environment and public health were made hostage in order to exert pressure, an unheard-of situation until now."[28] Leaving aside the question of whether or not the workers would be considered terrorists, they certainly appear to have committed a terrorist act, since there was no way to isolate the effects of the acid from the general population, nor did they attempt to do so. As mentioned above, rivers and water supply infrastructure such as reservoirs are particularly vulnerable to this type of environmental terrorism, since they are publicly accessible in many places.

More common than these kinds of attacks are "resource-as-target" attacks on water resources. One such attack might involve a large hydroelectric dam on a major river. Terrorists equipped with a relatively small conventional explosive might not be able to cause serious structural damage to the entire dam, but they might be able to flood the dam itself and interrupt power generation. Alternatively, damage to the spillway gates could cause significant downstream flooding.[29] On July 17, 1995 a spillway gate at Folsom Dam broke under the weight of heavy flooding, pouring 40,000 cubic feet of water per second from the Folsom Lake reservoir into the American river and forcing the quick evacuation of fishermen, rafters and other recreationists, and homeless people living along the river banks.[30] It took six to ten days for the water level in Folsom Lake to go down so that the spillway gate could be fixed, during which time 400,000 acre-feet of water were released downstream, draining Folsom Lake of 40% of its

27. Smith 1994, 1.
28. *Christian Science Monitor*, 21 July 2000, 8.
29. James Mumford, Director of Safety Programs, Northwest Region, US Bureau of Reclamation. Personal Communication, 31 January 2001.
30. *San Francisco Chronicle*, 18 July 1995, A1.

capacity. This amount could have supplied two million people with water for one year.[31] A similar incident occurred in early January 1997, when heavy rains overtopped the Don Pedro reservoir. Filled to 100% capacity, water operators had to open the spillway and let out flood waters at a rate of 35,000 cubic feet per second, 3½ times the capacity of the downstream rivers and canals.[32] While neither of these incidents were terror-driven, they illustrate how much damage can be unleashed by manipulating an environmental resource. Flooding is not the only outcome. After the immediate flood pulse, there are water quality problems, as water treatment plants are overwhelmed. Fresh water supply is lost, as is hydroelectric power, commercial fisheries and recreation. Intermediate flood damage is possible if buildings remain in the flood plain. Finally, there is the expense of rebuilding the dam.

This type of resource-as-tool attack is also already occurring. In July of 1999, engineers discovered a homemade bomb in a water reservoir near Pretoria, South Africa. The dam personnel felt that the 15 kg bomb, which had malfunctioned, would have been powerful enough to damage the 12 million liter reservoir, thereby depriving farmers, a nearby military base, and a hydrological research facility of water. Police recognized this action as deliberate sabotage and began searching the country's other reservoirs for similar devices.[33] Even a simulated terrorist attack on a water resources site, the destruction of the Lake Nacimento Dam, caused some panic in central California until the media was notified that the situation was merely a disaster preparedness drill.[34] And most recently, Palestinians attacked and vandalized water pipes leading to the Israeli settlement of Yitzhar[35] to force the Israelis out of the settlement.

Agriculture and Forest Sites

Forests and agricultural sites have not generally been identified as terrorist targets, but attention to this kind of target is growing, and the economic and political repercussions of damaging or destroying such a site can be significant. RAND terrorism expert Peter Chalk recently pointed out that such "agro-terrorism" can have devastating economic, environmental, and human health effects, and the USDA has allocated $39.8 million to examine this problem.[36] Forests and farmland are vulnerable to destruction by fire or commercially-available herbicides, which can destroy both the growing crop(s) and render the land incapable of regeneration. While it is debatable among scholars whether or not the application of Agent Orange during the Vietnam War was a terrorist act,

31. *San Francisco Chronicle*, 19 July 1995, A1.
32. *San Francisco Chronicle*, 6 January 1997, A1.
33. *Pretoria News*, 21 July 1999, 1.
34. *San Francisco Chronicle*, 27 October 2000, A1, A23.
35. *Jerusalem Post*, 9 January 2001.
36. *Jane's Americas News*, 9 February 2001, as found at www.janes.com/regional_news/americas/new/jir/jir010209_1_n.shtml.

56 • A New Vigilance: Identifying and Reducing the Risks of Environmental Terrorism

since it made no distinction between the Viet Cong and non-combatants, Operation Ranch Hand destroyed 36% of the mangrove forest area in South Vietnam and without extensive reseeding, it will not return to its natural state for perhaps a century.[37]

Weaknesses of agriculture/forest sites include lack of natural borders, allowing fire or pathogens to spread from the targeted area to other areas. Depending upon the specific site, natural borders like roads and lakes are infrequent. Fires can even cross barriers such as roads when fanned by high winds, and dry weather conditions can make forests, fields, and grasslands more susceptible to fire. In addition, certain resources such as old growth forests may have historical and prestige value above and beyond what ecosystem services these resources provide. California's redwood trees, for example, are thousands of years old and their destruction would entail a far greater loss than just the timber revenue.

A hypothetical resource-as-tool attack on an agriculture/forest site might be crop poisoning. A well-known example of this type of attack was the cyanide poisoning of some Chilean grapes in 1989. While this particular incident caused no identifiable sickness, it was psychologically and economically effective: it caused panic in supermarkets and ultimately cost the Chilean fruit export industry millions of dollars in lost revenue by destroying consumers' trust. Just before Christmas in 1994, over $1 million damage resulted from the threat of poisoned turkeys in Vancouver, British Columbia.[38] Psychological effects aside, poisoning a crop during processing would be much more physically efficient and would reach many more potential targets. In addition, the increasing use of genetically modified crops could result in a transgenic agent being introduced into the germline of a particular crop, contaminating it on a permanent basis.

A disturbingly common resource-as-target attack on an agriculture/forest site might be a wildland fire set in a national forest. Forest fires can cause significant damage. In May 2000, a prescribed burn in the forest near Bandelier National Monument burned out of control and threatened the Los Alamos National Laboratory and the nearby town of Los Alamos, resulting in the evacuation of 25,000 people.[39] The fire ultimately destroyed 47,650 acres, 220 houses and buildings, and resulted in a total damage estimate of $1 billion, for which the federal government was forced to compensate local residents $661 million.[40] A fire set near a major city (e.g., Arapahoe National Forest, near Denver; Angeles National Forest, near Los Angeles; or Tonto National Forest, near Phoenix) could result not only in loss of recreational use and possible timber revenue (lumber sales and replanting costs), but also in additional economic and

37. Buckingham 1982.
38. Smith 1998b.
39. CNN, 7 June 2000, as found at www.cnn.com/2000/US/06/07/control.fires.02/
40. ABC news, 20 May 2000, available at: abcnews.go.com/sections/us/DailyNews/alamos000520. html; and ABC news 21 July 2000, as found at abcnews.go.com/sections/us/DailyNews/alamos 000720.html.

human health damage to city residents from evacuation, smoke inhalation, and fire-related property damage, as well as subsequent post-fire flooding.[41]

In a recent Report to the President, the Departments of Interior and Agriculture pointed out that the wildfires of 2000 were particularly fierce for two reasons. First, a severe drought across much of the country resulted in particularly dry ground conditions, and second, more than a century of aggressive wildfire suppression policy has led to a large build-up of dead trees, brush and other fuel.[42] As early as 1995, the Departments of Agriculture and Interior issued a policy statement that "predicted serious and potentially permanent environmental destruction and loss of private and public resource values from large wildfires . . . Conditions on millions of acres of wildlands increase the probability of large, intense fires beyond any scale yet witnessed, . . . These severe fires will in turn increase the risk to humans, to property, and to the land upon which our social and economic well-being is so intimately intertwined".[43] The wildfire risk is compounded by population growth in the nation's most forested states, and increased development along forest boundaries,[44] making a forest fire a very attractive terrorist tactic.

Forests and agricultural sites have generally suffered greatly as environmental casualties during war, but have not often been sought out specifically as terrorist targets. However, they have served as resource-as-target sites for repercussions in civil conflicts. Recently, the ethnic Oromo minority in Ethiopia has claimed that the Ethiopian government set virgin forests afire in its territory to pressure the group into withdrawing demands for autonomy.[45] As recently as November 2000, the Israeli army destroyed over 400 olive trees belonging to Palestinians in response to Jewish settlers' claims that rock-throwing children were using the trees as cover.[46] This destruction clearly had an economic impact on the Palestinians as well. Such precedents contribute to the perception that these sites are valuable targets.

Mineral and Petroleum Sites

Sites involving non-renewable resources with high economic value make attractive targets for violence of every kind. Oil refineries serve as attractive military targets during wartime, depriving the enemy of energy. Vulnerable areas of mineral and petroleum sites include the extensive and necessary infrastructure for the processing and transportation of the resource. Oil derricks, wellheads, pipelines, loading terminals, and tankers are all vulnerable to fire or conventional

41. Soot left on the forest floor from wildfires repels water and can keep the ground from absorbing rainwater (AP, 20 May 2000).
42. Forest Service 2000, 3, as found at www.fs.fed.us/fire/nfp/president.shtml.
43. Ibid, 6.
44. *San Francisco Chronicle*, 30 May 2000, A3.
45. "Politics of Forest Fire," *The Sidama Concern*, March 2000. Available at www.sidamaconcern.com/scfiles_news/sidama_politics_of_forest_fire_5l.htm.
46. *San Francisco Chronicle*, 29 November 2000, C2.

58 • A New Vigilance: Identifying and Reducing the Risks of Environmental Terrorism

terrorist explosives. Attacks on this infrastructure can create extensive environmental damage before being contained. In addition, oil spills can interfere with the normal workings of power stations and desalination plants by fouling intake water.[47]

Mineral and petroleum sites are also particularly attractive targets because of the necessity of the resource to the health and growth of the national economy. Fossil fuels in particular have no readily available substitutes, especially on short notice and in necessary quantities.[48] An attack on a loading terminal at a main oil field can halt commerce for weeks, causing shortages in fuel and natural gas, and costing millions of dollars in higher prices. An attack on a site where a strategic metal is mined (e.g., vanadium or tungsten) can cause economic damage, and possible strategic concerns, by forcing mine customers to buy necessary supplies on the less-reliable and often more expensive spot market.

Oil pipelines in Colombia have regularly been the targets of attack. In 1997, over 45 separate attacks on the Cano Limon-Covenas pipeline, reputedly by leftist guerrillas from the National Liberation Army (ELN), caused Colombia's national oil company Ecopetrol to declare *force majeur* on all exports from the Cano Limon field.[49] In 1998, the ELN bombed the OCENSA pipeline, spilling over 30,000 barrels of oil and triggering a blaze that killed more than 70 people when the fire spread through nearby villages.[50] The Trans-Alaska pipeline has had its share of attention: an episode of the TV drama "Seven Days" included a terrorist attack on the pipeline, and in August of 1999, the Royal Canadian Mounted Police arrested a man in British Columbia who had planned to bomb the pipeline out of political and financial motives.[51]

Categorizing the attacks as resource-as-tool or resource-as-target attacks is sometimes difficult for these types of sites: a single attack can have both types of consequences. For example, a hypothetical mineral and petroleum site for an environmental terrorist attack would be the Alaskan oil fields. An exploded pipeline or wellhead would not only waste the oil (resource-as-target terrorism), but would befoul the delicate and fragile Arctic ecosystem (resource-as-tool terrorism). The most obvious example of the crippling disruption resulting from such an attack is the destruction of the Kuwaiti oil fields at the end of the Gulf War. While it remains debatable as to whether this was true terrorism or a legitimate act of war, the damage done from this attack was almost incalculable: approximately 6 million barrels of oil were burned *per day* until all the well fires

47. Dabbs 1996, 2.
48. Alternative energy sources are limited; after Three Mile Island and Chernobyl, nuclear power has never been fully embraced by the public as a safe method of energy, and renewables such as hydro, thermal, and wind power are limited by the generating capacity of current technology.
49. Energy Information Administration 2001.
50. *Golob's Oil Pollution Bulletin*, 27 November 1998, 5.
51. *Albuquerque Tribune*, 24 August 1999, available at www.abqtrib.com/y2k/082499_y2k.shtml; and *National Post*, 24 December 1999, available at www.nationalpost.com/content/features/millennium/122499mill4.html. According to accounts, he planned to buy oil and gas futures before the end of the year, bomb the pipeline (which he hoped would be blamed on a Y2K foul-up), then reap large profits after the resulting fuel shortage caused oil and gas prices to rise.

were capped, and the people of Kuwait suffered health and ecological problems for years afterward.[52]

Wildlife and Ecosystem Sites

Natural ecosystems are probably the least likely to be identified as terrorist targets. However, the damage that can be done at such sites rivals only water resource sites for gravity and long-lasting effects. Any ecosystem attack has multiple repercussions, and wildlife-intensive sites are vulnerable to perturbation and habitat destruction. These resources are damaged by killing wildlife outright, or by destroying or rendering unsuitable its habitat. This type of terrorist attack can occur in conjunction with other types (e.g., a forest fire not only renders the timber useless, but destroys a mature ecosystem and deprives species of habitat). The vulnerabilities of wildlife sites include the endangered status of species residing there, and the cultural heritage considerations that attach themselves to specific species, such as California redwood trees or Koalas.

While not common, examples of this type of ecosystem attack do appear. In the Galapagos Islands, 600 miles off mainland Ecuador, local fishermen angry at catch restrictions killed dozens of internationally protected Galapagos tortoises in 1996.[53] In May 2000, the fishermen made a threat uniquely dangerous to the delicate and complex ecosystem of the Islands: they threatened to release birds, cats, goats, and weed seeds on the islands if their demands were not met.[54] This is a particularly dangerous threat, and not an idle one. The inadvertent introduction of zebra mussels in the Great Lakes in the mid-1980s has fouled raw water intakes along the coastline, altered the energy balance of lakes and streams, caused extinction of other aquatic species, and disrupted navigation, boating and sport fishing all through the Great Lakes. The US Fish and Wildlife Service has estimated damage so far at $5 billion and Congress has spent $150 million on methods to eliminate them or control their spread, unsuccessfully.[55] Ecosystem destruction such as that threatened by the fishermen may be so severe that the area may be damaged beyond recovery.

Island archipelagos such as the Galapagos are not the only type of ecosystem vulnerable to terrorist attack. Coral reefs present another extremely attractive target. The International Coral Reef Initiative estimates that ten percent of coral reefs worldwide are now degraded beyond recovery, and another 30 percent are on the verge of significant decline.[56] More are being destroyed every year by fishing and coral mining. Weakened as they are by routine economic activity, a physical attack against a reef with poison or dynamite could severely impact a country's economic base. Similarly, the destruction of an endangered species, if

---

52. Hawley 1992, 14, 110ff.
53. *Globe and Mail*, 19 October 1996, D6.
54. *San Francisco Chronicle*, 10 December 2000, A27, A34.
55. Ludyanskiy et al. 1993.
56. NOAA 1994.

60 • A New Vigilance: Identifying and Reducing the Risks of Environmental Terrorism

concentrated in a few locations would result in a symbolic loss, if not a strategic or economic one.

Recommendations for Reducing or Managing Security Threats

In order to reduce the damage that can result from environmental terrorism, resource managers and security officials will have to consider new ways to deter terrorism and to protect natural resources. In combating environmental terrorism, democracies face civil rights obstacles that more authoritarian states do not. Since draconian crackdowns on the population are not acceptable,[57] liberal states may take specific legal steps to address more specifically the threat of environmental terrorism. Terrorists are currently treated as criminals, and the political aspects of their acts are often ignored. A clear example of this occurred just after the September 11 New York and Washington attacks as every American TV station and newspaper asked repeatedly, "How could anyone do this to us?" The reality, however, is that American policies and action abroad have earned the enmity of many people.

In addition, until recently, environmental crimes were ill-defined and not often prosecuted. Specific anti-ecocide laws would punish environmental terrorists under the criminal code while making clear society's condemnation of environmental destruction.[58] Likewise, there may be circumstances related to the scope or severity of attack under which extraterritorial application of domestic counter-terrorism law is applicable and appropriate.[59] This would allow the United States and other countries victimized by environmental terrorism to extradite terrorists or take other protective measures outside their own borders.

An alternative step would be the explicit reclassification of "terrorism" from crime to acts of (unjust) warfare. This appears to be the direction in which President Bush is taking the United States: bringing military resources to bear on terrorist apprehension and other counter-terrorism preparation. Terrorists could be tried under military justice.[60] Terrorism expert Walter Laqueur points out that "many terrorist groups have without hesitation attacked the police and, of course, civilians, but have shown reluctance to attack the military. They must have assumed that the military would be a harder target and that there would be massive retaliation."[61] However, the reclassification of terrorism from crime to war has an ideological downside. Aside from the social repercussions of restricted civil liberties a terrorist is currently a criminal—a vandal, perhaps a murderer, but still a criminal. By calling terrorism "war," terrorists are elevated to the status of soldiers and their grievances are legitimized as battles worth fighting and dying for.

57. Wilkinson 2000, 38; *New York Times*, 12 December 2001, A1.
58. Schofield 1999, 620.
59. Raimo 1999, 1490.
60. Crona and Richardson 1996, 354–355.
61. Laqueur 1999, 37.

However, the explicit involvement of the military in the responsibility for counter-terrorism preparation and response raises its own major concerns about the diffusion of responsibility. Already there are approximately 40 federal agencies involved in counter-terrorism response, led by the FBI and including the CIA, the EPA, the DOE, and others. Making counter-terrorism preparation and response another Operation Other Than War (OOTW) responsibility of the military further muddies the water with regard to civilian authority and speed of response. Furthermore, the United States has always made an effort to separate domestic law enforcement from military involvement. While domestic OOTW assignments for the military usually involve disaster relief, using the military as law enforcement means crossing the boundary between civil and martial law, something democratic societies do not tolerate in non-emergency situations.

Regardless of the agencies or laws that are involved, successful counter-terrorism preparation can only be enhanced by more communication between terrorism experts and more specific recommendations to federal, state, and local policy-makers. The Gilmore Commission, a congressionally-mandated counter-terrorism advisory panel, has recently issued its second annual report, and first among its key functional recommendations is the call for enhanced sharing of terrorism intelligence, threat assessments, and other information.[62] This information sharing should include research on choice of terrorist targets, not just motivation or type of weapon. Further research questions may include how to clarify the differences between crime, terrorism, and warfare, since the quasi-criminal, quasi-military nature of terrorism tends to blur these distinctions,[63] and an examination of which particular places around the world will be vulnerable to environmental terrorism.[64]

Finally, the most reliable way for a nation to protect itself against the disruption caused by environmental terrorism is to diversify resource use wherever possible. Multiple sources of food, water, and energy mean each individual source is less attractive as a target, and equitable distribution of resources among users contributes to reducing tension over resource scarcity. This may decrease the political motivation of terrorists who take action on behalf of the "oppressed." In addition, federal, state, and local governments can protect environmental resources *in situ* through more intensive and focused monitoring efforts, in conjunction with increased environmental data gathering, a sort of "early-warning" system to identify future environmental risks.[65]

As this paper goes to press, acts of purposeful environmental destruction continue,[66] and the current climate has given rise to fears of further attack: security has been stepped up at water and energy facilities all over the United

---

62. Gilmore Commission 2000, ix–x.
63. Devost et al. 1996, 2.
64. Chen et al. 1997.
65. William A. Nitze, 16 January 1997, Office of International Activities, Environmental Protection Agency. Speech before the World Affairs Council. As found at www.epa.gov/oia/sp8.htm.
66. For example, *Environment News Service*, 5 February 2001, available at ens.lycos.com/ens/feb2001/20011-02-05-01.html.

62 • A New Vigilance: Identifying and Reducing the Risks of Environmental Terrorism

States.[67] Terrorism itself is a constant and fearful phenomenon, as America has learned to its recent and terrible cost, and like the nine-headed hydra of ancient mythology, as soon as one group or method is terminated, more spring up to take its place. The choice of environmental resources as targets or tools of terrorism is consistent with both the increasing lethality of terrorism and the growing environmental awareness on the part of the public.[68] The prevention of environmental terrorism will require a new vigilance: it calls for a new understanding of both the nature of the threat, and the formulation of appropriate and effective responses.

References

Abbey, Edward. 1975. *The Monkey Wrench Gang*. New York: Harper Collins Publishers.

Baechler, Gunther. 1999. Environmental Degradation and Violent Conflict: Hypotheses, Research Agendas, and Theory-building. In *Ecology, Politics, and Violent Conflict*, edited by Mohamed Suliman, 76–112. London: Zed Books.

Beres, Louis Rene. 1995. The Legal Meaning of Terrorism for the Military Commander. *Connecticut Journal of International Law* 11: 1–27.

Buckingham, William A., Jr. 1982. *Operation Ranch Hand: Herbicides in Southeast Asia 1961–1971*. Washington: GPO. As found at cpcug.org/user/billb/ranchhand/ranchhand.html.

Centner, Christopher M. 1996. Environmental Warfare: Implications for Policymakers and War Planners. *Strategic Review* 24: 71–76.

Chalk, Peter. 2000. Grave New World. *Forum for Applied Research and Public Policy* 15. Available at forum.ra.utk.edu/spring2000/grave.html.

_____. 2001. The US Agricultural Sector: A New Target for Terrorism? *Jane's Intelligence Review*, 9 February 2001. Available online at: http://www.janes.com/regional_news/americas/news/jir/jir010209_1_n.shtml.

Chen, Robert S., Christopher Lenhardt, and Kara F. Alkire, eds. 1997. Consequences of Environmental Change—Political, Economic, Social. Proceedings of the Environmental Flash Points Workshop, Reston, VA, 12–14 November 1997.

Crona, Spencer J., and Neal A. Richardson. 1996. Justice for War Criminals of Invisible Armies: A New Legal and Military Approach to Terrorism. *Oklahoma City University Law Review:* 21: 349–407.

Dabbs, W. Corbett. 1996. Oil Production and Environmental Damage. American University Trade and Environment Database. Available at www.american.edu/projects/mandala/TED/projects/tedcross/xoilpr15.htm.

Devost, Matthew G., Brian K. Houghton, and Neal A. Pollard. 1996. Information Terrorism: Can You Trust Your Toaster? Available at www.terrorism.com/terrorism/itpaper.html.

Drake, C. J. M. 1998. The Role of Ideology in Terrorists' Target Selection. *Terrorism and Political Violence*10: 53–85. Available at www.st-and.ac.uk/academic/intrel/research/cstpv/publications.htm.

67. *Chicago Tribune*, 23 September 2001, 1; *San Francisco Chronicle*, 21 September 2001, A19, A21; and *San Diego Union-Tribune*, 19 September 2001, A3.
68. Centner 1996, 75.

Energy Information Administration. 2001. World Oil Market and Oil Price Chronologies: 1970–2000. U.S. Department of Commerce. Available at www.eia.gov/emeu/cabs/chron.html.

Federal Bureau of Investigation (FBI). 2000. Counterterrorism: FBI Policy and Guidelines. Available at www.fbi.gov/contact/fo/jackson/cntrterr.htm.

Forest Service. 1995. *Federal Wildland Fire Policy Memorandum*. Forest Service, U.S. Department of Agriculture. December 20, 1995. Available at www.fs.fed.us/land/wdfire1.htm.

_____. 2000. *Managing the Impact of Wildfires on Communities and the Environment. A Report to the President in Response to the Wildfires of 2000*. Forest Service, U.S. Department of Agriculture. September 8, 2000. Available at www.fs.fed.us/fire/nfp/president.shtml.

Freeh, Louis J. 1999. Statement for the record of Louis J. Freeh, Director, Federal Bureau of Investigation, on President's fiscal year 2000 budget before the Senate Committee on Appropriations, Subcommittee for the Departments of Commerce, Justice, and State, the Judiciary, and related agencies, Washington, DC. February 4, 1999. Available at www.fbi.gov/pressrm/congress/congress99/freehct2.html.

The Gilmore Commission. 1999. First Annual Report to the President and the Congress of the Advisory Panel to Assess Domestic Response Capabilities for Terrorism Involving Weapons of Mass Destruction. I. Assessing the Threat. Santa Monica, CA: RAND, 15 December.

_____. 2000. Second Annual Report to the President and the Congress of the Advisory Panel to Assess Domestic Response Capabilities for Terrorism Involving Weapons of Mass Destruction. II. Toward a National Strategy for Combating Terrorism. Santa Monica, CA: RAND, 15 December.

Gleick, Peter H. 1993. Water and Conflict. *International Security* 18 (1) Summer: 79–112.

_____. 1998. *The World's Water 1998–1999: The Biennial Report on Freshwater Resources*. Covelo, CA: Island Press.

_____. 2000. *The World's Water 2000–2001: The Biennial Report on Freshwater Resources*. Covelo, CA: Island Press.

Hawley, T. M. 1992. *Against the Fires of Hell: The Environmental Disaster of the Gulf War*. New York: Harcourt Brace Jovanovich.

Hoffman, Bruce. 1999. Terrorism Trends and Prospects. In *Countering the New Terrorism*, edited by Ian O., Lesser, Bruce Hoffman, John Arquilla, David F. Ronfeldt, Michele Zanini and Brian Michael Jenkins, 7–38. Santa Monica, CA: RAND.

Laqueur, Walter. 1996. Postmodern Terrorism. *Foreign Affairs* 75 (5) September/October: 24–36.

_____. 1999. *The New Terrorism: Fanaticism and the Arms of Mass Destruction*. New York: Oxford University Press.

Lee, Martha F. 1995. Violence and the Environment: The Case of 'Earth First!' *Terrorism and Political Violence* 7 (3): 109–127.

Lietzmann, Kurt M., and Gary D. Vest. 1999. *Environment & Security in an International Context*. Committee on the Challenges of Modern Society - Final Report, March. Report No. 232. North Atlantic Treaty Organisation.

Ludyanskiy, Michael L., Derek McDonald, and David MacNeill. 1993. Impact of the Zebra Mussel, a Bivalve Invader. *BioScience* 43 (8): 533–544.

MacKenzie, William R., Neil J. Hoxie, Mary E. Proctor, M. Stephen Gradus, Kathleen A. Blair, Dan E. Peterson, James J. Kazmierczak, David G. Addiss, Kim R. Fox, Joan B.

64 • A New Vigilance: Identifying and Reducing the Risks of Environmental Terrorism

Rose, and Jeffrey P. Davis. 1994. A Massive Outbreak in Milwaukee of Cryptosporidium Infection Transmitted Through the Public Water Supply. *New England Journal of Medicine* 331 (3) July 21: 161–167.

National Oceanic and Atmospheric Administration (NOAA). 1994. The State of the Reefs—ICRI's Major Concern. Available at www.noaa.gov/icri/state.html.

Raimo, Tyler. 1999. Winning at the Expense of the Law: The Ramifications of Expanding Counter-Terrorism Law Enforcement Jurisdiction Overseas. *American University International Law Review* 14: 1473–1513.

Rapoport, David C. 1999. Terrorism. *Encyclopedia of Violence, Peace, and Conflict, Volume 3:* 497–510. San Diego: Academic Publishers.

Robinson, Patrick. 1999. *H.M.S. Unseen.* New York: Harper Collins Publishers.

Schofield, Timothy. 1999. The Environment as an Ideological Weapon: A Proposal to Criminalize Environmental Terrorism. *Boston College Environmental Law Review* 26: 619–647.

Schwartz, Daniel M. 1998. Environmental Terrorism: Analyzing the Concept. *Journal of Peace Research* 35 (4) July: 483–496.

Smith, G. Davidson. 1998b. Single Issue Terrorism. Commentary No. 74. Canadian Security Intelligence Service. Available at www.csis-scrs.gc.ca/eng/comment/com_74e.html.

Smith, Velma. 1994. Disaster in Milwaukee: Complacency was the Root Cause. *EPA Journal.* Summer. Available at www.epa.gov/docs/epajrnal/summer94/06.txt.html.

Stern, Jessica. 1999. *The Ultimate Terrorists.* Cambridge, MA: Harvard University Press.

Wilkinson, Paul. 1996. Security and Terrorism in the 21st Century: The Changing International Terrorist Threat. Available at www.st-and.ac.uk/academic/intrel/research/ctspv/publications1a.htm.

_____. 2000. The Strategic Implications of Terrorism. In *Terrorism and Political Violence: A Sourcebook,* edited by M. L. Sondhi, 19–49. Indian Council of Social Science Research. India: Har-anand Publications.

Wolf, Aaron. 1998. Conflict and Cooperation Along International Waterways. *Water Policy* 1 (2): 251–265.

Zakin, Susan. 1993. *Coyotes and Town Dogs: Earth First! and the Environmental Movement.* New York: Viking Penguin.

[28]

When Terror Strikes, Who Should Respond?

AARON WEISS

During the past decade, concerns about possible terrorist acts involving weapons of mass destruction (WMD) led Congress and the President to adopt a comprehensive counterterrorism plan focused on preventing a chemical, biological, or nuclear attack and enhancing domestic preparedness. The agency of choice for domestic consequence management has been the Department of Defense. Of the $1.4 billion appropriated in the FY 2000 budget specifically for WMD response, over half went to DOD.[1] Overreliance on the military for domestic WMD protection, however, may diminish the military's warfighting capability and holds the potential for infringement of individual rights.

Presidential Decision Directive 39 (PDD-39), signed in 1995, and the Defense Against Weapons of Mass Destruction Act of 1996 are the cornerstones of the United States' WMD terrorism strategy. This strategy is divided into four elements: intelligence and warning; prevention and deterrence; crisis and consequence management; and acquisition of equipment and technology. While crisis management involves the criminal aspect of dealing with a WMD attack, consequence management (CM) involves treating victims of the attack, searching for survivors, ensuring the containment of victims who are infected or exposed, and cleaning up the attack area.

A number of agencies are involved in domestic preparedness. The National Security Council is the interagency consequence management coordinator; the Justice Department, through the FBI, handles crisis management and is responsible for preventing an attack; the Federal Emergency Management Agency (FEMA) is responsible for consequence management after an attack; and first-responders include local municipalities and state governments. But DOD has been assigned a disproportionate amount of domestic consequence management responsibilities. This is due to the national security threat of WMD terrorism and the historical reliance on the military to solve complex domestic issues. The assumptions that led to PDD-39 and the Federal Response Plan may no longer be applicable, however, as new information and analysis draw differing conclusions on the threat of WMD terrorism.

This article will discuss the Defense Department's role in domestic consequence management following a catastrophic terrorist attack. Catastrophic terrorism, weapons of mass destruction, and "superterrorism" all refer to the use of nuclear, chemical, or biological agents to bring about a major disaster with death tolls of ten thousand or higher.[2] The scope of this article will be limited to the discussion of superterrorism and not include other types of terrorism, such as conventional terrorism or small-scale chemical or biological weapons (CBW) terrorism. Pan Am 103, Khobar Towers, and the East African embassy bombings were incidents of conventional terrorism, for example, and the Aum Shinrikyo's sarin attack in Tokyo was an example of small-scale CBW terrorism. While the threat is no less serious, the low probability and unique political circumstances of an incident of nuclear terrorism exclude such weapons from this discussion.[3]

Bringing the Issue into Focus

Four events of the 1990s significantly sharpened the nation's perception of chemical-biological warfare and catastrophic terrorism. First, Saddam Hussein used his intermediate-range Scud missiles to demonstrate the paralyzing possibility of operating in a contaminated environment during the Persian Gulf War. Second, the World Trade Center bombing in 1993 demonstrated that foreign terrorists could not only operate on American soil, but could launch a chemical attack.[4] Third, the Oklahoma City bombing in 1995 proved that domestic terrorists could harm the nation. And fourth, the sarin gas attack in the Tokyo subway by the Aum Shinrikyo cult made chemical warfare a reality.

The United States responded to the threat of terrorism, particularly superterrorism, when President Clinton signed PDD-39 in June 1995, PDD-62 in May 1998, and the 1997 National Defense Authorization Act. The latter included the Defense Against Weapons of Mass Destruction Act of 1996, also known as the Nunn-Lugar-Domenici amendment.[5] The statute and presidential directives are the foundation of the nation's counterterrorism response and provide guidance to federal agencies.

Captain Aaron Weiss, USMC, is a contingency analyst in the Programs and Resources Department, Headquarters, US Marine Corps, Washington, D.C. Previous assignments were as the air traffic control officer-in-charge with a Marine Expeditionary Unit; an air defense officer in Cherry Point, North Carolina; and a student at the Naval Postgraduate School in Monterey, California. In addition to his M.S. from the Naval Postgraduate School, Captain Weiss recently graduated with an M.A. from Georgetown University's National Security Studies Program. His previous publications include a Chase Essay Contest honorable mention in the *Marine Corps Gazette* (1997).

Following the PDD-39 signing, other terrorist acts reinforced the belief that it is not a matter of *if*, but *when* terrorists will strike with weapons of mass destruction. As Senator Richard Lugar commented in 1995, "Americans have every reason to expect a nuclear, biological, or chemical attack before the decade is over."[6] The Centennial Park bombing at the 1996 Atlanta Olympics and conventional attacks on the Khobar Towers in Saudi Arabia and US embassies in Kenya and Tanzania demonstrated a willingness to attack Americans worldwide. Discovery of Saddam Hussein's WMD projects reinforced the American fear of a group capable of combining terrorism with a chemical or biological weapon.[7] In November 1995, rebels from the state of Chechnya placed a small, encased radiological device in a Moscow park, but did not detonate it. The device was supposedly placed there in order to prove to Russian officials that the Chechens possessed radiological agents and were willing to use them in order to secure the state's independence.[8] When a rare African bird virus was discovered in New York City in the summer of 1999, it took only a small stretch of the imagination to conclude that the outbreak could be the opening shot in a biological war. Whether the terrorists were international cults or individual nihilists such as the Unabomber, each act of terrorism was confirmation that the country was heading toward a day of reckoning—the use of weapons of mass destruction on American soil.

Additionally, political rhetoric concerning WMD attack was dramatized, exaggerated, and sensationalized in Hollywood films and popular literature. Examples included movies such as *The Rock*, *Executive Decision*, *Outbreak*, and *Twelve Monkeys*, novels such as Tom Clancy's *Executive Orders*, Richard Preston's *The Cobra Event* and *The Hot Zone*, and television episodes of the *X-Files*, *Millennium*, and *Chicago Hope*.

Chemical and biological weapons were perceived to be as devastating as a nuclear weapon at a fraction of the cost and technical expertise. While nuclear weapons require expensive materials, sophisticated facilities, and highly skilled scientists, chemical and biological weapons seemed to require very little by comparison. Meanwhile, modern technology had vastly increased the lethality of chemical and biological weapons and made US urban centers vulnerable. The confluence of several trends in the middle of the 1990s heightened the potential threat of chemical or biological attack. First, the expertise needed to produce highly sophisticated chem-bio agents appeared to be rapidly proliferating. Second, the technology and materials needed to manufacture and deliver the agents was up for grabs in the global economy. Third, the will to use WMD appeared to be increasing among rogue states and terrorist organizations. And last, it appeared that some support for WMD terrorism was state-sponsored, providing various organizations with security, resources, and expertise. The joining factor of these trends was American military superiority. Rather than face the United States on the conventional battlefield, adversaries were seeking unconventional or "asymmetrical" alternatives.

The capacity to manufacture chemical and biological agents seemed attainable and the lower-level expertise necessary was thought to be increasingly

"Overreliance on the military for domestic WMD protection . . . may diminish the military's warfighting capability and holds the potential for infringement of individual rights."

available. One fear among US policymakers following the collapse of the Soviet Union was that of a Soviet "brain drain" to terrorist nations and groups. Examples of this concern were reports of Iranians trying to recruit former Soviet scientists,[9] and the head of South Africa's chem-bio program traveling to Libya.[10] Meanwhile, the number of doctorates in life sciences awarded to foreigners in the United States had increased by over 30 percent since 1970,[11] and the relatively open atmosphere at US academic institutions was considered a conduit of technical information.[12] Thus, the fall of the Soviet Union, the quest for alternative methods of warfare, and the availability of US education in the sciences had created tens of thousands of technicians capable of producing highly sophisticated chemical and biological agents.

The most important factor in the creation of an American chem-bio response was the changing nature of terrorism itself. As the 1995 Tokyo subway attack indicated, the United States was witnessing the emergence of a new type of terrorism that was not connected to specific political goals.[13] The trend appeared to be moving away from attacking specific human targets such as a nation's officials and more toward indiscriminate killing.[14] Fanatical ethnic and religious organizations were not constrained by the same considerations as terrorist groups with political goals. With no need for legitimacy, the new breed of terrorist could easily cross the WMD line.[15] The emergence of terrorist groups with access to vast resources was another aspect of the changing face of terrorism. The Aum Shinrikyo cult and Osama bin Laden's organization were prominent examples. The Aum Shinrikyo operated a number of front companies, possessed assets in the hundreds of millions, purchased helicopters from Russia, trained pilots in the United States, and sought to procure weapons from Russia, Australia, Sri Lanka, Zaire, and North Korea.[16]

Though the United States abandoned and destroyed its biological program in 1972 following the ratification of the Biological Weapons Convention Treaty, the collapse of the Soviet Union revealed that the former USSR had remained engaged in chem-bio weapons production. According to a 1996 US General Accounting Office (GAO) report, "Upon its breakup in 1991, the Soviet Union bequeathed a vast array of weapons of mass destruction to Russia,

Ukraine, Belarus, and Kazakhstan. This legacy included about 30,000 nuclear weapons, 2,500 strategic nuclear delivery systems, and at least 40,000 metric tons of chemical weapons."[17] More shocking to policymakers was the discovery nearly five years later that Russia's bio-weapons facilities were still in operation.[18] Equally troubling was the fact that China was also engaged in chem-bio weapons manufacture. China's willingness to export weapons cast a sobering realization about the proliferation of WMD capabilities.[19]

Further evidence of state-sponsored capabilities came from the Middle East. Weapons inspectors in Iraq reported a more mature chem-bio capability than expected, while the CIA revealed that Egypt and Syria also maintained their own chemical weapons programs.[20] Similarly, the number of other states pursuing clandestine programs to develop unconventional weapons capabilities turned out to be much larger than commonly believed. At the time of the 1996 GAO report, 28 countries either possessed, likely possessed, or had clear intent to possess weapons of mass destruction.[21]

Properly prepared and disseminated, one kilogram of anthrax could kill thousands. A 1993 study by the Office of Technological Assessment concluded that a single airplane delivering 100 kilograms of anthrax spores by aerosol on a clear, calm night over Washington, D.C., could kill between one and three million people.[22] Critics pointed to the dearth of consequence management programs and the lack of detection capabilities required for a coordinated response.[23] The situation was described in 1996 by Senator Sam Nunn as "one of the most urgent national security problems America faces."[24] In that atmosphere, a call to arms was made to utilize the resources and organization of the military to mitigate the domestic effects of the WMD threat to the nation.

What Good is the World's Best Military if You Can't Use It?

The Defense Against Weapons of Mass Destruction Act of 1996 (the Nunn-Lugar-Domenici amendment to the National Defense Authorization Act for Fiscal Year 1997) advocated the training of first-responders to deal with a WMD terrorist incident. In 1997, the Nunn-Lugar-Domenici Domestic Preparedness Program began training first-responders—firefighters, police, and emergency medical technicians—in 120 cities across in the country. As part of the program, the military specifically was tasked to "develop and maintain at least one domestic terrorism rapid response team composed of members of the armed forces . . . capable of aiding federal, state, and local officials in the detection, neutralization, containment, disassembly, and disposal of weapons of mass destruction containing chemical, biological, or related material."[25] The Secretary of Defense designated the Secretary of the Army to serve as Executive Agent for the coordination of this mission and to develop a Domestic Preparedness Plan.[26]

Chemical and biological warfare was naturally seen as a national security issue and, as defender of the nation's security, the military was seen as the appropriate tool to manage domestic consequence management responsibilities. Writing in *Foreign Affairs*, national security experts Ashton Carter, John Deutch, and Philip Zelikow suggested that the threat of WMD use by terrorists against the United States was "a national security problem that deserves the kind of attention the Defense Department devotes to threats of military nuclear attack or regional aggression."[27] Congress and the executive branch evidently agreed and chose to tap the experience, organization, resources, and mission-oriented nature of the military to play a significant role in domestic consequence management. The Defense Department seemed to be the only agency that had the program management skills and resources to set up an initial consequence management program.[28]

And why not? Historically, the military has been used to solve or spearhead responses to a number of complex social issues. The military's organization, discipline, and mission-oriented culture have made it an attractive choice for policymakers, especially since the end of the Cold War. Furthermore, each of the services has special chemical warfare units that are specifically organized, equipped, and trained to respond to nuclear, biological, and chemical attacks. Seeing the military's obvious competence in the Gulf War, the government increasingly turned to the military to solve its problems. As a result, military forces have been diverted to civilian uses with an escalating commitment to formerly ancillary duties. In *Atlantic* magazine, author James Fallows summed up the perception of military competency: "I am beginning to think that the only way the national government can do anything worthwhile is to invent a security threat and turn the job over to the military."[29]

Even before the Cold War was over, Congress used the national security justification to involve the military in the "War on Drugs," a responsibility previously assigned exclusively to law enforcement.[30] The military also was used increasingly in domestic law enforcement, even extending to a regular military presence in high-crime areas of major metropolitan cities.[31] The military services were used for civilian law enforcement in 1992 when President Bush issued an Executive Order for the US Marines, Army, and the federalized California National Guard to restore order following the verdict of the Rodney King trial.[32] In 1994, Army support was provided to the Bureau of Alcohol, Tobacco, and Firearms during the siege and assault of David Koresh's Branch Davidian compound outside Waco, Texas.[33] The addition of border patrol operations in the American southwest[34] made it a *fait accompli* that the military had added the new mission of domestic law enforcement.

Additional non-combat domestic duties were added. In 1992, the US Army and Air Force assumed a domestic disaster relief mission when they responded to assist after Hurricane Andrew in south Florida[35] and after Hurricane Iniki in Hawaii a month later.[36] The Navy and Marines contributed to disaster relief by assisting in the Philippines following the eruption of Mt. Pinatubo in 1992 and again in 1994.[37] Although a legislative measure to use veterans' hospitals for the non-veteran poor was defeated, military medical assets were used to relieve hard-pressed urban hospitals.[38] With academically qualified servicemembers in both the enlisted ranks and the officer corps, scores of military units developed teaching relationships with local schools in an effort to stem declining education standards and student performance.[39] The military has even been called in to assist in environmental cleanup,[40] promote wildlife conservation,[41] rehabilitate public housing, rebuild bridges, and aid in other community projects.[42] Somewhat similarly, the Army and Army Reserve perform extended peacekeeping duties in Bosnia and Kosovo as auxiliary duties in a non-combat role. To meet the new domestic and non-combat missions, DOD has established a command and control element for a dedicated Joint Task Force for Civil Support (JTF-CS) resident in Joint Forces Command.[43]

Security at What Cost?

More than 85 years of experience in defending against biological and chemical weapons and 50 years of experience in nuclear defense made the DOD the most knowledgeable and resourceful organization available to deal with incidents involving such threats. PDD-39 made WMD consequence management a national priority and the Nunn-Lugar-Domenici amendment legally tasked DOD with providing assistance to agencies and responding to any terrorist attack. The challenge at hand was to design measures to adequately aid first-responders and to protect citizens without crossing the delicate line that separates providing sufficient assistance from a state of marshal law.[44]

The increasing role of the military in law enforcement, including the WMD consequence management role, is a historic change of policy. Since the passage of the Posse Comitatus Act in 1878,[45] the military had distanced itself from law enforcement activities and enforced a broad proscription against soldiers enforcing the law. Domestically deployed soldiers were told that "they could not and would not enforce the law—i.e., detain, arrest, or serve warrants or any other kind of process on civilians."[46] Exceptions to the Posse Comitatus Act include activities expressly authorized by the Constitution and the President's authority to use federal troops to quell domestic violence.[47] Upon receipt of a proper request from a state governor, the President can issue a proclamation that a breakdown in public order has occurred and is authorized to order the Secretary of Defense and Attorney General to quell the insurrection and restore public order. According to Army lawyer Thomas R. Lujan, "By the stroke of a pen within a single day, the underlying framework for the authorized use of military force within the United States can be completely changed."[48]

Following Congress's "declaration of war" on drugs some 20 years ago, military involvement in domestic law enforcement has dramatically increased and has challenged the clear limits of a civilian-controlled Army at the operational level.[49] The Nunn-Lugar-Domenici amendment changed Title 10 of the US Code to allow the military to intervene in domestic affairs, even permitting the arrest of civilians in extraordinary circumstances. Congress has blurred the formerly clear lines delineated in the Posse Comitatus Act and made the exception to the act—presidential authority—not only more commonplace, but expected in response to domestic emergencies.

Faced with complex social and public safety problems on one hand, and an energetic and capable military on the other, Congress and the President have increasingly turned to the military as a cost-effective and proficient solution. As a result, the armed forces have been diverted from their original purpose. Continued reliance on the active-duty military for ancillary missions, such as counter-drug operations and WMD consequence management, will almost certainly have the effect of degrading the nation's active military with regard to its raison d'être. Preoccupation with humanitarian and peacetime duties will leave the active-duty military unfit to engage a real military opponent. Each day spent preparing a metropolitan police force for consequence management is a day in which perishable warfighting skills are not maintained or improved.[50] Military analyst Harry Summers wrote that when militaries lose sight of their purpose, such as the Canadian military in the interwar period, catastrophe results:

> Instead of using the peacetime interregnum to hone their military skills, senior military officers sought out civilian missions to justify their existence. When war came they were woefully unprepared. Instead of protecting their soldiers' lives, they led them to their deaths. In today's post-Cold War peacetime environment, this trap again looms large. . . . Some today within the US military are also searching for relevance, with doctrinal manuals giving touchy-feely prewar and postwar civil operations equal weight with warfighting. This is an insidious mistake.[51]

In addition to the degradation of warfighting capabilities, emphasis on domestic preparedness may have a negative effect on the military's ability to protect itself. Five years after the Gulf War, DOD still had not reached adequate levels of force protection against chemical and biological weapons, even as PDD-39 tasked it with new missions. A General Accounting Office study in 1996 reported that "some military units designated for early deployment . . . did not have sufficient quantities or the needed sizes of protective clothing, and chemical detector paper, and decontamination kits in some instances had passed their expiration date."[52] In the follow-up report two years later, GAO "found shortages in individual protective equipment, inadequate chemical and biological agent detection devices, inadequate command emphasis on chemical and biological capabilities, and deficiencies in medical personnel training and supplies."[53]

This Is Not Your Father's Chem-Bio Threat

In the mid-1990s the WMD threat to the United States appeared frightening, credible, and possible—it seemed only a matter of time until an attack became a reality. However, the perceptions of the chem-bio threat may have outpaced the facts. Recent studies at the RAND Corporation, the Chemical and Biological Arms Control Institute, and the Monterey Institute of International

Studies (MIIS) have challenged some of the assumptions made in the last decade and have brought chem-bio terrorism into sharper focus. Their underlying theme: using chemical or biological agents is more difficult than previously thought and not very effective as a terrorist weapon. Therefore WMD counterterrorism policies, structures, and appropriations may be focused on the wrong threats and have minimal effect in deterring a chemical or biological attack or effectively responding if an attack actually occurs.

One main reason there have been so few examples of successful chem-bio terrorism is because of its technical complexity. Gaining access to specialized ingredients or virulent strains, as well as the knowledge required to handle them, is not as easy as once thought. For example, in addition to the difficulty of acquiring some of the microorganisms suitable for biological terrorism is the challenge of packaging the agent as a weapon in a way that it will survive the delivery process. The risk of contamination to the people handling the organisms is high, and the most lethal bacteria do not exist well outside the lab. Additionally, dispersing microbes and toxins over a wide area as an inhalable aerosol requires a delivery system that is technically unattainable for most terrorists. Dispersion is also highly dependent on, and easily disrupted by, environmental conditions. A low-tech terrorist could avoid environmental uncertainty by launching an attack in an enclosed space, such as the Aum Shinrikyo attack in the Tokyo subway, but such an attack would not generate mass casualties. An attack on an urban water system is also very difficult, because an incredibly large volume of chemical or biological agent would be needed to overcome the effects of dilution and chlorine.

So far, the FBI has not obtained evidence that any terrorist organization has succeeded in building a device capable of delivering a mass-casualty attack. Aum Shinrikyo, for example, failed in ten known attempts in Japan to conduct biological attacks with either anthrax or butulinum toxin.[54] Despite the cult's vast resources (approximately $1 billion) and access to trained scientists, it has been unable to overcome the technical hurdles associated with the acquisition, cultivation, and delivery of chem-bio weapons. The Director of Central Intelligence, George Tenet, recently testified that "the preparation and effective use of [biological weapons] by both potentially hostile states and by non-state actors, including terrorists, is harder than some popular literature seems to suggest."[55] In the United States, no mass-casualty attack with a chemical agent has ever occurred, and there has been only one successful small-scale incident of biological terrorism, when the Symbionese Liberation Army used cyanide-tipped bullets to assassinate a school superintendent in Oakland, California, in 1973.

The Center for Nonproliferation Studies in Monterey has attempted to bridge the gap between anecdotal and empirical knowledge. The center has compiled a database of 520 global chemical and biological incidents that occurred in the 20th century and has analyzed 263 cases that were terrorist (not criminal) cases. Their conclusion is contrary to conventional wisdom about the catastrophic nature of chem-bio terrorism. Actual attacks were few in number, small in scale, and generally produced fewer casualties than conventional bombs.

The 71 actual attacks using chemical and biological weapons, accounting for 27 percent of the global chemical and biological incidents in the last century, produced 123 fatalities and 3,744 injuries.[56] Of these, there was only one American fatality and 784 nonfatal US injuries, of which 751 were associated with a single incident of deliberate food poisoning by the Rajneeshee cult in Oregon in 1984.[57] Historically, traditional terrorists have eschewed chemical or biological weapons for several reasons, including unfamiliarity with the relevant technologies, the hazards and unpredictability of toxic agents, moral constraints, concern that indiscriminate casualties could alienate current or future supporters, and fear that a mass-casualty attack could bring down the full repressive power of the affected government.[58] As Brian Jenkins of RAND has noted, "Terrorists find it unnecessary to kill many as long as killing a few suffices for their purposes."[59]

In contrast, individuals and nontraditional groups that have sought to acquire chemical weapons or biological agents tend to be motivated by a fanatical religious, supremacist, or anti-government ideology, and often have a paranoid, conspiratorial worldview. Because the acquisition and use of such weapons requires several well-trained members, individuals pose a unique but minor risk. Even with ideological groups, however, the use of chem-bio agents is often too much for some members to stomach and consequently their plans are sometimes compromised.[60] The MIIS study provides evidence that despite political rhetoric or public perceptions to the contrary, a massive terrorist attack with chemical or biological weapons is not necessarily inevitable. While terrorists wish to convince citizens that they are capable of striking anywhere at any time, the studies conclude that terrorism involves predictable behavior and that the vast majority of terrorist organizations can be identified in advance.

As mentioned previously, another fear of WMD proliferation was through Soviet "brain drain." Yet there has been no open-source evidence indicating that WMD materials or knowledge has reached terrorist hands from the breakup of the former Soviet Union.[61] Though the potential proliferation of weapons and expertise has to be taken seriously, several factors mitigate the danger of chem-bio defectors. First, most chemical and biological scientists who departed the Soviet Union have emigrated to the United States, Britain, Israel, and Germany for commercial jobs. Second, there is no evidence to suggest that scientists have alternately gone to Libya, Syria, North Korea, or Iraq to sell their weapons expertise. Third, some confidence can be gained from the professionalism and ingrained security culture of the scientists. Last, many scientists have family and cultural ties that make living in Pyongyang, Damascus, or Tripoli less appealing than remaining in Russia. And even where isolated incidents have occurred, the individuals have been in contact with state officials, not terrorist organizations.

Even though state sponsorship would greatly reduce the technical hurdles terrorists might face in delivering a WMD attack, a number of factors reduce the likelihood of that happening. No evidence of a state-sponsored chemical or biological attack on the American homeland exists. State sponsorship of chem-bio weapons has been extremely rare and confined to highly trained, disciplined special operations units rather than terrorist cells. Rogue states fear potential retaliation upon discovery. Risking retaliation and global condemnation would make even the most marginalized nation reluctant to cross the threshold from conventional explosives to weapons of mass destruction.

Divesting the Active-Duty Military of Domestic Consequence Management

Just as serious analysis of the threat has come under scrutiny, so has consequence management. Rather than having an on-call federal agency flying in at a moment's notice, the first-responders to a WMD catastrophe will be local firefighters, hazardous materials (HAZMAT) teams, police, and emergency medical personnel. Local agencies will contain the scene, provide first aid, begin the investigation, and maintain order. As broader understanding of the chem-bio threat increases, the need for federal involvement—notably the involvement of the active-duty US military—should decrease. Training, expertise, and equipment will still be needed, but state and federal civilian agencies can provide this.

Federal efforts to combat terrorism are organized along a lead agency concept. The Department of Justice, through the Federal Bureau of Investigation, is responsible for crisis management of domestic terrorist incidents. State governments have primary responsibility for consequence management in cases of domestic disasters, including major terrorist attacks; the federal government, under FEMA, can respond to state and local requests for support under the Federal Response Plan. This plan outlines the roles, responsibilities, and emergency support functions of various federal agencies, including DOD, for consequence management.

There are numerous local, state, and federal organizations that can perform consequence management. For example, the General Accounting Office reports that over 600 local and state HAZMAT teams exist in the United States to assess and act on accidents involving highly toxic chemicals and other hazardous materials.[62] In addition, numerous federal organizations provide advice, technical experts, and equipment to local incident commanders. Air Force Colonel Robert P. Kadlec, M.D., a professor at the National War College who also served as the Senior Assistant for Counterproliferation in the Office of the Secretary of Defense, points to "the increased role of nontraditional agencies in national security issues. The threat of CBW has required a coordinated response across the federal spectrum and caused agencies heretofore unconcerned with national security issues, such as the Department of Agriculture, to snap to attention."[63]

As noted earlier, directing the federal consequence management effort is the National Security Council (NSC), which is the overall interagency coordinator for US policy on combating terrorism and federal efforts to respond to terrorist incidents. Under the NSC, the National Coordinator for Security, Critical Infrastructure, and Counterterrorism integrates the government's policies on unconventional threats to the United States. The Department of Justice has responsibility for crisis management in a WMD event. Its Hazardous Materials Response Unit (HMRU) provides laboratory, scientific, and technical assistance to FBI investigations. The FBI also provides training, acts as an advisory group to local agencies, and plans to have HMRU teams in 15 of its 56 field offices. On the scene of the attack, the Federal Emergency Management Agency acts in support of the FBI until the Attorney General transfers the lead to FEMA. Though state and local officials bear primary responsibility for consequence management, FEMA is in charge of the federal aspects of consequence management on the scene.

The Department of Energy maintains the Radiological Assistance Program, which provides 24-hour access to personnel and equipment for radiological emergencies. The department's Nuclear Emergency Search Teams consist of engineers, scientists, and other technical specialists. These specially trained teams are deployable within four hours with equipment to assist the FBI in handling nuclear or radiological threats. The Environmental Protection Agency (EPA) also prepares and responds to emergencies involving radiological substances. The EPA has approximately 270 on-scene coordinators available across the United States, two Environmental Response Teams, ten Superfund Technical Assessment and Response Teams, and 12 environmental labs—all supported by the EPA's National Enforcement Investigation Center. The Department of Transportation holds the responsibility for protecting airports and responding to terrorist attacks on transportation hubs. Within the Department of Transportation, the US Coast Guard is the lead agency on incidents that occur in coastal waters. The Coast Guard has three National Strike Force teams that are equipped to handle major oil and chemical spills, but can also handle terrorist events such as HAZMAT emergencies.

The Department of Health and Human Services is available for on-scene support with its Metropolitan Medical Strike Team. The Centers for Disease Control is the federal agency responsible for protecting the public health of the country through prevention and control of diseases and other public health emergencies. The US Treasury Department utilizes the Bureau of Alcohol, Tobacco, and Firearms (ATF) as the lead agency in investigating armed violent crime, arson, explosions, and large car bombs. The ATF has four National Response Teams that can arrive within 24 hours to major bombing and arson sites.

If, in addition to this extensive civil structure, the government continues to rely on the military services for WMD consequence management, then greater reliance could be placed on the military's reserve components. The Nunn-Lugar-Domenici legislation required DOD to develop a mobilization plan to integrate

> *"Preoccupation with humanitarian and peacetime duties will leave the active-duty military unfit to engage a real military opponent."*

National Guard and Reserve forces in consequence management. According to the plan issued in January 1998, the Army National Guard and US Army Reserve must be ready "to train local authorities in chemical and biological weapons detection, defense, and decontamination; assist in casualty treatment and evacuation; quarantine, if necessary, affected areas and people; and assist in restoration of infrastructure and service."[64]

The Army Reserve has a disaster recovery mission and is responsible to its local citizenry. It also has 63 percent of the chemical units in the US Army, including 100 chemical reconnaissance and decontamination elements stationed across the United States that can perform basic detection and decontamination operations.[65] The Army Reserve also has eight battalion and three brigade headquarters, 26 chemical companies capable of providing decontamination support to military units or municipalities, two chemical reconnaissance companies, the only deployable biological detection company, and individual expertise that can be deployed as needed.

The Army National Guard, operating in its traditional civilian assistance role, can be a unique and invaluable asset in a WMD emergency. Local understanding of the community combined with training with other federal response teams makes the Guard a front-line defender in WMD consequence management. National Guard units are located in cities and towns across each state and are the governor's primary military asset; each governor commands them until federalized by executive order. The National Guard would be essential in maintaining order following a chemical or biological weapons attack and has taken on an increasing consequence management role following the Nunn-Lugar-Domenici legislation. Twenty-seven National Guard Rapid Assessment and Initial Detection teams have been created to assist local and state authorities in assessing the situation surrounding a WMD attack. These units are located across the country and, according to the DOD plan, may eventually increase to at least one team per state.[66]

Finally, states and local municipalities have begun meeting the consequence management requirement with their own internal resources due to their increased understanding of terrorist capabilities. In a 1999 General Accounting

Office report, many state officials indicated that they maintained a reliable
consequence management capability and "that their own experienced technicians
can not only perform sufficient detection and identification to begin to handle
the situation, but also work in the stressful, dangerous environment."[67] States
discounted the use of federal assets in some areas because they would not arrive
in time to be effective, especially since the federal and military units do not
operate routinely with existing state programs. Also, state officials "dismiss the
idea of fully relying on federal assets because of concerns about their availability
and responsiveness if the state ever needed them."[68] For example, the WMD
consequence management effort in the City of Los Angeles is, by design, a
self-contained response entity. It is deliberately devoid of federal agencies and
resources due to a perception that a federal response will usurp local control
without guaranteeing a timely response.[69]

Conclusion

During the middle of the last decade, the nation appeared to be on the
brink of a superterrorism emergency, and the military was the only agency thought
to be capable of an immediate response. The sense was that "an incident will
happen: WMD will be used against Americans in their own country."[70] The United
States seemed vulnerable to terrorists with access to technology, materials, and
expertise. The US military's organization, discipline, and mission-oriented culture
made it an easy choice for policymakers who wanted immediate action to counter
the threat of chemical or biological warfare.

The nation and the military have responded. More than 40 federal and
600 local agencies now stand ready to react to a domestic WMD attack—or to
an overseas attack if necessary.[71] First-responder training is being conducted in
local municipalities, by state WMD units, and across the nation. As the United
States continues to prepare and train for a superterrorist attack, the seeming crisis
that required immediate military involvement is waning. The abating emergency,
changing in part due to more fully developed views of terrorists and their
capabilities, marks an appropriate time to wean the active-duty military from
WMD consequence management, and to turn those responsibilities over to
civilian agencies and the National Guard and Reserve forces.

The sense of immediacy that drove the need for a chem-bio response
structure has been reduced, and while the threat remains, the probability of attack
is not what it once seemed. Weighing the concerns of military effectiveness,
national security, overall public safety, and the nature of the WMD threat, the
use of active-duty military personnel to prepare for WMD consequence management is a poor allocation of national resources. The primary reason for having a
military is to fight and win the nation's wars. While it can be argued that a WMD
attack on American soil and citizens would be an act of war, the diversion of
military assets to consequence management is not the answer. Conversely,

increasing the consequence management mission by active-duty military may actually increase the threat to the United States by decreasing the military's ability to perform its primary role. Potential terrorists, correctly ascertaining that a WMD attack would redirect large numbers of active-duty forces to consequence management, might be able to divert US combat power and resolve away from their respective region of the world.

Even more troubling is the provision in the Nunn-Lugar-Domenici legislation that basically repeals the Posse Comitatus Act in times of national emergency. The precedent to disregard "a law generally considered a great bulwark in our democratic society"[72] and add domestic roles to the active-duty military suggests a disturbing trend toward infringement of individual rights that makes Charles Dunlap's 1992 *Parameters* article, "The Origins of the American Military Coup of 2012,"[73] seem eerily prophetic. During debate of Nunn-Lugar-Domenici, Representative Bob Barr stated, "The potential for abuse is frightening, especially when you consider the egregious abuses of federal power that led to the Waco tragedy."[74] In the end, the local citizenry—supplemented with good planning, training, and equipment—will be the most capable responders to confront, contain, and counter a WMD attack.

NOTES

1. US General Accounting Office, *Combating Terrorism: Observations on Federal Spending to Combat Terrorism*, GAO/T-NSIAD/GGD-99-107 (Washington: GAO, March 1999).

2. Ehud Sprinzak, "The Great Superterrorism Scare," *Foreign Policy*, No. 112 (Fall 1998), p. 116.

3. For the purpose of this article, WMD refers only to biological or chemical weapons.

4. Stefan H. Leader, "The Rise of Terrorism," *Security Management*, April 1997. Investigators theorize that the World Trade Center bombers laced the bomb with cyanide due to the large amount of cyanide and manuals found at the bombers' residences. The cyanide was subsequently vaporized in the blast.

5. Colonel Robert P. Kadlec, M.D., USAF, has coined the terms "pre-Cobra Event" and "post-Cobra Event" to apply to the flurry of activity after 1995, referring to the well-publicized response by President Clinton after reading Richard Preston's book by the same name.

6. Senator Richard Lugar, quoted in William C. Mann, "Terrorists with Doomsday Weapons a Growing Threat, Experts Warn," *The Atlanta Constitution*, 1 November 1995, p. A6.

7. Barbara Crossette, "Iraq Gives UN Fuller Details on its Germ Warfare Program," *The New York Times*, 23 August 1995, p. A1; Laurie Mylorie and James Ring Adams, "Saddam's Germs," *The American Spectator*, November 1995, pp. 60-62.

8. Glenn Guenther, "Analysis of the Nunn-Lugar-Domenici Amendment," master's thesis (Monterey, Calif.: Naval Postgraduate School, 1998), p. 17.

9. Judith Miller and William J. Broad, "The Germ Warriors: A Special Report; Iranians, Bioweapons in Mind, Lure Needy Ex-Soviet Scientists," *The New York Times*, 8 December 1998, p. 1.

10. Peta Thornycroft, "Poison Gas Secrets Were Sold to Libya," *Weekly Mail & Guardian*, 13 August 1998.

11. Robert Traylor, "All Fall Down," *New Scientist*, 11 May 1996, p. 33.

12. Barbara Crossette, "Expert Says Iraq Got Bomb Data from U.S.," *The New York Times*, 23 March 2000, p. A4.

13. Eric Croddy, "Urban Terrorism: Chemical Warfare in Japan," *Jane's Intelligence Review*, November 1995, p. 520.

14. Walter Laqueur, "Postmodern Terrorism," *Foreign Affairs*, 75 (September/October 1996), 26.

15. John F. Sopko, "The Changing Proliferation Threat," *Foreign Policy*, No. 105 (Winter 1996-97), p. 20.

16. David E. Kaplan, "Aum Shinrikyo" (1995), in *Toxic Terror: Assessing Terrorist Use of Chemical and Biological Weapons*, ed. Jonathon B. Tucker (Cambridge, Mass.: MIT Press, 2000).

17. US General Accounting Office, *Weapons of Mass Destruction: Status of the Cooperative Threat Reduction Program*, GAO/NSIAD 96-222 (Washington: GAO, September 1996), p. 1.

18. Bill Gertz, "China, Russia Still Producing Biological Weapons," *Washington Times*, 8 August 1996, p. A6; and Gertz, "16 Biological Sites Identified in the ex-Soviet Union," *Washington Times*, 3 March 1992, p. A3.

19. Judith Miller, "Evidence Grows on Biological Weapons," *The New York Times Magazine*, 3 January 1993, p. 33.

20. Tony Capaccio, "CIA: Iran Still Holding Limited Stocks of Biological Weapons," *Defense Week*, 5 August 1996, p. 1; Barbara Starr, "Egypt and Syria are BW Capable," *Jane's Defence Weekly*, 21 August 1996, p. 15; Seth W. Carus, *The Poor Man's Atomic Bomb? Biological Weapons in the Middle East* (Washington: Washington Institute of Near East Policy, 1991), p. 60.

21. US Congress, Congressional Research Service, *Nuclear, Biological and Chemical Weapon Proliferation: Potential Military Countermeasures*, Report No. 94-528S (Washington: GPO, 1994), p. 3.

22. US Congress, Office of Technology Assessment, *Proliferation of Weapons of Mass Destruction: Assessing the Risks* (Washington: GPO, 1993), p. 54.

23. Richard K. Betts, "The New Threat of Mass Destruction," *Foreign Affairs*, 77 (January/February 1998); Ashton Carter, John Deutch, and Philip Zelikow, "Catastrophic Terrorism: Tackling the New Danger," *Foreign Affairs*, 77 (November/December 1998); Laqueur, "Postmodern Terrorism."

24. *Congressional Record*, 26 June 1996. Senator Nunn gave this testimony on the Senate floor during the debate of the Nunn-Lugar-Domenici Amendment.

25. US Congress, *National Defense Authorization Act for Fiscal Year 1997, Title XIV: Defense Against Weapons of Mass Destruction, Subtitle A: Domestic Preparedness* (Washington: GPO, 1996). Also known as Nunn-Lugar II. In October 2000, this responsibility was transferred to the Justice Department (FBI).

26. DOD Directive 3025.15 designates the Department of the Army as executive agent for consequence management planning and implementation with responsibility to task service components and commit assets.

27. Carter, Deutch, and Zelikow, p. 81.

28. Major Adrian T. Bogart III, personal interview with Chief Resource Management Officer, Consequence Management Program Integration Office, US Department of Defense, 4 May 2000.

29. James Fallows, "Military Efficiency," *Atlantic*, August 1991, p. 18.

30. Charles Lane wrote in "The Newest War," *Newsweek*, 6 January 1992, p. 18: "The Pentagon resisted the [counternarcotics] mission for decades, saying that the military should fight threats to national security, and the police should fight crime."

31. K. R. Clark, "Spotlighting the Drug Zone," *Pentagram*, 30 January 1992, pp. 20-21.

32. Douglas Jehl and John M. Broder, "King Case Aftermath: A City in Crisis; Bush Pledges Enough Force to Quell Riots, *Los Angeles Times*, 2 May 1992, p. A1.

33. Edward Walsh, "GAO: Military Aid in Davidian Siege Proper; '93 Support to FBI, ATF Cost $1 Million," *The Washington Post*, 28 August 1999, p. A6.

34. H. G. Reza, "Military Silently Patrols U.S. Border," *Los Angeles Times*, 29 June 1997.

35. Mary Jordan, "Bush Orders U.S. Military to Aid Florida," *The Washington Post*, 28 August 1992, p. A1.

36. Melissa Healy, "Administration Rushes Storm Aid to Hawaii," *Los Angeles Times*, 13 September 1992, p. A1.

37. Bob Drogin, "In Mt. Pinatubo's Wake, Buried Dreams and Lives," *Los Angeles Times*, 18 October 1992; and Reuters, "Hundreds Flee Philippine Volcano," *Los Angeles Times*, 12 March 1994, p. A11.

38. Scott Shuger, "Pacify the Military," *The New York Times*, 14 March 1992, p. 25.

39. Kurt Streeter, "Soldiers on the Front Lines of Hope," *Los Angeles Times*, 25 December 1998, Metro section.

40. Anne Garfinkle, "Going Home is Hard to Do," *The Wall Street Journal*, 27 January 1992, p. 12; and Peter Grier, "US Defense Department Declares War on Colossal Pollution Problem," *The Christian Science Monitor*, 2 March 1993, p. 9.

41. Michelle Rushlo, "Military's Role in Species Conservation Grows," Associated Press, 17 May 2000.

42. Helen Dewar, "Nunn Urges Military Shift: Forces Would Aid Domestic Programs," *The Washington Post*, 24 June 1992, p. A17; and Philip A. Brehm and Wilbur E. Gray, *Alternative Missions for the Army* (Carlisle, Pa.: US Army War College, Strategic Studies Institute, 17 July 1992).

43. Statement of General Joseph Ralston, Vice Chairman of the Joint Chiefs of Staff before the 106th Congress, Committee on Armed Services, US Senate, 9 March 1999.

44. Guenther, p. 57

45. Posse Comitatus Act, section 1385, title 18, US Code, as amended, provides the following: "Whoever, except in cases and under circumstances expressly authorized by the Constitution or Act of Congress, willfully uses any part of the Army or the Air Force as a posse comitatus or otherwise to execute the laws shall be fined not more than $10,000 or imprisoned not more than two years or both."

46. US Department of the Army, "Domestic Disaster Assistance, A Primer for Attorneys," Judge Advocate General's School, Center for Law and Military Operations, Charlottesville, Va.

47. Under 42 U.S.C. 5170b, reference (f), "The President may authorize the Secretary of Defense to use DOD resources for performing . . . emergency work that may ultimately qualify for assistance which is essential for the preservation of life and property." Also, DOD emergency work cannot exceed ten days without specific authorizing action.

48. Thomas R. Lujan, "Legal Aspects of Domestic Employment of the Army," *Parameters*, 27 (Autumn 1997), 90.

49. See 10 U.S.C. Sections 371-378, codifying judicially created exceptions to the Posse Comitatus Act.

50. Barton Gellman writes in "Strategy for the 90s: Reduce Size and Preserve Strength," *The Washington Post*, 9 December 1991, p. A10: In "interview after interview across the services, senior leaders and noncommissioned officers stressed that they cannot be ready to fight without frequent rehearsals of perishable skills."

51. Harry Summers, "When Armies Lose Sight of Purpose," *Washington Times*, 26 December 1991, p. D3.

52. US General Accounting Office, *Chemical and Biological Defense: Emphasis Remains Insufficient to Resolve Continuing Problems*, GAO/NSIAD 96-103 (Washington: GAO, 29 March 1996).

53. US General Accounting Office, *Chemical and Biological Defense: Observations on DoD's Plans to Protect U.S. Forces*, GAO/NSIAD 98-83 (Washington: GAO, 17 March 1998), p. 1.

54. Sheryl WuDunn, Judith Miller, and William Broad, "How Japan Germ Terror Alerted the World," *The New York Times*, 26 May 1998, p. A1.

55. George J. Tenet, "The Worldwide Threat in 2000: Global Realities of Our National Security," Director of Central Intelligence testimony before the US Senate Foreign Relations Committee, 21 March 2000.

56. During the Tokyo subway gas attack, 4,500 of the 5,000 "injuries" were thought to be psychosomatic.

57. In 1984, members of the Oregon-based Rajneeshee cult deliberately contaminated restaurant salad bars in The Dalles, Ore., with salmonella bacteria, affecting 751 people with diarrhea. Their objective was not to kill people, but to sicken voters and keep them at home in order to throw the outcome of a local election in the cult's favor.

58. Jonathan B. Tucker and Amy Sands, "An Unlikely Threat," *The Bulletin of Atomic Scientists*, 55 (July/August 1999), 18.

59. Brian Michael Jenkins, *The Likelihood of Nuclear Terrorism* (Santa Monica, Calif.: RAND, P-7119, July 1985), p. 6.

60. In 1972, an eco-terrorist group called R.I.S.E. was thwarted in its plan to wipe out residents around Chicago with a disease pathogen. Other group members, in disagreement with the apocalyptic plan, informed the FBI.

61. John Parachini, "Combating Terrorism: Assessing the Threat," testimony before the US House Subcommittee on National Security, Veterans Affairs, and International Relations, 20 October 1999.

62. US General Accounting Office, *Combating Terrorism: Use of National Guard Response Teams Is Unclear*, GAO/NSIAD 99-110 (Washington: GAO, May 1999), p. 2.

63. Colonel Robert P Kadlec, M.D., USAF, interview with author on 26 April 2000.

64. US Department of Defense, *The Department of Defense Plan for Integrating National Guard and Reserve Components Support for Response to Attacks Using Weapons of Mass Destruction* (Washington: GPO, 1998).

65. US General Accounting Office, *Combating Terrorism: Use of National Guard Response Teams Is Unclear*, p. 14.

66. In 1999, Congress expanded from 10 to 27 the number of Civil Support Teams (CST) of National Guardsmen to deal with nuclear, chemical, biological, or other terrorist incidents. The Rapid Assessment and Initial Detection (RAID) team name was changed in March 2000 as a result of this legislation, but most contemporary literature still refers to them as RAID teams. For the purposes of clarity and consistency, this article refers to the National Guard units as RAID teams.

67. US General Accounting Office, *Combating Terrorism: Use of National Guard Response Team Is Unclear*, p. 9

68. Ibid., p. 10.

69. Kadlec interview, 26 April 2000.

70. Chris Seiple, "Consequence Management: Domestic Response to Weapons of Mass Destruction," *Parameters*, 27 (Autumn 1997), 133.

71. The US State Department is the lead agency for managing and coordinating counterterrorism policy and operations abroad.

72. Lujan, p. 84.

73. Charles J. Dunlap, Jr., "The Origins of the American Military Coup of 2012," *Parameters*, 22 (Winter 1992-93), 2-20. In his article, Dunlap writes from the future to explain how the military lost its fighting capability at the expense of domestic missions as well as its ties to Constitutional government.

74. Pat Towell and Karen Foerstel, "Anti-Terrorist Additions," *Congressional Quarterly*, 20 July 1997, p. 2062.

[29]

EPILEGOMENA TO A SILENCE: NUCLEAR WEAPONS, TERRORISM AND THE MOMENT OF CONCERN

Achilles Skordas*

ABSTRACT

The cardinal issue examined in the article is whether international law can be relevant to nuclear decision-making, in particular in view of the worldwide activities of terrorist networks and the eventual military response of the threatened democracies . To deal with this issue it is necessary to examine not only whether the Advisory Opinions of the ICJ on the nuclear weapons interpret international law correctly or not, but also what quality of expectations for a future conduct they evoke to the addressees. The Court had the obligation to select not the most accommodating or 'moralizing' course of reasoning, but that interpretative alternative, which would both optimize prevention and maximize stability in the international system. From that view, the wisdom of the two Opinions seems open to questioning. The 'gap' proclaimed by the Court, as well as the recognition of a 'right to self-preservation' of the state, have 'nationalized' the nuclear weapons question in the Post Cold War era. The Opinion for the UNGA can thus induce societies under strong internal and external pressure to wage a desperate 'exit' with nuclear weapons. This Opinion is doctrinally inconsistent and it raises implicitly fear into a normative standard. Bearing in mind that a general and complete prohibition would be ineffective, it seems that a third legal strategy would have served the cause of peace and stability far better. The Court could have explicitly recognized an entitlement of states to have recourse to a nuclear strategy under very restrictive conditions, in particular for the protection of those supreme national interests that also constitute major collective interests of the international community. The actual exercise of that entitlement would have been restrained by the obligation of the states to fully respect jus ad bellum *and* jus in bello *in all circumstances. The difference with the psychological background of the* non-liquet *is clear: the need to fully comply with international law and the decision not to surrender to the envisaged threat, are capable of mobilizing the species-specific resource of 'anxiety' – not of fear – and of awakening the 'moment of concern'. Unfortunately, the Court has 'fled' in the face of its own systemic function and adopted an Opinion that transmits the wrong message to the addressees, inducing them to an atavistic response to the threat.*

* Dr. jur. (Frankfurt/Main), Assistant Professor, University of Athens, Faculty of Law (skordas@law.uoa.gr), Visiting Research Fellow, Max Planck Institute for Comparative Public Law and International Law, Heidelberg. The author would like to thank Oren Gross, Assistant Professor, Tel Aviv University, for his comments on an earlier draft of this article.

192   *Achilles Skordas*

1 THE KILLING OF THE INNOCENT IN THE NEW NUCLEAR AGE

1.1 The Silence of the Court and State Survival

The ICJ Advisory Opinions on the threat or use of nuclear weapons[1] have been already extensively commented on in the legal literature; however, an existential issue of that kind can resurface, when intellectually challenging positions are seen in the light of new developments in international practice and in international relations. The opportunity has been given by two essays, the first by M. Koskenniemi titled 'The Silence of Law/the Voice of Justice',[2] and the second by M. Kohen on 'The Notion of "State Survival" in International Law'.[3] The new practice is the '*Final Report to the Prosecutor of the ICTY by the Committee Established to Review the NATO Bombing Campaign Against the Federal Republic of Yugoslavia*'.[4] The Report demonstrated the way in which the principle of proportionality is to be applied through the examination of eventual commitment of serious violations of the international humanitarian law during a 'high tech' armed conflict and illuminated the function of the proportionality principle in these circumstances. Furthermore, after the terrorist attacks of September 11, 2001 against the United States, the risk of the threat or use of nuclear weapons or of other weapons of mass destruction does not belong to the sphere of the unthinkable any more. Nuclear terrorism is an eventuality the international community cannot evade any more. A reassessment of the legal aspects is therefore necessary, more than ever.

Koskenniemi formulated an argument that deserves further attention. He maintained that the Court proclaimed a *non-liquet,* because it touched the limits of the capacity of legal language having to determine the conditions for the 'massive

---

[1] Advisory Opinion, *Legality of the Use by a State of Nuclear Weapons in Armed Conflict,* ICJ Reports (1996) 66 [Opinion for WHO]; Advisory Opinion, *Legality of the Threat or Use of Nuclear Weapons* , ICJ Reports (1996) 226 [Opinion for UNGA]. In para. 96 of the Opinion for UNGA, the ICJ stated that: 'Furthermore, the Court cannot lose sight of the fundamental right of every State to survival, and thus its right to resort to self-defense, in accordance with Art. 51 of the Charter, when its survival is at stake'. In the operative part of that Opinion, the Court formulated its final position as follows (2E, second paragraph): 'However, in view of the current state of international law, and of the elements of fact at its disposal, the Court cannot conclude definitively whether the threat or use of nuclear weapons would be lawful or unlawful in an extreme circumstance of self-defence, in which the very survival of a State would be at stake'. In that way, it recognized the existence of a gap in international law, which does not enable the Court to give a definite answer to the question put by the UN General Assembly.

[2] In L. Boisson de Chazournes /Ph. Sands (eds), *International Law, the International Court of Justice and Nuclear Weapons* (1999) 488–510. A first version of the essay was published with the title 'Faith, Identity, and the Killing of the Innocent: International Lawyers and Nuclear Weapons' (1997) 10 *LJIL* 137–162.

[3] In Biosson de Chazournes and Sands, *op. cit.*, 293–314.

[4] PR/PIS/510-E of 13 June 2000 (*ICTY Report on NATO Bombing Campaign*).

killing of the innocent'.[5] For Koskenniemi, the paradox of an absolute rule for the prohibition of nuclear weapons is that it can be 'softened' by a relative rule, which could provide grounds justifying the use of those weapons under specific circumstances; for instance, if such use would be the only means available to prevent a nuclear attack from a nuclear submarine. The limits of the potentially legitimate use of nuclear weapons could then be determined by the principle of proportionality. This would lead to a legal-technical analysis breaking a major taboo:

> By lifting the matter onto the level of judicial reason, the Court would have broken the taboo against any use of nuclear weapons. It would have opened a professionally honourable and perhaps even a tragically pleasurable way of addressing the unaddressable. The (massive) killing of the innocent would have become another contextual determinant, a banal 'factor' in an overall balancing of the utilities, to be compared with the equally banal factors of sovereignty, military objectives, and so on.[6]

Thus, he suggests that the emphasis must be shifted from the idea of law as an 'integral and closed system' to institutional morality and the person of the judge.[7] According to this point of view, the silence of the Court is fully justified. The professionalism of judges retreats before the need to move the killing of the innocent away from the realm of rationality 'to the realm of the incommensurate and the emotional'. The author concludes that in this particular point, the language of law becomes incompatible with the voice of justice: 'For the voice of justice to be heard, law must sometimes remain silent'.[8] He considers the Advisory Opinion for the UNGA as successful, given that the Court *had* to abstain from defining rules on a possible use of nuclear weapons. He defends this silence and criticizes what he calls 'modern law's totalising ambition'.[9]

Kohen has brilliantly criticized the central notion, upon which the *lacuna* of international law has been established by the Court, namely the notion of 'state survival' and 'self-preservation'. The author finds no convincing argument that the survival of a state is a right protected under international law, although the Opinion tends to this direction. Self-defence or the state of necessity in contemporary

---

[5] More than a quarter of a century ago, Fred Iklé had spoken of the 'mass killing of hostages', when he criticized the doctrine of retaliation against the population centres of the opponent, in 'Can Nuclear Deterrence Last Out the Century?' (1972–1973) 51 *Foreign Affairs* 267–285, in particular at 281. Iklé favoured instead a policy of 'smart bomb' technologies, *ibid.*, 282–285.

[6] Koskenniemi, *loc. cit.*, 496–497.

[7] Koskenniemi describes as follows Hannah Arendt's observation on the Eichmann process: 'For Arendt, the role of the President of the Court became crucial. Steering between the political excesses of the prosecution and the half-hearted technicalities of the defence, it was the President's moral intuition, his sense of justice and his acting as a moral agent in his own right, and not as an impersonal mouth of the law, that salvaged the Jerusalem trial and made it an act of justice instead of its contrary', *ibid.*, 506.

[8] *Ibid.*, 489. See also 507–510.

[9] *Ibid.*, 489.

194   *Achilles Skordas*

international law does not bring about a right to self-preservation of states. And he then remarks:

> As has been rightly pointed out, survival is an instinct, not a right. And when acting under instinctive pressure, states often violate international law.[10]

In an earlier essay, Kohen had differentiated between the policy of deterrence and the actual use of force: deterrence would then be lawful, but the use of nuclear weapons unlawful.[11] The advantage of that position is its conceptual clarity and the capacity conferred upon the observer to distinguish, in times of peace as well as in times of armed conflict, legal from illegal conduct. Considering, however, the fundamental function of legal norms to guide the conduct of the addressees, it is apparent that this interpretative approach destabilizes the conceptual horizon of the decision-makers. It permits nuclear powers to organize an extremely complex and sensible system on the eventual use of force; it enables them to develop first or second strike doctrines, flexible response or assured destruction strategies or to construct escalation ladders with the purpose of deterring a general war.[12] However, when the 'extreme circumstances' arise, it presents them with the clear-cut dilemma either to remain passive and face annihilation, or to commit the most serious international crimes. It also shutters the normative perspective of the non-nuclear weapon states because, if the nuclear power is law-abiding, it shall not be able to effectively protect third states relying on its nuclear umbrella. Rogue states or terrorist organizations will be encouraged by the compliance of a nuclear-weapons state to international law, to pursue their 'agenda' even with recourse to threat or use of chemical or nuclear weapons without fearing a commensurate retaliation. A nuclear power that does not abide by international law might be more trustworthy, because it can be expected to act at least for the protection of its own strategic and global interests. The preventive function of defence planning is thus impaired and any rationalization and conduct guidance the law is expected to promote is hopelessly abandoned. Consequently, uncertainty arising from the breakdown of norms is capable of placing the potential victim, once again, on instinct.

The state is presented in the ICJ Opinion as an entity with an existence and life of its own. The Court's terminology is reminiscent of those theories in the German discourse of early constitutionalism, which emphasized the biological and living aspect of the state as an organism. If the state is a being-within-history and has the potential to evolve, grow and develop,[13] it also faces the eventuality of physical end

[10] Kohen, *loc. cit.*, 313.
[11] Kohen, 'L'avis consultatif de la CIJ sur la *Licéité de la menace ou de l'emploi d'armes nucléaires* et la fonction judiciaire' (1997) 8 *EJIL* 355.
[12] See on these strategies L. Freedman, 'The First Two Generations of Nuclear Strategists', in P. Paret (ed.), *Makers of Modern Strategy from Machiavelli to the Nuclear Age* (1986) 735–778.
[13] See Böckenförde, 'Der Staat als Organismus – Zur staatstheoretisch-verfassungs-politischen Diskussion im frühen Konstitutionalismus', in E.-W. Böckenförde, *Recht, Staat, Freiheit* (2nd ed., 1992) 270.

Epilegomena *to a Silence* 195

or destruction. Moreover, the danger to the very survival of the state cannot be adequately defined without taking into consideration the element of fear, extreme hostility and existential struggle 'to the end' between the source of the eventual threat and the 'nation'.

1.2 The New Strategic Environment

International law, as well as the Court's Opinions, should be reinterpreted in consideration of the new political and strategic environment which has been shaped in the 90s.

In the *Millennium Report* to the UN General Assembly, the UN Secretary-General has openly questioned the utility of nuclear strategy after the end of the Cold War:

> When the bipolar balance of nuclear terror passed into history, the concern with nuclear weapons also seemed to drift from public consciousness ... Whatever rationale these weapons may once have had has long since dwindled. Political, moral and legal constraints on actually using them further undermine their strategic utility without, however, reducing the risks of inadvertent war or proliferation. . . . The objective of nuclear non-proliferation is not helped by the fact that the nuclear weapon states continue to insist that those weapons in their hands enhance security, while in the hands of others they are a threat to world peace. . . . Not only are the Strategic Arms Reduction Talks stalled, but there are no negotiations at all covering the many thousands of so-called tactical nuclear weapons in existence, or the weapons of any nuclear power other than those of the Russian Federation and the United States of America.

The Report concluded by proposing to convene a major international conference that would help to identify ways of eliminating nuclear dangers.[14] In the United Nations *Millennium Declaration*, the member states agreed to 'strive for the elimination of weapons of mass destruction, particularly nuclear weapons', but they did not take any decision on the procedure and kept all options open, including that of an international conference.[15]

An 'orderly' exit strategy from the possession of nuclear weapons is therefore still not in sight, as the difficulties for the ratification of the Comprehensive Test Ban Treaty amply demonstrate.[16] On the contrary, a 'disorderly' breakdown of the

[14] *Millennium Report*, A/54/2000, 53.
[15] UNGA Res. 55/2, 18 September 2000, no. 9, ninth paragraph. For some recent initiatives in disarmament see *Press Briefing on Disarmament Affairs*, 25 October 2000; for the draft resolutions on disarmament approved by the First Committee of the UN General Assembly, *Press Releases* GA/DIS/3189/26 October 2000 and GA/DIS/3191/30 October 2000.
[16] Press Release GA/DIS/3170/3 October 2000. A major setback for the efforts of disarmament was the rejection of the Comprehensive Test Ban Treaty by the US Senate on 14 October 1999, see *Keesing's Record of World Events*, 43239.

196   *Achilles Skordas*

current strategic structure cannot be excluded, as evidenced by the nuclear tests of India (11 and 13 May 1998) and Pakistan (28 May 1998),[17] in the unilateral approach towards the ABM Treaty, the prospects of militarization of outer space and the risks of nuclear proliferation. Members of the UN Secretary General's Advisory Board on Disarmament Matters have recently expressed their uneasiness about the possible dismantling of that structure, which could enhance the efforts of each state to ensure its own invulnerability. Such a development would lead to nuclear anarchy and destabilize the policies of deterrence which, although 'perverse', had sought to provide the necessary guarantees for the maintenance of peace over a long period of time.[18]

Nuclear strategy has entered an era of uncertainty after the end of the cold war and proliferation has facilitated the availability of nuclear weapons in comparison to the first nuclear age. Thus, both the threat and the eventual use of nuclear weapons would be nowadays more 'anarchic' than in the past and the consequences of crossing the nuclear threshold would have a considerable, even catastrophic, impact upon the foundations of the international system as a whole, although their physical impact would be more limited than during a whole-scale nuclear war of the bipolar age.

The proliferation of weapons of mass destruction, that is of nuclear, chemical and biological weapons, constitutes one of the gravest security risks in the post cold war era. Biological weapons in particular are easy to fabricate and to use and may kill hundreds of thousands of people. It had been observed, that state-sponsored terrorism or terrorism of non-state actors was capable of creating a climate of insecurity, in particular in the public opinion of the United States.[19] Moreover, a number of countries have already acquired or are in a position to acquire nuclear weapons and other weapons of mass destruction. Although a global nuclear devastation can be practically ruled out, it has also been contended that a lesser catastrophe, such as the destruction of a single population centre, has become more probable.[20] The reality of 11 September has therefore reaffirmed some of these nightmares. Other authors maintained even that the danger of the use of weapons of mass destruction against the USA and their allies is greater than any time since the Cuban missiles crisis. [21] The risks arising from an eventual breakdown of the non-proliferation regime are demonstrated in the fact that the permanent members of the Security Council seem to have little leverage upon the new nuclear powers [22] or upon terrorists.

The increased risks of proliferation of weapons of mass destruction are echoed

[17] See the Statements by the President of the UN Security Council S/PRST/1998/12, 14 May 1998 and S/PRST/1998/17, 29 May 1998, in which he 'strongly deplored' these tests in the name of the Council.

[18] Press Release GA/DIS/3168/29 September 2000.

[19] Laqueur, 'Postmodern Terrorism' (1996) 75(5) *Foreign Affairs* 24–36, Betts, 'The New Threat of Mass Destruction' (1998) 77(1) *Foreign Affairs* 26–41.

[20] Cropsey, 'The Only Credible Deterrent' (1994) 73(2) *Foreign Affairs* 14.

[21] Carter, Deutch, Zelikow, 'Catastrophic Terrorism – Tackling the New Danger' (1998) 77(6) *Foreign Affairs* 81.

[22] See Carpenter, 'Closing the Nuclear Umbrella' (1994) 73(2) *Foreign Affairs* 11, who refers to the limited influence of the United States. However, the same would be also true of the potential influence of the other traditional nuclear powers upon those states.

in the recent CIA Report *'Global Trends 2015: A Dialogue About the Future With Nongovernmetal Experts'*.[23] The Report anticipates an expansion of the nuclear capacities of India and Pakistan. Russia would increasingly rely on its shrinking nuclear arsenal to deter potential threats against the Russian territory, while China will have deployed 'tens to several tens of missiles with nuclear warheads against the United States', but also 'hundreds of shorter-range ballistic and cruise missiles for use in regional conflicts', some of which will have nuclear warheads. For the Report, 'by 2015, the United States, barring major political changes . . ., will face ICBM threats from North Korea, probably from Iran, and possibly from Iraq, in addition to long-standing threats from Russia and China'. The Report concludes that 'the risks of escalation inherent in direct armed conflict will be magnified by the availability of Weapons of Mass Destruction'.

Although the credibility of the US deterrence strategy extended to protect allied and friendly countries is openly questioned and although it is also hotly disputed, whether nuclear deterrence is appropriate for preventing the threats of the new nuclear age,[24] the traditional nuclear powers follow further the modes of thought shaped during the cold war.[25] It can be expected that nuclear deterrence will be maintained as part of a wider strategy of prevention, including conventional response, preparations for civil defence and institutional reform of the security, intelligence and defence apparatus.[26] The national missiles defence system planned by the United States could possibly constitute a non-nuclear deterrence of nuclear attacks, but it encounters strong international opposition.[27]

The new nuclear age is qualified by a deep change in the state-of- mind in comparison to the previous cold war era, which is accurately described in a recent essay by P. Bracken:

> Although similarities exist between the second nuclear age and the first (command and control problems, for example), there are also some striking differences. The single biggest one is the role of nationalism. The Cold War was a struggle waged with the icy rationality and cool logic that characterized the two superpowers' approach to nuclear weapons. There was no place for hysteria; indeed, one striking feature of even the most dangerous nuclear issues was that the two sides never really got angry at each other. But the second nuclear age is driven by national insecurities incomprehensible to outsiders whose security is no longer endangered. In the West, the politics of rage had no role in foreign policy. This cannot be said for disputes in Asia

---

[23] See in http://www.cia.gov/cia/publications/globaltrends2015/index.html.

[24] Carpenter, *loc. cit.*, 8–13.

[25] Iklé, 'The Second Coming of the Nuclear Age' (1996) 75(1) *Foreign Affairs* 128, Jost, 'France's Nuclear Dilemmas' (1996) 75(1) *Foreign Affairs* 108–118.

[26] See, for instance, Betts, *loc. cit.*, 26–41, Carter, Deutch, Zelikow, *loc. cit.*, 80–94, Perry, 'Defense in an Age of Hope' (1996) 75(6) *Foreign Affairs* 64–79.

[27] On the relevant discussion, see O'Hanlon, 'Star Wars Strikes Back' (1999) 78(6) *Foreign Affairs* 68–82, Thränert 'Auf der Suche nach dem Kompromiss', *Frankfurter Allgemeine Zeitung*, 3 June 2000, 11.

198   *Achilles Skordas*

between Pakistan and India, the two Koreas, or the Arab states and Israel. Having such emotional dynamics linked to the brandishing or use of ballistic missiles and weapons of mass destruction is something to be anticipated – and dreaded. Despite the economic opening of Asia and Western claims that globalization will somehow render national identity obsolete, nationalism is a rising force in Asia, where it broke the colonial grip. Nationalism is not viewed kindly in the West these days, where it is automatically associated with ethnic cleansing, extremism and xenophobia. Though this association is often untrue, nationalism will undoubtedly complicate the second nuclear age.[28]

Bracken gives a new perspective of nuclear proliferation:

Thus, what is now perceived in the West as a breakdown in nonproliferation policy is seen in the East as a push for national security. Asia sees no reason to accept a non-Asian monopoly on the military instruments needed to ensure order, and it projects a growing sense that reasonably wealthy countries must defend their own interests.[29]

The essay entitled 'Against Nuclear Apartheid' by J. Singh, Senior Adviser to the Indian Prime Minister published in *Foreign Affairs*, is characteristic of that perception.[30] Similarly, the Pakistani Foreign Secretary Sh. Ahmad has answered with an essay under the title 'The Nuclear Subcontinent – Bringing Stability to South Asia'.[31] Both authors contend that the proliferation of nuclear weapons enhances stability in their region. The slippery path of such justifications is apparent in Ahmad's argument, that 'Pakistan's nuclear tests were undertaken in self-defense',[32] an expression which is, in its legal dimension, semantically only short of equating nuclear tests with the use of armed force (but see art. 51 of the UN Charter). Even if the Indian tests would be qualified as a prohibited threat of the use of force, it is clear that Pakistan would have no right to self-defence under the Charter, but only the right to countermeasures or retorsion not involving the use of force.

R. Betts commented on the political-psychological consequences of a terrorist blackmail upon the population of the United States as follows:

Suppose a secretive radical Islamic group launches a biological attack, kills 100,000 people, and announces that it will do the same thing again if its terms

---

[28] Bracken, 'The Second Nuclear Age' (2000) 79(1) *Foreign Affairs* 155–156. Similarly, Luttwak stressed that during the Cold War 'there were many wars, but the remarkably deliberate and controlled behavior that became a new norm for nations around the world deterred the thoughtless escalation of confrontation and the eruption of war through sheer miscalculation', 'A Post-Heroic Military Policy' (1996) 75(4) *Foreign Affairs* 33.

[29] *Ibid.*, 149.

[30] J. Singh, 'Against Nuclear Apartheid' (1998) 77(5) *Foreign Affairs* 41–52.

[31] S. Ahmad, 'The Nuclear Subcontinent – Bringing Stability to South Asia' (1999) 78(4) *Foreign Affairs* 123–125.

[32] *Ibid.*, 123.

are not met. (The probability of such a scenario may not be high, but it can no longer be consigned to science fiction.) In that case, it is hardly unthinkable that a panicked legal system would roll over and treat Arab-Americans as it did the Japanese-Americans who were herded into concentration camps after Pearl Harbor. Stretching limits on domestic surveillance to reduce the chances of facing such choices could be the lesser evil.[33]

'Institutional' rage and fear are, therefore, common features in crises, in which the use of weapons of mass destruction might be evoked. Such a state-of-mind in political and judicial instances will have a direct impact upon the response of individual decision-makers in the course of such a major crisis.

At the beginning of the 20th century, the needs of military planning and the early mobilization of the military machine nullified any perspective for the political management of the crisis that led to the outbreak of the first world war.[34] The ICJ's Opinions give the opportunity to deal with the question, whether the quality of modern war technology under the political conditions of the new nuclear age minimizes the limits of legal reasoning, thus rendering the decision on the use or the threat of use of nuclear weapons an existential issue which cannot be treated in the categories of legality/illegality. The challenge for international law is the affirmation or denial of its capacity to offer an ultimate, even though imperfect, guidance for an 'exit' strategy from the nuclear dilemma under critical circumstances.

1.3 The Question of Legality Redefined

The cardinal position put forward in the present essay is that recognition by the Court of a conditional entitlement of states to have recourse to nuclear weapons in some extreme situations for the protection of major interests of the international community instead of concluding in favour of a *non-liquet*, would have been better suited to develop a preventive effect against the use of these weapons. To have reached that conclusion, the ICJ should have scrupulously adhered to the systemic rationale of its judicial-advisory function and should have stated the law unequivocally, taking, *inter alia*, into consideration that the two Opinions are addressed not only to the requesting organs but, primarily, to the UN member states.[35]

In that context it will be examined, why the *non-liquet* and the resulting inconsistencies of the Advisory Opinion are incompatible with the systemic function this category of judicial acts is expected to fulfill in the UN system of legal and political communication. The next issue is whether the incapacity of the legal system to process the question put to it by the UN General Assembly is to be

---

[33] Betts, *loc. cit.*, 39–40.

[34] H. Kissinger, *Diplomacy* (1994) 201 et seq.

[35] See Salmon, 'Who are the addressees of the Opinions?' in Boisson de Chazournes and Sands (eds), *op. cit.*, 27–35.

200 *Achilles Skordas*

attributed to an implicitly inferred conviction of the Court, that a prohibitory norm of international law would not have any practical preventive effect on decision-makers at the moment of nuclear crisis (see under 2). If both, *non-liquet* and a general prohibition, cannot effectively guide the conduct of the addressees, it should be examined, whether the approach proposed here would be better to deploy a preventive effect, in consideration of the principles enunciated in the *Report on NATO Bombing Campaign*. As a theoretical background, Martin Heidegger's distinction between 'anxiety' and 'fear' offers an interpretative 'pre-understanding' (*Vorverständnis*) of the relationship between norm and the new nuclear age' s state-of-mind (see under 3). Finally, we will return to the point of departure and look upon, what the institutional morality of a Court can mean, as juxtaposed to the personal integrity of its members and to political decision-making (see under 4).

2 *NON-LIQUET* VS GENERAL PROHIBITION

There are three possible interpretative alternatives as to the response of international law to the threat or use of nuclear weapons: either *non-liquet*, or a general prohibition, or a conditional entitlement. In the present chapter, we will examine the shortcomings of the first two alternatives, as they result from the Court's Opinions.

2.1 *Non-liquet* and Depoliticization

It has been argued that, in the WHO Advisory Opinion, the Court articulated a 'depoliticization' approach towards the activities of the specialized agencies.[36] Considering that radical functionalism demonstrates a generalized distrust towards the capacity of international organization to resolve political issues as such, including the threat to peace and security,[37] the Court's functionalism seems to be rather a moderate one.[38] What has to be examined, however, is, whether the Court's refusal to answer to the WHO's request is 'functionally equivalent' to the Court's silence to the request of the UN General Assembly and whether both responses reveal then a certain 'depoliticization attitude' of the Court towards the policy-making capacities of the international institutions.

The answer to the question, whether international courts have to fill the existing

---

[36] Klein, 'Reflections on the principle of speciality revisited and the "politicisation" of the specialised agencies', *ibid.*, 78–91.

[37] See G. Niemeyer, *Law Without Force – the Function of Politics in International Law* (1941) 379–402, in particular at 385.

[38] A moderate functionalism is represented, for instance, by M. Virally, 'La notion de fonction dans la théorie de l'organisation internationale', in *Mélanges offerts à Charles Rousseau* (1974) 277–300, where the author distances himself explicitly from the radical functionalist theories, see 281.

gaps, depends on the extensive or restrictive interpretation of the notion of *lacuna*[39] or on the expected acceptance of the judge's 'activism' by the addressees.[40] Article 65 paragraph 1 of the Statute recognizes in principle the discretion of the ICJ to refuse to give an advisory opinion, but, in practice, it is recognized that this discretion is to be exercised only exceptionally for 'compelling reasons'.[41] It has thus been maintained that, considering the consultative function as part of the judicial function, discretion seems to be very limited.[42] In the *Interpretation of Peace Treaties with Bulgaria, Hungary and Romania*, the Court stated that an advisory opinion 'represents *the participation in the activities of the Organization*, and, in principle, should not be refused'.[43] Under this assumption, the *non-liquet* in the Advisory Opinion should be looked at from the perspective of the function that the advisory opinions perform in the system of the United Nations. This system, in particular the relationship between the UN and the specialized agencies, has been adequately described in the Advisory Opinion to the WHO. The question is, whether the *non-liquet* is compatible with the rationale of that system, as described by the Court itself.

The Advisory Opinion for the WHO recalls that the international organizations enjoy international legal personality and operate under the 'principle of speciality'. They consequently exercise only those powers conferred to them by states through the constitutions of the organizations. Certainly, international organizations also possess the so-called 'implied powers'; [44] for the Court, such powers are, nonetheless, only recognized by them to the extent that they are necessary for the fulfillment of their objectives. The Opinion stresses that, to ascribe to the WHO the competence to address the legality of the use of nuclear weapons would mean to disregard the principle of speciality.[45] The implied powers rule constitutes one of the elements of teleological interpretation.[46] Implied powers should not be necessarily related with an extensive interpretation, but can also lead to a restrictive interpretation of the relevant provisions.[47]

The Court specified the legal status of the specialized agencies, among them the

---

[39] But see L. Siorat, *Le problème des lacunes en droit international* (1958) 251–252, who defines gaps in a rather restrictive way.

[40] See U. Fastenrath, *Lücken im Völkerrecht* (1991) 281–285, who defines gaps in a broad manner, *ibid.*, 213 *et seq.*; Aznar-Gomez, 'The 1996 Nuclear Weapons Advisory Opinion and Non-liquet in International Law' (1999) 48 *ICLQ* 13.

[41] S. Rosenne, *The Law and Practice of the International Court, 1920–1996* (1997, Vol. II) 1020–1029, Mosler, 'Art. 96', in B. Simma (ed.), *The Charter of the United Nations – a Commentary* (1994), margin number [hereinafter MN] 22–25; Opinion for UNGA, note 1 above, 234–238, paras 14–19.

[42] G. Abi-Saab, 'On Discretion – Reflections on the nature of the consultative function of the International Court of Justice', in Boisson de Chazournes and Sands, *op. cit.*, 36–50.

[43] ICJ Rep. (1950) 62, at 71, emphasis added.

[44] *Reparation for injuries suffered in the service of the United Nations*, ICJ Rep. (1949) 174, at 182. H. Schermers/N. Blokker, *International Institutional Law* (3rd edn, 1995) 158–163, paras 232–236.

[45] Opinion for WHO, see note 1, 78–79, para. 25.

[46] Ress, 'Interpretation', in Simma (ed.), *op. cit.*, MN 36.

[47] *Ibid.*, MN 36.

202 *Achilles Skordas*

WHO, as set out in the UN Charter. The Charter provides in articles 57 and 63 the method whereby such organizations are to co-ordinate their action with the United Nations itself and its organs. The Court justifies the principle of differentiation of functions with the coherence it brings to the relationship between the United Nations and the various autonomous and complementary organizations that are invested with sectorial powers.[48]

For the ICJ, if the WHO possesses, according to article 57 of the Charter, 'wide international responsibilities', those responsibilities are restricted to the sphere of public health and should not encroach on the responsibilities of other parts of the UN system. According to the Opinion, issues relating to the use of force, the regulation of armaments and disarmament fall within the competence of the United Nations, but not of the specialized agencies. In the opposite case, the concept of the specialized agency would be deprived of meaning.[49] Thus, there is no need for judicial guidance of the specialized agencies, if they do not possess the competence to take decisions on the issues in question.

The 'systemic rationale' argument is here convincing. The effectiveness of the UN system is based on the functional differentiation of several autonomous subsystems. Crossing and overlapping powers may lead to confusion of the limits between the several parts of the entire system and to the progressive erosion of the responsibility of each such subsystem.[50] This principle applies in the relationship between the UN and its specialized agencies, but it should also be taken into consideration by the principal organs of the UN when they create subsidiary organs.[51] For the Organization to comply with the principle of effective collective action,[52] the subsidiary organs must also have a structure suitable for their programme of action and possess specific powers, which should be functionally differentiated from the powers of other organs of the same system.[53]

The real issue here is not whether the specialized agencies are also competent to deal with questions having political aspects, but whether the fundamental political issue has been already dealt with and decided by the primarily concerned political organ (the General Assembly or Security Council). Through its decision, the political organ provides an orientation for the further action of specialized agencies. The request by the GA for an advisory opinion and the qualification of the Assembly's resolutions by the Court as not creating an *opinio juris* for the prohibition of nuclear weapons, demonstrated the ambivalence of the Assembly

---

[48] Opinion for WHO, see note 1, 80, para. 26.

[49] *Ibid.*

[50] See also Matheson, 'The Opinions of the International Court of Justice on the Threat or Use of Nuclear Weapons' (1997) 91 *AJIL* 419–420.

[51] See art. 7 paras 2, 22, 29 and 68 of the UN Charter.

[52] See art. 1, para. 1 of the UN Charter.

[53] For instance, the difficulties in co-operation and communication are especially evident regarding the powers of the UN system in the field of human rights, see Alston, 'The Committee on Economic, Social and Cultural Rights', in Ph. Alston (ed.), *The United Nations and Human Rights* (1992) 498–501; Opsahl, 'The Human Rights Committee', *ibid.*, 385–388.

towards the issue of disarmament and nuclear weapons. In that sense, it was the UNGA that was competent to take the necessary steps for activating the advisory mechanism.

If the central point of the Advisory Opinion to the WHO is that the 'systemic prosperity' is maximized, to the extent that the subsystems carry out their specific functions without interfering with the functions of the others, then it is clear, that the *non-liquet* in the Opinion for the UNGA does not contribute to the overall 'well-being' of the UN system and of the international community. From the point of view of the performance of the Court's function, the *non-liquet* leaves the GA as the competent organ and the member states without any effective legal guidance. The Opinion for the UNGA seems to contradict not only the Court's decision to give an answer to the request of the organ, but also the principles it affirmed in the WHO Opinion. Actually, if the Court was justified not to respond to a specialized agency, it had two response alternatives *vis-à-vis* the competent political organs: either it could refuse to respond for 'compelling reasons', including the existence of a gap in the law, if it considered that such an answer would not serve the 'best interests' of the international community; or, if it decided to give an answer, then it had to offer qualified legal advice to the competent political organs.

In fact, a 'depoliticization moment' exists in the Advisory Opinion, but it lies in the *non-liquet* itself, not in the rejection of the WHO's request. The Court was not called upon to decide on the lawfulness of a certain conduct on the basis of specific acts, but to draw the general lines of the (il)legality of the threat or use of nuclear weapons and to present the legal perspective of a hotly debated political issue. The Opinion did not have to 'usurp' political functions, provide simplistic answers, or prescribe the exact conduct of states during nuclear crises. Through its response, the Court could have formulated, *inter alia*, legal principles and criteria enhancing the political and legal discourse in the United Nations under the circumstances of the post cold war period; for instance, on the function of deterrence or its relationship with the maintenance or restoration of international peace and security; or on the conditions of eventual permissibility of the threat or use of nuclear weapons as armed or belligerent reprisals, if norms protecting the collective interest of the international community would be violated (genocide, threat or use of chemical or nuclear weapons by an aggressor state, nuclear terrorism).[54] The Court did neither deal with the issue, whether the illegitimate possession of nuclear weapons, in

---

[54] The Court did not deal with issues relating to the application of chapter VII of the Charter or with the threat or use of force by a state within its own boundaries, Opinion for UNGA, see note 1, 247, paras 49–50. The Opinion for the UNGA also stated that it does not have 'to pronounce on the question of belligerent reprisals save to observe that in any case any right of recourse to such reprisals would, like self-defence, be governed *inter alia* by the principle of proportionality', para. 46. On armed reprisals and the protection of collective interest, see P. Daillet/A. Pellet, *Droit International Public* (6th edn, 1999), para. 570, Tietje, 'Die Völkerrechtswidrigkeit des Einsatzes von Atomwaffen im bewaffneten Konflikt unter Umwelt- und Gesundheitsschutzaspekten – Zur Gutachtenanfrage der WHO an den IGH' (1995) 33 *Archiv des Völkerrechts* 296–299.

204 *Achilles Skordas*

deviation from the Non-Proliferation Treaty, would bear any consequence for the qualification of (il)legality of the eventual recourse to the threat or use of nuclear weapons.

The Advisory Opinion could have stressed the progressive loss of relevance of the deterrence in the new era for the relations among major powers, or the potential residual security benefits of possessing the weapons. The Court should have stated that in the transition period until the nuclear powers fulfill their duty 'to achieve ... nuclear disarmament in all its aspects',[55] the threat or use of nuclear weapons would be legal in exceptional circumstances, if such an action was necessary for the suppression of major and non-calculable risks to international security. Finally, it had the option of declaring the use or threat of nuclear weapons as illegal in all circumstances. In all those cases, it would have at least considered the international interest.

The recourse to the *non-liquet* and to the 'extreme circumstances of self-defense' without any further determination of criteria, have instead promoted the 're-nationalization' of the question of the legality of the threat or use of nuclear weapons. The Court reduced its perspective on the rationale of national concerns, instead of focusing on the 'concept of the political' in the international community. It is asked, of course, whether it could have been possible to induce the addressees of the Opinion to consider the major interests of the international community, without introducing a far-reaching exception to the prohibition of the use of force based on the 'extreme circumstances of threat to the international security'. The Court could have restrictively formulated an exception for self-defence, only when such interests would be *also* at stake, in consideration of the proportionality principle. The Opinion has given the wrong 'signal' in that respect: Falk argued, for instance, that eventually only an extreme circumstance of individual, but not collective, self-defence would justify recourse to a nuclear strike.[56]

2.2 Inconsistency and the Neutralization of Normative Expectations

Judge Higgins sharply criticized the lack of consistency in the Advisory Opinion. She held that the Court could have declined to give an opinion, if it considered that the question was not legal or it was very vague or it would have caused the Court to script scenarios or to 'legislate'. Nonetheless, after that alternative was put aside, the Advisory Opinion declared a *non-liquet* because of the prevailing uncertainty as to the present status of the law and the actual facts.[57] The inconsistency

---

[55] Opinion for UNGA, see note 1, para. 99.

[56] Falk, 'Nuclear Weapons, International Law and the World Court: An Historic Encounter' (1996) 71 *Die Friedens-Warte* 240. There can be observed, nevertheless, a slight difference in the attitude of the same author in (1997) 91 *AJIL* 68–69, where he seems more ambivalent on the legitimacy of the use of nuclear weapons for collective self-defence.

[57] See Dissenting Opinion of Judge Higgins (Opinion for UNGA), ICJ Rep. (1996) 583, para. 2.

aspect goes, however, beyond that point and it results from the structure of the
non-liquet itself.

The Opinion only imperfectly fulfilled the function of interpreting and stating
international law. Even though advisory opinions do not have formally binding
force nor do they produce *res judicata*, as judgments do (article 59 of the Statute),
they still have a precedential value with an *erga omnes* quality, since they state the
law authoritatively.[58] Therefore, the Court is committed not to give vague, evasive
or inconsistent answers. In the present case, the Opinion enables not merely different, but rather radically contradictory interpretations on fundamental issues. The
two Opinions have indeed clarified important aspects of international law relating
to decision-making in international organizations, to the law of armed conflict and
to environmental law. However, the Opinion for UNGA has failed to give a
satisfactory answer to the cardinal issue of the question put forward by the
Assembly, namely the relationship between *jus ad bellum* and *jus in bello* in cases
of the threat or use of nuclear weapons, with the result of further confusing the
addressees. This confusion not only has consequences at a political level, but it may
deform the normative expectations and distort the addressees' conduct respectively.

A basic contradiction refers to the qualification of the principles of international
humanitarian law as 'intransgressible',[59] a qualification which shows them close to
jus cogens, without identifying them with it. Actually the Court explicitly declined
to qualify the legal character of the rules of international humanitarian law as *jus
cogens*.[60] At the same time the Court allowed for the possibility that the international legal order may accept deviations from the *jus in bello*, even as an exception, when the survival of the state is at stake. The Court's sequence of syllogisms
may equally support two lines of thought. Either a breach of international humanitarian law could be envisaged under such circumstances, or the application field of
the *jus in bello* should be delimited on the basis of the principle of proportionality
and in the light of the interests protected by the *jus ad bellum*, namely the extreme
situation of self-defence.[61] This latter position was formulated in particular by
Judge Higgins.[62] Judge Fleischhauer considered *jus ad bellum* and *jus in bello* as two
systems of norms having an equal rank, therefore the smallest common denomina-
tor between the conflicting systems would have to be found.[63] Bothe and
Marauhn/Oellers-Frahm assume that only the extreme circumstance of self-defence

---

[58] M. Shahabuddeen, *Precedent in the World Court* (1996) 165–171, in particular at 170–171,
Rosenne, *op. cit.*, 989, 1045. But also see Roberto Ago, ' "Binding" Advisory Opinions of
the International Court of Justice' (1991) 85 *AJIL* 439–451.

[59] Opinion for UNGA, see note 1, 257, para. 79.

[60] *Ibid.*, 258, para. 83.

[61] J. Gardam, 'Necessity and Proportionality in *Jus ad Bellum* and *Jus in Bello*', in Boisson de
Chazournes and Sands (eds), *op. cit.*, 275–292, Matheson, *loc. cit.*, 430.

[62] Diss. Op. Higgins (Opinion for UNGA), ICJ Rep. (1996) 588–589, paras 21–24. For Judge
Guillaume, the state enjoys, for the use of nuclear weapons under threat to its survival, an
'excuse absolutoire', Sep. Op. Guillaume (Opinion for UNGA), *ibid.* 290, para. 8.

[63] Sep. Op. Fleischhauer (Opinion for UNGA), *ibid.*, 308–309, para. 5.

206 *Achilles Skordas*

might justify, as a last resort, the use of nuclear weapons; otherwise such a use would be illegal and would not be covered by the principle of proportionality, even if it produces minimal effects, as in the desert or the high seas scenarios.[64] For Condorelli, if a danger to survival would justify the use of nuclear weapons, the further question arises, whether it could also justify other deviations from international humanitarian law by states that do not possess nuclear weapons.[65] Akande constructed three different interpretative alternatives for operative paragraph 2E.[66] If consistent answers to these issues are possible, they certainly result from the authors' skill, not from the Advisory Opinion itself, which includes, besides the majority view of the *non-liquet*, two lines of thought, the one favouring the illegality in any circumstance and the one not excluding *a priori* the eventuality of a lawful threat or use of nuclear weapons under restrictive conditions.[67]

The Opinion does not, therefore, produce a coherent legal communication, but rather allows for the grounding of deviating and contradictory normative expectations.[68] If the rules of international law, as enunciated by the Court, establish contradictory expectations for the addressees, the regulatory force of the respective rules is weakened or even negated. Considering that, fortunately, no international practice on the actual use of nuclear weapons exists since 1945, the uncertainty arising from the *non-liquet* and from the inconsistencies among different levels of normative expectations may encourage the states concerned to fill the gap with the facts they will eventually produce at the moment of a nuclear crisis.

2.3 General Prohibition and the Absence of Prevention

There is a possible explanation for this ambivalence of the Opinion. If, due to the existential nature of nuclear decision-making, international law cannot have any

---

[64] M. Bothe, 'Nuklearstrategie nach dem IGH-Gutachten?' (1996) 71 *Die Friedens-Warte* 256–257, Marauhn/Oellers-Frahm, 'Atomwaffen, Völkerrecht und die internationale Gerichtsbarkeit' (1997) 24 *Europäische Grundrechte-Zeitschrift* 235.

[65] L. Condorelli, 'Nuclear Weapons: a weighty matter for the International Court of Justice – Jura non novit curia?' (1997) 37 *International Review of the Red Cross (IRRC) – Special Issue* 19–20. See also the critique of David, 'The Opinion of the International Court of Justice on the legality of the use of nuclear weapons', *ibid.*, 31, L. Doswald-Beck, 'International humanitarian law and the Advisory Opinion of the International Court of Justice on the legality of the threat or use of nuclear weapons', *ibid.*, 53–54, McCormack, 'A non-liquet on nuclear weapons – the ICJ avoids the application of general principles of international humanitarian law', *ibid.*, 88–89, Mohr, 'Advisory Opinion of the International Court of Justice on the legality of the use of nuclear weapons under international law', *ibid.*, 97, 100.

[66] D. Akande, 'Nuclear Weapons, Unclear Law? Deciphering the Nuclear Weapons Advisory Opinion of the International Court' (1997) 68 *BYIL* 203–211.

[67] See for these three lines of thought, Ouchi, 'The Threat or Use of Nuclear Weapons: Discernible Legal Policies of the Judges of the International Court of Justice' (1998–1999) 13 *Conn.J.Int'l.L.* 107–118.

[68] See also the criticism of Queneudec, 'ET à la CIJ: méditations d'un extra-terrestre sur deux avis consultatifs' (1996) 100 *RGDIP* 907–914.

visible preventive effect and cannot guide the conduct of decision-makers, it could be expected that these structural deficits would be mirrored in the judicial act itself. Thus, knowing that the capacities of the legal system have reached their limits, the judges feel free to express the deadlock in the Advisory Opinion. Inconsistencies and gaps are then deliberate signs demonstrating the malfunctioning of the legal communication, due to the incapacity of legal coding to process the issues under examination.

This, rather 'nihilistic' alternative on the effectiveness of international law is harboured by a remark in the dissenting opinion of Judge Weeramantry, where he described the nature of what he called 'nuclear decision-making':

> A decision to use nuclear weapons would tend to be taken, if taken at all, *in circumstances which do not admit for fine legal evaluations*. It will in all probability be taken at a time when passions run high, time is short and the facts are unclear. It will not be a carefully measured decision, taken after a detailed and detached evaluation of all relevant circumstances of fact. It would be taken under extreme pressure and stress. Legal matters requiring considered evaluation may have to be determined within minutes, perhaps even by military rather than legally trained personnel, when they are in fact so complex as to have engaged this Court's attention for months. The fate of humanity cannot fairly be made to depend on such a decision. . . . The weapons should in my view be declared illegal in *all* circumstances. [69]

The characteristics of a nuclear crisis are, according to the Judge, the shortage of time for crucial decisions, the expectation of serious loss to the national interest and the absence of exact information, concerning in particular the strategy of the enemy. The decision-making takes place under conditions of extreme stress, intense passions, pressure and very high risks. If this analysis intended to reproduce the nuclear dilemma during the cold war, it gives a poor idea of the overall legal and systemic factors containing the outbreak of nuclear war; the picture should have been supplemented by the strong preventive mechanisms developed by the two superpowers through international law, for instance the ABM Treaty, as well as by the impact the impersonal and 'impassionate' rationality of the bureaucracies administering the nuclear Leviathans of the two political-military blocks could exercise upon the individuals responsible for taking the final decision. If the remark of Judge Weeramantry meant to describe the dilemma in the new nuclear age, it is inconsistent with the Judge's normative conclusion that nuclear weapons should be declared illegal in any circumstances. Under the above factual assumptions, it is not evident, what the advantages of that normative alternative are. It is not clear, for instance, why any differentiated approach to the question of legality would have increased the risk of nuclear war in comparison to complete prohibition, if

---

[69] Diss. Op. Weeramantry (Opinion for the UNGA), ICJ Rep. (1996) 529–530, (V.6 of the Opinion), emphasis added.

208   *Achilles Skordas*

international law is not capable of guiding the conduct of the addressees due to the inherent nature of nuclear decision-making.

The preventive capacity of international law on the issue in question can be examined from another angle. In the Advisory Opinion for the WHO, the ICJ had stipulated that any policy of prevention of health risks, carried out by the WHO, must fall within its competence, which does not include the question of the legality of nuclear weapons.[70] Again Judge Weeramantry noted in his dissenting opinion that the Organization must take into consideration, when setting out its policies, mostly those dangers arising from lawful and not from illegal activities:

> The state of law, relating to any form of activity hazardous to human health, is WHO's legitimate concern, and though WHO may not have the power to alter the law, it has at least the right to know what the law is. The greater the hazard, the greater is WHO's right to information. If the hazard can be created legally, the duty of preparedness for that eventuality becomes all the greater.[71]

On that point it was observed that, as from the nature of its activities, the WHO must also take precautionary measures for health hazards, which are not necessarily foreseeable, such as epidemics or natural catastrophes.[72] Consequently, the Organization possesses the competence to undertake preventive action even in cases of non-foreseeable illegal activities. In that light, Weeramantry's argument is not convincing and the counter argument is supportive of the Court's position which stressed that the causes of the deterioration of health are numerous and varied and that the 'legal or illegal character of these causes is essentially immaterial to the measures the WHO must in any case take in an attempt to remedy their effects'. And then the Opinion stressed: 'Whether nuclear weapons are used legally or illegally, their effects on health would be the same'. Moreover, 'the legality or illegality of the use of nuclear weapons in no way determines the specific measures, regarding health or otherwise (studies, plans, procedures, etc.), which could be necessary in order to seek to prevent or cure some of their effects'. Finally, the Court clarified that the WHO is only competent to take actions of 'primary prevention', that is to systematically distribute information on the consequences of nuclear warfare[73].

However, a *caveat* is necessary here. The inherent logic of the cost-effectiveness of the activities of an Organization imposes the restriction that the Organization is committed to prepare such planning only in cases where the risk that the damage-entailing activity would occur is not *de minimis*. The obligation of prevention cannot extend to any non-foreseeable risk, legal or illegal, man-made or not. The degree of sufficient possibility for the realization of the risk may again depend on

[70] Opinion for WHO, see note 1, 76–78.
[71] Diss. Op Weeramantry (Opinion for WHO), ICJ Rep. (1996) 134, (III.4 of the Opinion).
[72] Marauhn/Oellers-Frahm, *loc. cit.*, 229.
[73] Opinion for WHO, see note 70.

the extent of the damage predicted and the importance of the legal interest put at risk (balancing the factors 'damage x probability').[74] By an eventual use of nuclear weapons, the predicted damage is expected to be extremely high, not only in view of the primary repercussions of the use of such weapons on human life, but also given the secondary health hazards related to environmental damage as well. Consequently, the planning of precautionary or damage-limiting measures would be justified even on a low probability risk, not however, if the probability would be negligible.

From the overall political activism which has led to the submission of the request, it is clear that the WHO expected an Opinion providing for a general prohibition of the threat or use of nuclear weapons. An answer from the Court would have therefore affected the planning of the Organization, on the pre-condition that the eventual prohibitive rule would develop a preventive effect of such a significance, as to preclude to the point of extinction the already limited, but real, possibility of recourse to such weapons. Under this assumption, the WHO would have legitimately raised the issue of (il)legality of the use of nuclear weapons – although the Court would not necessarily be committed to give an answer to the request. If international law prohibited any use of nuclear weapons in armed conflict, the WHO could ignore the eventuality of nuclear war in its planning, but only if the compliance pull of a prohibitive rule of international law could produce an additional and noticeable preventive effect beyond that arising from the knowledge of the devastating consequences of the use of those weapons.

The Court's flight to the *non-liquet* in the Opinion for the UNGA, combined with the rejection of the WHO's request, signifies that the WHO is not in a position to utilize the factors 'legality/illegality' in its planning, since no 'constant' may be established between law and nuclear decision-making. The rejection of the WHO's request in particular, if seen in the light of the Opinion for the UNGA, implies that any planning has to involve the eventuality of nuclear emergencies of different kinds, because the abstract normative qualification of legality or illegality is irrelevant with the *real risk* involved in the possession of nuclear weapons. Even the formulation in paragraph 2E, paragraph 1 of the operative part of the Opinion to the UNGA, that is that 'the threat or use of nuclear weapons would generally be contrary to the rules of international law applicable in armed conflict' is practically nullified by the *non-liquet*. As a matter of fact, the risk of a nuclear conflict is not *de minimis* and international law can do nothing about that.

It is an open question, whether the Court could have sufficiently taken into account two contradictory interests, the speciality principle and the enunciation of a prohibitory rule for nuclear weapons. From a first sight, this legal strategy is a 'mission impossible'. If international law would prohibit any threat or use of nuclear weapons, this prohibition should have to be accompanied by the assumption of a

---

[74] On the concept of risk in administrative law, see U. Di Fabio, *Risikoentscheidungen im Rechtsstaat* (1994). The author considers the formula 'Schaden x Wahrscheinlichkeit' as at least very narrow, *ibid.*, 54; it is not, nonetheless, inappropriate for giving a *prima-facie* idea for the balance of interests involved in the Court's Opinion.

preventive effect which, in its turn, would have justified the WHO's request and would have destabilized the speciality principle! Only one outcome from that dilemma seems to have been possible: the Court could have refused the WHO's request with a slightly differentiated argument, namely that any particular preventive impact of the prohibitory norm upon the decision to use nuclear weapons was real, but not specific, thus not *ex ante* separable from the preventive effects deployed by the general prohibitions of the use of force. With that answer, the Court could have still maintained the integrity of the speciality principle, without declaring the 'legality factor' as irrelevant. In other words, the Advisory Opinion to the UNGA could have declared the use of nuclear weapons as illegal in all circumstances; the Court could have declined to answer the request of the WHO, reasoning that the specific prohibition of the threat or use of nuclear weapons is directly drawn from the *jus ad bellum* and the *jus in bello* and thus any preventive effect would be already included in the general rules. In its turn, the WHO could have taken guidance for its further action from the Opinion for the UNGA.

The Court's final response, as it results from both Opinions, indicates that the judges declined to formulate a prohibitory rule, because they were not convinced that the rule in question would have been armed with any significant 'net preventive effect' in addition to the existing factual situation that results from the nature and the constraints of the nuclear strategy. Although the Opinion to the UNGA formally adhered to the Charter's rules on the prohibition of the use of force, it actually put the 'nuclear issue' into parentheses, as far as the effectiveness of international law is concerned.

Finally, had the Court declared the policy of deterrence also incompatible with international law, then the existence of the rule would have to go through a hard test: would the nuclear powers, as expected, refuse to comply with such a rule, and would they continue to possess nuclear weapons, they would continuously be in breach of the rule. It is an open question, whether a rule can withstand such a pressure from a contrary state practice.

The question, thus, remains, whether international law can effectively guide the conduct of the addressees under the third interpretative alternative, namely as a conditional entitlement to use nuclear weapons. In the Court's approach, international law 'gives up' at the crucial moment of a nuclear crisis. The view to be brought forward here is that international law could have sufficiently represented the 'moment of concern' as a 'way to prevention', if the Court had not given its preference to silence as a more accommodating course of reasoning.

3 THE CONDITIONAL ENTITLEMENT: PROPORTIONALITY AND THE MOMENT OF CONCERN

A conditional entitlement to have recourse to nuclear weapons can be established on the combined interpretation of article 2, paragraph 4 and article 51 of the Charter; such a recourse has to be consistent with the rules of *jus in bello*, as stipulated by the principle of proportionality. This entitlement should not be confused with the existence of a 'specific prescription authorizing the threat or use of nuclear weapons or any other weapon in general or in certain circumstances', which has been explicitly rejected by the Court.[75] The meaning of a conditional entitlement to recourse to nuclear weapons is not that international law specifically permits the threat or use of nuclear weapons; it merely indicates that, under restrictive conditions, resulting from the combined application *of jus ad bellum* and *jus in bello*, the threat or use of nuclear weapons can be lawful and this legality, contrary to the Court's Opinion, can be described *ex ante* in legal terms.

3.1 Proportionality and the *ICTY Report on the NATO Bombing Campaign*

The maximization of risk and uncertainty arising from the ambiguity on the legality of the threat or use of nuclear weapons, is described by Koskenniemi as follows: 'only fear – the irrational image of the Apocalypse – puts nuclear weapons in a special category, detaching them from the banal logic of causes and consequences, gains and losses'.[76] Nonetheless, in this sense, the guarantee for avoiding the nuclear holocaust depends on an extremely unstable balance between that fear and the fear of the annihilation of one's own nation: fear versus fear.

Even if law does not always prevent war or other man-made disasters, it has the capacity to make tragedies intelligible and calculable and, thus, part of the self-reflection of the addressees. Existential dramas cannot be re-experienced; however, they can be (re)constructed in the sense that, by describing an expected conduct, law prefigures the effects of the relevant actions and decisions. The contribution of the proportionality standard to prevention is that it balances interests and consequences and enables *alter* to comprehend the potential response of *ego* and then translates both actors' existential struggle into the legal language of reprisals, counter-countermeasures and international crimes. Viewing, as a whole, the situation that would evolve during a nuclear crisis, it can be reasonably anticipated that, in a protracted conflict, escalation that reaches the level of the use of nuclear weapons, even in the form of legitimate reprisals of some kind or of acts of self-defence, would lead, sooner or later, to the violation of *jus cogens* norms of international law.

Under the assumption of an entitlement to use these weapons in self-defence, the tremendous legal risks incurred by the decision-makers are apparent first and foremost through a legal-technical analysis based on the proportionality principle. Only then is it evident that any use of nuclear weapons is a balancing act at the edge of legality. The more rational and detailed the analysis of the different aspects of the entitlement becomes, including the potential legal consequences under the law of international state responsibility and international criminal responsibility, the more any predictability of the proportionality principle is led *ad absurdum* and the legal

---

[75] Opinion for GA, see note 1, para. 52.
[76] Koskenniemi, *loc. cit.*, 497.

212   *Achilles Skordas*

discourse deconstructs the presumed right and transforms it to an ultimate, but very questionable, guarantee for the stability of the international system.

The Opinion to the UNGA leads to another direction. Here, a clear demarcation must be made between an empirical approach based on the anticipation of real situations and emergencies that lead to the conclusion, as the Court correctly formulated it, that 'the threat or use of nuclear weapons would *generally* be contrary to the rules of international law applicable in armed conflict',[77] and the next paragraph of that same part establishing the existence of an entitlement on an alleged right to 'self-preservation'.[78] In the first paragraph, the eventuality of a *legal* recourse to nuclear weapons would result from a rather improbable coincidence of circumstances, whereby the word 'generally' describes that improbability. The actual normative standard is introduced in the second paragraph. Here the legal justification of the act in question would result from a novel and apocryphal normative standard, which would encourage a misguided interpretation and application of international law. It is therefore necessary to compare the 'self-preservation' standard, upon which the Court bases the '*non-liquet*', with the proportionality standard, which is inherent to any entitlement to threaten or use nuclear weapons.

The Report to the ICTY Prosecutor on the NATO Bombing Campaign against Yugoslavia has demonstrated the ample complexity of a proportionality-based legality assessment of the acts of belligerents during an armed conflict which is conducted with the most modern technological means. The Committee has drawn a number of fundamental principles, which, if seen in the light of the potential use of nuclear weapons, show the extreme limits and constraints of military planners.

The Committee examined the obligations of the belligerents to protect the natural environment and concluded that even when targeting legitimate objectives, it is necessary to avoid excessive long-term damage to economic infrastructure and to the natural environment. If the target is sufficiently important, a greater degree of risk to the environment could be justified. And then:

> The critical question is what kind of environmental damage can be considered to be excessive. Unfortunately, the customary rule of proportionality does not include any concrete guidelines to this effect.[79]

The Report underscored also that the notion of excessive environmental destruction is imprecise and the actual environmental impact, both present and long term, of NATO's air campaign was still unknown at the time the report was drawn.[80] It also stated that actions resulting in massive environmental destruction would be questionable, particularly when they did not serve a clear and important military objective.[81]

[77] ICJ Rep. (1996) 266, para. 104, under 2E, first para., emphasis added.
[78] *Ibid.*, 2E, second paragraph.
[79] *ICTY Report on NATO Bombing Campaign*, see note 4, para. 20.
[80] *Ibid.*, para. 23.
[81] *Ibid.*, para. 22.

The Committee examined then, whether the use of depleted uranium projectiles would be inconsistent with international law. It stressed the scientific uncertainties and the concerns on the impact of the use of such weapons and that perhaps in the future there would be a consensus that the use of such projectiles violates general principles of law applicable to the armed conflict. Referring to the ICJ Nuclear Weapons Opinion it stated the following:

> No such consensus exists at present. Indeed, even in the case of nuclear warheads and other weapons of mass destruction – those which are universally acknowledged to have the most deleterious environmental consequences – it is difficult to argue that the prohibition of their use is in all cases absolute.[82]

In the Report, the Committee developed a number of standards or tests enabling the judge to determine the legality of specific war acts. The evaluation of these standards has to follow on the light of the response of the so-called 'reasonable military commander'.[83] If the war acts have caused disproportionate civilian casualties and the attack has been undertaken with intention or recklessness, then the criminal responsibility for 'unlawful attack' is established. The commanders thus have the duty to do everything practicable to verify that they attack military objectives, to take all practical precautions in the choice of methods and means of warfare to minimize civilian casualties and to refrain from launching attacks expected to cause disproportionate civilian casualties or property damage.[84]

The measure of the 'reasonable commander', who makes the above evaluations on the field apparently fails by the use of nuclear weapons. The relevant decision is expected to be taken on the highest political levels and has to include an assessment of all possible factors and determinants. It is not at all clear, what kinds of precautions could be taken, or how it could be assured that civilian casualties were minimized.

As far as proportionality is concerned, the Committee formulated further its uneasiness by the interpretation and application of that principle:

> The main problem with the principle of proportionality is not whether or not it exists but what it means and how it is to be applied. It is relatively simple to state that there must be an acceptable relation between the legitimate destructive effect and undesirable collateral effects. . . . It is much easier to

---

[82] *Ibid.*, para. 26. NATO has admitted since March 2000 having used depleted uranium ammunition in Kosovo. For the time being, there is considerable uncertainty as to the effects upon health and environment: see for instance, the UNEP/UNCHS Balkans Task Force (BTF) Study '*The potential effects on human health and the environment arising from possible use of depleted uranium during the 1999 Kosovo conflict – A preliminary assessment*', October 1999; see also the WHO's statement of 8 January 2001, concluding that no rise of leukemia cases in Kosovo has been observed in the past four years, in: http://www.who.int/eha/disasters/index.shtml. Other information links also the eventually more dangerous uranium reprocessed from nuclear reactors to the NATO ammunition, see http://europe.cnn.com/2001/WORLD/europe/01/17/defence.uranium.02/index.html.

[83] *Ibid.*, para. 50.

[84] *Ibid.*, para. 28.

214 *Achilles Skordas*

formulate the principle of proportionality in general terms than it is to apply it to a particular set of circumstances because the comparison is often between unlike quantities and values. One cannot easily assess the value of innocent human lives as opposed to capturing a particular military objective.[85]

Moreover, the Report drew up an indicative list of unresolved issues on the application of the proportionality principle. This list comprises the balancing between the military advantage and the injury to non-combatants, the factors to be included or excluded in totalling the sums, the standard of measurement in time or space and the extent to which the military commander is obligated to expose his forces to danger in order to limit civilian casualties and damage to civilian objects.[86] Additional difficulties arise in connection with the legal principle of distinction between military objectives and civilians,[87] as well as with the evaluation of acts targeted against dual use facilities, that is facilities which can have both civilian and military uses, or of military facilities within or near densely populated areas.[88]

It could be argued that the Committee has done nothing other than follow the rationale of the Court in the Advisory Opinion on the *Legality of the Threat or Use of Nuclear Weapons*, to which it has even explicitly referred, and that, just as in the Opinion, it has stated gaps and uncertainties of the law of war. However, there exists a fundamental differentiation among indeterminacy of the legal principles, such as proportionality, and the 'gap' declared by the Court in the Nuclear Weapons Opinion. Despite their indeterminacy, general principles are among the sources of international law (article 38 paragraph 1b and c of the ICJ Statute), while in the Opinion for the UNGA the ICJ declared, through the *non-liquet*, that the legal system was incapable of performing the requested operation. The differentiation is not a theoretical one, given that states are bound by the indeterminate principles of international humanitarian law, so that international state or criminal responsibility may arise, if the belligerents commit actions which would be qualified as violations of these principles or rules. However, based on the *non-liquet* of the Advisory Opinion, states might reasonably contend that, under the 'extreme circumstances of self-defense', these principles should be applicable only to a limited extent.

The Report has given criteria for distinguishing the intention or recklessness from simple negligence in acts potentially qualified as violations of article 3 of the ICTY Statute, which, although indeterminate, constitute the basis of establishing the responsibility of military commanders.[89] Furthermore, in the *Kupreskic* Judgment, the ICTY has formulated the principle that discretionary powers to attack belligerents should be construed narrowly, so as to expand the protection of civilians, if cumulative attacks against military targets jeopardize excessively the

---

[85] *Ibid.*, para. 48.
[86] *Ibid.*, para. 49.
[87] *Ibid.*, para. 29.
[88] *Ibid.*, para. 51.
[89] *Ibid.*, para. 28.

lives and assets of civilians. The so-called 'Martens Clause' significantly facilitates the emergence of new customary rules on international humanitarian law, even if international practice is scant or inconsistent, and enables the criminal prosecution of persons having committed acts inconsistent with those rules.[90] Therefore, it is not despite, but rather because of the combination of indeterminacy *in* the legal principles – and not *beyond* them – with international state or individual criminal responsibility that the preventive effect of the law of war is deployed. The belligerents undertake the risk to determine themselves a humane course of action during warfare, taking into account the Martens Clause, so as to minimize 'collateral damage' and to comply with the requirements of international humanitarian law.

When reading the *Kupreskic* Judgment, one cannot avoid the impression that a potential prohibition of the use of depleted uranium could emerge through the customary law-creating process envisaged by the Martens Clause, without prejudice to the question of legality of the nuclear weapons themselves. The Prosecutor of the ICTY stated recently that if sufficient elements would exist, an investigation would be necessary, as to whether the use of the heavy metal constituted a war crime[91].

Although the factual impossibility of planning a 'legal' nuclear war from the beginning to the end has not been transformed into a prohibitive norm by the Court,[92] it should not have been abandoned to the realm of legal silence. The impossibility of conducting such a war should have been indicated by the Court, but the final conclusion should remain on the non-outspoken side of legal reasoning and be derived from the reflective capacity of the decision-makers themselves. What the Court said in the second subparagraph of paragraph 2E of the *dispositif*, namely that it cannot provide an answer for an extreme situation of self-defence, is a very accurate description of the planner's factual dilemma under the conditions of extreme pressure of a nuclear crisis. However, the Opinion raised this dilemma into a new emerging standard of international law, which can *as such* tempt a state to configure the standard and shape the presumed norm through force and facts.

3.2 Anxiety, Fear and Concern as Existential States-of-mind

Drawing upon Heidegger's famous distinction in '*Sein und Zeit*', we can argue that 'anxiety', not the mobilization of apocalyptical fear, is the appropriate state-of-mind for avoiding Armaggedon. In anxiety, *Dasein* does not flee in the face of a

---

90 ICTY, *Kupreskic* case, IT-95-16-T, Judgment of 14 January 2000, paras 521–536, see also Cassese, 'The Martens Clause: Half a Loaf or Simply Pie in the Sky?' (2000) 11 *EJIL* 212–215.

91 See http://europe.cnn.com/2001/WORLD/europe/01/14/balkans.uranium/index.html .

92 See, for instance, paras 6 and 7 of the General Comment 14 of the Human Rights Committee on 'nuclear weapons and the right to life', art. 6 of the International Covenant on Civil and Political Rights: '6. The production, testing, possession, deployment and use of nuclear weapons *should be* prohibited and recognized as crimes against humanity. – 7. The Committee accordingly, in the interest of mankind, calls upon all States, whether Parties to the Covenant or not, *to take urgent steps, unilaterally and by agreement*, to rid the world of this menace', (emphasis added).

216   *Achilles Skordas*

definite instrumentality within-the-world, or in the face of 'decision', as it happens in a state of fear, but it flees in the face of itself as Being-in-the-world: *'That in the face of which one has anxiety is Being-in-the-world as such.* . . . That in the face of which one is anxious is completely indefinite'.[93]

L.P. Thiele interprets as follows the essence of anxiety:

> Being at home connotes a peaceful belonging, while anxiety indicates an uneasy displacement. How are the two reconcilable? The answer, Heidegger intimates, is that existential anxiety, although disruptive of everyday familiarity, is confluent with a deeper ontological serenity. He writes that 'the anxiety felt by the courageous cannot be contrasted with the joy or even the comfortable enjoyment of a peaceable life. It stands – on the hither side of all such contrasts – in secret union with the serenity and gentleness of creative longing'. . . . Profound serenity prevails, however, only once one has learned truly to share the world with the intrusive intimations of thrownness and contingency.[94]

Anxiety reveals itself as care and concern. Care and concern – in the meaning of '*Sorge*' – is, for *Heidegger,* the fundamental characteristic of human condition', it is projecting, planning, anticipating, calculating; time is a major component of this conception, since concern can only be experienced in an open horizon.[95] Concern has the capacity of a second order observation and reflection beyond the limits of everydayness.

Anxiety through 'Being-in-the-world' and concern for the world possess a different quality than fear, although neither of them originates from any rationality 'inherent' in *Dasein*. If willing, wishing, urge and addiction are rooted in *Dasein* as care and concern,[96] and these future-oriented and species-specific states-of-mind are mobilized at the moment of decision, at the moment of concern, only then can nuclear war be prevented. They are the same phenomenological structures of *Dasein* that can induce decision-makers to wage a necessary showdown with a genocidal or racist-fundamentalist regime or with globally acting terrorist networks that threaten the foundations of international peace and security. In that sense, care should not be misconstrued as 'love' plus 'ethics':

> Care is occasionally mistaken to mean altruistic love and caretaking, something that excludes 'egoistic' or 'greedy' dispositions. Care may indeed disclose itself as a love for humans and nature. But that is not all care is. Because care permeates human being, modes of human being that are neither loving, nor necessarily authentic, are also aspects of care. Care does

---

[93] Martin Heidegger, *Sein und Zeit* (17th edn, 1927/1993) 186, para. 40; the above passage was taken from the American edition, *Being and Time*, 230–231 (trans. by John Macquarrie/ Edward Robinson, 1962).

[94] L.P. Thiele, *Timely Meditations – Martin Heidegger and Postmodern Politics* (1995) 178–179.

[95] See R. Safranski, *Ein Meister aus Deutschland – Heidegger und seine Zeit* (3rd edn, 2000) 182.

[96] Heidegger, *op. cit.*, 193–196, para. 41, *Being and Time, op. cit.*, 238–241.

not necessarily describe benign relations humans establish with each other or with other forms of life. Rather, care refers to the totality of human Being-in-the-world. Existence, falling, and facticity, all of which are constitutive of *das Man*, also pertain to care. Rather than indicating a specific ethical or emotional relationship, care, like guardianship, signifies the ontological state of worldliness.[97]

The 'moment of concern' is thus the moment of the Guardian, of humanity as 'shepherd of Being'.[98]

Fear would not be the appropriate psychological resource to face existential perils, since it would lead either to a flight in front of the threatening instrumentality, hoping to avoid the worse, or to a non-proportionate response under panic. In fear, the actors lose sight of the capabilities they still possess and mutual destruction might appear at the moment of existential crisis, as a more 'liberating' alternative than deliberation and balancing of multiple factors. Unlike the 'voice of fear', the 'moment of concern' does not pave the way to unconditional surrender or to the collective '*Freitod*'; it is instead the unique moment of 'resoluteness' ('*Entschlossenheit*') for life and of distancing oneself from it. If resoluteness means the *Dasein*'s authentic potentiality-for-Being, it is only in the anticipation of death that all the factical anticipatoriness of resolving would be authentically understood.[99] It is only in that anticipation that *Dasein* may be kept free from 'falling' in the worldly reality,[100] thus also into fear.

International law cannot certainly 'impose' anxiety or 'exclude' fear from the decision-maker's horizon. But it can describe the 'moment of concern' in normative categories and 'reveal' to those responsible the complex considerations of the existential dilemma, implicating the necessity to afford protection to the most fundamental interests of international society with the assumption of the most extreme risks. The moment of concern requires a nation to overcome its deepest wounds and to come to terms with the darkest moments of its past.

Israel's stance during the war for the liberation of Kuwait was representative for the concern and calculated self-restraint a state is capable of demonstrating towards an aggressor in an existential situation, taking into consideration the broader interests of the international community. Although it was not known at that time, whether the missiles launched by Iraq against Israel's civilian population carried chemical warheads, Israel abstained from any preventive or retaliatory strike with conventional weapons, in caretaking of the cohesion of the Coalition and of the United Nations.[101] The counter argument, that Israel already enjoyed the protection of the US defence shield, is not capable of altering that appreciation. The intrinsic semantics of the Israeli attitude can only be assessed in the light of the deep

---

[97] Thiele, *op. cit.*, 184.
[98] But see *ibid.*, 109, 184–185.
[99] Heidegger, *op. cit.*, 302, para. 61, *Being and Time, op. cit.*, 349–350.
[100] C. Graf von Krockow, *Die Entscheidung – Eine Untersuchung über Ernst Jünger, Carl Schmitt, Martin Heidegger* (1958) 76.
[101] See *Keesing's Record of World Events*, 37936, 37939.

218   *Achilles Skordas*

trauma of the willing defencelessness and fatalism of the Jewish people during the holocaust, so dramatically portrayed by Hannah Arendt in her account of Eichmann's trial.[102] In his recent autobiography Marcel Reich-Ranicki gives his own first-hand testimony of the life and death of the Warsaw ghetto's Jewish 'elite'. The suicide of Adam Czerniakow, chairman of the Jewish Council, offers an insight to the existential dead end of those who, responsible for the fate of the community, but powerless, had to become the executioners of their own people.[103]

The United States faced equally the risk of their troops being attacked by Iraqi chemical weapons. To prevent that possibility, the American leadership made an alleged indirect, but effective threat of the use of nuclear weapons, should the Iraqis employ their chemical arsenal. The important point is, however, that, according to existing information, the United States had decided in advance not to make use of those weapons.[104] Whether the 'moment of concern' will outbalance the fears and trauma of the attacks against New York and Washington D.C. during the anti-terrorist wars of the near future, will not be answered with words, but with deeds.

3.3 The Moment of Concern in Legal Interpretation

The semantics of the ICJ's Advisory Opinion for the UNGA operate in a com-pletely different direction. The *non-liquet* spoiled the complex communication channel, through which the 'groundlessness' of a legal justification of the use of nuclear weapons could be discovered and perceived by the participants themselves. The Court did exactly what it should have avoided and paternalistically disclosed the secret: international law cannot guide the conduct of the decision-makers in an existential situation. The consequences in real life are unfortunately more compli-cated than the sudden end of a mystery tale or a love story. The Opinion handled the states-addressees rather as 'biological' than as social systems. The Court con-sidered the states incapable of a complex second order observation and stated that the law cannot say if the use of nuclear weapons might be lawful or unlawful in an extreme circumstance of self-defence. The differentiated response alternatives, procedures and approaches, which modern states and their bureaucracies or the international organizations possess in order to manage ongoing major crises, are

---

[102]   See Hannah Arendt, *Eichmann in Jerusalem – A Report on the Banality of Evil* (1965) 112–134.

[103]   Reich-Ranicki describes as follows the content of the two letters left by Czerniakow: 'Auf dem Tisch fanden sich auch zwei kurze Briefe. Der eine, für Czerniakow's Frau bestimmt, lautet: "Sie verlangen von mir, mit eigenen Händen die Kinder meines Volkes umzubringen. Es bleibt mir nichts anderes übrig, als zu sterben". Der andere Brief ist an den Judenrat in Warschau gerichtet. In ihm heißt es: "Ich habe beschlossen abzutreten. Betrachtet dies nicht als einen Akt der Feigheit oder eine Flucht. Ich bin machtlos, mir bricht das Herz vor Trauer und Mitleid, länger kann ich das nicht ertragen. Meine Tat wird alle die Wahrheit erkennen lassen und vielleicht auf den rechten Weg des Handelns bringen" . . .', Marcel Reich-Ranicki, *Mein Leben* (13th edn, 2000) 250.

[104]   See Diss. Op. Schwebel (Opinion for UNGA) 1996 ICJ Rep. 324.

turned aside by the Court, which practically raises fear to a normative standard which can fill the gap of law.

The more 'instinctively', in Kohen's sense, and 'mechanically' a state responds to what it seems to be a 'mortal threat', the more chances it has to misinterpret aspects of its response as legally acceptable or justifiable in terms of a 'right' to self-preservation. It might be even rational for a political elite to act under the pressure or the alibi of a bellicose mood in a society which has been actually the victim of an abominable attack, with the expectation to mollify even the 'hard' standards of international law. Instead of offering the states the chance to recreate by themselves the normative impasse of an eventual use of nuclear weapons following the path of the proportionality principle, the Court supplied them with a margin of appreciation escaping legal control and offering an atavistic justification for the moment of crisis. The silence of the law lets then the voice of fear be heard.

Compliance with the principle of proportionality in a situation where the use of nuclear weapons would be evoked, seems feasible only in borderline cases. The advantages of modern technology in war, namely accuracy and the capacity to distinguish between combatants and civilians, are expected to be lost during a nuclear conflict, not necessarily because of the nature of the weapons themselves, but also because of the unforeseen development of the chain of events leading to a progressive loss of control over the conflict, during which uncertainty over the legality of specific acts or strikes would rapidly rise with the increase of complexity of the situation. Nonetheless, the conclusion that it is practically impossible to act in conformity with international law under such circumstances should be the outcome of the application of the regular methods of interpretation on the relevant principles and provisions of international humanitarian law. It should be based upon the assumption that, unless a specific rule for the prohibition of nuclear weapons has emerged, the legality of their use should be measured by the standards of international law, adapted obviously to the particular circumstances of such an existential situation.

Prevention is not credible and effective, unless the subjects of international law are 'let alone' to deliberate on the finalities of the proportionality standard, after the judge has particularized legal instruments and modalities of the overall process and has demonstrated the indeterminacy and non-predictability of the principles. To activate deliberation in the political decision-making process, international law should rather recognize that states have the right to threaten with, or to use nuclear weapons in self-defence and, *at the same time*, for the purpose of maintaining or restoring international peace and security, within the limits of necessity and proportionality – but they must conform both to *jus ad bellum* and to *jus in bello*.[105] In that perspective, international law does not renounce its guiding function at any moment of that process. Decision-makers should have been led by the Opinion to know that, if they use nuclear weapons, under any circumstances whatsoever, it would be expected of them to conform with any single aspect of the international

---

[105] This principle, which is introduced in para. 42 of the Opinion for the UNGA is 'neutralized', if not refuted, by para. 96, see also Gardam, *loc. cit.*, 285.

220   *Achilles Skordas*

humanitarian law and of the law of the UN Charter. The Court had to describe the different steps by the application of the proportionality principle and stress that any miscalculation would transform an intended act of defence to an act of aggression and would lead to the commission of crimes against peace, war crimes and crimes against humanity. In the twilight zone between law and natural situation, where rules exist, but are not fully operational, prevention is, that nuclear war can be legitimate. This is the ultimate rationalization and the last barrier to self-annihilation.

The problem with the Court's Opinion is not that it cannot be re-interpreted in another way that would better fit the spirit of international law and the maintenance of international peace and security. There exists here a discrepancy between a legal interpretation *ex post* versus legal interpretation *ex ante*: should nuclear weapons ever be used, it could be expected that the stigma of illegality would not be altogether erased from such an act, because an international judicial organ eventually dealing with such a case would be inclined to disapprove the use of nuclear weapons, at least to some extent. (It cannot even be excluded that the use of nuclear weapons would lead to the emergence of a customary rule of general prohibition). Nonetheless, here is not at issue any speculation about the future legal (dis)qualification of an actual use of nuclear weapons, but the present guidance of the future conduct of the addressees of international law during a nuclear crisis.

Under the circumstances of the cold war, the Court's Opinion would not have been capable of 'misleading' the enormous nuclear bureaucracies of the two superpowers which operated in the concern of the major collective interests they represented. It seems that the overall impact of *general* international law on the effective guidance of nuclear decision-making at that time would be minimal, due to the overlapping disciplines superimposed by the bipolar system. Nowadays, in view of the degeneration of that order and of the rapid development of international criminal law and of international responsibility for the various breaches of peace, the 'guiding capacity' of the *erga omnes* rules is increased. The silence of the Court is, on the contrary, capable of inducing states to wage a nuclear escape from a major crisis, with exclusive reference to their national stereotypical fears – real or presumed. A subsequent determination of illegality would be of little comfort to the international community.

Under the condition that the Court considered the general prohibition of the use of nuclear weapons as not founded on positive law or as non-effective, it had practically two alternatives: either it would permit the use of nuclear weapons under all relevant restrictions of international law, including necessity, proportionality and *jus in bello*, or it would permit it without further specifications, under a general justification clause, dressed as a gap in the law. What appears as silence of the Court, is nothing else than such a 'hidden' justification clause.

In the first alternative, the Court would have 'trapped' the addressees in the 'web' of legal reasoning, which would demonstrate the enormous risks of any such enterprise at every step and would clearly develop a preventive effect. To do that, the Opinion had to bear the cost of the explicit and very unpopular determination, that the entitlement to use nuclear weapons existed, but it should be exercised only in exceptional circumstances in regard to an existential threat for the international community as a whole and obviously for the state-actor itself; moreover, that by the qualification of the different aspects of legality, the illegitimacy of the acquisition of nuclear weapons should also be taken into account. The Statement of the President of the Security Council at the conclusion of the meeting held at the level of Heads of State and Government on 31 January 1992 was very clear: 'The proliferation of all weapons of mass destruction constitutes a threat to international peace and security'. Therefore, if the policy of deterrence is pursued in deviation from the Non-Proliferation Treaty, it would also constitute a presumption for an illegitimate threat of the use of force.

On the question of the threat or use of nuclear weapons, article 51 of the UN Charter should be repositioned within the system of maintenance and restoration of international peace and security, in which it systematically belongs. The interpretation would be more restrictive, because recourse to a nuclear strike would be legal only if the right to self-defence were to be effectively exercised for the protection of the supreme and conspicuous interests of the international community.

An unfolding international crisis threatening major interests of the international community (for instance, invasion and occupation of resources vital for the functioning of the international economy, genocide following an invasion, or 'post-modern' terrorism threatening the foundations of the international political and economic order, nuclear aggression), could justify, depending on the circumstances, recourse to nuclear strategy by third states. Article 51 should be interpreted so as to enable the threat or use of nuclear weapons in such existential situations for the international system. This would constitute a case of legitimate collective self-defence, even if the target has not already committed an armed attack but has engaged in an irreversible course of action for that purpose or even if not all formal conditions for the application of article 51 of the UN Charter would be met – for instance, the victims decline from invoking the right to self-defence due to the irresistible force or pressure of the invader.

The role of the law of international state responsibility and the law of international criminal responsibility has to be stressed. The principles of necessity and proportionality do not only operate for the qualification of legality on the level of the primary rule of either *jus ad bellum* or *jus in bello*, but are also relevant for the determination of the legal consequences on the level of the rules of state and criminal responsibility. If the balancing of the interests in question would imply that the use of nuclear weapons was, under the circumstances, necessary for the suppression of a major threat to international peace and security, but not proportionate in view of its specific effects,[106] this would probably result in the mitigation of the legal consequences under the law of international state responsibility, but not in the qualification of the act as legal. This could be the case, for instance, if a nuclear weapons state takes measures to prevent an imminent nuclear terrorist attack against itself or against another state and this preventive strike results in widespread destruction

---

[106] For the differentiation between necessity and proportionality, see R. Ago, 'Addendum to the eighth report on State responsibility' (1980) II(1) *YbILC* 69–70.

222 *Achilles Skordas*

in the state-target. Recourse to a nuclear strategy for the protection of exclusively national interests would also not justify a determination of legality, but it would eventually imply, under exceptional circumstances, at the most mitigation of some of the legal consequences of the illegal act. Similarly, armed reprisals with the purpose of putting an end to major violations of international law would not be qualified as legal, but could, nonetheless, result, under the same conditions, into a mitigation of state responsibility. The separation of necessity from proportionality in the sense that the military response against the threat is necessary, but the way armed force is used proves to be non-proportionate, may become a structural feature of future warfare – hopefully not of nuclear warfare, but possibly of humanitarian interventions. The Kosovo intervention is in that respect an exemplary case.

A political leadership evoking the eventual recourse to nuclear weapons in an existential situation of regional conflict dominated by extreme passions and fear would have to balance all these factors. Under the realist assumption that decision-makers in a fervent nationalist political environment or in 'societies under fear' could be demagogues susceptible to 'crossing the Rubicon' of armed conflict, but they are not suicidal, cold-blooded war criminals, the complexity of the legal evaluation would constitute a factor awakening the moment of concern.

Instead, the Court chose to recognize an exception from the normal operation of the legal system founded on an extreme danger to the survival of the state. Thus, international law seems not to bind the conduct of the addressees to some plausible and comprehensible normative standard, but, on the contrary, it relates the application and interpretation of the rules of international law with a factual situation, which is raised to the rank of the self-justifying standard of 'self-preservation'. The Court 'saved its face' and avoided explicitly admitting the existence of an entitlement to have recourse to nuclear weapons but, simultaneously, through a Pilatus-proper *non-liquet*, conferred upon the states the legal justification to do so. This is not the best way to provide guidance and to induce addressees to comply with international law; indeed, this is not an example of institutional morality.

4 CONCLUDING REMARKS: ON JUDICIAL MORALITY AND POLITICAL DECISION

Although institutional morality depends heavily on the person representing the institution, as *Koskenniemi* is right to point out,[107] incongruities between personal roles and institutional functions can be observed. The openness and frankness displayed by the fourteen individual opinions in the ICJ Opinion on Nuclear Weapons, as well as the confrontational character of the voting, as revealed by the narrow majority dependent on the President's casting vote with which the Advisory Opinion was adopted, constitute rare examples of personal independence and judicial integrity.

[107] Koskenniemi, *loc. cit.*, 500–507.

Nonetheless, judicial morality goes beyond that and requires the judge to carry out, to the end, the duty of interpreting and implementing the law. Institutions communicate with their addressees through acts and it is through the wisdom and consistency of these acts that their appeal, thus their success or failure, is measured; this is why it is not particularly useful to calculate the number of judges who have directly or indirectly expressed themselves for or against a comprehensive prohibition, but it is necessary to interpret the judicial act itself. The judge's professional ethics require her or him to protect the autonomy of the communicative act of the system he or she serves against strong pressures by other antagonistic systems of communication, such as the political or the economic one or even the system of moral values. The de-differentiation of international law from politics and the abdication of legal discourse from its guiding function in favour of a calculated ambiguity which refuses to select among interpretative alternatives and proclaims a gap, constitutes a setback from the principle of the differentiation of tasks between the diplomatic-political and the jurisdictional spheres.

The international adjudicator is bound by his or her own systemic function to render international law transparent and to draw the lines which divide the legitimate from the illegitimate action. The judge is committed to formulate the pertinent rules and clarify the normative expectations of the addressees. In any way, the judge is bound to adopt, as far as possible, consistent decisions. An inconsistent decision or opinion renders probable the reciprocal neutralization of conflicting normative expectations and risks to undermine the authority of law. Even if the absence of consistency and the presence of contradictions are inherent features of any legal order, it is the task of judicial function to promote the harmonization of its principles and not to reproduce its systemic weaknesses.

The Advisory Opinions on Nuclear Weapons constitute a demonstration of the contradictions in the implementation of the principle of differentiation of functions in international organizations. International adjudication has a major role to play in the regular development of that process. The principle of separation of functions as a general guiding principle of international organization, referring both to the relations among co-operating international organizational structures, as well as between judicial and political functions within the same international organization, does not depoliticize the international judge.

On the contrary, she or he has to build a clear idea of the checks and balances in the international community and of the driving forces behind it. It also requires him or her to clarify rules as well as consequences of the acts of states or of other subjects of international law, sometimes to eliminate barriers to transboundary communication and, finally, to enable actors to assume responsibility, consistently with the evaluations and standards of their respective system, within the limits provided by the international legal order. If the international society is to be viewed as an extremely complex mega-system, which cannot be geared by any single centre, but may be influenced by a plurality of authority sources, it is a constituent part of the international judge's 'ethos' to assume a cosmopolitan perspective, thus to be tolerant of different cultural perspectives and political traditions, and then to set with precision and flexibility workable standards for the interpretation and

224   *Achilles Skordas*

application of *the* international law as part of the common 'civilization' of mankind.[108] Moreover, self-consciousness of one's own system's rationale and respect of the other systems' boundaries and spheres of action constitute necessary conditions for the maintenance of the delicate equilibrium that would guarantee the effectiveness of the international decision-making mechanisms.

Dissent and 'informed decision', taken in principle by the political instances – as the Court indicated, when it unanimously recognized the obligation of states to reach disarmament through negotiations,[109] not any easy-to-achieve moral consensus, fear or 'taboo', is the response of contemporary society towards the evaluation of existential risks and decisions. Although, in the present case, there exists, according to the Court, an obligation of states to achieve nuclear disarmament in all its aspects, the transition passes through the challenging path of consecutive political decisions reforming military structures and doctrines or implementing alternative security arrangements. If, as the Opinion has stated, the obligation to reach disarmament is an obligation of result, states keep control of the tempo and modalities of the overall process. International law guides the conduct of states and international organizations through general principles illuminating the complexity of the issues in question and the multiplicity of factors that have to be considered.

Ronald Dworkin argued, referring to biotechnology, that to play God means to play with fire; he stressed that this is exactly what mortals have done since the time of Prometheus. The alternative would be an irresponsible escape from the unknown[110] and, we should add, obscure. Or, as Carl Schmitt has put it, '*ohne Blitz kein Licht, ohne Angst kein Blitz, ohne Finsternis keine Angst*'.[111] The nuclear age is still far from being over – for better or for worse, for more peace and stability or for more chaos and destruction, that is the question.

[108] Here we should distinguish between 'culture', which represents philosophy, art, religion or literature of regional communities and 'civilization', representing the universal and common political and legal structural elements of international society, see Reese-Schäfer, 'Postmoderne Gerechtigkeitsdiskurse im Spannungsfeld von Universalismus und Kulturrelativismus', in H. Münkler/M. Llanque (eds.), *Konzeptionen der Gerechtigkeit – Kulturvergleich-Ideengeschichte-Moderne Debatte* (1999) 271–274.

[109] See Opinion for the UNGA, see note 1, 267, para. 2F of the oper. part.

[110] Die Zeit, Nr. 38/1999, in http://www.ZEIT.de/archiv/1999/38/199938.genetik_.html on file on 14 December 1999.

[111] 'Without flash, no light; without anxiety, no flash; without obscurity, no anxiety', in Carl Schmitt, *Glossarium – Aufzeichnungen der Jahre 1947–1951* (Freiherr von Medem ed., 1991) 30 July 1949, 251.

Name Index

Abraham, Itty 38
Adams, S.A. xx, 43–7
Ahmad, S. 350
Ahronheim, J. 243
Alexander, S.M. 219
Alibek, K. 162
Ames, T. 204
Anderson, Elizabeth L. 281
Anderson, Jeffry L. xx, 15–33
Arendt, Hannah 370
Arreguin-Toft, A. 8
Asahara, Shoko 190
Atkinson, R. 138

Backschies, J.R. 216
Baily 141
Baker, Douglas A. 99, 142
Baker, Howard 291
Banderet, Louis E. 219, 220
Barker, P. 197
Barletta, Michael xx, 85–90
Barsky, A. 198
Bartholomew, R. 199
Basayev, Shamil 139
Baskin, S.I. 217, 218
Bassoon, Wouter 162
Baum, A. 201
Beckwith, J. 164
Beers, Charles J. 83
Bennett, P. 196, 204, 208
Beres, L.R. 254
Berezuk, G. 202
Bermudez, J.S. jr 155, 162
Bertollini, R. 199
Betts, R.K. 196, 247, 248, 253, 254, 350–51
bin laden, Osama 176, 178, 181, 189, 261, 264, 269, 271, 272, 282, 289
Birchard, K. 200
Bison, J. 204
Bleich, A. 197, 198
Bolton, John 299
Bongo, Omar 38, 39
Bonner, R. 166
Booth, William 199
Borus, J. 198
Boss, L. 199

Bothe, M. 357
Boutwell, Jeffrey xiii, xiv
Bracken, P. 349–50
Bravo, M. 202, 206
Bray, M. 132
Brennan, R. 196, 206
Brewin, T. 205
Brix, K. 200
Broad, W.J. 154, 162, 163, 165, 167
Brown, M. 200
Brownfeld, A. 8
Bush, George W. 35, 39, 40, 85, 86, 88, 90, 224, 229, 242, 283, 284, 291, 292, 293, 294, 297, 298, 301, 320
Buyer, Steven 40

Calogera, Francesco xiii
Cameron 136, 138, 139, 141
Caplan, Arthur 244
Carvalho, A. 198
Cerasoli, D.M. 219
Chalecki, Elizabeth L. xiv, 305–23
Chalk, Peter 8, 9, 315
Chambers, William 80
Chandler, R.W. 216
Cheney, Dick 36
Cherwell, Lord 37
Christopher, G.W. 247, 254
Churchill, Winston 37
Chyba, Christopher F. xviii, 5, 6, 115–28
Cirincione, J. 2, 6
Clancy, Tom xiii, 79, 81
Clinton, Bill 130, 261, 272, 283, 292
Clooney, George 79
Cockburn, Andrew 82
Cockburn, Leslie 82
Cockerel, C.J. 132
Cohen, William 271, 272
Cole, L.A. 233
Coles, D. 204
Collina, Tom Z. xix, 3, 291–303
Collins, D. 198, 201
Collins, Larry xiii, 79, 82
Collins, T. 3
Condorelli, L. 358
Connolly, C. 10